Major General John Alexander McClernand

Major General John Alexander McClernand

Politician in Uniform

Richard L. Kiper

The Kent State University Press
Kent, Ohio, and London

Library of Congress Catalog Card Number 99-22750
ISBN 0-87338-636-1
Manufactured in the United States of America

06 05 04 03 02 01 00 99 5 4 3 2 1

Library of Congress Cataloging-in-Publication Data
Kiper, Richard L., 1945–
Major General John Alexander McClernand : politician in uniform /
Richard L. Kiper.
p. cm.
Includes bibliographical references (p.) and index.
ISBN 0-87338-636-1 (cloth : alk. paper) ∞
1. McClernand, John A. (John Alexander), 1812–1900. 2. Generals—
United States Biography. 3. United States. Army Biography.
4. Politicians—Illinois Biography. 5. United States—History—
Civil War, 1861–1865—Campaigns. I. Title
E467.1.M374K57 1999
973.7'092—dc21 99-22750
[B]

British Library Cataloging-in-Publication data are available.

Dedicated to

Private 1st Class Brian John Williams
3 May 1950–7 April 1970

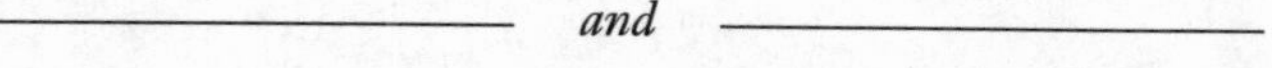

and

Specialist 4th Class Bernard George Brantmeier
18 July 1949–25 June 1970
Company D, 2d Battalion, 3d Infantry
199th Infantry Brigade
Republic of Vietnam

Contents

Maps

Preface

On the eve of the American Civil War in 1861, the United States Regular Army numbered about 1,100 officers and 15,000 enlisted men, scattered across the United States and the western territories. By the end of the war almost 2,667,000 men would serve as regulars or volunteers to preserve the Union.[1] Not only did rapid expansion of the military require enlisted men, but also a large number of officers were needed to command the newly activated companies, regiments, brigades, and divisions. Lower-level officers usually were elected by the men of the unit. Others would assume command as a reward for having raised an organization. Generals, however, were appointed by the president. To meet the need Lincoln sought professionals, but politics also played a major role in selecting men for those coveted positions. Political support for the war was critical in the early stages, and appointment of a favored son to a generalship could go far in cementing a state's—particularly a border state's—loyalty. Among those early appointments to brigadier general was John Alexander McClernand, congressman from Illinois and resident of Springfield, Lincoln's home town.

John Alexander McClernand's life spanned a tumultuous period in the history of the United States. It was a time of exploration and expansion, of conquest and settlement, of growth and progress, of immigration and mobility, of unity and sectionalism, of enslavement and subjugation, of civil war and unification. It was into this turbulent age of crisis, compromise, and conflict that John McClernand was born. His life bridged the years from the second war with England in 1812 to the defeat of Spain and the acquisition of Cuba and the Philippines. It embraced the struggles with the Indians in the northwest and in Florida, and the war against Mexico. He was a congressional contemporary of figures such as John C. Calhoun, Henry Clay, Daniel Webster, Stephen A. Douglas, Sam Houston, Horace Greeley, and Jefferson Davis. He knew and served presidents from Polk to Cleveland in his second term. Yet it was to be the tragedy of America's civil war that brought McClernand to political prominence. The question of slavery propelled him into the national limelight as he sought a political solution to the growing differences between North and South. That effort having failed, the outbreak of war launched McClernand on a career as a military figure. He served with

Ulysses S. Grant, William T. Sherman, David Porter, and James McPherson during the great campaigns of the western theater. As both a politician and a soldier, McClernand, the frontier child of a Scottish immigrant, would be embroiled in the momentous events of nineteenth-century America.

John McClernand has become a footnote in the story of the American Civil War. His role prior to the war was that of politician; during the war it was that of soldier. With respect to the latter, historians generally have viewed him as a secondary figure who contributed little, other than controversy, to the ultimate Union victory in the West. T. Harry Williams has characterized him as "vain," "insubordinate and incompetent." Bruce Catton described him as a "misfit . . . clearly not up to the command of an army corps." Robert Leckie wrote that he was "selfish and pompous." Geoffrey Perret characterized his generalship as "inept" and as having "demonstrated no talent for command." He wrote: "As a commander, the man was simply hopeless." All, to include James McPherson, recognize that he was ambitious, and most modern historians believe that it was his ambition that ultimately led to his fall from grace. Most also grant that he was courageous. A few, such as Allan Nevins and Shelby Foote, acknowledge that McClernand may not have received the credit he deserved. Nevins and Herman Hattaway allude to the possibility of a conspiracy to prevent him from receiving that credit. Many assert that McClernand's personality led to his undoing.[2]

These views lead to many questions. Was John McClernand a good general, or was he incompetent? Did he perform militarily any better or worse than professional soldiers? Was he the "troublemaker and malcontent" that Catton asserted, or was there resentment against his success that led to jealousy and criticism? If such resentment existed, did it lead to a conspiracy against the former politician? Or was McClernand in fact incompetent, insubordinate, overly ambitious, and jealous of the success of professional soldiers? Answers to these questions provide a realistic evaluation of a complex individual who rose to high rank in the Union army. They also lead to greater understanding of the events in the western theater of the American Civil War.

Acknowledgments

Completion of this work would not have been possible without the assistance of many individuals. I am deeply indebted to Professor Theodore Wilson of the University of Kansas, whose guidance and constructive suggestions were critical. I owe Dr. William G. Robertson of the United States Army Command and General Staff College a special debt, because it was his suggestion that I research this topic. The willing and cheerful assistance of Ms. Cheryl Schnirring and the staff of the Illinois State Historical Library enabled me to locate useful manuscripts, microfilm collections, and photographs that were indispensable to my research efforts. The staff of the Combined Arms Research Library, Fort Leavenworth, Kansas, readily assisted me in locating material both through the in-house collections and from external sources that were critical to completion of this work. Particularly helpful were the historians and guides at the Vicksburg, Shiloh, and Forts Henry and Donelson National Military Parks, and the Arkansas Post National Memorial. They were instrumental in assisting me to understand the flow of the campaigns and battles. Conversations with historians Mr. Edwin C. Bearss, Mr. Warren Grabau, and Mrs. Jacqueline Wright resulted in a great amount of useful information. Correspondence and conversations with Mr. McClernand Crawford, great-great-great-grandson of John Alexander McClernand, provided insight into aspects of the subject's character that is unavailable elsewhere. These conversations also led me to numerous other sources for information. The talent of Barbara Baeuchle, who drew the maps, should be readily obvious.

Special appreciation is given to my wife of over thirty-one years, Diane. She endured the trials associated with researching and writing this book. Her patience, understanding, love, devotion, and assistance made production of this work truly a joint effort.

1
From Congressman to General

Newly settled Breckenridge County, Kentucky, was an unlikely place for a medical doctor from Scotland to locate, but in the late 1700s Dr. John McClernand left his native land for Antrim, Ireland, and then for Philadelphia. Departure from his adopted land was possibly hastened by participation in the United Irishman Revolt—an armed rebellion against British rule. After a short stay, he moved west to Kentucky and met Fatima Seaton Cummins, a widow whom he soon married. On 30 May 1812 their only child, John Alexander, was born. Young John could trace his lineage to clan Clernand, which had been prominent during the reign of Malcolm I of Scotland. According to clan lore, his ancestor had fought with the king and had been recognized for exceptional bravery in battle. The Clernand crest depicted a hand, which indicated faithfulness, a dagger, which symbolized bravery, and a bird, which signified quickness in action. Those qualities displayed on the clan crest and the legacy of his ancient ancestry might be said to characterize the life of the newborn American.

At age four John and the family moved from Hardinsburg, Kentucky, to a farm near Shawneetown, Illinois. After his father died, Fatima, who was a good businesswoman in her own right, supported herself and young John. By age sixteen the boy had completed the formal education then available, but William J. Gatewood, an Illinois state senator, saw great potential in the teenager and began to tutor him in French and Latin. John also began to read law books in the Shawneetown office of Henry Eddy. He was admitted to the bar in 1832 and went into practice with Albert G. Caldwell.[1]

In April 1832 trouble flared along the western border of Illinois, when Black Hawk, leader of the Sac and Fox tribes, crossed the Mississippi River into the state. The governor called out the state militia, and on 16 June 1832 John McClernand enlisted as a private in the company being formed by Capt. Harrison Wilson from Gallatin County. Shortly thereafter he became an assistant quartermaster on the staff of Brig. Gen. Alexander Posey, when several militia units were organized into a brigade. During his three months of service the young soldier was recognized for a daring exploit: he carried a dispatch from Posey across a hundred miles of hostile territory. The war ended at the Battle of Bad Axe, Wisconsin, in August 1832, and John returned to his home in Shawneetown. He was mustered out on 14 August.[2]

After the war McClernand was afflicted with ill health. To regain his strength he began an active life of a trader along the Ohio and Mississippi Rivers. By 1835 he had returned to his hometown, where he established and edited the first democratic newspaper in the town—the *Gallatin Democrat and Illinois Advertiser*. Although the paper went out of business shortly thereafter, his name became widely known in the area. John McClernand then entered politics.[3]

In 1836, at age twenty-four, McClernand was elected to the Illinois legislature in Vandalia for the first of three two-year terms. He gained statewide exposure when he was appointed to a committee, of which the prominent politician Stephen A. Douglas was also a member, to investigate charges against a fellow Democrat, President Andrew Jackson, relating to Jackson's effort to abolish the National Bank. McClernand's report vindicated the president on all charges. One other individual who would figure prominently in McClernand's future—the Whig Abraham Lincoln—also sat in the Tenth Assembly of the legislature.[4]

The Tenth Assembly is notable in Illinois history for having voted eight million dollars for a "System of Internal Improvements," which included building rail lines, improving waterways, and constructing the Illinois and Michigan Canal. Although Lincoln and McClernand supported the internal improvements bills, the two politicians were at odds over another measure that required the state to demand payment of revenue from the federal government "in specie." Both spoke extensively on the issue, with McClernand favoring the measure and Lincoln opposing it. The larger issue, though, was whether there should be a state bank. Lincoln would introduce a bill supporting it; in contrast, McClernand, a fellow representative wrote, "has commenced an uncompromising War against all the Banks in the World." In a letter to the *Sangamo Journal* after an exchange on Illinois banking problems and the specie question, Lincoln referred to his opponent as someone who "after half an hour's gabbing" had "in substance said nothing." A fellow assembly member, Democrat Usher Linder, disagreed. In his view, McClernand was "a young man of great fluency of speech."[5] An issue would soon arise, though, that would force Lincoln and McClernand to speak out "in substance."

By the mid-1830s the Missouri Compromise reached in 1820 was beginning to unravel. One issue was whether Congress could abolish slavery in the District of Columbia. Another was whether Southern states had the right to control slavery within their borders. Many slaveholding states had passed measures asserting that right. Kentucky's resolution declared that she "can never permit another State to assail her local institutions." The measure approved in Virginia clearly stated that such rights had been provided by the Constitution. Alabama requested that all states stop the "malignant deeds of the abolitionists calculated to destroy our peace and sever this Union." Several Northern states issued proclamations in regard to the resolutions, and in December 1836 an Illinois House committee was established to prepare a response. John McClernand was a member and was thus forced to confront the issue of slavery.

On 12 January 1837 the committee issued its report. The report stated that abolitionists were "reprehensible" and that their actions were "misguided and incendiary." It declared that "the right of property in slaves is [made] sacred to the slave-holding States by the Federal Constitution," of which "they cannot be deprived . . . without their consent." The same doctrine applied to the District of Columbia. The Illinois House adopted the response. In March 1837, however, Lincoln filed a protest in which he sought to clarify his position. He agreed with the provision that only the states could abolish slavery within their borders, but he differed with the majority about the District. In his view only Congress had that right. Thus was framed a critical constitutional issue of the era—popular sovereignty versus the power of the central government. McClernand was in the camp of the former.[6]

In 1838 McClernand chose not to run for reelection to the legislature; Thomas Carlin, nominated for governor, offered the office of lieutenant governor to his fellow Democrat. The state constitution, however, required a minimum age of thirty, so McClernand, age twenty-six, had to decline. Carlin was elected and then sought to appoint his youthful political ally secretary of state. This move touched off a major controversy in Illinois politics.

Alexander P. Field, the incumbent secretary of state, had held the post since 1829. The Illinois constitution did not recognize a governor's right to remove an appointee, and the Senate refused to confirm Carlin's nominee. McClernand sued, and on 22 July 1839 the Illinois Supreme Court ruled in favor of Field. During the legal battle, Abraham Lincoln represented the company that stored Field's official papers. Stephen A. Douglas represented McClernand.[7] Following the court decision, because of his advocacy of the Illinois and Michigan Canal construction project Governor Carlin appointed him to the canal commission, and he served as its treasurer.[8]

During the protracted struggle over the nomination, McClernand's name was prominent in Illinois newspapers. The *Chicago Daily American* characterized the politician as "a young gentleman of very fine talents and manners" but also as "a sufficiently shrewd archer to have two strings in his bow." There was also a hint of scandal, for the shrewd politician may have violated his oath to keep the canal route secret so as to prevent land speculation. Writing to Henry Eddy, a director of the Bank of Illinois, McClernand had advised Eddy that land in the Lockport region could double in value in the near future. Although the canal eventually did run through Lockport, near Chicago, no conspiracy was proven.[9]

The *Sangamo Journal*, a Whig newspaper in Springfield, was vehemently critical of McClernand's ambitions. "Mr. McClernand does not seem disposed to give up any office which he may hold until he secures a better," the paper editorialized. The following month the paper again attacked the politician: "Col. McClernand is anxious to do away [with] the principle of holding one office for life [in reference to his objections to Field's longevity as secretary of state]—though he appears to have no great objection to hold different offices all his days."[10]

In 1839 John McClernand attended the State Democratic convention in Springfield, and in 1840 he, along with Lincoln, was reelected to the Illinois legislature after a two-year absence. During the session McClernand led the opposition to a Whig-sponsored attempt to disenfranchise unnaturalized aliens (most of whom voted Democratic) residing in Illinois. He argued that such an act violated the state constitution, which allowed white males who had lived in the state for more than six months to vote. His feisty remarks about the judicial system resulted in a challenge to a duel from Supreme Court Justice Theophilus Smith, who was the only Democrat on the four-judge court. A time and location was set, but the honorable justice failed to appear.[11]

During the 1840–1841 legislative session, McClernand and Lincoln clashed over the issue of voter fraud. While both sought to curb the practice, the question of how to do it produced the contention. Lincoln proposed a committee that would give the Whigs a majority. McClernand amended Lincoln's proposal by declaring that the issue should be referred to a committee with a Democratic majority. McClernand's amendment passed, simply because the Democrats held the majority in the assembly.[12]

Throughout 1840 he campaigned for Martin Van Buren's reelection as president, while Lincoln espoused the candidacy of the Whig William Henry Harrison. Both sought the position of presidential elector, and they met in debate several times. Their debate in a Methodist church in Mount Vernon was characterized as "spirited." McClernand was by then becoming well known throughout the southern part of the state. His scholarly preparation and the theatrical delivery of his speeches had earned him the sobriquet of "Grecian Orator." The *Sangamo Journal* again displayed its Whig leanings in publishing a letter "in which it is stated that John A. McClernand is using up A. Lincoln in his addresses to the people. Abraham Lincoln used up by John A. McClernand? Bah!" On a less contentious occasion that fall, the two rivals attended a grand ball in Springfield to celebrate the relocation of the state capital from Vandalia to the central Illinois town. Nevertheless, the two remained political rivals, and debates between them during the legislative session, especially over the question of whether there should be a state bank, were "peculiarly sharp and personal." McClernand finished fourth in the balloting for elector and Lincoln tenth. The Illinois popular vote went to Van Buren; the top five vote-getters in the elector race cast their votes for him.[13]

In 1842 the voters of Gallatin County returned John McClernand to a third term in the Illinois legislature. The session was most notable as an indication of McClernand's continuing rise in stature within the Democratic party of Illinois. Four candidates emerged to fill the United States Senate seat occupied by Richard M. Young. Supreme Court judges Sidney Breese and Stephen Douglas (who had been appointed to the court in 1841), Young, and John McClernand vied for the nomination. Not until the nineteenth ballot did the nomination go to Breese; McClernand, who the *Sangamo Journal* had described as having "a singular propensity for office," was a distant third. The following year Samuel McRoberts, the other United States senator from Illinois, died in office, and McClernand again sought the governor's appointment to fill the vacancy. Again it was denied him. The reason given by the *Alton Telegraph* was that he "was guilty of the sin of residing in the south."[14]

Southern Illinois's proximity to the slaveholding states of Kentucky and Missouri made the people of the area particularly sympathetic to the proslavery stance of their Southern and western neighbors. The Illinois constitution, adopted prior to the state's admission to the Union in 1818, had allowed French slaves and indentured servants who had been brought into the territory to remain in those conditions. Although it had prohibited the future introduction of slaves, it did allow slaves to be used in the salt springs near Shawneetown, the area where John McClernand was raised. Additionally, the region commonly known as "Egypt" had economic and social ties to the South, for many of its citizens were immigrants from Kentucky, Tennessee, North Carolina, and Virginia. Cairo, Illinois, was the center of trade with the South along the Mississippi, Tennessee, and Cumberland Rivers.

The Fugitive Slave Act of 1793 had long held that Southern slave owners could recover runaways who crossed into free states. In 1842, however, that act had been modified by a United States Supreme Court decision, *Prigg v. Pennsylvania*, in which the court ruled that states could enact "personal liberty laws" to prevent state officials from enforcing the Fugitive Slave Act. During the 1842–1843 session of the Illinois legislature, a bill was introduced that required any negro in the state to provide proof of freedom or face confinement for one year. Gustave Koerner, member of the House, used a parliamentary maneuver to object to the bill because of his concern that it infringed on personal liberty. It was his opinion that Southern members of the body held a majority that would ensure passage of the legislation. He reasoned they would do so because "that part of the State was really much overrun by negroes from Kentucky and Missouri, and they were, no doubt, a very annoying and a very troublesome set." McClernand countered Koerner's objection with a warning that if the bill were not passed, southern Illinois would be faced with a "most dangerous population." He then charged that Koerner appeared to favor abolitionism. The bill was referred to committee and there died. Nevertheless, it was an indication of the sectional differences that inflamed the United States. It was also another step in John McClernand's personal involvement with the slavery question.[15]

In May 1843 the Shawneetown politician pursued another opportunity for national office. The 1840 census had added four seats to the Illinois congressional delegation. Democrats at the Second District convention nominated McClernand for the House of Representatives, to run against the Whig Zadoc Casey, also a Black Hawk War veteran. McClernand campaigned as a "selfmade man" and easily defeated his opponent in the August general election. In December he and Stephen A. Douglas, who had won the House seat from the Fifth District, took their seats in the United States Congress.[16]

In addition to pursuit of national office, McClernand was involved in another form of pursuit. Mary Todd, who in November 1842 had married Abraham Lincoln, had a close friend, Sarah Dunlap, from Jacksonville, Illinois. Douglas had courted Sarah since soon after his arrival in Illinois in 1833. The *St. Clair Banner* described Sarah as "exceedingly fair . . . her neck and forehead . . . as alabaster, her eye . . . dazzling, her hair . . . shining—while all that poets fancy, or writers of romance conceive, is more than realized in her beautiful countenance!" It was John McClernand, though, who won her hand. They married in November 1843 and together set out for Washington.[17]

Freshman congressman McClernand made his first floor speech in January 1844, in defense of President Van Buren and in favor of a measure to rescind a fine imposed on former president Jackson during the War of 1812. The measure passed. Other issues with which he dealt concerned the distribution of public land, the granting of rights-of-way to the Great Western Railway Company, and the provision of funds for lakes, harbors, and rivers. His oratory on the subjects at hand was so intense that at one point silence had to be imposed on him by sustained use of the gavel.[18]

The election of 1844 saw McClernand returned to the House, with 99 percent of the popular vote. In the fall he campaigned in Illinois in favor of James K. Polk. His oratory received wide coverage: the *Sangamo Journal* ridiculed his speeches, while the *Illinois State Register*, a Democratic newspaper, characterized them as "sensible, patriotic, eloquent, and statesmanlike." Illinois and the nation went with Polk. The following year McClernand's name was mentioned for governor, but he declined, saying that he had "no disposition whatsoever to aspire to or occupy the station."[19]

Washington in 1845 and 1846 was beset with questions regarding Texas and Oregon. In a floor speech in January 1846, McClernand made clear where he stood on issues regarding the borders of the United States. He was an expansionist and opposed any compromise with Great Britain that would lead to surrender of territory south of the line 54°40' north latitude. "The great mountains of the East and West were the granite bands formed by the Almighty hand to bind the numerous States which were to spread out in beautiful and glorious prospect over the intervening space together as one firm and cemented UNION. It is for England to count the cost and dread the consequences of an unjust war with the United States," he warned. In May the Prairie State representative voted to approve Polk's message declaring war against Mexico. The following month he spoke in full support of war with Mexico and briefly addressed military policy. The war, he said "should be prosecuted vigorously and effectively. . . . Let the young Samson of the West beware that he is not shorn of his strength by being insulated from the Pacific." McClernand realized that a war to expand Texas would benefit the South, but he believed that as a quid pro quo the South would then support Northern aims in Oregon. He miscalculated the level of Southern aid he could command as a result of his advancement of claims on Texas, and he was chagrined by Polk's acceptance of the forty-ninth parallel as the northern border of Oregon.[20] Expansion and slavery continued to mix in a volatile concoction that eventually engulfed both the nation and John McClernand.

In August 1846 the Illinois congressman won a third term in Congress, with no opposition in his district. Douglas was concerned that at the last minute McClernand might oppose him for a Senate seat, but such was not to be. In the House, Abraham Lincoln took his seat for the first time. Mary Lincoln wanted to be reunited with her friend Sarah McClernand, and she pleaded with her husband to take her with him. Mary wrote, "The irresistible

Col. Mc. cannot do without his wife" and had brought Sarah with him, but, she continued, "I expect you would cry aloud against it." Abraham was not persuaded, and Mary remained in Springfield.[21]

Whether slavery would be allowed in the territories became as contentious as the issues of slavery in the states and in the District of Columbia. Expansion westward was continuing, and the question of slavery in regard to that expansion had to be faced. McClernand was a die-hard expansionist. "Extension and expansion is the condition of our political existence," he declared; "To fix arbitrary bounds on the republic would be to cage the eagle in its upward flight." In early 1847 he clearly articulated his stance on the question of slavery in the territories acquired through expansion. He reiterated that Congress "could not constitutionally in any way interfere with the institution of slavery in the slave-holding States," because it was a local matter. He added, though, that "in the case of the Territories of the United States the case is different. In regard to them, the jurisdiction of this Government is supreme."[22] This would not be his last speech on the subject.

The end of the war with Mexico brought renewed questions about slavery in newly acquired lands. In 1846 David Wilmot introduced an amendment to a bill to authorize payment to Mexico for land. The amendment, later known as the Wilmot Proviso, legislated that "neither slavery nor involuntary servitude shall ever exist in any part of said territory." His argument was based on Article IV of the Constitution, which stated: "The Congress shall have Power to . . . make all needful Rules and Regulations respecting the Territory . . . belonging to the United States." The leading opponent of the proviso was John C. Calhoun, who argued that Congress had no right to prohibit citizens from migrating to the territories with their slaves. Such differences led McClernand to write his friend Charles Lanphier, editor of the *Illinois State Register,* in January 1848 that "we are in a national crisis."[23] The issue was to be a prominent one at the Democratic National Convention in May.

McClernand voted against the Wilmot Proviso and did not support its inclusion in the Democratic platform. In order to "purge away the rank inflammation of politics and religious fanaticism" that surrounded the issue, he wanted the "barn burners" and "fire brands" excluded from the 1848 national convention. In the midst of the crisis, Douglas and Senator Lewis Cass of Michigan formulated what became known as the "doctrine of popular sovereignty." The doctrine had as its objective to get the divisive question out of Congress by permitting the residents of a territory to decide for themselves whether the area would be organized as slave or free.

In the convention Calhoun argued that the Constitution required Congress to protect slavery in the territories; therefore, Congress could not prohibit slavery in those territories. McClernand disagreed with Calhoun's interpretation of the Constitution and saw Douglas's popular sovereignty doctrine as the most practical way to resolve the question. He wrote Lanphier that "we should refer the question of slavery in the Territories . . . to the people immediately interested. This would be but an affirmance of the right and the capacity of the people to govern themselves." To underscore this position he, along with Lincoln, voted against an amendment proposed by Douglas to extend the line of the Missouri Compromise to the Pacific Ocean. Such an extension would automatically have made the Oregon Territory free soil. McClernand pointed out the inconsistency of Calhoun's argument: by wanting Congress to protect the rights of slaveholders, Calhoun was arguing for congressional interference with the issue in the territories. At the same time, Calhoun did not believe Congress could interfere with the right of the people to determine whether slavery would exist in those territories.[24]

Serving in the House did not satisfy McClernand's ambition. In 1848 he explored the possibility of running for a U.S. Senate seat in the fall elections. His father-in-law, James Dunlap, informed him that he would have some backing from Democrats, but Charles Lanphier urged caution. In February McClernand accepted a draft for his House seat from his Shawneetown constituents and in November returned to Congress. The election for Senator, though, was held in January, and McClernand allowed himself to be considered for the position. He finished third in the balloting, but a question of the eligibility of the winner, James Shields, threw the contest into the Illinois Senate. Finally, on the twenty-first ballot, Shields was declared the winner. It was to be John McClernand's last attempt to move over to the Senate.[25]

Inability to capture a senatorial position did not diminish McClernand's political ambition. Within the House the most powerful position was that of speaker. When Congress convened in December 1849, McClernand suddenly found himself in the thick of the race for that coveted spot. Initially he had supported Howell Cobb of Georgia, but after fifty-eight ballots McClernand himself was second. At that point, trailing by forty votes, he withdrew and asked that his fellow representatives bestow their votes "upon some other member more worthy to receive them, and more likely to be elected." The reason offered was that "he would avoid rather than court its weighty responsibilities." The actual reason was that the House was so split both across party lines and within the parties themselves on the slavery issue that the possibility that paralysis would become the norm in that body was very real. Although he did not say so, McClernand probably foresaw that in such an environment the speaker would have little influence. The speakership went to Cobb.[26]

On 29 January 1850—a momentous day in the United States Senate—Henry Clay introduced several measures that eventually became the Compromise of 1850. Inextricably linked to the measures were the questions of whether to admit California as a free state, whether to restrict slavery in territorial governments to be organized in Utah and New Mexico, and whether to abolish slavery in the District of Columbia. Tensions ran high. During the debates McClernand, whom Alexander Stephens described as "a gentleman whose general courtesy and urbanity of manner secured him the personal respect of all," met with the two Georgians, Stephens and Robert Toombs. He proposed a meeting at the home of Speaker Cobb to discuss a resolution of the impasse. McClernand, who became chairman of the Committee of the Whole in the House during the debate, assured his fellow House members that he and fellow Illinoisan Douglas understood each other perfectly and would work in concert to secure whatever compromise the group could reach. On 25 March Douglas, who was chairman of the Senate Committee on Territories, introduced a bill in the Senate, and on 3 April McClernand did the same in the House. The two measures proposed that California be admitted as a free state, that Utah and New Mexico be organized as territories without restrictions as to slavery, and that no attempt be made to abolish slavery in the District.[27]

Debate over Clay's resolutions proved acrimonious. McClernand wrote Lanphier that the contest over California would be "violent"; he began to carry two revolvers and a bowie knife. He realized clearly that disunion could easily result from the turmoil. He consistently reiterated the stance that slavery was a local issue, but one that was entitled to national protection. He deplored talk of disunion. In a floor speech he urged his colleagues to "rescue the Union from the perils that threaten it," and he cautioned that the slavery issue might "dissever the Union itself." "The insensate idea of peaceable disunion" is a "fatal delusion," McClernand warned. He cautioned Governor Augustus French of Illinois to "prepare for the storm" and to "provide against portentous violence." Both Illinois senator James Shields and Springfield representative Thomas Harris supported attempts to prevent disunion and hoped for compromise. McClernand's constituent A. G. Sloo wrote the congressman that if he prevented dissolution, "he could be a heart throb away from being president in 1852."[28]

John McClernand attempted to play the role of compromiser throughout a debate in which no real compromise was possible. He had "regular combat with the free soilers and abolitionists in the House" and was accused of being a "slave propagandist," which Representative William Sackett of New York defined as being a "friend of bondage." Although he was "as much opposed to the existence of slavery as any one," he also opposed abolitionism, believing that the Constitution recognized slavery. He declared that he would "be glad to see slavery prohibited everywhere," but he concurred in the concept that slaves were property and were not equal to whites. He implored the abolitionist camp to seek "a formal and peaceful alteration of the Constitution." The question, he said, was "whether law or violence shall prevail"; popular sovereignty was an attempt to bridge the gap between the two. Free soilers, though, could not accept that solution, for it allowed slavery in areas outside the slaveholding states. Abolitionists maintained their belief that slavery was morally abhorrent. Southerners were concerned that decisions in the territories would be made only when antislavery forces held the majority. They were even more concerned that the North would simply refuse to enforce provisions of the Fugitive Slave Act, which had been embodied in the Compromise.[29]

Accolades were bestowed on the luminaries of the Thirty-first Congress—Henry Clay, Daniel Webster, John C. Calhoun, and Stephen A. Douglas—for their roles in drafting a compromise. In fact, however, the measure that eventually passed both houses was essentially the one drafted by John McClernand and Douglas. Two years earlier McClernand's father-in-law had written him that "Mr. Clay has gotten ahead of you and . . . has stolen your thunder." That was indeed the case. John McClernand feared for the future of the Union. As an ardent supporter of the Constitution, he knew the slavery question had to be settled on the basis of that document. The problem was one of interpretation, with seemingly irreconcilable differences between the camps. Compromise had to be found, and it was, for a while at least. The fiery orator became a mediator, a negotiator. His role, however, was primarily behind the scenes. In the end, he had achieved little renown. He had lost a bid for the speakership. His flirtation with a Senate seat had come to naught. In June he wrote Lanphier that he intended to quit the House at the end of his term and, after eight years in office, return home. On 1 August the *Illinois State Register* printed the formal announcement.[30]

McClernand returned to Illinois, but at Cairo he had an extremely close call. A drunken pilot who boarded the same boat as the congressman got into an argument with a crewman. The pilot drew a pistol, which discharged. The ball missed McClernand by about an inch; powder from the shot was embedded in his face. After that incident, his trip was uneventful.[31]

In 1851 John and Sarah moved to Jacksonville, a few miles west of Springfield, and he began to engage in land speculation. The following year he chaired the Democratic State Convention and was appointed a presidential elector. At the national convention in Baltimore he was offered as a favorite-son candidate but supported Douglas for the office. The nomination went to Franklin Pierce, and throughout the fall McClernand campaigned actively for him. After the election McClernand expected to be offered a ministerial position in Spain or Mexico, but such a reward was denied him. The probable reason was that McClernand originally had supported Douglas for the nomination. In his appointments after being elected president, Pierce tried to appease the many factions of the Democratic party, but no one who could be considered a friend of Douglas received an appointment. McClernand returned to his law practice in Illinois.[32]

The Compromise of 1850 brought four years of relative peace in the slavery debate, but in 1854 storm clouds again built up, as the question of how to organize the territories of Kansas and Nebraska became a major issue. Clinging to the doctrine of popular sovereignty, Douglas proposed, in what became known as the Kansas-Nebraska Act, that the people of the two territories determine for themselves whether they would be organized as slave or free. As both lay north of 36°30' and in large part within the borders of the Louisiana Purchase, a decision for slavery would violate the Missouri Compromise of 1820. In essence, Douglas's proposal voided the Compromise—a prospect that generated intense criticism throughout the North. Opposition within the Democratic party led Douglas to declare that anyone who did not support the bill was not a true Democrat. McClernand broke ranks with his fellow statesman, whose oratory he declared to be "simply an act of senseless and outrageous proscription." He refused, he said, to "bend the knee to Baal" or worship a "Little Giant."[33] The dispute between the Illinois Democrats was not over the essence of the Kansas-Nebraska Act but rather over Douglas's declaration that support of the act was the only true proof of party loyalty.

The Missouri Compromise had provided political cover in Egypt for McClernand's antislavery convictions. He was able to compromise over the question of New Mexico, because for the most part it lay south of 36°30'. California would be a free state, and the people of Utah would decide their future. The Kansas and Nebraska territories, however, lay entirely north of the Compromise line. The question, thus, lay squarely before him. How could he oppose the extension of slavery north of 36°30' while also upholding the right of the people in the territories to decide the question for themselves? He concluded that popular sovereignty took precedence, and in that respect he stood with Douglas. Many in the North, however, castigated Douglas for what they considered a proslavery position. In their view his bill, as an abrogation of the Compromise, would result in the extension of slavery.

Abraham Lincoln joined with McClernand to speak against Douglas throughout the state, but for different reasons. Lincoln argued that the measure could extend slavery; McClernand's concern was that using the Kansas-Nebraska Act as a test of party loyalty was "inimical to the harmony and success of the democratic party." He was not anxious to chain his political future to a position that many in the North viewed as proslavery and antithetical to the Democratic party. In his speech at Alton he declared that he had "opposed from first to last the principles and policy of the Missouri line" but that he was "utterly opposed either to making the repeal or the restoration of the Compromise a democratic—a party test." Still, although he continued to speak out against the "party test" and to attend anti-Kansas-Nebraska speeches by Lincoln, McClernand maintained his personal ties to Douglas, even riding in the same carriage with him to the Illinois State Fair in early October.[34]

In January 1856 Thomas Harris, who had won McClernand's vacated congressional seat, wrote Lanphier about the possibility of the former congressman running for governor. With insight into McClernand's character, Harris expressed concern that if he were elected governor, there might be some difficulty controlling his actions. McClernand did not run. Instead, that summer he moved from Jacksonville to Springfield and opened a law office with Elliott B. Herndon. For the next few years he spent most of his time practicing law, occasionally opposing Lincoln in court, sometimes serving as his co-counsel, and at other times recommending clients to him. He remained active in state Democratic politics, as chairman of the State Democratic Central Committee. After James Buchanan's nomination he spoke at numerous rallies on his behalf. He also maintained a correspondence with Douglas, who after the election invited him to Washington for Buchanan's inaugural.[35]

For his support of the president's campaign, McClernand expected to receive an appointment as minister to Russia. Both Harris and Douglas pushed the nomination with Buchanan. The *Illinois State Journal*, formerly the *Sangamo Journal*, wrote, in a change from its usual lively commentary on McClernand, that such would be a "distinguished compliment to our fellow townsman." Buchanan, however, chose not to make the appointment, and McClernand remained in the practice of law.[36]

Slavery was again thrust into the foreground when the United States Supreme Court ruled in March 1857 that the Missouri Compromise was unconstitutional. Three months later the proslavery territorial legislature in Kansas, sitting at Lecompton, drafted a constitution that allowed for slavery in the territory. This measure conflicted with the Topeka Constitution, passed in 1855, which prohibited slavery. Douglas wrote McClernand to express his concern that Democrats "must stand firmly by the principle . . . which guarantees the right of the people . . . to form and regulate their own institutions." The question was which constitution reflected the will of the people. Soon Douglas sided against the Lecompton measure, which was supported by the Buchanan administration and many Southern Democrats. Buchanan seemed to take the position that it was necessary that Kansas be a Democratic state even if it was a Democratic slave state. In January 1858 McClernand, as chair of the Illinois Democratic Organizing Committee, introduced a resolution in support of Douglas's anti-Lecompton stance. The next month he published a broadside that firmly declared his adherence to the principle of popular sovereignty and warned that Buchanan was urging the use of force "to subjugate the people of Kansas." He urged Douglas: "Agitate! Rouse the people! If we can prevent a present defeat we will secure ultimately an overwhelming victory."[37]

Douglas wrote that he was with McClernand "heart and soul," but such support was not unanimous in Illinois. The *Illinois State Journal* reprinted an editorial from the *Chicago Press and Tribune* that castigated McClernand's stand and predicted that the people of Illinois would give "no more moral weight" to his declarations than to "an untranslated proclamation of the Emperor of China." Douglas could not forestall the Senate from supporting the Lecompton measure, but the resolution failed in the House. Not until the Southern states seceded would Kansas gain admission to the Union.[38]

By 1858 the rift between McClernand and Douglas had healed. On the nation's birthday the Springfield lawyer spoke on Douglas's behalf in Chicago. The next day he gave a rousing patriotic speech in Springfield. Throughout the summer he continued to speak out for the Democratic party and for Douglas's candidacy for the Senate. In the fall he formed a Democratic club in Springfield as a counter to the Young Men's Republican Club. He could not, however, secure support for his own return to the House of Representatives. Some reports alleged that he was despondent. The *Illinois State Journal* was gleeful: "His few friends fear that he may commit suicide," it reported.[39]

John McClernand did not commit suicide. Instead, according to E. L. Baker, editor of the *Journal*, a few days later he vented his anger on the editor himself. Baker wrote that the two met near the town square and that McClernand "commenced a violent assault" upon him with a cane. He then took a pistol from his coat and declared, "If you want to take it up, I'll put a hole through you." Bystanders intervened, and the fracas ended.[40] Nothing came of the incident, but it indicated the volatility of Illinois politics as the end of the decade approached. The incident also confirmed that the former congressman was not one to shy from controversy or to take criticism lightly.

Lincoln and McClernand continued to face each other on numerous occasions. In January 1858, in a case before the Illinois Supreme Court, McClernand represented the Democrats in the state legislature against the Republican governor, who was defended by Lincoln. The court ruled in Lincoln's favor. A year later they met again in a courtroom on opposite sides of a case, but later that month the two joined to give toasts in celebration of the one-hundredth birthday of the poet Robert Burns. In August they were again in opposition, in a murder trial.

Thomas Harris, who had won election to the Sixth Congressional District seat, died suddenly, and McClernand became a candidate for the vacancy. The *Illinois State Register* gave its full backing to the Democrat. The *Journal* opposed him, sarcastically describing his speeches as "a gorgeous oratorical panorama (without any extra charge for the imaginary barrel-organ accompaniment)." Lincoln often spoke on behalf of the Republican candidate, John M. Palmer. The campaign was extremely bitter, with the *Journal* referring to McClernand's "imbecility" and editorializing that he was "wholly unable to exhibit the smartness of even a village politician." The split within the party between those who had supported Buchanan and those who had backed Douglas was still evident. There was no doubt in the voters' minds that a vote for McClernand was a vote for Douglas; not until the eighteenth ballot did McClernand secure the nomination.[41]

On 8 November McClernand defeated Palmer in a landslide. The chief cause for the Republican disaster was the fallout from John Brown's raid on Harpers Ferry. McClernand had characterized Palmer as an abolitionist and one who supported the Brown plot. The Republican position, he had declared, was tantamount to "proclaiming war against the people of the South." The future victor had hammered at the theme of popular sovereignty, which, coupled with the Brown raid, resonated strongly with the Illinois populace.[42] Fear of abolitionism and slave uprisings gripped the South. The raid had a decided impact on the nation, the Thirty-sixth Congress, and John Alexander McClernand.

Immediately after convening, the new Congress was thrown into turmoil over the question of the speakership. The position was particularly important in the Thirty-sixth Congress, because neither the Republicans nor Democrats had a clear majority. Thus, the twenty-seven members of the American party became crucial to the formation of any coalition. Douglas wanted the House to elect a speaker who could draw together his own Democratic anti-Lecompton supporters, Democratic pro-Lecomptonites, and Southern moderates. The Democratic nominee was Thomas S. Bocock; McClernand was designated as floor leader to push through the nomination. His immediate objective, he wrote Lanphier, was to keep Illinois Democrats "within the party organization and to conciliate Democrats of all shades of opinion so far as practicable." His ultimate goal was to hold the party together so that Douglas could secure the Democratic nomination for president.[43]

In the acrimonious debate over the issue, McClernand was recognized as a conciliator. He realized that compromise was essential in a body so split by factionalism. "Whether from the North or the South," he declared, "we are members of the same common party; standing upon the same platform of principles and devoting our energies and efforts to the same common purpose." In his mind only the principle of popular sovereignty could defuse the volatile slavery question which permeated debates. Inevitably his name was mentioned for the speakership, but he declined in order "to set an example of self denial." Nevertheless, such Southern Democrats as Jefferson Davis of Mississippi, J. B. Ashmore of South Carolina, and Howell Cobb of Georgia supported him. As he had other battles, he lost this one. He could not overcome opposition from Republicans and American party loyalists who opposed him because he was a Democrat, or from some Democrats and Southerners who clung to the Missouri Compromise line rather than McClernand's popular sovereignty.[44]

McClernand had lost the speakership, but he had gained in stature. Two Illinois Republicans, Gustave Koerner and Lyman Trumbull, observed that Illinois Democrats had "neither principle nor talent, saving McClernand." This was a far cry from Trumbull's 1842 characterization of the politician as a "milk and water democrat." That derisive term had been coined by Illinois governor Thomas Ford to describe a "timid, moderate, and accommodating" individual who would never contradict, advocate, or offend, but would "agree for the time being, to anything, and with anybody." Thaddeus Stevens, the radical Republican from Pennsylvania, expressed his admiration for McClernand: "What he desires, he is not afraid to vote for." In public the Illinoisan was conciliatory. Privately, though, he was furious: "You have no conception of the d—d villany and wicked and dastardly persecutions to which we are subjected by the ultraists," he wrote Lanphier. Aware of his friend's temper, Lanphier warned, "Give 'em hell" but "keep cool." McClernand wrote to a constituent, John Henry, of his growing despair: "Our country for the first time is in serious danger of civil commotion."[45]

McClernand and Douglas had failed to hold the Democratic party together during the speakership fight. Douglas favored popular sovereignty. Buchanan accepted the Supreme Court decision that slaves were property and could be taken into the territories. McClernand was cautiously optimistic that Douglas could secure the nomination at the Democratic convention, to be held in Charleston, because the Southern delegates would support him "on the second or third ballot." As the date of the convention approached, though, McClernand became increasingly concerned. To Lanphier: "The present struggle is growing more and more vehement. The fight is hand-to-hand."[46]

McClernand was not a member of the Illinois delegation to the convention, but he attended to lobby for Douglas. The split within the party became evident when a fight over the platform erupted. The Douglas platform stressed popular sovereignty but would allow the Supreme Court to resolve slavery disputes in the territories. Southerners refused to accept any platform that did not guarantee protection of slave property in the territories. When agreement could not be reached, delegates from eight Southern states walked out. The fate of the Democratic party was sealed. McClernand was dejected, for he knew Douglas could not win the presidency with the party divided. The newspaperman Murat Halstead observed McClernand "seated mournfully" outside the meeting site: "There was Col. McClernand, with peaked face, running to hooked nose, sadly playing with his watch-guard."[47]

McClernand returned to Springfield, where, despite the outcome at Charleston, his popularity remained high. On 19 May he reiterated his support for Douglas and that evening was serenaded by the Union Band outside his home. At the convention, which adjourned to Baltimore, Douglas received the Democratic presidential nomination. The previous month the Republicans had nominated Lincoln. In June McClernand received the Sixth District Democratic nomination for another term in the House. Despite their political differences, that spring Lincoln and McClernand were co-counsels in a patent case. They lost. It was the last case Lincoln ever tried.[48]

During the remainder of the summer and fall, McClernand stumped the state in support of Douglas. By various accounts his eloquence was unsurpassed, as he compared Douglas to "the Eagle" and on another occasion "to our Savior, Julius Caesar, and George Washington." The *Journal* continued its attack upon the House nominee, to whom it referred as "by mistake, the representative of this district" and representative of "the Douglas Faction of the Sham Democracy." In September the newspaper repeated a story in the *Carlinville Spectator* accusing McClernand of corruption for selling government documents. "He is wealthy and even sports a carriage," it added. The charges were false, and the editor of the *Spectator* apologized. The *Register* continued its support: "A vote for John A. McClernand is a vote against negroism, negro equality, abolitionism, Lovejoyism, Lincolnism, and every other foul ism." McClernand's support for Douglas was unabated, and, after a rally in Springfield on 18 October, the McClernands held a reception at their home for Judge and Mrs. Douglas. Mary Todd Lincoln wrote, "They expected hundreds, but they only numbered thirty. This rather looks as if his greatness has passed away."[49]

In November John McClernand won reelection to Congress for a sixth term by five thousand votes, and Abraham Lincoln won the presidency. McClernand returned to a Congress in which "the absorbing, almost exclusive question of discussion here is 'secession' and 'disunion.'" He told Lanphier that he believed "most of the senators and representatives of the South . . . are fatally bent on disunion." If war came, Illinois and other northwestern states must remain in the Union. In a speech to the Democratic Association of Washington, he attempted to moderate the intense feelings in the city. He declared that he deplored Lincoln's election "as a great national calamity" but that he could not agree "that his election is sufficient cause for breaking up the country." It was the nation's duty "to acquiesce in his election; if not in respect to him, in respect for the people and the constitution itself."[50]

In the charged atmosphere of the Capitol McClernand continued to moderate the proceedings. He introduced a resolution calling for a committee of one representative from each state to find a solution to the threat of disunion. A Virginia representative submitted a similar resolution, envisioning a committee of thirty-three members; McClernand withdrew his resolution, to avoid conflict with the one from a crucial Southern state. The Senate created a similar Committee of Thirteen, which also sought a means to prevent Southern secession.[51]

Neither committee was able to reach agreement on measures acceptable to the South, although on 18 December 1860 a proposal introduced by Senator John J. Crittenden appeared to offer some hope. Among other provisions, the Crittenden Compromise would extend the line of the Missouri Compromise to the Pacific; slavery would be protected south of the line and prohibited north of it. Even though the proposal violated the principle of popular sovereignty, the Illinois representative attempted to gather support for it in an effort to prevent disunion. On 20 December, however, South Carolina seceded, and McClernand realized that peaceful dissolution of the Union was not possible. He wrote Lanphier that Illinois "ought to hasten to arm herself." A few days later he wrote: "Civil war is immediately impending. Arm and organize our militia." Upon hearing of the demand for the surrender of Fort Sumter, he blasted his fellow Democrat Buchanan to Lanphier for failure to send support to the fort: "The curses of all future ages will be upon him. God's grace could scarcely save him from endless and infinite damnation. War is upon us." Finally, resentful, frustrated, and angry that war appeared so imminent and compromise so hopeless, he yelled at William Barksdale of Mississippi, "Come on! Come on! Now we are ready to meet you, and settle it quickly."[52]

Despite the flash of passion, McClernand still hoped for compromise to avoid war. To his colleagues he spoke of the Union, the Constitution, and reconciliation: "Let us all . . . rally in favor of the integrity of the Constitution and the Union." Thirteen years earlier he had declared that he could not support a line that separated slave and free states. He had feared that such would "hasten the dissolution of the Union." If the Crittenden Compromise was the only means to reach a settlement, though, he was willing to forego his "strong objections to a geographical line, and adopt the plan of adjustment recommended by [the] committee."[53]

Preservation of the Union was foremost in McClernand's mind. In a passionate speech on the House floor he denied "the constitutional right of any State to secede from the Union." War would be a tragic consequence for the nation. "I do not desire war. I would avoid it by all honorable means. . . . Such a war would be fratricidal, unnatural, and most bloody." He attempted to defuse the question of blame by arguing that "both sections have been driven into excesses." Still seeking compromise, he called upon all to "merge the partisan in the patriot, and, coming up to the altar of the country, generously sacrifice every angry feeling and ambitious aim for the welfare and glory of the country." For his part, he was willing to forego his insistence upon the primacy of popular sovereignty and accept any recommendations that the two congressional committees or Crittenden proposed if it meant war would be avoided.[54]

At a Democratic convention in Springfield, he reiterated that the Union had to be preserved and protected. Back in Congress he declared his support of any measure that might save the country, but in truth he would accept only a compromise that would appeal to Southern moderates and not allow the fire-eaters to take control of the party. To Lanphier he wrote, "If we become entangled with disunionism we will be lost as a party." When anti-Douglas Illinois Republican William Kellogg introduced a compromise measure, McClernand "dramatically struck hands with Kellogg at a climax, when he said he was willing to join conservative men of all parties to save the country." The move brought hearty applause from the House and the gallery. Historian Carl Sandburg would conclude that this action greatly enhanced McClernand's standing among his constituents.[55]

As the situation in South Carolina and throughout the nation deteriorated, McClernand returned to Illinois. His passion for the Union was unabated. In a speech to the Illinois legislature, he declared that "this was no time for partizanship [*sic*]—all men must stand by their government and their flag." In another speech he declared that he was "no partisan of Mr. Lincoln. Yet placing country before party I would cordially support him as Chief Magistrate of the Nation to . . . put down the rebellion." At Springfield he declared that he "would sacrifice party on the altar of the country." Apparently his influence and oratory were effective. Several constituents wrote favorably about his stance, as did Lincoln's law partner, William Herndon. Frequently he advised Republican governor Richard Yates about the conditions in southern Illinois, where McClernand still had considerable influence. His reputation as a moderate and a compromiser over the slavery issue was such that Yates believed he could use him to secure the loyalty of Egypt.[56]

Despite the rhetorical excesses during the campaign of 1860, relations between the president and John McClernand had remained respectful. Although the Democrat once spoke of Lincoln's "want of personal beauty," personal attacks proved the exception. McClernand acknowledged Lincoln as one of the foremost debaters in the country and, after the election, publicly expressed support for the new president's efforts to maintain the Union. The two were acquaintances but not friends. They met socially, but there is no indication they were ever in one another's home. Their wives were devoted friends, but that relationship did not extend to the two political opponents. Their political views were disparate except on the central goal of maintaining the Union. How to do that, though, was rapidly becoming not a political question but a military one.[57]

In April 1861 John McClernand wrote a letter that presaged many over the next several years. To Lincoln—his townsman, his president, his commander in chief—he sent a proposal for military operations. He called for the nation to "take up arms" and move against Texas. He asserted that a land invasion of that state, coupled with a naval attack upon her coast, would quickly force her back into the Union. In May he and Yates proposed to Lincoln and the general in chief, Winfield Scott, a plan to fortify New Madrid, Missouri; Memphis, Tennessee; Corinth, Mississippi; and Columbus, Kentucky.[58] These schemes revealed the strategic naivete of John McClernand, whose only military experience comprised a few months in the Black Hawk War. The first proposal required land and naval forces that the United States did not have, and Texas was not a decisive objective, as events of the war would prove. As for the second, any force at Corinth would be isolated, and occupation of Columbus would violate Kentucky's effective neutrality. Confederates had already begun constructing fortifications at New Madrid and Island No. 10 along the Mississippi River, and a Union force at Memphis would be cut off by guns from those two positions.

These proposals revealed several things about John McClernand. First was his brashness. He had no hesitation about proffering his opinion on a subject about which he knew nothing. Second was his assertive leadership. He was a party leader in Illinois and had been extremely influential in Congress. Leadership in formulating strategy was required and he was eager to provide it. Third was his energy. McClernand engaged in political crises at home and in Washington; yet he could still marshal enthusiasm for military affairs. Fourth was his patriotism. Maintaining the Union was critical; political differences paled in comparison. Fifth was his confidence in his own influence. He had met with presidents and congressmen; on many occasions his advice had been heeded; he had no reason to believe Lincoln would not heed it. Finally they showed he was a man of vision. His overall plan was not one of short-term gain but of long-term consequence. It was a means to achieve the objective of restoring the Union. The war had to be ended and the Union preserved. One other character trait would soon become evident, though it was not reflected in his proposals of the spring of 1861—ambition.

Stephen A. Douglas died on 3 June 1861. His political ally John McClernand eulogized him as one of the leading Democrats of the era. "A great man has fallen," he declared. He compared Douglas to "Homeric heroes," Plato, and Demosthenes; he characterized him as a "patriot and statesman." Douglas's wife, Adele, desired that her husband be buried in Washington, but McClernand, along with Yates and three other prominent Illinois politicians, pressed her to bury him in his adopted state. She relented, and he was buried in Chicago.[59]

Spring and summer 1861 were difficult times for John Alexander McClernand. The Charleston convention had been a disaster, and then, on 8 May, his wife Sarah died. She had been ill for at least two years with tuberculosis. Her friend Mary Todd Lincoln had often expressed concern about Sarah's health in letters to a mutual friend. Finally that debilitating malady, coupled with complications from the birth of a daughter—Sarah—on 28 April, led to her death at age thirty-six. Upon hearing of her death, Mary Lincoln wrote, "I was grieved to hear of Mrs. McClernand's death. Her friends & orphan children will never cease to miss her." Baby Sarah would die in July. The couple had had six children, and their father would outlive five of them. Only Edward, who would accompany his father on military campaigns, graduate from West Point, rise to the rank of brigadier general, and receive the Medal of Honor, would survive his father.[60]

During that summer of grief McClernand met a man who would exert a decisive role in his future. On 19 June he and fellow Illinois Democratic congressman John Logan appeared at Camp Yates, outside Springfield. There they were introduced to an obscure colonel who commanded the 21st Illinois Infantry Regiment. The regiment had enlisted for thirty days only, and that time was up. On 3 May Lincoln had called for three-year volunteers, but only about half of the 21st Illinois had responded. The two politicians asked the regiment's colonel, Ulysses S. Grant, if they could address the men. Grant knew of McClernand's strong stance in support of the Union and allowed the two to speak. Both gave rousing patriotic speeches, and the men of the regiment reenlisted for three years. Neither Grant nor McClernand could have known at that moment how intertwined their lives would become.[61]

Lincoln, Yates, McClernand, and Logan knew that southern Illinois—Egypt—was important strategically and politically to the Union. Secessionists were active in the southern towns of Carbondale and Jonesboro and in Pike County, west of Springfield. Anti-Union feelings were so intense that there existed, the *Chicago Tribune* reported, the possibility of a division in the state so that "the southern portion may be tacked on to the Southern Confederacy." The *Cairo City Gazette* proclaimed that "the sympathies of our people are mainly with the South." Governor Yates expressed his concern that "secession is deeper and stronger here than you have any idea." Mary Logan, wife of Congressman John Logan, wrote of sentiment in the region: "The theory of States' rights had so impregnated the minds of the people that they were unable to divest themselves of the feeling that the people of the South really owed their first duty to their States, and not to the Government of the United States." A gathering at Marion protested Lincoln's call for troops, and the *Jonesboro Gazette* objected to the possibility of Union troops being stationed in the region. Efforts were undertaken to raise troops for the South. Such was the value of the region that a law associate of Lincoln wrote, "The Union could not have endured the loss of Egypt."[62]

One of the major reasons for his statement was trade. In 1840 more trade along the rivers that bordered southern Illinois went south than went north. By 1860 the eastern trade had taken precedence, but the volume of commerce with the South was greater than it had been twenty years earlier. The *Cincinnati Enquirer* wrote that the prosperity of the people along the Ohio River was bound up with the Southern trade. The paper opposed any "agitation" that would "disturb" trade arrangements. Southerners recognized the importance of the rivers, and in February a convention in Alabama proposed that the Mississippi be closed to traffic from the North. The secession of Louisiana and Mississippi ensured that the South would in fact control commerce on the river. Douglas, in late April, had decried how the "great river has been closed to the commerce of the world."[63]

The "great river" was critical to the Union cause. In March 1860 McClernand had met with President Buchanan to urge him "to stay the course of secession, which was rebellion." The congressman was not only concerned about the Union but also was representing the concerns of his constituents. If the Mississippi River were "to pass under foreign jurisdiction," it would doom the northwest "to an inferior rank as a nation." In May 1861 McClernand had written Secretary of War Simon Cameron after visiting Lincoln and discussing with him strategy with respect to the river. While he acknowledged that most of the trade from the northwest was with the East, he reminded Cameron that there also had been extensive commerce, particularly in corn, with the South. Southern actions to block that commerce along the Mississippi were causing economic loss among corn growers of his state; he asked that Cameron develop a plan for the government to buy the excess.[64]

McClernand and Douglas were not alone in their views of the importance of the river. William Tecumseh Sherman, who also would figure importantly in McClernand's future, wrote his brother-in-law in June that the "Mississippi River is the hardest and most important task of the war."[65] General in Chief Scott also recognized its importance and proposed a major effort to secure that north-south waterway. The "Mighty Mississippi" would not only be important to southern Illinois and Ohio River towns; it would also be the centerpiece of future military operations in the West. The river's course, and those of Grant, Sherman, and John McClernand, would collide within the year.

Governor Yates appointed Orville Browning to fill Douglas's unexpired term. Browning and McClernand returned to Washington in early July, stopping in Fort Wayne for dinner with members of the Kentucky delegation. A few weeks later Browning met with the Illinois congressional delegation in the room of the other senator from Illinois, Lyman Trumbull. The task before the group was to propose men to be commissioned as brigadier generals. Only the president could make such appointments, and Lincoln was besieged with requests. Two Illinoisans, John Pope and Stephen Hurlbut, had already received appointments. The delegation believed Illinois merited nine such commissions and recommended seven additional names to Lincoln. The next day Browning delivered the names to the president, who selected three: Ulysses Simpson Grant, Benjamin Mayberry Prentiss, and John

Alexander McClernand. On 30 July Lincoln notified Secretary of War Cameron of his desires. Of the first group of thirty-seven brigadiers appointed that summer, Pope would rank thirteenth in seniority, Grant nineteenth, Hurlbut twenty-sixth, Prentiss twenty-ninth, and McClernand thirty-third.[66]

Of that first group of thirty-seven, two declined appointment. Of the remainder, twenty-three had attended West Point, and twenty-two had graduated. Twenty-one designees had served in the Mexican War; one had fought Indians, and two (including McClernand) had been in the Black Hawk War. Four nominees had had military experience in the present war. Two were West Point graduates with no combat experience. Five of the appointments were made purely for political purposes.[67]

John McClernand joined 187 other Civil War generals appointed directly from civilian life with little or no military experience. In that first group, Jacob Cox from Ohio had helped organize the Republican party. Franz Sigel was appointed to gain support of the German population in the North. Robert Schenck had served four terms in Congress as a Whig and had campaigned for Lincoln. Stephen Hurlbut was a Republican member of the legislature in Lincoln's home state. James Cooper was a U.S. senator from Maryland. Lincoln appointed him to help ensure the loyalty of that state. Others would follow. Nathaniel Banks, speaker of the house and governor of Massachusetts, would feel the brunt of numerous military defeats. Francis P. Blair, who helped save Missouri for the Union, would serve under Grant and Sherman and do quite well. Benjamin F. Butler, a Massachusetts Democrat with a considerable following, would cause outrage in New Orleans and fail to act decisively near Richmond. Daniel Sickles would lose a leg at Gettysburg and would often be at odds with his superiors—a trait that would also dog the new brigadier general from Illinois, John McClernand.[68]

On 7 August, after Congress adjourned, McClernand visited the president to be presented his commission. The appointment letter authorized him to raise four infantry regiments, four cavalry companies, and two artillery companies. Lincoln's comment to his new general on that occasion spoke clearly to the reasons behind the appointment. "Keep Egypt right side up," he urged the general. McClernand was the most powerful politician in Illinois. His loyalty to the Union was beyond question. His influence in southern Illinois, along with that of John Logan (who within a year would be appointed a brigadier), was considerable, and Lincoln counted on him to keep the region in the Union fold. Lincoln's secretary, John Nicolay, wrote that no Democrat in the state, except Logan, "could bring such a decided and valuable support to the Union cause as McClernand." He had demonstrated courage during the most turbulent period since the founding of the republic. He had sought compromise in the face of extreme demands for abolition or "negro equality." His intelligence, charisma, and eloquence were known throughout Illinois, and his influence with Southern politicians had been remarkable. John McClernand, a lifelong Democrat, would be an extremely valuable ally in the upcoming struggle.[69]

John McClernand and John Logan served Lincoln well in southern Illinois; Egypt did not turn out to be a problem. During the war, although 3,538 men from Illinois eventually were drafted, volunteers filled all quotas from Egypt. Nonetheless, Lyman Trumbull agreed that "there was considerable opposition at first" to the war. McClernand attributed that opposition to the low prices farmers were receiving for their products and the high rates they were having to pay to ship them to markets. Actually, opposition to war policies continued in Illinois until Union victories at Vicksburg and Gettysburg, coupled with Lincoln's growing popularity, caused Copperhead sentiment to be replaced with pro-Union and pro-Republican views. Rumors of secret societies such as the Knights of the Golden Circle circulated in Illinois throughout the war, but none could be substantiated. One study of the societies has labeled the rumor as a "subversive bogey-man . . . intended solely to aid Republicans in defeating Democrats at the polls." Although no small measure of praise must go to Douglas for his April 1861 speech in Springfield that united Republicans and Democrats against the rebellion, McClernand's fiery pro-Union speeches and his and Logan's influence were valuable to the Union cause. To Josiah Grinnell, Republican House member from Iowa, Lincoln said, "There is General McClernand from my state, whom they say I use better than a radical." He knew his Illinois man, he declared.[70] How well he knew him remained to be seen.

2
A Taste of Battle

On 7 August 1861 John McClernand received the official news of his appointment to the rank of brigadier general. Five days earlier, though, the *Illinois State Journal* had reported McClernand's commission, and in glowing terms. The newspaper trumpeted the value of this Illinois son to the Union cause and asserted that McClernand had the "head to plan a battle and invent strategy," despite the fact that the Illinois politician had had no command experience. His appointment, the editors asserted, would meet with "almost universal satisfaction."[1] Whether that sentiment extended to official Washington remained to be seen.

McClernand's friend and political colleague Illinois senator Orville Browning met with Lincoln and the general in chief, Winfield Scott, on behalf of the newly appointed brigadier general. From there Senator Browning saw the acting secretary of war, Thomas A. Scott, and he extracted a letter from Scott to Governor Yates. This letter requested Yates to "afford . . . McClernand all the facilities in your power for arming and equipping his brigade for service, at the earliest date possible."[2]

Brigadier General McClernand interpreted Acting Secretary Scott's letter as authority from the seat of national government to leapfrog over all other Illinois commanders, who had been awaiting arms and equipment for months. Betraying patterns of behavior that would surface in the future, McClernand convinced himself that he had personal authorization from the president and a directive from the general in chief to arm his brigade and deploy it as soon as humanly possible.

Undoubtedly Lincoln, Winfield Scott, and Thomas Scott did not intend the letter to be interpreted in that sense. On 5 April 1861 the regular army numbered only 17,113 men. Within a month public responses to a barrage of proclamations swelled the army to 156,861. Throughout the North units were being formed, and commanders and politicians were clamoring for the wherewithal to field their respective forces. Governors of northeastern states were able to obtain an initial supply of arms from the numerous arsenals in that region. Others were not so fortunate. The War Department attempted to bring order out of the growing chaos. The solution was to distribute the available weapons "pro rata to the troops called for from each State."

Due to the shortage, states were competing with one another to obtain what weapons could be found, and the effect was to drive up the cost. Union manufacturers suddenly had to gear up to meet the avalanche of demands pouring in from the federal government as well as from the states. Lincoln's secretaries, John Nicolay and John Hay, later wrote that the federal government was in those days beset by confusion and disorganization as bureaus sought to meet the overwhelming demands suddenly thrust upon them. To cut through the "knotty tangles of red tape," "impatient governors and State agents, and irrepressible colonels and captains" brought their requests for assistance directly to Lincoln. A letter from the War Department to Illinois governor Yates might reduce the pressure upon the president for equipment, but it would exacerbate the inflationary costs of weapons. Not until late 1861 would the War Department be able to standardize procedures. After that, states could contract for weapons only with specific authorization.[3]

Finding arms for the thousands of men who volunteered for and were mustered into Federal service posed a major problem for Union commanders. McClernand attempted to solve that problem for his own command through personal arrangements with contractors. One such deal produced four thousand British-made Enfield rifles and two batteries of artillery for his brigade. Beginning in 1855 U.S. government arsenals had produced the U.S. Model 1855 rifled musket as the standard infantry weapon, but production rates had not anticipated the dramatically increased need for such weapons six years later. Consequently, many infantrymen were armed with whatever weapon they had brought with them or that could be procured by their commanders. In many cases entire units were armed with old smoothbore muskets, which had little value on the modern battlefield. On the other hand, the Enfield (the standard weapon of the British army since 1855) was considered by some experts to be superior to the American rifled musket.[4] When McClernand saw an opportunity to acquire such fine weapons, he jumped at the chance.

To Messrs. Tellson and Shepherd, contracting agents in New York, McClernand wrote enthusiastically that the Enfield agent in the United States could deliver the four thousand rifled muskets within sixty days at a cost of nineteen dollars each. He urged Tellson and Shepherd "to give immediate and practical attention hereto." To cover payment, he obligated the government of Illinois and cited the letter from Secretary Scott to Governor Yates as authorization for the federal government to reimburse the state of Illinois—certainly a liberal interpretation of that document.[5]

McClernand departed from Washington for Illinois on 12 August, along with Browning and others heading home. The new general had not left all of his requests for arms in the hands of only one agent. Illinois representative Philip B. Fouke, who soon was to command a regiment in McClernand's brigade, had reported that the general's request for weapons would "be placed behind those already contracted for." Prior to McClernand's departure from Washington, therefore, he charged Fouke to contract for two batteries of James rifled cannon as well as Sharps carbines and pistols for the cavalry. Fouke assured his future commander that the weapons would arrive at his encampment before the men of his brigade reported.[6]

Governor Yates acted on Secretary Scott's request that he assist in arming and equipping McClernand's brigade. On 20 August he directed the assistant adjutant general of Illinois to appoint Capt. James Dunlap, McClernand's father-in-law, to equip the units that would join McClernand.[7] However, McClernand was to badger his fellow politician for months on the subject of arms and equipment for his brigade.

Although Congress had passed "an act to indemnify the States for expenses incurred by them in defense of the United States," the problem of payment had been made more acute by the financial requirements imposed upon the state of Illinois to fill the regiments being formed. To meet his immediate requirements, McClernand continued to use his personal influence; he wrote directly to the quartermaster general of the army, Montgomery C. Meigs, to request that an account of twenty-five thousand dollars be established for him to draw upon to field his brigade.[8]

Headquarters of the Army Special Orders No. 141, dated 21 August 1861, assigned McClernand and his brigade to the Western Department, commanded by Maj. Gen. John C. Frémont. Known as "The Pathfinder" for his exploration of the West, Frémont had served in the army, had been governor of California, had been elected to the United States Senate, and had been an unsuccessful candidate for president in 1856. Lincoln had appointed him major general in July 1861 and sent him to department headquarters in St. Louis. Also ordered to report for duty to Frémont was Brig. Gen. Ulysses S. Grant. Grant was to command the District of Southeast Missouri, which included the forces at Cairo, Illinois.[9] From that date until mid-1863 the future of the soldier John McClernand would be inextricably linked to that of Grant, then virtually unknown.

McClernand immediately began a correspondence with his new commander. On 24 August he wrote Frémont a general request for supplies for his regiment. The old soldier replied that the proper course was to submit a detailed requisition to the quartermaster of the Western Department.[10] Such a response must have been an affront to a powerful politician accustomed to communicating directly with leading figures of the day. He had much to learn about the ways of the United States Army.

Three days later McClernand sent Maj. Mason Brayman, a fellow Illinois lawyer who had been appointed as his assistant adjutant general, to meet with Frémont in St. Louis. Brayman, reflecting McClernand's political sensibilities, asked that his brigade not be ordered into active service until completely armed and equipped and that it not be divided but be ordered into service as a unit. Brayman reported back that Frémont, who had significant political connections himself, appreciated "the special powers under which you are acting" and would allow McClernand sixty days to prepare his command for deployment as a brigade. He also reported that Frémont was anxious to begin a campaign down the Mississippi River and that he had "immediate need" of McClernand's men.[11]

In fact, the department commander did not allow McClernand his promised sixty days. Instead, on 27 August Frémont ordered his newly appointed brigade commander to relocate immediately. Aware of lingering secessionist sentiments in southern Illinois, Frémont saw the advantage of posting the former congressman in that region. He also directed McClernand to deploy a portion of his command at points along the Illinois Central Railroad and on the Mississippi bank opposite Commerce, Missouri. McClernand alerted his regimental commanders and prudently sent a staff officer to coordinate with the commandant of the camp at Cairo to prepare for the arrival of his men. McClernand himself departed for Cairo on 29 August. Making clear that a major push was underway, Frémont also ordered Grant to Cape Girardeau. As senior officer in the field, Grant would command the operation.[12]

What had prompted the sudden change? Earlier that month Maj. John McDonald of the 8th Missouri (Union) Infantry had reported to the Western Department commander that four thousand Confederates were at Benton, Missouri, and 1,500 more were near Commerce. Frémont saw the possibility of concentrating his forces, defeating the gathering Rebels, and then occupying Columbus, Kentucky.[13]

In August, however, Union forces were prohibited from occupying Columbus, because Kentucky had declared itself neutral the previous May.

Columbus commanded the Mississippi River from its high banks, but invasion and occupation of a neutral state could be politically disastrous either to the Union or Confederate cause in the West. Frémont was thus compelled to await a Southern move.

The Rebels refused to accommodate the Union desire for an offensive against their forces scattered in eastern Missouri. On 1 September Grant informed Frémont that intelligence had revealed that Confederate forces north of Bird's Point had begun a withdrawal about four days earlier. To verify the report, Grant asked McClernand to order Col. W. H. L. Wallace, Union commander at Bird's Point, to reconnoiter toward Charleston. Two days later Frémont informed Grant that he had received similar reports of Confederate withdrawals.[14]

While troop movements were taking place across the river, McClernand, having reached Cairo on 1 September, remained in camp. Col. Richard Oglesby, the camp commandant, was aware of McClernand's presence in the town, but the two had had no contact. Having been assigned to command the District of Southeast Missouri, Grant determined to establish his headquarters at Cairo. He arrived on 4 September and inquired of Oglesby why McClernand had not assumed command. Oglesby replied that he did not know. McClernand's orders to proceed to Cairo with his brigade did not specify whether he was also to take command of that post, although he would be the ranking officer. By the testimony of his postwar memoirs, Grant impatiently demanded that the new brigadier take command at once.[15]

Clearly Grant was annoyed with this politician-general for not having taken command as the senior officer present. Immediately after his conversation with Oglesby, he issued General Orders No. 3, which stated that McClernand was to command not only the post of Cairo but also the forces at Bird's Point and Mound City. Subsequent recollections notwithstanding, however, McClernand can hardly be blamed for failure to take command at Cairo. Not until 2 September did Frémont authorize him to do so. McClernand received that order on 4 September and at once notified Frémont and Oglesby that he would assume command; on that same date he responded to an inquiry from Grant that he had received Frémont's directive and would take command. Oglesby and McClernand agreed to a change of command at 8:00 A.M. the following day.[16] Nevertheless, such a conflict could not bode well for future relations between the two Prairie State generals.

On 3 September, Confederates under Maj. Gen. Leonidas Polk committed what proved to be a serious political blunder. The Rebels invaded Kentucky and, the following day, occupied Columbus. That action removed any

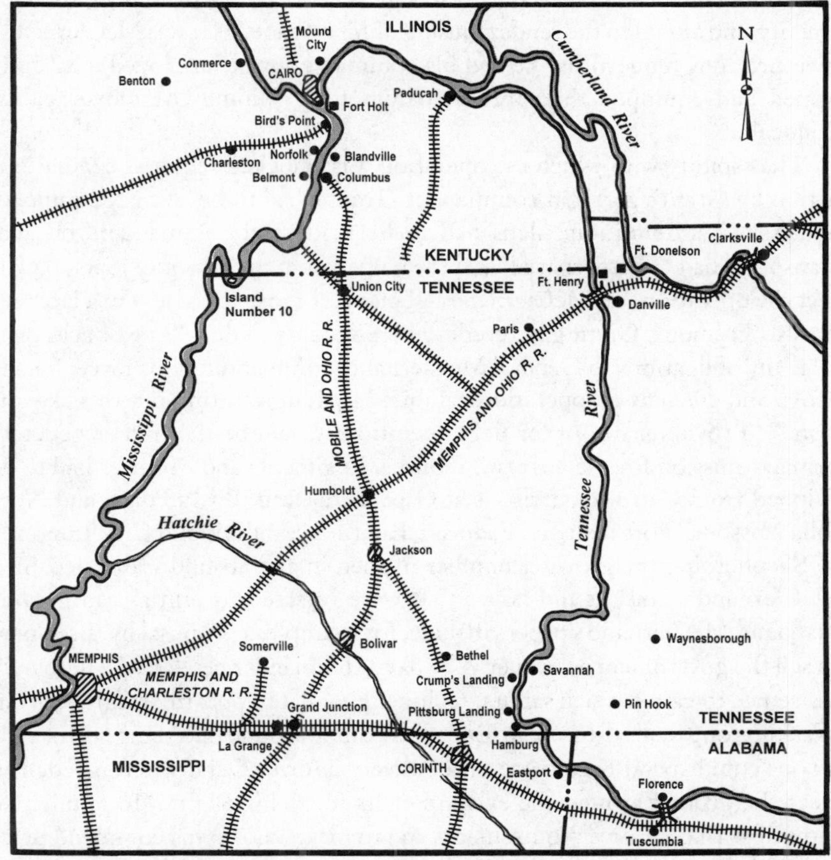

Western Theater Area of Operations

obstacle to a Union advance into this border state. Grant immediately determined to seize Paducah, which controlled access to the Tennessee River. McClernand, now in command of all forces remaining near Cairo, sent a reconnaissance party to the Kentucky shore. Grant accompanied the expedition, and by 8:30 A.M. the following morning, Paducah was in Union hands.[17]

Grant had met no resistance at Paducah, and the *Illinois State Journal* hailed the operation. The paper showered praise equally on Grant and McClernand, but clearly McClernand's role had been that of a provider of troops rather than a commander in combat. On 4 September, the same day that Grant prepared to attack Paducah, Frémont directed that McClernand not "be detailed from Cairo on any distant service, but . . . to remain there or vicinity, and attend to the rendezvousing of his brigade."[18] It was McClernand's own previous request that he and his command not be employed until fully armed and equipped that prevented him from joining the move against Paducah.

The rapidity with which the operation was launched required expeditious action by Grant's garrison commander. Troops had to be alerted, equipped, and issued ammunition; plans had to be made and commanders briefed; transports had to be prepared; and the navy had to provide gunboats to protect the operation. To McClernand fell many of those tasks, and in a later report to Frémont, Grant gave credit where credit was due: "I must acknowledge my obligations to General McClernand, commanding this force, for the active and efficient co-operation exhibited by him in fitting out this expedition."[19] Providing troops for field operations would be the Illinois general's primary mission for the next two months. Regiments and batteries had to be shipped from Cairo to garrisons at Cape Girardeau, Bird's Point, and Norfolk, Missouri; Fort Holt and Paducah, Kentucky; and Mound City, Illinois.[20]

Shepherding the growing number of men in and around Cairo occupied McClernand's time, as did issues that were referred to him as camp commandant. McClernand's papers include, for example, a proposal by three men to sell the government a steamer. The navy commander needed McClernand's assistance to care for sick sailors. Colonel Fouke, temporarily returned from Washington, wanted to use prisoners to ditch around the tents so that his troops could spend time more productively in drill. Details were needed to clear the ground around the encampments for fields of fire. To familiarize himself with defensive requirements and to make known his command presence, McClernand made periodic visits to troops in the field. Personal visits to observe his command would become routine throughout his career.

The new post commandant was finding that military service did not always engender the glory that he expected. On 10 September McClernand wrote Lincoln that "as commandant of this post and its dependencies my duties are most onerous." Indeed, little glory was to be had solving problems of bad bread, unfit ammunition, tents in poor condition, requests for furloughs and disability discharges, requests for relief from court-martial duty, and requisitions not submitted in the proper format.[21] While solutions to such concerns were essential to the efficiency of the army, they were not the basis of newspaper headlines. It was military victories that brought favorable headlines and that yielded both promotion and political influence. In comparison, garrison duties were "most onerous."

The new general also corresponded with Washington on personnel matters. In letters and telegrams to the general in chief and to Lincoln he requested that Alexander Bielaski and 1st Lt. James H. Wilson be appointed aides-de-camp to assist him in carrying out his duties. Bielaski would be appointed; Wilson, whose father had been McClernand's commander in the Black Hawk War, would not, but he would play a major role in McClernand's fate in the summer of 1863.[22]

Many of the soldiers at Cairo undoubtedly found a certain action of their commander as onerous as he found garrison command. In early September McClernand expressed concern to Grant about the effects of drinking upon the soldiers. Grant responded by issuing a general order that authorized commanders to arrest anyone frequenting "the lowest drinking and dancing saloons."

With that order Grant enclosed a letter sent from Mr. Henry Smith of Cairo to Frémont. The letter, McClernand apparently concluded, called into question his conduct in dealing with inappropriate activity in the vicinity of his encampment. His defensive reaction was to become characteristic of those in similar situations during the course of his military career.

McClernand wrote Grant a bristly memorandum reminding his commander that he had requested that Frémont not deploy his command until it was fully prepared for service. Had his wishes been met, his command would have been removed from the vices of Cairo—it would still be near Springfield. Second, he reminded Grant that immediately upon arrival he had suggested that martial law be declared in the city so that establishments that contributed to discipline problems could be closed, but his fellow Illinoisan had refused. Third, he disclaimed any responsibility for the situation, by emphasizing his role in preparing troops for the move against Paducah. Fourth, McClernand implied that the true culprits were his predecessors, who had failed to nip the problem in the bud. He concurred in Grant's general order and he too would issue one, to discourage behavior that would be "subversive of good conduct and military discipline." McClernand was acting as a politician, for a professional soldier's response would have been simply the concluding statement.

Grant's and McClernand's initial actions addressed only drinking and the resulting fraternization between officers and enlisted men. Further complaints from Col. Michael Lawler about demoralization that resulted from "houses of ill-fame" and from Capt. Adolph Schwartz about the "beastly use of intoxicating liquors" finally, on 9 October, produced an order from McClernand that "the tippling and other disorderly houses of the city and vicinity" be closed. However, as soldiers from time immemorial have been known to do, the blue-coated men in Cairo would continue to indulge their desire for spirits. Finally, in late November, the general issued another order "absolutely prohibit[ing] the sale, barter or exchange" of "intoxicating drinks and beverages" within the city of Cairo.[23]

Whatever the effect of such draconian action on morale, the most severe problem that faced McClernand's command continued to be the shortage of effective weapons. On the day he arrived at Cairo, McClernand wrote Frémont that he was sending an officer to St. Louis "for the purpose of receiving and bringing forward such arms as you may be prepared to send." Two days later Frémont telegraphed Grant that he was sending 2,500 weapons to Oglesby and five hundred to McClernand. This was totally inadequate. To form a brigade of four infantry regiments and four cavalry companies required about four thousand infantry and 320 cavalry weapons.[24]

McClernand did not simply wait for the state or federal government to meet the needs of his brigade. On 7 September and again two weeks later, McClernand reminded the Illinois assistant adjutant general of Acting Secretary Scott's order and of his need for four thousand rifled muskets. To ensure that the Enfields he believed he had contracted for did in fact arrive, he dispatched Lawler—who had complained that his regiment had only five hundred old flintlock muskets—to Springfield. A few days later he also sent Col. Napoleon B. Buford to Springfield to see Yates. Buford carried a letter in which McClernand implored the governor to "send arms, particularly Enfield rifles which I have caused to be sent to you." He added a personal note: "I make no merit of the sacrifices I have made in entering the military service. Duty required it and that is enough; but in entering the Service expected to be enabled to make my service reliable to my country and honorable to my State. . . . I cannot do it without arms." Such conceit couched in terms of humility contained a veiled threat: if arms were not provided, it would not be Brig. Gen. John McClernand who would be at fault. The best Buford could do, however, was obtain the governor's promise to provide rifled muskets for one company in each regiment.[25]

McClernand kept his immediate superior in the chain of command informed of his dire need for arms. On 17 September he informed Grant that he had only two thousand weapons for the 3,068 men in his brigade. Most of the arms, he said, were unfit for service, the cartridges were useless, and the bulk of his cavalry was unarmed. To ensure that his difficulty was known, McClernand sent a similar letter to Frémont. Grant recognized his brigade commander's plight and wrote the Western Department commander to add his own voice to that of McClernand. Frémont agreed to provide arms as soon as possible, primarily because he wanted Grant to prepare his command for a move down both banks of the Mississippi. (Earlier that month Grant had suggested such a move toward Belmont, Missouri, and Columbus, Kentucky, but the cautious Frémont had wanted to wait for a more propitious moment.) Information that Confederates were moving toward Columbus and Belmont prompted Frémont to ship two thousand more rifled muskets to McClernand on 28 September. The Illinois politician turned general remained dissatisfied. On 30 September he observed that only half his men were armed, adding, "Our strongest safeguard is formed in the ignorance of the enemy as to our true condition."[26]

Meanwhile, from Washington Fouke wrote McClernand that he had confirmed the order for four thousand Enfields; the arms would "be advanced on the governor's order." Yates was expected in Washington any day, and Fouke hoped to complete the transaction upon his arrival. Still relying upon his political connections, McClernand then urged Fouke to see the quartermaster general (Meigs), the secretary of war, and the president, three men who he was confidant would "favor the most speedy outfit of my brigade." A typically self-serving paragraph in his letter requested that Fouke inform the president "of the amount of work I am doing here, and my part in organizing . . . transportation for the different expeditions." He also brazenly declared that if equipped with sufficient weapons, his brigade alone could have captured the Confederates, who had withdrawn from eastern Missouri in September. McClernand's desperation about the difficulty of obtaining weapons was evident in the oratorical conclusion of his missive to Fouke: "Persevere! Persevere! Persevere and triumph! If you don't I cannot say what will become of us."[27]

Yates would agree only to the provision of artillery, carbines, and pistols and not the infantry rifled muskets. There were too many requests for too few available weapons, and the Illinois governor was unable to meet the demand. Fouke informed McClernand that the general would have to consult the governor himself on the matter. He added, "For Gods sake order me back!"[28] The issue of weapons for McClernand's brigade was far from settled.

John McClernand was only one of many politicians bombarding the War Department and the president with requests for weapons. Gov. Oliver P. Morton of Indiana, Gov. Samuel P. Kirkwood of Iowa, and Gov. William Dennison of Ohio were three influential officials who believed their needs outweighed those of others and had asked Lincoln to remedy their difficulties in arming soldiers from their states. Lincoln and Secretary of War Stanton replied that they were doing the best they could. In a separate letter Lincoln wrote the adjutant general of the army, Lorenzo Thomas, that "Gen.

McClernand has shown great energy and industry . . . and since has effected certainly as much as any other Brig. Genl. in organizing forces."[29] Certainly he had demonstrated great energy and industry in organizing forces, but he had yet to taste battle.

Most of September was spent in efforts to deduce Confederate intentions. McClernand sent to Frémont a stream of intelligence reports in which he informed him of Rebels near Columbus and Paducah. He coordinated with Col. W. H. L. Wallace at Bird's Point for a reconnaissance to Norfolk, Missouri, and forwarded to Frémont reports of Confederates in the vicinity. McClernand warned his subordinate to use caution, and he sent reinforcements and a gunboat to assist in the defense of Norfolk. Whether from political instincts or from recognition of the value of praise from a superior officer, he also complimented Wallace: "I am pleased with your zeal, activity, and prudence."[30]

Union soldiers had several minor contacts with Confederate forces during September and October, but few casualties resulted. Rebels burned part of a railroad bridge between Bird's Point and Charleston, and McClernand dispatched the 11th and 20th Illinois Regiments in pursuit. He cautioned Col. C. Carroll Marsh, commander of the 20th Illinois, to try to get the Rebels to attack him in his entrenchments, for soldiers behind earthworks were inherently superior to those attacking across open ground. He also took another action, one that indicated that he understood the necessity to coordinate operations.

A reconnaissance by Col. John Logan, the important Illinois congressman, had revealed that "a strong Secessionist" by the name of Shelby Thompson had stocked a considerable amount of corn and cordwood on his farm. On 30 September, the same day that Marsh was sent after the bridge burners, McClernand ordered Logan to seize goods of value to the Confederacy at Thompson's farm. Eleven miles separated the two operations, but unless Marsh was aware of Logan's presence, there was risk of a clash between the two friendly forces. Wisely, McClernand cautioned his subordinate "not to mistake [the men of Logan's force] for the enemy."[31] It appeared the former politician was learning his new craft.

On 14 October, "for the better convenience of administering the duties of this military district," Grant reorganized the forces within the District of Southeast Missouri into five brigades. Although the order stripped McClernand of the forces at Bird's Point, it increased his command from four to six infantry regiments. The general did not take the order as a slight, for he promptly wrote Grant that he "acknowledg[es] the compliment paid him . . . and trusts that the future will justify the confidence reposed in him."[32] One of the regiments added was the 18th Illinois Infantry, commanded by Col. Michael Lawler. Lawler had requested this assignment because his men were "personally acquainted with General McClernand and have full confidence in his abilities to command. Most all of the men composing his brigade are our neighbors and kinsmen."[33] Such a request was testimony to McClernand's popularity and the respect accorded him. As with many political generals, however, command over one's constituents posed substantial challenges.

How did officers who had been politicians before the war and had relied upon their popularity for reelection now resolve the conundrum of enforcing discipline among friends and neighbors? The 31st Illinois Volunteer Infantry, commanded by John Logan, was a prime example of this problem. Many of the soldiers in the regiment continued to call Logan "John." The *Jonesboro (Illinois) Gazette* believed the regiment's strength derived from the fact that all except twelve men were Democrats, as was Logan. The newspaper's presumption was that similar political views would cause Logan to "command the entire confidence of his men." After the war he might need their votes. Such arrangements, however, often were sources of friction between professional soldiers and political appointees.[34]

To organize forces for the Union, McClernand and Logan again called upon their oratory and popularity, as they had done when Grant's regiment reenlisted the previous June. Sixty miles north of Cairo another regiment refused to reenlist. The two former politicians traveled to the unit. Displaying the same oratorical prowess that had carried him to national office, McClernand called on the soldiers to "stand by the flag." Logan urged them to "fear not death, but dishonor." All reenlisted, and Lincoln's appointment of favored politicians as generals and colonels bore fruit for the Union cause.[35]

As a brigade commander in the field, McClernand found that his duties differed significantly from those of the commander at Cairo. The secretary of the treasury, Salmon P. Chase, had issued a directive on 3 September that prohibited vessels from carrying goods to or from states in rebellion. To enforce that edict, McClernand dispatched several expeditions down the Mississippi River to seize property that could be used by Confederate forces. As reports of Confederate troops in the vicinity continued to trickle in, he sent troops, accompanied by gunboats, to reconnoiter. One such reconnaissance resulted in a reprimand from the Illinois general to the commander of the 2d Illinois Cavalry for "not infrequently making unauthorized demands upon the inhabitants with threats of violence if not complied with."[36]

Two months of limited combat had provided John McClernand the opportunity to learn the rudiments of his new trade. Administration, reconnaissance, security, discipline, coordination—tasks that were second nature to military professionals—were new to the political professional. As a lawyer and former congressman, McClernand had the advantage of understanding logic and paying attention to detail, order, facts, and deadlines. No school existed, however, to prepare generals appointed to their position directly from civilian life for the responsibilities and duties inherent in martial service.

How, then, were newly appointed officers to learn their trade? In 1835 Gen. Winfield Scott had published *Infantry Tactics Or Rules for the Exercise and Manoeuvres of the United States Infantry*, in three volumes. This work served as the basic tactical manual for officers who served in the Mexican War and continued to be published through 1861. In 1855 William J. Hardee revised the first two volumes of Scott's work and published it as *Rifle and Light Infantry Tactics for the Exercise and Manoeuvres of Troops When Acting as Light Infantry Or Riflemen.* This latter work, known simply as Hardee's *Tactics*, became the primary training manual for the novice officer corps in both Civil War armies. In November 1861 McClernand received twenty-eight copies of the manual for his brigade. Such was the need for the manuals that in 1862 and again in 1864 Congress appropriated funds to purchase "books of tactics and instructions for volunteers."

In 1862 Maj. Gen. Henry Wager Halleck published *Elements of Military Art and Science*, which had a chapter on tactics and an impressive bibliography for those who desired to read more on the military art. Unfortunately, most of the works on the list were in French and German. Another source of information on the military art was the Army Regulations, with which amateur officers had to familiarize themselves. Dr. John Brinton, the surgeon of Grant's command, wrote, "In the evenings I spent a good deal of time in studying up my 'Army Regulations,' which is one of the best things an officer can do." Reading regulations and drill manuals took the volunteer officer only so far. T. W. Higginson wrote in the September 1864 issue of *Atlantic Monthly* that an officer's "best hints were probably obtained by frankly consulting regular officers, even if inferior in rank." The soldier who knew how to transform a mob of eager but raw volunteers into a trained and disciplined organization became a prized commodity.[37]

There is no direct evidence that John McClernand read Scott's, Hardee's, or Halleck's publications, other than the acknowledgment that copies of Hardee's *Tactics* had been received at his headquarters. Still, too many accounts of Civil War participants who admit to their reliance on those manuals have survived to permit the conclusion that this politician was simply lucky or possessed an innate appreciation for military maneuver. No member of his staff had military experience. Therefore, the surmise seems justified that McClernand gained his basic knowledge and understanding of military operations through study of tactical writings.

One trait was coming to the fore that could be detrimental in a hierarchical system like the military: while the general understood the lines of authority from himself to those below him, he failed to grasp the significance of such lines from himself to those over him. This limitation may be explained partially by Frémont's order of 9 September to McClernand, who remained at Cairo, to "keep me minutely informed" of the situation at Paducah. Although Grant had accompanied the expedition, he remained an intermediate link in the chain of command. Grant, though, had muddied the water by twice authorizing subordinates to communicate with Frémont directly.[38] At any rate, McClernand apparently viewed Frémont's order as authority to correspond with him directly on any subject.

McClernand's political power had enabled him to correspond freely with congressmen, governors, and presidents without regard to a chain of command. For success in the Union army, it was imperative that he recognize the primary hierarchy and learn to subordinate himself to those in authority. Politicians, in contrast, retained office based upon electoral victories; constituents had to be pleased, and accomplishments had to be publicized. McClernand's letters to Lincoln and Yates tended to reflect the mind-set of a politician. Unless he could harness his tendency to communicate outside the chain of command and restrain his need for appreciation and approval, his future in the highly structured environment of the military was likely to be short.

All was not drudgery at Cairo. McClernand had his son Edward with him, and Grant used that circumstance as leverage with his own wife, Julia, to get her to allow his son Fred to join him also. (Fred would accompany his father throughout the Vicksburg campaign, and Edward would go on to a distinguished military career.) Richard Oglesby and W. H. L. Wallace, fellow Illinois lawyers and commanders of two of McClernand's regiments, dined with the general, and on 20 October they all attended a review of the 18th Illinois Regiment.[39]

In late October, Illinois representative Elihu B. Washburne inspected the defenses of Cairo. On 31 October the House Select Committee on Government Contracts, of which Washburne was a member, held a hearing in Cairo about the quality of arms being furnished to the soldiers. McClernand and Grant used the opportunity to complain about the lack of weapons. At its conclusion Washburne wrote Chase that Grant was "one of the best officers in the army" and that McClernand was "doing admirably." Following up, upon his return to Washington, Washburne submitted his fellow Illinoisans' complaints directly to the president. Lincoln responded to McClernand that he understood the problems he faced and that the government was doing all it could. "The plain matter of fact is," he wrote, "our good people have rushed to the rescue of the government faster than the government can find arms to put into their hands."[40] McClernand's influence extended only so far.

The week before the hearing, Grant had himself gone to Springfield to plead with Yates for additional arms. He reported to McClernand that his "mission to Springfield was only partially successful. The Governor has neither Artillery nor small arms at present at his disposal." As a result, Grant informed Frémont, the lack of arms and equipment left Union forces unprepared for a forward movement.[41]

A "forward movement" against the enemy was exactly what McClernand craved. "The season is at hand," he had written Frémont in September, "when troops can move south with comfort and safety." He claimed that "an adequate and well equipped army" could defeat the enemy in the region. He offered an analysis of the strategic situation, arguing that the Rebels were vulnerable, in that the massing of "Union armies near Washington and in North Carolina prevent the enemy from massing in front of us."[42] This would not be the only time the novice general presumed to offer advice on the design and conduct of campaigns for the Union army.

Grant's trip to Springfield had been preceded by a short journey to St. Louis to consult with Frémont. Grant notified McClernand that he would command in his absence. In a fawning reply that exaggerated the responsibilities during Grant's three-day absence, McClernand acknowledged "the obligation imposed by the confidence which you are pleased to repose in me. While I cannot expect to equal, or even approximate the merit of your military administration you may rest assured that I will do all in my power to justify your expectations of me and to insure success."[43] Grant, not given to bombast, exaggeration, or excessive praise, was probably bemused by the former politician's purple prose.

During Grant's absence McClernand ordered all soldiers who were performing hospital duties to return to their regiments. Such details absented soldiers from drill, and McClernand, frustrated by the effects, decided to end the practice. His priority was training, and hospital details interfered with training. This created a conflict with the medical director, Dr. John Brinton, a Philadelphia surgeon who would serve with Grant through most of the war. He complained to Grant upon his return, and the district commander canceled McClernand's order. This could have created a great deal of resentment against the doctor, but the general, although annoyed, accepted the order and later magnanimously referred to Brinton as "a real gentleman."

Brinton's proximity both to Grant and McClernand endows his views of the two men with credibility. Writing many years later, he praised Grant's nobility and character. His insights also provided an accurate reflection of John McClernand's character. He described him as "a clever lawyer and shrewd politician," and as "one possessed of a certain amount of influence." McClernand's problem was that he never "exactly comprehended what a real general was . . . nor do I believe he ever eliminated the idea of politician." In Brinton's estimation, McClernand was jealous of Grant, but such an observation, while certainly true later in the war, does not fit the actions of the former Illinois congressman in the fall of 1861.[44]

Grant, too, wanted to move south. On 28 August Frémont had ordered a force to occupy Belmont, Missouri, directly across the river from Columbus, Kentucky. The occupation was completed on 2 September, but on 4 September, in consequence of the Confederate occupation of Columbus, Grant ordered the force withdrawn. Nevertheless, he continued to conduct reconnaissances along the Missouri bank of the Mississippi in anticipation of an eventual offensive down the river. On 16 September Grant ordered another reconnaissance toward Belmont, a move confirmed by Frémont on 28 September.[45] The little village—no more than three buildings and a steamboat landing—was beginning to draw considerable attention.

On 1 November Frémont ordered Grant to prepare for a major offensive. Reports of a sizeable Confederate force about sixty miles west of the Mississippi led to the dispatch of two separate Union contingents in an attempt to trap the Rebels. While this operation was under way, Frémont telegraphed Grant to "make demonstrations" north of Columbus "without, however, attacking the enemy," in order to prevent Confederates there from reinforcing their compatriots in Missouri and Arkansas. Grant promptly notified Brig. Gen. Charles F. Smith at Paducah that he was to march toward Columbus. He also summoned McClernand to meet with him at his headquarters at 10:00 P.M. on 5 November.[46]

Orders from McClernand alerted subordinate commanders, but that was not all that flowed from the Illinois general's pen. Four days earlier Maj. Gen. George Brinton McClellan had been appointed general in chief of the Union armies, succeeding the aged Winfield Scott. Violating the principle of chain of command, McClellan had dispatched a telegram to McClernand asking for information about his force. McClernand immediately promised a "full account of everything important connected with the enemy," adding a request: "Please give me a chance to do something."

His "full account" stretched to fourteen pages plus six enclosures. The missive congratulated McClellan upon his assumption of command, extolled "the brilliant and honorable career of Lieut. Gen. Scott," commented upon the ongoing operation west of the Mississippi, reported the enemy strength in Columbus, and argued the proposition that "thirty-thousand well-armed men, and the river force," could push the Rebels back to Memphis. "But," McClernand added, "the forces here are *not well armed*, nor in any way prepared for an advance movement. With arms, Illinois alone can advance to New Orleans." As it was, the men then preparing for an expedition toward Columbus would not "be armed with weapons which provide any service."[47] He thus added the general in chief to those to whom he had complained about the lack of adequate weapons. McClernand's concerns about equipment may not have been exaggerated. Grant's strength report of 31 October 1861 indicated that the First Brigade had 3,628 enlisted men present for duty; yet, for the upcoming operation McClernand would be able to provide only 1,830.[48]

The former politician's "chance to do something" came not from McClellan but from Grant. On 5 November Grant had six separate columns in motion on both sides of the Mississippi in compliance with Frémont's order. Undoubtedly Frémont's directive and Grant's subsequent movements were the subjects of a meeting that evening. John McClernand must have been ecstatic over the possibility of finally going into action against the Rebel army.

At 4:00 P.M. on 6 November, Grant's First Brigade, under McClernand, and the Second Brigade, commanded by Col. Henry Dougherty, began loading onto transports. That evening the steamers and gunboats tied up along the Kentucky shore in an attempt to deceive Confederates at Columbus as to their true destination. About 2:00 A.M. Grant received word from W. H. L. Wallace that Rebel reinforcements were crossing the river from Columbus to Belmont. This intelligence convinced the district commander to attack Belmont.[49]

In compliance with Frémont's order to "make demonstrations," Grant immediately issued orders to sail at 6:00 A.M., with McClernand's brigade in advance. By 8:30 the force of 3,114 men had disembarked about three and one-half miles north of Belmont. "The early autumnal morning was delightful," Dr. Brinton would recall. Neither Grant nor McClernand had personal knowledge of this area, so intelligence regarding terrain, road networks, and enemy dispositions was critical. The pilot of the *Belle Memphis*, Charles M. Scott, knew the area, as did Capt. Adolph Schwartz of McClernand's staff. The latter had participated in the brief September occupation. Manifesting what was to become a constant trait throughout the war, McClernand accompanied the reconnaissance toward Belmont and observed personally the

Battle of Belmont (7 November 1861)

Union Organization—Brig. Gen. Ulysses S. Grant
McClernand's Brigade, Brig. Gen. John Alexander McClernand

27th Illinois Infantry, Col. Napoleon B. Buford

30th Illinois Infantry, Col. Phillip B. Fouke

31st Illinois Infantry, Col. John A. Logan
Dougherty's Brigade, Col. Henry Dougherty
7th Iowa Infantry, Col. Jacob G. Lauman
22d Illinois Infantry, Lt. Col. Harrison E. Hart
Cavalry
Dollins's Company, Capt. James J. Dollins
Delano's Adams County Company, Lt. James K. Catlin
Artillery
Chicago Light Battery, Capt. Ezra Taylor

Confederate Organization
First Division, Western Department, Maj. Gen. Leonidas Polk
Forces at Belmont, Col. James C. Tappan
Reinforcements, Brig. Gen. Gideon J. Pillow

terrain his brigade would traverse. Upon his return to the main body, he ordered two cavalry companies to "scour the woods along the road to Belmont" and keep him informed of what they found. McClernand ordered his three infantry regiments toward Belmont, with the cavalry in advance.[50]

McClernand's reconnaissance had taken him along the Bird's Point Road to within a mile and a half of the Confederate defenses. There he found a large cornfield, fronted by a bayou with only a few crossings. Facing his first battle as brigade commander, McClernand conferred with Grant, who initially had remained behind with the reserve, and then directed his three regimental commanders to deploy on a line that faced toward the Confederate position. In keeping with standard tactics of the time, McClernand ordered his subordinates to deploy skirmishers in front of the main body. The aim was to develop—to determine the precise location and strength of—the Confederate position. As the brigade line advanced across the bayou and into the thick woods beyond, it became disorganized and misaligned. Disregarding the danger, McClernand rode forward, realigned the regiments, and continued the advance.[51]

About one hundred yards beyond the bayou, Col. Napoleon Buford's 27th Illinois Infantry encountered Confederate cavalry. Realizing that the battle was developing to his right, McClernand immediately ordered Col. Philip Fouke's 30th Illinois to support Buford. The advance continued, but delayed by thick woods, heavy underbrush, and swampy ground, the regiments of the First Brigade were unable to keep their alignment. McClernand, who stayed with the forward troops, personally directed Buford to fall back so that Fouke and the 31st Illinois, under Col. John Logan, could align themselves with the 27th.

Union regiments attempted to march through the thick timber and deep ravines as they had been taught to do back on the parade grounds of Cairo, but they became increasingly disorganized. Occasionally a Rebel bullet or shell found its mark, and the sight of comrades suddenly falling dead further increased the anxiety in the ranks. Finally, the officers abandoned the drill decreed in Hardee's *Tactics* and ordered the men to "take trees and fight Indian fashion." According to one regimental historian, the men's advance became more orderly as "their nerves grew stronger."[52]

Hearing fire persisting on the Union right, McClernand ordered Buford to shift in that direction "to feel the enemy and engage him if found." Although this maneuver had the effect of outflanking the Confederate position, it created a gap in the Union line. Fortunately, the 22d Illinois and 7th Iowa, which had originally been deployed on the Union left, shifted to the right and momentarily filled the gap that Buford had left. These regiments were commendably marching to the sound of the guns, but their final position placed them in the center of the Union line. Logan then occupied the extreme left. Buford's maneuvering put more distance between his regiment and the rest of McClernand's brigade. The resulting situation would have taxed the command ability of even the most seasoned general.

McClernand, the novice soldier, faced a critical juncture. He immediately ordered Logan to extend his line to the left, and he brought up two artillery pieces to reinforce the position. Meanwhile, on the right, Buford had found a road that flanked the entire Confederate position and led directly into the Rebel camp near the river. Within minutes the entire Confederate line was forced back by pressure from the front, the right, and the left.[53]

By later testimony, McClernand had remained in the front ranks, exhorting the 30th and 31st Illinois to victory. As those two regiments reached a small rise that overlooked the Confederate camp, McClernand and the regimental commanders spied the 27th Illinois to their right. The general immediately recognized the favorable position of the Union forces and ordered an attack all along the line. Logan later wrote, "In this charge I saw General McClernand, with hat in hand, leading as gallant a charge as ever was made by any troops unskilled in the arts of war." During this charge McClernand's horse was wounded under him, and his harness was hit by several bullets.[54] The Illinoisan would continue to exhibit such courage and boldness throughout his military career.

Reaching the enemy camp, McClernand quickly ordered an artillery battery to fire on Confederates who had fled north and were regrouping. If left unmolested, those soldiers could have cut off the Union retreat to their transports.[55] As the firing dissipated, Union soldiers "swarmed around the flagpole, cannon and tents like bees around an overturned hive." Above the captured camp the Stars and Stripes was "unfurled in the face of the foe, and defiantly supplant[ed] the mongrel colors." Order evaporated as "officers and soldiers . . . delivered flowery speeches to their comrades who cheered themselves hoarse." With theatrical flair, McClernand himself led the crowd in three cheers for the Union. The celebration continued, as the 22d Illinois band appeared and played "Yankee Doodle," "Dixie," and "The Star-Spangled Banner."[56] One officer would write that "the inspiration of those moments infused me with a willingness to join the angels and march on to glory right then and there." Discipline among the inexperienced bluecoats disintegrated, and men and officers became "demoralized from their victory" and began to "pick up trophies." Grant attempted to stop the plundering but was powerless to do so. McClernand should have recognized the precarious position of his brigade and enforced discipline, but instead he contributed to the disorder. The only means to restore order was to burn the camp. Grant gave the order, and McClernand passed the mandate to his regiments.[57]

While the revelry among the Union troops continued, Leonidas Polk, the Confederate commander at Columbus, ordered the 11th Louisiana and 15th Tennessee to cross the river, absorb the remnants of the Rebel units involved in the battle, and flank the Union army.[58] He hoped to turn defeat into victory, but Grant quickly got his command in motion toward the waiting transports.

Suddenly appreciating the danger to his command, McClernand instructed Capt. Ezra Taylor to direct the fire of his artillery battery toward the gathering Confederates; he then ordered Logan to attack and "cut their way through them." Confederate infantry parted to the left and right as Logan's regiment, leading the breakout, pushed through a sea of gray. Despite "galling fire," McClernand remained mounted as he directed the withdrawal of his brigade. One shot grazed his head, and his horse received another wound.[59]

Despite the efforts of Grant and McClernand, the retreat became a rout when the volunteers—still amateurs—suddenly found themselves running a gauntlet of fire. Observing the scene, McClernand realized that Buford's 27th Illinois was nowhere in sight. He sent his adjutant, Maj. Mason Brayman, to find it, but without success. McClernand himself then twice rode back over the field of battle amid the fire of Union and Confederate alike, but he also failed to locate his missing regiment.[60]

In the confusion Buford had become separated from the main body of the Union army. He had then marched his regiment north until he encountered the bayou and the road along which he had marched and deployed that morning. As he continued toward the steamboat landing, however, he had heard firing and realized that Confederates were between his command and safety. He then again turned north, reaching the river about three miles above where the force had disembarked earlier. In the fading light, Buford and his command saw the Union boats steaming north.[61]

Back at the landing, McClernand realized the gravity of the situation. He alerted Cdr. Henry Walke, who commanded the gunboats, that Rebel soldiers were in pursuit and that the army had to load quickly onto the steamboats. That morning, after the initial disembarkation, Grant had stationed five companies to protect the landing; when the retreating Federals reached it, however, these companies already had boarded the transports rather than protect the arriving troops. James Catlin's cavalry company, though, was about to embark. McClernand acted. He grabbed Catlin and told him to take his men and "watch the enemy." Within minutes the confused masses of McClernand's and Dougherty's brigades burst from the woods and cornfields and rushed toward the transports. Behind them came gray clad soldiers seeking revenge for the defeat of their comrades a few hours earlier. Bullets rattled off smokestacks and passed through deckhouses, but soldiers and sailors, using axes to chop the mooring lines, soon got the boats away from the landing and into the channel. From their decks, however, they could see those who had not made it aboard being marched off into captivity.[62]

What about Buford? He now faced two choices: either march north until he reached Bird's Point—a distance of about twelve miles—or attempt to catch and hail the departing transports. He borrowed a horse from a farmer and sent his adjutant, Lt. Henry A. Rust, in pursuit of the boats. McClernand, meanwhile, had requested Commander Walke's gunboat to search for the missing regiment. Unable to remain inactive, the brigade commander then ordered the captain of the steamer *Chancellor* to land; and along with two staff officers, he disembarked himself to look for the soldiers. Almost immediately they met Rust, and soon the 27th Illinois was aboard the transports and gunboats. By midnight the fleet and army were safely back at Cairo.[63]

At best, the Battle of Belmont could be considered a draw. The Union won the morning round; the Confederacy won the afternoon engagement. Newspapers North and South reported shock at the losses, although the figure of 386 killed and wounded reported by Grant was small in comparison to those of future encounters. Within two days of the battle, both the *Chicago Tribune* and the *St. Louis Missouri Daily Democrat* had called Belmont a defeat. Senator James Harlan of Iowa called for Grant to be relieved of command for having committed an "egregious and unpardonable military blunder." Even Western Department headquarters cast blame on the expedition commander for exceeding the scope of his orders to "make demonstrations . . . without . . . attacking the enemy." "General Grant did not follow his instructions," wrote the assistant adjutant general, McKeever, to Frémont. "No orders were given to attack Belmont or Columbus."[64]

While Grant was being castigated, opinions regarding McClernand's performance were quite different. Illinois papers reported that it was McClernand who had saved the day, Grant having bungled the attack. The *New York Herald* glamorized McClernand's role. A front-page story reported that he set "his boys an example of heroism by plunging headlong into the rebel ranks and making himself a road of blood." Newspaperman Charles Dana reported that "General McClernand led [his] men with conspicuous bravery throughout the action." (By 1863 Dana's opinions of the Illinois general would be radically different.) The *Chicago Evening Journal* wrote that McClernand was "among the bravest of the brave." The former politician no doubt relished such favorable press.[65]

To his father, the evening after the battle, Ulysses Grant wrote a short account of the fight. In it he made a telling assessment of McClernand's performance. McClernand, he wrote, had "acted with great coolness and courage throughout, and proved that he is a soldier as well as statesman." In his first report to Western Department headquarters Grant alluded to his subordinate's prominence in the battle, observing that "Gen. McClernand & myself had a horse shot under us." Commander Walke also attested to that fact in his official report. In his own final report Grant added further praise of the bravery of his subordinate: "General McClernand was in the midst of danger throughout the engagement and displayed both coolness and judgement."[66] Reports of remarkable courage would be the norm during General McClernand's military career.

Not everyone shared this high opinion of McClernand's performance. From Cairo after the battle, Henry Whitney, a former law associate of Lincoln, wrote that Grant "was perfectly imperturbable" and that McClernand, although "a man of great intellect, undaunted courage and aggressiveness, was nervous and fidgety . . . at the scoring . . . in the Northern newspapers." Iowa newspapers, amazingly, accused both Grant and McClernand of cowardice and claimed they had remained apart from the actual fighting.[67]

Grant was stung by criticism of his generalship at Belmont. Yet despite that criticism, he continued to stick by and defend his subordinate. Again he wrote his father, on 29 November: "All who were on the battle field know where Gen. McClernand and my self were and it needs no resort to the Public press for our vindication."[68] It appeared that all was well between the two men from Illinois.

At Grant's headquarters the assistant adjutant general, John Rawlins, made clear his opinion of McClernand: "God damn it," he supposedly yelled, "it's insubordination! McClernand says—. McClernand did—. After his great victory McClernand—. The bastard! The damned, slinking, Judas bastard!"[69] Rawlins's opinion of McClernand never changed. The extent to which it may have influenced Grant can only be surmised.

McClernand wasted no time informing the general in chief, George McClellan, about the "terrible battle." On 8 November he provided a brief report to his fellow Democrat, who was the rising star in the eastern theater. While he acknowledged that "Genl. Grant was in chief command," he made sure that McClellan knew of his own role in the recovery of the forces left behind after the transports departed. He also held a review and published a lengthy congratulatory order that lavished praise on his men for "their gallantry and good conduct" over "a concealed enemy of superior numbers."[70] While such orders can raise morale, extol valor, and celebrate victory, they can also serve to inflate the extent of a triumph or the role of the commander. Often over the next year and a half John McClernand would use bombastic congratulatory messages to ensure that his personal role in battle was acknowledged and that the accomplishments of his command were noted. In June 1863 such an order would have a devastating effect on his future. Aside from McClernand's rhetoric, the true state of his command after Belmont is best stated by Matthew Jansen, a soldier in the 27th Illinois: "We are not yet veterans, only recruits after all."[71]

A letter from Lincoln to McClernand two days after the battle seemed to reinforce the prevailing opinion that McClernand, not Grant, was responsible for whatever Union success had been achieved at Belmont. Lincoln wrote to the brigade commander, not to the expedition commander. "You have had a battle, and without being able to judge as to the precise measure of its value, I think it is safe to say that you, and all with you have done honor to yourselves and the flag and service to the country. Most gratefully do I thank you and them."[72]

McClernand quickly responded to his benefactor. "Accept my grateful acknowledgment for your kind commendation," he wrote. He then took advantage of their rapport to provide the commander in chief advice on conditions in the western theater. Success had been rare because of the lack of a unified command. In a veiled critique of Frémont, he postulated that had such a command existed, rather than the "district and independent commands[,] . . . a combined and simultaneous attack . . . upon Columbus as well as Belmont would probably have resulted in the reduction of both of the latter places."[73]

Although McClernand was buoyed by Lincoln's flattery and the praise from newspapers, his joy was tempered by a personal loss. Capt. Alexander Bielaski, his aide-de-camp, had been killed at Belmont. In his official report the general spoke glowingly of the Polish immigrant, who had once proposed that the Union cavalry be armed with lances in the manner of European horsemen. The day after the battle, McClernand sent a personal note to Bielaski's widow, in which he assured her that her husband had "died as a hero covered with glory." The general would act as kindly throughout the war when those close to him fell in battle.

Mrs. Bielaski wanted to have her husband's body returned, and she asked her pastor, Rev. L. P. Clover, to recover it. There began a running series of accusations in the *Illinois State Journal* as to what the general had or had not allowed. At first McClernand refused to allow Clover to travel to the battlefield because of the confused situation, but he did send a note to General Polk to ask him to look for Bielaski's body. Clover, indignantly, informed the general that the people of Springfield would be displeased with his lack of charity. The general's impolitic reply reflected the confidence that the Union victory had instilled in him: "What has Springfield to do with a military command?" The *Journal* editorialized that Clover might be a secessionist and was not to be trusted. Ironically, Springfield would have much to do with McClernand's military future. The rhetoric notwithstanding, Bielaski's body was recovered, and his funeral was held in Springfield on 12 November.[74]

Back at Cairo, McClernand settled back into the routine of army life. Daily drills and reviews continued. The general had to deal with issues of defective ammunition, bad bread, the costs of improvements to the camp, indiscriminate firing by soldiers in his command, requests for reports of items captured at Belmont, the treatment of the wounded, the need for new barracks to accommodate the 48th Illinois Infantry (due to arrive in camp), the transfer of prisoners of war, and details of guards and pickets.[75] The latter issue would become a theme McClernand raised repeatedly during his military service. In any military organization, duties have to be performed for which adequate manpower is not available. Guard duty and fatigue details are only examples of the endless demands for men with which commanders have to cope. Such duties, however, detract from the effectiveness of unit training, have no value for individual training, and can be destructive to morale. In December 1861 at Cairo, McClernand's brigade was required to furnish about 17 percent of its strength in details, which included loading and unloading supplies from vessels for transshipment to other posts and for the navy. He appealed to Grant for relief. Grant ordered the other posts to furnish men to meet the daily fatigue requirements at Cairo.[76] Such an action by a political appointee to improve conditions in the command raised McClernand's stature in the eyes of his commanders and his men.

Inspections were a fact of life for Civil War soldiers, and the battle-tested general understood the value of such customs. Whether officers paid attention to detail, whether equipment was clean, serviceable, and sufficient, and whether the men knew the requirements of their positions could be determined from an inspection. Not only did the brigade commander inspect the regiments, but also he called upon the regimental commanders to do the same for subordinate units. In December 1861, the chief of artillery of the Department of the Missouri inspected two of McClernand's batteries.[77] Such inspections provided insight into the condition of a command, gave the commander an opportunity to interrogate the soldiers about their conditions, and allowed the men of the brigade to see their commander. These actions by John McClernand and other commanders paid dividends on the battlefield, where a commander's visibility often determined the fate of the struggle.

Inspections were essential, but so, too, were quality weapons. Not until 9 November did Yates notify McClernand that he was sending him the Enfield rifled muskets for one company in each regiment that had been promised in September. This did not satisfy McClernand, who wrote Yates that he was sending Capt. James Dunlap, his quartermaster, to Springfield. He reiterated that he had contracted for four thousand Enfields but needed the governor's authorization for payment. In an approximation of blackmail, he informed Yates that if the state of Illinois would not purchase the weapons, he would "arrange with the men to take it out of their monthly wages." Debate over Belmont was then raging, and the seasoned politician knew how to make the most of the controversy. "Our victory at Belmont would have been more complete if our arms had been effective," he told the governor. Yates had no desire to be blamed for Illinois casualties caused by lack of weapons.[78]

Fouke left Cairo for New York shortly after the battle and on 20 November telegraphed McClernand that he needed authorization to release weapons for shipment. Yates agreed to contract for the Enfields. Unfortunately, approval came too late: the United States government claimed a monopoly over all purchases of Enfields and also the power to determine how they would be distributed. Fouke was able to obtain three hundred cavalry pistols and some carbines along with two field guns, but the problem of infantry weapons remained.[79]

During Washburne's visit to Cairo at the end of October McClernand had given him a memorandum for General Meigs in regard to his need for weapons. The memorandum actually landed at department headquarters, and it engendered a sharp rebuke to McClernand for going out of channels.[80] The general, however, persisted in doing all he could to arm his command.

His efforts began to bear fruit in early December. On 7 December Grant received four thousand rifled muskets. From this store the 18th Illinois in McClernand's brigade received 384. Grant, himself concerned about the lack of modern weapons, informed headquarters that his command still required five thousand more.[81]

Persistence was a characteristic that had both positive and negative influences on McClernand's military career. Once he embraced a cause, he pursued it doggedly, and that proved the case with weapons for his brigade. Telegrams flowed between the general and Fouke in Washington and the arms agent, J. M. Wardwell, in New York. On 4 December, Fouke said that he still had not received Yates's authorization. Wardwell wired McClernand that the secretary of war would authorize shipment only at Yates's request. The agent then telegraphed the Illinois state treasurer, who refused to pay for the guns. Immediately McClernand wired back that the governor would pay. He again sent Dunlap to Springfield on 18 December to plead his case and to enlist the assistance of two influential friends, Judge William Thomas and Jesse K. Dubois, in bringing pressure on Yates. Finally, on 14 January 1862, Fouke wired that four thousand rifled muskets were being shipped to McClernand's men. They were to arrive eleven days later and soon would be put to use.[82]

In November a political problem interrupted McClernand's military duties. The general had incorrectly believed that his acceptance of a commission had terminated his congressional term. His error had left the Sixth District with no representative, for Governor Yates had called no election, because officially the seat was not vacant. Finally, the problem was resolved. McClernand resigned his position in Congress, and Yates called for an election.[83]

On 9 November, while McClernand was continuing his efforts to obtain weapons, a major change took place in the West. Maj. Gen. Henry W. Halleck, known as "Old Brains" to his army colleagues, replaced Frémont. "The Pathfinder" had made political enemies of the Missouri governor and the postmaster general, Montgomery Blair, and had angered Lincoln by issuing his own "emancipation proclamation." When he failed to achieve military success, Lincoln had reassigned him to a command in the Shenandoah Valley. Simultaneously, a new administrative entity, the Department of the Missouri, replaced the old Departments of the West, the Cumberland, and the Ohio. The boundaries embraced Missouri, Iowa, Minnesota, Wisconsin, Illinois, Arkansas, and Kentucky west of the Cumberland River. Lincoln and McClellan were reluctant to extend the limits of the command to the Alleghenies because of the influence of Don Carlos Buell, who continued to command east of the Cumberland. Halleck suspected the reason he was not given a wider command was that Secretary of War Stanton distrusted him. Prior to the war the two had become involved in a legal dispute in California, during which Stanton had suspected Halleck of perjury. Although Halleck was wary of the lingering effects of this encounter, Stanton's biographers, Benjamin Thomas and Harold Hyman, conclude that the secretary did not allow his personal feelings to interfere with his professional judgment. Grant's command was redesignated the District of Cairo.[84]

Halleck had graduated from West Point in 1839. He had subsequently published several works on national defense and on military art and science and had translated Henri Jomini's commentary on the Napoleonic wars. He had resigned from the army in 1854. Then had followed a successful career as a lawyer and businessman. At the outbreak of the Civil War, at Winfield Scott's urging, he had been appointed major general, to rank behind only Scott himself, George McClellan, and John Frémont. In contrast, Grant had entered the Academy the year Halleck had graduated and spent eleven years on active duty, during which he participated in the Mexican War. After his resignation he had failed at numerous business ventures, and at the beginning of the war, he had even difficulty obtaining a commission. By war's end, though, Grant would be Halleck's boss.[85]

In late November Grant and McClernand were agreed that a new department with headquarters at Cairo, independent from that of Halleck, should be established. Grant apparently proposed such a reorganization to Congressman Washburne during his visit to Cairo in late October. Grant believed Cairo well suited for a site from which to launch operations against the Confederacy. Cairo, situated at the terminus of the Illinois Central Railroad and at the confluence of the Ohio and Mississippi Rivers, had been a trading center, and it possessed wharves that could be utilized by the Union navy. The navy controlled the inland waterways, and Grant could use its flotillas to carry his army into Kentucky and Tennessee as well as directly south along the Mississippi River. In his letter to Lincoln on 22 November, McClernand too proposed a separate department comprising "the immediate valley of the Lower Mississippi, including Southern Mississippi and South Western Ky," under "an energetic, enterprising, and judicious commander." There can be little doubt who McClernand had in mind as that commander.[86]

McClernand broadcast the seeds of the idea of a separate department. In a letter to Ohio representative Samuel S. Cox, he broached the notion of "a new military department embracing the immediate valley of the Lower Mississippi." "The people of the Upper Mississippi," he wrote, must be allowed "unshackled navigation of that river to its mouth." He did not propose himself as commander of such a department, but his subsequent actions clearly indicate that he desired to be independent. Although Grant had borne the brunt of the criticism for Belmont, he had shared what little glory came from the affair. McClernand was ambitious. Ambition was best served by sharing glory with no one and being subordinate to no one.

Cox replied that he would argue for a new command on the floor of the House. McClernand did not wait for that event. He also wrote Logan, who had returned to Washington after Belmont, about a new department. On 27 December Logan discussed the concept with Lincoln and afterward wrote his friend that he was "satisfied that he is favorable to establishing a department at Cairo." The president would, of course, first have to consult with General in Chief McClellan.[87]

Again, in early January 1862 McClernand proposed to his fellow Illinois politician a command "more responsive to Illinois needs than a quasi foreign pro consulate"—a reference to Halleck in Missouri. A few days later the congressman replied to the ambitious McClernand, bringing into the open an issue that was to come to control the general's worldview—perhaps to the point of paranoia—for the remainder of his life. Congressman Logan reiterated that he had "on all occasions been pressing the necessity of a separate

Dept at Cairo and at one time thought there was a fair prospect for success, but am fearful that there is too much West Point controlling things here. I shall see Lincoln again to morrow and will again urge our claims. I think if a dept could be established there your promotion would be almost certain as the Prest. is certainly your friend."[88]

Those three points—a separate command, the influence of West Point officers, and Lincoln's friendship—were to shape McClernand's military career.

In January 1862, West Point graduates dominated key staff positions in Washington and commanded many of the military departments throughout the country. McClellan himself was a West Pointer, and four of the five principal staff bureau chiefs were United States Military Academy graduates. In the field, West Point graduates headed the Departments of the Missouri, Ohio, and Pacific, and the Departments of New Mexico and Kansas.

At the outbreak of the war, 638 West Pointers already had regular army commissions, returned to the regular army from civilian life, or accepted commissions in volunteer regiments. Eighty more officers would graduate and join the army during the war. Lincoln's initial call for seventy-five thousand troops, issued 15 April, by itself called for 3,549 officers. With over two thousand regiments eventually formed, Academy graduates would constitute only a small percentage of the Union officer corps. Their influence, though, far outweighed their numbers, as they rose to higher-level commands than their previously untrained counterparts. It was with those trained professionals that McClernand (and other political generals) would encounter difficulties.[89]

Grant's concern was not with command arrangements but with the lack of armaments for his command and the shortage of soldiers to fill the regiments. Well aware of his subordinate's influence with the Illinois governor, he determined to use that relationship to advantage. On 22 November he ordered McClernand to Springfield "for the purpose of laying before the Governor of the State the importance of filling regiments now actually in service, and arming them . . . in prefference [*sic*] to regiments yet to be called out."[90] The former representative was busy using his influence with Senator Orville Browning of Illinois to the same end. Browning saw Yates on 23 November and wrote the general that he had "called his attention to the deficiencies in men in the several regiments of your brigade."[91]

McClernand had to delay his trip a few days, because of Grant's absence from Cairo. On 27 November, however, he met with Fuller, the state adjutant general, and Governor Yates to explain the necessity to fill his brigade, which at that time was at 80 percent strength. He outlined the Confederate threat that faced Illinois soldiers near Cairo, the inability of inadequate Union forces to launch an offensive, the burden of detailing soldiers to assist in providing supplies to nearby posts, and the difficulty of detaching soldiers for recruiting duty. He also raised an issue that was to vex professional soldiers in the Union army for the remainder of the war.

For patronage reasons, governors appointed colonels, who were then entitled to raise regiments, normally from their local areas. When regiments were depleted, rather than fill them, governors appointed new colonels to raise new regiments. Existing regiments had to fill deficiencies by sending recruiters to their hometowns to persuade men to enlist. This practice increased the popularity of wartime governors, but professional soldiers decried such methods, because they failed to take advantage of the experience gained by soldiers in veteran regiments. New recruits and their officers had to relearn the lessons that old soldiers had been taught on bloody battlefields. McClernand pointed out that existing regiments "have gained military experience and comparative expertness," but his logic was not enough to persuade the governor. The problem of understrength regiments would continue to bedevil the Union army.[92]

Lack of men was not an excuse to forego training or halt operations. Grant was to state in his memoirs that after Belmont, "the troops under my command did little except prepare for the long struggle which proved to be before them." McClernand's brigade took part in several limited operations. In November he sent about 1,200 men into pro-Union Crittenden County, Kentucky, as a show of force. An infantry and cavalry force reconnoitered toward Columbus and along the west bank of the Mississippi during November and December. These forces were to seek out Confederate forces and to break up illicit trade being carried on along the river. He sent one cavalry detachment to the old Belmont battlefield, because of a rumor that Confederates had emplaced heavy artillery there. The troopers found nothing.[93]

While at Cairo, McClernand maintained close links with constituents and fellow politicians. He wrote a personal note to Mrs. W. H. M. Osborn, to thank her for the articles sent to the sick and wounded after Belmont. From Mr. N. W. Mince, who was taking care of his affairs in Springfield, he learned that his house was being well taken care of. Mince congratulated him upon the recent victory but urged him "not [to] expose [himself] to the murderous fire of the enemy again." In the mistaken belief that he still held a seat in Congress, William Barnes of Jacksonville and Wallace Stockdale of Springfield requested appointments to the Naval Academy. Senator Lyman Trumbull asked McClernand to provide a letter of recommendation for his son Walter to the Naval Academy.[94]

On 17 December, McClernand began a correspondence with the commander of the newly created Department of the Missouri, Henry W. Halleck. His first letter chronicled his history since being appointed brigadier general, informed Halleck of the strength of his command, listed his duties, alluded to the detrimental effects of too many fatigue details, and urged that the brigade's requisitions for arms be filled. Two days later the persevering general sent a similar letter to Brig. Gen. Samuel Sturgis at Halleck's headquarters. A disappointing Christmas Eve reply stated that Halleck had no arms to give.[95]

Although he was concerned primarily with the military situation, events of a political nature did not escape McClernand's notice. He was particularly attuned to how the political winds were blowing in southern Illinois. After all, political acuity and the respect he enjoyed among southern Illinois Democrats were prime reasons why Lincoln had given him a brigadier's commission. In early December he discussed with Logan and Fouke, both of whom had been congressmen prior to the war, the possibility of resuming their seats. The rationale for his proposal that Fouke and Logan return to Congress was, he apprised Lincoln, the political situation in Illinois. "There are two factions," he wrote, "one consisting of Ultra discontented Republicans, and the other of *quasi*-Secessionists being apostate democrats, who if the war should continue eighteen months will unite in common measures of opposition to the war policies of the Government." In the general's view, Fouke and Logan were "true Union men" who would "cooperate with the Union men in [Congress], in support of a vigorous prosecution of the war." This letter made clear the stand that McClernand had taken before the outbreak of hostilities on the purpose of the war. He told Lincoln that the "Ultra discontented Republicans" sought "to substitute a new issue for the war, viz. the abolition of slavery." To him the purpose of the war in December was the same one he had spoken of in January—not "the abolition of slavery" but suppression of the rebellion. A few days later he received from Lincoln's secretary, John Hay, authority for the two to return to Congress. Although both were Democrats, they had become strong supporters of the president's war efforts. Fouke was to return to Washington and resign his commission in April 1862. Logan chose to remain with the army; he resigned his congressional seat in April, and by war's end he would be one of the most respected combat commanders in the Union army.[96]

In a letter to Congressman Cox, McClernand expressed the same views. He decried those who were "blind to the real condition of things," who "prate about Compromise and peace." "The real issue," he declared, "was submission to rebellion or the repression of it." "Make a great speech in favor of a vigorous prosecution of the war," he urged, and "remember me in such ways as your friendship and good judgement shall dictate."[97] Perhaps, he hoped, Logan, Fouke, and Cox could stave off any attempt to expand the war's objectives.

In all, John McClernand had to be pleased about accomplishments during the year. He had completed the transition from congressman to general. He had "seen the elephant" at Belmont, and he had done well. The benefits of personal reconnaissance, visibility to the troops, concern for his men; the qualities of decisiveness, boldness, courage; the difficulties of managing a command, of equipping regiments, of enforcing discipline—these were the necessities of military service to which he had been exposed. He had learned much, but he had not acquired self-discipline. His habit of corresponding outside the chain of command had, if anything, intensified. He had exhibited emotional bombast when he should have been restrained. Nevertheless, his political influence remained and, perhaps as a result of military victory, had even grown with congressmen and President Lincoln alike. Lincoln himself had written directly to the brigade commander and complimented his performance. Newspapers and constituents were favorable. "I am told you do all the work, the headwork for the department there," his admirer Henry Quigley wrote from Springfield. Not everyone shared that rosy view. Mary Logan, wife of John Logan, wrote her husband that he would never receive the "merited credit" he deserved. McClernand, she wrote, was a "man of so little hard sense and so aristocratic and over bearing and [is] suspicious of you. He will never do you justice."[98] It had been a good year for John McClernand, if not for the nation, but 1861 had planted not only the seeds of future military success but also those of professional disaster.

3
Penetrating the Confederacy

Confederate strategy in the West in January 1862 was defensive. President Jefferson Davis believed that above all he had to hold on to the territory of the Confederacy, for loss of territory might endanger the chance of receiving foreign recognition. His commander in the theater, Gen. Albert Sidney Johnston, faced the difficulty of holding a line that ran, in the east, from the Cumberland Gap near the juncture of the Virginia, Kentucky, and Tennessee borders; through Bowling Green, Kentucky, which protected approaches to Nashville; to a western anchor on the Mississippi River at Columbus, Kentucky. Intersecting this defensive line were the Tennessee River, which ran south from Paducah through Kentucky and Tennessee into Alabama, and the Cumberland River, which connected the Ohio River to Nashville.[1]

The geography of the region between the Appalachian Mountains and the Mississippi River was ideally suited to the principle of unity of command, under which all military forces are commanded by one individual. The Appalachian Mountains formed a natural boundary between forces in the eastern theater and those in the western theater. The Mississippi River formed another natural barrier, which would channelize operations west of the Appalachians. For the South, the individual in command west of the Appalachians was Johnston. For the North, however, there was no similar arrangement. The order that had established Halleck's Department of the Missouri had also created the Department of the Ohio, under Brig. Gen. Don Carlos Buell. The effect of this departmental structure was to make Halleck and Buell coequal commanders, whose departments were separated by the Cumberland River. Directives for coordinated operations against Johnston would thus have to emanate from Washington.[2]

A cursory glance at a map of the western theater reveals the strategic importance of the two rivers that bisect the region. In September, Brig. Gen. Charles F. Smith, who had been the commandant of cadets at West Point when Grant was a cadet and thereafter one of Grant's subordinates, pointed out to Brig. Gen. Lew Wallace, later author of *Ben Hur*, the importance of the Tennessee and Cumberland: "These are lines leading into the heart of the seceding states." In November the chief engineer of the Department of the Ohio, who also recognized the importance of the waterways, wrote Halleck calling for a "great movement by land and water, up the Cumberland and Tennessee Rivers."[3]

Lincoln had a different idea. Concerned about protecting loyal citizens of eastern Tennessee, he wanted Buell to launch an operation into that region of the state. The departmental commander disagreed. On 27 November, Buell proposed to the general in chief, McClellan, a plan to move toward Knoxville in the east, in compliance with Lincoln's desires, but also to send a column toward Nashville and a naval force up the Tennessee and Cumberland. His plan called for Halleck to demonstrate against Columbus. Two weeks later he proposed that any operation in eastern Tennessee be scrapped and that all forces move up the two rivers. McClellan then ordered Halleck to cooperate with Buell, to send an expedition up the Cumberland, and to demonstrate against Columbus to prevent that garrison from reinforcing the Confederates in eastern Tennessee.[4]

Buell and Halleck grasped the strategic advantages of using the two rivers to attack into the Confederate heartland, but Halleck was ambivalent. In a meeting with Brig. Gen. William T. Sherman and Brig. Gen. George W. Cullum, Halleck laid a map on the table and asked:

> "Where is the rebel line?" Cullum drew the pencil through Bowling Green, Forts Donelson and Henry [on the Cumberland and Tennessee rivers, respectively], and Columbus, Kentucky. "That is their line," said Halleck. "Now, where is the proper place to break it?" And either Cullum or [Sherman] said, "Naturally the centre." Halleck drew a line perpendicular to the other, near its middle and it coincided nearly with the general course of the Tennessee River; and he said, "That's the true line of operations."[5]

Despite his appreciation of that line, Halleck believed he was too committed in Missouri to attempt an operation into Tennessee. More fundamentally, though, the proposed operation conflicted with his understanding of Baron Antoine Henri Jomini's principles of warfare. In letters to Buell and Lincoln on 6 January 1862, Halleck expressed grave reservations about the prospective advance: "To operate on exterior lines against an enemy occupying a central position will fail, as it always has failed, in ninety-nine cases out of a hundred. It is condemned by every military authority I have ever read."[6] By 20 January, however, he had reconciled some of his objections. He informed McClellan that an offensive up the Cumberland and Tennessee was a "feasible plan" but warned that an advance by Buell should not be attempted simultaneously.[7]

Grant recognized the necessity to control the twin rivers and the advantages of an offensive. In mid-January he met with Halleck to discuss such a campaign. It is possible that he and McClernand had discussed that concept, as well as the creation of a department at Cairo, as early as November. In a letter to Congressman Washburne, Grant wrote of a "plan proposed by Gen. McClernand and myself."[8]

Although no record of their "plan" has survived, subsequent events suggest that an operation into Tennessee that utilized the rivers may have been the design. McClernand had frequently written of an advance down the Mississippi and of a strong attack against Columbus. Throughout his military career he envisioned operations using the main rivers in the western theater as axes of advance into the Confederate heartland. At this point in the war, he and Grant were both located at Cairo, and there was little sign of the tensions that eventually would darken their relationship. It is conceivable that the two Illinois generals discussed a future offensive using the strategically important waterways in Kentucky and Tennessee and that such an operation was the "plan" to which Grant referred.

Before any plan could be implemented, McClernand had to complete the organization of his brigade. In early January 1862 that still had not been done; one cavalry and one artillery company remained to be filled. The general complained to Lincoln, questioning whether his authority had been revoked, and grumbled that he was forced to compete for recruits with other units. Lincoln surely must have found these issues trivial in comparison with other matters he faced. McClernand had authorization to organize his command, and he could have dispatched his own recruiting officers. To fill his brigade required his own initiative, not that of the president of the United States.[9]

Problems regarding the organization of his brigade were suddenly cast aside on 8 January, when McClernand received an order from Grant to be prepared to move to Fort Jefferson and Elliott's Mill, Kentucky. Halleck, under pressure from Washington, had authorized Grant to demonstrate toward Columbus "to prevent reinforcements from being sent to [Brig. Gen. Simon Bolivar] Buckner," the Confederate commander at Bowling Green.[10]

With action imminent, the brigade commander wasted no time in issuing the necessary orders for the regiments at Cairo to prepare to march. Direc-

Forts Henry and Donelson Campaigns, February 1862

Union Organization

District of Cairo, Brig. Gen. Ulysses S. Grant

First Division, Brig. Gen. John Alexander McClernand

First Brigade, Col. Richard J. Oglesby

Second Brigade, Col. W. H. L. Wallace

Third Brigade, Cols. William B. Morrison (wounded) and Leonard F. Ross (effective 10 Feb.)

Second Division, Brig. Gen. Charles F. Smith

First Brigade, Col. John McArthur

Second Brigade, Brig. Gen. Lew Wallace (effective 14 Feb.)

Third Brigade, Col. John Cook

Fourth Brigade, Col. Jacob G. Lauman (effective 10 Feb.)

Fifth Brigade, Col. Morgan L. Smith

Third Division, Brig. Gen. Lew Wallace *(effective 14 Feb.)*

First Brigade, Col. Charles Cruft

Second Brigade (attached to Third Brigade)

Third Brigade, Col. John M. Thayer

Confederate Organization

Fort Henry, Brig. Gen. Lloyd Tilghman

Heiman's Brigade, Col. Adolphus Heiman

Drake's Brigade, Col. Joseph Drake

Fort Donelson, Brig. Gens. John B. Floyd and Gideon J. Pillow (second in command)

Pillow's Division, Brig. Gen. Bushrod R. Johnson

Buckner's Division, Brig. Gen. Simon B. Buckner

Forrest's Cavalry Brigade, Col. Nathan B. Forrest

---

tives went out establishing embarkation times and locations and which boats to load. To ensure commanders were accountable, McClernand ordered them to report to him their state of readiness. That the soldiers and the officers had served for only a few months and were still undisciplined was evidenced by the many blankets and overcoats left in encampments rather than carried on the soldiers' backs. The men would soon regret such shortsightedness in the bleak January weather.[11]

Belmont had taught Grant and McClernand a lesson in regard to control of the river—the Confederates had been able to move reinforcements across the Mississippi unhampered by Union gunboats. That movement had brought recognition of the potential disaster awaiting transports without gunboat protection. Consequently, McClernand wisely requested that Grant provide gunboat escort for the steamers conveying Union soldiers. Grant replied that he had already done so.[12]

On 10 January, McClernand's regiments arrived at Fort Jefferson. Prudently, he had directed his cavalry to move there first, in the event Confederates were nearby, and then to establish pickets on the roads to Columbus to prevent the main command from being surprised. Security of the force was his foremost concern, and he ordered commanders to ensure guards were posted and awake, that noise discipline was enforced, and that no one left camp. The seriousness with which the brigade commander viewed violations of such provisions was made evident to all when he added to the order: "These offenses are so dishonoring to the army . . . and sacredness of the Cause in which the volunteers of Illinois are engaged . . . that the law will be enforced and offenders shot."[13]

Aboard the transport *Emerald* was Dr. Brinton, who had earlier had the sharp disagreement with McClernand. That the general bore no grudge against him was evident. Because Brinton was in great discomfort from boils, McClernand magnanimously allowed him to remain on board rather than go ashore with the troops. As he departed, he told the boat's captain: "Take good care of my doctor." Brinton later wrote that he "was very much touched by his consideration."[14]

McClernand provided Grant a report of his actions the following morning. In it he made a most interesting request for "a full supply of engineering and intrenching implements," to include axes, shovels, and spades.[15]

West Point graduates since 1830 had been lectured by Dennis Hart Mahan on the principles of Jomini and the merits of field fortifications. In 1836 Mahan had published *A Complete Treatise on Field Fortifications*, which became the textbook for cadets on the subject. The text asserted that entrenchments would enable volunteer militia to defend a position as well as regular soldiers. Subsequent editions appeared in 1846, 1852, 1860, and 1862. In his *Elements of Military Art and Science*, Halleck, West Point class of 1839, showed himself to be a strong supporter of field fortifications.[16] But McClernand was not a West Point graduate. His only combat experience with field fortifications had been at Belmont, where the Confederate camp had been surrounded by abatis, which had obstructed the Federal advance, but no entrenchments. Nevertheless, clearly he recognized their value, for he had urged Marsh in September to entice Confederates to attack him in his entrenchments.

One of the regimental commanders who accompanied him on the march was a West Point graduate. Napoleon Buford, class of 1827, had been a cadet prior to Mahan's tenure, and thus he had been exposed to Gay de Vernon's *Treatise on War and Fortification*, which had been the U.S. Military Academy textbook on fortifications until 1830. De Vernon advocated field fortifications when conducting both offensive and defensive operations. He also strongly favored field fortifications for encampments.

Three other regimental commanders had fought in Mexico during the Mexican War. Although neither the Americans nor the Mexicans had employed field fortifications extensively in Mexico, American soldiers had faced them at Monterrey, Churubusco, and Chapultepec. The casualties sustained had given the Americans an appreciation for their potential effectiveness.

In addition to those four officers who had some experience, either academic or practical, with field fortifications, McClernand was accompanied by an engineer, Lt. Henry C. Freeman. The presence of these officers and McClernand's lack of formal military education and his minimal combat experience make it highly likely that they had influenced him to request entrenching tools. If so, their influence indicates the general's willingness to accept advice in areas where he recognized his shortcomings. Whether he would continue to heed their advice remained to be seen.[17]

For the next three days, cavalrymen of the First Brigade reconnoitered south toward Elliott's Mill and west toward Blandville. On 12 January a cavalry detachment moved to within two miles of Columbus. McClernand ensured that Grant was fully informed of his movements.[18]

Again, the Illinois general displayed his recognition of the need for army-navy cooperation. On 11 January, McClernand communicated with Cdr. William D. Porter to alert him that he had learned Confederate vessels were moving north along the Mississippi. The intelligence report was accurate, and Porter had a running fight with several steamers that afternoon. The next day, McClernand requested Porter to fire a few shots into the Confederate positions near Columbus to distract them from his own movements.[19] The experience he was gaining in joint operations would be of immense benefit the following year.

Supply problems worried McClernand throughout the operation. Grant had directed his subordinate to take five days' rations, but transportation shortages and poor road conditions, which Grant characterized as "intolerable," had made him unable to do so. The result was that many in the command were "absolutely destitute of provisions." To solve the problem McClernand either confiscated livestock from Rebel sympathizers or purchased supplies from loyal citizens.[20] At this early stage of the war, McClernand and his men were learning how to live off the land. It was a practice that would become far more prevalent as the war continued.

Halleck's order to Grant for the operation had specified that in order to prevent Confederate reinforcements from being sent eastward, "he was to make a great fuss about moving all [his] forces" and to "give [his] men a little experience in skirmishing." Grant and McClernand had met the evening of 8 January, and Grant had undoubtedly explained what he wanted his brigade commander to accomplish. As he moved southeast toward the Cumberland River from Fort Jefferson, McClernand allowed his cavalry to probe toward Columbus, while he marched the main body first south to Blandville, then southwest to Milburn, and finally north to Lovelaceville. Throughout the operation he took great pains to ensure that his column was protected from surprise attack by the Confederates at Columbus.[21]

On 18 January Grant wrote his subordinate commander that "the object of the expedition [has] been accomplished," and by 21 January the First Brigade was back at Cairo. As during the Belmont expedition, McClernand had been able to practice his craft under field conditions. He had absorbed new lessons regarding leadership, logistics, security, deception, maneuver, the effects of weather, and army-navy coordination and cooperation. But Halleck had forbidden Grant to bring on a general engagement, and that meant no opportunity for McClernand to make favorable headlines. The campaign did make the newspapers, but editors were not unanimous in their views of it or of the former politician. The *New York Times* characterized the operation as "an immense humbug," asserting that McClernand's column had returned "without having accomplished a single thing of importance." Its rival *New York Herald*, however, reported more favorably that "the most active part taken in this grand reconnaissance was done under the command of General McClernand."[22] The general would soon ensure that its true results were known.

After his return to Cairo, Grant left for St. Louis to present his plan to capture Fort Henry on the Tennessee River. The district commander placed McClernand in charge during his absence. It was a golden opportunity, and the general wasted no time. "Being in temporary command" of the district, it was his "duty to submit" a report of the expedition to Halleck, even though Grant was then meeting with the department commander. The report alluded to Grant only three times, while it covered in minute detail the actions of McClernand and his command. He closed by recommending "a renewed advance of our forces," either to attack Columbus or to occupy the region between that town and the Tennessee River. He presumptuously signed the report "John A. McClernand, Brigadier-General, Commanding District of Cairo."[23]

Unbeknownst to McClernand, Grant and his plan had been unceremoniously dismissed by Halleck. To have received then such advice from a novice political general could have done little to improve Halleck's opinions of such officers in general or John McClernand in particular. Halleck, thenceforth, never viewed the Illinois general with anything other than disdain.[24]

Four days later, McClernand wrote an account of his exploits to Lincoln. It was more than a narrative, however: he implored the president to give him twenty-five thousand men to take Columbus. "Our men are disappointed in not being allowed to march upon Columbus," and the moral effect was discouraging. This was a direct attack upon Halleck's generalship, but he did not stop there. "I am tired of delays and inaction," he declared. "We should fight and push forward, and push forward and fight again." He concluded, "I feel an assurance that you sympathize with these views."[25]

Indeed, Lincoln did sympathize with McClernand's views. For months he had been urging McClellan, Halleck, and Buell to advance. Finally, exasperated by the lack of compliance, the president issued on 27 January "President's General War Order Number One," which called for a "general movement of the land and naval forces" on 22 February 1862.[26]

Preparations for a general movement in the West were under way. While McClernand was demonstrating east of Columbus, Charles F. Smith had marched a force to Calloway on the Tennessee River, from where he had boarded a gunboat to examine Fort Henry farther up river. He reported to Grant that "two iron-clad gunboats could make short work" of the fort. He also noted that Fort Donelson was only twelve miles distant, on the Cumberland River.[27]

President Jefferson Davis realized that the Tennessee and Cumberland Rivers had to be defended to prevent their use by the Union army and navy as an unimpeded avenue of approach into the heart of the Confederacy. The ideal location for forts to block the river would have been in Kentucky south of Paducah, where the two rivers were only three miles apart; the two forts and their garrisons would thus be within supporting distance of one another. Kentucky, however, in early 1861 had been neutral, and Davis had been loath to take any action to jeopardize that status. Consequently, Confederate engineers had looked in Tennessee for favorable locations to construct the needed forts.

Mr. Adna Anderson, a prominent civil engineer, had first surveyed the terrain along the Cumberland near Dover, Tennessee, in May 1861. He had selected a site on a hill that rose seventy-five to a hundred feet above the river at a bend, where guns could be located to fire directly on boats that attempted to pass the fort. The fort would be named Donelson, after Brig. Gen. Daniel S. Donelson, a West Point graduate and speaker of the Tennessee House of Representatives at the outbreak of the war.[28]

Anderson had moved west to the Tennessee, surveyed its shore, and found a site for the second fort. At this point, Gov. Isham Harris intervened. He replaced Anderson with Maj. Bushrod Johnson, a West Point graduate, whom he named state engineer. Johnson ignored Anderson's findings and positioned the fort at a bend in the river. Anderson had done the same on the Cumberland, but Johnson had unfortunately failed to consider the effect that a rise in the river might have. The fortification would be called Fort Henry, in honor of Tennessee senator Gustavus A. Henry.[29]

Work on the two forts progressed slowly during the summer of 1861, but it sped up considerably when in September Union gunboats ascended the Tennessee to within thirty miles of Fort Henry.[30] In mid-November Gen. Albert Sidney Johnston, commander of the Confederate Western Department, ordered Brig. Gen. Lloyd Tilghman to command the forces at Henry and Donelson. After he inspected the area, Tilghman recommended to Johnston that another fort be constructed on the high ground along the west bank of the Tennessee. Such a work would command the river and Fort Henry. Construction on Fort Heiman, named for Col. Adolphus Heiman, a Prussian member of the 10th Tennessee Infantry Regiment, began.[31]

The tenacity for which Grant would become known later in the war was evident even at this early point. On 28 January, after having been rebuffed in St. Louis, he again sought Halleck's approval for an operation against Fort Henry. Flag Officer Andrew H. Foote, who commanded the gunboats near Cairo and whom Grant "consulted freely upon military matters," wired Halleck that he and Grant were "of the opinion that Fort Henry . . . can be carried with four iron-clad gunboats and troops." The next day Grant sent another message to the department commander requesting permission to attack Fort Henry.[32]

Finally, on 30 January Halleck telegraphed Grant, "Make your preparations to take and hold Fort Henry." He followed up the telegram with written instructions to take the fort and cut rail communications in the vicinity. What had induced him to change his mind was a telegram from McClellan the previous day informing him that Confederates appeared to be shifting fifteen regiments from northern Virginia to Kentucky.[33]

McClernand, meanwhile, was occupied with mundane matters. The mail had brought news that his city and county taxes were due immediately, that the roof of his house in Springfield had a leak, and that the plaster, carpet, and piano were in danger of being ruined by the rain. He also received a letter

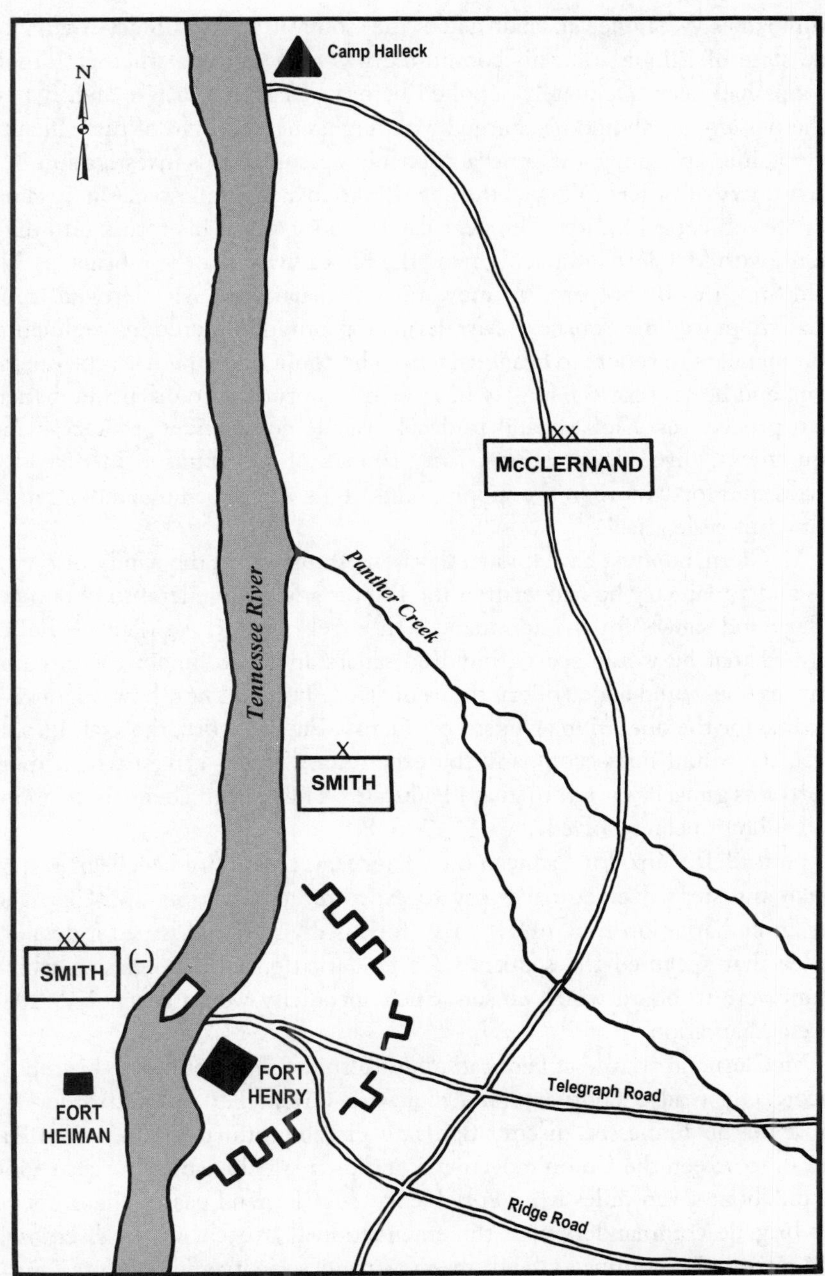

Vicinity of Forts Henry and Heiman, February 6, 1862

from James W. Singleton, chairman of the Committee on Military Affairs for the state of Illinois, that his committee was to determine whether Illinois troops had been adequately supplied before being sent to war and, if not, whether anyone should be charged with negligence. In light of his difficulty in obtaining weapons, the general probably welcomed this investigation.[34]

A flurry of orders followed the decision to invade Tennessee. On 31 January Grant alerted Smith. The next day he reorganized his forces into divisions, with McClernand to command the First Division, of two brigades. He told Smith to be prepared to move on 3 February and McClernand to be ready to move on 2 February. McClernand promptly ordered his regimental commanders to report to headquarters so he could brief them on the operation, and he sent for the master of river transportation to discuss embarkation procedures. McClernand told his brigade commanders to take camp equipment, three days' rations, forty rounds of ammunition in cartridge boxes, and forty more in the supply trains. This was to be no demonstration but a full-scale attack.[35]

McClernand must have known that something was in the wind, for on 27, 28, and 30 January he had written the Illinois adjutant general to obtain artillery and sabers for his command. On 2 February, Col. Allan C. Fuller replied that he would send a hundred sabers and that "under the circumstances" he would add artillery to his division. It would not, however, arrive in time for the operation against Fort Henry. Furthermore, the 55th Illinois Infantry would not accompany the expedition; "being armed with almost worthless guns, it was left to guard Paducah." The issue of adequate weapons had still not been resolved.[36]

Grant left Cairo for Paducah on 2 February, having told McClernand to "take any steps deemed necessary to expedite embarkation." McClernand set an embarkation time of 2:00 p.m. for his division and issued a detailed order that specified the sequence for embarkation and designated which units were to board which vessels. Such specificity would certainly "expedite embarkation."[37]

McClernand arrived at Paducah mid-afternoon on 3 February (his report incorrectly read 2 February) and met with Grant. He received orders to move up the Tennessee, disembark his cavalry about thirteen miles from Paducah to screen the Union movement, and then land his entire force at Pine Bluff, about seven miles from Fort Henry. McClernand passed the order to his brigade commanders with the emendation that each was to disembark and dispose his command "with the view to its security and comfort." Supplementary orders were issued to establish picket lines to prevent surprise and to protect the artillery batteries.[38]

With a "hurricane of cheers long continued and the rivalry of bands playing," the expedition left Paducah the night of 3 February. Grant, demonstrating full confidence in his subordinate's ability, did not accompany the force but remained behind to supervise the embarkation of the remainder of his army.[39]

At 4:30 A.M. on 4 February, McClernand disembarked his command at Itra Landing on the Tennessee shore about eight miles north of Fort Henry, sent out cavalry patrols—one of which he accompanied—and issued detailed orders for the encampment of his brigades. He properly directed that artillery be emplaced to maximize fields of fire; that guards be established; that baggage trains be positioned so as not to interfere with road movement or tactical deployment; and, most significantly, that infantry camps be located to facilitate "immediate formation into line of battle . . . fronting the enemy." This last directive indicated McClernand's awareness of the need to be alert constantly for enemy activity and to be prepared for battle.[40]

Grant decided to establish his lodgment closer to Fort Henry, preferably south of the swollen Panther Creek to eliminate the difficulty of crossing that obstacle. A reconnaissance, however, revealed that such an encampment would be subject to artillery fire from the fort. He therefore directed that McClernand reembark his division and move to Bailey's Ferry, just north of Panther Creek. McClernand issued the necessary orders. The soldiers reembarked and then disembarked at the new location four miles north of the fort. Immediately he sent his cavalry to reconnoiter the countryside and moved his infantry to occupy the commanding bluffs inland from the river. The general christened the new encampment "Camp Halleck."[41]

McClernand made a personal reconnaissance of the terrain to his front, with an eye toward an expected movement to invest the fort; he realized that he had to control the road where it crossed Panther Creek. A small Confederate force at that point could severely disrupt a Union advance. Prudently, he ordered an artillery battery and two infantry regiments to protect the crossing site.[42]

The division commander spent the next day reconnoitering the terrain between his encampment and the fort as well as the fort itself. He reported to Grant that enemy steamers had been observed arriving at the fort with reinforcements. He suggested that Grant send gunboats south of the fort to sink the transports and prevent more soldiers from landing.[43]

Grant arrived that evening and met with McClernand, Brig. Gen. Charles F. Smith, who commanded the Second Division, and Flag Officer Foote on board *Cincinnati.* Lt. Comdr. S. Ledyard Phelps, captain of the gunboat *Conestoga*, came aboard with a Confederate torpedo that he had lifted from the river. The officers gathered around to observe while the boat's armorer unscrewed the cap. As the cap loosened, a "loud sizzling noise" erupted. McClernand and Smith threw themselves to the boat's deck, while Foote and Grant ran for the boat's ladder. The sailors who witnessed this event roared with laughter, for the noise had been only the gases generated by the wet powder in the torpedo. Once the senior commanders of the expedition had composed themselves, they all had a "hearty laugh" over the incident.[44]

At the meeting's conclusion, Grant issued a complete operations order. McClernand was to have his First Division occupy a blocking position between Fort Henry and Fort Donelson to prevent the former garrison from escaping and the latter from reinforcing. It was then to prepare to assault Fort Henry. Two brigades from Brigadier General Smith's division were to attack Fort Heiman, on the west bank of the river. His Third Brigade was to march due south against Fort Henry in support of the First Division. The operation was to begin at 11:00 A.M., 6 February. Foote was to bombard Fort Henry from the river.[45]

McClernand promptly notified his subordinate commanders of the upcoming operation. He then ordered his brigades to fill their haversacks with two days' rations and to reconnoiter the ground between the two forts. Two orders, one designating the order of march and a second providing McClernand's concept for the operation, followed. Neither order, however, specified how the brigades were to arrange themselves astride the road between the two forts or what would be the signal for the attack. The novice general had not yet learned the necessity of putting such details in writing.[46]

Grant's order had contained a phrase that struck a nerve with his First Division commander. Grant had directed McClernand to "move at 11 O'Clock, A.M. to morrow under the guidance of Lieut. Col. McPherson." James McPherson was a West Point officer who would rise to the rank of major general and command of the Army of the Tennessee before being killed near Atlanta. Perhaps because he was suspicious of West Pointers or because McPherson was only a lieutenant colonel, McClernand sent a note back to Grant to clarify that portion of his order: "Of course, the words 'guidance of Lt. Col. McPherson' were not intended to interfere with my authority as commander."[47] Grant probably had no such intention, for his order had implied merely that McPherson was to guide McClernand to the road between Henry and Donelson. The suspicious politician, however, wanted to ensure that his command prerogatives were not usurped. This would not be the last instance when conflict arose between McClernand and McPherson.

Brig. Gen. Lloyd Tilghman quickly realized that his position at Fort Heiman was untenable. Without heavy artillery, the fort was useless against the Union fleet. With Smith's brigades bearing down on them, the garrison would be lost unless evacuated. Consequently, during the evening of 4 February, Tilghman ordered the garrison to abandon the fort and join the command at Fort Henry.[48]

Heavy rains overnight made life miserable for Union and Confederate soldier alike. Fort Henry's poor siting became readily apparent, as the rising Tennessee River began to fill the enclosure. Tilghman assessed his situation and at mid-morning decided the only prudent course was to abandon Henry also and consolidate his forces at Fort Donelson, twelve miles to the east.[49]

At 10:50 A.M. Foote's gunboats got under way toward Fort Henry. Ten minutes later McClernand's infantry began to slog through the mud toward the Rebel position. Neither the division commander nor his superior had taken into account the effect of rain and mud on the rate of march. According to Col. John Logan, the road was "reduced to the consistency of soft porridge of almost immeasurable depth." Consequently, by 12:30 P.M., when Foote opened his bombardment of the fort, McClernand had covered only about four of the eight miles toward his blocking position.[50]

At 2:00 P.M. Tilghman hauled down the Confederate flag and surrendered the fort and eighty-four men to Foote. Grant arrived an hour later. Not until about 2:30 P.M. did McClernand's division reach its assigned position, too late to prevent the escape of almost 2,500 Confederates. Although his 4th Illinois Cavalry exchanged volleys with the Rebel rear guard and brought away thirty-eight more prisoners, McClernand had failed to prevent the escape of the Rebel garrison. Newspaper reporter Dana wrote that McClernand's delay had been "unavoidably caused by the high water, bad roads, and difficult character of the country." He would not so generously absolve the Illinois Democrat of blame in future reports. Nevertheless, the professional Grant and the politician McClernand had much to learn about the effect of weather on military operations.[51]

Grant ordered McClernand to establish defensive positions around the fallen fort, and then he telegraphed Halleck: "Fort Henry is ours. I shall take and destroy Fort Donelson on the 8th."[52] He did not in fact begin such a movement for several days, but the message to Halleck indicated that Grant intended to exploit his victory and give the enemy no time to react.

As after Belmont, McClernand wasted no time informing Grant, Governor Yates, and even Lincoln of his command's role in the victory. Failing to account for the delay caused by the rain, he wrote Grant that his "rapid advance" and the Confederate "apprehension of being cut off from retreat" had been as responsible for the surrender as had been the bombardment from the gunboats. He did acknowledge that he had been unable to block the enemy's retreat. He boasted, though, that his division "was the first of the land forces to enter the fort"—in fact, an inconsequential feat.[53]

Yates received a letter in which McClernand thanked him for the sabers he had recently received and maintained the subservient pose he had often adopted with the governor. He wrote, "I also have to thank you for the kindness, courtesy, and honorable confidence—the timely support and energetic cooperation which I have received at your hands." McClernand certainly knew how to ingratiate himself with those who might influence his future. He also notified the Illinois adjutant general that he intended to present a captured artillery piece to Yates.[54]

On the same day, he sent Lincoln a letter that maximized his own role in the recent campaign. Although acknowledging Foote's services, he misrepresented his own failure to cut off the enemy retreat, writing that he had "hastened forward" to engage or pursue the enemy. "My division was the first into the Fort and was the only one that pursued the enemy," he boasted. He did not mention that his had been the only division on the east side of the river. To ensure that Lincoln did not miss the importance of the victory he stated, "This is perhaps the most complete victory achieved during the war."[55]

Perhaps he was too flushed with victory or too much the politician pandering to other politicians. Most likely he was incapable of accepting that he was Grant's subordinate, for he now took a step for which he had no authority. In his battle report to Grant on 6 February, he informed his commander that "as a just tribute" he had renamed the captured Confederate position "Fort Foote." He also notified the naval commander that he had done so, "as an acknowledgment of the consummate skill" displayed in the fight.[56]

Grant ignored the redesignation of the fort, although McClernand continued to use it in his personal correspondence. Twice within a matter of days the politician had named locations for someone other than his immediate commander. To name his encampment "Camp Halleck" could only have been meant to flatter the new department commander. Certainly Foote was entitled to credit for the capture of Fort Henry, but Grant should have been the one to change the name of the fort in his honor. McClernand had clearly overstepped his bounds, and the fact that Grant ignored the name change indicated what he thought of his subordinate's action.

While the infantry occupied defensive positions around Fort Henry, McClernand's cavalry reconnoitered toward Fort Donelson. With two days' rations in their haversacks, the cavalry rode to within about a mile of the fort on the Cumberland River. To Grant McClernand sent the locations of enemy pickets, condition of the roads, and rumors of gray-clad reinforcements.[57]

During the course of his brief period of military service, John McClernand had become increasingly concerned to ensure that his command was protected from surprise. Perhaps the narrow avoidance of disaster at Belmont had instilled in him respect for the unexpected. At Camp Halleck he had been careful to ensure that pickets were out and cavalry on patrol. His diligence continued after the battle; he demanded that his brigade commanders report whether pickets were in position "to guard against surprise."[58] The security of his command would become almost an obsession, but a lack of perimeter security was to be the prime reason for near disaster two months later.

Glory at Fort Henry had fallen primarily on Foote and Grant. McClernand was anxious to move on to greater exploits. On 9 February he sent a lengthy recommendation to his superior in which he detailed a campaign against Fort Donelson. His division would lead the army. On an accompanying diagram, he sketched locations for his infantry brigades and supporting artillery outside the fortification and proposed a method of attack. He ignored the fact that Grant had a second division available to participate in the operation.[59]

The next day Grant notified his division and brigade commanders to meet with him on board *New Uncle Sam* at 3:00 P.M. The question was whether to march immediately against Fort Donelson or to await reinforcements. Grant asked each general for his views. Charles Smith said simply. "There is every reason why we should move without the loss of a day." McClernand then read a lengthy paper that was probably the proposal submitted to Grant the day before. He, too, favored an immediate movement.

Brigadier General Wallace, who attended the meeting, wrote critically of McClernand's performance. "It had been better for him, probably, had he rested with a word to that effect. . . . The proceeding smacked of a political caucus, and I thought both Grant and Smith grew restive before the paper was finished; then, as if in haste to preclude argument instantly that the reading ended, Grant turned to me, nodding, and I said, 'Let us go, by all means; the sooner the better.' Fast as called on, then, the others responded yes." Although Wallace believed that McClernand "was rapidly acquiring the art of war," it was his opinion that Grant had already determined the course to be followed. In Wallace's view, McClernand's sermonette was "offensive" to Grant and was the basis for the "unpleasantness" that subsequently developed between the two generals from Illinois.[60]

If Grant found McClernand's oratory "offensive," McClernand had no animosity toward his commander. On that same day McClernand had written his old friend Elihu Washburne in support of Grant's endorsement of Charles F. Smith as brigadier general. Smith's appointment had not been confirmed by the United States Senate, because of suspicions about his loyalty as well as opposition from several politically appointed generals, one of whom was Lew Wallace.[61] The fact that Smith was a West Point graduate indicated that McClernand had not yet totally developed the intense dislike for West Pointers that was to characterize his later career.

After adjournment of the meeting on board *New Uncle Sam*, Grant issued orders for his divisions to be ready to move early on 12 February. They were to travel light, taking forty rounds of ammunition and two days' rations. By separate orders a third brigade of four regiments was added to McClernand's command. Grant ordered the navy to steam to the Cumberland in support.[62]

McClernand immediately issued a warning order to his brigades and then, after receipt of Grant's operation order, issued his own. Grant's order was strikingly similar to what McClernand had proposed earlier. The First Division would lead; two brigades would advance along the Ridge (or Dover) Road, and one would follow the Telegraph Road. Smith's Second Division would follow along the Ridge Road. McClernand was to halt two miles from Fort Donelson, connect the two wings of his command, and await further orders. Smith was to send one brigade into the town of Dover to block a Confederate retreat in that direction.[63]

The First Division order specified the order of march of the entire command, gave an instruction to form a continuous line, stressed the necessity of emplacing the artillery in a commanding position, and issued a directive to camp with a "view toward defensiveness." The only fault in the order was that it did not specify how the three brigades were to align themselves when they reached the vicinity of Fort Donelson. Such an omission could lead to confusion in the face of the enemy. By separate correspondence McClernand ordered Cols. W. H. L. Wallace and Richard Oglesby, his two lead brigade commanders, to reconnoiter toward Donelson.[64]

The Confederate departmental commanders were in a quandary. Grant had penetrated their defensive line and was obviously poised to strike at Donelson. Buell's army remained a threat to Bowling Green, and Polk was practically isolated at Columbus. Were Donelson to fall, the Confederate supply depot at Clarksville, Tennessee, and the city of Nashville would be vulnerable to attack. Gen. P. G. T. Beauregard urged Johnston to concentrate most of his forty-eight thousand men against Grant. Instead, Johnston ordered a general retreat to a new line near Nashville. Bowling Green would be abandoned, and only small garrisons were to be left at Columbus and Clarksville. He predicted that Donelson would soon fall.[65]

Brig. Gen. John B. Floyd, who had been President Buchanan's secretary of war, commanded Fort Donelson. His second in command was Brig. Gen. Gideon J. Pillow, who had faced Grant and McClernand at Belmont. Two subordinate brigadiers, Bushrod R. Johnson and Simon B. Buckner, commanded the left and right wings of the entrenchments, respectively. Col. Nathan Bedford Forrest and his cavalry joined the garrison the evening of 10 February. About fifteen thousand Confederates would face Grant's army, also a force of about fifteen thousand men.[66]

Fort Donelson would be a far tougher nut to crack than had been Fort Henry. Its parapet sloped from sixteen feet thick at the base to eleven feet thick at the top. A moat twelve feet wide and six feet deep encircled the walls. Rifle pits, abatis, ditches, and flooded streams added to the strength of the defenses. Two batteries well sited along the Cumberland River protected the fort from bombardment by Union gunboats.

Grant suddenly grew impatient and, shortly before noon on 11 February, ordered his command to begin the march toward Donelson that afternoon rather than the next day. The brigades began to move at about 4:00 P.M. and camped about four miles from the Rebel fort four hours later. The weather was warm, and soon the roads were lined with discarded blankets, coats, and knapsacks. Union commanders failed to prevent the practice. The still-raw Union soldiers and officers had forgotten the lessons of January. Soon they would again have cause to regret their lack of foresight.[67]

McClernand had his men up and moving at dawn, 12 February. Screened by the 4th Illinois Cavalry, McClernand's division slowly moved toward the waiting Confederate army. To ensure that the advances of his separated brigades were coordinated, McClernand had the lead brigade commanders maintain frequent contact with each other. At noon, Wallace found the Telegraph Road blocked by an impassable stream. He located another road that led south and soon joined Oglesby and the Third Brigade, commanded by Col. William R. Morrison, moving along the Ridge Road.[68]

Shortly before being joined by Wallace, Oglesby's advance guard had encountered Forrest's dismounted cavalry blocking the march along Ridge Road. After a sharp skirmish in which he was in danger of being outflanked, Forrest withdrew.[69]

Not until about 2:00 P.M. did Grant and McClernand meet. The district commander provided direction as to how he expected his subordinates to deploy their divisions against the fort. Shortly before, McClernand had directed a reconnaissance of the area to the right of his advance and had begun to deploy his brigades along a ridge that ran parallel to the Confederate outworks. Scouts from the 2d Illinois Cavalry reported the results to McClernand, who, aware of the importance of their observations, accompanied his scouts to headquarters. Grant ordered his division commander to continue the movement, allowing the lead brigade of the Second Division to form to the left of the First Division facing Fort Donelson. Scattered skirmishing continued throughout the day, and by evening four Union brigades were arrayed against the Cumberland River fortress.[70]

The Union line did not completely encompass the Confederate position. McClernand realized that a sizeable gap existed between his right and the river. If that situation continued, Floyd would be able to escape or to envelop the Union right. To protect against the latter possibility, the First Division commander ordered Oglesby to entrench so as to increase the strength of his defensive position.

A gap also existed in the center of McClernand's line, where Indian Creek separated Wallace from McClernand's other brigades. Because such a gap invited a Confederate attack to penetrate the Union line, he notified Grant that he would abandon the heights to the left of the creek in order to close the hole. He also ordered Oglesby to shift farther to the right to occupy Dudley's Hill, which offered good observation toward the river. By early afternoon McClernand had his division united and deployed along the Wynn's Ferry Road, with its right anchored on Dudley's Hill near the Forge Road. Cavalry patrolled the low ground between Dudley's Hill and the river to alert McClernand to Confederate movements in that sector.[71]

Since daybreak 13 February, Capt. Frank Maney's Tennessee Battery had harassed Union infantrymen who showed themselves atop the ridge along which ran Wynn's Ferry Road. Finally, McClernand ordered Capt. Jasper Dresser's Battery D, 2d Illinois Light Artillery, to return fire. The Confederate battery ceased fire for a time, but it opened up again, and Lt. George Gumbart's Battery E joined the fray. Two other Union and two more Confederate batteries also joined in.[72]

Oglesby's men had come under fire from Maney's battery the day before as they deployed along Wynn's Ferry Road. Confederate infantry that supported the battery had also fired upon the Union soldiers, inflicting several casualties. Obviously his command was in range of the Confederate gunners, and by 12:30 P.M. McClernand had had enough. Without authority from Grant, the impetuous general ordered an attack by his Third Brigade against the position occupied by Maney's battery and Colonel Heiman's brigade. Col. William Morrison's Third Brigade had only two regiments (the third regiment had been left to guard Fort Henry), so McClernand attached the 48th Illinois from the Second Brigade to provide more firepower.[73]

Carl von Clausewitz, the noted German military theorist, had postulated earlier in the century that "defense is the stronger form of warfare." He had written, realistically, that "it is a risky business to attack an able opponent in a good defensive position." His contemporary, Henri Jomini, agreed and

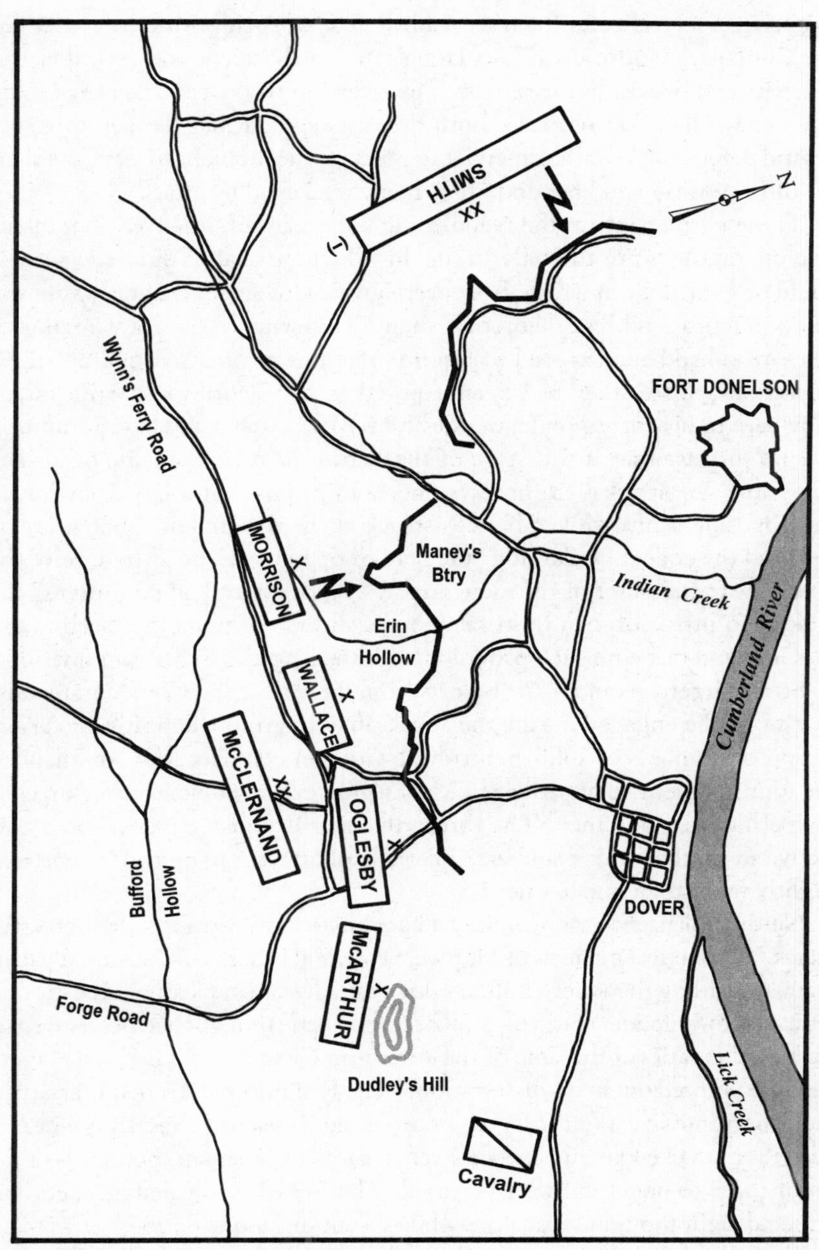

Fort Donelson, Afternoon, February 13, 1862

enunciated several rules for the establishment of such positions. Generally, the Confederate position at Fort Donelson met all except one critical factor: there was no provision for retreat. The river was to the rear, and the Union navy controlled that obstacle. Both theorists agreed that the key to a successful defense was for the defender to perceive the moment to leave the shelter of his position and fall upon the enemy weakened by attack.

These participants in the Napoleonic wars realized, however, that offensive operations were the only means by which tactical or strategic success could be gained. Both wrote about prerequisites for an attack, but Jomini was more practical and less theoretical than Clausewitz. West Point graduates since 1830 had been exposed to Jomini's theories of offensive and defensive operations, just as they had been exposed to his theories of fortifications. Nowhere in his correspondence does John McClernand allude to Jomini, so it is no surprise that at this stage of the war his plan violated one of his key provisions for attack—"to observe and hold in position a large portion of the opposing army, while a blow is struck at the remainder." Such a provision had the effect of enlarging "the field of operations," so as to deceive the enemy as to the point of the main attack.[74] Since Grant had not ordered the attack, no provision had been made for a diversion in another sector, and McClernand made no such provision with the brigades in his own division.

Strength returns and battle reports from the Union and Confederate units that would be engaged during the attack do not permit a definitive determination of numbers of soldiers involved. Colonel Heiman, who commanded the four regiments that protected Maney's battery in a defensive redan, estimated he had 1,600 men. The three attacking Union regiments had a collective strength of 1,907 soldiers. The ratio of attacker to defender, thus, was slightly more than one to one.[75]

Neither Clausewitz nor Jomini had postulated force ratios for a successful attack. The tactical manuals of Hardee, Scott, and others were essentially drill manuals. Although modern military doctrine advocates at least a three-to-one (attacker-to-defender) ratio of combat power, little thought had been given to such mathematics at the time of the American Civil War. As Edward Hagerman has pointed out in his dissertation, "The Evolution of Trench Warfare in the American Civil War," fifty-eight thousand Russians at Sevastopol in August 1855 attacked an entrenched French force of nineteen thousand—a ratio of three to one—and were repulsed. The French had rifled muskets and inflicted eight thousand casualties while sustaining about 2,700.[76]

Tactical thinking prior to and during the early years of the Civil War had merely asserted the importance of the offensive and maintained that a powerful assault by trained soldiers would overwhelm defensive works. Ratios for a successful attack were no more than opinion. One Union general, Jacob D. Cox, had written, "One rifle in the trench was worth five in front of it."[77] Others would express different opinions. In this case, however, McClernand chose to attack an entrenched position, manned by men with rifled muskets, with a ratio of about one to one and without a diversionary attack. Such an amateurish decision could lead to only one result.

Union troops advanced to within forty yards of the Confederate redan but were unable to proceed farther. For an hour they held their position under withering fire from the entrenched graybacks. Observing the plight of the three regiments pinned down on the slopes before the Confederate position, McClernand turned to the 45th Illinois and ordered it into battle. At best, the addition of that regiment could have increased the force ratio to only one and one-half to one. Having suffered 142 casualties, the four regiments withdrew to Wynn's Ferry Road.[78]

Earlier that day, Smith too had ordered an attack, also without Grant's approval, against the Confederate right by two of his brigades. It too was unsuccessful; yet Grant made no mention of this abortive attempt by his old West Point commandant either in his official reports or in his memoirs. Only the political general McClernand was to be castigated in writing for attacking "without orders or authority."[79]

That night three inches of snow fell, and many Union soldiers regretted discarding their overcoats and blankets on the march from Fort Henry. The temperature fell to below zero.[80] Dawn brought the arrival of Lew Wallace and reinforcements from Fort Henry. Grant immediately organized a third division under Wallace and posted it in the line between McClernand and Smith. He explicitly ordered Wallace not to take any offensive action. This strengthened the Union line and made it more difficult for the Confederates to achieve a breakout, but establishing the line meant that there could be no reserve. Grant's plan then was to contain the Rebels in Fort Donelson and, as at Fort Henry, allow the gunboats to pound them into submission.[81]

During the day McClernand ordered numerous reconnaissances, one of which he accompanied, of the land between his right and the river. He feared the Confederates would be able to break out of the encirclement along that avenue, because he had insufficient troops to man it completely. He requested reinforcements, and at about 5:00 P.M. Col. John McArthur's First Brigade of Smith's division was ordered to move to McClernand's support. The Illinois general stationed the newly arrived brigade on his extreme right, with two regiments on Dudley's Hill. The darkness, however, prevented a thorough examination of the ground. McArthur later claimed he was "without instructions" from McClernand. If true, it indicated a decided laxity in leadership on the part of the politician. Units positioned on the extreme flanks of an army are critically important; if turned or routed, the entire army is in danger of defeat.

McClernand had no general reserve (though McArthur and Oglesby on the extreme right each posted one regiment as a brigade reserve). Even without a reserve, however, the division commander had insufficient troops to establish a continuous line between Dudley's Hill and the river. He elected to cover the ground with the 2d and 4th Illinois cavalry.[82]

At 3:00 P.M. Foote got under way with six gunboats to attack the river batteries. The defense prevailed here as well. At 4:30 P.M. the gunboats broke off the action after sustaining losses of ten killed and forty-four wounded, including Foote. Two boats were damaged so severely that they were unable to participate in further operations against the fort. Two others also received extensive damage. Although they remained near Fort Donelson, they fired only from long range. That night Grant wrote his wife Julia, "The taking of Fort Donelson bids fair to be a long job."[83]

While Grant was writing home, Confederate generals were meeting to discuss the situation at Fort Donelson. From Johnston, Floyd had received a message that gave him no cause for optimism. "If you lose the fort, bring your troops to Nashville if possible," the department commander had written.[84] To move to Nashville required the Confederates to break out of the near encirclement on the Union right—the area between McArthur's brigade under McClernand's control and the Cumberland River.

About 1:00 A.M. the council broke up after a decision to attack at 5:00 A.M. In a colossal blunder, the four principal Confederate generals left the meeting with different ideas as to what the mission actually was. John Floyd, Simon Buckner, and Bushrod Johnson believed the Confederates were to force their way through the Union lines and retreat toward Nashville. Johnson, however, expected the actual retreat to begin at night, to allow the commands involved in the attack to reorganize themselves. Gideon Pillow believed the mission to be to "cut up" the Union force and "ultimately . . . to retire from the post."[85] Such confusion was a prelude to disaster.

The attacker-to-defender ratio, if the Rebels struck the Union flank brigade, would be slightly more than four to one. Furthermore, the Confederates had an advantage that added considerably to the combat power they could throw against the sleeping Union soldiers—surprise. Grant's attitude pervaded the army. "I had no idea," he later wrote, "that there would be any engagement on land unless I brought it on myself."[86] It would not be the last time the Union general would be surprised by an unexpected enemy attack.

Shortly before dawn, Grant received a request from Foote to meet with him, on board his flagship because his wounds prevented him from coming to Grant. Leaving an order that his division commanders were to maintain their positions and "to do nothing to bring on an engagement," Grant rode to the landing over frozen, almost impassable, roads. He left no one in command during his absence.[87]

At daybreak, 15 February, Confederate skirmishers from the 26th Mississippi Infantry encountered pickets from McArthur's brigade. The brigade commander quickly assessed the situation and deployed his regiments to counter the Confederate advance. Oglesby almost immediately arrived on the scene, recognized the obvious attempt to turn the Union right, and quickly redeployed his brigade to connect with McArthur, who was refusing (bending back) his right and falling back in the face of the onslaught.[88]

By 8:00 A.M. McClernand's situation was serious. Five Confederate brigades—nearly six thousand men—had slammed into the Illinoisan's flank. Several Union regiments had exhausted their ammunition and were forced to retire after a defense described by Floyd as "obstinate." Gray-clad soldiers were lapping around McClernand's right, which was by then at a ninety-degree angle to his main line. To hold he required reinforcements. McClernand sent Maj. Mason Brayman, his adjutant, to Lew Wallace for help. Wallace, under orders from Grant not to bring on an engagement, listened to Brayman's report that "the whole rebel force in the fort massed against [McClernand] in the night" and that he needed "immediate help." Wallace sent a messenger to notify Grant, only to learn that the commanding general was absent. A second messenger from McClernand appeared and implored Wallace to come to the division's aid. "The whole army is in danger," he added. Forced to make a decision, Wallace ordered a brigade under Col. Charles Cruft to march to the sound of the guns.[89]

Between 9:00 and 10:00 A.M. Cruft reached the area of the fight, along the Wynn's Ferry Road. McClernand ordered him into line, but as a reserve. Wallace was infuriated by this move (and was still angry forty years later—in his autobiography he castigated the First Division commander for it). To him, putting Cruft in reserve meant that McClernand "was not in need," as had been reported. In actuality, McClernand's order was proper. His front was collapsing, the entire Union line was in danger of being rolled up, and the units that were still fighting were almost out of ammunition. By deploying Cruft's fresh brigade in line of battle behind the front he allowed its commander a few moments to align his regiments, seek cover, and be prepared to meet the onrushing Confederates.[90]

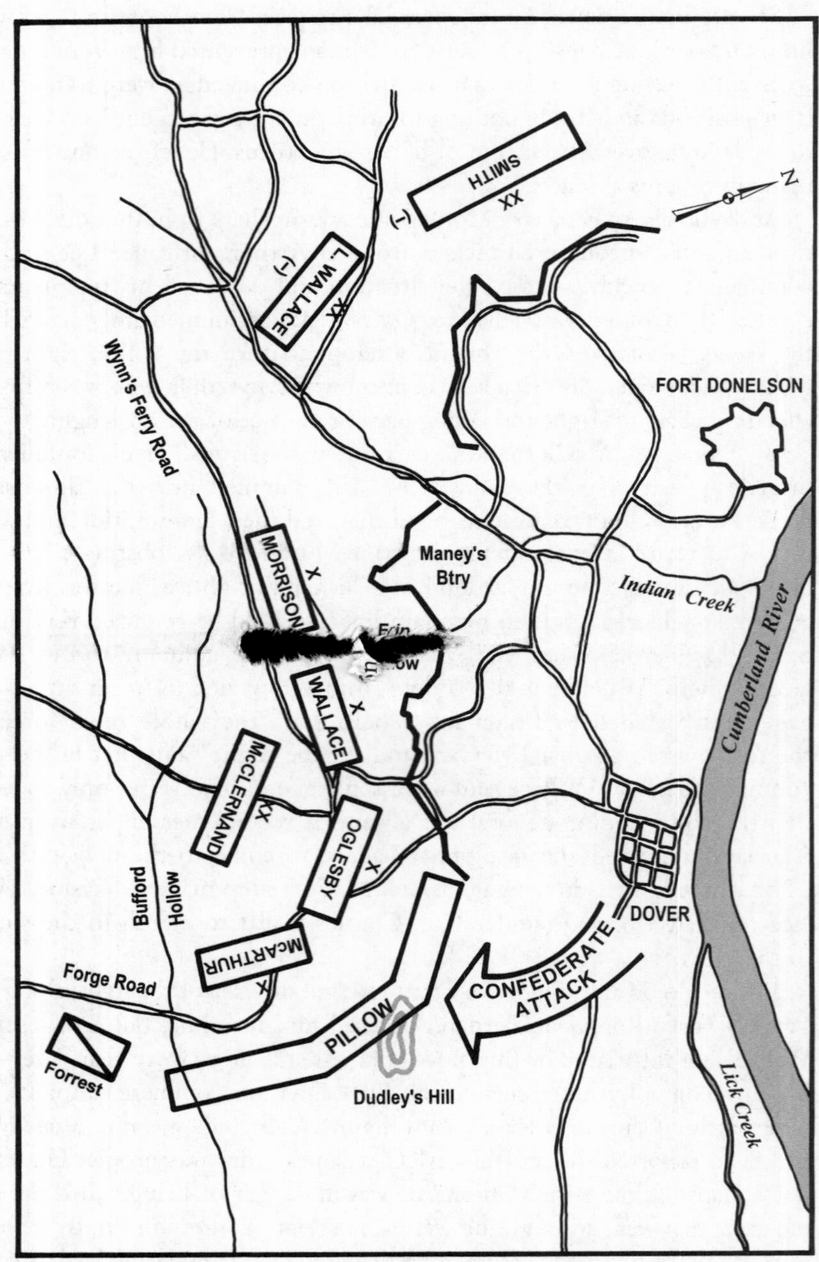

Fort Donelson, 9:00 a.m., February 15, 1862

As Confederate regiments shifted to McClernand's right and threatened to envelop his refused flank, the battle developed into a brigade and regimental fight. The division commander could only beseech them to hold as long as possible and ask for help. On the extreme right, the overwhelming gray flood drove McArthur back. Oglesby's left was driven back, but W. H. L. Wallace filled the gap and organized a counterattack. As so often happens in the fury of combat, McClernand's order for Cruft to deploy was not executed, because of the pressing events on the right. A messenger from an Illinois regiment begged for help, and Cruft moved toward the threatened flank. As the Union dam began to break, some regiments withdrew precipitously, others attempted an orderly withdrawal, while yet others tried to shift laterally to maintain a cohesive front.

Oglesby and McArthur withdrew about a mile to Bufford Hollow, and the opportunity for a smashing victory by the Confederates was at hand. Nathan Bedford Forrest's cavalry harassed McClernand's flanks and inflicted heavy casualties. Soldier-politician John Logan had fought his regiment well and had not withdrawn it with the remainder of Oglesby's brigade. Instead, Logan established a line with Cruft and W. H. L. Wallace on the ridge east of Bufford Hollow. Wallace, under attack by a Rebel brigade that had sallied from the redan protecting Maney's battery, notified McClernand that he needed reinforcements desperately.[91]

At about 10:30 A.M. the Rebels renewed their vicious assaults, and soon Logan's 31st Illinois and most of Cruft's brigade were driven back into the hollow. W. H. L. Wallace fell back along the Wynn's Ferry Road with most of his brigade, but his right-most regiment was driven back with Logan toward Bufford Hollow. Pillow later wrote that McClernand's division had "contested the field most stubbornly." Nevertheless, the road to Nashville lay open.[92]

As panic-stricken men fled along the Wynn's Ferry Road, they passed through Lew Wallace's remaining brigades. It quickly became apparent to Wallace that a crisis was occurring to his right. Without orders, he sent his remaining seven regiments to stiffen the line that McClernand was attempting to form against the onrushing tide. As he did so, he met W. H. L. Wallace for the first and only time. The two commented as to how their names had "been the cause of great profanity in the post office."[93]

Meanwhile, McClernand had formed the remnants of his brigades at a right angle to the Wynn's Ferry Road but with a gap between the ridge on which the road lay and the bulk of his command, near Bufford Hollow. He deployed skirmishers to cover the intervening ground and cavalry to patrol forward of the Union position. Lew Wallace's regiments appeared at about

1:00 P.M., formed along the Wynn's Ferry Road, and then slipped right to join McClernand's men.[94]

Thirty minutes later Grant arrived, to find Lew Wallace and McClernand conversing about the situation. According to one source, McClernand disgustedly muttered to Grant, "The army needs a head," to which Grant replied, "It seems so." Was this a rebuke from the amateur general of the professional for his absence from the field? McClernand began to explain the situation to the army commander, who, until his return from meeting with Foote at about noon, had been unaware that his army was on the verge of destruction. Grant interrupted him and ordered his two division commanders to retake the Wynn's Ferry Road before nightfall. He then rode to the Union left to direct Smith, who had sat idle while the battle raged to his right, to attack that portion of the Confederate line that had been weakened by the massive assault.

In his autobiography, Wallace claimed that he had led the counterattack to recover McClernand's lost positions. According to Wallace, McClernand had told his fellow division commander that he was unable to retake the road. Wallace had inferred that McClernand wanted him to lead the attack. At that moment a brigade from General Smith's division had arrived, as a result of the earlier summons for help from McClernand. Wallace wrote that McClernand released the brigade to him for the attack. In his own report, the First Division commander made no reference to a desire for Wallace to conduct the attack. Both individuals had huge egos, and no third-party reports confirm either account. Wallace, though, clearly indicated in his official report of the battle that he believed McClernand had slighted his command. Such an actual or perceived slight was probably the foundation for Wallace's desire to enhance his status at the expense of John McClernand.[95]

By this time the First Division had suffered approximately 1,500 casualties among the almost eight thousand who had awakened that cold, snowy morning. McArthur had four hundred additional casualties. Wallace had seven regiments that had not been engaged, and the Fifth Brigade of Smith's division added two more, over seven thousand fresh men in all. McClernand's men had been fighting and retreating steadily for more than five hours in the face of an attack by six brigades. It would be uncharacteristic of John McClernand voluntarily to concede command of an operation to another. In no other instance during the war was he to do so. The situation the afternoon of 15 February, however, was truly desperate. If Wynn's Ferry Road remained under Confederate control, the door to Nashville and safety for many of the fort's defenders would be open.

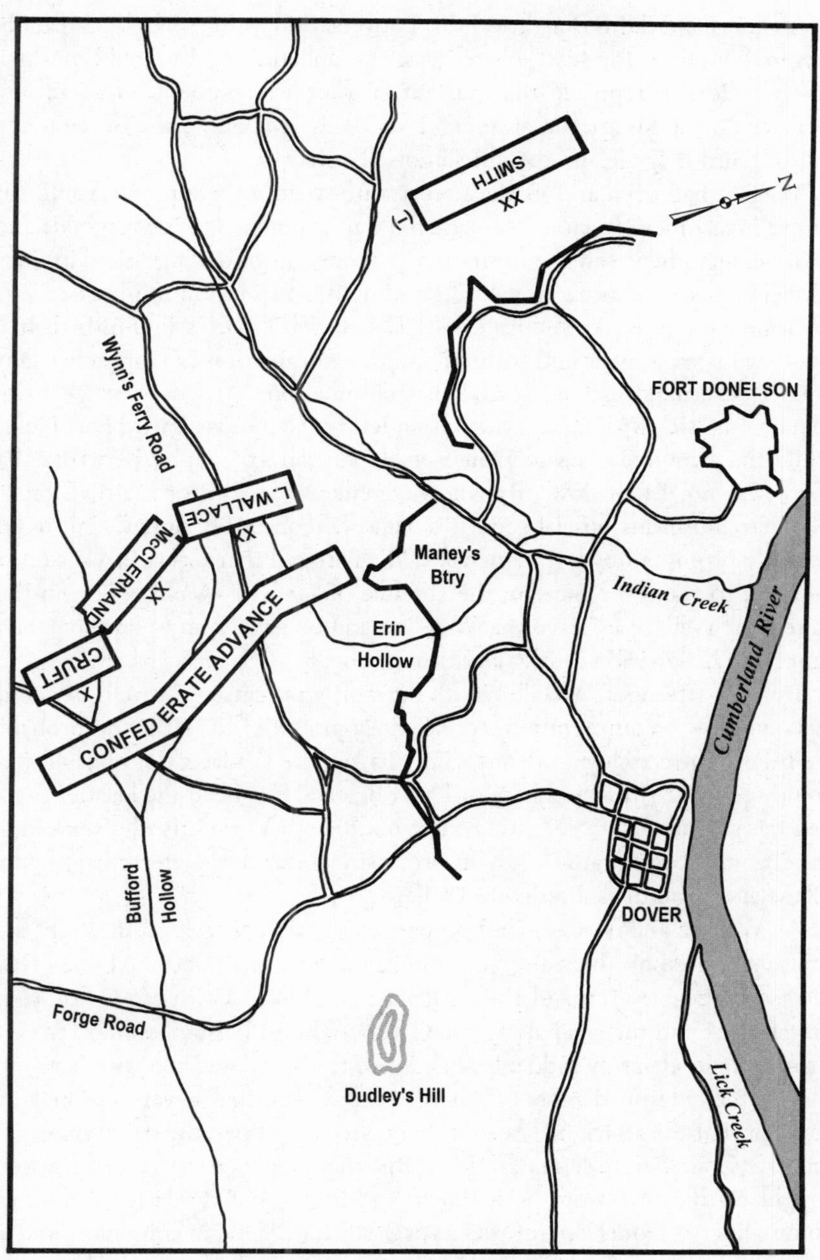

Fort Donelson, 1:00 P.M., February 15, 1862

McClernand did not mention this conversation in his report. Instead, he credited Wallace for his "spirited assault" and praised his "skill and gallantry." He also reported that he sent "five or six regiments" to reinforce Wallace during his assault, although he actually sent only the two regiments in his Third Brigade and the 4th Illinois Cavalry.[96]

Wallace had been an Indiana state senator before the war and would run for political office afterward. During the war he pursued his own agenda and, as did many others, saw the future political benefits of distinguished military service. On several occasions he allowed political ambition to interfere with his military duties. At Paducah, he had believed Charles F. Smith to be a Southern sympathizer and had opposed his nomination as a brigadier general. McClernand had supported that nomination. Wallace wrote his wife that he was "sick with rage" when Grant left him behind to guard Fort Henry while the army marched to Donelson. In his autobiography he wrote that there was not "a shadow of acknowledgement" to him or his division by McClernand in his official report. That is demonstrably untrue, but it was possibly prompted by a statement by McClernand that Cruft had made the decision to reinforce him "in the absence of General Wallace." From that statement Wallace inferred that McClernand believed him to have been absent from his division during a critical period.[97]

By mid-afternoon McClernand's division was scattered, tired, demoralized, and low on ammunition. A realistic appraisal of the situation probably led him to the conclusion that it would have to be Wallace, not himself, who could recover the lost roads. His Third Brigade had been the least engaged and was still an effective fighting force but his other two brigades were in no condition to counterattack. To his professional credit he deferred command of the assault to the subordinate Wallace.

As Wallace and McClernand prepared to counterattack on the right and Smith gathered his division to assault on the left, there occurred one of the most inexplicable events of the American Civil War. With the Union right driven back and the road along the Cumberland to Nashville open, the entire Confederate army suddenly abandoned the battlefield and withdrew into the Fort Donelson defenses. Gideon Pillow, who had never accepted the concept that the attack had been designed to force open the door for an immediate Confederate retreat, ordered Buckner to return to the fort. Buckner sought clarification from both Pillow and Floyd, but the latter, the senior commander at Donelson, refused to override his second in command, and by nightfall the entire Confederate garrison, except for the 1,300 who lay on the field of battle, had withdrawn to their positions of that morning. Wallace and portions of McClernand's division pressed ahead until an order from Grant recalled them to the positions they had held at dawn. Smith, meanwhile, had gained a portion of the Confederate outer works on the Union left.[98]

As the Union soldiers settled into their positions for the night, Wallace's division occupied the extreme right of the Union line. McClernand was to his left. Wallace's position, however, did not extend to Dudley's Hill, as had McClernand's that morning. The door to Confederate safety at Nashville was still ajar.[99]

That night Floyd called another council of war and decided to cut his way out of Donelson the next morning. Reports from Forrest and a local inhabitant indicated accurately that Union pickets did not cover the road from the fort. Inaccurate reports, however, led the assembled Confederate generals to believe that the "woods were perfectly alive with troops" and that the "decidedly unfavorable" condition of the road would make a breakout impossible. That was enough for the mercurial Floyd: he decided to surrender the command. Forrest would have none of it and announced he would cut his way out. Floyd turned over command to Buckner, and he and Pillow crossed the river to safety. (A few days later Gen. Bushrod Johnson would simply walk away while unguarded. About 1,200 men would escape capture.)[100]

Buckner, meanwhile, sent to Grant a message proposing "the appointment of Commissioners to agree upon terms of capitulation of the forces and fort under my command, and in that view suggest an armistice until 12 o'clock to-day." Grant's reply left no doubt as to his view of terms and an armistice: "No terms except an unconditional and immediate surrender can be accepted. I propose to move immediately upon your works." Grant had notified McClernand, Wallace, and Smith to be prepared to renew the assault. It would not be necessary, for Buckner had no choice. He had "to accept the ungenerous and unchivalrous terms" that Grant proposed.[101]

Grant ordered McClernand's division to occupy the southern end of the captured works and Smith's division to occupy the northern end. Both generals were ordered to provide details to collect property captured as a result of the surrender. Wallace was to return with two brigades to hold Fort Henry.[102]

"Unconditional Surrender" Grant suddenly became a household name when the news of Donelson's surrender reached the North. Union folk in Northern cities celebrated wildly the recent victories. Reports that the general had smoked during the battle led to huge quantities of cigars being sent to him. Other reports, however, were not so congenial to the veteran soldier. The *Cincinnati Commercial* accused him of having been "inexcusably absent from the field," and it assigned to him responsibility for McClernand's men being "needlessly slaughtered." Despite such criticism Grant had won two major victories in ten days and had cracked the Confederate defensive line in the West. On 19 February the United States Senate rewarded him with promotion to major general, to date from 16 February.[103]

McClernand, too, received his share of favorable publicity for the victory. The *Chicago Times* reported that the men of his division had "stood their ground so manfully" and "bore the brunt of the battle." The *Illinois State Journal* praised him as well and printed a letter from the general's aide: "General McClernand was continually with his command, exposing his person day and night to shell, shot, and even to the enemy's rifles." McClernand too received a promotion to major general.[104]

As at Belmont, at Fort Donelson McClernand's personal presence and influence on the battlefield had contributed substantially to Union success. Charles Dana wrote that he "behaved with the most conspicuous gallantry." Even a detractor, Lew Wallace, commented on his bravery. James Wilson, who later was to be a severe critic of the Illinois general, wrote that he "was an officer of undaunted courage" who "would be in the thick of the fight. It was regarded as certain," he added, "that McClernand would make a gallant resistance."[105]

John McClernand, the political general with no schooling in the military art, was indeed "rapidly acquiring the art of war." By 16 February 1862 he had been involved in two major battles and had participated in the Union victory at Fort Henry. During the first critical hours on 15 February, McClernand had displayed traits that would have been approved even by professional soldiers. He had properly placed total trust in his three brigade commanders, plus Colonel McArthur from Smith's division. In reality there had been little he could do directly, but he resisted the temptation to take charge and try to manage their battle. His place had been to think ahead. He had realized the danger to the Union army and had concluded that unless he was reinforced quickly, the entire line might collapse. His call for help from Wallace, and Wallace's willingness to ignore Grant's injunction not to bring on a battle, had saved the army from possible defeat.

He must be faulted for not having insisted that his command dig in, although some units did so on their own. McArthur's assertion that he did not receive a comprehensive briefing from McClernand also indicates that the novice general had not fully learned the necessity for coordination among commands. In the future he also would need to ensure he was completely familiar with the terrain and that his subordinates had a clear understanding of their commander's concept for defense. Critical to his future and the success of his command would be whether the Confederate army would allow him the luxury of continuing to learn before confronting him with a disaster.

On 17 February, the day after the surrender, McClernand issued a congratulatory order to his division for its conduct at Forts Henry and Donelson, as he had done after Belmont. The wording that the division had "led the way in the valley of the Lower Mississippi, the Tennessee and the Cumberland" was meant to praise the soldiers and inspire them to future glory, but the words could also be taken as a not-so-subtle reference to his own role as division commander. The next day he sent a copy of the order to Lincoln, with a letter that cast doubt on the performance of other officers: the victory covered "a number of serious mistakes," and the First Division "was not properly supported." Also as he had done after Belmont, he offered advice to the president about future operations: the army "should now push on to Memphis and Nashville."[106]

Ten days later he sent Grant his official report of the battle. He also sent a copy to Lincoln. In a further letter to the president he boasted that "of all our land forces mine were the first to reach Camp Halleck, Fort Henry, Fort Donelson, and Clarksville." McClernand's case for the first three claims was based on his division's having been first in the order of march.[107]

Clarksville fell to Foote's gunboats on 19 February, and the next day Grant, McClernand, and W. H. L. Wallace visited the city. Wallace would describe it as a "pleasant trip" that included a march through the streets with two infantry companies from Wallace's brigade (McClernand's division), accompanied by the band of the 11th Illinois Regiment. That was the basis for McClernand's claim that his men were the first to reach Clarksville. Charles F. Smith's division occupied the city on 21 February.[108]

In his report, filled with hyperbole, McClernand asserted that he had suggested to Grant on the afternoon of 15 February that the army make "a simultaneous assault at all points" and that Grant had accepted that suggestion. Grant denied that assertion. Lew Wallace, who had been present at the discussion, indicated that the idea for an attack on both the left and right flanks had been Grant's.[109]

Elsewhere in his report the former politician claimed that his division had borne "the brunt and burden of the battle" and had "sustained much the greatest loss." While it is true that the First Division suffered the greatest number of casualties and had borne a disproportionate share of the fighting, it was the entire army that gained the victory. In the same paragraph as the quotes above, McClernand listed the spoils from the surrender and wrote, "Our trophies corresponded with the magnitude of the victory." The implication was that his division alone had earned the "trophies" of prisoners, weapons, and stores.[110]

Grant forwarded the report to Halleck, but he wrote in his letter of transmittal, "I transmit herewith the report of the action of the First Division. . . . I have no special comments to make on it, further than that the report is a little highly colored as to the conduct of the First Division and I failed to hear the suggestions spoken of about the propriety of attacking the enemy all around the lines on Saturday. No suggestions were made by General McClernand at the time spoken of."[111]

Although in it McClernand congratulated Grant "as the respected commander of a victorious army," the report obviously did not meet with Grant's full approval. In a letter to Halleck's chief of staff, Grant had praised McClernand and Wallace for their presence "in the midst of danger." In letters to Illinois representative Washburne, though, he mentioned neither general. On 21 February Grant wrote that Smith, who had not seized the initiative as had Lew Wallace, should be promoted to major general, and the next day he wrote that John Logan, who had been wounded three times on 15 February, should be promoted to brigadier general. He did not mention either of his other two division commanders—John McClernand or Lew Wallace. At Lincoln's request, Washburne submitted the names of all brigadiers at Donelson, and it was the president who directed they all, including Grant, be promoted.[112] It is impossible to know whether the fact that Smith was a West Point graduate and the other two division commanders were not had any bearing on Grant's recommendation. His recommendation regarding Logan was probably based on that soldier's wounds and the sterling performance of his regiment during the battle.

Henry Halleck, the student of Jomini, recognized the opportunity Grant had presented him. The Union army had driven into the center of the western theater. Confederate forces on the extremities at Columbus and Bowling Green were vulnerable. On 10 March, Halleck presented his intentions to McClellan: "Reserves . . . will now be . . . sent to the Tennessee. That is now the great strategic line of the Western campaign."[113]

4
Into the Heartland

The loss of Forts Henry and Donelson left the Confederate army in a difficult situation. Union forces had effected a strategic penetration that threatened to cut off Maj. Gen. Leonidas Polk's army at Columbus, Kentucky, from that of Gen. Albert Sidney Johnston at Murfreesboro, Tennessee. On 24 February, Maj. Gen. Don Carlos Buell's Federal forces occupied Nashville, from where he could keep an eye on Johnston. Gen. P. G. T. Beauregard arrived from the eastern theater and took command of the scattered Confederates near Corinth, Mississippi. Union gunboats roamed the Tennessee River all the way to Florence, Alabama. If Halleck acted quickly, he could unite the forces under Grant and Buell and mass against either Johnston or Polk before they could move to aid each other. Unfortunately for the Union cause, Halleck was not the type to act quickly.

Although he had fallen ill, McClernand continued to direct the occupation and reconnaissance of the area around Fort Donelson. He also continued his pattern of complaining to Grant about the number of men that had to be provided for details. On 17 February he wrote that six hundred men were on detail and picket duty without shelter during rain and snow. As an indication of how Grant felt about such complaints, he replied that such duties were equitably distributed between divisions and advised his subordinate to use soldiers who had not participated in the recent battle: "A few days hard work is not going to bust fresh men."[1]

Grant, who had been designated on 15 February as commander of the District of West Tennessee, directed McClernand's division to guard the roads between the Cumberland and Tennessee Rivers. Accordingly, McClernand ordered his cavalry to reconnoiter the area and to "bring in any enemy property found." Perhaps as a reflection of his lack of military expertise, the division commander's order initially left arrangements for the mission to the three brigade commanders. Subsequent orders, however, were more specific. In these he specified the time for the operation to begin, the route to be followed, and the action to be taken to interrupt Confederate rail and telegraph communication. He further directed the brigade commanders in regard to the extent of their picket lines and warned them against being surprised by enemy forces.[2]

Unfortunately, McClernand's order to bring in "any" enemy property ran afoul of Department of the Missouri General Orders and the Confiscation Act of 6 August 1861, which contained instructions for the seizure of private property. Private property could be seized only if needed "for the subsistence or transportation of [Union] troops," if the owner were "in arms against the United States," or if the property afforded "aid and assistance to the enemy." A rebuke from Grant followed for the "embarrassment" violations could cause. In a reply in which he apparently attempted to distance himself from such actions, McClernand responded that his orders had been to seize "enemy property" and that he condemned and denied complicity in any violation of his instructions. Well he should deny it, for General Orders No. 8 required that "the officer highest in command [would] be held accountable" for violations.[3]

The novice general also had to concern himself with administrative matters. On 25 February a soldier appeared at Grant's headquarters with a furlough granted by McClernand. Army regulations and District General Orders No. 9, however, required that furlough requests be sent to the higher headquarters and not be presented in person by the soldier seeking the furlough.[4] It was a minor incident, but one that indicated that the division commander was still learning proper military procedures.

As of 26 February McClernand had received no orders for further movements beyond Fort Donelson. In a letter that day to Grant, the Illinois general suggested a course of action that was to lead to the greatest controversy of his military career. He wrote, "I have, from the breaking out of the rebellion, attentively and carefully studied the immediate valley of the Mississippi as a principal field of military operations. These considerations may occasionally be supposed to afford some assurance of the efficiency of my command if employed in that field."[5] McClernand was not just suggesting the creation of a separate department or a general concept of operations, as he had in his letter of last December to Congressman Cox. He was now proposing, through military channels, that his command be employed in active operations in that region. Along the course of the Mississippi lay the course of John McClernand's future.

As a division commander, McClernand was not directly involved in high-level strategic decisions, although that did not constrain him from offering such advice. Henry Halleck, however, was concerned not about McClernand's future but about his own. Even after the fall of Donelson, he feared that the Confederates would unite to destroy Grant's army. While Halleck vacillated and asked for reinforcements, Grant, with a greater appreciation for the strategic situation, urged that he be allowed to occupy Clarksville and then quickly seize Nashville. Finally, on 20 February, Halleck ordered Buell to move up the Cumberland toward Nashville. Grant, however, received no orders as to what operations he should conduct.[6]

McClernand spent his time ordering reconnaissances along the Tennessee River to determine where troops could be embarked for future operations. The results, which revealed that several main roads were impassable because of high water, he dutifully reported to Grant.[7]

On 27 February McClernand accompanied Grant to Nashville, which had recently been occupied by Buell. There the former congressman visited the widow of President James K. Polk. She later wrote him to ask that he attempt to locate her nephew, who had been captured at Fort Donelson, and he attempted to do so upon his return to his command.[8]

Throughout his military career, John McClernand would exhibit concern for the soldiers under his command. Perhaps this was because, as a politician, he realized that many of those soldiers would return to Illinois after the war, and they would then not be soldiers but voters. Also, during the next few years he would command men from other states—states with governors whom he knew personally, governors who could be influential should he desire to return to the national political stage. In March 1862 he was concerned that those soldiers were sick and needed fresh beef and potatoes. To Grant he complained about the situation but expressed confidence that the district commander would attend to "this serious evil." Grant replied that forty thousand pounds of potatoes were being shipped from Cairo to Fort Donelson, and apparently realizing the seriousness of his subordinate's complaint, he also wrote Halleck that his command was suffering for want of beef.[9]

As the war progressed and incompetent commanders fell by the wayside, soldiers benefited as their welfare became a prime consideration for commanders from army to company level. Units that had enlisted together and were commanded by local men had a common bond that caused health and morale to be foremost. Such army commanders as George B. McClellan and William S. Rosecrans were notable for their concern for the welfare of their soldiers. McClellan was affectionately known as "Little Mac" to his men, but his insistence on massive amounts of supplies to support them (and his consistent tendency to overestimate the enemy facing him) led Lincoln and others to question whether he had more concern for his army than for fighting the Confederates. Rosecrans, known as "Old Rosy," was often seen among the troops inquiring about their welfare and the quantity and quality of food being provided to them. Both generals, though, would prove that taking care of the soldiers was only part of a commander's responsibility. They still had to win on the battlefield. When they could not, they were removed.[10]

On 1 March, Halleck ordered Grant to move up the Tennessee to destroy the railroad bridge near Eastport, Mississippi, and the rail junctions at Corinth, as well as at Jackson and Humboldt, Tennessee. Grant was then to return to the vicinity of Paris and Danville, Tennessee. Halleck made no mention of seeking out and attacking the Confederate army, and he cautioned that Grant was to retreat rather than risk a major battle.[11]

The next day Grant ordered McClernand to prepare two brigades to embark upon the expedition. In turn, the division commander selected the Second and Third Brigades, allocated the necessary wagons, and directed the units to be prepared to move upon further orders. The detailed order was issued the following day. In it McClernand specified the order of march and the time of movement—7:00 a.m., 4 March.[12]

Unbeknownst both to Grant and McClernand, a maelstrom was swirling around the district commander, one that would soon engulf the commander of the First Division. At his headquarters in St. Louis, Halleck was caught between demands for information from the general in chief, George B. McClellan, and a lack of information from Grant. In his reports to McClellan he attributed to his subordinate "neglect and inefficiency," passed along rumors of drunkenness, and accused him of leaving his command without authorization. Finally, on 4 March, he replaced Grant with Maj. Gen. (by which rank Halleck referred to him) Charles F. Smith. Not until 15 March did the brouhaha subside, when Halleck backed down in the face of a demand from Washington that he either drop the matter or prefer charges.[13]

McClernand learned on 6 March that Grant, in obedience to Halleck's order, had placed Smith in command of the movement up the Tennessee. McClernand, however, outranked Smith as a brigadier general and therefore believed he should have been given the command. In a letter to Grant he angrily complained that "I rank him as a brigadier and cannot recognize his superiority without self-degradation, which no human power can constrain me to do." What he did not know was that Smith had been nominated for promotion to major general on 3 March and that in the telegram to Grant the next day Halleck had given Smith the rank of major general (although he did not have the authority to do so—that authority was reserved to Washington).[14]

In another letter to Grant on 9 March, McClernand alluded to an interview with his fellow Illinoisan. Probably during that meeting he raised the question of who ranked whom. Grant by then either knew Smith had been promoted or was acting on the information received in Halleck's letter, for he had addressed a message to him as "Major General" on 5 March.[15]

Also on 9 March, McClernand, two of his brigade commanders, and eight staff officers sent a letter to Grant in which they expressed their "gratitude and respect" for the "uniform urbanity and kindness you have extended to us." They urged him to use the letter for whatever purpose he chose.[16] This was a remarkable letter that could have had no ulterior motive. The praise for Grant's successes at Belmont, Henry, and Donelson was apparently heartfelt. Grant had been relieved, and McClernand had no way to know whether he would eventually be reinstated. This communication is a clear indication that at this point in McClernand's career and in his relationship with Grant, he had for his senior only respect, admiration, and subordination. As further evidence, McClernand, when he learned that Grant had been restored, sent him congratulations and added, "I hope soon to see you with us."[17] By the end of the year, however, his attitude would be markedly different.

To comply with Grant's order to move up the Tennessee, McClernand had to move two brigades of his division from Fort Donelson back to the vicinity of Fort Henry. The First Brigade, commanded by Col. Richard J. Oglesby, remained at Fort Donelson. McClernand encamped near Metal Landing, about a mile south of Henry and ordered that five days' rations be prepared. The division (less the First Brigade) began to embark steamboats on 5 March and completed the loading the next evening. Confusion as to his mission caused McClernand to express his concern to Grant: "Having no instructions to guide me hence I will await them." The ensuing instructions were to disembark at Pine Landing, a few miles farther south.[18]

On 5 March Halleck changed the mission. Rather than return to Paris and Danville, the army was to encamp at Savannah, Tennessee, just north of Pittsburg Landing.[19]

Ill health and equipment problems continued to bedevil the men of McClernand's First Division. At Pine Landing, surgeons from the Third Brigade protested that the lack of fruit and potatoes was "beginning to tell fearfully upon the energies and health of the men." McClernand then made an urgent request to his commissary officer to provide the needed food. He also requested that haversacks and canteens be provided to reduce shortages of those items in his command.[20]

In his mind the question of command had not been resolved, and McClernand still deferred to Smith, because of Grant's order. On 8 March he recommended to Smith that the army disembark at Hamburg, which, a reconnaissance had revealed, was closer to Corinth than was Eastport. He prudently ordered his command to load the transports "preparatory for a forward movement." He then asked that his division be allowed to lead the army. Smith's order, however, placed McClernand's division third, behind those of William T. Sherman and Stephen A. Hurlbut.[21]

In a blizzard of field orders, McClernand directed the order of movement of his Second and Third Brigades on the transports (the First was to march to Fort Henry and remain there); provided instructions to be followed if the boats were attacked; issued extremely specific guidance for actions upon landing; and established the order of march in case a forward movement was ordered. The general's instructions for landing were a model for such operations. In them he carefully specified where each brigade was to land, how many skirmishers were to be set out, the size of the reserve, the mission of the cavalry, and finally, instructions for the artillery and baggage train. The First Division would be prepared for any eventuality.[22]

McClernand's two brigades began to move up the river on 10 March, and McClernand himself arrived at Savannah the next day.[23] En route, however, another controversy arose over rank and command authority. During embarkation, soldiers from McClernand's and Hurlbut's divisions had become intermixed on one of the transports. Hurlbut, who ranked McClernand as a brigadier, informed him that he had taken charge of the boat and would return it to him when his command disembarked. The Illinois politician took great exception to this action, because the boat had originally been assigned to McClernand's command. In a sharp response to Hurlbut, McClernand wrote, "Your communication assumes authority to command me. You will pardon me for respectfully denying your right to do so. I am commander of a division and so are you, and like you am responsible to Maj. Gen. Smith."[24]

Although Hurlbut, in his reply, stated he did not wish to argue over authority and returned the boat to McClernand's control, he ensured that the politician understood the authority that dates of rank imposed. "Your remark that you only consider yourself liable to orders from the Major General you will find erroneous. Either of the officers of your own rank senior to you have *the right* to give you orders. The officers apparent are Genl. Sherman and myself." He added, "I advise that you meet this . . . in the spirit offered, kindness and with a desire that the public service may not suffer by any useless controversy."[25] Such controversies, however, would plague John McClernand throughout his military career.

On 13 March, Smith and McClernand met on board the steamer *Leonard.* McClernand was ordered to land his brigades at Savannah and occupy the surrounding country. The division commander did so and provided his commander a sketch of his position. He also informed him that intelligence indicated that Rebel cavalry was in the vicinity. He further reported that men in his command were not being paid promptly and that they were short of clothing.[26]

Security of the force was a primary concern to the division commander. Both to protect the army from surprise and to locate enemy soldiers, McClernand dispatched cavalry patrols over the next several days. He wisely alerted two infantry regiments to provide support should the patrols encounter an enemy force. Scouts found water high and roads impassable, due to the downpours that had occurred during the month. On 17 March cavalry scouted about eighteen miles to the southeast and reported that two hundred Confederate cavalrymen had been in the vicinity the night before. Soldiers from Brig. Gen. Lew Wallace's Third Division scouted west toward Purdy. William T. Sherman's Fifth Division reconnoitered south to the area between Corinth and Eastport.[27]

While these operations were occurring, the Forest City Union Association of Cleveland, Ohio, met and passed a resolution thanking "Gen. J. A. McClernand for the able, gallant and patriotic manner in which he has officiated on the Mississippi, Cumberland, and Tennessee rivers and to the gallant officers and soldiers under his command." He wrote back deferring "all credit to the brave officers and men whom it has been my good fortune and honor to command." He concluded, "I claim none for myself." The astute politician knew how to respond to praise. The Association sent a similar proclamation to Grant, who also responded kindly.[28]

McClernand corresponded also with the Hon. James W. Singleton, chairman of the Illinois Constitutional Convention. In January Singleton had inquired about the status of equipment being furnished for Illinois units. McClernand had replied that only through Governor Yates's intervention had he been able to secure enough supplies to embark on the expedition to Forts Henry and Donelson. This not only further cemented his relationship with the governor but ensured the support of the Convention delegates: "A body like that you represent gives the soldier a new life, and inspires him with fresh courage to fight the battles of the Constitution."[29] Although such a missive can rightly be viewed as self-serving and political, other portions indicate the seriousness with which the general viewed shortages of equipment, arms, and clothing. Throughout his military career, McClernand would consistently seek to ensure his men were well fed, adequately clothed, and properly armed, even if it meant using his political connections.

After being restored to command, Grant reported to Halleck that fifty to sixty thousand Confederates were rumored to be in the vicinity of Corinth and Eastport. Halleck urged caution "so as not to bring on an engagement." Having been named commander of the Department of the Mississippi on 11 March—a department that included Buell—he ordered Buell and his command from Nashville to Savannah.[30]

Grant arrived at Savannah on 17 March and surveyed the dispositions of his command. Wallace's division was at Crump's Landing, six miles from Savannah. Sherman's and Hurlbut's divisions were encamped at Pittsburg Landing, two miles farther up river. Oglesby's brigade departed Fort Henry on 15 March and joined McClernand ashore at Savannah, while Smith's division remained on transports in the river. Grant, who believed that the Rebels were massing near Corinth, immediately ordered his entire army, except McClernand's division, to concentrate at Pittsburg.[31]

While Grant was arranging his divisions, McClernand was busy reconnoitering the countryside east of the Tennessee River. On 18 March he dispatched a combined cavalry, infantry, and artillery force under the Third Brigade commander, Col. Leonard F. Ross, toward Pin Hook and Waynesboro, Tennessee. The aggressive general cautioned Ross not to allow himself to be surprised and authorized him to pursue if an enemy force was encountered and withdrew. All the force found was 150 sacks of flour. McClernand's report to Grant, though, provided valuable information about the countryside, the sentiments of the people, and the absence of enemy forces.[32]

McClernand also continued to complain about what he believed was the excessive number of men he was required to furnish daily for details. He wrote Grant's assistant adjutant general that he had only 4,350 men in the division yet had to furnish soldiers for the quartermaster and commissary sections. He reminded higher headquarters that he also had to furnish his own guards and pickets. The expedition east of the river further reduced the number of men available for details. The requirements, however, did not lessen.[33]

On 20 March Grant ordered McClernand to send two of his brigades to Pittsburg. The third was to remain at Savannah as a garrison until other units arrived to relieve it. McClernand duly selected the First and Third Brigades to embark and sail to join the other divisions at the Landing. The embarkation was delayed, because only two boats were available for the brigades, and only one at a time could unload at Pittsburg. McClernand ensured that his commander was kept informed of his situation. He also directed Ross, who would land first, to position his brigade so that the follow-on force could "encamp in proper force and continuous to it."[34] This would ensure that no gaps occurred in the line and that the division would be in

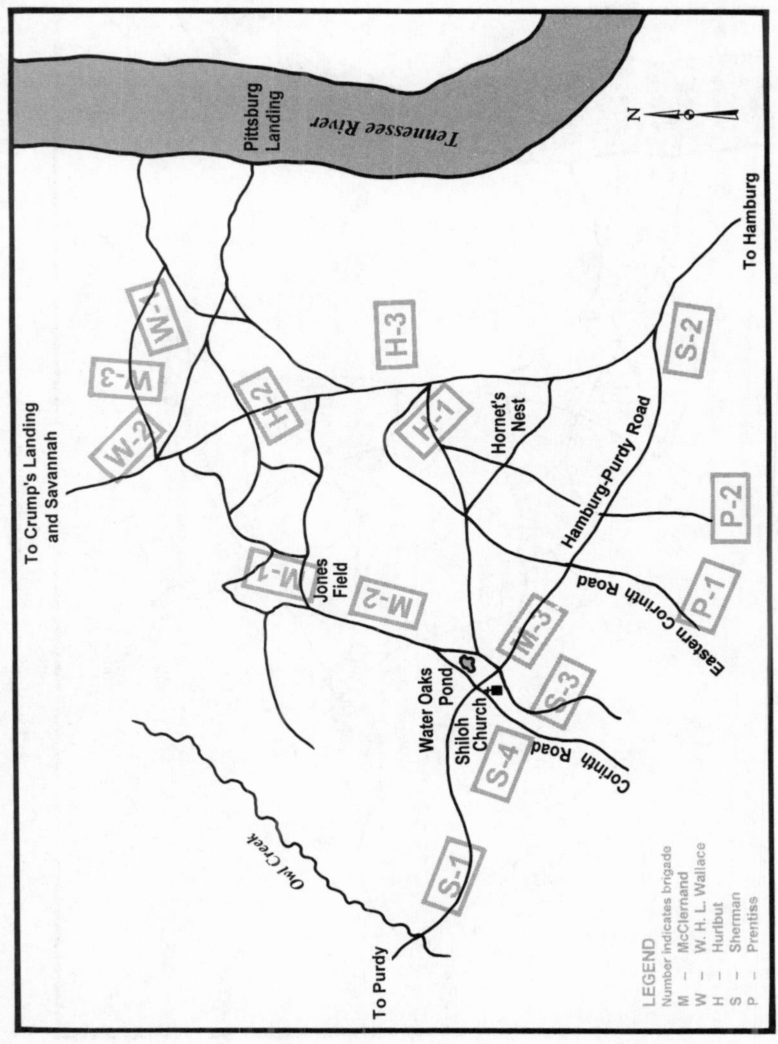

Union Encampments Prior to Battle (Shiloh)

position to repel an attack. Unfortunately for the Union army, such dispositions were not implemented.

By 25 March McClernand's, Hurlbut's, Sherman's, and Smith's divisions were encamped between Pittsburg Landing and Shiloh Church. Grant, however, had disposed these divisions in a bizarre manner. McClernand's First and Second Brigades were aligned at a ninety-degree angle to Sherman's line.

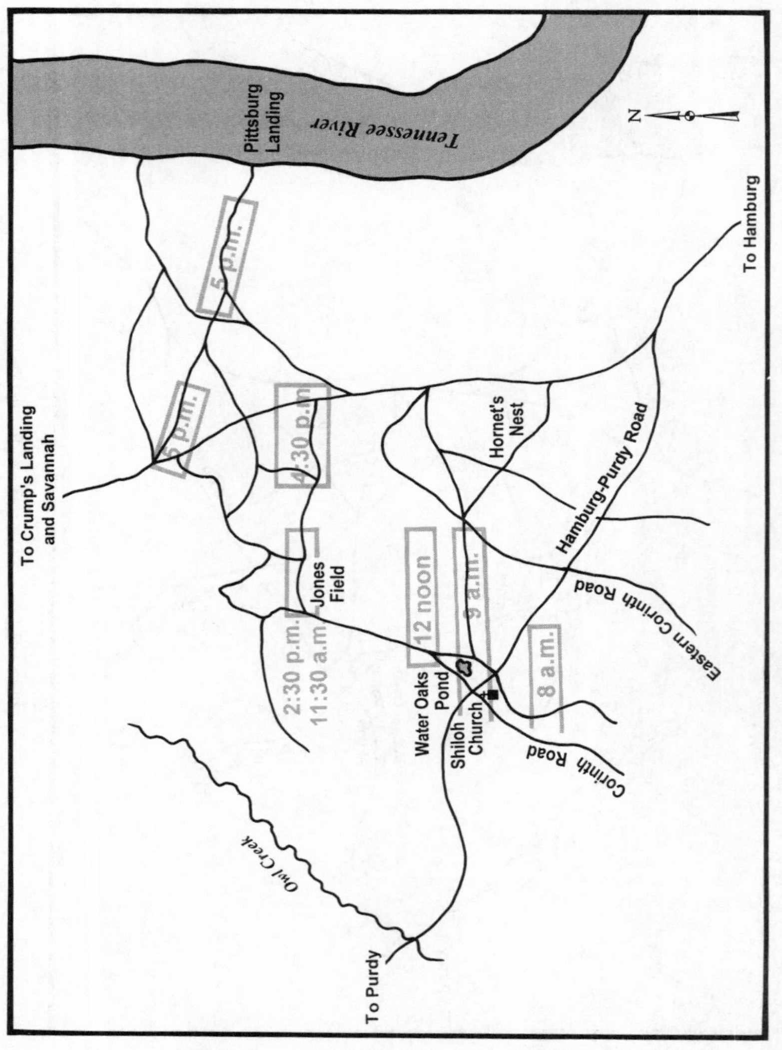

Locations of McClernand's Division, April 6, 1862

To their front were encamped two of Sherman's brigades, with their center on Shiloh Church. His First Brigade was to the west, with a flank on Owl Creek. The Third and Fourth Brigades encamped near Shiloh Church. His Second Brigade was to the east, to protect the army's flank near the Tennessee River. McClernand's Third Brigade was to the rear of Sherman's Third Brigade. The Sixth Division, commanded by Brig. Gen. Benjamin M.

Prentiss, would have filled the gap between Sherman's brigades had they not been forward of his line. Smith (who was soon replaced by W. H. L. Wallace, due to an injury) was in position near the landing to McClernand's rear. Hurlbut's three brigades were scattered to the east of McClernand. Lew Wallace's division was deployed between Crump's Landing and Purdy.[35]

This flawed deployment meant that there was no connected battle line and that Union soldiers would mask the fire of other bluecoats to their rear. No one expected a Confederate attack, and not even the forward line had thrown up breastworks. Only McClernand was concerned about the vulnerable position of the Union command. On 27 March he expressed his concern to Grant and suggested that "the various camps here should be formed upon some general and connected plan. Such a precaution might be necessary to avoid confusion and self destruction in case of a possible night attack."[36] Had Grant heeded his subordinate's misgivings, the momentous events to come might have taken an entirely different course.

In 1864 Sherman would write that Smith, not Grant, was responsible for the deployment on the ground. Sherman would assert that his division was posted only as a picket line and that "McClernand and Prentiss were the real line of battle." Smith, of course, by then was dead and could not defend himself. McClernand had returned to Illinois and, because of subsequent events, was in disfavor. Clearly, Sherman's letter was an attempt to minimize his own role in the disaster, making his division only "the outlying pickets." Grant had by then become the general in chief.[37] The implication was that the fault for the disaster lay with Smith and, perhaps, with McClernand and Prentiss for not having conducted a more adequate defense. The record is clear, however, that there was no "real line of battle" and that Grant had ample opportunity to correct the dispositions if he had found them to be faulty. McClernand expressed concern, but his fears were ignored.

The issue of rank that had simmered between McClernand and Smith reached a boiling point on 26 March. By Special Orders No. 36, Grant appointed Smith, "the senior officer of the forces at Pittsburg[,] . . . to command that post." Smith then directed McClernand to provide a detail of privates. The feisty general immediately informed Smith that he was to receive orders only from Grant, and he protested to Grant that he outranked Smith as a brigadier general. He had heard rumors that Smith had been promoted to major general, he added, but he also heard rumors that he too had been promoted. (In fact, he had been promoted on 24 March, but the official correspondence had not yet reached him.) If Smith actually outranked him, he would submit to his authority; if not, however, he could not recognize him as his superior officer. Smith also wrote Grant and expressed confusion over the question of rank.[38]

Grant solved the immediate problem by moving his headquarters from Savannah to Pittsburg. He then wrote Halleck and asked for a resolution. Halleck referred the question to Secretary of War Stanton. Finally, on 5 April, Halleck provided Grant a list of officers recently promoted to major general. Even though both had the same date of rank, on that list McClernand outranked Smith.[39]

With the rank controversy resolved, Grant chose to spend much of his time at Savannah. Perhaps because it was only eight river miles from Pittsburg, he designated no one to be in command during his absence. The fact that he remained unequivocally in command places the responsibility for the upcoming events squarely upon his shoulders.

Rank was not the only controversy in which McClernand was involved during March. On the 28th, Grant wrote his subordinate that complaints had been lodged against McClernand's command for having "carried off with them to Pittsburg a number of Negroes, belongin [*sic*] to Citizens of this place and vicinity." Such action was a violation of general orders, and Grant demanded that the guilty parties be charged. McClernand replied that he would investigate promptly, but his lawyer training was evident in his response. He informed Grant that without knowledge of who had lodged the complaint and without identification of the negroes, it would be difficult to determine the status of the individuals.[40]

The next day the division commander again wrote his superior about this issue. In this letter McClernand stated that he had attempted to obey all orders concerning "properly disposing of negroes found within our lines," but that military officials were not competent to make proper determination of ownership of slaves. He, therefore, proposed that a civilian tribunal be established to make such determinations. He then assured Grant that any individual within his command found to be in violation of orders regarding "confiscating property (including slaves)" would be investigated.[41]

Although McClernand was engaged in operational and administrative matters, politics remained an essential element in his correspondence. Illinois governor Richard Yates had not forgotten his political ally. On 26 March he wrote McClernand about political conditions in Illinois and the general's own political fortunes in his home state: "I thought I could see a little feeling among certain ones of your own party not to give you full credit for your great services but . . . the masses of the democratic party and all the republicans . . . have the warmest feelings for you." On a personal note, he added, "Let me assure you that I miss no occasion to do you justice, and that it affords me pleasure to do so."[42] The general would indeed provide the governor many occasions to do him justice in the future.

Battle of Shiloh (6–7 April 1862)

Union Organization
Army of the Tennessee, Maj. Gen. Ulysses S. Grant
First Division, Maj. Gen. John Alexander McClernand
First Brigade, Cols. Abraham M. Hare (wounded) and Marcellus M. Crocker
Second Brigade, Col. C. Carroll Marsh
Third Brigade, Col. Julius Raith (mortally wounded) and Lt. Col. Enos P. Wood
Second Division, Brig. Gen. W. H. L. Wallace (mortally wounded) and Col. James Tuttle
Third Division, Maj. Gen. Lew Wallace
Fourth Division, Brig. Gen. Stephen A. Hurlbut
Fifth Division, Brig. Gen. William T. Sherman (wounded)
Sixth Division, Brig. Gen. Benjamin M. Prentiss (captured)

Army of the Ohio, Maj. Gen. Don Carlos Buell

Confederate Organization
Army of the Mississippi, Gens. Albert Sidney Johnston (killed) and P. G. T. Beauregard
First Corps, Maj. Gen. Leonidas Polk
Second Corps, Maj. Gen. Braxton Bragg
Third Corps, Maj. Gen. William J. Hardee
Reserve Corps, Brig. Gen. John C. Breckinridge

McClernand was anxious to obtain an independent command, where the glory would be his alone. As a division commander he was vastly overshadowed by army, district, and department commanders. He hoped his patron President Abraham Lincoln would help. At the end of March he forwarded directly to the president his report of the battle at Fort Donelson, "unofficially and for your personal information." In it he warned Lincoln that a major battle was in the offing between "the hosts gathering and marshaling" at Pittsburg Landing and at Corinth. Additionally, he included therein a request: "If you will give me an independent command, in an active and contested field, I will try and reward your confidence."[43]

By 3 April, three Confederate corps under Gen. Albert S. Johnston had gathered at Corinth. One was Polk's command, which had abandoned Columbus on 2 March. Buell's movement from Nashville was lethargic; he was still forty-five miles from Savannah.[44] Near Pittsburg Landing, McClernand's men and those of the other divisions, 37,331 strong, drilled, cleaned equipment, conducted reviews, and attempted to remain dry during the incessant rain. McClernand asked for reports about the condition of horses and equipment and took time to write a congratulatory note to the recently promoted Brig. Gen. W. H. L. Wallace. Neither he nor the other division commanders ordered their soldiers to entrench. A Confederate attack was not anticipated.[45]

Sherman reconnoitered toward Eastport and encountered a few mounted Confederates, but he failed to locate the 40,335 Rebels near Corinth. On 3 and 4 April, Sherman's outposts clashed with Confederates from the 1st Alabama Cavalry about four miles from Shiloh Church on the road to Corinth. Both Sherman and McClernand reported the encounters to Grant. Despite these incidents, Sherman on 5 April wrote Grant, "I do not apprehend anything like an attack on our position."[46]

Grant planned to deploy Buell's Army of the Ohio at Hamburg, about four miles south of Pittsburg. One division of that force was expected at Savannah on 5 April. About 1:00 P.M. on 4 April, McClernand sent a cavalry battalion to scout the road to Hamburg and also Bark Road, which ran southwest toward Corinth. Apparently the battalion scouted only the area near the Tennessee River, for in the early afternoon of 4 April the Confederate division of Maj. Gen. William J. Hardee was arriving at Mickey's farmhouse, about four miles from the intersection of the Bark and Corinth Roads and about seven miles from Sherman's division at Shiloh Church. From Savannah Grant wrote to Halleck, "I have scarcely the faintest idea of an attack (general one) being made upon us, but will be prepared should such a thing take place."[47]

Unbeknownst to the encamped Federals, four Confederate corps had moved within cannon shot of the bluecoats. On Sunday morning, 6 April, Johnston had deployed his army to strike Grant's men at Shiloh Church with the intent to turn the Union army and force it away from the river. At about 5:00 A.M. a Union patrol stumbled upon the gathering Confederates, and a sharp fight broke out. Prentiss alerted his advanced division and began to awaken his men and deploy them for battle. Reports reached Sherman, but he discounted the possibility of Rebels being near—that is until his orderly was killed beside him. His reaction: "My God, we are attacked!"[48]

Soldiers of McClernand's 43d Illinois were awake early on that Sunday. Fearful of an attack, the regimental commander, Col. Julius Raith, had had his men load their weapons the night before. No attack ensued, but the weapons remained loaded throughout the night. To ensure they would fire, Raith had requested that McClernand allow his men to discharge their weapons. The division commander agreed, but before all companies had completed the firing, noise of fighting to the front reached their ears.[49]

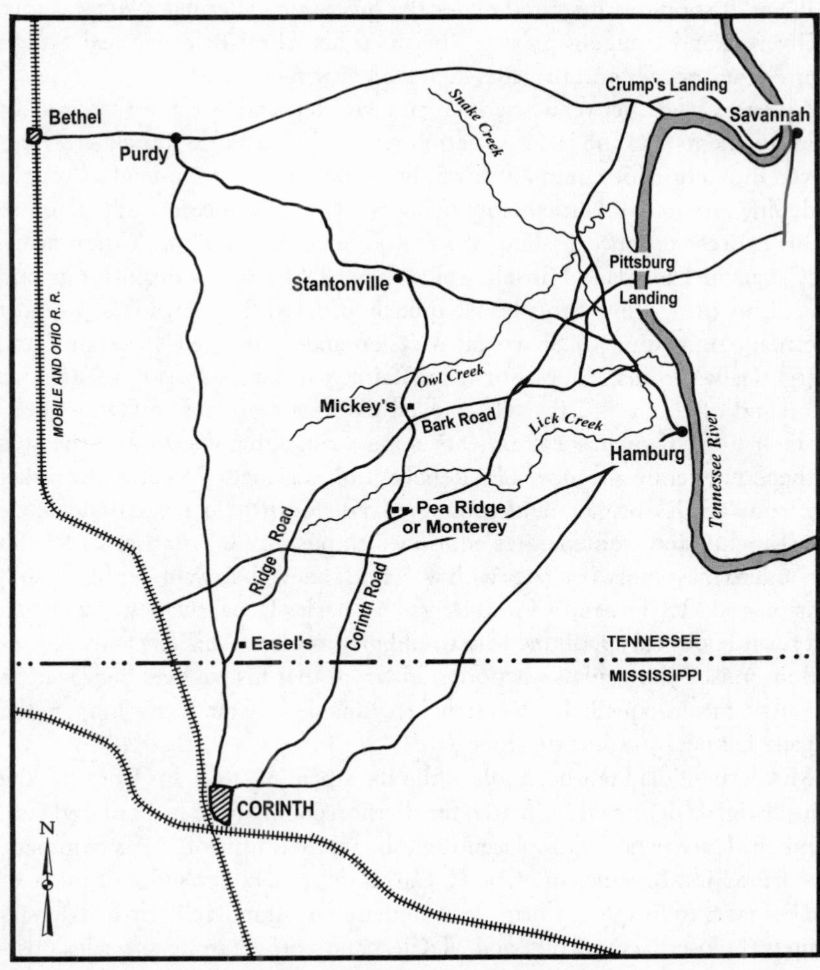

Area between Pittsburg Landing and Corinth

Sherman and his brigade commanders hastily attempted to deploy their men to stem the onrushing gray tide, but against four massed corps, any success was only temporary. Although the terrain favored the defense, Sherman gradually gave ground until by 9:00 A.M. his division had been pushed back from Shiloh Church to a line along the Hamburg-Purdy Road.[50] Screaming soldiers waving the Stars and Bars slammed into Prentiss's Sixth Division as well, and it soon disintegrated under the onslaught. Sherman's left was thus uncovered, and a huge gap existed between his Third Brigade, near Shiloh Church, and his Second Brigade, deployed near the river.[51]

Couriers raced between Sherman and McClernand as the former sought reinforcements and the latter situation reports. The battle immediately devolved into a brigade commander's fight as the forward commanders sought to deploy into line of battle before being consumed by the gray tide. Because of his expressed concern about the faulty deployment of the Union army, McClernand had made himself well aware of Sherman's dispositions and that of his own Third Brigade. He quickly ordered that brigade to support Sherman. According to Sherman, McClernand responded "promptly and energetically" to his request for help. Raith, who was suddenly thrust into command of the Third Brigade, moved his four regiments a few hundred yards forward of their encampments along a ridge that overlooked the area of the Confederate advance. The Rebel assault was met by a blaze of musket fire from Raith's brigade and soon wavered. Raith held his ground tenaciously, while the Confederates continued to push back Prentiss, on Raith's left, and to mass more brigades with which to renew the assault on Sherman's division and McClernand's Third Brigade. Charles Dana, the newspaperman and future political appointee who would play a role in McClernand's fate, at Shiloh praised the general's actions and wrote that his soldiers displayed "a gallantry rarely equalled." Nevertheless, unable to stand any longer, the brigade fell back in some disorder.[52]

McClernand had not been idle while the storm raged to his front. As the Third Brigade deployed for battle, the division commander had ordered Col. Abraham Hare, who had replaced Oglesby (away on furlough) as commander of the First Brigade, and Col. C. Carroll Marsh, commander of the Second Brigade, to form their brigades and march to support Sherman. Marsh's camp was closer to the front, and McClernand's orders to his brigades positioned Marsh first, to serve as a base upon which the other brigades would form. Hare would form on Marsh's left and Raith on his right. McClernand had been warned by one of his staff officers of the continuing Confederate advance and met his brigades as they arrived near the Purdy Road. He personally directed them into position. As Sherman's Third Brigade began to stream back, Raith filled in to the right of the Second Brigade.[53]

As Sherman was forced back from Shiloh Church, his brigades fell in with the line McClernand had established, thus creating a continuous position from Owl Creek to the Eastern Corinth Road. At about 9:00 A.M., Johnston's Confederates slammed into this newly established line, in what Sherman described as a "furious attack on General McClernand's entire front."[54]

Unfortunately for the men of the First and Fifth Divisions, Prentiss's Sixth Division no longer existed. What remained of it, along with Brig. Gen. Stephen Hurlbut's Fourth Division and Brig. Gen. W. H. L. Wallace's Second Division, had occupied a sunken road that would become known as the Hornets' Nest. The result was that the Federal line formed a lazy inverse V to the left of McClernand's left-most regiment—the 8th Illinois Infantry. From that regiment a gap of several hundred yards existed across an open field in front of the sunken road.

About mid-morning Grant arrived on the field, his breakfast at Savannah having been interrupted by reports of the developing battle. He conferred with Sherman and then rode off in the direction of McClernand. In 1872 McClernand would write that at no time during the battle did he see Grant, although Grant did confer with Sherman and Prentiss, who had joined the Union soldiers gathering at the Hornets' Nest. Apparently the army commander realized the precariousness of the Union position and the critical gap that separated the 8th Illinois from the sunken road, for he ordered the 15th and 16th Iowa to report to McClernand to reinforce his line.[55]

It was too late: two gray brigades suddenly appeared on Marsh's left. For five minutes the two opponents traded fire, but soon McClernand's line began to give way as Confederates penetrated between the First and Second Brigades and swept the remnants of the Third Brigade from the field. Within moments regiments began to break, and soon large portions of the Illinois general's right and center brigades were heading toward the rear. Hare, on the left, stood only a few minutes longer before his brigade too was caught in the destruction of the Union line.[56]

Disaster seemed imminent, but fortunately for the Union men, Hurlbut, in response to Sherman's plea for help, had dispatched a brigade under Col. James C. Veatch, and it had just taken a position to McClernand's rear when the blue stream from their front began flowing through it. Two of Veatch's regiments melted, but two others stood fast, thus delaying the surging Rebels. Soon, however, they too joined the mob streaming toward Pittsburg Landing.[57]

The collapse of Raith's, Marsh's, Hare's, and Veatch's brigades resulted in a major penetration of the Union line. The sunken road position held, but McClernand's and Sherman's left flank was open. The only option was to withdraw. McClernand ordered his command to establish a new line about two hundred yards to the rear. His difficulty in ensuring that this order was carried out cannot be exaggerated. By 11:00 A.M., as the Union line was disintegrating, regiments and brigades were becoming scattered across the battlefield. Raith had been mortally wounded. Confederates were pushing

Sherman's and McClernand's front and had enveloped McClernand's left. Simply to locate commanders was almost impossible. "The scene was fearful," Illinois officer George Carrington would write. Nevertheless, the First and Second Brigades were able to establish a line on a ridge to the rear of their Purdy Road position. Three regiments of the Third Brigade had withdrawn from the battle because they were out of ammunition. The 43d Illinois failed to receive McClernand's order to withdraw and was routed by onrushing Rebels.[58]

Sherman and McClernand had succeeded in establishing the new position to try to hold the Union right flank. Confusion within the Confederate corps, which were hopelessly entangled, allowed them a few precious moments to arrange the remnants of their own regiments. Despite the respite, the Confederate push against McClernand's left was too strong, and this line too collapsed. About noon, most of the two divisions withdrew north about six hundred yards to Jones Field, but part of McClernand's First Brigade fled to the northeast toward the landing.[59]

W. H. L. Wallace's adjutant, Capt. Israel P. Rumsey, was to be highly critical of McClernand's conduct during this phase of the battle. According to Rumsey, McClernand withdrew his left flank, which left Wallace's right at the Hornets' Nest exposed. Rumsey wrote that he "plead with McClernand to throw his left forward, but he refused." By the time he returned to Wallace, Hurlbut had collapsed, and Confederates were swarming through the gap on Prentiss's right.[60]

Such criticism does not accord with the facts. By the time Rumsey saw McClernand, Col. Jesse Hildebrand's brigade of Sherman's division, to Raith's front, had long since been destroyed. Raith's brigade had been scattered across the battlefield. The combined corps of Bragg and Polk had simply been too much for the Union divisions to withstand. Once McClernand's left had been driven back, the Confederates were free to hold the gap between the Union right (Sherman and McClernand) and center at the Hornets' Nest. That cauldron became a magnet that attracted increasing numbers of gray-clad infantry, who began to encircle the beleaguered bluecoats. McClernand's only hope to save the remnants of his command was to refuse his left and attempt an orderly withdrawal, even if that action meant exposing the men in the Hornets' Nest to increased Confederate fire.

At Jones Field, McClernand and Sherman were able to rally portions of their divisions to reestablish the Union right. The historian of the 55th Illinois Infantry would credit McClernand with "pugnaciously keeping up a . . . resistance creditable to himself and the cause." The Confederate attack slowed, and McClernand saw an opportunity to retake the lost ground. With the command "*Forward!*" the fiery general initiated a counterattack with a portion of his Second and Third Brigades. To his right, Sherman and the remnants of his command joined the advance. If successful, the counterattack could relieve the pressure against the sunken road. Back to the area of his initial headquarters McClernand drove the Confederates. Union casualties mounted, as Rebel reinforcements reached the scene. The increased resistance soon forced Sherman back, thus exposing the right flank of McClernand, who had no choice except to retreat. By 2:30 P.M. most of his command was back at Jones Field, except for what was left of the First Brigade, which had retired to the northeast and was out of contact with the division.

Although the "fine charge"—as characterized by Sherman—had delayed the Confederates for an hour, the two Union divisions were no longer cohesive fighting forces. Both had been reduced to confused groups of men with decimated chains of command. Regiments were separated from brigades and brigades from divisions. The Union right had been badly mauled in an endeavor that Lew Wallace was to refer to as "useless valor." Nevertheless, Sherman and McClernand stitched together a line that held until about 4:00 P.M., when the dam at the Hornets' Nest broke and Federal and Rebel alike came streaming toward and through the position.[61]

Where was McClernand during the day? Regimental and brigade reports of the fighting are replete with references to McClernand at the front issuing orders to form line of battle, pull out of line to obtain ammunition, support artillery batteries, and eventually, retreat to form a new line. During the counterattack from Jones Field, Lt. Col. Thomas E. G. Ransom observed McClernand "bravely rallying and pushing forward an Ohio regiment" (probably the 53d Ohio from Sherman's destroyed brigade), and he was observed by the commander of the 43d Illinois "present in the thickest of the fight." From the vicinity of his old headquarters, McClernand directed unit movements to try to hold his forward position until he had personally to give the order to retreat.[62]

A withdrawal in the face of the enemy or under enemy pressure is an extremely difficult maneuver even with experienced soldiers and officers. While many of McClernand's men had fought at Donelson and had been faced with a similar situation there, they were still too raw to fall back in a completely orderly manner, especially when confronted by such an overwhelming force. Nevertheless, McClernand and his officers managed, despite the incessant noise, the thick black-powder smoke, and the rampant confusion, to establish several successive defensive lines during the withdrawal. Thick vegetation and water-filled creek bottoms further hampered the Illinois general's control of the situation. Yet despite these difficulties, at the end of the day the First Division retained some semblance of its organization and combat capability.

In the thick of the fight throughout, the Illinois general had displayed "great coolness and courage" under fire, had appreciated the tactical situation, had recognized the extreme consequences of the storm that had broken over the Union army that Sunday morning, and had done everything he could to save his division and the army.[63] If the army was defeated, it would not be because of the political general John Alexander McClernand.

What of the relationship between Sherman and McClernand during the battle? Sherman later reported that he and the Illinoisan acted "in perfect concert" as they struggled to maintain the line. Grant would write that McClernand told him on the day of the battle "that he profited much by having so able a commander supporting him." Indeed, McClernand himself praised Sherman: "To him is due great credit for the gallant, skillful, and important part he took in it."[64]

These comments probably reflect the situation accurately. The Union plight was desperate, and the commanders undoubtedly knew a defensible position had to be established or the entire command could be driven into the river. As division commanders, McClernand and Sherman were coequal; although Sherman was junior in rank to McClernand, neither technically was in support of the other.[65] Their reports indicate that neither sought to establish a senior-subordinate relationship with the other but that both acted in accordance with the critical nature of the situation.

By 1872, however, McClernand was to have a different view of the situation. As mentioned, he would write that he never spoke to Grant. He would also write that Sherman's division had lost its organization and occupied no definite positions, and that "Sherman was without any real command."[66] This assessment certainly cannot be accepted as correct, because of conflicting evidence. It is, undoubtedly, based on events that transpired in the years between 6 April 1862 and 11 January 1872.

Adam Badeau, who joined Grant's staff in February 1864, in his biography of Grant was to sound an entirely different theme. He wrote that Sherman

> in reality, commanded McClernand's division, as well as his own; for McClernand, who possessed both energy and courage, was a novice at soldiering, and with great good sense, sought and followed the advice of the man who was his junior in rank, but his superior in all military knowledge and experience; and Sherman, without stopping for any

> considerations of jealousy or pique, advised McClernand constantly and efficiently.[67]

It strains belief that McClernand "sought and followed" Sherman's advice. There is no evidence that McClernand previously had sought advice from Sherman; nor is there any indication in Sherman's letters either to his wife or brother that such was the case.[68] Furthermore, prior to Shiloh McClernand actually had more combat experience than Sherman, who had heard shots fired in anger only during the one-day First Battle of Bull Run. (Although Sherman had served in the Seminole War in Florida, he had not participated in any fighting.) Published in 1867, Badeau's account was probably influenced by subsequent events and must be examined carefully in light of those events.

McClernand's line near Jones Field was shattered by the mass of infantry, cavalry, and artillery fleeing to the rear. Sherman and the First Division commander quickly conferred and began to establish a new line along the Hamburg-Savannah Road. This line would be critical, for on its right was the bridge over Owl Creek, which Lew Wallace would need to bring his command to the battlefield. Both generals pieced together whatever units they could find to defend against the oncoming Confederates. Pandemonium reigned, as regiments from one division found themselves commanded by generals from other divisions. McClernand threw the 7th Illinois from the Second Division in as his reserve. Col. James Veatch, also from the Second Division, subordinated his brigade to McClernand's command as they strove to establish a last line of defense. McClernand ordered Colonel Marsh to gather all stragglers and place them into line. He also found two Ohio regiments (probably the 81st and 53d), which he sent into gaps in his newly created line.[69]

By nightfall Sherman and McClernand had established a defensible position on the Union right. The remnants of the Second Division and portions of the Fourth Division were to their left. The Sixth Division no longer existed. Wallace's Third Division began to arrive about 7:30 P.M. The advance division of Major General Buell's Army of the Ohio reached Pittsburg Landing around 5:00 P.M., pushed its way through the mass of frightened humanity milling about at the landing, and formed on the Union left, with the Tennessee River on its flank. The Confederate attack had spent itself. The two armies slept on their arms as a cold rain fell during the night.[70]

Newspaperman Henry Villard arrived at Pittsburg Landing with Buell's lead division. What he found was "an immense, panic-stricken, uncontrollable mob . . . with no sense of obedience left." Villard later met McClernand

and Hurlbut and described them both as "political generals" who "sought glory as much through army correspondents as by feats of war—if not more." He added, however, that "they [had] established a fair record as commanders." Years later B. H. Liddell Hart would credit Sherman and those two "political generals" with bringing "a measure of order" to the frightened, confused, and disorganized mass of blue that sought refuge along the river bank.[71]

Gen. P. G. T. Beauregard awoke the morning of 7 April to the sound of cannon booming near the river. Unbeknownst to him, Buell's army, although discovered by Bedford Forrest's cavalry, had crossed the Tennessee during the night and was now attacking the Rebel right. As Buell hammered the weary Confederates, Grant sent Lew Wallace's fresh division and what remained of Sherman's, McClernand's, Hurlbut's, W. H. L. Wallace's, and Prentiss's divisions against Beauregard's left and center.[72]

Late Sunday evening Grant had ordered McClernand "to assume command of all detached and fragmentary corps in [his] vicinity." These had included regiments from both Sherman's and Hurlbut's divisions, which were intermixed with those of his own. On 7 April Sherman's division was checked momentarily by a Confederate counterattack near Jones Field, but McClernand's combined force outflanked the Rebels and forced them to withdraw.[73]

As McClernand's attack reached the vicinity of the site of his original headquarters, the 53d Ohio Infantry received a volley that caused it to break for the rear. Marsh and McClernand tried to rally the men, but to no avail. The First Division wavered but then stood firm; McClernand would unselfishly credit Marsh with that and also for the subsequent action that resulted in reoccupation of his camps near Water Oaks Pond. Sherman would later describe the fighting here as "the severest musketry fire I ever heard."[74]

Close cooperation continued between Sherman and McClernand. About 2:00 P.M. Confederates attempted to envelop the First Division left. "Here one of the severest conflicts ensued that occurred during the two days," wrote McClernand in his official report. Having recognized the threat, the general shifted to the left, but not quickly enough to prevent the line from falling back "in great confusion." McClernand would candidly report that "a repulse seemed inevitable." The two regiments from Buell's Second Division that suddenly "came up at my request and succored me" drew praise from McClernand in his official report. The Confederates were driven back "in disorder" after a forty-minute fight, and McClernand's men soon passed through the former camps of the Third Brigade. By 4:00 P.M. the Union right had reached Shiloh Church, and the Confederate army was in full retreat. Grant did not pursue.[75]

On the morning of 8 April McClernand and the other commanders surveyed the battlefield. It had been a costly victory. The First Division alone had sustained 1,742 casualties—about 25 percent of its effective strength—while the entire Union army suffered 13,047 killed, wounded, and missing. Grant's Army of the Tennessee was a shambles, and Buell's Army of the Ohio had been bloodied, but the Confederates had lost heavily too, and they were in retreat toward Corinth. The incredible loss of life was brought home vividly to the First Division commander when he entered his tent, which had been held by Confederates the night before. In it he found one dead Confederate soldier slumped on his field table and another upon his cot. As they scoured the countryside during the next several days, McClernand's men would locate additional Union and Confederate dead and take several more Confederate prisoners.[76]

The general's compassion again shone through in the week following the battle. The division commander found time to inquire about Raith's wound. Its seriousness prompted him to order his brigade commander to be taken to Savannah to receive better attention, and he directed one of his officers to ensure that Raith received the best possible care. Despite these efforts, Raith died on Friday.[77]

On Tuesday, Grant ordered the 5th Ohio Cavalry to "ascertain if the enemy have retreated." McClernand and Sherman were ordered to provide infantry to support the cavalry if necessary. McClernand cautioned his First and Second Brigade commanders to place pickets in advance of their brigades and for the two to work in conjunction with one another.[78] He did not intend to be surprised again.

That day Grant issued a message of congratulations to his command for the victory at Shiloh. He assured them that "future generations . . . will enjoy the blessings of the best government the sun ever shone upon preserved by their Valor."[79] Such a message, issued by John McClernand over a year later, would have a dramatic impact.

Aware of the disaster that had nearly befallen his army, Grant issued a general order on 9 April that scored the lack of discipline and state of unpreparedness that had existed in the Union army prior to the battle. In the order he directed pickets and cavalry outposts be established to guard against surprise. McClernand issued a field order to relay the same instructions to his division. Also, Grant the previous day had complained to McClernand about "promiscuous firing by some of your Division," which, he reminded his subordinate, army orders prohibited. McClernand acknowledged that such firing had occurred, although he added that it had been more prevalent in other units. He promptly issued a field order on the subject; the order allowed weapons to be fired between 9:00 and 10:00 A.M. to ensure they functioned properly.[80]

These incidents provide insights into McClernand's military qualifications and character. The amateur McClernand had issued no orders about pickets prior to the battle (though neither had the professional Grant). McClernand had expressed concern about the dispositions of the Union army, but both Sherman and Grant had displayed confidence that the army would not be attacked. Neither Sherman, Grant, nor any of the other professional soldiers had attempted to fortify their positions.

When confronted with a violation of general orders, McClernand admitted it but then attempted to cast his guilt in terms of degree and the violations of other commanders. A man of stronger character would have simply acknowledged responsibility. "Promiscuous firing" is an indication of lack of discipline. Not only is it a waste of ammunition, but also there is the strong possibility of soldiers being injured. Still, McClernand, the inexperienced soldier, recognized the necessity to ensure that the weapons within his command were functional. Rain had fallen for days prior to the battle, and mud had permeated everything. A schedule of regular test-firing would ensure the weapons were not fouled and also ensure that nearby units did not mistake the sudden burst of musketry for an attack. McClernand's action in this regard, although a strong indication of how much the general had learned since being appointed to his position, indicated that he had not completely adopted the ways of the soldier.

On 11 April Halleck arrived at Pittsburg Landing and took overall command of both the Army of the Tennessee and the Army of the Ohio. Two days later he issued his own order to congratulate the victors of the battle. He also warned Grant that he must deploy his force so as to be able to resist any attack. The cautious Halleck would make no movement until he was satisfied that his army had recovered from the fighting on 6 and 7 April.[81]

As he had done on 26 February, McClernand on 11 April inserted himself into the decision process concerning the proper course of action for the army. He wrote Grant that he believed that the Confederates would abandon Virginia and concentrate in the lower South, to maintain control of that region. He therefore recommended that the army either entrench and reinforce to defeat a concerted Confederate attack or immediately move against the beaten Rebels to its front. McClernand was wrong in his assessment of Confederate strategic intentions. He failed to appreciate the importance of Virginia and the iron mills of Richmond to the survival of the Confederacy. Halleck chose the first course of action McClernand suggested; the army would not begin a general advance until 29 April.[82]

Congressman John McClernand, 1842.
Courtesy of the Illinois State Historical Library.

Cairo, Illinois, September 1861. Brig. Gen. John McClernand stands directly in front of the pillar (*center*). Brig. Gen. Ulysses S. Grant, with his hands in his pockets, is to his right.
Courtesy of the Chicago Historical Society.

Headquarters of the Army of the Potomac near the Antietam Creek battlefield, 3 October 1862. Major General McClernand is on President Abraham Lincoln's (*at center*) right. Major General McClellan, army commander, is the second person on Lincoln's left.
Courtesy of the Library of Congress.

From left: Allan Pinkerton, President Lincoln, Major General McClernand at McClellan's headquarters near the Antietam Creek battlefield, 4 October 1862.
Courtesy of the National Archives.

Post–Civil War law office of John McClernand and A. M. Broadwell on the east side of the public square in Springfield, Illinois. *Courtesy of the Illinois State Historical Library.*

"General McClernand's Grand March" was composed by Louis M. Rink in 1862.
Courtesy of McClernand Crawford.

West Point cadet Edward McClernand, ca. 1867. Born in 1848,
Edward graduated West Point in 1871, received the Medal of Honor in 1877,
retired as a brigadier general, and died in 1926.
Courtesy of McClernand Crawford.

John Alexander McClernand, ca. 1887.
Courtesy of the Illinois State Historical Library.

McClernand (at right) sat for this 1899 portrait with (from left) son-in-law Henry W. Butler, grandson William J. Butler, and great-grandson Henry W. Butler II. *Courtesy of McClernand Crawford.*

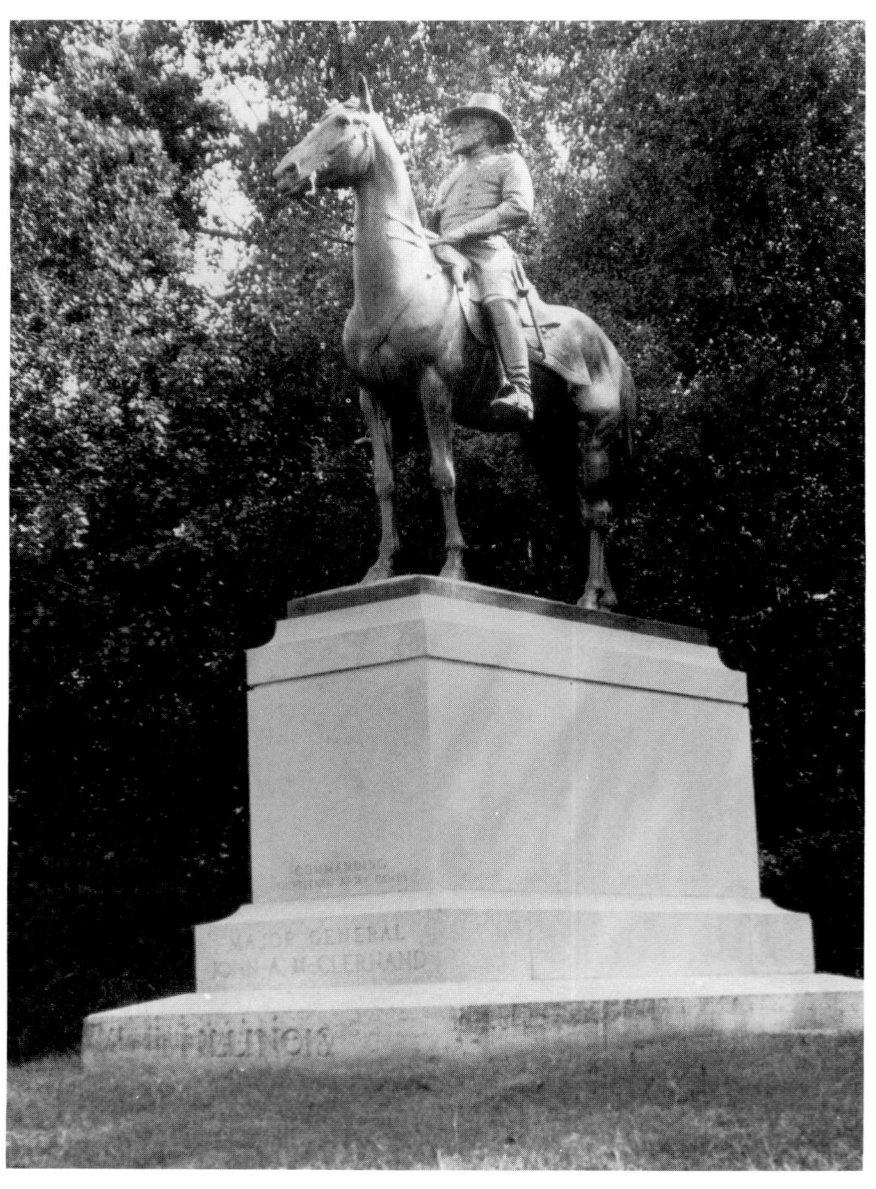

This statue of Major General McClernand at the
Vicksburg National Military Park was dedicated on 15 October 1919.

During those weeks McClernand immersed himself in the details of commanding an army division. He asked for reports on the condition of his artillery and for estimates of the amount of clothing and equipment his men would require for the upcoming campaign. He was particularly concerned about the lack of hospital tents, which the recent battle had proven were necessities for the surgeons. He had his command scour the battlefield to collect arms and ammunition, which he turned over to the army ordnance officer. In compliance with an order from Halleck, he established a regimen of drill and inspections to prepare his troops for future combat and to check the condition of the men and equipment. Obviously influenced by the events on the morning of 6 April, he specifically directed that "special pains . . . be taken to instruct sentinels in their duties."[83] He had learned his lesson about the element of surprise.

McClernand's political patron, Gov. Richard Yates, reached the Shiloh battlefield on 14 April, "accompanied by an army of surgeons and nurses and immense quantities of necessary hospital stores." It made good press for the governor, and for three days he made his presence known to Illinois soldiers. He spent time with his fellow politician, who came to see him. What they discussed is unknown, for Yates wrote only that "I have talked much with [him]," but it is not unreasonable to suspect that McClernand laid the idea of an independent command—the idea he had already broached with Lincoln—before Yates.[84]

On the day that Yates arrived, Grant issued a general order that was to have a significant effect on McClernand's career, although neither knew it at the time. In this order Grant directed that all official communications be sent through the chain of command. McClernand dutifully promulgated the order to his division.[85]

That same day, John McClernand made a mistake that he had made before, that he was to make again in similar occurrences, that would engender the wrath of Ulysses Grant, and that eventually would end his military career. He sent directly to Lincoln a self-serving report that exaggerated the role of his command: "My division, as usual, has borne or shared in bearing the brunt." He also took direct aim at Grant's generalship after the battle: "It was a great mistake that we did not pursue him Monday night and Tuesday."[86] While his division had indeed "borne or shared in bearing the brunt" at Fort Donelson and Shiloh, to insinuate that fellow generals had not borne their shares of the burden could only have unfavorable consequences for himself should they learn of his telegram. Although a pursuit may have inflicted irreparable damage on the Confederates, whether the Union army had been capable of pursuit Monday or Tuesday was an open question. To criticize his immediate commander, Grant, to the president for not having made a pursuit was not only insubordinate but also very foolish.

On Monday evening after the battle, Grant had telegraphed Halleck that a heavy fight had developed for two days but had resulted in "a complete repulse of the enemy." Two more telegrams the next day had advised his superior that the enemy had been "badly routed" and that his cavalry was in pursuit. Halleck notified Stanton, but neither general presumed to act outside of the chain of command to notify Lincoln directly.[87]

On 9 April Grant provided a lengthier letter about the two-day battle. Significant is his praise of Sherman. He added that singling out Sherman meant "no disparagement . . . to the other division commanders," whom he mentioned by name. All, he wrote, had "maintained their places with credit to themselves and the cause."[88]

Undoubtedly Sherman had performed well during the battle, but certainly his failure to detect Confederate movements to his front, his discounting of reports from his cavalry and infantry of Rebels in the vicinity on 4 and 5 April, and his unwillingness to accept reports of their presence early on 6 April had contributed significantly to the debacle. These errors were to be erased: Halleck telegraphed Stanton a few days later that "it is the unanimous opinion here that . . . Sherman saved the fortune of the day on the 6th instant, and contributed largely to the glorious victory on the 7th." Unmentioned were Buell and Lew Wallace, whose fresh troops had tipped the balance decisively in the Union favor. Also unmentioned were the accomplishments of the other division commanders.[89] Whether McClernand or the other commanders knew of Grant's letter or Halleck's telegram is unknown. It is suspicious in light of future events that Sherman alone among the division commanders in Grant's Army of the Tennessee was a West Point graduate.

In the weeks following the battle, limited tactical operations occurred within the First Division sector. Only the cavalry was involved, watching the Union army's right flank along Owl Creek to prevent surprise by Confederate forces. On 22 April Grant ordered McClernand to strengthen the force guarding the creek, to a brigade. The division commander took his responsibility seriously; he personally examined the area along the Purdy Road where it entered the Union flank and ensured that Grant was aware of Confederate activity.[90]

On 23 April Halleck finally ordered the armies in the Department of the Mississippi to move forward, about two miles, on the following day. Grant's army would constitute the right wing, Buell's the center, and Maj. Gen. John Pope's the left. McClernand was to build a bridge across Owl Creek; he responded with a vague order that directed a forward movement but neglected to specify the exact locations where each brigade would encamp. In a separate directive to Brig. Gen. Leonard F. Ross, who had resumed command of the Third Brigade, he stated that "I am so pressed with business that it is impossible for me to superintend the final location of my new camping ground"; he asked Ross to perform that duty. While this was not an unusual request, it was unusual that McClernand, the division commander, would believe he had to offer a reason to his brigade commander to perform an assigned mission.[91]

During his army tenure McClernand had learned the necessity of security and sanitation. He provided directives to all his commanders to ensure that the requirements of both were accomplished. Shiloh had taught him a lesson about surprise, and the rigors of camp life had taught him the necessity of preventing disease.

McClernand's infantry scouts reported that Rebels had obstructed the road about six miles from the creek with felled trees. The next day his cavalry reported that the Confederates had also destroyed a bridge along the road, probably over Turkey Creek.[92]

On 26 April McClernand ordered his First Brigade to conduct a reconnaissance in force "for the purpose of learning more efficiently the distance and disposition of the enemy." His order to the new brigade commander, Col. Michael K. Lawler, specified that he was merely to reconnoiter to the front, engaging the enemy only if he believed he could drive him back. In no case was he to advance farther than three or four miles, so that he could be reinforced if necessary. The actual mission of Lawler's force of six infantry regiments and four cavalry companies was to destroy a Confederate force at Pea Ridge (also known as Monterey), southwest of the Union position, that was harassing McClernand's pickets.

This aggressiveness by the Illinois general soon led to questions. Upon learning of this expedition, Grant queried McClernand as to who had authorized such a movement. McClernand replied that he believed that Col. James B. McPherson, Grant's engineer, had authorized him to "feel in my front and advance my camp if it should be found safe to do so." Obviously embarrassed by Grant's implied censure, McClernand stated he would withdraw the force.[93] This incident was a second seed that would bear bitter fruit between McPherson and McClernand in the months ahead.

McClernand's combativeness was only slightly reduced. On 27 April he dispatched another cavalry patrol, which found two negroes "skulking about" just beyond his picket line. After he questioned them, McClernand reported to Grant that the negroes had said Confederate cavalry was at Pea Ridge, and he asked for instructions. He also met with Grant, who apparently gave him permission to send Lt. Col. William McCullough's cavalry on a reconnaissance toward that location. McCullough's men killed three Confederates and picked up two more negroes, who reported that a man living in the vicinity was giving information to the Rebels about Union movements.[94] McClernand, who was developing a keen sense of the need for intelligence, reported this to Grant also.

Special Field Orders No. 31, Department of the Mississippi, dated 28 April 1862, made official the reorganization that Halleck had announced on 23 April. The order added that a reserve would be established from the three corps, but it named no commander for it. Two days later Special Field Orders No. 35 announced McClernand as the commander of the reserve. The order also announced that Grant would function as Halleck's second in command. Halleck had questioned Grant's ability on several occasions, and perhaps such an arrangement would allow him to keep a close eye on his subordinate. Grant asked for an explanation; Halleck evasively replied that "if you believe me your friend you will not require explanations; if not, explanations on my part would be of little avail." This meant that Grant's role during the upcoming operation would be minimal.[95] The department commander, his second in command, and the three forward corps were now all commanded by West Pointers. McClernand, the political general who had fought his division with considerable skill at Shiloh, was relegated to command of the reserve, which would follow behind the advance.

Halleck's reorganization produced a confused chain of command. Grant was second in command of the entire army, but he was also to retain command of the Army of the Tennessee, which constituted the right wing. Halleck's order, however, stated that George Henry Thomas, another West Point graduate, would command the right wing. On 1 May Grant issued an order in which he took command of the reserve. During the month ahead, McClernand would receive orders from Halleck, Grant, and on one occasion, even from Buell. Not until 12 May did Halleck direct Grant not to exercise control over the right wing or the reserve.[96]

On 29 April Halleck's entire command began a general advance toward Corinth, a key rail center in northern Mississippi. The sick who could accompany the march moved with the column; the others were left in hospitals. To ensure that the adjacent division commander, Hurlbut, was aware of his movements, McClernand notified him that he was withdrawing his pickets. The First Division led the advance of the right wing. That evening the division halted at Mickey's White House, about four miles from Monterey, along a branch of Lick Creek. McClernand reported that the stream was unfordable and would have to be bridged. His command would remain between Mickey's and Monterey until 11 May.[97]

Both Yates and McClernand knew the political value of maintaining close ties with Illinois soldiers. On 11 May the Illinois governor again visited his political crony and his constituents, this time at Monterey. He received a division review and praised the men "for their patriotic devotion, the luster they had shed upon Illinois, and their soldierly appearance and expertness." McClernand in return complimented the governor "for his untiring efforts to promote the soldier's welfare."[98] Probably during this visit McClernand again discussed with Yates the possibility of an independent command that he had mentioned to Lincoln in late March. Although there is no direct evidence, future events give cause to believe that Yates and McClernand also discussed at this point the possibility of the general assisting in raising troops in his home state.

Never would McClernand forget his political roots. Throughout his military career he would maintain contact with those who had supported him politically prior to the war. In late May he wrote Yates, and he also corresponded with Sen. Lyman Trumbull, about the possibility of an appointment for the senator's son to the United States Naval Academy.[99] These two politicians would play major roles in the future of John McClernand.

McClernand wisely relinquished command of his division after being named commander of the reserve. To perform both tasks would have taxed even the most experienced commander. His reserve command then consisted of a division commanded by Maj. Gen. Lew Wallace (replaced by Brig. Gen. Henry M. Judah on 3 May), a second commanded by Brig. Gen. Thomas L. Crittenden, and a third division (McClernand's former division) to be commanded by Brig. Gen. John A. Logan.[100] This organization, however, would change during the upcoming campaign.

To be certain that his subordinates understood his expectations, McClernand issued numerous orders. Commanders were informed that they alone were responsible for the "good order and police of their camps," that they were to have at least two hundred rounds of ammunition on hand for each soldier, and that they were to ensure that their commands were supplied with all necessary ordnance, quartermaster, and medical supplies.

The latter was critical, because the torrential rains and mud that the army had encountered for months had led to outbreaks of pneumonia and typhoid fever. Grant issued specific instructions that hospital tents would be used only for hospital purposes and not for general housing. He warned against surgeons leaving the sick without proper care and emphasized that commanders who failed in this regard would be arrested. Finally, McClernand directed officers to inspect the preparation of food to guarantee that it was cooked properly.[101] After Shiloh, John McClernand and Ulysses Grant knew the value of men with rifled muskets. They could not afford to lose soldiers to sickness deep in Confederate territory.

Halleck's movement from Shiloh toward Corinth was excruciatingly slow. Lew Wallace had estimated that no more than five days would be required to complete the march of twenty miles and capture Corinth. Apparently, McClernand too expected a rapid pursuit of the defeated Confederates, for he ordered his division commanders to keep five days' rations on hand "to meet the contingencies of short-notice to march." There would be no such contingencies. Four weeks later, Beauregard would evacuate the city without a fight.[102]

McClernand's primary mission during the advance was to protect the Union right flank from attacks by any Confederates operating from near Purdy. Halleck would not allow himself to be surprised as Grant had been. The reserve commander directed Lew Wallace to provide cavalry to reconnoiter in that direction, and he took the unusual step of communicating directly with Hurlbut, one of Sherman's subordinates, to make him aware that there was Union cavalry operating near his division, thereby precluding a clash between blue-clad infantry and cavalry. He made certain that Grant, his immediate superior, was aware of his actions.[103]

On 3 May, Halleck ordered the reserve to move to Monterey, to keep guards posted at the crossings of Owl and Snake Creeks, and to remain in supporting distance of the right-wing divisions. Halleck had received word that Confederates were moving toward Purdy a "considerable force" that would threaten the Union flank. McClernand's responsibility was to locate that threat and prevent it from operating against Thomas's wing. He responded by again sending McCullough's cavalry to the west, where it encountered and drove off a small band of Confederate cavalry.[104]

Despite Halleck's insistence that Grant did not command the reserve, McClernand continued to correspond directly with Grant, and Halleck issued orders to the reserve through his second in command.[105]

McClernand was beginning to feel a certain amount of frustration. His correspondence contained muted complaints about the size, disposition, and mission of his command. He asked for more cavalry, because that available to him was insufficient to cover the area he had been assigned. He deployed much of his infantry to rebuild the road back to Pittsburg and the bridges across the streams swollen by incessant rain. Crittenden's division had been lost to McClernand, and his two remaining divisions were insufficient to guard the sixteen-mile flank from Pittsburg to Easel's, Tennessee. In response to his request he received eighty-six troopers, many of whom were unarmed. Wisely, McClernand kept Sherman, who commanded the division on the extreme right flank of the army, informed of his plight and the location of his pickets.[106]

Only one incident marred the reserve commander's performance during the movement to Corinth. On 24 May Grant queried him as to why pickets had twice failed to examine the passes of his personal escort as Grant and his party moved along the road to Pittsburg late at night. McClernand replied that he had discussed the matter with his division commanders to ensure that passes were checked.[107]

By 27 May the line the reserve had to cover stretched for three additional miles. McClernand's instructions from Grant were to continue to protect the Union right and to inform him and the division commanders if the presence of a large body of the enemy was detected. Grant, Sherman, and McClernand were in constant communication, as Sherman provided intelligence about Confederates on the flank and McClernand reported skirmishes with Rebel guards along the Mobile and Ohio Railroad. McClernand reported that a repatriated Union surgeon had estimated that 146,000 Rebels were in Corinth.[108]

On 30 May, as the Union army was preparing to conduct a siege of Corinth, Beauregard evacuated the city. Halleck directed his wing commanders to occupy the Confederate entrenchments and to send scouts to ascertain the enemy's movements. McClernand was to continue to watch the Union right flank.[109]

Grant characterized his own role during this campaign as that of "little more than an observer."[110] The same could be said of McClernand, for he had done little more than provide divisions or brigades for the wing commanders to employ.

On 1 June McClernand vented his frustration in a letter to Halleck. He complained that his position had "been one of actual inferiority, if not practical subordination, to that of other officers inferior to me in rank." As evidence he cited the fact that his command was smaller than that of the other major commanders. He asked whether he had been relegated to a secondary role because he was not a professional soldier. He hastened to add that his complaint was not filed in a "spirit of egotism or vain-glory," but that he only sought justice.[111]

Halleck responded three days later. He informed McClernand that he was "entirely mistaken" if he believed his position as commander of the reserve was a subordinate position, and he reminded his subordinate that his new command was twice as large as the single division he had previously commanded.[112] This response did not satisfy the Illinois general. Having failed to obtain redress through military channels, he would soon turn to the avenue he knew best—his political connections.

Meanwhile, Beauregard's army remained a formidable force, and Halleck had to determine what to do about it. In characteristic fashion, he did little. He allowed a brief pursuit by Pope, but he became more concerned with protecting his supply line than with defeating the Confederate army.

Halleck ordered McClernand to send one division by way of Purdy toward Bolivar to secure the railroad bridge over the Hatchie River. McClernand designated Wallace's division for the operation. His order to his division commander focused on supply procedures. He told Wallace to draw his support from Pittsburg or Crump's Landing but authorized him to furnish "proper vouchers" to civilians from whom he had to purchase provisions. McClernand continued to keep his fellow Illinoisan, Grant, informed of his movements.[113]

On 5 June Halleck, concerned that Pope and Buell might need to be reinforced, ordered McClernand to halt his march toward Bolivar. The next day McClernand directed Lew Wallace to send one brigade toward Jackson, Tennessee, to investigate a report that eight hundred Confederate cavalrymen were in that vicinity. McClernand informed the department commander of his actions.

He also requested more cavalry. Grant had ordered McClernand to send three companies of cavalry to Sherman. The reserve commander complained of this directly to Halleck rather than confront Grant. The controversy invoked consternation in Sherman, who asked Grant to "remind McClernand of the importance of seeing such orders of transfer obeyed promptly." Such seemingly minor issues eventually would become major imbroglios.

The next day the Union force drove the Confederates out of Jackson and took possession of the town, "their dinner, a number of animals, and a quantity of commissary and quarter-master's stores." The aggressive politician then sent part of Wallace's command to Somerville to secure the Memphis and Ohio Railroad at that point. He also found time to write Judge Collamer of Vermont to urge the appointment of Col. Thomas Ransom, a graduate of Norwich University, as brigadier general.[114]

For the next few weeks, McClernand coordinated the operations of the two divisions that remained in the reserve. Logan and Wallace chased Rebel cavalry, which was burning Confederate cotton to prevent it from being converted into Union clothing; they also protected rail and telegraph lines and rebuilt bridges that connected Corinth with points north and west. On 17 June Wallace entered Memphis to defend it against rumored attacks.[115]

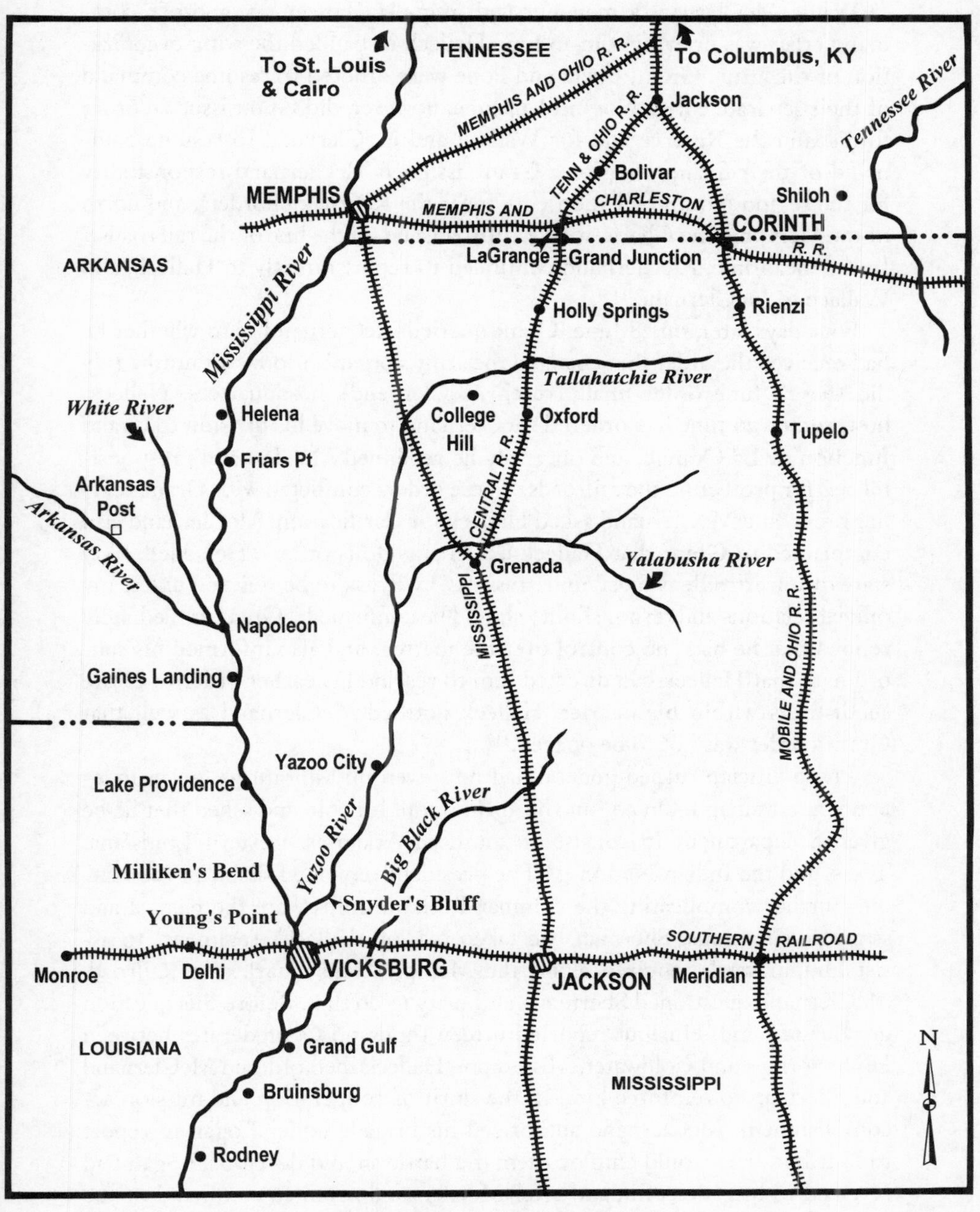

Area of Operations, the Army of the Tennessee

While McClernand's men pursued gray-clad horsemen, another command crisis was brewing. On 10 June Halleck disbanded the wing organization of the army; Grant, Buell, and Pope were ordered to resume command of their separate corps. Not until 24 June, however, did Grant issue an order to disband the Reserve and for Wallace and McClernand to resume command of their former divisions. Grant assigned McClernand responsibility for the region "south of Union City [near the Kentucky border], and north of the Memphis and Charleston [Rail]Road; and on the line of the rail roads." In the meantime, McClernand continued to report directly to Halleck, and Wallace to McClernand.[116]

Four days later, on 28 June, Grant queried McClernand as to whether he had received the order that changed the army's organization. Not until 2 July did the 24 June order finally reach McClernand's headquarters. Halleck, however, on 26 June had ordered McClernand to move his division to Grand Junction or La Grange, and on 3 July he redefined McClernand's responsibilities for protecting the railroads. These orders conflicted with Grant's earlier order, and McClernand asked Halleck for clarification. McClernand also complained to Grant that Halleck had changed his orders. He added, "My state of uncertitude is most embarrassing. I will ask to be relieved unless my official relations and responsibility should be confirmed." Grant immediately replied that he had "no control over the matter" and also informed his subordinate that Halleck had directed him to rescind his earlier order to create subdistricts within his district. Halleck notified McClernand as well that Grant's order was not to be obeyed.[117]

The politician turned general had not given up aspirations for an independent command. On 20 June he again wrote Lincoln and asked that he be given a department to consist of southern Arkansas, western Louisiana, Texas, and the Indian Nation.[118] The president remained silent on the matter. Further complicating the command relationships were the tactical and strategic situations. Sherman had taken two of Wallace's regiments to assist him in work required along the Memphis and Charleston Railroad. McClernand questioned Sherman's authority to do that. Before this question got out of hand, Hurlbut reported fifteen thousand Confederates between Holly Springs and Coldwater, Mississippi. Halleck then ordered McClernand and Sherman to reinforce him. In the spirit of cooperation and mission accomplishment, McClernand authorized his brigade under Logan to report to Hurlbut, who would employ them if a battle should develop. (Logan had reverted to brigade command after McClernand resumed command of the division.) Halleck then ordered Sherman to take command of all forces involved in the operation.[119]

As if the situation in southern Tennessee was not complicated enough, a major strategic crisis now added to the confusion. In Virginia, Maj. Gen. George B. McClellan had been driven back from the gates of Richmond by the duo of Robert E. Lee and Stonewall Jackson. This had produced, in Halleck's words, "another stampede in Washington" and an order to McClernand on 30 June to take his entire division to Washington. Halleck concluded the directive with: "You go to a new theater. Success attend you." McClernand immediately started one brigade north and notified Halleck he would start the others as soon as rail transport was available. The next day, however, Lincoln and Stanton stopped the movement, for fear that it would lead to the loss of western Tennessee and the abandonment of another operation, against Chattanooga. Despite his desire to escape to the East, McClernand recognized the strategic importance of the Mississippi River Valley. To Halleck he wrote, "I am rejoiced. The Mississippi valley is worth forty capitals."[120] Indeed, the Mississippi Valley would be of utmost importance to John Alexander McClernand's career.

The crisis in Virginia prompted Lincoln to issue a call for three hundred thousand volunteers on 1 July. The quota for Illinois would be 26,148. The next day McClernand wrote Yates and invited him again to visit the Illinois troops. He also wrote Grant and asked that he be allowed to see the governor of Illinois about deficiencies in his command, specifically problems about recruiting. He deemed it "essential to the efficiency of [his] command and the good of the service."[121] Apparently Grant believed otherwise, for he issued no order to allow him to travel to Illinois.

Not to be stymied by Lincoln's failure to respond to his 20 June letter, McClernand continued his campaign to get out from under Halleck and Grant. On 9 July he requested that U.S. representative Elihu B. Washburne of the Illinois congressional delegation intervene on his behalf, to argue that he be allowed to reinforce McClellan with two divisions of Illinois troops. He included with the letter a petition to the Senate and the House of Representatives that he be allowed to reinforce McClellan.[122] As a bonus, such a move would in effect elevate McClernand to the status of a corps commander.

On 11 July the command structure in the West underwent a notable change: Henry Halleck was ordered to Washington to become general in chief of the Union army. Five days later, Ulysses Grant became commander of the District of West Tennessee, to include the Army of the Mississippi and the Army of the Tennessee.[123] McClernand, as commander of the District of Jackson, Tennessee, and of the First Division, Army of the Tennessee, would report directly to Grant.

Halleck had squandered the opportunity to press the advantage gained at Shiloh. Bragg had escaped, and his army remained intact. Portions of Halleck's once formidable force were now sent to Chattanooga, to Columbus, Kentucky, and to Helena, Arkansas. Grant was forced onto the defensive.

Railroad communications were a primary concern of the Union commanders. To protect the railroads, Grant on 15 July adjusted his dispositions so as to establish a defensive line westward from Corinth to Memphis and northward through Bolivar and Jackson to Columbus. McClernand disposed his command along the Tennessee and Ohio Railroad north from Grand Junction to Jackson and along the Mobile and Ohio Railroad to Humboldt. He deployed his cavalry on reconnaissance missions to the south and southeast of Grand Junction. The infantry was concentrated at Bolivar, in accordance with Grant's orders. For the next several weeks he kept his commander informed on almost a daily basis of Rebel movements in his area of responsibility.[124]

At Grand Junction the north-south Tennessee and Ohio Railroad intersected the east-west Memphis and Charleston Railroad. Nevertheless, Grant's defensive concept for the region dictated that troops be withdrawn from Grand Junction in order to hold a line north of the railroad along the Hatchie River. McClernand was extremely reluctant to abandon such a key junction and, in a series of telegraphic exchanges with Grant, finally gained the concession of being allowed to post a cavalry force there. That concession may have been won by his having sent Halleck a copy of his protest; "Old Brains" had then wired Grant to establish an outpost there if it "can be safely kept up."[125] Such a maneuver could have done little to enhance the relationship between the two generals from the Prairie State.

The difficulty McClernand faced was that of a force of almost eight thousand men present for duty, only about 530 were the highly mobile cavalry necessary to counter the Confederate horsemen, under Col. Joseph Wheeler. While the Union forces were retrenching, the Confederates were preparing a cavalry raid that would strike Bolivar and Jackson, defended by McClernand's soldiers.

On 25 July Wheeler set out for the Union posts. For a week he destroyed telegraph lines, burned cotton and railroad bridges, tore up rail lines, and generally raised havoc in the Union command. Brig. Gen. Leonard F. Ross initially reported that five hundred Rebels were involved in the raid—an estimate that was remarkably accurate. By 27 July, however, his estimate had grown to two thousand infantry and five thousand cavalry.[126]

With his infantry scattered, McClernand could do little except direct his cavalry detachments to reinforce Ross. In a stream of telegrams, the division commander kept his department commander and his other principal subordinate, Brig. Gen. John Logan, informed of Confederate movements. For the next three days, McClernand attempted to orchestrate a coordinated attack on the Confederate raiders, but to do that he needed more cavalry. He asked Grant for help in obtaining more mounted soldiers and also carbines and revolvers for the troopers he had.[127]

He also turned for assistance to the arena in which he, perhaps, felt more comfortable—the political arena. On 25 July McClernand telegraphed Andrew Johnson, Military Governor of Tennessee, about the possibility of raising a force to assist him in guarding the western part of the state. He had known Johnson from their service together in the House. The governor replied that he could raise a thousand men but that McClernand would have to provide much of the equipment. The general forwarded the exchange to Grant. He continued to correspond with Johnson throughout August, and in September Halleck authorized the volunteers to be mustered in.[128]

The pace at the headquarters of Grant, McClernand, and Logan was frantic. The three commanders were all communicating with one another while also trying to pinpoint the elusive Rebels. McClernand complained to Grant that his cavalry force was insufficient to hold the defensive line Grant had established along the Hatchie River. Logan complained to McClernand that he, Logan, had insufficient force because McClernand had ordered his men to Bolivar rather than allow him to deploy them from Jackson, which was closer to the Confederate route. Grant sent one message, which consisted only of five questions about the Rebels.[129]

Frustration boiled over in the volatile Illinoisan when he learned that the raiders had destroyed bridges south of Jackson that he had ordered be protected. For some time the telegraph lines hummed with recriminations from McClernand and defensive replies from Logan as to why forces were not available to protect the crossings. That issue passed when the division commander sought to maneuver his infantry to cut off the Rebels, who by 30 July were retiring to Holly Springs, Mississippi.[130]

The pugnacious McClernand chafed under his inability to move offensively against the Confederate forces. He wrote Grant: "My wish is . . . to pass from the defensive to the offensive." The *Illinois State Journal* published a private letter from McClernand to an unnamed individual in which he castigated the government for its adherence to a "defensive policy illustrated by digging and ditching." He proposed that the Union "throw a million of armed men into the field and by aggressive blows crush the rebellion at all points, and in the quickest possible time."[131]

By 1 August, however, Wheeler's men were safe behind Confederate fortifications in Jefferson Davis's home state. In a highly fluid situation, McClernand's men had been unable to force a decisive confrontation with the gray-clad intruders. In his report to Grant, McClernand somewhat overstated the result by stating that "the enemy fled precipitously and escaped capture."[132]

In actuality, there was little McClernand could have done to prevent the damage inflicted by the Confederate raiders. With little cavalry and over sixty miles of front to defend, he had been at the mercy of Wheeler's cavalry, which had been able to pick the least defended parts of the line to penetrate the Union front. The Union army could not guard every mile of track or wire but had to concentrate on those points where the railroad crossed rivers and telegraph lines terminated. It also had to keep a wary eye out for Bragg's army, which was still a powerful force. The exact dispositions of McClernand's command cannot be determined, but undoubtedly some of the fault for the destruction must rest on that commander's shoulders. A sufficient infantry contingent should have been posted at each bridge along the railroad at least to delay a Confederate attack until reinforcements could arrive. Outposts could have been established between those contingents to provide warning of intruders. Still, however, the Confederates could have attacked at any point at any time. The initiative had lain not with Grant and McClernand but with Bragg and Wheeler.

McClernand's discontent with his subordinate position in the western theater increased greatly during the slow march toward Corinth. In July he wrote Sen. Orville Browning of Illinois, who had been appointed to fill the unexpired term of Stephen A. Douglas, with an extraordinary request. He asked that the senator persuade the War Department to allow him, plus all of his Illinois soldiers, to be sent to the East. On 16 July Browning presented this petition to Stanton, who sought to distance himself from any dealings with those two politicians. He stated that only Halleck had the authority to make such a disposition.[133]

Neither McClernand's March letter to Lincoln nor his July missive to Browning had achieved the results he desired. In August he again wrote Lincoln, but this time he requested a leave of absence. Lincoln forwarded the request to Stanton, who then sent it to Halleck, who responded in a blistering letter later that month: "Permit me, Genl, to call your attention to the fact that in sending this application directly to the president, instead of transmitting it through prescribed channels, you have violated the Army Regulations. This is not the first instance of this kind, for I remember to have reminded you of this Regulation some months ago."[134]

Interestingly, the day before McClernand wrote Lincoln, Grant had also written the president directly, to request that several officers be promoted to brigadier general.[135] No censure from Halleck resulted from that correspondence. Unfortunately, the Illinois politician neither heeded the advice nor took to heart the rebuke that Halleck, the professional soldier, proffered. The result would be the downfall of John Alexander McClernand.

While McClernand schemed, Grant received new marching orders for August from the new general in chief. He was to move his army to protect the rail communications, centering his defense at Bolivar and along the Hatchie River. He was then to launch an offensive into northern Mississippi and western Tennessee to "clean out" the Rebel forces operating in those regions. Not until November, however, would Grant launch such an offensive, for other Confederate operations required him to reduce further the number of divisions available to him and to deal with the pesky Rebel partisans that were becoming increasingly active in western Tennessee.[136]

Reports of Confederate movements continued to flow into McClernand's headquarters—reports that he dutifully forwarded to Grant. Rebel troops were reported to be leaving Tupelo, Mississippi, for Chattanooga, Tennessee. Others were rumored to be preparing to move to LaGrange along the railroad, and activity was reported in Fayette County, Tennessee. Guerrillas were heard to be drilling in Benton County just across the border in Mississippi. McClernand urged Grant to concentrate his army at Bolivar and attack. Sherman, too, suggested an attack upon the Confederate railroads; the department commander declined the proposals.[137] First Division soldiers skirmished with Confederates throughout the month. McClernand maneuvered his forces based upon intelligence received, but he was unable to concentrate a force sufficient to destroy the Rebel raiders.[138]

During this period of relative inactivity, the relationship between the two Illinois generals began to show more signs of the rancor by which it would eventually be characterized. Several incidents occurred in which there was considerable disagreement and even signs of hostility between the two men. The first occurred on 4 August, when McClernand angrily informed Grant that Col. Josiah W. Bissell was investigating destruction of government property within his district. Clearly annoyed, McClernand wrote that "if Col Bissell ever invades my district again and usurps authority which belongs to me and not to him, he will be made to answer in a very exemplary way for it." Bissell replied that he had acted on the mistaken belief that he had McClernand's permission.[139] The tone of McClernand's letter undoubtedly alerted Grant both to his subordinate's volatile temper and his jealousy over his command prerogatives.

Another dispute occurred on 12 August. Grant, on 28 July, had ordered McClernand to send troops to Bolivar to defend against a threatened Confederate attack. A telegram from Grant on 12 August (not available) apparently questioned McClernand's compliance. McClernand replied that he had complied with that order but had taken the additional step of establishing an outpost line along the Hatchie River, to provide early warning of Rebel movements. A second order from Grant (not found, but probably of 29 July) had directed his subordinate to retain forces at Jackson, and another telegram on 12 August implied that McClernand had withdrawn soldiers from that location without orders. McClernand replied he had done nothing "which subsequent reflection condemns. If I have," he added, "I am ready, as ought to be held, to answer for it."[140]

Confederate operations confirm that both Grant and McClernand should have been concerned. On 11 August Gen. Braxton Bragg ordered Maj. Gen. Earl Van Dorn to join Maj. Gen. Sterling Price and "to press the enemy closely in West Tennessee." Price, who commanded the District of the Tennessee, envisioned the two forces first seizing Corinth, Mississippi, and then driving north to Paducah, Kentucky. Van Dorn subsequently proposed uniting between Corinth and Grand Junction—the area immediately south of McClernand's position. On 30 August, Confederate cavalry struck the railroad north and south of Bolivar. McClernand had responded to Grant's 28 July order by sending Lawler's brigade to Bolivar, but he had gone further and sent two regiments northwest of Bolivar to protect crossings of the Hatchie. He also kept four regiments at Jackson, and that apparently was the source of the conflict: Grant had ordered "most of the troops" to be sent to Bolivar. The next day he had countermanded that order, but he must have believed that McClernand had defied him by his failure to send those four regiments that remained at Jackson, plus the two along the outpost line, to Bolivar. McClernand claimed that he notified Grant of his reasons for disposing his troops in such a manner, but the fact that he had failed to comply exactly with Grant's orders must have irritated the department commander and could only have made worse the growing antagonism between the two generals.[141]

The third incident began on 13 August, when McClernand telegraphed Grant that Maj. Gen. Edward O. C. Ord was at Bolivar "in the Exercise of some military function." As Bolivar was within McClernand's geographic district, he wanted to know by whose authority Ord was there. There ensued an acrimonious exchange between the two Illinoisans—an exchange that may have poisoned further the relationship and served as a catalyst for events yet to come.[142]

Grant replied to his subordinate's query, "Your views seem to conflict with mine. My view of this matter is, and it will have to govern until higher authority decides against me, that I command all the troops that are within . . . certain limits. All commanders under me command troops and not territory."[143]

McClernand was outraged. In a letter to Grant he defended his actions: "You speak of conflict of views. I have never claimed to command a district of fixed and definite limits." He asserted that Grant's order to protect the railroads from Humboldt to Bethel and Bolivar allowed him to divide his district and to assign troops and a commander to each subdivision to control the countryside contiguous to the rail lines. McClernand had previously queried Brig. Gen. Grenville M. Dodge, who commanded another section of railroad, about the possibility of establishing a boundary between them to ensure the territory was covered adequately. He asserted to Grant that this action had not intended to usurp Grant's authority over any territory but to enhance the cooperation between two of his subordinates. He then challenged Grant's specific comment about his authority over all troops within his district. In an emotional display of defensiveness he wrote, "Pardon me for saying, that this is a boast of authority uncalled for by anything I have said or done. In no instance have I gainsayed [*sic*] your authority. Whoever told you so falsifies the truth. My actions disprove the charge." He concluded that his only purpose in writing was to vindicate his conduct.[144]

In early August McClernand clashed again with an officer who would later play a role in the Illinoisan's demise. Recently promoted Brig. Gen. James B. McPherson had become superintendent of railroads for Grant. On 4 August McClernand telegraphed Grant that private goods were being shipped over the rails in preference to military stores. In a strong response, McPherson replied that although some goods were indeed being smuggled along the line, he had "labored diligently" to ensure only government freight was being shipped. He added that McClernand himself had twice requested that private goods be shipped. His final sentence indicated the anger McPherson felt over the charge: "In future shall pay no attention to communications or complaints written by Officers who know nothing about the circumstances and who misstate facts or attempt to convey false impressions."[145] McClernand had made an enemy: McPherson would not forget.

McClernand had one other political card to play. On the same day he wrote Lincoln and asked for a leave of absence, he also wrote his friend Governor Yates in Illinois. "I think I could offer some information and assistance in regard to the refilling of our old regiments," he wrote. "Ask the Secretary of War to order me to visit you at Springfield for that purpose." Yates instructed his secretary to "write Secretary of War earnestly . . . write be glad if can come."[146] To McClernand Yates replied that he had done as his crony had requested. He added that he had told Stanton that McClernand's "co-operation & assistance will be of great benefit to us, at this time. I hope the order will be made at once."[147]

Illinois was important. Not only was it the president's home state, but also, as noted, on 4 August it had been subjected to a call for 26,148 more volunteers for the Union cause. Growing Democratic sentiment and the persistent Copperhead movement in the state would not allow the Federal officials to deny a request from the influential governor. Consequently, on 25 August the general in chief ordered that "General J. A. McClernand will repair to Springfield, Ill., and assist the Governor in organizing volunteers." That same day Grant notified his subordinate by telegraph of the order. Two days later Special Order No. 174 made the directive official.[148]

5
Return to Illinois

On 28 August, McClernand turned over command of his division to Brig. Gen. Leonard F. Ross and started for Springfield, arriving two nights later. The following day McClernand informed Gov. Richard Yates he was reporting "for the purpose of assisting in organizing the new troops raised and to be raised in the State of Illinois" but that he would serve in any capacity in which he might be useful.[1]

Recruiting in Illinois in response to Lincoln's 2 July 1862 call for troops had lagged. In Chicago, for example, the six recruiters averaged fewer than one recruit each week. City men were reluctant to forego high wages for low army pay. In rural areas, married men were unwilling to enlist unless they were assured their families would be cared for while they were gone. In August, Illinoisans faced the additional obstacle of the fall harvest. Unless farmers could be persuaded to enter the army, either from a spirit of patriotism or fear of the draft, the state's quota would not be met. The threat of a draft now enticed men to arms, however, because of the stigma attached to being conscripted. Despite some hesitancy, by mid-August patriotic fervor had attracted so many to the national colors that the state was unable to provide adequately for the assembled multitudes.[2]

McClernand assumed his new duties with enthusiasm and a well organized plan for fulfilling his responsibilities. As Yates was the commander of the Illinois militia, as well as the senior politician in the state, McClernand informed him of the steps he was taking to organize and muster units. He directed his staff to address the myriad details involved in raising and outfitting large numbers of troops—establishing encampments; organizing the units; procuring ordnance; training artillerymen; providing medical support as well as clothing, blankets, and camp equipment; and, of course, obtaining the blank forms, stationery, and instruction books so essential to modern warfare. He recommended that troops be concentrated at no more than four locations, in order to maximize efficiency. He asked about barracks, transportation, and weapons. On 2 September he reported to Yates that he was sending an officer to assist in organizing a regiment in Williamson County. This prompted Yates to request that McClernand detail members of his staff to instruct new regiments forming at eight other locations, one in each of the Illinois congressional districts.[3] In short, McClernand's actions reflected his experience in the western theater and the recognition that readying soldiers for the battlefield required not only training but also extensive administrative and logistical preparation.

While attending to the details of organizing units, McClernand also had to contend with acquaintances who asked for his assistance to obtain positions in the army. For example, in September the superintendent of public instruction in Springfield wrote to recommend two men for commissions. A colonel of a regiment in McClernand's former command wrote to ask for his backing for promotion to brigadier general. Another wrote to request a discharge. Not all requests were of a personal nature; the colonel of another regiment in McClernand's former command petitioned for assistance in replacing casualties. Each request required his personal attention; one resulted in a letter from McClernand to Lincoln to seek discharge for an influential individual in Illinois.[4]

For three weeks McClernand issued orders to subordinates about aspects of organizing the units, received reports on training regimens, and provided status reports to Yates. From his combat experience, McClernand recognized the necessity for adequate training. His aide at Camp Duncan, Illinois, reported that he had established a training schedule for the 101st Illinois Regiment consisting of early-morning instruction for officers followed by squad and company drill. Officer instruction was held again after lunch, followed by battalion drill and a dress parade. As a result of this training, the regiment had "rapidly improved in both discipline and drill."[5] Lt. Harl Christie informed McClernand that the 123d Illinois had excessive numbers of men on leave, thus reducing the effectiveness of its training; McClernand reported this to Yates and requested he issue an order prohibiting such practices. He also reported that generally units were making satisfactory progress, but he singled out ones in which members were not attending drill. McClernand requested that Yates order them to comply with the instructions of his officers.[6]

While McClernand was attending to his military responsibilities, he did not forego opportunities to cultivate his political roots. Upon his return to Springfield, he had been heartily welcomed for his war deeds, and a few days later the same occurred at Illinois College, in nearby Jacksonville. Shortly afterward he addressed a crowd in Chicago. According to the account of this speech that appeared in the *Chicago Tribune*, he said, "Any commander who relies wholly upon STRATEGY must fail. We want the right man to lead us; a man who will appoint a subordinate officer on account of his merits, and not because he is a graduate of West Point. Neither Ceasar [*sic*] nor Cromwell were graduates of West Point."[7]

McClernand's prior immediate commanders had been West Pointers—Halleck and Grant—and he had fought alongside another West Pointer, Sherman, at Shiloh. His exact motives for making such statements are unknown; however, there can be little doubt that he realized that his clashes with Grant and the perception that Halleck stood between him and Lincoln could have a significant effect on his military ambitions. Furthermore, his sense of not having received the credit he deserved for his service motivated him to continue a direct correspondence with Lincoln in order to achieve the recognition he believed he merited. Halleck himself had received considerable criticism for his slow movements after Shiloh, and McClernand possibly seized upon that criticism as a means to extol the merits of a war based on the offensive rather than on maneuver.

Coincidentally, in November Lincoln penned a memorandum that addressed the same issue. "The army," he wrote, "like the nation, has become demoralized by the idea that the war is to be ended, the nation united, and peace restored, by strategy, and not by hard desperate fighting."[8] Although there is no direct evidence for the subject having arisen at the time, it is quite possible that McClernand had discussed the issue of strategy with Lincoln when he visited the president in late September 1862.

On 22 September Yates, indicating his confidence in McClernand's political and military abilities, ordered, "Please repair to Washington City, without delay, to assist me in regard to matters affecting the organization of the new levies of troops in this State."[9] McClernand left that night. Armed with a letter of introduction from Yates, McClernand had the entree to the political circles he so desperately sought.

In a meeting on 26 September in Governor Yates's hotel room, McClernand outlined to Secretary of the Treasury Salmon P. Chase his proposal for carrying the war to the heart of the Confederacy by opening the Mississippi River and then interdicting Southern railroad communication links. Chase recorded that the Illinois general "made a very favorable impression on me." The secretary then sent a note to McClernand that he would arrange an interview with Lincoln so that McClernand could present his ideas personally. When Stanton saw Lincoln on 27 September and asked him his opinion of McClernand, Lincoln responded that while McClernand was "brave and capable," he was "too desirous to be independent of everybody else."[10] This observation reflected Lincoln's insight into the character of John McClernand.

On 28 September, McClernand submitted a lengthy letter to Lincoln in which he detailed his proposal for opening the Mississippi River and laid out his strategic vision for future operations. The first step would be to seize Vicksburg. To achieve that, he proposed landing a force at Drumgould's Bluff, on the Yazoo River north of Vicksburg.[11] Such a move had merit, as it would place Union forces in position to cut the Jackson-Vicksburg railroad and to move against Vicksburg itself from the rear. (In December this was precisely the plan that Sherman would attempt, but the effort would end in his repulse at Chickasaw Bayou, only a few miles from Drumgould's.) Other aspects of his plan—operations west of the Mississippi, from New Orleans, against Mobile, and eventually toward Atlanta—would also be implemented in future movements of the Union army in the West.

Opening the Mississippi was hardly a new idea. McClernand himself had addressed the significance of that waterway even before he had been appointed brigadier general. Gen. Winfield Scott had proposed in his 1861 Anaconda Plan that very strategy. In May 1862, Assistant Secretary of the Navy Gustavus Fox had written of the importance of the Mississippi in a private letter to Comdr. David Dixon Porter; he had later referred to opening the river as "the imperative act." Halleck and Stanton, in an exchange of correspondence in June, had discussed an operation against Vicksburg, although Halleck believed that campaigning in Arkansas had a higher priority. The general also hoped that the navy alone would be able to force the surrender of that citadel. In July 1862, naval forces under Adm. David Farragut and Flag Officer Charles Davis made an unsuccessful attempt to do just that.[12]

At a cabinet meeting on 3 August 1862 Secretary Chase and Secretary of the Interior John P. Usher had raised the matter and had even urged that a special force be raised for the purpose of taking Vicksburg, but the project had been dropped until McClernand arrived in Washington.[13]

McClernand visited Lincoln on 30 September and was invited to accompany him to Sharpsburg, Maryland. There Lincoln was to meet with Gen. George B. McClellan, whose Army of the Potomac had forced the Confederate Army of Northern Virginia under Gen. Robert E. Lee back south of the Potomac River. At a cabinet meeting on 6 October, after Lincoln's return from the Antietam Creek battlefield, Stanton proposed organizing a Mississippi expedition, with McClernand in command. According to Chase, "the President seemed much pleased."[14] Given McClernand's 28 September letter to Lincoln and his habit of communicating directly with the president, it is probable that McClernand had campaigned for an independent command and movement against Vicksburg while accompanying Lincoln.

Halleck, however, was unconvinced of McClernand's qualifications for such an important command. Chase wrote in his diary: "He [Halleck] said he is brave and able but no disciplinarian; that his camp was always full of disorder; that at Corinth he pitched his tents where his men had been buried just below ground, and with dead horses lying all around. The cause of the evil was that his officers and men were his constituents." The general, however, had never issued a written censure to McClernand for these breaches.

Secretary of the Navy Gideon Welles, too, wrote that McClernand "is not of the Regular Army, and is no favorite, I perceive, with Halleck." The implication was that Halleck was partial to professional soldiers. Lt. James H. Wilson claimed to have told McClernand that "Halleck would probably be against him," but he gave no indication of why.[15] The answer undoubtedly goes back to Halleck's previous association with McClernand in the western campaigns of 1862. Also, as a professional soldier, Halleck understood the need for discipline. In McClernand he saw this quality lacking.

Upon his return to Washington from Sharpsburg, McClernand made repeated requests for Secretary of War Edwin Stanton's assistance with the Vicksburg operation. On 10 October he proposed an expedition of twenty thousand (the number he had proposed to Lincoln in his 28 September letter was sixty thousand) and requested two officers as division commanders and four officers for brigade commanders. Not until 11 October, however, did Stanton inform Halleck that McClernand would call on him to discuss the details of the expedition and to receive instructions. Subsequently, McClernand proposed to Stanton for the expedition a new organization, which would consist of twenty-four thousand infantry, three hundred cavalry, and 1,600 artillerymen organized into ten batteries and a siege train. The following day he sent a similar proposal to Halleck. In neither letter did he mention that he would command the expedition. Apparently McClernand did not meet with Halleck as Stanton had arranged, for there is no mention of such a meeting in any of McClernand's correspondence. Given his later penchant for recounting the details of the events surrounding his rear-area assignment, it is difficult to accept that he would intentionally have excluded any reference to a meeting with Halleck.[16]

Why would Lincoln entrust such a critical expedition to a general possessing so little in the way of formal military credentials? Influential groups in the western theater were by mid-1862 displaying signs of discontent with the course of the war. Blockage of the Mississippi was producing severe strain on the commercial interests of the region. That outlet for goods was closed, and shippers had increased dramatically their rates for moving goods eastward by river and railroad. The embargo of trade to the South had caused economic ruin in border cities along the Ohio. The *New York Times* editorialized about the necessity to open the Mississippi: "Each individual member of the expedition will feel a personal interest in its success, because to a certain extent the pecuniary prosperity of every one of them will be found dependent on the unobstructed navigation of the Mississippi River."[17]

Lincoln's Republican administration was in disfavor in the western region, and Democrat McClernand's influence in the area was considerable. Lincoln could surely trade on that influence by authorizing McClernand to raise troops to open the Mississippi, thus appealing to local sentiments, and also give McClernand himself the command, thus appealing to McClernand's ambition. Stanton even wrote McClernand that his "personal influence" was being "relied on for the increased force" necessary to conduct the Mississippi operation.[18]

Also, McClernand's military record at Belmont, Forts Henry and Donelson, and at Shiloh indicated a steadiness under fire, a willingness to expose himself to danger, and reasonable skills of command. By October 1862, such professional soldiers and West Point graduates as Irvin McDowell (who had been routed at First Bull Run), George McClellan (who had retreated from the gates of Richmond), and John Pope (who had been defeated at Second Bull Run) had failed to make any gains in the East. Only in the West had a string of successes been achieved, and the politician turned general John McClernand had been associated with most of them. His reputation was widespread, as another article in the *New York Times* indicated: "Gen. McClernand has inspired the whole West with enthusiastic faith in his courage, untiring energy and military skill."[19] As he considered the situation along the Mississippi, Lincoln surely must have recognized the possibility of combining his political ally's military and civic reputation to the advantage of the Union cause.

McClernand remained in Washington for several weeks. Elsewhere, events that would affect the Mississippi expedition were transpiring. In April 1861, Lt. David Dixon Porter, United States Navy, had met with Lincoln to discuss a joint expedition to seize Fort Pickens at Pensacola Bay, Florida. Although the expedition later failed, it had brought Porter to Lincoln's attention.[20] On 15 October 1862 Porter again found himself in Lincoln's presence, but this time as an acting rear admiral in command of the Mississippi Squadron.

According to Porter, the two men had a conversation concerning Vicksburg and McClernand, a conversation that revealed much about Lincoln's opinion of McClernand as well as the effects of McClernand's correspondence with Lincoln. The president told Porter that his mission was to move against Vicksburg, and he asked his recommendation regarding who should command the land troops. Porter responded that Grant, who commanded the department, should be overall commander but that Sherman would probably command at Vicksburg. Lincoln responded, "Well, Admiral, I have in mind a better general than either of them; that is McClernand, an old and intimate friend of mine." When Porter stated he did not know McClernand, Lincoln exclaimed: "What! Don't know McClernand? Why, he saved the battle of Shiloh. . . . He is a natural-born general." Porter expressed concern about entrusting the expedition "to anyone except a scientific military man," but Lincoln told him he should cooperate with McClernand and then gave him a note of introduction to discuss the matter with the general. After that discussion Porter recorded that McClernand expected to take Vicksburg in a week.[21]

There are difficulties with this account. According to the diary of Secretary of the Navy Welles, Admiral Porter himself also resented West Pointers (the "scientific military men" of the day) and dreaded any association with them, calling them "self-sufficient, pedantic and unpractical." In his biography of Porter, Richard West argues that Porter agreed to cooperate with McClernand primarily because he was not a West Point graduate. According to West, Porter had little use for West Pointers Halleck or McClellan. John Hay, Lincoln's private secretary, would recall that McClernand was an acquaintance of the president's but not "the old and intimate friend" as Porter claimed Lincoln had said, the two having been political opponents. Porter also stated he was leaving Washington to meet with Grant at Cairo, but the two did not actually meet until late November.[22]

Although Welles recognized Porter's professional abilities, he was skeptical about his character. To his diary in August he confided his views of the naval officer: "David was not always reliable on important matters, but amplified and colored transactions where he was personally interested. . . . I did not always consider David to be depended upon if he had an end to attain, and he had no hesitation in trampling down a brother officer if it would benefit himself."[23] He later wrote that he was "incapable of gratitude, and is eaten up with selfish ambition. Those who know Porter well are aware he can certify to almost anything."[24] The admiral's views of McClernand must, therefore, be viewed with a jaundiced eye.

Nevertheless, on 21 October McClernand received confidential orders from Stanton for the expedition down the Mississippi.

> Ordered, That Major-General McClernand be, and he is, directed to proceed to the States of Indiana, Illinois, and Iowa, to organize the troops remaining in those States and to be raised . . . and forward them . . . to Memphis, Cairo, or such other points as may hereafter be designated by the general-in-chief, to the end that, when a sufficient force not required by the operations of General Grant's command shall be raised, an expedition may be organized under General McClernand's command against Vicksburg. . . .
>
> The forces so organized will remain subject to the designation of the general-in-chief, and be employed according to such exigencies as the service in his judgement may require.[25]

To this Lincoln appended a handwritten note: "This order, though marked confidential, may be shown by Gen. McClernand, to Governors, and even others, when, in his discretion, he believes so doing to be indispensable to the progress of the expedition. I add that I feel deep interest in the success of the expedition, and desire it to be pushed forward with all possible despatch, consistently with the other parts of the military service."[26]

These are remarkable orders! Obviously Lincoln's personal endorsement added a degree of urgency and importance to McClernand's mission, and, placing the most favorable interpretation on this missive, McClernand eagerly accepted what he took to be his role as an independent commander. If studied carefully, however, the orders were ambiguous. No copy was sent to Grant, although Vicksburg lay in his department, but the orders manifestly allowed Grant to use the forces McClernand was fielding. Nor was Halleck immediately informed, for as late as 11 December he would write Maj. Gen. Samuel Curtis, commanding the Department of the Missouri, that instructions regarding the expedition had not been provided to him.[27] Although McClernand certainly believed otherwise, the orders did not call for McClernand to have an independent command, only to command an expedition against Vicksburg. The last paragraph also allowed Halleck to divert the forces assigned to McClernand if made necessary by unforeseen circumstances. In effect, both Halleck and Grant had veto power over the expedition. McClernand, however, as revealed by his subsequent correspondence, believed he was under the direct authority of the president, operating independently. The glory of taking Vicksburg would be his.

McClernand left Washington on 21 October, and the following day he met with Gov. Oliver P. Morton of Indiana in Indianapolis to inform him of Lincoln's directive. He arrived in Springfield on 24 October and met with Yates the following day. He then sent Maj. Walter B. Scates, Illinois assistant adjutant general, to meet with Gov. Samuel J. Kirkwood of Iowa to explain to him Lincoln's desires.[28] On 28 October McClernand assumed the duties of inspector general for the state of Illinois and immediately informed Stanton that five regiments were prepared to move.[29] In a flurry of activity the same day, he queried Scates on the details of raising and preparing troops for movement, and he received from Col. Allen C. Fuller, Illinois adjutant general, a report about the status of units then mustering.

In this and subsequent correspondence, McClernand showed remarkable organizational talents and an understanding of the myriad details involved in such undertakings. He asked for numbers of soldiers, about weapons available and sources for those required, about deficiencies, whether money was available for disbursing bounties and advance pay for soldiers departing, about uniform requirements, and for the names of officers in charge of the mustering sites. Those regiments reported as ready to move he ordered to do so immediately.[30] On 29 October he was spurred to even greater zeal by two telegrams from Stanton that requested that he "get the troops forward as fast as possible. . . . The importance of the expedition on the Mississippi is every day becoming more manifest."[31]

On 30 October Fuller reported that three additional units were ready to move; McClernand telegraphed the commanders of five others asking why they were not ready. On that day and the next he sent aides to inspect the delinquent units and provide him personal reports. Responding to Stanton's urging, he advised Governor Morton on the 30th of the urgency of forwarding units and asked to know which ones were ready.[32]

McClernand's feverish activity continued into November. He informed Governor Kirkwood that the fleet to support the expedition was ready but that he needed another regiment of cavalry. Kirkwood's adjutant general informed the general that three regiments were on the move, ten were almost ready, and a regiment of cavalry would be raised. Additionally, McClernand urged his officers to arrange transportation for Illinois regiments that were ready, and he ordered the commanders of those he believed slow in complying with marching orders to report to him personally to explain the delays. All of these movements were reported to Stanton. On 10 November McClernand was able to state that he had either completed the organization of, had forwarded, or was mustering twenty infantry regiments, six artillery batteries, and six cavalry regiments from Illinois, as well as twenty-two infantry regiments from Indiana and Iowa.

This was an impressive effort, and the same level of activity continued throughout the month. He continued to attend to the details of carbines and holsters and revolvers, but the problem that consumed the greatest amount of his time was pay for the soldiers, for until the men were paid, they could not be moved from their encampments.[33]

While McClernand was organizing and forwarding units from Indiana, Iowa, and Illinois, Grant and Sherman were preparing to conduct operations in Mississippi. On 16 October Grant, by War Department General Orders No. 159, had been appointed commander of the Department of the Tennessee, which included Memphis—the very city to which McClernand was forwarding troops. On 12 November Sherman, commander of the District of Memphis, ordered his units organized into two divisions of five brigades, with the brigades comprising many of the units McClernand had forwarded.[34] For what purpose?

McClernand's proposed expedition was hardly a secret, despite the confidential nature of his original orders. On 29 October, Col. William S. Hillyer, Grant's aide, had informed Sherman of reports that McClernand would go to Helena, Arkansas, and lead an expedition from there.[35] The *New York Times*, the *Illinois State Journal*, and the *Louisville Journal* had speculated about the purpose of the forces McClernand was raising and the date the expedition was to commence. On 17 November the *State Journal* even reported that McClernand would command the expedition.[36] That Grant was aware of this is certain.

Among those who knew of the expedition was Lt. James H. Wilson, who reported to Grant's headquarters as chief topographical engineer in early November. The previous month Wilson had met McClernand in Washington, and McClernand had told him of the Mississippi expedition. Wilson had pointed out that "Halleck would probably be against him and in favor of giving Grant . . . the chief command." McClernand responded that he "realized Halleck was against him" but that he had the support of Lincoln and Stanton.[37]

Wilson relayed all of this to Grant. In addition, he pointed out "McClernand's intimacy with Lincoln" and that the general "had been specially authorized to organize and command an expedition for the specific purpose of capturing Vicksburg and opening the Mississippi." According to Wilson, this was the "first authentic information" Grant had received about the proposed expedition. Wilson would also assert that it was at his urging that Grant decided to take command personally along the river.[38] Of course, it was not until January that Grant actually determined to do so.

On 9 November Brig. Gen. James M. Tuttle, commander of the District of Cairo, notified Grant that units were arriving there "with a kind of loose order to report to Gen. McClernand."[39] That Grant had not been officially informed of McClernand's mission is clear from a 9 November message in which he specifically stated that he was unaware of orders directing units to report to McClernand. Grant conjectured that if such orders were in effect, their scope would be limited to reporting to McClernand only as Illinois inspector general.[40] The following day he sought an explanation from Halleck about the rumors of an operation against Vicksburg: "Am I to understand that I lay still here while an Expedition is fitted out from Memphis . . . ? Am I to have Sherman move subject to my order or is he & his forces reserved for some special purpose?" Halleck responded, "You have command of all troops sent to your department, and have permission to fight the enemy where you please."[41]

This reply placed Halleck squarely behind Grant and gave the latter absolute control over military operations in his department, in effect circumventing any effort by McClernand to conduct an independent operation against Vicksburg. To Sherman on 14 November Grant explained that "the mysterious rumors of McClernand's command" had forced him to ask Halleck for clarification of the situation. Grant having received that clarification, Sherman was to move his forces toward Oxford, Mississippi.[42]

On 24 November Sherman wrote his brother that "McClernand is announced as forming a grand army to sweep the Mississippi," and in a comment that revealed his opinion of the Illinois general, he groused, "The truth is, he is in Springfield, Ill., trying to get elected to the U.S. Senate." Sherman and Wilson were aware of McClernand's mission. Grant and Sherman had met at Columbus, Kentucky, only a few days before Sherman wrote his brother. Wilson claimed to have told Grant of the upcoming operation. There can be no doubt that Grant knew what was transpiring.[43]

Porter, too, would recollect informing Grant of McClernand's expedition when the two first met at Cairo in late November, which was after Grant had made his decision to move into Mississippi. According to Porter, the two discussed a plan in which Porter would support Sherman in a landing on the Yazoo River. Porter expressed a desire to cooperate with Grant until McClernand arrived.[44] If Porter's account was correct, Grant had definite cause to be concerned about what was transpiring in Washington and what McClernand's role was to be.

McClernand made no effort to communicate with Porter following their October meeting in Washington, even though Porter's headquarters was at Cairo, Illinois. On 21 October Porter queried Assistant Secretary of the Navy Gustavus Fox as to McClernand's whereabouts. "Hurry him up," he wrote. "We can't be idle 'till spring."[45]

On 29 October Porter wrote to Welles that he was prepared to move toward Vicksburg. Welles passed the communication to Stanton on 5 November. Perhaps because of recent changes in the command arrangements over the navy (previously Halleck had been able to issue orders to naval squadrons on the inland waters), on 15 November Halleck inquired of Assistant Secretary Fox when Porter would "be ready to operate down the river on Vicksburg." Apparently, Stanton had not informed Halleck of Porter's status. That same day Secretary Welles informed Porter that Halleck had indicated McClernand would be prepared to move in about three weeks. Porter was to cooperate with that army commander.[46]

On 21 November, Porter ordered Capt. Henry Walke to enter the Yazoo River, determine where McClernand could land troops, and hold the area until the army arrived. Three days later Porter wrote Sherman that the Navy Department had advised him to be ready to conduct with McClernand an attack on Vicksburg in three weeks.[47] This indicated that Porter was well aware of the details of McClernand's plan, proposed in Washington, to land at the Yazoo. It also indicated that Sherman knew precisely what was going on.

On 12 November and again on 5 December, Porter informed Fox that still he had heard nothing from McClernand, and on 7 December Halleck authorized Grant to request Porter to cooperate with his movements. Porter informed the Navy Department that Grant had requested his assistance, that he would be ready to move on the 13th, and that he had still heard nothing from McClernand.[48]

McClernand's failure to maintain close contact with Porter was a blunder. Porter claimed to have told Lincoln he was disparaging of nonprofessional generals, although he did not care for West Point ones. Welles specifically stated that Porter preferred to be associated with "a citizen general."[49] That McClernand was not a West Pointer should have been a point the Illinoisan could cultivate to gain Porter's support. As a politician McClernand was well aware of the necessity to further relationships with potential allies. In January 1863 and afterward, Porter, however, would ally himself with the two most prominent and successful West Pointers in the western theater—Sherman and Grant—against McClernand.

On 14 November Grant notified Sherman that he should be prepared to move his command to the vicinity of Holly Springs and to combine with

Grant's forces for a march through central Mississippi against the Confederate army. Eight days later, Grant ordered his subordinate to move to Holly Springs. Accordingly, two days after Porter sent his missive about cooperating with McClernand, Sherman departed from Memphis with two divisions; he met Grant at Oxford, Mississippi, on 5 December.[50] Two days later, Grant asked Sherman to meet with him to discuss the idea of Sherman returning to Memphis. Undoubtedly, the two also discussed the ramifications of McClernand's arrival in the theater, for the following day Grant wired Halleck that Sherman "will command the expedition down the Mississippi" and that he would cooperate from Oxford. He ordered Sherman to Memphis and directed him to "assume command of all the troops there, and . . . move with them down the river to the vicinity of Vicksburg and . . . proceed to the reduction of that place."[51] On the 9th, however, from Halleck came a message that must have seemed cryptic indeed to Grant: "The President may insist upon designating a separate commander; if not, assign such officers as you deem best. Sherman would be my choice as the chief under you." Grant wired back that Sherman had already departed—a message somewhat cryptic in its own right.[52] While Sherman had in fact moved from Oxford, he certainly had not departed Memphis to attack Vicksburg.

Why the change in plans? Clearly there were operational reasons for such a move. With two powerful forces, Grant expected that the weaker Confederates would be unable to concentrate sufficient forces to defeat either arm. Grant recognized that the objective was Vicksburg, not necessarily the Confederate army, for Vicksburg was the key to the control of the Mississippi River. If Confederate forces could be destroyed or captured along with the city, so much the better. Grant's mission would be to prevent other Confederate forces from reinforcing Lt. Gen. John C. Pemberton in Vicksburg while Sherman took the city. All this made sense strategically, but there was another reason for the change: John Alexander McClernand.

Grant's opinion of McClernand is well established. After Wilson reported for duty with Grant in early November, he had a conversation with Grant's adjutant general, Maj. John A. Rawlins. While Rawlins praised McClernand's courage, he "denounced his ambition, his jealousy, and his disposition to intrigue with the politicians in Washington."[53] Given the close relationship between Rawlins and Grant, these comments undoubtedly also reflected the latter's views. Grant would record in his memoirs that in early November "he did not think the general selected [McClernand] had either the experience or the qualifications to fit him for so important a position" and that he "feared for the safety of the troops entrusted to him."[54]

In a 9 December telegram to Halleck, Grant stated he had learned that McClernand would arrive soon. He told Halleck: "The enterprise would be much safer in charge of [Sherman]." On 14 December he telegraphed Halleck that "I would regard it as particularly unfortunate to have . . . McClernand . . . sent to me. [He] is unmanageable and incompetent."[55] In his memoirs Grant wrote:

> My object in sending Sherman back was expedited by a desire to get him in command of the forces separated from my direct supervision. I feared that delay might bring McClernand, who was his senior and who had authority from the President and the Secretary of War to exercise that particular Command—and independently. [Grant did not actually learn of this officially until 28 December.] I doubted McClernand's fitness; and I had good reason to believe that in forestalling him I was by no means giving offence to those whose authority to command was above both him and me.[56]

Although Grant's thoughts as expressed in his memoirs must generally be read with caution, in the case of McClernand the above statements reflect Grant's sentiments in 1862. On 14 December Sherman wrote his brother from Memphis that he was to organize forces "as may be assigned from Helena, and to proceed to Vicksburg." Adam Badeau, who later joined Grant's staff, wrote after the war that Grant "was still anxious lest McClernand should obtain the command of the river expedition, and therefore had hurried Sherman to Memphis."[57] Clearly Grant did not want McClernand to command such an important expedition. Whether he was "giving offence" to higher authorities (Halleck, Stanton, and Lincoln) is problematical.

In his memoirs Sherman was to acknowledge that "the preparations were hasty in the extreme," but, he would explain, speed was necessary "to reach Vicksburg as it were by surprise while General Grant held in check Pemberton's army."[58] He does not mention whether McClernand's imminent arrival had any bearing on the extreme haste.

Stanton had crafted the 21 October order to McClernand to allow maximum leeway for the authorities in Washington, to include Halleck, to limit his authority. Stanton had also sent two telegrams to McClernand, on 28 and 29 October, that stressed the urgency of raising troops and gave every indication of the administration's full support of him.[59] Certainly Lincoln had doubts, but for political reasons he had still seen fit to give a command to

McClernand. At best, McClernand enjoyed less than wholehearted support from the entire command structure, from Grant through Lincoln.

McClernand had not been idle since his return to Springfield in late October. Although he set aside a few hours to have Mr. G. K. Smith paint his portrait, he continued to attend to the details of organizing and forwarding units for active service. He questioned Governor Morton of Indiana and the adjutant general of Iowa on locations and mustering status of units, and he queried the Illinois adjutant general for reports of unit status. He addressed continuing problems of pay, equipage, and transportation, and, once they were taken care of, ordered the units moved expeditiously. All troop movements he reported to Stanton and Halleck. He also reported intelligence he had acquired regarding the number of Confederates at Vicksburg and the fortifications being strengthened at Port Hudson, Louisiana. In this same dispatch he proposed using gunboats to ferry soldiers across the Mississippi below Vicksburg. This correspondence reveals a great deal about McClernand's abilities as a soldier, for in May 1863, that was precisely the plan effected by Grant to place Union soldiers in a position to strike Vicksburg.[60]

While forwarding troops, McClernand on 10 November was also urging Stanton to speed the execution of the expedition.[61] Probably McClernand suspected something was awry, for on 13 November, two days after Halleck notified Grant he would command all troops in his department, McClernand stated to Stanton, "I infer that General Grant claims the right to . . . control all the troops sent to Columbus and Memphis."[62] Was McClernand aware of Halleck's directive?

Because of his prominent position in Illinois politics and his years of service in the nation's capital, McClernand had connections with numerous individuals in positions to know what was transpiring. Governor Yates was in Washington when McClernand wired him on 20 November: "Please see the Secretary of War and learn the status of the enterprise." Yates visited Lincoln that same day and discussed problems that still remained with the arms furnished to Illinois troops. Whether the subject of McClernand's command was raised is unknown, but a few weeks later Halleck informed Grant of the possibility of Lincoln naming an independent commander for the expedition.[63]

Six days later, McClernand wrote Lyman Trumbull, U.S. senator from Illinois, asking "what is said and being done with regard to me and the enterprize [*sic*] with which my name has been lately connected." Trumbull replied on 1 December that Stanton had spoken favorably of the expedition.[64]

On 1 December he also wrote Stanton stating that most troops had departed Indiana, Iowa, and Illinois, and that his staff could perform all the remaining details. He then specifically asked to be sent forward to command the expedition. The same day that he contacted Trumbull, McClernand also wrote the other Illinois senator, Orville H. Browning, and asked that he determine whether there was any move to supersede him. Browning wrote back on 2 December saying he had seen Lincoln and that "both he and Secretary of War are very anxious for you to have the command of the expedition, and intend to stand by you. . . . Go ahead, you are in no danger."[65]

Browning's assurances did not soothe McClernand. On 5 December he wrote Governor Morton suggesting that he, Yates, and Kirkwood go to Washington and urge that the expedition immediately be ordered to proceed.[66] Having heard nothing for a week, he wrote both Lincoln and Stanton and urged them to send him forward with the expedition. Three days later, Stanton replied that he believed Halleck had issued the order but he would see him "and have the matter attended to without delay." The next day McClernand wrote Halleck, referred to his 1 December letter, and asked to be sent South "in accordance with the order of the Secretary of War of the 21st of October giving me command of the Mississippi expedition."[67] Clearly frustrated by the lack of response to his queries, on 16 December he again sent a letter to Browning, in which he accused Halleck of thwarting the wishes of the president and secretary of war.

> I am satisfied that the President and Sec of War favor me as the commander of the Expedition, but I am persuaded the Genl in Chief is my enemy—personal enemy and senselessly so.
>
> I think I understand the Genl in Chief as well as any man living. I think he designs to give the command of the Expedition to Sherman whom he unjustly gave the credit of the victory at Shiloh. I say *unjustly* in no disparaging or unfriendly sense to Genl Sherman, but simply in vindication of truth.[68]

At 9:00 A.M. on that same day, McClernand, now almost frantic about the delays, wired both Lincoln and Stanton: "I believe I have been superseded." He asked for clarification. On 17 December Stanton first replied that he was surprised by McClernand's telegram and later the same day, wired that Halleck had issued no order superseding him. The next portion of the reply must have struck McClernand like a thunderbolt: "The operations being in General Grant's department, it is designed to organize all the troops of that department in three army corps, the First Army Corps to be commanded by you, and assigned to the operations on the Mississippi under the general supervision of the general commanding the department. General Halleck is to issue the order immediately."[69] This was the first mention to McClernand that he would command a corps under Grant rather than have an independent command.

The following day, Halleck issued General Orders No. 210, which organized Grant's army into four corps and assigned McClernand command of the Thirteenth Army Corps. Sherman was to command the Fifteenth Army Corps. In a missive to Grant the same day, Halleck wrote: "It is the wish of the President that General McClernand's corps shall constitute a part of the river expedition and that he shall have the immediate command under your direction." Apparently, in deference to McClernand's political muscle, Lincoln could not afford to alienate the Democrat, despite the military leadership's misgivings, but he seized the opportunity to ensure McClernand was well supervised. Grant recorded in his memoirs, however, that "this interfered with my plans, but probably resulted in my ultimately taking the command in person. Dispatches were sent to him [McClernand] the same day in conformity." Grant followed on the 22d with General Orders No. 14, assigning specific units to the Thirteenth Corps.[70]

Grant's 18 December dispatch "in conformity" might have mollified McClernand, because it clearly gave him command of the river expedition. Although Sherman's corps would constitute a part of the expedition, McClernand was the senior commander by date of rank. Unfortunately, McClernand did not receive the order until he reached Memphis on 29 December. Not having heard from Grant by the 23d, he wired Stanton that he had still not been relieved from duty in Illinois. That evening Stanton wired back: "You are relieved of duty at Springfield, and will report to General Grant for the purpose specified in the order of the General-in-Chief."[71]

The period 11 November to 23 December 1862 has the trappings of a conspiracy against McClernand. Although the Illinois general had performed his mission well, he had been unable to obtain the orders necessary for him to take the field with his soldiers. In his report to Stanton on 24 December he summarized the number of units he had fielded and forwarded: fifty-two infantry regiments, five cavalry regiments, and six artillery companies. Still being mustered were eight infantry regiments and four artillery companies.[72] This was a considerable accomplishment, and having put the majority of the units in the field, McClernand was anxious to join them. He dutifully requested orders, but every request appeared to be stymied. Was there, in fact, resentment among the West Point officers who controlled his future? In particular, did Halleck want to block McClernand until it was too late for him to interfere with operations against Vicksburg? Was Lincoln having second thoughts about McClernand's military capabilities? Why did Stanton not intervene before 23 December to have McClernand ordered from Springfield? What was Grant's role in delaying McClernand's active involvement in the endeavor?

Unquestionably, there was an effort in Washington to prevent or delay McClernand from taking command of the Mississippi River expedition. As mentioned, Secretary of the Navy Gideon Welles had recorded in his diary Halleck's opinion of McClernand, though he had added, "the President entertains a good opinion of him." He also entered the assessment of the postmaster general, Montgomery Blair: "Blair alluded . . . to the fact that McClernand was crowded aside; said there was a combination to prevent his having that command."[73]

Neither Grant nor Sherman, both West Pointers, thought much of McClernand. Another West Point graduate, Union general James B. McPherson, who would also command one of Grant's corps during the Vicksburg campaign, wrote Grant on 20 December: "In consequence of orders . . . placing General McClernand in charge of the expedition under you I would, if in your place, proceed to Memphis and take command of it myself." The day prior, Grant had informed McPherson that McClernand would "have the chief command of the Vicksburg expedition, but under my direction."[74] Obviously McPherson, who had clashed with McClernand in August, believed him unfit for direct command of the expedition.

Halleck certainly doubted McClernand's fitness for command, and he was in a position to delay his assumption of that command. Halleck was not singling out McClernand for criticism, for he detested all political generals. In November 1862 he explicitly stated his opinion in a letter to Brig. Gen. John M. Schofield, another graduate of West Point: "If you could be here for a few weeks you would see how difficult it is to resist political wire-pulling in military appointments. Every Governor, Senator, and Member of Congress has his pet generals to be provided with separate and independent commands. I am sick and tired of this political military life."[75] Undoubtedly, he cast McClernand as a "pet general."

Until informed officially of McClernand's status, Halleck could claim ignorance of the whole affair. Unquestionably he knew of McClernand's orders, having been directed by Stanton to meet with McClernand before the orders were issued. Halleck had also received McClernand's letter advising him of how he would organize such an expedition. Also, as previously cited, Welles claimed on 15 November that Halleck said McClernand would be ready to move in about three weeks.

McClernand made little effort to inform Halleck of his ultimate objective, communicating with him only to inform the general in chief of the troops he had mustered. Not until 22 December did Halleck indicate to McClernand that he would be included in the expedition against Vicksburg, and then the general in chief did it only by forwarding a copy of the telegram that informed Grant. McClernand assumed Halleck knew or believed that as an independent commander he should report only to Stanton. That he believed "Halleck was against him" and was an "enemy" must have played no small part in the lack of correspondence. His comment to Browning on 16 December that he believed Halleck wanted to give command of the expedition to Sherman appears to have been prescient.

Halleck and Grant were, by contrast, in continuous communication. Halleck informed Grant, in answer to his inquiry, that Grant commanded all troops in his department, and that this would include units forwarded by McClernand. On 25 November Halleck had approved Grant's request for Sherman's forces to move in concert with him into northern Mississippi, and on 8 December Grant informed Halleck that Sherman would command the expedition down the river.[76] The latter took place eight days after McClernand had first requested authorization from Stanton to leave Illinois. On 9 December Halleck sent a message to Grant stating that the president "may insist upon designating a separate commander." Nine days later Halleck informed Grant that McClernand would command the forces on the river, but not until five days after that did Stanton authorize McClernand to assume his command. By then it was too late, for on 20 December Sherman departed from Memphis with his entire command. Included in that command were eight infantry regiments and one artillery battery that had been mustered into service and sent to Memphis during McClernand's tenure in Illinois.[77] Clearly, Halleck and Grant wanted little to do with McClernand and probably blocked his departure for Vicksburg as long as possible.

No evidence exists that Lincoln was reconsidering his 21 October order to McClernand. Lincoln was on record as being concerned about McClernand's desire for independence and was surely aware, particularly as he was a lawyer, of the implications in the caveat in that order, which made McClernand's forces subject to the ultimate control of Halleck. Welles recorded in his diary that Lincoln "started from his chair" when Blair remarked that "there was a combination to prevent [McClernand] from having that command."[78] Stanton then assured Lincoln that it was not the case. Although the 21 December order from Halleck stated that the president desired McClernand to have "immediate command" of the river expedition, it also recognized

McClernand's subordination to Grant as department commander—"under your direction."

Stanton's reply to McClernand's queries regarding being superseded did not reflect a change in command arrangements, because McClernand remained in command of the forces to constitute the expedition—but also under command of Halleck, as specified in the 21 October order, and under Grant as department commander. However, because of his desire to be independent and his belief that the 21 October order gave him that independence, McClernand certainly would have thought otherwise.

Stanton's role is difficult to ascertain. The secretary of war had voiced his encouragement, and McClernand had stated he was satisfied with Stanton's support. Nothing in Stanton's diaries reveals his thoughts on this issue. Even though McClernand queried him on 12 December, and Stanton replied three days later that he believed Halleck had sent the orders and he would "have the matter attended to without delay," not until 23 December were the orders actually issued. Additionally, Stanton apparently did nothing to force Halleck to give sole command of the Mississippi expedition to McClernand, and he acquiesced in the order assigning him to command a corps. In both instances it can be argued that he was abiding by the wishes of the president to give McClernand an important command, as well as ensuring that the affair remained under the ultimate control of the general in chief.

Certainly Porter's role in the downfall of McClernand has to be examined carefully, for the two officers had similar unflattering qualities. Stanton characterized the admiral as a "gas bag . . . blowing his own trumpet and stealing credit which belongs to others." Although Welles recognized Porter's courage and professional abilities, he too characterized him as "selfish," "scheming," "untruthful," ambitious, and as exhibiting "a great deal of duplicity."[79] According to Welles, Lincoln did not have complete confidence in Porter, even comparing him to McClellan, who was always requesting more men, because the admiral was always requesting more vessels.[80] Porter's actions in 1863 have to be scrutinized in light of these unfavorable traits.

Although McClernand exerted considerable energy and displayed admirable organizational ability during his assignment in Illinois, the extent of the credit due him must be examined. His mission from Governor Yates was to "assist in organizing the new troops raised and to be raised in the state." His mission was not actually to raise the troops, although undoubtedly his personal reputation among many of the influential men of the state assisted in their ability to recruit soldiers. Even his order of 21 October only assigned him the responsibility "to organize the troops . . . to be raised." By his own words, that also included mustering them into Federal service. At no time did he acknowledge responsibility to raise troops, although he did allude to problems in doing so in correspondence to Stanton.[81]

John McClernand was the senior officer responsible for organizing and mustering troops; however, of the almost four months that he had that mission, he was in Washington for one (22 September–24 October). He was, therefore, in Illinois only three weeks prior to leaving for Washington and for only two months before steaming south to join his command at Memphis. These dates call into question the influence that he personally could have had on the mustering effort.

As a result of the July and August calls for troops, Illinois furnished 58,689 men. This included fifty-nine infantry regiments and six artillery batteries. Only New York and Pennsylvania furnished more. From 31 August, the day after McClernand arrived in Springfield, through 23 December, the day he departed for Memphis, forty-four regiments and two batteries were mustered into service. Of these, thirty-three infantry regiments entered Union service during McClernand's first month in Illinois, but only five regiments and two batteries entered after his return from Washington. Of the thirty-three, nine were mustered in within four days and eighteen within the first week of his arrival.[82] Realistically, McClernand could not have been responsible for recruiting, organizing, or mustering the first nine that entered the army and could have had only a slight effect on the remaining nine. This leaves only fifteen regiments upon which his direct influence could have reasonably been exerted prior to his departure for Washington. Of the five that entered service after his return, one entered the next day and one three days after that. Again, his direct influence could have been only minimal, if not nonexistent.

Nevertheless, there is an army axiom that states the commander is responsible for everything a unit does or fails to do. Although not physically present in Illinois during the entire period of his assignment, McClernand's correspondence indicates his aptitude for organizing units and preparing them for field duty. During his tenure, McClernand accomplished the mission he was assigned, and forty-four infantry regiments joined the Union cause. Eight would serve with Sherman at Chickasaw Bayou and with the Illinois general at Arkansas Post. Six others would participate in the Vicksburg campaign. The effectiveness of his efforts in Illinois cannot be discounted.

Having on 23 December received orders to proceed, McClernand arrived at Memphis six days later. The 23d was doubly important to the politician turned soldier, for on that date he also married Minerva Dunlap, sister of his deceased wife. The ceremony took place in Jacksonville, Illinois, with Governor Yates in attendance. On the return to Springfield, the train on which they were riding struck a horse and jumped the track. After a two-hour delay, the journey continued on to Cairo, where the McClernands were to catch a boat for Memphis. There the general would take command of the Mississippi River expedition. At Cairo he requested two guns and ammunition to be placed on *Tigress*, the boat on which he, his wife, and staff would be traveling to Memphis. He arrived at Memphis to find the city devoid of troops, Sherman having departed nine days earlier.[83]

Waiting for McClernand at Memphis was the 18 December message from Grant that assigned him command of the Thirteenth Army Corps. Ironically, the 18th was also the date that Confederate Brig. Gen. Nathan Bedford Forrest had launched a raid north of Jackson, Tennessee, a raid that resulted in the destruction of portions of the railroad between Jackson and Columbus, Kentucky. Forrest also cut the telegraph lines that linked Grant with the War Department and all other forces in the West. Communications were not fully restored until the last few days of December.[84]

Loss of communications was not Grant's only problem, for on 20 December Maj. Gen. Earl Van Dorn raided Grant's major logistical base at Holly Springs, destroyed tons of supplies, and brought one arm of Grant's pincers movement on Vicksburg to a complete halt. Although Grant was well aware that his communications had been cut, he made no effort to contact Sherman using messengers to ensure that he did not lead the expedition to the Yazoo. The Confederates, therefore, were able to mass forces against Sherman while Grant was withdrawing from northern Mississippi. Sherman did, however, learn of the raid on the 21st, while at Helena, but he put little faith in the report.[85] Perhaps his judgment was clouded by the realization that if he halted, McClernand would arrive to take command.

Van Dorn's raiders continued to raise havoc with Union communications, by cutting the lines north and west of Bolivar, Tennessee, and burning several more railroad trestles on the 23d. Not until Christmas Day did Grant write to the Union commander at Memphis, forwarding a copy of the 18 December order and attempting to alert McClernand to his situation. McClernand did not receive this communication either. On 28 December Grant again wrote him at Memphis, to explain that the train carrying the message had been unable to get past Jackson, Tennessee, because of the destruction by Confederate raiders.[86]

That same day, McClernand wrote to Grant to express disappointment that Grant was not at Memphis. He included copies of his October orders with Lincoln's endorsement, the telegram that expressed Lincoln's desire that McClernand command the river expedition, the orders to leave Springfield to conduct the expedition, and an extract of a message from Stanton emphasizing the importance of the campaign.[87] This was the first time Grant had seen the specifications of McClernand's original orders.

McClernand also wrote Lincoln, venting his anger about the situation and charging that a conspiracy against him existed. "Left here by myself, I shall have to run the gauntlet of the Mississippi in a command steamer in order to reach my command at Vicksburg. Either accident or intention has so conspired to thwart the authority of yourself and the Secretary of War and to betray me, but with your support I shall not despair overcoming both." McClernand would continued to believe this charge of conspiracy for the remainder of his life. Not only had he been reduced from commander of the expedition to a corps commander, but the entire force he had recruited had gone ahead to attack Vicksburg without him.

In a calmer moment, he asked Lincoln to promote three members of his staff, one of whom was his father-in-law, James Dunlap. Lincoln approved the requests, and Dunlap was promoted to lieutenant colonel on 1 January 1863.[88]

McClernand did not receive Grant's 28 December letter. It arrived after he departed from Memphis to catch up with his command and Sherman. Unbeknownst to him, the previous day Sherman had suffered a defeat by Confederate forces under Brig. Gen. Stephen Lee at Chickasaw Bayou, north of Vicksburg on the Yazoo, and had been forced to reembark his command and withdraw.

6
Victory in Arkansas

McClernand departed from Memphis on 30 December. En route to the Yazoo, he stopped at Helena, Arkansas, to confer with Brig. Gen. Willis A. Gorman, commander of the Eastern District of Arkansas. One subject was the reduction of Arkansas Post.[1]

France had established Arkansas Post as a trading post along the Arkansas River in the late 1600s. The Spanish had constructed a fort, Fort Carlos, there in 1781, and the post had continued as a major trading center. Following the sale of Louisiana to the United States, Arkansas Post had become the territorial capital of Arkansas and had remained so until 1820, when the capital moved to Little Rock. The move had devastated the economy of the region to such an extent that when John James Audubon visited the place in the 1820s, he described it as poor and practically deserted except for a few Indians.[2]

A former soldier in Napoleon's army, Frederic Notrebe, had immigrated to the United States in 1809, had begun marketing cotton at Arkansas Post in 1819, and had built a cotton gin there in 1827. The post again had taken its place as a prominent river trading center; brick buildings, including a state bank, had appeared. When the state bank system failed, however, Arkansas Post had again fallen on hard times. Once again, it had been practically abandoned in 1855, when the capital of Arkansas County was moved to DeWitt, twenty miles north.[3]

The lack of Confederate defenses along the rivers of Arkansas was demonstrated in June 1862, when Union forces moved up the White River and captured a Confederate battery at St. Charles, Arkansas. Soon thereafter, Maj. Gen. Theophilus H. Holmes, commander of the Confederate Trans-Mississippi Department, directed Col. John A. Dunnington to establish defenses to protect Little Rock and the Arkansas River Valley. Dunnington selected the site of the abandoned Arkansas Post to build a fortification that the Confederates referred to both as Fort Hindman and Arkansas Post.

Dunnington, formerly of the Confederate States Navy, recognized that the fort could also serve as a base for Confederate naval vessels, one from which they could interfere with Union navigation on the Mississippi, only fifty miles away.[4]

Gorman's predecessor, Brig. Gen. Alvin P. Hovey, had believed eight thousand Confederates were stationed at Arkansas Post. These he had regarded as a threat to his base at Helena, and in November 1862 he had led a force to eliminate that threat. A combination of low water in the Arkansas and orders to return to Helena against the possibility of operations elsewhere had forced Hovey to abandon his attempt to destroy the post. Most of Hovey's forces, about half the garrison at Helena, had then joined Sherman for the unsuccessful attempt to take Vicksburg by way of the Yazoo River.[5] Maj. Gen. Samuel R. Curtis, commander of the Union Department of the Missouri, however, still kept a watchful eye on the Confederates at Arkansas Post. Had Holmes realized the precarious situation at Helena, he might have launched an attack against that Federal garrison and thereby possibly prevented Sherman's attack up the Yazoo and even McClernand's forthcoming movement against Arkansas Post.[6]

Arkansas Post took on new significance in late December 1862. Brig. Gen. Thomas J. Churchill, commander of the garrison, had stationed pickets at the junction of the cutoff between the Arkansas and White Rivers as well as at the junction of the Arkansas and Mississippi. From them he received continuous reports of gunboats and transports moving on the Mississippi. On 29 December, he received a report that an unarmed transport, *Blue Wing*, towing two coal barges, was near the mouth of the White. Guerrillas fired on the transport; the captain beached it and surrendered. Capt. L. M. Nutt, commander of an independent Louisiana cavalry company, brought the boat, laden with ammunition, into Arkansas Post that afternoon.[7] The ammunition would be employed against its former owners a few weeks hence.

In a driving rainstorm on 2 January 1863, Sherman met with Porter on board *Black Hawk*, anchored in the Yazoo River. The admiral informed Sherman that McClernand had arrived at the mouth of that river, about five miles north of Vicksburg. According to Porter, the two discussed a possible attack on Arkansas Post, although Sherman stated in a message to Grant only that he intended to retire to Milliken's Bend and return the navy transports to Memphis. Sherman told Porter that he had heard rumors that McClernand was there to supersede him.[8] Evidence from newspapers, personal reports, and meetings with Grant suggests that Sherman had been aware of this prior to leaving Memphis. Sherman's statement to Porter lends credence to the theory that Grant and Sherman may have conspired to prevent McClernand from taking command until the capture of Vicksburg was a fait accompli.

The following day, McClernand asked Sherman to meet with him on board *Tigress* to determine a course of action. Sherman had learned of the capture of *Blue Wing*, possibly from Porter or a letter from Gorman, and of course McClernand was aware of the incident from his meeting with Gorman. Sherman was to assert that in their meeting McClernand had only a vague plan to open the Mississippi by "cutting his way to the sea" and that the Illinois general objected to Sherman's proposal to attack Arkansas Post. Sherman believed such an attack would prevent future losses to Union shipping—exactly what Dunnington sought to inflict. The two did agree on one matter, and that was the necessity for Sherman to withdraw his forces from the Yazoo. According to Sherman, McClernand then proposed that the two consult Porter about the possibility of an attack up the Arkansas River. Sherman wrote Porter that the three of them should discuss the matter.[9]

Late in the evening of 3 January, McClernand, Sherman, and Porter met aboard the latter's flagship. The meeting was as stormy as the weather, but Sherman's and Porter's accounts differ as to who was responsible for the vehemence. Porter would claim that McClernand was discourteous to Sherman, who then left the cabin. Sherman was to write that it was Porter who was overly forceful with McClernand—he described his tone as "curt"—and that Porter threatened not to support any attack against Arkansas Post unless Sherman commanded the army. Sherman, by his account, then asked Porter to meet in a forward cabin. There, Porter later said, he told Sherman he would not allow McClernand to be rude to the general. Sherman would record that he told Porter harmony in the command was critical. They then joined McClernand, and according to Porter, McClernand then asked if the admiral objected to his accompanying the expedition; according to Sherman, it was Porter who asked McClernand if he objected to the admiral accompanying the expedition. Also, by Sherman's account, Porter stated he had not liked McClernand from the time they first met in Washington in October 1862. Porter, however, in his memoirs would write that he had told Assistant Secretary of the Navy Gustavus Fox, shortly after that meeting, that he had no opinion of McClernand.[10] As McClernand never wrote of the incident, it is impossible to determine the accuracy of either account. What is notable, though, is that there was a high degree of discord among the senior leaders on the Mississippi. These overtones of disharmony may explain future events in the military career of John McClernand.

Both Porter and Sherman agreed that an attack on Arkansas Post was the primary subject discussed at the meeting, but who actually proposed the expedition is disputed by Porter. Unquestionably, McClernand had indicated the great importance he attached to the Post during his meeting at Helena.[11] When the general raised the subject, Porter countered that such an attack had actually been Sherman's idea, proposed the day before. In a letter four years later, Sherman would claim that it was his idea to attack Arkansas Post and that it took "two days to prevail on McClernand to make the move." Whether Sherman had discussed such an idea with Porter prior to the meeting is questionable, as are many of Porter's recollections. On 3 January Sherman, in the same letter to Porter in which he proposed the three commanders meet, also proposed "to go right up and clear out the Post of Arkansas and Little Rock," citing the capture of *Blue Wing* as justification.[12] It is possible that the letter was the first mention of such a campaign to Porter. Porter's hostility to McClernand is indicated by a letter to Rear Adm. Andrew H. Foote, dated 3 January. "McClernand," he wrote, "has just arrived and will take command. Sherman, though, will have all the brains."[13] Was the ambitious Porter attempting to cast his lot with Sherman, whom he perceived to be a rising figure in the western theater?

During this verbal encounter, McClernand consulted maps of the region and decided that he would take the entire force to capture Arkansas Post. Such a large army, supported by Porter's gunboats, would provide overwhelming superiority for the Union forces. As he was the senior commander, McClernand announced that he would command the foray.

In a dispatch to Stanton that same day, McClernand characterized Sherman as "a brave and meritorious officer" who "has probably done all in the present case [the attack at Chickasaw Bayou] that any one could have done." The Illinois general went on to say that he "would not detract anything from him, but give him all credit for good purposes, which unfortunately failed in execution."[14] Certainly McClernand was being magnanimous toward Sherman, for this letter also indicated McClernand's outrage at the delay in the order allowing him to leave Springfield; it also accused Halleck of issuing orders that allowed Grant and Sherman to move against Vicksburg without him. In McClernand's mind he had been deprived of the command that was rightfully his, as established by the order of 21 October. By stating that he would accompany the joint effort against Arkansas Post, McClernand clearly established that he was in command and intended to exercise the authority granted him by the War Department.

Sherman greatly resented McClernand's arrival and assumption of command. In letters to his wife, Sherman characterized the appointment as "absurd" and opined that Lincoln "will get his fill before he is done." He declared that the president was "dead set to ruin me for McClernand's personal

Battle of Arkansas Post (10–11 January 1863)

Union Organization

Army of the Mississippi, Maj. Gen. John Alexander McClernand

First Corps (Thirteenth Corps), Brig. Gen. George W. Morgan

First Division, Brig. Gen. Andrew J. Smith

First Brigade, Brig. Gen. Stephen G. Burbridge

Second Brigade, Col. J. W. Landrum

Second Division, Brig. Gen. Peter J. Osterhaus

First Brigade, Col. Lionel A. Sheldon

Second Brigade, Col. Daniel W. Lindsey

Third Brigade, Col. J. F. DeCourcey

Second Corps (Fifteenth Corps), Maj. Gen. William T. Sherman

First Division, Brig. Gen. Frederick Steele

First Brigade, Brig. Gen. Francis P. Blair

Second Brigade, Brig. Gen. Charles E. Hovey

Third Brigade, Brig. Gen. John M. Thayer

Second Division, Brig. Gen. David Stuart

First Brigade, Col. Giles A. Smith

Second Brigade, Col. Thomas Kilby Smith

Confederate Organization

Post Commander, Brig. Gen. Thomas J. Churchill

First Brigade, Col. Robert R. Garland

Second Brigade, Col. James Deshler

Third Brigade, Col. John W. Dunnington

glory." To his brother, Sen. John Sherman, he wrote that he would submit gracefully, but the tone of the letter was deeply indignant. In a second letter, though, he was far more blunt: "I never dreamed of so severe a test of my patriotism as being superseded by McClernand." Lt. Col. Marcus Spiegel of the 120th Ohio Infantry wrote his wife that it was rumored that Sherman had exclaimed that "he would go to H—l or Vicksburg before McClernand came." Nevertheless, in an announcement to his soldiers, Sherman recalled how they had supported him and stated his expectation that they would "give him [McClernand] the same hearty support and cheerful obedience."[15]

Porter's recollections must again be considered in light of others' opinions of him. Welles was concerned with his "defects and weaknesses," which included a tendency to exaggerate his reports. He also questioned Porter's willingness to play a subordinate role in any campaign that required him to support the army. Throughout the Vicksburg campaign, Porter's dispatches would extol the role of the navy but often question the performance of the army. Welles was not alone in his view, for Sen. Orville Browning found Porter to be "very gassy. His own exploits constitute the staple of his conversation." Nevertheless, Porter would continue to advance in rank, eventually becoming superintendent of the Naval Academy.[16]

On 4 January 1863 McClernand issued General Orders No. 1, by which he assumed command of the Army of the Mississippi (his designation, not one approved by the War Department) and divided it into two corps. The Thirteenth Corps (redesignated First Corps), with two divisions, was to be commanded by Brig. Gen. George W. Morgan, and the Fifteenth Corps (redesignated Second Corps), also consisting of two divisions, was to be commanded by Maj. Gen. William T. Sherman. McClernand's force thus totaled 31,753 soldiers.[17] It was that army that McClernand would lead against Arkansas Post.

What military significance did the Post have? Was it worth sending such a large force with naval support to capture it? Certainly Sherman thought so. The day after the meeting with Porter and McClernand, Sherman wrote Grant that he had suggested to McClernand that the Confederate fort be destroyed to reduce interference with Union traffic on the Mississippi. Two days later he wrote his brother that destroying Arkansas Post would eliminate a Confederate force that could threaten the rear of the Union army.[18] While, in a letter to Grant, Sherman justified the move against Arkansas Post, his motives are somewhat suspect. In his memoirs he would write that his relief by McClernand following his failure "raised the usual cry . . . of 'repulse, failure, and bungling.'"[19] He had been defeated at Chickasaw Bayou. Perhaps a victory would redeem his reputation.

McClernand listed his reasons for the attack in his "after action" report of the expedition. Essentially, they totaled four. First, destruction of Arkansas Post would eliminate the threat to Union communications along the Mississippi River. Second, Grant's and Sherman's withdrawal from the vicinity of Vicksburg had allowed that city to be reinforced; McClernand's Army of the Mississippi could not attack Vicksburg successfully without the support of the Army of the Tennessee, whereas in early January there was no plan for another coordinated attack on Vicksburg by the two armies. Third, Maj. Gen. Nathaniel Banks was to have moved up the Mississippi from New Orleans to pressure Vicksburg from the south, but no word had been received from him; there was no reason for McClernand to believe that Banks would reach the vicinity of Vicksburg before he returned from the Arkansas River. Fourth, this large Union force would be idle at Milliken's Bend while it awaited further orders.[20] By using the available troops, McClernand could reduce the threat from Arkansas Post against river traffic and ensure that the Union soldiers were gainfully employed. It remained to be seen whether a successful campaign would redeem Sherman's reputation after failure at Chickasaw Bayou and establish McClernand's worth as an independent commander.

Was Arkansas Post a decisive objective for the Union army? Certainly the capture of *Blue Wing* and gunfire directed by Confederates at other Union boats on the Mississippi had demonstrated that there was a threat from Arkansas Post. In addition to the Post, there were several other bases from which Confederates attacked Union boats. Cap. J. H. McGee, who commanded an unattached and independently operating company of Arkansas cavalry, captured and destroyed three steamboats, two flatboats, and twelve coal barges on the Mississippi near Memphis between 6 January and 16 February. On 24 February two Confederate steamers sank the Federal ironclad *Indianola*, operating from Fort DeRussy on the Red River.[21]

Although these attacks were certainly irritants to the Union navy, they could hardly be characterized as decisive. The Union navy dominated the Mississippi River, and such losses were clearly acceptable. Yet, as Grant himself later admitted, "five thousand Confederate troops left in the rear might have caused us much trouble and loss of property while navigating the Mississippi."[22]

Sherman, too, was concerned that troops from Arkansas Post could interfere with traffic along the Mississippi. He reported to Grant in January that the capture of *Blue Wing* was "a mere sample" of the havoc that could result were Arkansas Post not eliminated. After its destruction Sherman continued to justify the attack: "We were compelled to reduce it. Its importance to the enemy cannot be doubted." Striking a personal note, he wrote to his wife: "This relieves our Vicksburg trip [meaning Chickasaw Bayou] of all appearances of a reverse." In fact, Illinois papers were blaming Sherman for the repulse at Chickasaw Bayou. He went on to say that its capture made him "feel much less uneasiness about our communications."[23]

Was the Post a threat to Union ground operations in the vicinity of Vicksburg? Ideally, Confederate forces in the Trans-Mississippi would cooperate with those in Mississippi to launch coordinated attacks against Union forces separated by the Mississippi River. After Grant withdrew from northern Mississippi following the attack on Holly Springs and consolidated his army on the Louisiana side of the river, Confederates should have been able to harass the Union force and make it difficult for Grant's army to move through the region or to make an amphibious assault from the Louisiana shore to the

Mississippi bank. This, however, would have required an overall Confederate commander in the theater—a commander more aggressive than Holmes.

The Trans-Mississippi Department had been created in May 1862 by the merger of the Department of Texas, District of Arkansas, and several scattered Louisiana districts. On 1 October 1862, Confederate forces in Mississippi and east Louisiana had been organized into the Department of Mississippi and East Louisiana, under Maj. Gen. John C. Pemberton. The boundary between the two departments was the Mississippi River. On 24 November 1862 Gen. Joseph E. Johnston was given overall command of Pemberton's department, Gen. Braxton Bragg's Department No. Two in western Tennessee, and Lt. Gen. Edmund Kirby Smith's Department of East Tennessee. This reorganization, however, left Johnston and Holmes as coequal commanders who both reported to Richmond.[24]

Lack of Confederate unity of command in the vicinity of Vicksburg reduced the possibility of any coordinated effort against the Union army. On 21 December 1862, President Jefferson Davis informed Holmes that he saw gaining control of the Mississippi River as one of two principal Union goals (the other being the capture of Richmond), but he failed to establish a command structure that would provide forces and a single commander to frustrate that Union objective. In his letter Davis stressed that Holmes should cooperate with Pemberton and reinforce the armies under Johnston, who would concentrate them against the Union forces. Rather than order this, however, Davis only stated that he hoped Holmes would be able to do so.[25] Holmes believed that he had to retain the Arkansas River Valley or the entire Trans-Mississippi would be lost, and he could not spare any soldiers to aid Pemberton or Johnston. The Confederate War Department then several times ordered Holmes to reinforce Pemberton with ten thousand troops, but Holmes stalled, writing that any move to reinforce Vicksburg would mean the abandonment of Arkansas. Finally, on 11 December, the Confederate War Department capitulated to Holmes: "You must exercise your judgment in the matter; . . . it is impossible at this distance to judge of your necessities, but . . . if you could give aid it was hoped you would do so."[26]

Davis, the West Point graduate and former United States secretary of war, could not bring himself peremptorily to order Holmes to subordinate his forces to Johnston or to have him reinforce Vicksburg. The president relied on his department commanders to make decisions affecting their commands and would not interfere with their decisions if they objected to guidance from central authority. In Davis's words, "A large discretionary power is necessarily vested in the several Departmental commanders." Holmes made no effort to reinforce Vicksburg or harass Union forces in eastern Arkansas and northeastern Louisiana; nonetheless, Davis left him in command until March.[27] By then it was too late for the Confederates to counter the large Union force opposite Vicksburg.

Were Confederate forces in the Trans-Mississippi region a threat to Union operations on the west side of the Mississippi opposite Vicksburg? In late 1862 Richmond believed the Trans-Mississippi Department had fifty to fifty-five thousand troops available to protect Arkansas and reinforce Vicksburg. Actually, however, there were only about half that number in Arkansas, with about nine thousand more in western Louisiana. The effectiveness of those forces, even if united, was certainly questionable. Confederate forces in the region had suffered continuous setbacks leading to the loss of Missouri. Defeats at Pea Ridge in March 1862 and at Prairie Grove in December had cleared organized Confederate forces from northern Arkansas. Also, defection of Creek and Cherokee allies on Arkansas's western border with the Indian Territory had increased the vulnerability of that region.[28] Additionally, Holmes, the department commander, was weak, if not incompetent. If properly organized and led, a large Confederate force could indeed have caused considerable problems in the Union rear. There is no reason to believe, however, that the large Union army across from Vicksburg could not have defeated any organized Confederate attacks.

McClernand's greatest defender regarding his point about cooperating with Banks was Sherman himself. In what he described as a "semi-official" letter, Sherman told Grant that he was certain McClernand's army would return to the vicinity of Vicksburg before Banks could arrive for a coordinated attack.[29] (In fact, Banks never reached Vicksburg, and Port Hudson did not fall until July 1863.) Before departing Memphis, McClernand learned that Grant's move south had been blocked. Without additional forces, the capture of Vicksburg would be impossible. Sherman had tried and failed, and, without either Grant or Banks, any further attempt to seize the Confederate fortress would prove futile.

At the time McClernand, Sherman, and Porter agreed to attack Arkansas Post, the three Union armies that could threaten Vicksburg were widely separated. Banks was south of Port Hudson, Louisiana; Grant was withdrawing from northern Mississippi toward Memphis; and McClernand was only a few miles north of, although across the river from, Vicksburg at Milliken's Bend. Until at least two of those three forces could unite, an attack on Vicksburg was out of the question. Even then, the winter rains would cause great difficulty for the army as it attempted to move overland in the swampy bogs bordering the river. Clearly, a long campaign was in the offing.

What was McClernand's force to do in the meantime? An attack on Arkansas Post would not only achieve a military objective but also, as McClernand stated, keep the troops occupied for the foreseeable future. Grant certainly could not argue with this philosophy, for in his memoirs he stated that one of the reasons he began digging canals to attempt to bypass Vicksburg was "to divert the attention . . . of my troops"—he "never felt great confidence that any of the experiments resorted to would prove successful."[30]

McClernand, therefore, was left with the alternatives of attempting another assault on Vicksburg with small probability of success, taking his army back to Memphis, or finding a Confederate force to attack. Sherman had been defeated at Chickasaw Bayou, and there was no reason to believe another attack would succeed; Grant himself later stated that a retreat to Memphis would have been interpreted as a defeat; and the Arkansas Post project had some military merit.[31] It can only be concluded, therefore, that McClernand's judgment in the matter of what to do with the army in January 1863 was based on sound military principles. However, it is also probable that in making the decision, McClernand saw an opportunity to achieve a military victory as an independent commander, with possibly favorable political consequences.

By General Orders No. 3, dated 4 January 1863, Sherman alerted his corps for further operations.[32] That same day, the expedition to destroy Arkansas Post got under way: the Army of the Mississippi embarked on fifty transports, accompanied by thirteen rams and gunboats plus Porter's command flagship *Black Hawk*.[33]

The following day McClernand issued orders to his corps commanders for the attack on Arkansas Post. The orders issued by the political general were clear and contained much of the detail that Sherman and Morgan needed to deploy their forces. McClernand acknowledged that his intelligence on the Post might be faulty; therefore, he specifically directed his subordinates to use their initiative to overcome unforeseen events. He informed them about the river route to the Post, established the order of march along the river and upon debarkation, and instructed the disembarked forces to travel light. Shiloh was still a fresh memory, and he reminded the commanders to provide for the security of the force, using skirmishers and cavalry patrols. He gave specific instructions as to where the corps were to be aligned prior to any assault and ordered the two commanders to ensure that their units formed a unified front. The events of Fort Donelson, too, were still vivid, and he issued instructions as to how to cover ground for which there was insufficient infantry available. To prevent being surprised by a

Confederate force moving toward Arkansas Post from the direction of Little Rock, McClernand ordered that a contingent of infantry, cavalry, and artillery be disembarked across the river from the Post to establish a blocking position to interfere with Confederate reinforcements.[34] For an amateur, with this order McClernand got the campaign off to a good start.

In the selection of a river route for the army to move from Milliken's Bend to Arkansas Post, deception had been a primary consideration. By leaving the Mississippi at the mouth of the White River and traveling up that stream a distance, the Union force might be able to deceive the Confederates into believing it was actually moving farther north, to attack the Rebels at St. Charles. There existed, however, a cutoff that connected the White and the Arkansas, by which the fleet could enter the latter and move rapidly toward the Post. *Conestoga*, sent on a reconnaissance of the route, reported plenty of wood along the banks for fuel. The vessel had no trouble navigating the waterways. Porter provided the army commander with charts of the route, so that he would have no difficulty in directing the movement.[35] The admiral also provided McClernand the latest intelligence on the Post, which he had obtained from what he described as a "refugee." The report stated that about seven thousand Confederates occupied the fort (about two thousand more than were actually there).[36]

As the senior commander of the expedition, McClernand must be credited with exceptional leadership in the early stages of the expedition. The objective was clearly defined; a force large enough to overcome the resistance expected based on the intelligence available was assembled; deceptive measures to confuse the enemy were implemented; account was taken of the logistical requirements of the fleet; a feasible tactical plan to reduce the Confederate fort was developed; and a plan was made to provide for the security of the attacking force. McClernand and the Union army were ready.

One potential problem existed: McClernand was operating in another commander's department. Established along geographical or state boundaries, the Union departmental configuration was little different from that of the Confederates. In September 1862, the Indian Territory, Missouri, Arkansas, and Kansas had been consolidated into the Department of the Missouri, under Maj. Gen. Samuel R. Curtis. Operations west of the Mississippi River had to be coordinated with him. On 16 October, Grant had been assigned as commander of the Department of the Tennessee, which included Vicksburg and northern Mississippi. Just as with the Confederates, the Mississippi River served as a boundary between the two departments; therefore, Grant had no jurisdiction over Curtis.[37] Unlike the Confederates, however, Curtis responded to directives from Halleck as early as 3 November and again on 7 January to reinforce Grant across the Mississippi. As Arkansas Post lay within Curtis's department, McClernand, even if operating independently, would be operating in his jurisdiction—a sensitive undertaking.

Curtis was aware of McClernand's desire to capture Arkansas Post, from the conversation at Helena on 30 December, and he was concerned himself about that Confederate force as a threat to Helena. Undoubtedly, he welcomed McClernand's letter of 8 January informing him of the move against the fort. This letter had had two purposes: first, to inform Curtis of operations within his department, and second, to coordinate McClernand's move against Arkansas Post with Curtis's proposed move toward Little Rock. Both purposes reflect favorably on McClernand's professional sensitivities.[38] By 11 January Curtis, Gorman, and Brig. Gen. Clinton Fisk had organized a force to move into the interior of Arkansas in conjunction with McClernand's move. Those commanders too realized Vicksburg was "too big a boo" for them until the scattered Union forces could be concentrated.[39]

If the joint expedition was to succeed, cooperation between McClernand and Porter was critical. Although the initial meeting between the two on 3 January had been less than harmonious, the actual conduct of the campaign began with close coordination between the army and navy commanders. McClernand provided Porter a copy of the instructions given to Sherman and Morgan, and Porter, as noted, provided McClernand charts and intelligence that were available to him. By the time they reached the mouth of the Arkansas, on 8 January, the two were in continuous contact regarding the state of the river, the advisability of steaming at night, prospective landing points near Arkansas Post, signals for moving the fleet, and care of the wounded.[40] Probably based upon his experiences with joint attacks on Forts Henry and Donelson, as well as at the near disaster at Shiloh, McClernand recognized the need for cooperation between the two services; he worked to establish the relationships necessary to ensure a successful campaign.

As he awaited the start of the operation, the Illinois general had time to reflect upon the events of the past year. In his mind, victory in the West had been within the grasp of the Union forces since the success at Fort Henry. Yet, one event after another had transpired to snatch certain glory from the Union army in the West and, of course, from himself. To him, Forts Henry and Donelson, Shiloh, the Corinth campaign, and the reversals at Holly Springs and Chickasaw Bayou had been caused not by Confederate strategy but by incompetence on the part of Maj. Gen. Henry W. Halleck, general in chief of the Union armies. His anger boiled over in a 7 January letter to Lincoln in which he accused Halleck of "willful contempt of superior authority," "incompetency," and of being "personally hostile to very many, if not all, of our officers who are not West Point graduates." McClernand urged the president to relieve him from command.[41] Lincoln did not relieve Halleck. McClernand would write other epistles in which he would express his views about Halleck, Grant, and West Point officers in general. Despite the insubordination, Lincoln would allow the contentious politician to retain his position.

Unfortunately for the former congressman, it was not until 8 January that he wrote Grant to inform him of his plans to attack Arkansas Post. When he did, McClernand stated his reasons for the expedition and his plans for his army following the expected success.[42] Grant did not receive this report until, probably, three days later, as his communications had been interrupted by Confederate cavalry raids. The Tennessee department commander reached Memphis on 10 January after the failed attempt to move against Vicksburg from the interior of Mississippi. In a dispatch to Porter, Grant stated he had heard nothing official since 22 December, which was prior to Sherman's defeat at Chickasaw Bayou. He wrote McClernand that his requirements had to be "guessed at" but that he was forwarding reinforcements, because "this expedition must not fail." Undoubtedly Grant was referring to an expedition against Vicksburg, as he at that time was unaware that McClernand, Porter, and Sherman were poised for an attack on Arkansas Post.[43]

Also on 10 January, Brig. Gen. Fisk, commander of a volunteer brigade assigned to the Department of the Missouri, wrote General Curtis from Memphis. His comments provide further evidence of the lack of respect in which McClernand was held by fellow officers. Fisk wrote, "General McClernand is to command the down stream force. This arrangement causes much bitterness among us generals, who are all ambitious of doing brave deeds in opening the Mississippi. I am quite discouraged."[44] Fisk himself had had no military experience prior to the war and afterward ran for political office. Whether he was bitter because he would not have a prime position in the attacks on Vicksburg, was looking to reap the political benefits of successful war service, or simply doubted McClernand's ability is a matter of speculation. Whatever the reason, it is obvious that McClernand's unfavorable reputation had spread throughout the western theater.

Fisk was not alone in his opinion. Col. Thomas Kilby Smith, one of Sherman's brigade commanders, wrote his mother that "the advent of McClernand is deprecated" and referred to him as a "political general."[45] Smith had fought at Shiloh but was a lawyer and, like Fisk, had had no military experience prior to the Civil War.

A correspondent for the *Illinois State Journal* confirmed the general atmosphere within the command in regard to McClernand. His arrival was seen as "an unhappy turn. No one thinks McClernand is the man for the place." That report was not quite accurate, for Lieutenant Colonel Spiegel had written his wife prior to the attack on Chickasaw Bayou that he believed it was being launched because "Sherman wants the glory alone." En route to Arkansas Post he wrote her that he knew little of McClernand, but "I have nevertheless most implicit confidence in him, while for our old Commander [Sherman] I had nothing but contempt and detestation and looked upon him as utterly unfit to lead an Army."[46] Such conflicting moods did not bode well for a campaign against a fortified Confederate position.

Upon receipt of McClernand's 8 January letter, Grant fired off a blistering response, dated 11 January, to his maverick general.

> Unless absolutely necessary for the object of your expedition [Vicksburg] you will abstain from all moves not connected with it. I do not approve of your move on the Post of Arkansas while the other is in abeyance. It will lead to the loss of men without a result. So long as Arkansas cannot re-enforce the enemy east of the river we have no present interest in troubling them. It might answer for some of the purposes you suggest, but certainly not as a military movement looking to the accomplishment of the one great result, the capture of Vicksburg.
>
> Unless there is some great reason of which I am not advised you will immediately proceed to [Milliken's Bend] and await the arrival of re-enforcements and General Banks's expedition.[47]

That afternoon Grant wired Halleck that "General McClernand has fallen back to White River, and gone on a wild-goose chase to the Post of Arkansas."[48] Clearly Grant was focused on the main Union objective of capturing Vicksburg. What Grant did not know was that Banks, whom he had not heard from since 16 December, was not in a position to cooperate against that river fortress.

Meanwhile, McClernand had wired Grant on the 10th that he was within three miles of Arkansas Post and was moving against that fort.[49] McClernand's first military venture as an expeditionary force commander was beginning.

Brig. Gen. Thomas J. Churchill's five thousand Confederates at Arkansas Post had not been idle. Scouts from the post had reported on 8 January that a Union gunboat was at the cutoff between the White and Arkansas rivers sounding the water's depth. Sgt. William Heartsill of the 2d Texas Cavalry

Regiment had remarked that "the atmosphere begins to smell a little gunpowderish around here."[50] The following morning Capt. Samuel J. Richardson, commander of Company F, 2d Texas Cavalry, had reported that the fleet had entered the Arkansas. A light rain fell throughout the night as the Confederate soldiers awaited the Yankee attack.[51]

Arkansas Post, or Fort Hindman, was positioned on a bluff overlooking a bend in the river. About three hundred feet on a side, the fort had casemates with eight- and nine-inch guns facing the river. A line of rifle pits extended from the fort to a swamp about seven hundred yards west. Several other artillery pieces were within the fort and along the trench line. The Confederates had also driven piles into the river bottom to impede navigation.[52]

On the evening of 9 January 1863, the joint expedition reached Notrebe's Farm, about three miles from Arkansas Post, but in the darkness and rain the men did not begin disembarking until 4:00 a.m. In pursuance of McClernand's plan to establish a blocking position between the post and Pine Bluff, however, one brigade, commanded by Col. Daniel W. Lindsey, did disembark on the opposite bank during the night; it moved to a position on the Arkansas River above the fort. McClernand had failed to achieve surprise, for Churchill's pickets at the mouth of the cutoff had reported the movement of the Union fleet into the Arkansas. Upon receiving the report, the Confederate commander had posted two brigades in rifle pits about one and a half miles from the fort in the direction of the Union fleet. One brigade was held in reserve, although several of its companies were posted as skirmishers forward of the pits. Three cavalry companies were sent to watch the Federals as they landed. Sherman and Morgan completed disembarking around noon.[53]

As the troops were going ashore, McClernand—ever the orator—rode up to the 55th Illinois Infantry, raised his hat, and shouted, "May your gallantry on this occasion equal, if not exceed, your gallant conduct at Shiloh!" Although the men of this regiment had resented McClernand for replacing Sherman, they responded to their fellow Illinoisan with three cheers as they marched away.[54]

Early that morning McClernand had conducted a personal reconnaissance of the site of the impending battle, and Porter's gunboats had begun a bombardment of the Confederate forward rifle pits. After a few hours, the Rebels were forced to withdraw. Mindful that this was a joint operation, McClernand had alerted Porter to Sherman's proposed location so as to prevent the gunboats from firing into friendly Union forces. Sherman, meanwhile, had begun marching his corps in accordance with McClernand's plan to circle the fort; his right flank would rest on the Arkansas River. Morgan was to follow, join with Sherman's left, and then anchor his own left on the

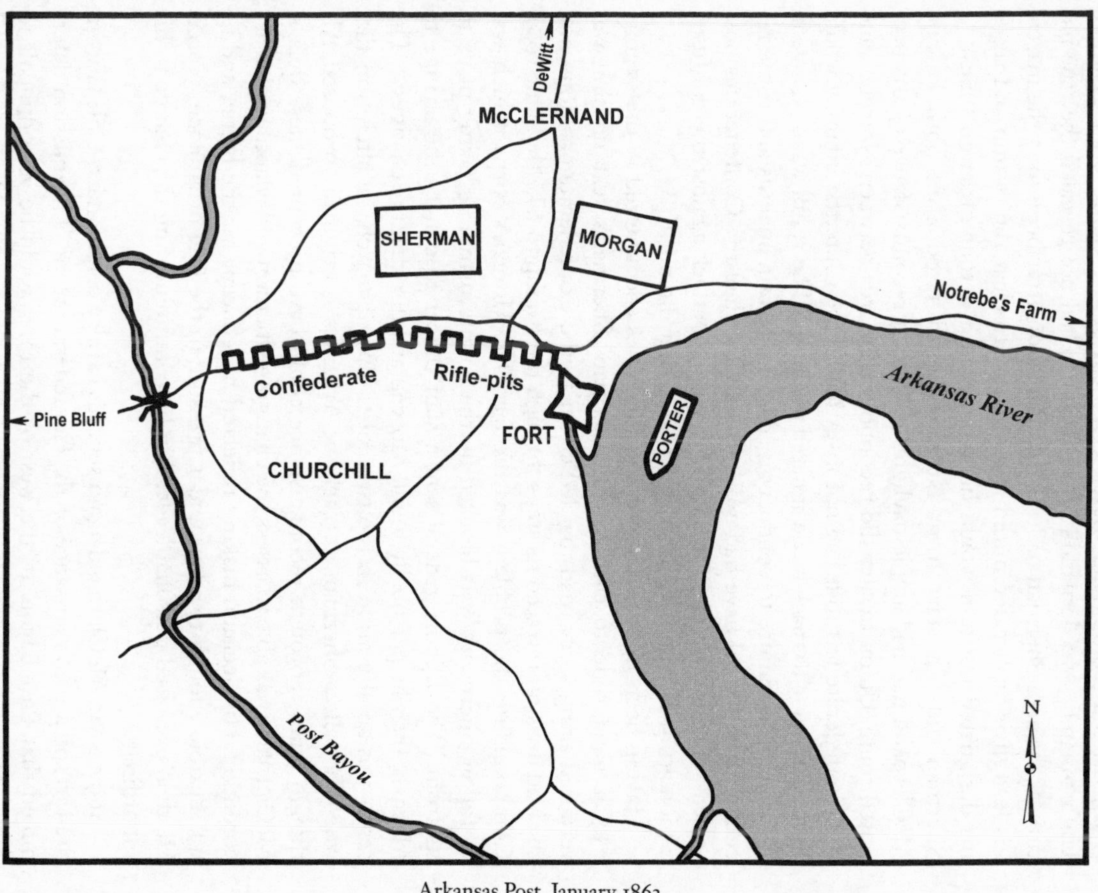

Arkansas Post, January 1863

Arkansas, thus completing the envelopment of the Confederate position. Unfortunately, McClernand's reconnaissance had not revealed the true nature of the area Sherman had to cross, and soon after beginning the march, his lead division became mired in a swamp. To clear the swamp and reach his designated position would have required a detour of seven miles. As Sherman did not start from Notrebe's until 11:00 a.m., both he and McClernand had had ample daylight to direct a reconnaissance of the proposed route. Union cavalry did reconnoiter the area between Notrebe's and the Confederate left, but had not investigated the route the infantry would have to traverse to reach its designated positions. The result was a change in the plan. This failure to conduct an adequate terrain analysis and route reconnaissance could have had a disastrous effect had the Confederates possessed sufficient forces to launch a preemptive attack against the confused Union army. Fortunately for McClernand, they did not.[55]

Having been informed about the difficulties encountered in the swamp, McClernand rode to confer with Sherman. Sherman's rear division was rerouted along a dry road that led closer to the Confederate positions, and the lead division retraced its steps through the swamp to take the same road. Compounding the problem was the fact that Morgan's corps, which was to follow Sherman's, was blocked by the countermarching taking place to its front. The Illinois general sent a staff officer to convey the change to Morgan; then he personally found Morgan and directed the changes.[56] The result was an alteration in the two corps' line of march, an alteration that would not allow Sherman to reach the Arkansas as originally proposed. Although more thorough reconnaissance could have prevented these delays, McClernand was able to assess the changing situation and adapt his plan accordingly. His decision making reflected his concept for the battle, and he was flexible enough to adapt under pressure in the face of an enemy force. He then exercised personal leadership by communicating the change to his subordinates.

At 9:00 p.m. McClernand again sent his cavalry commander, Col. Warren Stewart, on a reconnaissance of the Confederate front. This mission determined that Post Bayou, to the west of the fort, would be very difficult to cross. This report, however, conflicted with an account by Morgan after the battle, that he examined the bayou and was able to cross it with ease. This points out the importance of a thorough reconnaissance, if time permits. Based on Stewart's report, McClernand then directed Sherman to move to the bayou and anchor his right on it. Sherman's divisions reached their new positions around 2:00 a.m., after marching most of the day. Morgan moved into position on Sherman's left and, supported by Porter's gunboats, forced the Confederate pickets to withdraw. Both Union corps prepared for the next day's battle.[57]

Several years later, Porter would write that at about 3:00 P.M. on the 10th he received a message from McClernand, who "had accompanied the expedition, it was supposed[,] merely as a spectator." There could in fact have been no doubt in Porter's mind that McClernand was more than a spectator—that he was, in fact, the senior army officer present and had assumed overall command of the expedition. Porter would record that the message stated that Sherman was in position and that the gunboats should commence their bombardment of the fort.[58]

This recollection is considerably different from the chronology of events established by other commanders and from Porter's report immediately after the battle. In that report Porter wrote: "At 2 o'clock McClernand told me the troops would be in position to assault the main fort. . . . At 5:30 P.M. General McClernand sent me a message that everything was ready . . . , but no assault took place." Brig. Gen. Charles E. Hovey, a brigade commander in Sherman's corps, reported that it was 2:00 P.M. when he was ordered to reverse his march through the swamp and return to the river.[59] As McClernand had personally ascertained that Sherman could not reach his assigned position, there is no logical reason for him then to have informed Porter that Sherman was in position to attack.

As darkness approached on 10 January, McClernand did order Porter to begin a bombardment in order to divert Confederate attention from the Union infantry moving in their front, not as preparation for the main attack. In his report McClernand stated, "Promptly complying, the admiral . . . opened a terrific cannonade upon the fort." Both Union corps commanders confirmed in their reports that Porter conducted a bombardment in the late evening.[60] It can only be concluded that Porter's later writings are either the result of a very faulty memory or are nothing more than an attempt to slander John McClernand.

During the early light of 11 January, Sherman and Morgan positioned their corps for the assault on Arkansas Post. By ordering Sherman to anchor his right on Post Bayou, McClernand precluded a Confederate attack aimed at enveloping the right of the Union army. The depth of the bayou also made it difficult for the Confederates to withdraw to the west once the Union attack began. To ensure that the two corps were tied together, McClernand sent Sherman a message that Morgan would be on his left. There followed a series of messages among the key commanders to ensure the attack was coordinated between all the arrayed forces. At 10:00 A.M. Sherman met with McClernand to report that he was prepared to attack. At the same time, the army commander sent Morgan a message that the gunboats would signal the attack. He also sent an order to Porter to report when he was ready to support the attack.[61] Shortly thereafter Morgan reported that he had placed artillery near the Confederate fort and was also prepared for the attack. At 11:20 A.M. McClernand notified Porter that "my whole force is disposed for attack and await your advance attack on the fort."[62]

Around 1:00 P.M. Porter's bombardment of the Rebel fort began, and minutes later the infantry initiated the main attack.[63] This too had been closely coordinated by McClernand; he had ordered his corps to advance after a thirty-minute bombardment. The signal for Porter to shift his fire away from the attacking infantry was to be the shouts of the advancing soldiers.[64] Considering the state of communications during the period and the quantity of smoke that would obscure the battlefield, this was probably the only solution to the problem of preventing friendly casualties by naval gunfire.

During the morning McClernand had moved his headquarters from *Tigress* to a position near the juncture of his two subordinate corps and approximately nine hundred yards from the fort. He informed Sherman of his location, and that is where the two met around 10:00 A.M. Although his headquarters was in a wooded area, the ground between McClernand and the fort had only a few scattered trees to obscure observation. The army commander stationed a man in a tree to report the army's progress to him.[65]

It is fundamental that a commander should position himself where he can best control his forces. Command in the American Civil War was difficult, because of the lack of effective control measures. Essentially, during a battle a commander either led from the front or, at higher levels, communicated with his subordinates by messenger. By establishing his headquarters where he did, McClernand had put himself in a position to communicate rapidly with both of his corps commanders as well as to get immediate reports from his observer of what was occurring, although the observer's view would be hindered by smoke. In fact, during the fight McClernand's subordinates kept him informed, and at one point he even directed reinforcements be sent to General Morgan.[66] Certainly communicating with Porter was far more difficult, and the arrangements made were probably the best that could be effected under the circumstances.

By 5:00 P.M., McClernand's force of thirty-two thousand soldiers had overwhelmed and captured the Confederates in Arkansas Post. Churchill's losses were 4,791 captured, sixty killed, and seventy-five to eighty wounded. In addition, the Confederacy lost five thousand muskets and eighteen cannon of various calibers. Union losses in killed and wounded were far greater: 134 killed, 898 wounded, and 29 missing. Porter's casualties totaled thirty-one.[67] These figures reflect the traditional difficulty encountered by infantrymen attacking across open ground against a fortified position and cannot be construed as a reflection on McClernand's generalship. In fact, they reflect a respectable Confederate-to-Union loss ratio of 4.5 to 1.

The original ground tactical plan devised by the Union army commander was sound. Completely encircling the fort with his two corps and using the fleet to control the river side of the fort would have left no escape for the Confederates. It would also have prevented Confederate use of their rifle pits, because the Union soldiers could have easily enveloped them. The Rebels' only hope would have been for another force to break through to them. Based on the size of the Union army, however, this would have been a very difficult proposition. (A Confederate relief force did attempt to intervene, but upon reaching Pine Bluff—twenty-five miles distant—it learned of the fort's surrender.)[68]

Unfortunately, the swamps encountered by Sherman and the difficulty of crossing Post Bayou prevented this plan from being implemented. The only feasible alternative was the frontal assault actually made against the fort and rifle pits, utilizing the overwhelming combat power of the Union army and the enfilading fire from the naval gunboats. With few exceptions, frontal assaults would continue to be the norm throughout the Civil War. McClernand cannot be faulted either for his plan or the results of the battle.

Accounts of the events immediately following the surrender of Arkansas Post lend credence to the theory that Sherman and Porter were instigators of an effort to cast McClernand in an unfavorable light. McClernand, in his official report, wrote that Churchill surrendered the fort to Brig. Gen. Stephen G. Burbridge, whose brigade made the direct assault on the Post. Burbridge said the same in his report. McClernand continued that he then arrived at the fort and received the formal surrender from Churchill; Churchill, in his own report, does not mention to whom he surrendered. At some point, McClernand then returned to *Tigress*, where Sherman found him. In his memoirs Sherman reported the exuberant McClernand exulting over the victory: "Glorious! Glorious! My star is ever in the ascendant! I'll make a splendid report. I had a man up a tree."[69]

The reason for Sherman's visit was that McClernand had directed Brigadier General Morgan to command the captured fortification, for it was Morgan's corps that had assaulted the Confederate position; to Sherman he had assigned command of the area outside the fort. Sherman was probably upset about this, because his corps had suffered the greater number of casualties, in his assault against the two Confederate brigades occupying the rifle pits extending west from the fort. Also, Sherman had led the failed attack on

Chickasaw Bayou, and a headline that credited his corps with the capture of Arkansas Post could go a long way toward removing the stigma of that defeat.

A few days after the battle Sherman, in a letter to his brother, insinuated that McClernand's official report was inaccurate and that his own reflected the true state of events. He also made a most telling comment about his motives: "Mr. Lincoln intended to insult me and the military profession by putting McClernand over me. . . . Only in times like these all must submit to insult and infamy if necessary."[70] There is, in fact, little difference between the two battle reports, and McClernand's praised Sherman's "usual activity and enterprise."[71] There is no evidence that Lincoln intended insult by appointing McClernand to command. In early February, Sherman sent a copy of his report of the battle to Grant and asked him to forward it to Halleck so that he could "see the truth amid the cloud of falsehood and defamation by which I have again been enveloped."[72]

Political appointees were a fact of life in the Civil War, and as has been seen, Lincoln needed McClernand's influence. By date of rank he was senior to Sherman; therefore, when sent to the vicinity of Vicksburg, he would have to be placed in command. Sherman recognized this fact, however galling, and subordinated his personal feelings to the need for harmony. To his credit, there is no evidence that he voiced his opinion of McClernand to his subordinates—only to his wife, brother, and Grant.

Porter, in contrast, continued his campaign against McClernand. He believed Sherman had not received the credit he deserved. Both in his memoirs and in his *Naval History*, Porter blasted McClernand's leadership and extolled that of Sherman. Porter wrote that Churchill surrendered to Sherman (clearly untrue) and that only then did McClernand assume command of the army (again clearly untrue)—a "most ungenerous thing for him to do." Porter also wrote that McClernand "actually had nothing to do with the management of the army, and was down four miles below the fort during the operations. Sherman was virtually the military commander."[73] These statements are also untrue, for the evidence establishes the fact that McClernand was in command and issuing orders as the commander, that Sherman followed those orders, that McClernand personally managed the forces at Arkansas Post during the two-day battle, and that he was present on the battlefield during the final assault.

To Assistant Secretary of the Navy Fox, Porter wrote on 16 January, "I think it is a great misfortune that McClernand should have superseded Sherman who is every inch a soldier. . . . McClernand is no soldier, and has the confidence of no one. . . . Sherman used to help me think, but now I have to think for McClernand and myself also." Porter also accused McClernand of poor planning and failure to keep everyone informed of upcoming operations: "McClernand tells no one what his plans are (having none) nor tells me what he would like me to do."[74]

Again, the evidence does not support these charges. From the night of 3 January, when McClernand first met with Porter and Sherman, until the surrender of Arkansas Post, the record is replete with correspondence from McClernand to the admiral informing him of the army's movements and seeking to coordinate naval fire support. The navy escorted the army transports and reconnoitered the river routes, and Porter himself provided McClernand charts of those waterways. What the evidence does support is a charge that Porter sought to gain the maximum credit for the navy and himself for operations on the western waters.

Porter also claimed to have sent a message to Grant that urged him to take command personally of the entire force. No such message has been located, although Grant in his memoirs mentions having received such a recommendation from Porter and Sherman. (On 17 January 1863, Sherman wrote Grant and urged him to "join us and direct our movements."[75] It is probably to this letter that Grant is referring.) Porter claimed that he "anticipated no good results from McClernand's commanding the army, that it was unjust to Sherman, that I was certain McClernand and myself could never co-operate harmoniously."[76]

Even after the initial meeting on *Black Hawk* on 3 January, there appeared, however, to have been excellent cooperation between the army and navy commanders. Immediately after the battle McClernand sent a message to Porter in which he congratulated him "upon the efficient and brilliant part taken by you . . . in the reduction to-day of the Post of Arkansas" and acknowledged the "harmonious and successful co-operation of the land and naval forces." In his official report, McClernand briefly mentioned the effective naval contribution, but certainly not to the extent that their effectiveness warranted.[77] Undoubtedly this upset Porter, as on 11 and 14 January he wrote the fleet captain, Capt. A. M. Pennock, commander of the naval station at Cairo, that the army had not taken the post by assault and that "McClernand tries to make it appear that the army did its share; but they never attempted an assault until we had dismounted every gun, and then the rebels repulsed them." A few weeks later, he wrote in a similar vein to Sen. James W. Grimes, stating that "it was a naval fight altogether."[78] There is an element of truth in Porter's comments, but the casualties in the Union army belie the assertion that the army did less than its share. It appears from this correspondence that Porter was doing his own share of headline grabbing.

These epistles also contradict the message Porter sent to McClernand shortly after the fort fell: "I congratulate you that we have disposed of this tough little nut, the capture of which is alike creditable to the Army and Navy. . . . I shall be ready to co-operate with you again tomorrow."[79] Apparently Porter, and perhaps Sherman as well, was offering cooperation to the commander's face while at the same time waging a sub-rosa campaign to have McClernand, the politician soldier, replaced—and the sooner, the better.

McClernand's conduct following the battle was professional, notwithstanding any giddiness at the victory, as described by Sherman. Not only did McClernand congratulate Porter for the navy's role in the victory, but he also wired Grant announcing success and advising him that Porter had "efficiently and brilliantly cooperated."[80] The following day he issued a congratulatory order to the soldiers; although bombastic and filled with hyperbole, it nevertheless demonstrated McClernand's recognition that such declarations were necessary to instill high morale in the army. Porter, as a professional sailor, did the same, although his message was somewhat more subdued and made a veiled suggestion that the victory actually belonged to the navy. On 14 January McClernand wired news of the victory to Curtis, in whose department Arkansas Post was located.[81]

In this latter communication, McClernand also spoke of continuing up the Arkansas River to Little Rock. The evening of the surrender of Arkansas Post, McClernand requested that Porter sound the river toward Little Rock, with the obvious intent of continuing on to that Confederate city. *Monarch* reported it could only ascend twelve miles before the water became too shallow for further progress.[82] McClernand, therefore, was forced to forego an attack against the state capital.

The surrender of the Confederate fort did not end McClernand's responsibilities as commander. At 2:00 A.M. on 12 January, about eight hours after the surrender, McClernand ordered Sherman to sweep the road toward Little Rock for the enemy. Sherman found no one, as the surrender had been complete; ideally, however, such a pursuit should have been conducted immediately to prevent any possible escape.[83]

McClernand also attended to other immediate requirements following the victory. He ordered Sherman and Morgan to begin boarding the Confederate prisoners onto the Union transports, to provide details to bury the dead (specifically observing that unburied men and horses were a detriment to the health of the command), and to begin removing the piles from the riverbed to facilitate possible further naval operations. Sgt. William Heartsill was placed on *Conway*. Reflecting continuing coordination between the army and navy commanders, Porter offered to have a gunboat accompany the steamers (officially under army control) carrying the prisoners to St. Louis. He also informed the general that he would station a gunboat above the fort to prevent any Confederate naval foray against the transports. He was particularly concerned about the Rebel ram *Pontchartrain*, which was known to be at Little Rock, although in fact the shallow river prevented her from moving.[84]

On 13 and 14 January McClernand continued to supervise destruction of Arkansas Post. Sherman informed him that he would complete demolition of his assigned portion of the fort by nightfall. A hard rain, though, made destruction more difficult; the casemates would not burn. The commander ordered Sherman to return to Notrebe's landing and embark his corps. He informed Morgan of Sherman's move, ordered him to continue to demolish the fort, and cautioned him to guard the passes across the bayou, to prevent a Confederate attack. He also rebuked the commander of the 34th Iowa for leaving weapons where the Confederate prisoners could seize them. He sent Stewart's cavalry up the Arkansas to search for Confederates who had fired at a Union boat.[85]

McClernand had to make a decision. Porter had reported that the depth of the Arkansas River would not allow for a campaign toward Little Rock. Brigadier General Gorman, commander of the Eastern District of Arkansas, queried him as to whether he intended to attack Little Rock or remain at Arkansas Post; he also asked whether he knew of any other Confederate forces in the vicinity. McClernand informed Curtis and Gorman that he might remain at the post for two or three days and see whether rising water would permit a move against Little Rock. Sherman, too, favored a move against that Confederate city; he viewed the attack on Arkansas Post as a diversion that would allow Curtis and Gorman to move against other Confederate forces in Arkansas. McClernand wrote Grant that he was sending the prisoners to St. Louis but that he himself desired to go to Little Rock; if the depth of water did not allow that, he would complete the destruction of the Post and return to Napoleon, at the mouth of the Arkansas.[86]

A move deeper into Arkansas would have indeed been a wild goose chase. As stated, Confederate forces in Arkansas were disorganized, scattered, and commanded by an incompetent general. Curtis was fully capable of dealing with those forces without McClernand's help. The most critical factor in such a move was the depth of the Arkansas River. Had McClernand and Porter been able to reach Little Rock and then been stranded by falling water, the entire thirty-two thousand men of the Army of the Mississippi, plus

Porter's Mississippi Squadron, would have been marooned and unavailable for any move against the primary objective of Vicksburg. It is fortunate for the Union cause that the depth of the Arkansas did not allow such an operation to begin.

A signal event interrupted McClernand's dreams of further glory. On 14 January McClernand received Grant's message of 10 January, which stated unequivocally his disapproval of the fact that he had not heard from McClernand. McClernand replied in his defense that he had sent several dispatches to Grant informing him of his plans and had heard nothing from him. McClernand's ambitions and relations with Grant were to become a victim of Van Dorn's raids, which had interrupted Union communications. Grant's missive would accelerate the downward spiral in the relationship between the two Illinois generals.

No animosity emerged in McClernand's reply, although Grant's message must have stung, particularly in light of his recent victory. He informed Grant he would immediately return to Napoleon and would await the reinforcements Grant promised. He would ask Porter to provide gunboat protection for the transports that carried those reinforcements, the *Blue Wing* affair obviously being on his mind. He also informed Grant that he had ample supplies to continue any movement Grant might direct. In compliance with Grant's order, McClernand instructed Fisk's brigade to join him at Napoleon.[87]

McClernand could not have known how furious Grant was over the diversion of troops for what he considered a "wild-goose chase." In response to Grant's complaint to Halleck, the general in chief authorized him to relieve McClernand and either assign the next-ranking officer to command or take command himself. Rawlins then drafted an order from Grant for McClernand to turn over his command to the officer next in rank.[88] Grant, however, presented with an opportunity to rid himself of the political general, chose not to fire McClernand. Instead, on 13 January he sent a less inflammatory message to his fellow Illinois general in which he acknowledged receipt of his dispatch regarding his imminent attack on Arkansas Post. He also acknowledged that he had not heard from Banks since 16 December. In a more conciliatory tone, he requested that McClernand return to Milliken's Bend. To get the expedition against Vicksburg back on track, Grant also wired Halleck that he was assembling his forces and requested Curtis to reinforce McClernand with all available troops.[89]

Had McClernand at this point simply obeyed Grant's request and then attempted to reconcile his differences with his commander calmly and professionally, he might have prevented the disaster that befell his military career a few months later. Instead, McClernand fired off letters, not only to Grant but to President Abraham Lincoln as well. To Lincoln he wrote:

> I believe my success here is gall and wormwood to the clique of West Pointers who have been persecuting me for months. How can you expect success when men controlling the military destinies of the country are more chagrined at the success of your volunteer officers than the very enemy beaten by the latter in battle? Something must be done to take the hand of oppression off citizen soldiers whose zeal for their country has prompted them to take up arms, or all will be lost.
>
> Do not let me be destroyed, or, what is worse, dishonored, without a hearing. [H]ow can General Grant at a distance of 400 miles intelligently command the army with me? He cannot do it. It should be made an independent command, as both you and the Secretary of War, as I believe, originally intended.[90]

With this remarkable correspondence he enclosed a copy of his letter to Grant:

> I take the responsibility of the expedition against Post Arkansas, and had anticipated your approval of the complete and signal success which crowned it rather than your condemnation.
>
> Had I remained idle and inactive at Milliken's Bend with the army under my command until now I should have felt myself guilty of a great crime. Rather had I accept the consequences of the imputed guilt of using it profitably and successfully upon my own responsibility.
>
> The officer who, in the present strait of the country, will not assume a proper responsibility to save it is unworthy of public trust.[91]

Undoubtedly, McClernand was smarting from the delay in being allowed to leave Illinois, from his perception that victories had slipped away because of Halleck's incompetence, and from Sherman's absconding with his soldiers (as McClernand saw it) at Memphis and leading them into an unsuccessful attack at Chickasaw Bayou. To receive then a rebuke from Grant for a complete Union victory was too much for McClernand's ego, particularly when other generals—Sherman and Gorman—had sanctioned the expedition. Yet this emotional appeal to Lincoln, and the reply to Grant, which bordered on disrespect, could only be detrimental to McClernand's future.

Lincoln responded on 22 January:

> I have too many *family* controversies (so to speak) already on my hands, to voluntarily, or so long as I can avoid it, take up another. You are now doing well—well for the country, and well for yourself—much better than you could possibly be, if engaged in open war with Gen. Halleck. Allow me to beg, that for your sake, for my sake, & for the country's sake, you give your whole attention to the better work.
>
> Your success upon the Arkansas, was both brilliant and valuable, and is fully appreciated by the country and government.[92]

McClernand should have realized from this letter that Lincoln would not back him in a confrontation with his senior military commanders. Lincoln had enough problems as it was with political generals—Nathaniel P. Banks, John C. Frémont, Benjamin F. Butler—and he did not need the additional headaches that getting involved in the McClernand-Grant-Halleck affair would bring. In effect, he attempted to defuse the situation, by appealing to his fellow Illinoisan's vanity and patriotism. Apparently, McClernand was concerned about his future, for he wrote to a friend, "I may be standing on the brink of official ruin." A political crony of McClernand visited the army the following month and deduced that the issue between McClernand and Grant was one of jealousy. In his view, they were "both democrats and both trying to be great men."[93]

Meanwhile, McClernand had to resolve an embarrassing situation at Arkansas Post regarding the numerical designations of his corps. On 18 December, Grant had dispatched two orders to McClernand. The first had designated the forces for Grant's Army of the Tennessee and the second, General Orders No. 210, had officially numbered the four corps under Grant's command. In the latter, McClernand's corps was designated the Thirteenth and Sherman's the Fifteenth; but, probably due again to the Confederate cavalry raids in Grant's rear, the order never reached McClernand. On 12 January Sherman published his General Orders No. 2, which stated that his corps would be designated the Fifteenth, rather than the Second, as numbered by McClernand when he assumed command on 4 January. McClernand saw this on 14 January and inquired of Sherman by what authority he had done it. Sherman replied that he had received a copy of General Orders No. 210 and had acted in accordance with it. He furnished McClernand a copy and McClernand promptly redesignated his subordinate units accordingly.[94]

This incident smacks of a deliberate attempt by Sherman to embarrass his commander. Since Sherman had received no forwarding directive from McClernand regarding renumbering the corps, he should have questioned him about the discrepancy between McClernand's 4 January order and the 18 December War Department order. To renumber his corps unilaterally, while certainly authorized by the War Department, can only be construed as petty, provocative, and insensitive to McClernand's prerogatives as expedition commander. Given Sherman's overt dislike for the Illinois politician, such an action was not surprising.

Sherman's anger at, if not outright jealousy of, the political general was manifest in several letters he wrote immediately after the victory on the Arkansas. To his wife, Sherman characterized McClernand as "unfit and . . . consumed by an inordinate personal ambition." He told his brother that the general would unfairly receive the credit for the victory. Years later he would refer to McClernand as "the meanest man we ever had in the west—with a mean, gnawing ambition, ready to destroy everybody who could cross his path."[95] The poisonous relationship between the two generals would continue as the Union army began to prepare for and carry out its next operation in the western theater.

McClernand and his Army of the Mississippi left the destroyed Arkansas Post. It was a different army from the one he had met at the mouth of the Yazoo. It was "in splendid spirits and with the demoralization induced by Chickasaw Bluffs thoroughly cured." Kilby Smith, though, believed McClernand had only reaped "the harvest that had been sown by Sherman." In accordance with Grant's order, McClernand assembled his force at Napoleon on 16 January. The next day Grant met him there, along with Porter and Sherman.[96]

The commander of the Department of the Tennessee must have been surprised by what he learned, for on 17 January Sherman wrote Grant and defended the campaign against Arkansas Post. (This is the letter mentioned above, in which he urged Grant to take command.) He cited the capture of *Blue Wing* as evidence of the danger to Union communications and the rumored size of its garrison. Tellingly, however, he added: "I only fear

McClernand may attempt impossibilities." To his brother, Sherman stated that he had actually proposed the operation against Arkansas Post. Porter had reported that "the success at Arkansas Post had a most exhilarating effect on the troops" after their defeat at Chickasaw Bayou. In his memoirs Grant wrote, "I was at first disposed to disapprove of this move . . . but when the result was understood I regarded it as very important." Sherman recorded in his memoirs that when Grant received a full explanation for the expedition, "he could not but approve." Porter, too, stated that "the importance of this victory can not be estimated."[97] The only new information Grant had regarding the reasons for the campaign was that Sherman had advocated it, as well as McClernand. Does this sudden change in Grant's attitude lend credence to McClernand's charge that a "clique of West Pointers" was, indeed, against him?

Whether in fact there was such a conspiracy is impossible to ascertain. McClernand was no favorite with such West Pointers as Grant, Sherman, and McPherson, but neither was he admired by non–West Point graduates like Gen. Clinton Fisk, Gen. Thomas Kilby Smith, or Adm. David Dixon Porter. Ironically, both West Point graduate Gen. Samuel Curtis and nongraduate Gen. Willis Gorman (both Mexican War veterans) were able to communicate and operate effectively with McClernand. Military competency was not the issue. There were West Point graduates who proved to be incompetent and nongraduates who became competent commanders.

The issue is McClernand and his ambition and his vanity. The Arkansas Post campaign provides a glimpse into these aspects of McClernand's character, but this glimpse reveals an individual who kept one eye on his political future and one on the military present. He had powerful friends in Congress and in Northern statehouses. His influence with a president from the opposition political party was substantial. Politicians had used military service as a stepping-stone to higher office for almost a century, and so it would be following the American Civil War. To achieve political aspirations, however, meant achieving military successes. McClernand sought to do that not by subordinating himself to Grant but by obtaining an independent command, where the glory would be his alone. Success at Arkansas Post should have been his, for it was his generalship and his plan that won the battle. But McClernand saw his victory slip through his fingers, as Grant first disapproved and then came personally to take command on the river.

McClernand's success against Arkansas Post was widely reported in the *Illinois State Journal* and the *New York Herald*, and he received a letter of congratulations from Illinois governor Yates.[98] Lincoln also commended him for his success, which he called "both brilliant and valuable." To buttress his position, McClernand asked Yates for support. Yates responded that he might go to Washington personally "to see that you are sustained in your views."[99] Perhaps these missives, together with his military victory at Arkansas Post, gave McClernand confidence to face Grant in a showdown at month's end. What he could not have known was that the Arkansas Post campaign would be his only opportunity to command an independent operation.

7
Prelude to Vicksburg

While the controversy over command simmered, military planning and operations still had to be conducted. On 17 January McClernand issued General Orders No. 11, ordering the movement from Napoleon to Milliken's Bend. The directive, which reflected considerable attention to detail, established the order in which the transports would move, the time the fleet would depart (twelve o'clock noon, 18 January), directed that each boat have enough fuel for the trip, and arranged signals to begin the move. McClernand also requested that Porter dispose his gunboats to protect the transports, and he ordered corps commanders to ensure that guards were placed while boats were gathering wood.[1]

Other details in the Army of the Mississippi also required McClernand's attention. Upon assuming command of the army, McClernand had assigned command of the First Corps (Thirteenth Army Corps) to Brig. Gen. George W. Morgan. He wrote Grant on 18 January that Sherman's corps had eight more regiments and seven thousand more men than did Morgan's, and so he requested reassignment of one brigade from the former to the latter—a recommendation that Grant did not implement. He also expressed his concern to Grant about the lack of supplies; he was particularly worried about the shortage of ordnance, operating as they were at the end of such a long line of communications.[2] In another letter he requested assistance to raise the effectiveness of his cavalry, which was "miserably armed and badly mounted."[3] As a partial remedy, McClernand consolidated all cavalry from both corps under one command.[4]

Also on 18 January, McClernand, because of a change directed by Grant, issued a new order to his corps commanders to disembark at Young's Point, not Milliken's Bend, and to find places to camp that would command the approaches into the area, with the Thirteenth Corps on the right, Fifteenth on the left. The mission: "protecting operations in cutting a canal across the point opposite Vicksburg."[5]

How to capture the Confederate bastion was the question of the day. Shortly after arriving at Milliken's Bend, Grant and his three senior generals examined the Vicksburg defenses and discussed the options. These included a direct assault, turning the Confederate defenses by way of the Yazoo, and moving south of the fortress and attacking it from that direction.

From Napoleon, Grant wired Halleck that he was considering a plan that would eventually lead to the fall of Vicksburg: "What may be necessary to reduce the place I do not yet know, but since the late rains think our troops must get below the city to be effective."[6] Grant had no intention of returning the army to Memphis, as he believed that would be interpreted as a defeat. Nonetheless, Vicksburg was a formidable obstacle. Not only was the city defended by a Confederate garrison, under the departmental command of Lt. Gen. John C. Pemberton, but the geography of the region greatly aided the defense. The rains to which Grant referred were causing the Mississippi to rise at the rate of two and a half inches each day.[7] At that rate, the bottomland of Louisiana across from Vicksburg would soon be under water. Sherman had been defeated in his attempt to secure a foothold near Vicksburg north of the city; Grant had been forced to turn back from his attempt to reach the eastern side of the fortress. As he would write in his memoirs, "The problem was to secure a footing upon the dry ground on the east side of the river from which the troops could operate against Vicksburg." To do that, the Union army had to get across the Mississippi. His decision was to bypass the city to the south. In a magnanimous gesture that gave credibility to McClernand's strategic vision, Wilson declared "that McClernand might have had [this] idea from the first."[8]

To cross the river would require boats. Somehow Grant had to get Porter's fleet past the Vicksburg batteries so they could ferry the army across the water. During the summer of 1862, Union general Thomas Williams had attempted to dig a canal across the base of DeSoto Peninsula, formed by the Mississippi on the Louisiana shore across from Vicksburg. When completed, the Union navy would have been able to bypass the city completely without having to encounter its formidable batteries, which controlled the river. Although the canal reached a depth of thirteen feet, the river fell faster than the canal could be dug, and the operation had to be abandoned.[9] To Halleck on 20 January Grant proposed renewing work on the canal begun by Williams with minor corrections to its course. He also stated that he intended to continue attempts to land forces on the Mississippi shore near the Yazoo River.[10]

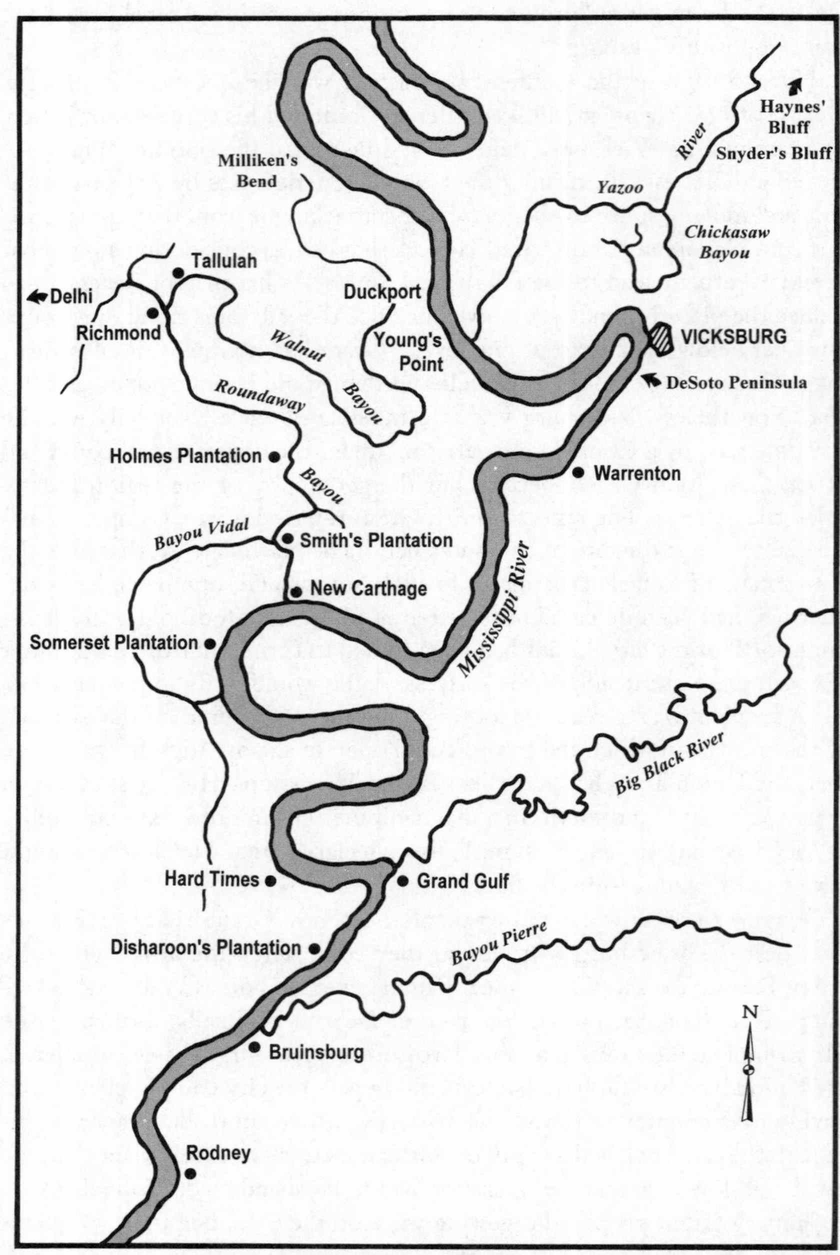

Area between Milliken's Bend and Bruinsburg

The day prior, Secretary of the Navy Welles had written Porter that "the President is exceedingly anxious that a canal from which practical and useful results would follow should be cut through the peninsula opposite Vicksburg. The Department desires that this plan may be tried whenever you deem it expedient and can have the cooperation of the army."[11] On 25 January Grant received a message from Halleck to the same effect: "Direct your attention particularly to the canal proposed across the point. The President attaches much importance to it."[12] As mentioned in his memoirs, Grant thought of the canal attempt as an experiment in which he had little confidence, but the army commander was reluctant to lie idle until spring, when maneuver in the swampy region would become easier.[13]

Even before receiving Halleck's directive regarding the canal, Grant had ordered McClernand to begin work on it.[14] The Army of the Mississippi arrived at Young's Point on 21 January. McClernand immediately ordered a reconnaissance down the river to the site of the old canal, and he continued examining the region the next day. He had appreciated the naval contribution at the battles in Tennessee and Arkansas, and now he requested Porter to provide support from the gunboats should his scouts meet any Confederates. McClernand reported to Grant that he had established a defensive line along the old canal. He also reported that three thousand Confederates were encamped near Delhi, Louisiana, about forty miles to the rear, and that another force was reported about eighty miles south of Vicksburg. Furthermore, he informed Grant, he would determine whether the old canal was suitable for enlargement or whether a new canal had to be dug. He then directed Sherman to begin work to enlarge the old cut.[15] On the same day, Grant wrote that he was attempting to obtain picks and spades for the work.[16]

This correspondence indicates that McClernand understood his mission and the importance of an attempt to bypass Vicksburg. His actions during these few days indicate an understanding of the military principles of reconnaissance, intelligence, logistics, and obedience to orders. There is no indication of animosity toward Grant, or of Grant toward McClernand, but there must have been a chill between the two notwithstanding, for the command arrangements had still not been resolved.

For the next week McClernand continued to direct operations in eastern Louisiana, and he continued to inform Grant of what he was doing. Recognizing that the Confederates controlled the Mississippi between Port Hudson and Vicksburg, which also gave them access to the Red and Ouachita Rivers, McClernand informed Grant that he would place a battery a few miles below Vicksburg to interfere as much as possible with Confederate river traffic. He also directed the cavalry to reconnoiter toward Richmond,

Louisiana, about thirteen miles west of Young's Point, in the direction of the reported Confederate force at Delhi. Anticipating rain and a need to move men and wagons closer to the canal, McClernand ordered Sherman to put the roads in the area in good condition.[17]

Then the rains began. Sherman informed McClernand he had to corduroy roads across the swamps, which were becoming impassable. McClernand became so concerned about the rising water that he directed that the transports that were to have been returned to Memphis be retained "until all danger of inundation is passed." On 26 January McClernand wrote Grant that the Mississippi was continuing to rise and had caused three breaks in the levee below the lower end of the canal. Another occurred at Young's Point. The enemy became not the Confederates at Vicksburg but the Father of Waters, which threatened to do what the Rebels had been unable to do—drive the Union army back to Memphis.

McClernand was constantly determining the number of shovels available, not to dig the canal but to repair breeches in the levees. On 26 January, Grant wrote Halleck to express his concern about the flooding. Two days later Grant arrived to assess the situation.[18] What he found was not encouraging. Despite the efforts of McClernand's and Sherman's soldiers and the rising waters in the main channel, the water in the canal was only five feet deep, too shallow for use. On 31 January he informed Halleck that "prospects not flattering by the canal of last summer."[19]

The problem was one of engineering. In 1848 the state of Louisiana had attempted a similar project, which had failed because it had been so sited that the river current could not enter the upper opening of the canal. An officer in the 97th Illinois, Victor Vifquain, now came to the same conclusion and provided McClernand a report and a sketch of how to modify the existing effort to take advantage of the river current. McClernand, pursuant to Grant's order to dig the canal, ordered Sherman to try it. McClernand also requested that Porter position a tug so as to increase the flow of water into the canal. Porter responded that a tug would not work but that stern-wheelers or side-wheelers might;[20] however, he was in fact pessimistic about the project, calling it in a letter to Welles "simply ridiculous." He told Welles that McClernand's idea to use tugs to increase the flow would not work and that he had informed Grant that the canal had to be repositioned.[21]

McClernand too had little faith in the venture. He informed Grant on 30 January that if the modifications he was attempting did not work, "the uselessness of the present canal will have been demonstrated." He proposed making a new cut elsewhere and obtaining dredging machines to make the work easier.[22] Throughout the endeavor McClernand, despite his misgivings as well as Grant's (which he expressed in his memoirs), made every effort to comply with his commander's directive and intent, and he loyally made suggestions about how to make the canal effort succeed.

As success of the canal endeavor appeared less and less likely, Grant began exploring other routes to bypass Vicksburg. On 30 January he wrote McClernand that he had heard that a route could be found from Lake Providence (about sixty miles north of Young's Point) through Tensas Bayou, the Ouachita and Black Rivers, and then into the Mississippi. He wanted a brigade detailed to dig a canal from the Mississippi to Lake Providence "as soon as possible." Immediately, McClernand issued comprehensive instructions for a brigade to meet the steamers that would carry them from Young's Point to the vicinity of the lake. He informed Grant of what he had done and also proposed an alternative should that not work, although the alternative would have meant a considerably longer route.[23]

The canal, however, was not McClernand's only concern. On 25 January he had received a report that Union boats on the Mississippi were being fired on from the vicinity of Greenville, Mississippi, between Vicksburg and the Arkansas River. McClernand requested that Porter send a gunboat "to punish the attack" and told Porter "nothing has proved so effectual a remedy as the punishment inflicted by you."[24] This is truly generous praise from the Union general, considering that Porter had been writing disparagingly to Welles and others about McClernand's conduct of the Arkansas Post campaign, even stating "the fighting at the Post was done by the navy."[25] There is no indication that McClernand was aware of Porter's comments.

McClernand also had to concern himself with reports of guerrillas operating in the area. Sherman reported that five transports had landed Confederates on the Louisiana shore south of his position. McClernand then informed the captains of the army transports as well as Generals Morgan and John McArthur, whom Grant had assigned to him on 15 January, of the possibility of attack.[26]

The corps commander also dealt with other problems inherent in such a large-scale operation. He directed Sherman to reposition one of his brigades to provide a continuous front for defense. He sent out foraging parties for fresh beef and coordinated with Porter to provide gunboat protection for them along the river. He also continued to seek reports on the availability of transportation, entrenching tools, camp equipment, and animals.[27] These are the kinds of responsibilities with which every commander must be concerned, whether professional soldier or political appointee. McClernand's conduct here cannot be faulted.

Although he was a tough politician and a soldier, McClernand had a humane, compassionate side. George Morgan had served him well as a corps commander, but he had fallen ill during the campaign. In a personal letter to him, McClernand expressed concern and told him to attend to restoring his health. In the meantime, he replaced him with Brig. Gen. A. J. Smith. A more telling incident occurred 23 January, when Col. Warren Stewart was killed near New Carthage. Stewart had served on McClernand's personal staff prior to commanding the cavalry. Three days later McClernand wrote Richard Yates, governor of Illinois, to extol Stewart's virtues and request that he be buried with full military honors in a cemetery plot that adjoined his own, near Springfield. In a separate letter to Yates marked "private," McClernand enclosed a blank check and asked Yates to purchase a plot for Stewart's burial. "Please fill up the check with the sum required for that purpose," he wrote.[28]

That McClernand also possessed a strong temper is attested to by one of his staff officers, Henry Clay Warmoth (who became governor of Louisiana in 1868 and was subsequently impeached). Twice in April Warmoth incurred McClernand's wrath; he characterized McClernand as "dictatorial, disagreeable, and unreasonable" and contended that McClernand "acted the Damned fool" when he swore at him for an alleged offense. Warmoth was not alone in this view of the Illinois general. Capt. William L. B. Jenney of Sherman's staff also had been the recipient of McClernand's ire, when he questioned an order from the Illinois general to blow up a portion of the canal across from Vicksburg. Jenney characterized McClernand's rage as "customary."[29]

Congratulations on the success of the Arkansas Post campaign certainly assuaged his temper, though. Compliments continued to be received at McClernand's headquarters from politicians, soldiers, and civilians. From Yates: "You cannot imagine with what delight I heard of your brilliant success at Arkansas Post and everybody speaks of it as a brilliant affair." From Maj. Gen. Samuel R. Curtis, commander of the Department of the Missouri, came two messages: "I heartily . . . congratulate you on the complete sweep," and another saying it was "successful and exceedingly creditable to you." From W. D. Sanders, a professor at Illinois College near Springfield: "I cannot refrain from congratulating you upon the brilliant success of your expedition to Arkansas Post." And from Lt. Harl Christie, who was in Washington carrying dispatches from McClernand to Stanton: "The whole North is elated at your complete success at Post Arkansas. . . . You are in the lead in the Southwest." From another friend, N. W. Mince, in Springfield: "The deed . . . adds new and able laurels to your increasing fame. Your friends and all true patriots rejoice." Sen. Lyman Trumbull of Illinois wrote, "We are all looking with great interest to your operation before Vicksburg."[30]

This enthusiastic praise undoubtedly quickened the pulse of the former politician. Did McClernand believe that he was to be the savior of the Union, that he alone could now redeem victory from a recent string of Union defeats? In December, Maj. Gen. Ambrose Burnside had been defeated decisively at Fredericksburg, Virginia, and Sherman had been beaten at Chickasaw Bayou; Grant had been forced to withdraw from northern Mississippi, and Maj. Gen. William Rosecrans had achieved only a draw at Stones River, Tennessee (although Bragg had then withdrawn to Murfreesboro). The victory at Arkansas Post was a boost to Union morale when operations on all other fronts were failing. Perhaps the Illinois Democrat believed that his victory now guaranteed him the support of Lincoln and the War Department. Coupled with his political connections, he was, he no doubt believed, in a very strong position.

There was other, more official, correspondence as well. On 3 January McClernand had written Stanton to express outrage at the events that had led to Sherman's departing Memphis with his troops before he could arrive.[31] Four days later he wrote Lincoln and charged Halleck with "wilful [*sic*] contempt of superior authority" and angrily questioned Halleck's military competence.[32] Not until 24 January did Stanton provide a lukewarm response, which did not address the issue McClernand raised: "I think you need no new assurance of the sincere desire of the President and myself to oblige you in every particular consistent with the general interest of the service, and I trust that the course of events will be such as will enable the Government to derive the utmost advantage from your patriotism and military skill."[33] Assurance, however, was exactly what McClernand did need, for events were about to take a turn entirely different from what he expected.

As early as 20 December 1862, Maj. Gen. James McPherson, then commanding the right wing of Grant's army, had urged Grant to take command of the expedition rather than have McClernand lead it. Upon his return to Memphis, Grant wrote Halleck on 20 January that his meeting with his subordinates had revealed "there was not sufficient confidence felt in Gen. McClernand as a commander, either by the Army or Navy, to insure him success." Five days earlier he had confided to McPherson that he intended to command the expedition down the river. Grant then informed Halleck he intended to take command personally of the river operations against Vicksburg.[34]

For military operations, unity of command—all forces under a single commander with the authority to direct those forces—is a basic principle of war. Although such principles had not been codified in 1863, Grant recognized the necessity of such authority if he was to maneuver successfully against Vicksburg. He therefore on 20 January requested that Union forces on both banks of the Mississippi be placed under a single commander for the duration of the operation.[35]

The following day Grant received a directive from Halleck: "By direction of the President, Major-General Grant will assume the command of all troops in Arkansas which may be within reach of his orders."[36] Grant now had command of both sides of the river. He then attached the District of Helena, commanded by Brig. Gen. Willis Gorman, to McClernand's Thirteenth Army Corps. He informed McClernand of the additional force but cautioned him not to move them from their present position. Remarkably, considering his previous vehement objections to the Arkansas Post campaign, Grant informed Gorman that he was concerned about Confederate forces on the Arkansas and White rivers and that "it is necessary . . . to break up all their forces on those two rivers."[37] Did this vindicate McClernand's judgment and his operation against Arkansas Post?

On 28 January McClernand received a letter stating that Grant wanted to meet with him the next day.[38] Although this meeting is not mentioned in official records, apparently the meeting did occur, and the subject probably was command arrangements within the Department of the Tennessee. McClernand later stated that he understood from their meeting on 29 January that "my relations to the forces here would continue undisturbed."[39] It is quite probable that if such a conversation occurred, Grant meant as *commander of the Thirteenth Corps*, while McClernand meant as *commander of the river expedition*. Rather than command a glorious victory at Vicksburg, he was now only to be a commander of various garrisons along the Mississippi.

On 29 January McClernand forwarded the orders announcing the new command arrangements to Sherman and Gorman, as well as to Brig. Gens. A. J. Smith and John McArthur.[40] The delay between the time Gorman was assigned to McClernand (22 January) and the date that McClernand communicated with him is unusual. McClernand had discussed the Arkansas Post expedition with Gorman prior to its execution and had communicated with him after it. On 25 January he had forwarded to Stanton a report from Gorman about the latter's continuing operations on the White River.[41] Based on McClernand's penchant for obtaining unit strengths and dispositions, as well as his desire to exercise command, it is highly unlikely that he would not have contacted Gorman during the interval. Nor does it appear that Gorman contacted him following his own receipt of Grant's order. This delay can only be attributable to the fact that McClernand's Army of the Mississippi was on the move from Napoleon to Young's Point during this period.

The thirtieth of January 1863 was a significant date in the military career of John Alexander McClernand. On that day McClernand sent Grant a message challenging his authority:

> I understand that orders are being issued directly from your headquarters directly to army corps commanders, and not through me. As I am invested, by order of the Secretary of War, indorsed by the President, and by order of the President communicated to you by the General-in-Chief, with the command of all the forces operating on the Mississippi River, I claim that all orders affecting the condition or operations of those forces should pass through these headquarters; otherwise I must lose a knowledge of current business and dangerous confusion ensue.
>
> If different views are entertained by you, then the question should be immediately referred to Washington, and one or the other, or both of us, relieved. One thing is certain, two generals cannot command this army, issuing independent and direct orders to subordinate officers, and the public service be promoted.[42]

From McClernand's viewpoint, confusion about the command arrangements was understandable. General Orders No. 159, 16 October 1862, had given Grant command of the Department of the Tennessee, which included northern Mississippi and the portions of Kentucky and Tennessee west of the Tennessee River. On 21 January 1863 Grant was given command of troops in Arkansas "which may be in reach of his orders." Grant, as department commander, had issued orders to McClernand since 18 December. Although no Headquarters of the Army order specifically authorized Grant to include eastern Louisiana in his command, McClernand never challenged his authority to do so, *as department commander*. In fact, on 30 January McClernand acknowledged that Special Orders No. 22 allowed Grant to extend his "command as far west from the Mississippi River as [his] orders may reach." Only when Grant began issuing orders directly to corps that McClernand believed constituted his independent command for a river expedition against Vicksburg did he raise the most strenuous objections.

War Department General Orders No. 210, 18 December 1862, designated McClernand as commander of the Thirteenth Army Corps and Sherman as commander of the Fifteenth Army Corps. Grant's instructions of the same date stated Sherman's corps would accompany McClernand. There was no question that McClernand would have command of Sherman, because of seniority, and McClernand believed he had presidential authority as well to do so, by virtue of the 21 October order to organize an expedition under his command against Vicksburg. Clearly, McClernand viewed himself as an army commander, not just a corps commander, operating under Grant as department commander.

Grant responded immediately to McClernand's challenge. By General Orders No. 13, 30 January 1863, Grant took personal command of the Mississippi River expedition. Sherman reverted to command of the Fifteenth Army Corps and McClernand to command of the Thirteenth Army Corps, with the additional responsibility of "garrisoning the post of Helena, Ark., and any other point on the west bank of the river it may be necessary to hold south of that place."[43]

McClernand did not accept the order gracefully. Upon receipt of this memo, he wrote Grant and (in a way that Grant characterized as "highly insubordinate") again questioned his authority, pointing out that in McClernand's interpretation, General Orders No. 13 conflicted with his initial order to command the Mississippi River expedition. In his view, garrisoning the west bank of the river would require most of his corps; therefore, "while having projected the Mississippi River expedition, and having been by a series of orders assigned to the command of it, I may be entirely withdrawn from it."[44]

A few days later he wrote Governor Yates to inform him that "Genl. Grant has relieved me of my command." He defended his operation up the Arkansas River, declaring that he had found a "defeated and disheartened [Union] army," which he had then led to victory. He decried the fact that Grant had "censured the expedition. I am persecuted in a thousand ways," he declared. He believed the president to be unaware of what had transpired and implored Yates to "do what you can for me."[45]

What McClernand had overlooked was the caveat in the 21 October order, a proviso stating he would command those troops "not required by the operations of General Grant's command." This gave Grant the leverage he needed to control McClernand. Also, McClernand apparently was not aware of Halleck's response to Grant's "wild-goose chase" telegram, in which the general in chief had authorized Grant to relieve McClernand and to take command of the expedition himself. Grant replied to his fellow Illinois general that "I have seen no order to prevent my taking immediate command in the field." The department commander also informed McClernand that he would add about seven thousand soldiers to his corps to assist garrisoning the river posts. This he subsequently did on 8 February, by adding two divisions from the Department of Eastern Arkansas to the Thirteenth Corps. On 28 March a third division was joined to his command.[46] McClernand responded on 1 February that he would "acquiesce in the order for the purpose of avoiding a conflict of authority in the presence of the enemy," but he asked that his protest be transmitted to Halleck, Stanton, and Lincoln.[47] That same day Grant forwarded the matter to the leaders in Washington, stating again to them his opinion of the politician general: "I have not [*sic*] confidence in his ability as a soldier to conduct an expedition of the magnitude of this one successfully."[48] None would intervene on McClernand's behalf.

To his credit, McClernand on 30 January, in the midst of this controversy and before he responded to Grant, issued General Orders No. 20—under authority of the Thirteenth Army Corps, not the Army of the Mississippi, in which he assumed command of the corps. The order designated Brig. Gens. Peter J. Osterhaus and Andrew J. Smith as commanders of the Ninth and Tenth Divisions, respectively. McArthur's division returned to the Seventeenth Corps, under McPherson.[49] To his discredit, apparently not trusting that Grant would forward his communications, McClernand also wrote Lincoln directly: "Please cause it to be signified to me whether Genl. Grant or myself will have *immediate* command of the Miss. river Expedition."[50]

Continuous rain and rising water provided McClernand with a rationale for another attempt to operate independently of Grant. On 21 January, General Curtis had written McClernand that Arkadelphia, Arkansas, was "the great store house and arsenal of the rebels in the west," that both clothing and ammunition were manufactured there. He believed that its destruction would cripple Rebel forces in the Trans-Mississippi Department.[51] McClernand liked the idea. On 1 February he proposed such a plan to Grant. The alternative, he stated, was to "be driven away by high water in a few hours." The following day he provided a copy of his proposal directly to Lincoln. In an attached letter he complained about the futility of the canal project.[52] Considering that Lincoln himself favored the project, this was not a politically astute comment by the Illinoisan. He should have known better.

On 14 February he offered several proposals to Lincoln, among which was an attack on Vicksburg from the vicinity of the Big Black River, east of the city—the direction from which Grant would eventually achieve success. Another proposal was simply to invest the city and starve it into surrender—in fact, the end result of Grant's operation. A third was to postpone a move on

Vicksburg and use the army to secure Arkansas and northern Louisiana. Well aware of the political situation, McClernand pointed out to Lincoln that the result of such victories would undermine the peace party and "the rising storm in the Middle and Northwestern States."[53] If Grant learned of this correspondence, it could only have increased his desire to get McClernand under control. Lincoln did not respond.

Also on 14 February, Brig. Gen. Benjamin M. Prentiss, who had replaced Gorman as commander of the District of Eastern Arkansas, wrote McClernand that he favored another expedition up the Arkansas River "if it will not interfere with the effort to take Vicksburg." The next day McClernand again wrote Grant about a move to disperse a reported Confederate force of ten to fifteen thousand at Pine Bluff, upriver from Arkansas Post. He proposed twenty thousand men from the Thirteenth Corps for the operation. His rationale was that it would clear Confederates from the west bank of the Mississippi. Grant's response indicated he had had enough of diversions: "I see but one objection to it. The objection is that all the forces now here to operate with are assigned to looking to the one great object, that of opening the Mississippi." Nevertheless, perhaps anticipating a future opportunity, McClernand directed Prentiss to "collect, *quietly*, all information you can obtain about rebel forces at Pine Bluff."[54]

Five days later Prentiss responded with an estimate of the Confederate situation considerably different from that initially reported. He now reported that there were only two thousand demoralized troops at Pine Bluff and, although ten thousand were at Little Rock, only six thousand were considered effective. Even this estimate was high, for Kirby Smith, upon taking command of the Confederate Trans-Mississippi Department, would later report to Jefferson Davis that in Arkansas there were only two divisions, with less than five thousand effectives in each. Rather than have Grant continue to base decisions on the previous faulty intelligence, McClernand reported Prentiss's revised figures to him and offered his services as leader of an expedition to capture or disperse them.[55] Clearly it would have been in McClernand's best interest for him to exaggerate the Confederate threat: that would not only have added justification for the Arkansas Post expedition but also might have induced Grant to launch another campaign to destroy the gathering Rebels. Nonetheless, McClernand subordinated ambition to truthfulness.

Grant did not respond to these further attempts to entice him to launch an operation into central Arkansas. Any such operation would have been a diversion from the objective of capturing Vicksburg. Coincidentally, Samuel

Curtis, who commanded the Department of the Missouri, proposed to Halleck and McClernand a move into western Arkansas. Halleck's reply encapsulated the Union strategy for the West in early 1863, and it applied to McClernand's proposal as well as to Curtis's. He wrote that Union control of the Mississippi would separate the Confederacy, its armies, and its supplies; that it would simplify supplying the Union forces arrayed along the river; and that it would facilitate further operations against Port Hudson and into the interior of the Trans-Mississippi.[56] The Confederates in Arkansas were no threat to Grant's operations against Vicksburg, unless they could be concentrated. In fact, Confederate general Richard Taylor, who commanded in Louisiana, had essentially conceded that region to the overwhelming Union force encamped along the Mississippi. Also, as Prentiss reported, the number of Confederate effectives was considerably less than the one hundred thousand soldiers Grant had available under his command. McClernand's proposal, therefore, can only be construed as an attempt to add to his laurels as reported in Northern newspapers after Arkansas Post, to remove himself and his corps from Grant's immediate presence, and to enhance his stature for future political campaigns. As late as 19 March, though, McClernand was still writing to Grant about the possibility of operations in Arkansas.[57]

To his letter to Lincoln on 2 February McClernand appended a note: "Sickness, including smallpox, prevails in the camp."[58] The memoirs of both Grant and Sherman attest to the abysmal conditions that existed in the Union camps. Grant wrote that "troops could scarcely find dry ground" and that "malarial fevers broke out among the men." Sherman wrote, "The waters of the Mississippi . . . continued to rise and threatened to drown us."[59] The water and the sick became primary concerns for the Thirteenth Corps commander. The shortage of surgeons contributed to the poor condition of the soldiers. A particular problem that was brought to McClernand's attention was that the artillery batteries had no medical personnel. McClernand referred the problem to Grant, who acknowledged there were not enough surgeons available and suggested that the batteries obtain medical assistance from the infantry regiments to which they were attached. On 2 February, the corps commander ordered his division commanders to designate surgeons to treat the sick of artillery and cavalry units attached to them.[60] Additionally, McClernand ordered that "all camps be kept clean of filth" and that commanders "give their personal attention to draining the camps."[61]

As his concern about the spread of smallpox increased, McClernand appointed B. B. Brashear, surgeon of the 16th Ohio, as acting medical director for the corps. McClernand ordered him to inspect the camps and hospitals and recommend solutions to the hygiene problem. Brashear immediately surveyed the situation and determined that the number of sick was overwhelming the available surgeons. For example, in the 114th Ohio there were 307 sick and only one surgeon; the corps had an average of eighty-two sick for each surgeon. He also found that commanders were not accepting responsibility for the health of their commands, although he acknowledged there were "no provisions against a continuous rain like that which is falling." He reported inadequate drainage and filth. He had also found that hospital tents were being used for officers' quarters and kitchens. McClernand then ordered that all hospital tents be turned over to division quartermasters within forty-eight hours. In what was undoubtedly a popular suggestion among the troops, Brashear also recommended the soldiers be given ale or beer, as it "would have a beneficial effect upon their health."[62]

McClernand also prevailed on Grant to request state governors to send help, and, utilizing his own political connections, he wrote the governors of Ohio, Indiana, Illinois, Wisconsin, and Kentucky asking them to fill the medical personnel vacancies in regiments from their states. By 11 March the Wisconsin governor had filled one vacancy, asked for volunteers to fill others, and had sent the state surgeon general to inspect all state regiments assigned to McClernand.[63]

Despite the weather, work on the canal and levees continued, but at a cost to the Thirteenth Corps in sickness and exhaustion. On 2 February, McClernand, concerned about the welfare of his men, requested that his corps be relieved of the requirement to provide an additional eight hundred men each day for canal work. Three days later Grant, although demanding that the work "be pushed forward with all possible dispatch," relented and assigned the additional requirement to Sherman.[64]

Little combat occurred during the winter in eastern Louisiana. McClernand's time was spent primarily in caring for his soldiers and administering his command. He continued to seek information on the quantity of equipment available; he required that the number and condition of weapons, to include artillery, be reported monthly, along with quantities of ammunition on hand.[65] He also had to investigate discipline problems in the 131st Illinois Infantry. One case involved the requisition and sale of excess government rations, in violation of a general order, and the other concerned the regimental commander, Col. George W. Neeley. The latter case had resulted from an incident in which a soldier in the 131st fired a weapon against orders, with Neeley present. Neeley, perhaps taking a page from McClernand's book, then wrote Lincoln to state he was being relieved by McClernand for political reasons.[66] Finally, the better to observe the health of the corps and the status of equipment, McClernand directed his inspector general to conduct formal inspections of each brigade during mid-February. The inspections continued until 1 April.[67]

These are actions of a professional soldier. Although he had had minimal military experience prior to the Civil War and no formal military training, McClernand understood the requirements of command. The welfare of the soldiers (many of whom, of course, were his constituents) was as important as the mission. If the soldiers were not healthy, they would be ineffective both in the work on the canal and in combat. If equipment was not cared for and arms and ammunition were not available, battles and lives could be lost. These were lessons that McClernand had learned in the year and a half since being appointed a brigadier general. Despite the atrocious weather and his skepticism regarding the canal endeavor, McClernand continued to perform his duties as corps commander very effectively.

On 12 February Grant visited the operation at Lake Providence to determine how work was progressing on the canal from the river to the lake. McClernand, as the next senior officer, was left in command near Vicksburg. The following day Porter reported about eight hundred Confederates on the river near Greenville. Taking the initiative, McClernand immediately ordered A. J. Smith to provide one infantry brigade, artillery, and cavalry to attack the enemy force. He also ordered Col. Lewis Parsons, officer in charge of river transportation, to provide transports and asked Porter to provide gunboats for protection. McClernand did not accompany the force but only ordered Smith to inform him when the expedition began. He set a time limit of one week. The force departed the next day.[68]

Prospects for Union success in eastern Louisiana continued to be dim as February turned to March. On the first day of the month, Maj. Gen. James McPherson, whose corps had been attempting to clear the Lake Providence route, wrote Grant that he was apprehensive about the success of the experiment. Grant directed that "the work on the canal in front of Vicksburg . . . be prosecuted day and night until its completion" and ordered McClernand and Sherman to provide half of their effective commands to work on it.[69]

Nature intervened in the execution of this order. By 7 March the river was rising at such a rate that the Thirteenth Corps was ordered to move to Milliken's Bend, "occupying the highest ground." McClernand accordingly ordered the two division commanders with him at Young's Point to embark first those troops most threatened by the impending flood. He also told them to send no more details to work on the canal until further notice.[70]

McClernand's attention at Milliken's Bend was divided between pursuing a new scheme to bypass Vicksburg and providing for the welfare of his command. Upon arrival at the new encampment, still concerned about the state of health in the corps, he directed Smith and Osterhaus to provide for latrines and drainage around the camp. He also ordered that private property not be seized and that civilians be prevented from moving freely through the Union lines. The corps inspector general and medical officer continued to conduct inspections as they had at Young's Point. In one regiment they found conditions "very unsatisfactory" and soldiers "wholly disqualified for duty." In another, "few of the arms are in good condition." Conditions in yet others were rated "moderate"; in one, they were "highly creditable." The corps commander continued his efforts to account for all hospital tents in order to shelter the sick. Such concern for the welfare of his men led one Ohio soldier to refer to McClernand as "the distinguished commander of our corps," and another to mention him as "that gallant soldier and splendid field officer."[71]

McClernand knew that when the winter passed, his soldiers could again expect to face the Confederate army, either in Louisiana or across the river at Vicksburg. The months of digging, rain, mud, and sickness had taken their toll on the military proficiency of his command. To face the spring, he had to resume training. Consequently, on 30 March he ordered that drill be resumed. Companies and regiments were to drill in the morning; in the afternoon, the brigades would drill, building on the morning's training. Brigade commanders were charged with the responsibility to carry out this order.[72]

For months now the Union commanders had been obsessed with finding a route to bypass Vicksburg. The canal project and the Lake Providence venture held little prospect of success. Grant, therefore, determined to attempt a different approach to Vicksburg, by way of the Yazoo Pass and various bayous north of the city. By 10 April, the Yazoo Pass attempt had come to naught. On 18 March Grant returned from a visit to Porter and conveyed to McClernand that he thought the route through Steele's Bayou had an excellent chance of success. McClernand ordered his cavalry to Tallulah, Mississippi, "to ascertain whether there is a practicable land route from Tallulah to Bayou Washington and to enquire whether there is any navigable connection between that bayou and the Yazoo."[73] Grant told his corps commander to be prepared to embark his entire force should they be needed as reinforcements. McClernand passed the order on to his division commanders the same day.[74]

However, the Illinoisan's resentment at his treatment by Grant continued to simmer. Grant was sending orders to Prentiss, who was actually part of McClernand's command, but who was deeply involved in the Yazoo Pass operation. On 19 March McClernand expressed his outrage to Grant: "I have the immediate command of all the forces operating on the Miss. river, but in fact you exercise immediate as well as general command." Grant replied, "I think you are mistaken. Feeling anxious to get news from [the Yazoo Pass force] promptly I directed Gen. Prentiss to forward me all reports direct, but did not mean this should preclude the same reports from being sent to you also."[75] This was similar to the issue that had prompted McClernand's outburst almost two months earlier. Certainly Grant had the authority to require Prentiss to send him reports directly, and under other circumstances this could have been simply a misunderstanding about the routing of those reports. McClernand, however, probably saw it as more than a misunderstanding, for military protocol demanded that reports be sent through the chain of command unless specific arrangement had been made otherwise. He certainly had not been persuaded that Grant had full authority to exercise direct command over operations on the Mississippi, and he undoubtedly believed that the 21 October order carried greater weight than did Grant's authority as department commander. This issue would continue to fester and to infect the relations between the two senior commanders in the bayous across from Vicksburg.

Despite these efforts to find a solution to the Vicksburg problem, the Union army remained mired in the Louisiana mud. The canal project was not going to work. Engineering design flaws and floods had conspired against Grant. The Lake Providence route had failed, because of a plethora of stumps in the waterways and harassment from Confederate partisans. By the end of the month, the Yazoo Pass–Steele's Bayou expedition too would fail. With the coming of spring, the Union army was no closer to taking Vicksburg than it had been in the latter months of the previous year. Newspapers were beginning to question Grant's competence. One Union soldier recorded that the Northern press was "clamoring for a forward movement and demanding that [Grant] be removed and McClernand . . . be given his command," a sentiment reflected in the *Chicago Times*.[76] A correspondent with the *Cincinnati Gazette* reported, "There never was a more thoroughly disgusted, disheartened, demoralized army than this is, all because it is under such men as Grant and Sherman." The *Gazette's* editor forwarded the report to Secretary of the Treasury Chase, adding his own opinion of Grant: "Our noble army of the Mississippi is being wasted by the foolish, drunken, stupid Grant. I have no personal feeling about it, but I know he is an ass."[77] Such sentiments were echoed by Murat Halstead of the *Cincinnati Commercial*, who wrote Chase that Grant "is a jackass in the original package." Chase warned Lincoln that such sentiments could not be disregarded.[78] Even Stanton was suspicious of Grant's ability. Governors Morton of Ohio and Kirkwood of Iowa wrote Stanton that the peace movements in their states were gaining momentum as a result of the lack of Union military success. Halleck wrote Grant that Lincoln "seems to be rather impatient about matters on the Mississippi."[79] Options were being exhausted. To McClernand's credit, however, he continued to seek a route south through the meandering bayous and streams of Madison Parish to a point below Vicksburg where the Union forces could finally cross.

On 29 March, Grant directed the Thirteenth Corps commander to ascertain whether a land or water route existed from Milliken's Bend to New Carthage. He also informed Porter that he intended to find a route through the bayous to New Carthage and then launch an attack across the river at Grand Gulf, Mississippi. McClernand then ordered Brig. Gen. Peter J. Osterhaus, commander of the Ninth Division, to prepare a regiment to assemble with four days' rations at the corps headquarters the following day. He also ordered Lt. Col. John Mudd, his cavalry commander, to provide a regiment of cavalry. On 31 March the 69th Indiana Infantry and 3d Illinois Cavalry assembled, their mission being "to open a practicable communication for our forces via Richmond, La., between this camp and New Carthage." Detailed instructions from the corps commander provided guidance on land and water routes through the bayous, use of the cavalry to seize contraband cotton, issuance of receipts for forage, and the location of potential defensive positions along the route. He also added a section of artillery to accompany the force. As a result of these orders, there could be no doubt about Osterhaus's mission.[80]

Later that day, Col. Thomas W. Bennett, commander of the force, reported that the bridge across Canal Bayou on the main road was out but that he had located another, at the Gibson plantation. McClernand ordered Brig. Gen. Eugene Carr, commander of the Sixteenth Division, to extend his pickets to protect the bridge.[81] Coincidentally, Lt. Col. James Dunlap, the corps assistant quartermaster, reported that about five hundred negroes, "generally in a destitute condition," were outside the Union lines. He suggested putting them to work in exchange for food. McClernand immediately directed Dunlap to use them to repair the road and bridges toward Richmond.[82] Maintenance of the roads and bridges through the swamps, bayous, and lowlands would become a major task for the soldiers and commander of the Thirteenth Corps.

Another problem McClernand suddenly faced was what to do with the cotton that was being confiscated in the area. As early as 1 March, McPherson had notified Grant that persons who claimed to own cotton were requesting permits to ship it to Memphis. Grant replied that the Treasury Department had limited trade on the Mississippi and that he had required permits to be issued by the provost marshal for freight being shipped. On 28 March reports reached McClernand that two men were forcing local citizens to sell cotton to them. He ordered Mudd to investigate. He found speculators were driving off families and claiming that their cotton had been abandoned. He concluded that "a general system of plunder prevails in the neighborhood." Mudd also found cotton being loaded on the steamer *Louisiana*. The owner claimed he had a permit from Grant but was unable to produce it. (On 6 April, after an investigation, the cotton was released to the owner.) McClernand's instructions to Mudd as well as to Bennett, who had also discovered baled cotton in the region, were that it "be brought in . . . for the use of the United States." He also directed Osterhaus to seize cotton found near Richmond.[83] Failure to act as decisively as McClernand did here regarding contraband cotton would bedevil another political general, Nathaniel P. Banks, during his expedition up the Red River in 1864.

While conducting military operations, John McClernand, always the politician, continued to maintain his political connections throughout the early months of 1863. Several letters passed between him and John Van Buren, son of the former president. Lucian Chase, who had served with McClernand in Congress, wrote from New York that "your history is well known here. It is such men who carry the destinies of the country upon their shoulders." In mid-March, McClernand sent to Governor Yates a piece of a cannon destroyed at Arkansas Post, "as an humble testimonial of the esteem and admiration of the brave men whose valor wrested it as a trophy from the enemy." Yates wrote back that he equated that victory with Fort Donelson, "in which that officer [McClernand had] also prominently participated."[84]

Others, though, had a different view of the former congressman. In his memoirs Sherman was to write of an occasion in early April when he was at Grant's headquarters with Charles Dana, Major General McPherson, Lieutenant Colonel Rawlins, and Lt. Col. James Wilson, the latter two assigned to Grant's staff. This was the same Wilson whom McClernand earlier had requested that Lincoln appoint to his own staff. The subject was McClernand, and the consensus was that he "was still intriguing against General Grant in hopes to regain the command of the whole expedition."[85] In December, McPherson had suggested to Grant that he command any expedition against Vicksburg rather than McClernand. Wilson characterized McClernand as "ambitious," "highstrung," and "a man of hasty and violent temper." He reported that Rawlins "denounced his ambition, his jealousy, and his disposition to intrigue."[86]

Sherman continued also to have little regard for McClernand. To his wife he characterized the Thirteenth Corps commander as a "dirty dog" who was "envious and jealous of everybody who stands in his way" and was concerned only with his personal glory. To her he declared his intent not to serve under McClernand should Grant be removed and McClernand installed in his place. He was convinced that if Grant was not careful, the politician would succeed him.[87] His experience with the Illinoisan at Arkansas Post had been enough, even though McClernand had won a victory in that campaign that only Sherman supported. Kilby Smith, one of Sherman's brigade commanders, again wrote his mother of his esteem for Sherman and his disdain for McClernand: "He is out of place here."[88] The interpersonal relations within the high command of the Army of the Tennessee had the potential for disaster.

Charles Dana, the newspaperman who had reported on the Battle of Shiloh, was at Grant's headquarters because he had been charged by Stanton with the responsibility to investigate payments made to and by the government in the Western armies. At least that was what was written in his instructions. What was not written was that the commissioner was to report on Grant, "to enable Mr. Lincoln and himself to settle their minds as to Grant."[89] In other words, Dana, with a new title of assistant secretary of war, was to be a spy for the president and secretary of war. Henry Villard, correspondent for the *New York Tribune* and a contemporary of Dana's, later wrote that Dana often showed "strong, bordering on malignant, bias" and conveyed impressions "hastily, flippantly, and recklessly."[90] Vicksburg was not to be the only time Dana stoked the fires of controversy.

Dana reached Milliken's Bend on 6 April. In his memoirs, he too wrote of a meeting with Grant, Sherman, and Porter regarding the upcoming attempt to cross the Mississippi. Dana recorded in a letter to Stanton, "I have remonstrated so far as I could properly do so against intrusting so momentous an operation to McClernand." This comment brought a rebuke from the politically astute Stanton, who suggested that he "carefully avoid giving any advice in respect to commands that may be assigned, as it may lead to misunderstandings and troublesome complications." Dana replied that his suggestion would be "scrupulously observed."[91]

Dana had never met McClernand before he joined Grant's army, and there is no indication in his memoirs of his ever speaking to McClernand. The meeting or meetings referred to by Sherman and Dana are clear evidence of at best hostility, at worst a conspiracy, against McClernand. Rawlins and Wilson were confidants of Grant; nonetheless, for senior generals to question the competence of the second-ranking officer in the Army of the

Tennessee in the presence of these junior officers was highly improper. Not only did it undermine the authority of McClernand, but also it called into question Lincoln's judgment in having appointed him. In present-day parlance, such conversations are "prejudicial to good order and discipline."

On 29 March, Grant had written Maj. Gen. Stephen Hurlbut, commanding the Sixteenth Corps at Memphis, about a request from McClernand to have the 18th Illinois Infantry (one of Hurlbut's regiments) assigned to his own corps. In the note the army commander included an interesting statement: "Feeling every desire to gratify General McClernand in every possible [way] consistently with the good of the service."[92] Nowhere does Grant expound on that statement, but certainly McClernand believed that Grant was in fact not gratifying him. On 20 March he had written a friend in New York that he was experiencing "a sea of trouble. West Point men have proved themselves better West Point partisans than Genls. We want a representative man. . . . We have not found him in the class of professional soldiers. I believe we will only find him among Statesmen." He went on to charge others with jealousy for his success at Arkansas Post and castigated "mere military men" who were incapable of succeeding in "revolutionary emergencies."[93] His opinion of professionals in general and West Pointers in particular was undoubtedly reinforced by a letter he received on 4 April from his former chief of staff, Adolph Schwartz: "I am informed that Halleck is a bitter enemy of yours, and that he will oppose any appointment to an independent command."[94]

McClernand continued his own sub-rosa campaign against Grant. On 15 March he wrote Lincoln a scathing letter about Grant's drunkenness: "On the 13th of March, 1863, Genl. Grant I am informed was gloriously drunk and in bed sick all next day. If you [are] averse to drunken Genl's I can furnish the name of officers of high standing to substantiate the above."[95] Two days later he wrote Yates an insubordinate letter denouncing Grant's leadership and imploring the governor to visit the command: "Time is passing & the Republic is dying of inertia. The fall and winter have passed, and the spring is now passing, and nothing decisive has been done in this quarter. Can't you prevail upon the President to send some competent commander? For our country's sake do. My situation is intolerable. Come down and see us. Bring Gov. Morton, and Kirkwood if you can—at all events, come yourself."[96] This ugly struggle between Grant and McClernand, a struggle that reached from the bayous of Louisiana to the capitol in Illinois and the White House in Washington, would continue throughout the campaign.

Within the Union command, there was no consensus about the proper course of action. Sherman in particular believed the army should return to

Memphis and undertake a new movement toward Vicksburg through northern Mississippi—a movement that had once come to naught due to Van Dorn's and Forrest's raids. Grant, though, would not accede to any move that appeared to be a retreat. McPherson too opposed the plan. Wilson reported that McClernand had favored a move to turn Vicksburg from the south ever since the two had talked in Washington the previous September. Sherman felt so strongly about his position that on 8 April, after McClernand had occupied Richmond, he asked Grant to have each corps commander provide his opinions on the developing campaign: "Unless this be done, there are men who will, in any result falling below the popular standard, claim that their advice was unheeded, and that fatal consequences resulted therefrom." In his memoirs, Sherman stated that this "was meant particularly to induce General Grant to call on General McClernand for a similar expression of opinion."[97] Even as late as 23 April, after the navy had passed Vicksburg, Sherman still opposed the operation and wrote his wife, "I have no faith in the whole plan."[98] This mistrust and strife within the highest levels of command was a disadvantage of the Army of the Tennessee, but only if the Confederates could take advantage of it.

Upon arriving at Richmond, Bennett encountered a small Confederate force across the bayou and drove them off. McClernand had urged him to move rapidly toward New Carthage and attack "boldly" any Confederates he met. The corps commander joined his lead regiment at Richmond that evening. Bennett's cavalry reported that the area between Richmond and New Carthage was under water except along the road. A few of the bayous required bridges, and the road needed to be repaired in places, but generally the route would accommodate the army. He also pushed his cavalry west toward Delhi and Monroe, reporting that there were no Rebel soldiers there "to speak of" but that his troopers had met a body of enemy soldiers near New Carthage.[99]

Engineers reported that the water route from Milliken's Bend to Richmond was navigable, but that Roundaway Bayou was only three feet deep from Richmond to New Carthage, too shallow for steamers to transport men and equipment. They also reported a good news–bad news situation. The bad news was that levee breaks caused by the rising Mississippi River and by Union engineers' blasting the levee to gain access to Lake Providence had flooded most of the countryside. The good news was that as a result the Confederates would have great difficulty assembling an attack against the advancing Union column.[100]

The two Thirteenth Corps divisions not advancing toward New Carthage had the task of digging a new canal to connect the Mississippi with Walnut

Bayou at Duckport. The intent was to enable the fleet to enter Walnut Bayou at that point, navigate to Roundaway Bayou, and finally exit into the river below Vicksburg. Grant ordered the corps to provide two thousand men daily to work on the canal. Upon his return from Richmond late on 1 April, McClernand notified Grant that he would comply with the order to his subordinates to provide the detail, but he also reported his situation: that he was repairing the road to New Carthage, and that the land route would probably accommodate the army better than another canal; that he was constructing a two-hundred-foot bridge at Richmond; and that he was building barges to carry equipment through the bayous. On his own initiative, McClernand also ordered his engineer to determine whether a water route could be produced by cutting the levee at Milliken's Bend. It was ruled impracticable. The Duckport canal venture was abandoned in early May, when falling water on the Mississippi rendered the project impractical.[101] In these endeavors McClernand's conduct continued to be proper and professional. He complied with his commander's order, but he also provided additional information of which Grant had been unaware. The result was that Grant reconsidered his decision based on McClernand's firsthand knowledge of the situation.

McClernand provided daily intelligence to Grant about the situation between Richmond and New Carthage. On 3 April he conducted a personal reconnaissance of the area between Smith's plantation and New Carthage, a distance of one and one-half miles. He was fired upon at New Carthage by a Confederate detachment. Thinking that his escort was about to run, the fiery general shouted, "Damn you, stand fire, don't you run, stand fire, damn you!" The escort was not running but seeking shelter behind the levee. Lieutenant Colonel Warmoth, who accompanied the general, reported they all had a good laugh over the incident after they had withdrawn.

The corps commander also reported he was sending boats down Roundaway Bayou from Richmond to determine its navigability to New Carthage. He had engineers examine the possibility of another land route, one that would require either filling or bridging crevasses in the levee. Grant had planned to embark troops at New Carthage to assault Grand Gulf, but McClernand reported that there was little dry ground available except about two miles west of New Carthage; this would entail only a short march prior to embarkation. In this dispatch to the army commander, McClernand loyally praised the "activity and zeal" of Osterhaus, Bennett, and Capt. William F. Patterson, who was responsible for the engineering efforts.[102]

By 4 April, McClernand's command was spread over thirty miles, from Milliken's Bend to New Carthage, but the lead units of the Army of the

Tennessee were now within two miles of the Mississippi River south of Vicksburg. Two missions remained to be accomplished: the majority of the army had to be moved south before the Confederates could react, and Porter had to get his boats past Vicksburg in order to ferry the soldiers across the river.

On 5 April McClernand began moving the remainder of his Ninth Division from Milliken's Bend and establishing supply depots along the route. In warfare, effective communications are essential; therefore, he also directed that signal posts be established to open telegraph communications from Milliken's Bend to Smith's. The problem of crossing the flooded area between Smith's and New Carthage still remained, so McClernand ordered his engineer to determine whether a road on piles could be built over the water.[103]

Although his corps was on the move, McClernand still understood the necessity of inspecting the soldiers and of letting them see their commander. Accordingly, he arranged to review a division on 8 April. Grant, of the same mind, indicated he desired to inspect two divisions on the 9th. Therefore, on 9 April, the soldiers of the Tenth and Fourteenth Divisions were formed, and Grant and McClernand reviewed both commands.[104]

One incident, however, marred the otherwise excellent operation that McClernand was conducting from Milliken's Bend. Inexplicably, he left about a thousand sick and stragglers behind without providing shelter or medical attention for them. Grant let him know that this was unacceptable. For a change, the general made no excuses. In late April he would issue orders to ensure the mistake was not repeated.[105]

Confederate activity increased during the first week of April. McClernand's forces were fired on by Rebel soldiers at Bayou Vidal, near Smith's plantation, and also near Richmond. A cavalry patrol near Delhi met about four hundred Confederates. Fortunately for the strung-out Union army, Lt. Gen. John C. Pemberton, Confederate commander of the Department of Mississippi and East Louisiana, which included Vicksburg, could not confirm reports of McClernand's movements. To the confused Rebel leader, the enemy appeared to be "constantly in motion in all directions." Even had he been able to ascertain Grant's intentions, the Southern command structure and Union gunboats between them rendered cooperation between Confederate forces across the river almost impossible.[106]

McClernand did not let this activity deter him from his main effort, which was to lead the Army of the Tennessee south of Vicksburg. Nineteenth-century armies, like modern ones, required extensive logistic support, and the Army of the Tennessee was no exception. Foreseeing his requirements, McClernand ordered his quartermaster to "use all possible dispatch" to procure mules, wagons, and harnesses for the movement of his corps to New

Carthage. He began moving ammunition to New Carthage for the impending assault crossing of the river, and he recommended to Grant that ammunition be sent by gunboat or protected barge past the Vicksburg batteries.[107] On 11 April one brigade of the Fourteenth Division left Milliken's Bend to relieve the detachments of Osterhaus that were guarding the road south. A few days later the Twelfth Division, commanded by Brig. Gen. Alvin P. Hovey, joined the Thirteenth Corps from Arkansas; by 15 April it was encamped at Holmes's plantation, about halfway between Richmond and New Carthage. McClernand then informed Grant that his entire corps would be assembled between those two locales, but he cautioned his commander that it would be necessary to send a regiment to hold Richmond after his own regiment withdrew.[108]

In light of the history of the relations between Grant and McClernand, why was the Thirteenth Corps commander chosen to spearhead the attack? Certainly he was the senior commander, and that alone would be grounds for him to lead. Apparently, however, the real reasons were luck, terrain, and weather. Flooding had forced Grant to disperse his army. In mid-March McPherson was the northern-most corps at Lake Providence; McClernand, in the center, was bivouacked at Milliken's Bend; and part of Sherman's corps was at Young's Point. All were digging canals, but only McClernand's channel appeared to be having success. Furthermore, there was an overland route from Milliken's Bend to Richmond, which was a key position on the proposed water route to New Carthage. Perhaps Grant hoped that Sherman's expedition to find a bayou route north of Vicksburg would obviate the necessity to use McClernand, but by late March Sherman and Porter had reached a dead end in the tangled waterways of Steele's Bayou. The Thirteenth Army Corps, therefore, was the logical choice to lead the movement to New Carthage. From Milliken's Bend until the Union army crossed the Mississippi, it would always be in the lead.

The Thirteenth Corps movements were preliminaries to the riverine assault crossing of the Mississippi. Several other operational decisions still had to be made. First, as noted, Porter had to run a sufficient number of transports and gunboats by Vicksburg to carry the Union soldiers across the river. Second, Grant had to determine where on the Mississippi shore to land the forces that were to cross. Third, Lincoln and Halleck had to decide whether Grant's army should then move against Vicksburg or turn south to assist Banks in the capture of Port Hudson.

On 12 April, Grant informed the War Department that Porter would make his attempt to run the batteries about three nights later. On the night of 16 April, the sky over the Mississippi in front of Vicksburg was lit by flares, bursting shells, and burning boats as eleven Union navy vessels made the attempt. One transport and several barges were lost, but on 22 April several more vessels were able to pass. Grant now had the means to cross the river. Porter's comment to Gustavus Fox at this point was indicative of his opinion of McClernand: "We arrived at Carthage in good time to keep McClernand from trouble." Mrs. Grant and Mrs. McClernand, who had arrived at Milliken's Bend in late March, viewed the procession.[109]

As the Union commanders surveyed Confederate defenses along the river, they observed strong fortifications at Vicksburg, at Warrenton (just south of the city), and at Grand Gulf, about thirty miles below Vicksburg. Nature herself had reinforced the defenses, with a line of bluffs that extended from north of Vicksburg to Grand Gulf. An assault at Warrenton would allow Pemberton to reinforce the garrison quickly at the first sign of a Union attack. The result could be disastrous for Grant and the Union cause. Grand Gulf, however, was at such a distance that, if surprise were achieved, the Confederates would be unable to shift troops from Vicksburg in time to affect the Union crossing. Also, once the Union army began its inland advance from Grand Gulf, its left would be protected by the Big Black River and its right by Bayou Pierre.

On 12 April McClernand asked Grant whether Grand Gulf would be the objective of the river crossing or whether he should ascend the Big Black River to where it intersected the road network into the interior of Mississippi. Grant replied that he "should get possession of Grand Gulf at the earliest practicable moment." He repeated this directive six days later but added that McClernand should take no risks and should entrench until the army was concentrated on the east bank of the river.[110] This would be the first in a series of orders to McClernand urging caution. Their effect would be felt in mid-May at Champion Hill.

The aggressive corps commander, however, did not believe caution was in order. He strained to advance. On 18 April in a letter to Grant, he emphasized that the time was ripe to seize Grand Gulf. In his view, if the army moved "at once," Vicksburg would soon fall. The next day he again urged Grant to move rapidly, otherwise "Grand Gulf may become another Vicksburg or Port Hudson." He implored the army commander to give him "a dozen good transports" so he could "strike the enemy before he could fortify." He added that "the loss of a few transports in running the blockade" would be outweighed by the advantage to be gained from a speedy move. Even Porter agreed with McClernand; he expressed his concern that "left to themselves, they [the Grand Gulf garrison] will make this place impregnable."[111]

Both Grant and McClernand recognized that an amphibious assault against a defended position is a difficult military operation. McClernand realized that as the spearhead of the army, he had to land as many soldiers as possible as rapidly as possible to establish a lodgment for the follow-on forces. Grant realized he could not leave one corps isolated, with the major obstacle of the Mississippi River between that corps and the remainder of his army. To provide reinforcements required pontoons to cross the bayous and flooded lowlands, as well as boats to cross the river. Grant, on 18 April, had assured his subordinate that he would send a pontoon train forward to provide bridging for the bayous. McClernand also had begun construction of fixed bridges across the waters on the Louisiana side, and he urged Grant to get enough steamers and barges, at least a dozen, below Vicksburg to allow him to cross his entire command at once.[112] To facilitate rapid loading of the transports, he had to position his corps along the Mississippi rather than have them strung out along Roundaway Bayou. On 19 April, with the arrival of the steamer *Forest Queen*, the tug *Ivy*, and several barges, he began shuttling Osterhaus's division eight miles south from New Carthage to Judge John Perkins's Somerset plantation. He also directed Osterhaus to determine whether a land route existed between New Carthage and Somerset, to facilitate the movement of wagons and troops. McClernand ordered his Fourteenth Division, commanded by Brig. Gen. Eugene A. Carr, to occupy the vacant positions at New Carthage, and he instructed the Twelfth Division, commanded by Brig. Gen. Alvin P. Hovey, to move from Richmond to Holmes's plantation, about halfway to New Carthage. A. J. Smith's Tenth Division was to keep the road open until relieved by James McPherson's Seventeenth Corps.[113]

A successful river crossing would require close army-navy cooperation. Although Porter had several times expressed disdain for McClernand, he never failed to support the corps commander during a joint operation. The admiral, based on a personal reconnaissance, had misgivings about the strength of the Grand Gulf defenses, but he declared his intention to attack anyway. He asked McClernand to send troops to assist in case he was able to bombard the Confederate works into submission.[114] McClernand agreed and issued an order to Osterhaus at 11:00 P.M. on 22 April to "immediately embark" his division and assault Grand Gulf, but only if he believed navy gunboats had inflicted sufficient damage on the Confederates to allow a successful landing. Wisely, he authorized Osterhaus to disembark at Perkins's plantation if the gunboats could not silence the Confederate batteries. So that all would be aware of his intentions, the corps commander then informed both Porter and Grant of his actions.[115]

Mud, flooding, lack of ammunition, and shipping all caused delay, and Osterhaus was not embarked until 10:00 A.M. the following day. Porter again examined Grand Gulf and reported to McClernand at noon that there were now two more fortifications than he had seen the day before. McClernand then accompanied Porter to see for himself. Grant also reconnoitered the enemy position and wrote Sherman "that if an attack can be made within the next two days, the place will easily fall."[116] For once, Grant and McClernand were of the same mind.

Confederate forces were still in the neighborhood, and McClernand had to deal with them as well as with the problems of getting across the river. On April 15, as Osterhaus was closing on Smith's plantation, his advance pickets encountered the 1st Missouri Infantry Regiment that had crossed the river from Grand Gulf. The pickets were forced back until reinforcements drove the Missourians away. Two days later, McClernand requested Porter to shell a Rebel camp at Perkins's plantation, but Confederate cavalry quickly returned, and Osterhaus had to drive them away as well.[117]

McClernand recognized the vulnerability of his forces until they could concentrate, and he knew the importance of securing dry land on the Louisiana shore as an embarkation point. Rebel attacks on the Union soldiers as they tried to board the boats to assault Grand Gulf would greatly complicate an already difficult operation. To protect the Union assembly area, he prudently ordered Carr to designate two regiments to guard the approaches to Perkins's.[118]

A second flotilla ran the Vicksburg batteries on 22 April, and, according to Dana, Union vessels south of Vicksburg now had a capacity of transporting about twelve thousand soldiers, or two of McClernand's divisions; Grant figured he could transport only ten thousand.[119] The plan at that time still was for a direct assault on Grand Gulf, which would require intensive fire support from the gunboats and overwhelming infantry to overrun the defenses. Moving the soldiers across the river rapidly thus became a primary consideration. To conduct the required ferry operations quickly, all soldiers needed to embark from a location as close as possible to Grand Gulf along the Louisiana shore. Although the move from New Carthage to Perkins's had reduced the overall distance, the latter was still about fifteen river miles from Grand Gulf. The return trip would be against the current, which would greatly slow efforts to reinforce the first wave. The only alternative was for the army to continue to move south along the Louisiana shore to get closer to Grand Gulf.

On 24 April McClernand ordered Osterhaus to reconnoiter south, both to find a suitable embarkation point and to determine if it might be possible to move up Bayou Pierre on the Mississippi side and assault Grand Gulf from the rear. He reported to Grant that Hard Times, only three miles from Grand Gulf, might be a suitable assembly area for the assault.[120]

After floundering in the mud for all of February and March, the Thirteenth Army Corps had covered thirty miles in four weeks and was preparing to cross the mighty Mississippi to attack the Confederates at Grand Gulf. Despite the difficulties that McClernand's men had to overcome, Porter continued his attacks on McClernand, writing Assistant Secretary of the Navy Fox that "it seems to me they have done nothing but encamp, and then move a mile or two." He attributed the slowness to unnecessary baggage and to McClernand, who, "wrapped in his dignity, scorned all advice."[121]

Grant's movement order had in fact specified that baggage be limited. McClernand had even chastised Osterhaus for the "large and cumbersome quantity of unauthorized baggage" with his division.[122] Dana was astonished to learn that McClernand's wife was accompanying the move. He wrote Secretary of War Stanton that he believed her presence and accompanying baggage was delaying the advance of the army.[123]

Grant wrote Halleck on 27 April that "moving troops from Smith's plantation has been a tedious operation; more so than it should have been."[124] In his memoirs, Grant acknowledges the difficulty of McClernand's march, which required construction of four bridges about two thousand feet long against strong currents, but nowhere does he explain what he meant by his comment to Halleck.[125] Was he laying the foundation for future action to be taken against the politician?

Until late April, McClernand's command of his corps and conduct of the campaign was exemplary. Despite his continued belief that overall command should be his, he performed his duties professionally, skillfully, and loyally. Grant's orders to him had indicated the importance of rapidity—"get possession . . . at the earliest practicable moment." McClernand's orders to his subordinates clearly indicated that he understood the necessity of speed—"immediately embark," "hold in readiness for prompt embarkation."[126] Porter's letter to Fox indicated little understanding of the terrain over which the Union army had to move, of the necessity to lay corduroy roads and build bridges, and Dana's assertion that movement was retarded by Mrs. McClernand and her baggage perhaps attributes too much to a minor issue. Yet in the closing days of April, the political animal within McClernand leaped to the fore and, while not causing a delay, did create the impression of it.

Gov. Richard Yates joined his Illinois soldiers at Perkins's plantation in late April. Although Grant makes no mention in his memoirs of Yates's being with the army, Wilson would declare that McClernand requested that Grant allow him to delay embarking his corps so that he might hold a review for Yates. Wilson gave no indication of Grant's response, although Dana wrote Stanton that Grant either late 25 April or early 26 April had ordered McClernand "to embark his men without losing a moment." Instead, at about 4:00 P.M. on 26 April, McClernand did hold his review, with a brigade of Illinois troops. Both the governor and the general gave rousing speeches that attested to the valor of the "brave and noble boys" from Illinois and urged them on to Vicksburg. Yates was honored with a fifteen-gun salute. Dana wrote to Stanton on 27 April that the salute had been fired "notwithstanding that positive orders had repeatedly been given to use no ammunition for any purpose except against the enemy. What course General Grant will take under these circumstances I have no idea." In fact he took no immediate action, but the army commander was not pleased with the actions of his subordinate general.[127]

Meanwhile, by 27 April the divisions of Hovey, Smith, and Carr had been assembled near Perkins's.[128] McClernand ordered his division commanders to select separate places along the river so that all divisions could embark simultaneously, rather than attempt to load at only one spot. Dana reported to Stanton that the "steamboats and barges were scattered about in the river" and "that there is much apparent confusion in McClernand's command." He also again reported the presence of McClernand's wife.[129] As Dana was not a trained soldier, it is possible that the movement of several divisions of soldiers to various assembly areas and the scattered transports appeared as confusion, when actually it was an indication of McClernand's foresight in providing for rapid embarkation. According to Dana, Grant drafted a letter of reprimand to McClernand concerning the conditions at Perkins's, delays in boarding, and excess baggage. The next day, however, Grant found conditions improved and so did not give the letter to his corps commander. Dana's report to Stanton is the only mention of this incident.[130]

The twenty-seventh day of April 1863 was one of great activity within the Thirteenth Corps of the Army of the Tennessee. Grant ordered McClernand, who would command the assault on Grand Gulf, to embark his corps for the attack. There remained some question in Grant's mind, however, as to whether the transports could run the batteries at Grand Gulf as they had at Vicksburg. In the eventuality that they could not do so without receiving severe damage, he warned McClernand that he might have to disembark his troops on the Louisiana shore short of Grand Gulf and then march overland to a point south of the Confederate position, where the infantry would be ferried over the river. McClernand issued a subsequent order to Carr, who would be on the left of the assault, and to Osterhaus, who would be on the right, as well as to Hovey, who would constitute the reserve. Speed was critical, for the troops on the Mississippi side of the river would be vulnerable to Confederate counterattack until they were reinforced. To ensure that the second wave would be embarked with minimum confusion, McClernand prudently specified which returning transports would be allocated to the second-wave divisions of Smith and Hovey. By 10:30 P.M. the two assault divisions, minus two infantry regiments and some cavalry, were loaded.[131]

Those two regiments were responding to another Confederate threat to interfere with Union attempts to cross the river. While investigating a suitable route from Perkins's to Bayou Pierre, Osterhaus's force had encountered Confederate cavalry near Choctaw Bayou and Lake Bruin. To replace those regiments in the assault on Grand Gulf, Grant authorized McClernand to attach one brigade from A. J. Smith's division to Osterhaus. The remainder of Smith's division was to move along the route reconnoitered by Osterhaus's detachment "to a point opposite or near and below Grand Gulf."[132] Upon reaching that destination, Smith would be in position to board the transports and cross the river rapidly to reinforce the first wave of infantry assaulting Grand Gulf.

On the morning of 29 April, Porter's gunboats began a terrific bombardment of the Confederate positions at Grand Gulf, while McClernand's two divisions waited for the signal to disembark and attack. At 7:50 A.M., the fleet opened fire. At 1:15 P.M., however, Porter, having sustained considerable damage, realized he would be unable to silence the batteries and withdrew.[133] Unless those batteries were put out of action, the vessels conducting the amphibious assault would be destroyed before they reached the Mississippi shore.

A new plan was needed, and quickly. McClernand had considered the problem of how to gain a foothold on the Mississippi shore for some time. On 12 and 24 April he had suggested to Grant that transports ascend the Big Black River and land infantry, which could then attack north to Warrenton or south to Grand Gulf. Dana reported to Stanton that Porter considered this plan too risky, probably on account of difficulty of maneuver in the narrow confines of the Big Black.[134] But on 24 April McClernand had also proposed a plan by which his command would march across the point of land in Louisiana north of Grand Gulf to a location opposite the mouth of Bayou Pierre, south of Grand Gulf. From there they would cross the river after the transports and gunboats had run the Grand Gulf batteries as they had done at Vicksburg. Another option he urged Grant to consider was a frontal attack, which would require intensive, accurate fire support from the gunboats.[135]

For once Porter disagreed with Grant, and he expressed his belief to the army commander, to Secretary of the Navy Welles, and to Assistant Secretary Fox that twelve thousand Confederates defended Grand Gulf and that Grant "cannot do what he expects." He also proposed a landing at Bayou Pierre.[136]

Although McClernand did not believe the Confederate defenses were as strong as Porter depicted, he knew from battlefield experience against strongly defended positions the inherent superiority they provided over attacking soldiers. A fundamental tenet of tactics is to seek the flank of the enemy and attempt to force him out of his defensive positions. Certainly that was Grant's plan for the Vicksburg campaign, and McClernand and Porter saw the wisdom of applying that strategy at Grand Gulf.

Following the naval bombardment on 29 April, Grant too realized he could not effect a landing in the face of the Confederate guns. The day prior, McClernand had proposed Hard Times to Grant as an assembly area for the forces that would conduct the assault.[137] Grant had approved, but after the unsuccessful bombardment, he ordered the Thirteenth Army Corps to disembark at Hard Times and march overland to Disharoon's plantation, a route that McClernand had reconnoitered on 28 April. As dusk approached, Porter's fleet began the hazardous journey past the Confederate guns at Grand Gulf. By 10:00 P.M., the fleet was south of the Rebel position. Grant informed Halleck that he would land on the east bank of the river the next day.[138]

Sunrise on 30 April 1863 saw the soldiers of McClernand's Ninth, Tenth, Twelfth, and Fourteenth Divisions sleeping on the ground at Disharoon's.[139] Dana, continuing his campaign against McClernand, had written Stanton late the night before that he doubted whether McClernand would promptly load his corps on the transports, "though General Grant has given the most urgent orders." By 8 A.M. that morning, however, the transports were loaded with the first wave of the assault force, and by noon about seventeen thousand soldiers of Maj. Gen. John Alexander McClernand's Thirteenth Army Corps were ashore at Bruinsburg, Mississippi.[140]

8
Springtime in Mississippi

As John McClernand stood on the east bank of the Mississippi River and watched his Thirteenth Army Corps cross, he must have felt a deep sense of pride and accomplishment, punctuated by visions of the future. After months of struggling through the bayous of Louisiana, the Union army was now south of Vicksburg, on the same side of the river as that Confederate citadel. McClernand's corps had led the crossing and was poised to strike into the heart of Jefferson Davis's home state of Mississippi. The Illinois soldier had battled West Point generals and Washington politicians, and he alone now stood on the Mississippi shore. Sherman was north of the city, conducting a demonstration at Snyder's Bluff. McPherson was still on the Louisiana side of the river. Grant watched the amphibious operation from Porter's flagship *Benton.* This exploit would make wonderful headlines.

McClernand's forces were unopposed as they landed near Bruinsburg. Pemberton had become confused by the various Union operations in his vicinity and was unsure as to where the Union main effort actually was. Col. Benjamin H. Grierson's cavalry had left LaGrange, Tennessee, on 17 April and was nearing Baton Rouge as the Thirteenth Corps was landing. As Confederate John Taylor confided to his diary, the raid had "kicked up a thundering ruckus," which, in combination with other Federal movements, distracted Pemberton from the real Union threat on the river south of Vicksburg.[1] The bayou expeditions north of Vicksburg had convinced him that Union forces still might attack from that direction. Although Pemberton had assigned to Brig. Gen. John S. Bowen the defense of Grand Gulf, about fifty miles south of Vicksburg by river, he knew Grant could land anywhere south of that point. To defend everywhere would mean stripping Vicksburg of defenders; he could spare only 5,164 men and fifteen guns for Bowen. Although he asked for help from Gen. Edmund Kirby Smith in the Trans-Mississippi Department, it would not be forthcoming.[2]

Union Organization (30 April 1863)

Army of the Tennessee, Maj. Gen. Ulysses S. Grant

Thirteenth Army Corps, Maj. Gen. John Alexander McClernand
Ninth Division, Brig. Gen. Peter Joseph Osterhaus
Tenth Division, Brig. Gen. Andrew J. Smith
Twelfth Division, Brig. Gen. Alvin P. Hovey
Fourteenth Division, Brig. Gen. Eugene A. Carr

District of Eastern Arkansas, Maj. Gen. Benjamin M. Prentiss
Thirteenth Division, Brig. Gen. Leonard F. Ross

Fifteenth Army Corps,
Maj. Gen. William T. Sherman

Sixteenth Army Corps,
Maj. Gen. Stephen A. Hurlbut
(stationed at Memphis, Tenn.)

Seventeenth Army Corps,
Maj. Gen. James B. McPherson

Compounding the Confederate commander's problem was the demonstration launched by Sherman north of the city. Although Sherman had been defeated in late December by Stephen Lee, and Porter's fleet had been blocked in the bayous north of the city in March, Pemberton could not afford to allow Sherman's Union corps to operate unmolested within striking distance of his northernmost defenses. His only recourse was to issue orders for various commands to be prepared to reinforce threats to the integrity of the defensive position in Mississippi. Unfortunately for Pemberton and the Confederacy, the threats were too numerous and the Confederate forces too few.[3]

By noon, 30 April, most of McClernand's men were ashore. Only then was it realized that the troops had consumed the rations issued on 27 April. The corps's wagons had been left at Somerset plantation, and no one had thought to ensure that the soldiers had the normal three days' rations prior to the assault. Consequently, the advance was halted while rations were ferried over and distributed, enough to last five days.[4] McClernand alone must bear responsibility for that oversight. In Illinois he had demonstrated his ability and willingness to immerse himself in the details of his command. Now, however, he had overlooked this detail, and it would allow the Confederates a few precious hours to move into position at Port Gibson.

About 4:00 P.M., McClernand notified Grant that he was "pushing forward" to seize the bridge over Bayou Pierre on the road to Jackson. If that bridge could be seized intact, it would speed the movement of the entire army.[5]

Dana did not recognize McClernand's attempts to move speedily against the enemy. He reported to Stanton that although the operation was proceeding smoothly, "had any other general than McClernand held the advance, the landing would certainly have been effected at daylight."[6] What Dana failed to appreciate was that although McClernand "held the advance," Grant held the reins of the army.

Grant's order of 27 April had specified that artillery and men be embarked. He had made no mention of cavalry. Because of the limited transportation, McClernand had ordered his men to take eighty rounds of ammunition and to leave the wagons behind. He also left his cavalry on the west bank and, thus, was now advancing blindly in enemy territory.

Generally, cavalry preceded any advance of a large body of troops, to alert the force to any enemy presence. In this instance, McClernand's lack of cavalry was due not to negligence but to the expectation that the corps might have to fight to secure a beachhead for the army. For such an operation infantry firepower would be needed, not cavalry. Cavalry loaded onto the limited transports would have occupied space that could be utilized more efficiently by Union infantrymen. Only after most of McPherson's Seventeenth Corps had crossed would McClernand's small cavalry contingent rejoin his command.[7]

At 4:00 P.M. the Thirteenth Corps moved out. Carr led, followed by Osterhaus, Hovey, and Smith. Rather than advance directly on Port Gibson by way of the Bruinsburg Road, the corps turned right near Windsor plantation and took the longer Rodney Road. This route could only have been directed by McClernand. The explanation for such an indirect route can be related to terrain. About a mile past Windsor, the Bruinsburg Road crossed James Creek, which entered the Mississippi near Bruinsburg. High water from months of rain undoubtedly had swollen James Creek, as it had the bayous of Louisiana. No bridge crossed the creek, and McClernand would have had to take precious time to construct one. Quite possibly he would have faced the same problem further on, where Widows Creek crossed the road. The southern route, however, had the advantage of crossing both creeks farther along their traces, where the water would be lower and the fords more passable. Although it cannot be determined exactly, McClernand probably learned of these conditions from slaves at Windsor or by sending a patrol east along the Bruinsburg Road.[8]

At around 12:30 A.M., after a twelve-mile march, Carr's scouts encountered skirmishers at the house of Mrs. A. K. Shaifer. The house sat at a crossroads between the main road from Port Gibson to Rodney and a smaller one that angled northwest to intersect the main road from Port Gibson to Bruinsburg. The Rebels fell back a short distance. Carr, who was unfamiliar with the rugged terrain in the area, decided to await daybreak before continuing the engagement.[9] With this movement the Thirteenth Corps had secured on the eastern bank of the river a lodgment with ample space in which to land the remainder of the army.

After setting his corps in motion, McClernand and his staff remained at Windsor plantation, owned by the widow of Smith Coffee Daniell, until about 2:00 A.M., when he rode toward the front. He arrived at daybreak, consulted with his commanders, and conducted a personal reconnaissance of the area. He quickly realized that control of the Bruinsburg and Rodney Roads, along with the road that connected the two near Shaifer's, was critical to preventing the Union forces from being flanked by Confederates.[10] Accordingly, he ordered Carr to deploy a force to block an attack into the Union rear and also to continue to press the main enemy body along the Rodney Road. Upon the arrival of Osterhaus and his 3,900-man division, McClernand ordered him to protect the Union left along the Bruinsburg Road. These movements were accomplished none too soon, as Brig. Gen. Edward D. Tracy had moved his Alabama brigade of 1,500 men into position astride the Bruinsburg Road in Carr's rear. As Osterhaus soon appeared to have the situation well in hand, McClernand turned his attention to the larger battle brewing on the Union right.[11]

Shortly after 5:30 A.M., Hovey's division arrived on the field, and McClernand ordered him to deploy his men along Magnolia Church Ridge. Carr's blue-clad soldiers were able to make only slight gains against the graybacks, who were aided considerably by the junglelike terrain. In response to a call for help from Brig. Gen. William Benton of Carr's division, Hovey's brigades joined Carr about one hour later. While this was occurring, Brig.

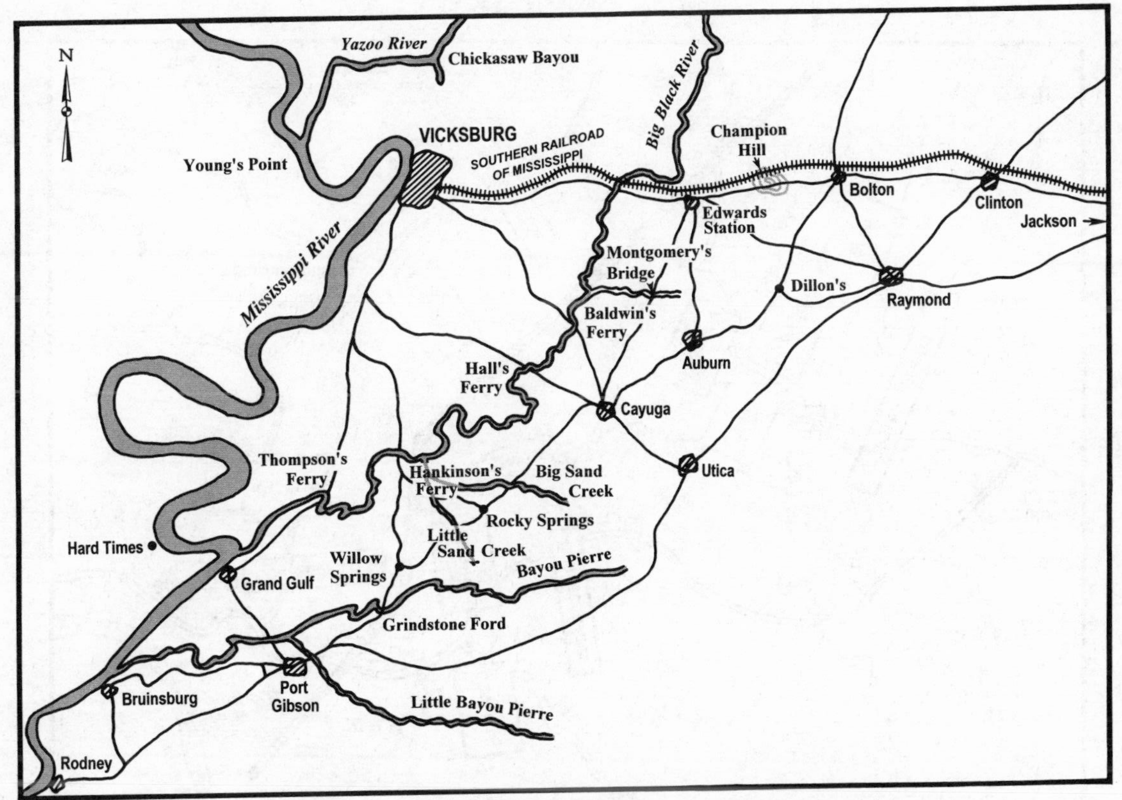

Area of Operations of the Army of the Tennessee in the Vicksburg Campaign

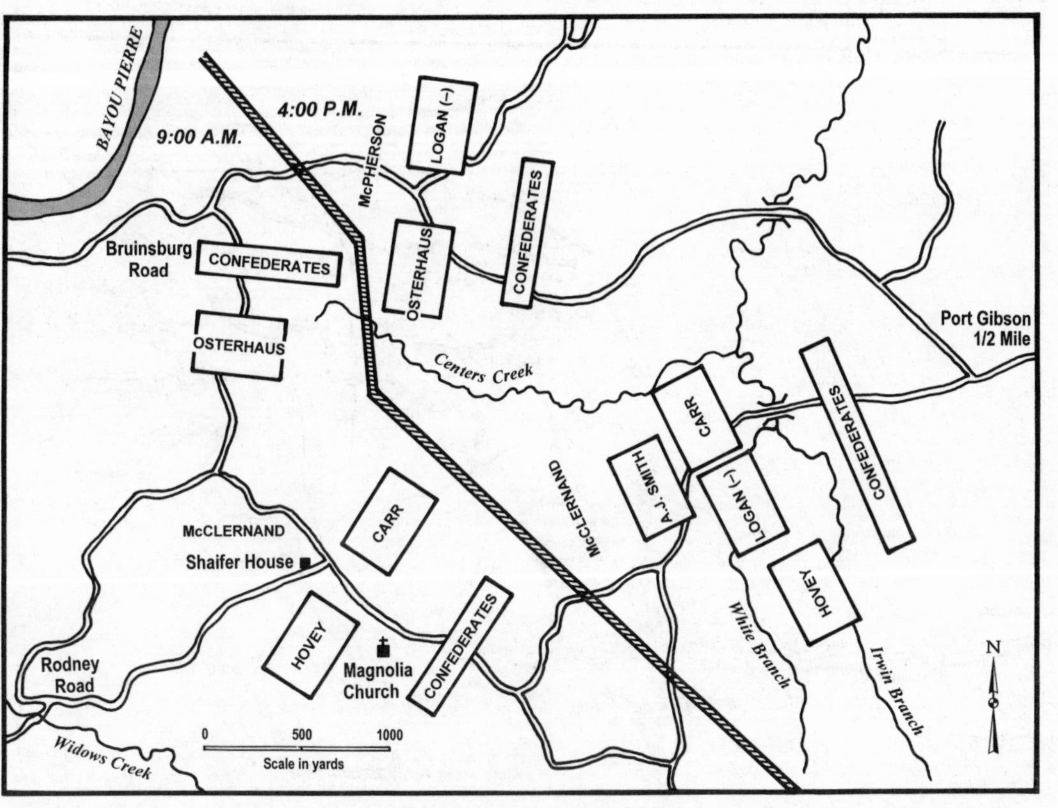

Battle of Port Gibson, May 1, 1863

Gen. A. J. Smith's division began to arrive, and McClernand ordered his brigades to join those of Carr and Hovey on the Union right. The corps commander had thus massed almost thirteen thousand men against a force of no more than 1,100 Confederates. The usual ratio for a successful attack is three to one, and McClernand's force along the Rodney Road clearly exceeded that. Perhaps the corps commander recalled the result of his attack against prepared Confederate positions at Fort Donelson. He would be certain everything was in order before ordering an advance.[12]

Grant arrived on the field at 10:00 A.M., met McClernand, and inspected the dispositions. Despite the numerical superiority on the right, the army commander later wrote that the Union forces were making little progress. On the left, Osterhaus was attempting to find a way through the thickets in order to launch a coordinated attack on the Confederate line. Unfortunately, he then grew cautious and called for reinforcements despite numerical superiority.[13] Dense brush and lack of cavalry prevented either Osterhaus or McClernand from ascertaining whether the Confederate flanks might be turned. Indeed, Widows Creek on the Confederate left and Bayou Pierre on the Rebel right hindered any attempt to envelop those flanks. In fairness to Osterhaus and McClernand, it must be recognized that the Confederates occupied exceptional defensive terrain. The cleared ridge tops provided excellent observation, but in the steep vine-tangled ravines between the ridges, the view was limited to only a few feet. Grant characterized the landscape as "the most broken country I ever saw."[14]

Soon after the two generals met, McClernand ordered an advance against the Confederate left, commanded by Brig. Gen. Martin Green. The overwhelming force soon drove the Rebels back from Magnolia Church. McClernand was ecstatic. Grant and Governor Yates joined the corps commander at the church, where Hovey's soldiers greeted them with the "wildest enthusiasm." The two politicians made brief speeches, with McClernand exclaiming that it was a "a great day for the northwest!" All considered the victory "a glorious achievement." Upon spotting Brigadier General Benton, whose brigade had had a significant role in the victory, McClernand clasped his hand and congratulated him on the performance of his command. As reported by one of McClernand's staff officers, "Gen. Benton's bosom heaved with emotions of joy, and [he] could speak only with difficulty."[15]

As Green fell back, he encountered Col. Francis Cockrell and Brig. Gen. William Baldwin, who were deploying their brigades along the Rodney Road to delay the Union onslaught. After the speeches and necessary reorganization, McClernand pushed his divisions forward through the canebrakes and ravines. As they reached the top of a ridge that fronted the new Confederate position, the Yankee soldiers were blasted back by artillery fire from the recently arrived Rebels.[16]

Unable to locate the Confederate flank, McClernand decided to mass his formations on a narrow front—twenty-one regiments over eight hundred yards—and batter his way through. Grant had responded to his corps commander's "frequent requests for reinforcements" by sending a brigade from McPherson's lead division to support each wing of McClernand's command. At about 2:00 P.M., Brig. Gen. John D. Stevenson reported to McClernand, and his brigade immediately went into the line. A sudden Rebel counterattack against the Union right was stopped by Carr, Burbridge, Stevenson, and Hovey, all of whose forces rapidly shifted to counter the threat.[17] Although McClernand greatly outnumbered the Confederates, the ravines and thick undergrowth still prevented him from determining the exact size of the force he faced or its exact location. At 4:00 P.M., while he halted to determine what to do next, Baldwin launched another counterattack. Union artillery fire finally turned the tide and drove the Confederates from the field. McClernand, however, failed to coordinate the advance of all forces under his command, and Stevenson suddenly found himself several hundred yards in advance of the main Union line. Realizing his predicament and uncertain as to the intentions of the Rebels, he retired to the line occupied by the other Union brigades. As darkness fell, the Confederates began an unmolested retreat to the north bank of Bayou Pierre.[18]

Meanwhile, at about 7:00 A.M., Osterhaus had attacked the waiting Rebel brigade. Col. Isham Garrott, Tracy having been killed, masterfully shifted his men to plug holes where the Union forces were making headway. In this deadly chess match, Osterhaus sought to counter by rearranging his regiments as he tried to find his way both through the almost impenetrable ravines as well as the Confederate line. At 2:30 P.M. Green's command, which had been driven from the field by McClernand's main attack, arrived in Garrott's rear and quickly formed into line. A lack of coordination, though, between the two Rebel leaders prevented the reinforcements from being used to best advantage.

In midafternoon Osterhaus resumed his attack, but again it became disorganized due to the difficult terrain. By 5:30 P.M., however, the overwhelming Union strength had been brought to bear, and the Confederates finally abandoned the fight and withdrew to join their comrades north of Bayou Pierre.[19]

The battle at Port Gibson had been a difficult affair for both sides. McClernand, who commanded the advance guard of the army, had encountered the enemy in a meeting engagement and had promptly developed the

Union Organization

Vicksburg Campaign

Army of the Tennessee, Maj. Gen. Ulysses S. Grant
Thirteenth Corps, Maj. Gen. John Alexander McClernand
Fifteenth Corps, Maj. Gen. William T. Sherman
Seventeenth Corps, Maj. Gen. James B. McPherson

Confederate Organization

Battle of Port Gibson—Brig Gen. John S. Bowen

Green's Brigade, Brig. Gen. Martin E. Green
Tracy's Brigade, Brig. Gen. Edward D. Tracy (killed) and Col. Isham W. Garrott
Baldwin's Brigade, Brig. Gen. William E. Baldwin
Cockrell's Brigade, Col. Francis M. Cockrell

Battle of Champion Hill—Lt. Gen. John C. Pemberton

Loring's Division, Maj. Gen. William W. Loring
Bowen's Division, Brig. Gen. John S. Bowen
Stevenson's Division, Maj. Gen. Carter L. Stevenson

Battle of Big Black River

Green's Brigade, Brig. Gen. Martin E. Green
Vaughn's Brigade, Brig. Gen. John C. Vaughn
Cockrell's Brigade, Col. Francis M. Cockrell

Vicksburg—Lt. Gen. John C. Pemberton

Smith's Division, Maj. Gen. Martin L. Smith
Bowen's Division, Maj. Gen. John S. Bowen
Forney's Division, Maj. Gen. John H. Forney
Stevenson's Division, Maj. Gen. Carter L. Stevenson

situation in, essentially, two separate fights. Despite a lack of intelligence regarding Confederate strength, he was able to stabilize the battle until the army commander arrived with additional forces. Although outnumbered significantly, Bowen had held off McClernand and McPherson for almost the entire day. McClernand would later be charged with having displayed "an excess of caution," but he had managed the fight as well as possible under existing conditions.[20]

In an engagement like Port Gibson, the advantage is with the defender. Bowen was able to establish positions on defensible terrain, whereas McClernand not only did not know the size of the opponent but had to contend with exceptionally difficult terrain. Perhaps he could have enveloped the Confederate left, had he been aware that the Natchez Road ran nearly parallel to the Rodney Road about half a mile to the east. An attack from that direction, however, would have forced the Union soldiers to advance in the canebrake of the beds of White and Irwin Branches, an almost impossible task.

Grant himself understood the difficulty of the terrain along the Rodney and Bruinsburg Roads and the advantage such terrain held for the defender: "The country in this part of Mississippi stands on edge. . . . The sides of the hills are covered with a very heavy growth of timber and with undergrowth, and the ravines are filled with vines and canebrakes, almost impenetrable. This makes it easy for an inferior force to delay, if not defeat, a far superior one."[21] As at Arkansas Post, McClernand may have let his enthusiasm for the success of his corps overcome his responsibilities to direct the last stages of the battle. Certainly it is important to recognize the soldiers who participated and to reward those who performed particularly heroic deeds, but doing so before his corps had consolidated its position on the battlefield and established defensive positions for the night was imprudent. Bowen had managed his defense well and had staggered the Thirteenth Corps several times with effective counterattacks. McClernand should have been directing his division commanders and preparing for future Confederate attacks instead of addressing Hovey's forces at Magnolia Church. The politician in the Illinois Democrat would not die.

Wilson was aware that McClernand had been near the front throughout the battle, and he characterized the Union corps commander as having "behaved with his usual gallantry." He believed the victory would make possible a rapprochement between Grant and his corps commander. Rawlins agreed, and the two asked that Grant personally congratulate McClernand on the victory. Both staff officers were surprised when he refused. Grant was still angry about what he believed to be the delay in crossing the Mississippi resulting from the review held for Yates on 26 April. Grant also believed McClernand had disobeyed orders during the battle. Wilson wrote that Grant had directed the corps commander to conserve artillery ammunition but that McClernand had replied that he was the one fighting the battle and would use whatever ammunition he believed was appropriate. It was Wilson's opinion that Grant then decided to watch McClernand closely. According to Wilson, after that the army commander rarely met with his subordinate or sent him written orders. To Wilson fell the responsibility to deliver messages to McClernand and to observe his cooperation with the other corps commanders.[22] Such command arrangements were likely to have disastrous consequences.

Humidity, heat, exhaustion, and darkness forced a halt to the Union advance. As the soldiers of the Thirteenth Corps encamped for the night, Grant provided McClernand his instructions for the next day: "Renew the attack at early dawn and if possible push the enemy from the field or capture him."[23] McClernand moved at sunrise, encountered no opposition, and occupied the town of Port Gibson by midmorning. The corps commander dispatched Col. Henry Warmoth to inform Grant that the town was in Union hands. He did not find the army commander until Grant himself had entered the town. Upon providing his report, Warmoth was the subject of a good laugh by Grant's staff for his report of the obvious.[24]

Retreating Confederates had destroyed the bridge over Little Bayou Pierre east of the town, so further pursuit was impossible until a new span could be completed. Lieutenant Colonel Wilson, in his report, claimed to have made repeated requests to McClernand for a brigade to assist in constructing a new bridge. McClernand understood the necessity to rebuild the span and informed Grant it would be done "at once." Inexplicably, the soldiers did not arrive for several hours, and the bridge was not completed until midafternoon. Grant then sent McPherson's corps to secure a crossing over Bayou Pierre at Grindstone Ford. The bridge there had been damaged, and Wilson called on McPherson for assistance in repairing it. McPherson was, as McClernand had been, several hours late in sending pioneer troops, yet Wilson's report was to be far less critical of McPherson than McClernand. As the report was not written until 30 May, perhaps subsequent events in Mississippi account for the difference in tone.[25] The crossing of Bayou Pierre by McPherson's corps marked the first time since 30 March that McClernand's Thirteenth Army corps had not led the Army of the Tennessee.

While Grant was crossing Bayou Pierre, Pemberton was transferring his headquarters from Jackson to Vicksburg. This put him closer to his forces and greatly facilitated communications with them. When he learned of Grant's movements, he ordered Grand Gulf abandoned and Maj. Gen. William W. Loring to send a small force to disrupt McPherson's attempt to secure a bridgehead over Bayou Pierre. They were too late. While McPherson's corps moved on to Hankinson's Ferry, McClernand's men, fatigued from the fighting, rested in Port Gibson throughout 2 May. Early the next morning Grant directed his Thirteenth Corps commander to leave one brigade to guard the new bridge at Port Gibson, another to patrol the road between Port Gibson and Grindstone Ford, and to march the remainder of his corps to Grindstone. To Carr, his Fourteenth Division commander, McClernand issued detailed instructions to watch the entire line of Bayou Pierre. It would not do to have the Confederates strike the Union left flank and possibly drive a wedge between McPherson's lead corps and the remainder of the army.[26]

Just as he set out, McClernand was notified by Grant that an Alabama regiment had been observed north of Port Gibson and that he should conduct a reconnaissance in that direction. Almost simultaneously, Carr reported a force of eight thousand Confederates somewhere between Port Gibson and Grand Gulf, but he had determined they were retreating. Nevertheless, McClernand warned Grant, who was on his way to Grand Gulf, that he should be careful as he approached the town in order to prevent capture. McClernand also replied that he would send two regiments to prevent the Confederates from interfering with the Union movement. The remainder of his corps marched toward Willow Springs, where they encamped for the night.[27]

Having learned from his experience on 30 April of suddenly finding his corps without rations, McClernand on 3 May notified Grant that he would be out of subsistence the next day. Feeding the army would be a major consideration for Grant throughout the coming campaign, but on 3 May it was McClernand's problem. He reminded Grant that he had no wagons, due to the army commander's directive to leave them behind, but he recommended a possible solution—to determine if the Big Black River, which entered the Mississippi near Grand Gulf, was navigable. That would allow provisions to be transported by boat to the advancing army. Porter previously had vetoed Grant's suggestion to send a gunboat up the Big Black, so McClernand's idea was rejected.[28] To make up for the lack of rations coming across the river, the men would have to forage for supplies during much of the upcoming operation.

Grant spent the night at Grand Gulf and contemplated his next move. After months of difficulties and increasing criticism from the Northern press, he "was on dry ground on the same side of the river with the enemy." The enemy occupied both Vicksburg and Port Hudson, near Baton Rouge. Should he turn north against the former, or south and cooperate with Maj.

Gen. Nathaniel P. Banks's force against the latter? In his memoirs he would record his dilemma: "Up to this time my intention had been to secure Grand Gulf as a base of supplies, detach McClernand's corps to Banks, and cooperate with him in the reduction of Port Hudson."[29] What was his thinking?

In March, Grant had suggested to Banks a cooperative movement against Vicksburg. Before Porter ran the Vicksburg batteries, Grant would have Banks capture Port Hudson and then move his army and his transports north. Grant could use those vessels to ferry the Army of the Tennessee across the Mississippi without exposing Porter's boats to the guns of Vicksburg. In fact, Lincoln on 2 April suggested to Halleck that Grant and Banks cooperate against Vicksburg. Halleck added that Lincoln "seems to be rather impatient." Such a move would have two other advantages. First, it would open a supply line from New Orleans to Grant's army, south of the river fortress. The second, left unspoken, was that it would get McClernand out of the way.

On 14 April Grant again wrote Banks that he would send him a corps by the 25th. Undoubtedly, Grant was still considering sending McClernand, who informed Grant that he was in a position to cooperate with Banks. Dana, however, reported to Stanton that Grant would go to Port Hudson personally and take McPherson's corps with him; McClernand would be left behind to garrison Grand Gulf.[30] In either case, McClernand would be rid of Grant, and vice versa. If he were to reinforce Banks, McClernand would be serving under a politician like himself, who might have a similar outlook on military service. But he would still not be independent, for Banks would outrank even Grant until 1864. If McClernand were to remain at Grand Gulf, perhaps he could operate independently for several months.

While at Grand Gulf, Grant finally heard from Banks. He was on the Red River and would not be near Port Hudson until 10 May, and then with a force too small to capture the fortification. To await Banks would delay further the capture of Vicksburg and give Pemberton even more time to strengthen its defenses and receive reinforcements. Grant could not wait. He wrote Halleck, not mentioning Port Hudson but simply informing him that he would "not stop until Vicksburg is in our possession."[31] He could not shed McClernand so easily.

Grant's plan was to move his army northeast toward the Southern Railroad of Mississippi that connected Jackson and Vicksburg. By using the Big Black River to screen his left flank, he would reach that railroad somewhere between Bolton and Edwards Station. There he would achieve a central position between the two Confederate cities and would be able to concentrate against a foray from one town while blocking any movement from the other. McPherson's corps would move along the road closest to the river, McClernand's on the road from Willow Springs to Rocky Springs; Sherman, who on 1 May had been ordered to return from his demonstration near Haynes' Bluff, was to divide his corps between both roads. The commander of the Thirteenth Corps issued detailed orders for his divisions and included in them the vital information as to the location of McPherson's corps, which would be moving almost parallel to the Thirteenth a few miles to the west. Such information could preclude the possibility of the two forces clashing and inflicting casualties on one another.[32]

Grant ordered no movement on 4 May. The Thirteenth Corps was to reconnoiter the road toward Jackson to determine the presence of enemy forces. Grant's usual aggressiveness was tempered by his belief that sixty thousand Confederates were in the Vicksburg–Grand Gulf–Haynes' Bluff–Jackson area. To counter them he had only thirty thousand bluecoats.[33]

From his headquarters at Willow Springs, McClernand spent most of 4 May querying Grant about rations and wagons and providing him intelligence regarding the enemy. Early that morning Grant informed his corps commander that Grand Gulf would be the supply base for the army. McClernand reminded him that he still had no wagons to move supplies forward and that he was almost out of rations. He complained that priority of movement across the Mississippi was being given to Sherman, while he was forced to supply his entire corps with only three wagons. He asked Grant to detail a hundred wagons from McPherson to convey rations to his men. He reminded Grant he was deficient in cavalry because of Grant's orders before crossing the Mississippi. Furthermore, as he was unable to move the arms collected at Port Gibson, he informed Grant, they would have to be left behind or destroyed.

There was more to McClernand's correspondence than simply concern about logistics: he also reported enemy movements in the area. A sizeable Rebel force was reported to be just north of the Big Black, and four steamers were supposedly at Hall's Ferry, about twelve miles from Willow Springs. He ordered Osterhaus to send a force to destroy them and, as he had done on the Louisiana side, even accompanied the detachment part of the way. On 5 May Osterhaus reported the vessels had been moved farther up the Big Black. The next day, McClernand notified Grant that a prisoner had reported eighty thousand Rebels at Vicksburg but that neither Edwards Station nor Jackson was fortified.

Other details occupied his attention. He expressed concern to Grant about safety for the wounded as they were moved by ambulance from the front back to Grand Gulf. Also, and despite rather leisurely movements since

1 May, soldiers still straggled from their commands. To remedy this problem, he directed commanders to appoint details to round up everyone who fell out of ranks and return them to their units. Except for the problem of rations at Bruinsburg, McClernand continued to pay attention to the logistical details of managing his command, as well as remaining attuned to the operational details of searching for the elusive enemy.[34]

Meanwhile, Dana continued to send Stanton derogatory reports regarding McClernand. Since 12 April he had been criticizing the corps commander's performance to the secretary of war. Although Stanton's rebuke on 16 April temporarily silenced the criticism, by 27 April Dana was again launching his attacks. His dispatch of 5 May was particularly vicious. "But for the exceeding incompetency of General McClernand, and the delay thence arising, the movement from Bruinsburg in this direction must have resulted in the capture of 5,000 instead of about 700 rebels."[35]

There was no factual basis for Dana's charge. True, failure to ensure rations were issued prior to the amphibious assault had delayed McClernand's advance for four hours, but he had still pushed ahead to Port Gibson until after midnight. He had fought and won a battle against an enemy force in terrain that greatly favored the defense, and he had followed Grant's orders and moved only as fast as Grant desired the army to move. Any delay should actually be attributed to Grant, who was undecided about whether Vicksburg or Port Hudson should be the objective, and who was attempting to find a solution to the difficult problem of supplying his army in enemy territory. In essence, Dana's personal dislike for McClernand, probably influenced by officers on Grant's staff, affected the accuracy and tone of his reporting to Stanton. Those reports undoubtedly found their way to Halleck and Lincoln.

The Illinois political general had demonstrated many times that he would not be rolled over by real or imagined enemies, and Dana's missives were no exception. On 6 May he again wrote Lincoln a letter in which he extolled his role and that of his men. He complained about Halleck. Although he struck out one sentence—"Such personalities are too small"—he left another: "I can see nothing to justify such invidiousness."[36] Even deep in Rebel territory, McClernand's feud with the Union high command continued.

In accordance with Grant's orders, McClernand reached Rocky Springs on 6 May. The following day he reported his dispositions to Grant. The corps commander was well aware that the Confederates could use the many streams in the region as obstacles to delay the Union advance. Accordingly, after a personal reconnaissance of the area to his north, he posted pickets to watch Hall's Ferry, placed a brigade across Big Sand Creek to secure that bridgehead, and encamped the remainder of the Ninth Division and the

Fourteenth Division on the near side. He placed Hovey's Twelfth Division along Little Sand Creek to reinforce the other divisions if necessary and to guard against any Confederate forays from the direction of Utica.

He also continued to stress his lack of wagons for providing food and ammunition to his corps, and he blamed Sherman, whose corps was then crossing the Mississippi, for appropriating steamers that should have been used to ferry the wagons of the Thirteenth Corps. Most importantly, he reported to Grant that Confederates "in strong force" appeared to be reinforcing and fortifying Edwards Station. He added, "The political consequences of the impending campaign will be momentous."[37] It was, indeed, a gratuitous comment.

Grant responded by directing the Thirteenth Corps to move on 8 May to Auburn—about eleven miles distant—with one division and to place the others between Auburn and Baldwin's Ferry, about seven miles to the northwest. McPherson was to move his corps east of McClernand's. This maneuver placed the Thirteenth Army Corps on the left flank of the advancing Army of the Tennessee, with the responsibility of preventing any Confederate attacks from the west. As Pemberton's Confederates were concentrated to the north and northwest of the Union force, this was indeed a heavy responsibility.

Grant also responded to McClernand's demands for logistical support. Grant directed his subordinate (McClernand) to supply each man with three days' rations and to send wagons and teams back to Grand Gulf along with a statement of his requirements. He was not to move toward Auburn until this had been accomplished. Sherman would protect the movement of supplies in the rear.[38]

Early on 8 May, Grant changed McClernand's route. Instead of moving to Auburn, the corps was redirected along the Telegraph Road toward Edwards Station. This simple change indicated the difficulty of operating in a region unfamiliar to the Union army. Grant directed the corps to take the Telegraph Road north about one-half mile beyond Cayuga. McClernand responded that a local negro had said the road actually went north about seven miles beyond Cayuga, even beyond Auburn. He also provided Grant valuable intelligence that Confederates were massing along the Southern Railroad of Mississippi between Edwards Station and Bolton.

The army did not move that day; instead, Grant and McClernand reviewed Osterhaus's, Carr's, and Hovey's divisions. One of McClernand's staff officers wrote, "The woods reverberated with their shouts of applause." It was a similar review for Governor Yates that had led to Dana's reports to Stanton alleging unwarranted delay. This review, however, prompted no similar missive. Early the next morning, McClernand sent a party to reconnoiter the road network near Cayuga.[39]

Logistics continued to hamper the movement of the Thirteenth Corps as well as that of the entire army. The army could obtain some subsistence from the countryside, but ammunition and additional rations had to come overland by wagon from Grand Gulf. Not until 2:00 P.M. on 8 May did ammunition wagons leave Grand Gulf for McClernand's corps, and rations were not expected until the following morning. McClernand queried Grant as to whether he should move forward anyway or wait until he had sufficient rations. If he was not to move, he informed Grant, he would send a detachment to reconnoiter Hall's Ferry, about eight miles away by road.[40]

The Thirteenth Corps did not move on 9 May, either; logistical shortcomings again delayed the march. Although a wagon train had arrived late the evening before, the rations would not be distributed throughout the corps until early on the 10th. At that time McClernand informed Grant he would comply with his latest order, to move toward Five Mile Creek. The only movement, however, was A. J. Smith's division, which rejoined the corps at Big Sand Creek after having been in reserve along Little Sand Creek.

McClernand continued to provide intelligence to the army commander. One report placed ten thousand Confederates to the south at Utica and another small force, which had since retired, at Cayuga. Both forces were actually scouting parties, attempting to locate the Union army and determine its line of march.[41]

By early 10 May, Thirteenth Corps haversacks and cartridge boxes were full; the soldiers broke camp and moved out. McClernand established his headquarters at Cayuga, and forward elements occupied positions along Five Mile Creek. Grant instructed his fellow Illinoisan to remain in position in order to allow McPherson and Sherman to draw abreast of the Thirteenth Corps, which would continue to protect the left of the army. These moves would position the Army of the Tennessee about twelve miles from the Southern Railroad. He also was to scout toward Fourteen Mile Creek, about seven miles closer to the Confederates forming at Edwards Station.

McClernand continued to complain about the lack of transportation. Finally Grant had had enough. In a sharp rebuke, he noted that the available transportation, "to say nothing of the large number of mules mounted by soldiers, would carry . . . five days' rations . . . if relieved of the knapsacks, officers, soldiers, and negroes now riding. You should take steps to make the means at hand available for bringing up the articles necessary for your corps." He went on to note that the Thirteenth Corps was being treated no differently in this matter than the others.[42]

After the short move of 10 May, the Thirteenth Corps halted again for a day, as instructed, while Sherman and McPherson marched their corps to bring them closer into an east-west alignment with McClernand. In accordance with Grant's directive to reconnoiter toward Fourteen Mile Creek, McClernand dispatched a combined-arms force of infantry, cavalry, and artillery to determine enemy positions as well as ascertain possible locations for a corps encampment near the creek. The forces probed the road north toward Edwards Station and northeast toward Raymond. The party moving north encountered the enemy about a half mile from the creek and decided to withdraw. Grant was moving cautiously and had written Halleck that his movements toward the creek were being conducted "without bringing on a general engagement." Confederate pickets along the Raymond Road scattered at the approach of the Union men. These reports convinced Grant that Pemberton was expecting the Army of the Tennessee and was picketing stream crossings to determine the line of approach. Both McClernand and McPherson reported that water was scarce in the area. The Confederates could, therefore, be expected to deny the water in Fourteen Mile Creek to the Union soldiers as long as possible.[43]

McClernand did not neglect the army's left flank, for which he was responsible. Further reconnaissance uncovered a road that the Confederates were attempting to open between Baldwin's Ferry and Hall's Ferry, along Big Black River. Such a road would enable Pemberton to move a sizeable force quickly against the Union flank and rear. McClernand suggested to Grant that units be detached to guard those ferries against that possibility. He also suggested that the entire army shift left and move closer to the river and farther away from Jackson.[44]

Grant was not ready to abandon his broad-front approach to the Confederates gathered along the Southern Railroad. He did, however, heed McClernand's warning and directed Sherman to station a regiment at Hall's Ferry and McClernand to guard Baldwin's Ferry. He also ordered the Thirteenth Corps to move along two roads toward Fourteen Mile Creek—one being the main road between Auburn and Edwards Station, the other to the west of that road. In effect, the division moving along the western road would serve as a flank guard for the entire army.[45]

McClernand issued orders for movement on 12 May. The objective would be Fourteen Mile Creek. Hovey was directed to lead out at 4:00 a.m., followed by Carr and then Osterhaus. The comprehensive order also specified the order of march for the trains and ambulances, and it provided for guards to prevent their capture or destruction. Hovey was to command all the cavalry, which was to protect the column from surprise. Smith's Tenth Division was to move along the westernmost road and protect the corps from attack across Big Black River, specifically at Baldwin's Ferry. To ensure that the

Thirteenth Corps formed a continuous front with Sherman's Fifteenth Corps, McClernand informed his division commanders that Sherman's left would tie in with his right along the road from Auburn to Edwards Station.[46]

About 5:30 A.M., Hovey's division stepped onto the road to Edwards Station. Each man carried eighty cartridges, double the normal amount. Confederates had contested Osterhaus's scouts at Fourteen Mile Creek the day before, and McClernand wanted to be prepared should they again try to block his way. The 2d Illinois Cavalry preceded the infantry and, indeed, encountered Rebel fire south of the creek. Reinforcements from Hovey's two lead brigades finally drove the Confederates back across the creek at Whitaker's Ford at 11:00 A.M. McClernand so notified Grant and indicated that he intended to establish a bridgehead with one division north of the creek. This message probably crossed the one from Grant to his corps commander requesting him to push one division across the creek. Grant also ordered him to establish communications with Sherman so as to preclude gaps in the Union front and to prepare fords for crossing the stream the next day. Uncharacteristically, McClernand included in his message a statement that he believed "this course of action will meet with your approbation."[47] Perhaps he sensed that he was out of favor with the army commander.

Smith's division encountered a Confederate outpost at Montgomery's Bridge across Fourteen Mile Creek as it advanced along the corps's left flank. Smith captured the bridge intact and established a strong bridgehead north of the stream. The bulk of his division bivouacked south of the bridge.[48]

McClernand's dispositions the night of 12 May were in full compliance with Grant's orders and were tactically sound. On the left, Smith was protecting the crossing at Montgomery's bridge with a small force but keeping most of his force south of the stream to guard against any attack from Baldwin's Ferry. The other divisions of the Thirteenth Corps were across the obstacle of Fourteen Mile Creek, preparing fords for the wagons that were following. They were in an excellent position to continue the march toward Edwards Station, only four miles distant.

Grant suddenly changed the plan. On 12 May McPherson encountered and defeated a determined Confederate force at Raymond. Unfortunately for the Confederates, Pemberton believed those Union forces were only a weak feint; they were actually an entire corps. On the Union side, this turn of events forced Grant to reconsider the situation. A Confederate force of unknown size had attacked his right flank; there were reports that Rebel reinforcements were arriving in Jackson; the city was a significant communications hub; and there was intelligence that Joe Johnston was soon to take command of all forces near the Mississippi capital. Considering all this, together with reports from Sherman and McClernand, Grant realized he was between two Confederate armies. He would first take on Johnston to secure his rear and then march against Pemberton.[49]

Couriers rode rapidly to the three corps commanders with new orders for the 13th. McPherson was to move at 4:00 A.M. for Clinton and Jackson, "to take the Capitol of the state and work from there westward." Sherman was to march through Raymond toward Jackson, so that two corps would be available for the fight. McClernand was to march three of his divisions to Raymond as a reserve. His fourth division was to go to Auburn to escort and protect wagons that were moving up from Grand Gulf.[50]

Adam Badeau would later assert that Grant had actually decided upon this course of action as early as 7 May and that Sherman and McPherson understood the army would probably move toward Jackson. McClernand, however, was not informed of this possibility. According to Badeau, Grant placed McClernand on the left of the army so that his would not be the corps conducting the operation against the Mississippi capital. This was done because "Grant feared to entrust McClernand with an independent expedition, which the movement against Jackson seemed likely to prove. McClernand was sure always to claim the most important position or command, but as he was now really nearer the great bulk of the rebel army, he had no reason to complain." In his memoirs, however, Grant was to state that it was not until McPherson's victory at Raymond on 12 May that he decided to attack Jackson. Prior to that he had intended only to get to the railroad and then drive west to Vicksburg. As the campaign turned out, Grant directed the movements of Sherman and McPherson against Jackson, so there was no "independent expedition" by anyone.[51] Nevertheless, Badeau's comment indicates McClernand's status within Grant's headquarters.

McClernand notified Grant he would comply "promptly" with his new orders but added a concern that his flank and rear would be vulnerable to attack from Confederates along the Southern Railroad. To protect his withdrawal, McClernand issued a detailed order that directed Hovey's division to feint toward Edwards Station. While Confederate attention was drawn to that movement, Carr and Osterhaus would begin the march to Raymond. After they crossed Bakers Creek, about two miles to the east, they would establish a defensive position to await Hovey. The trains would take a roundabout route to prevent them from interfering with troop movements. The corps escaped unscathed from its exposed position, with only Hovey's rear guard having clashed with Confederate patrols. Smith destroyed Montgomery's Bridge, to slow any Confederates who attempted to follow his division.

McClernand was also concerned about the detachments that had been posted to watch Baldwin's Ferry.[52] Should he remove them, thus depriving him of early warning of Confederate movements, or should he leave them and risk their capture? He decided to withdraw them. This was a justifiable decision. Clearly Grant believed the main threat to be from Johnston at Jackson. As he would be moving away from Pemberton and his army at Edwards Station and Vicksburg, Grant apparently believed that distance would work to his advantage. McClernand had expressed concern about his flank and rear, which were actually the flank and rear of the entire army, but Grant did not respond to this concern and did not direct that any measures be taken to continue to guard the crossings. Although McClernand had the implied task of protecting the army's rear, Grant should have given more explicit directions as to whether to continue to watch Big Black River or employ cavalry patrols to provide early warning. Apparently Grant concurred with McClernand's decision, for he never commented otherwise.

The reorientation of his corps was a remarkable accomplishment. McClernand had about fifteen thousand men in his three forward divisions, but he was faced by Confederates totaling about twenty-two thousand. A withdrawal in the face of the enemy is an extremely dangerous undertaking, one that must be accomplished with secrecy, deception, and tactical acumen. Had McClernand not conducted the operation with the skill he in fact displayed, the rear of the Army of the Tennessee could have been wrecked. Grant would write that "McClernand withdrew from the front of the enemy . . . with much skill and without loss, and reached his position for the night in good order."[53] This was indeed high praise for a commander who had been the target of so many negative judgments during the campaign.

Carr and Osterhaus reached Raymond about midnight, but Hovey, in the rear, halted at Dillon's plantation, along with McClernand's headquarters.[54] From Raymond, one road ran northeast to Clinton and one east to Jackson. Grant ordered Sherman to Jackson and McPherson, who had reached Clinton that afternoon, also toward the state capital. McClernand was to send one division to Clinton to destroy the railroad, one to a point three or four miles beyond Mississippi Springs toward Jackson, and one to Raymond, from where it could reinforce in either direction. These moves were to commence before dawn, 14 May. The divisions of A. J. Smith (Thirteenth Corps) and Francis Blair (Fifteenth Corps) were expected to be within one day's march of the Thirteenth Corps by the evening of that day.[55]

To ensure that Grant was aware of his dispositions and intentions, McClernand notified the army commander of the receipt of his directive and that his divisions would maintain contact with one another to prevent the Confederates from slipping between them. He also informed Grant of the location of the trains being guarded by Smith and Blair, as well as of his order to withdraw the guards from Baldwin's Ferry. Intelligence indicated that Rebels were massing at Edwards Station, and McClernand so advised Grant.[56]

Communications within an army in the face of an enemy are critical, and McClernand obviously understood this principle. This message communicated his present situation, his future intent, critical information regarding supplies for the entire army, and vital intelligence regarding the enemy presence. Although McClernand occasionally committed lapses in attention to detail, such a communication indicated that this general had a good grasp on the importance of keeping his commander informed of the situation.

In a driving rainstorm, soldiers of the Thirteenth Corps began the trek toward Jackson and Clinton. On this mud march Carr was able to cover only about six miles toward Jackson, and Osterhaus only about four miles toward Clinton. McClernand described the endeavor as "the most fatiguing and exhausting day's march that had been made."[57]

Meanwhile, McPherson and Sherman, after marches of about four miles and six miles respectively, encountered Confederate forces on the roads to Jackson. At about 3:00 A.M. Johnston had ordered an evacuation of the city. Delays caused by the storm and swollen streams had allowed most of the Confederates to retire before Union forces arrived. By 4:00 P.M. the two Union corps had forced the rear-guard brigades, commanded by Brig. Gens. John Gregg and William H. T. Walker, out of Jackson.[58]

Grant had now driven off one of the two armies he faced, but Pemberton remained not only as a threat to his rear but also as the obstacle to be overcome if Vicksburg was to be seized. If the remnants of Joe Johnston's force could unite with Pemberton, Grant could find himself in a difficult situation, deep in enemy territory. That junction had to be prevented. Accordingly, he notified McClernand "to make all dispatch," moving his corps toward Bolton "by the most direct road."[59] Such a move would place the Thirteenth Corps squarely on the main road between Vicksburg and the Mississippi capital. Clearly, speed was essential if the Union army was to arrive at the road before Johnston could join Pemberton.

McClernand ordered his divisions to march toward Bolton "by the most direct and practicable route." Remembering his logistical requirements, he told A. J. Smith to "send all the supplies of the Thirteenth Army Corps to Bolton." He then informed Grant that he had issued the necessary orders.[60] Early on 15 May divisions of the Thirteenth Corps began to move, and by 9:00 A.M. Osterhaus was in possession of the town. Evidently Grant was pleased with McClernand's movement, for in his memoirs he was to state that the general had "moved promptly." Uncharacteristically, Badeau described McClernand's move similarly.[61]

McClernand continued to concentrate his corps between Raymond and Bolton. Reconnaissance reported twenty-five thousand Confederates near Edwards Station, eight miles to the west. McClernand ordered his divisions to deploy on the three roads that ran east-west from Jackson to Edwards. These routes placed each division within supporting distance of the other, enabled the corps to advance on a broad front to seek the enemy, and, if he was encountered, to bring maximum combat power to bear. By midnight on 15 May, Hovey was near Bolton on the Jackson Road, Osterhaus and Carr were encamped along the Middle Road west of Raymond, and Smith and Blair had reached Raymond. At that point, McClernand, whose headquarters was at Bolton, had approximately twenty-one thousand Union soldiers available to oppose the Confederates at Edwards Station.[62]

Grant's orders for the following day reached the Thirteenth Corps commander that evening. Unsure of Rebel strength, Grant ordered McClernand to "march so as to feel [out] the force of the enemy . . . without bringing on an engagement unless you feel entirely able to contend with him." Grant also ordered Blair, in effect, to be attached to McClernand for the next day's move. Two of Sherman's three divisions were still in Jackson, destroying the railroad, buildings, and equipment that could be of value to the Confederacy. McPherson had retraced his steps from the capital toward the west, but only one division had reached Bolton that evening. The other halted east of Bolton. If Pemberton struck suddenly, John McClernand would have the only coherent force available to stop a Rebel advance.[63]

McClernand's order to his division commanders for the march on 16 May was extremely detailed. It specified the times at which all were to move-Smith and Blair at 5:00 A.M., the others at 6:00 A.M.—the route each was to take, disposition of the trains, the objective for the movement, and his own location; finally, it directed that each division maintain lateral communications with the others. Every division commander thus knew where the others would be as the corps advanced along the three routes toward Edwards.[64]

The corps commander also informed Grant of his plans and suggested that McPherson be deployed north of the Southern Railroad to block Rebels from fleeing the coming battle in that direction. This was not an outrageous suggestion. In his message on 14 May that informed McClernand of the fall of Jackson, Grant had noted that he expected the defeated Rebels to move north and then back west to link up with Pemberton at Vicksburg. It was not illogical to anticipate Johnston's actually turning south and falling on the

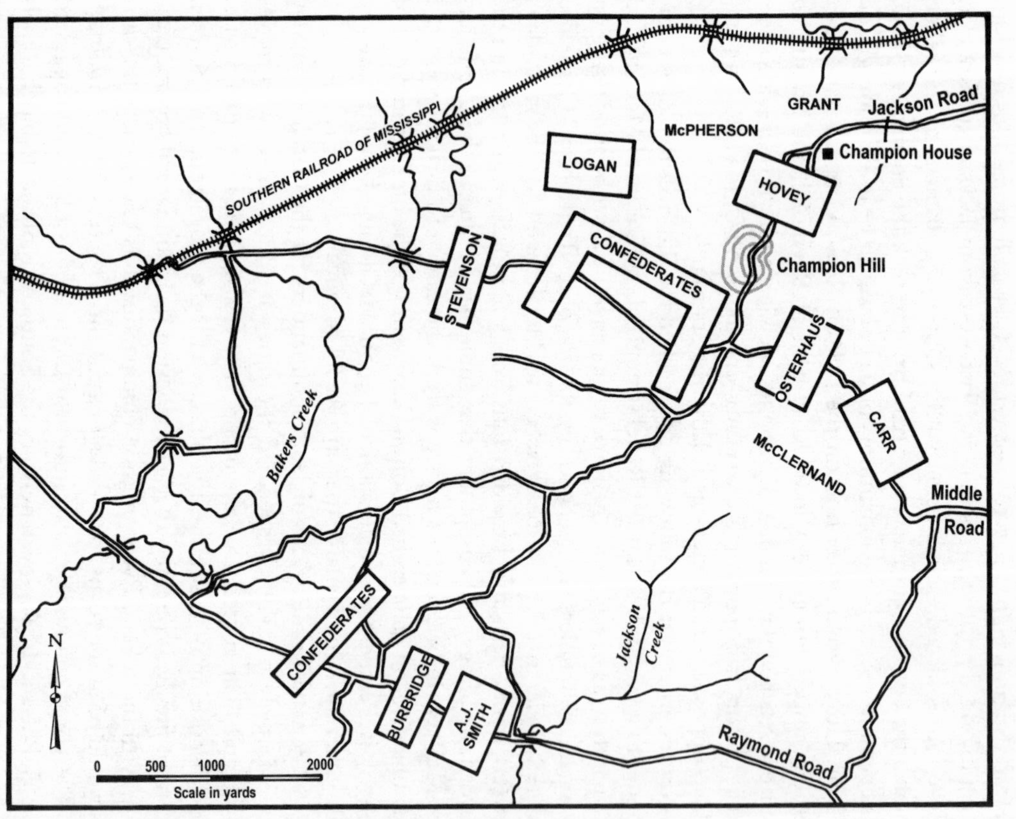

Battle of Champion Hill, May 16, 1863

flank of the Union army between the Mississippi capital and the river fortress. Grant, however, issued no specific instructions for this possibility. Instead, he directed McPherson to move Loring's division with that of Hovey along the northernmost road. Incredibly, Pemberton wrote later that on 16 May he intended to march his army toward Clinton by way of a road north of the railroad.[65]

Early on 16 May Grant received a report that Pemberton had about twenty-five thousand Confederates between Bolton and Vicksburg—a report that was very close to the twenty-three thousand he actually had. At 5:40 A.M. Grant, who was at Clinton, notified McClernand that the enemy had been confirmed as present at Edwards Station. Again he told his corps commander to "feel the enemy" but not to "bring on a general engagement till we are entirely prepared." A second message to McClernand ordered him to have Blair support Osterhaus, "moving forward cautiously." In his memoirs Grant would reiterate that McClernand was "to move cautiously."[66] Whether this directive was because Grant did not want McClernand to become decisively engaged for fear of what his subordinate might do, or whether the army commander was unsure of the enemy dispositions and wanted to gather more forces before a major fight, is unclear. At any rate, there is no question that Grant was concerned about the prospect of facing Pemberton and continuously instilled in his lead corps commander his desire that he exercise extreme caution during the advance.

McClernand's corps was already on the march when its commander received Grant's message. At 6:00 A.M. McClernand rode to McPherson's headquarters to discuss the upcoming battle. He also presented his idea that McPherson should be prepared to hit the Rebel flank and rear after the Thirteenth Corps had driven them back. Although the Seventeenth Corps commander ordered his divisions forward, he also sent a short message to Grant: "I think it advisable for you to come forward to the front as soon as you can."[67] Undoubtedly, McPherson neither trusted McClernand to command the battle nor desired to serve under the Illinois politician.

Shortly after 7:00 A.M. Smith's division encountered Confederates along the Raymond Road. To ensure the divisions on the north knew of Smith's fight, McClernand notified Hovey and McPherson and again suggested he move his divisions north of the railroad and be prepared to attack the Confederate forces in the flank after Hovey had engaged them. Mindful of Grant's order, he urged Hovey to move forward "cautiously but promptly." Osterhaus soon became engaged along the Middle Road. With two of his three forward divisions in contact with the Confederates, and Blair moving to support Smith, McClernand directed Carr to remain as a reserve.[68]

The noise of combat along the Union front continued to increase. Hovey encountered Confederates under Brig. Gen. Stephen D. Lee at about 9:00 A.M. At 9:45 A.M. McClernand received a dispatch from his division commander reporting that Confederate soldiers were strongly posted to his front and asking whether he should bring on a general engagement. McClernand immediately queried Grant: "Shall I hold, or bring on an engagement?" Blair notified Grant that he was "feeling the enemy cautiously" and was attempting to determine the exact locations of Osterhaus, Carr, and Hovey. The corps commander responded to Hovey that he had asked Grant for further instructions, but that he should take advantage of the developing situation "without bringing on a general engagement."[69]

Grant arrived in the vicinity of Hovey's battle along the Jackson Road about ten o'clock. Fifteen minutes later the army commander ordered McClernand to "close up all your forces as expeditiously as possible, but cautiously." He also warned McClernand that information gathered indicated the bulk of the Confederates to be south of Hovey's position. This would place them in the vicinity of the Middle and Raymond Roads. Grant's fear was that Pemberton would be able to slip around the Union flank and get into the army's rear.[70] In fact, Pemberton was indeed attempting to slip around the Union right, not to attack Grant but to join Johnston, who was falling back from Jackson.[71]

Caution characterized Union actions all along the front. In the north, Hovey had developed the Confederate position, but Grant had warned him not to attack until McPherson's lead division, commanded by Maj. Gen. John A. Logan, could support him. McClernand in the center was uncertain of his next move, because of Grant's admonition to exercise caution. On the left, A. J. Smith had halted at Jackson Creek to repair the bridge, and he told Brig. Gen. Stephen Burbridge, his lead brigade commander, to halt until other Union forces were at hand.[72] These delays allowed the Confederates to deploy their outnumbered forces in the most desirable positions to block the Union avalanche.

Despite the terrain and a tenacious defense, Hovey's and Logan's divisions launched ferocious attacks from the north. One of Logan's brigades swept around the Confederate left and crossed the Jackson Road, an action that blocked the Rebel escape route to the west. The Rebel left had been forced back across Champion Hill by Hovey, but a determined Confederate counterattack drove the Union forces back almost to Grant's headquarters. McPherson, unaware that Logan occupied the key Confederate escape route, ordered him to reinforce Hovey's regiments, which were being swept away by the gray tide. A fresh division from McPherson's corps slammed into the exhausted Confederates and soon drove them back over the crest of the hill.[73]

McClernand was in a dilemma. The dense terrain and numerous steep gullies not only prohibited him from extending a continuous line to connect Smith on the left with Osterhaus in the center and Hovey on the right but also prevented him from seeing more than fifty to a hundred yards in any direction. He knew Hovey was heavily engaged but that both McPherson and Grant were present to direct that portion of the battle. Smith was engaged in the south, but Grant had responded to McClernand's request for orders in that regard with another directive to be cautious, plus a warning that the Confederates must not be allowed to envelop the Union left. McClernand ordered Blair and Carr to cover the ground between the Middle and Raymond Roads to prevent the Rebels from penetrating the Union lines in that area, but he still had no definite order to launch a full-scale attack. A slow, cautious advance would place the Union force in an advantageous position to locate the shifting Confederates and stop their attempted envelopment. Even so, the dense terrain prohibited effective employment of artillery and cavalry.[74] An all-out attack could actually be disadvantageous, as it would destroy any cohesiveness along the line, would be unsupported by artillery, and could result in meeting Confederates in prepared positions. In the tangled woods, the Confederates would have a distinct advantage.

Finally, at 12:35 P.M., two and one-half hours since Grant's previous instructions, Grant ordered him to attack the enemy "in force if an opportunity occurs." According to Grant, he sent several such messages to McClernand to urge him to attack. Unlike all previous messages from Grant, this one did not specify caution, but it did have the fateful word "if." Even at this critical point in the battle, Grant could not muster the resolution necessary explicitly to order an attack. Upon receipt of it, McClernand, however, did give a positive order to Smith, Osterhaus, Carr, and Blair to "attack the enemy vigorously." Smith and Osterhaus would lead; Blair and Carr would support.[75]

McClernand's attack occurred about 2:30 P.M. In the Union center, Osterhaus advanced against the center of a disorganized Confederate line that was also being pressed hard by Hovey and McPherson. After a personal reconnaissance, Osterhaus inexplicably halted and asked for reinforcements. McClernand committed two brigades from Carr's division, and Osterhaus again advanced. He continued until he met the Union drive coming from the north, at about 4:00 P.M. In the south, West Point graduate A. J. Smith continued to sit idly while the battle raged to his right. His inaction allowed two Confederate brigades to shift from Smith's front to reinforce the desperate troops facing Hovey and Osterhaus. Even after McClernand dispatched his order to attack, Smith remained in position until about 5:00 P.M., with only the brigade of Brig. Gen. Lloyd Tilghman to his front. Burbridge was furious. In his opinion Smith's corps "could have captured the whole rebel force opposed to us."[76] Whether Smith never received McClernand's order to attack or simply ignored it remains a mystery. His inactivity, though, may have cost Grant the opportunity to destroy the Rebel army then and there. An aggressive attack before the two brigades moved to reinforce those facing Hovey and Osterhaus might have allowed those two Federal divisions to punch through the Confederate line. An attack after they had moved might have allowed Smith to turn north and roll up the entire Rebel army.

In his report dated 6 July Grant wrote, "The delay in the advance of the troops immediately with McClernand was caused, no doubt, by the enemy presenting a front of artillery and infantry where it was impossible, from the nature of the ground and the density of the forest, to discover his numbers." In his memoirs, however, he would take a different tack and blame the army's failure to destroy Pemberton's force on McClernand's failure to advance promptly: "Had McClernand come up with reasonable promptness," he wrote, "I do not see how Pemberton could have escaped with any organized force." Twice he would assert that he repeatedly ordered McClernand to attack, but to no avail. Wilson, too, condemned McClernand's actions. In his view, the corps commander had not "been as active and aggressive as he should have been" and "was so slow and cautious that he did practically nothing."[77]

The timing of McClernand's attack order is important because of these comments. Unquestionably, had McClernand attacked vigorously by 2:00 P.M. with both Osterhaus and Smith, the Confederate army would have been destroyed. Smith easily could have overrun the small force facing him and moved swiftly to cut off the escape route to Vicksburg. Osterhaus could have hit the disorganized Confederates in the center with a devastating blow that, coupled with Logan's position astride the Jackson Road on the Confederate left, quite probably would have led to an encirclement of two Confederate divisions. It appears, however, that McClernand did not receive Grant's attack order until at least 2:00 P.M.; allowing for the time needed to direct his own divisions to attack, it was probably closer to 2:30 P.M. before Osterhaus began moving. Why did it take so long for McClernand to react to Grant's 12:35 P.M. order? Is Grant's criticism justified?

Numerous descriptions of the battlefield indicate the great difficulty of cross-country movement in the vicinity of Champion Hill. Furthermore, commanders could never be certain of where their subordinates were at any given moment. Nor could couriers be certain of where the opposing lines were; they could as easily stumble into the enemy as into friendly forces. Maps were either sketchy or nonexistent. Even the map produced by Grant's chief engineer after the battle failed to include the Middle Road, which was the route of Osterhaus's advance. The area between Jackson and Vicksburg was populated primarily by yeoman farmers, so there would have been few slaves (who would willingly provide directions). In all probability, couriers used the main road network to convey messages between the three columns. This entailed a trip of about ten miles along the roads leading back to Bolton. At a gallop, a horse could cover that distance in about an hour, if the courier knew the way. If he had to ask directions or make turns, of which there were several between the Jackson and Middle Roads, it would take longer. The courier also would have to negotiate his way past troops on the road, which would slow him further. As he approached either McClernand's or Grant's vicinity, additional time would be required to locate the commander. It is for that reason that it can be assumed that Grant's message did not reach McClernand until at least 2:00 P.M. Likewise, it is reasonable to assume that McClernand's 9:45 A.M. message to Grant did not reach him until about 11:15 A.M. Grant did not reply to it until 12:35 P.M. Although it is not crystal clear, from McClernand's report it appears that it was about 2:30 P.M. when he ordered Osterhaus and Smith to attack.[78]

Grant later wrote, "Had I known the ground as I did afterwards," Pemberton would have been destroyed.[79] Undoubtedly this is true, and the Vicksburg campaign would have ended at Champion Hill. Grant should not be harshly criticized for not knowing his way in enemy territory, and McClernand should not be harshly criticized for exercising caution after repeated instructions from Grant to do so.

Although he had been warned by Grant to exercise caution, McClernand still must be criticized for the way he handled his corps even given that restriction. When ordered to attack and did so with Osterhaus and Carr, he should have pushed Osterhaus forward more aggressively. He also should have utilized Carr more effectively, by combining his weight with that of Osterhaus and smashing through Confederate resistance. That Carr's casualties totaled only three wounded indicates how poorly used his division had been. McClernand did not know that Smith was not executing his order, but he could have sent other couriers to ensure that it was being carried out. He did not; Smith failed to push forward, sustaining only twenty-five wounded, and Pemberton's army escaped. Unfortunately for McClernand, his actions at Champion Hill would leave a bitter taste in Grant's mouth.[80]

Relentless Union pressure along the Jackson and Middle Roads caused Pemberton to order a retreat at about 4:00 P.M.[81] After the smashing defeat,

Pemberton withdrew his greatly diminished force about ten miles, to the Big Black River. There he intended to hold the bridge where the Jackson Road crossed that stream until Maj. Gen. William Loring's division, which had become separated during the battle, arrived. McClernand and McPherson pursued, with Carr's relatively fresh division leading the pursuit. Carr and Osterhaus halted about 8:00 P.M. at Edwards Station. Smith and Blair, who McClernand had ordered to hasten forward, bivouacked about three miles southeast of there. Hovey remained behind to bury the dead and tend to the wounded. Grant directed Sherman to march northwest toward Bridgeport to prevent a Confederate withdrawal in that direction, a move about which McClernand had earlier expressed concern.[82]

McClernand continued his aggressive pursuit by rousing Carr and Osterhaus at 3:30 A.M. By contrast, McPherson did not begin his march until six o'clock. As Carr moved toward the river, dawn revealed Confederates dug in on the east side of the Big Black, with that unfordable obstacle in their rear. McClernand immediately ordered him to deploy his brigades north of the railroad and Osterhaus to deploy on the south side. He ordered Smith's division to extend the Union line to the left of Osterhaus. As Grant observed the action, Brig. Gen. Michael K. Lawler suddenly led his brigade in a charge that collapsed the Confederate left. The entire Rebel line disintegrated, as soldiers ran for the railroad bridge and an improvised boat span that crossed the Big Black. In Grant's words, the enemy had been "terribly beaten." His praise, however, was for Lawler, not McClernand.[83]

Carr had no praise for his corps commander, either. In late July he was to assert to Grant that "the battle was fought and won by my division" and that McClernand neither gave him any orders during the day nor came to the front until Grant arrived. Carr had made no mention of this in his initial report to Grant, and Osterhaus wrote no report of the battle. McClernand's role, therefore, is difficult to assess. Carr's relationship with his superior had at times been "disagreeable," and he believed his command had never received the credit it deserved. A careful reading of McClernand's reports, however, indicates otherwise. At Port Gibson the corps commander had reported that Carr's division attacked with "vigor and celerity." At Champion Hill he credited Lawler, of Carr's division, with having "cast the trembling balance in our favor." He also praised Lawler for the victory at Big Black River, though he gave little mention to Carr. McClernand wrote at length of the role of Carr's brigades during the attack of 22 May but, again, mentioned Carr only briefly. He concluded his report, however, with a recommendation that Carr and the other brigadiers be promoted. Although it is impossible to state for certain, it is possible that Carr, who was a West Point graduate and

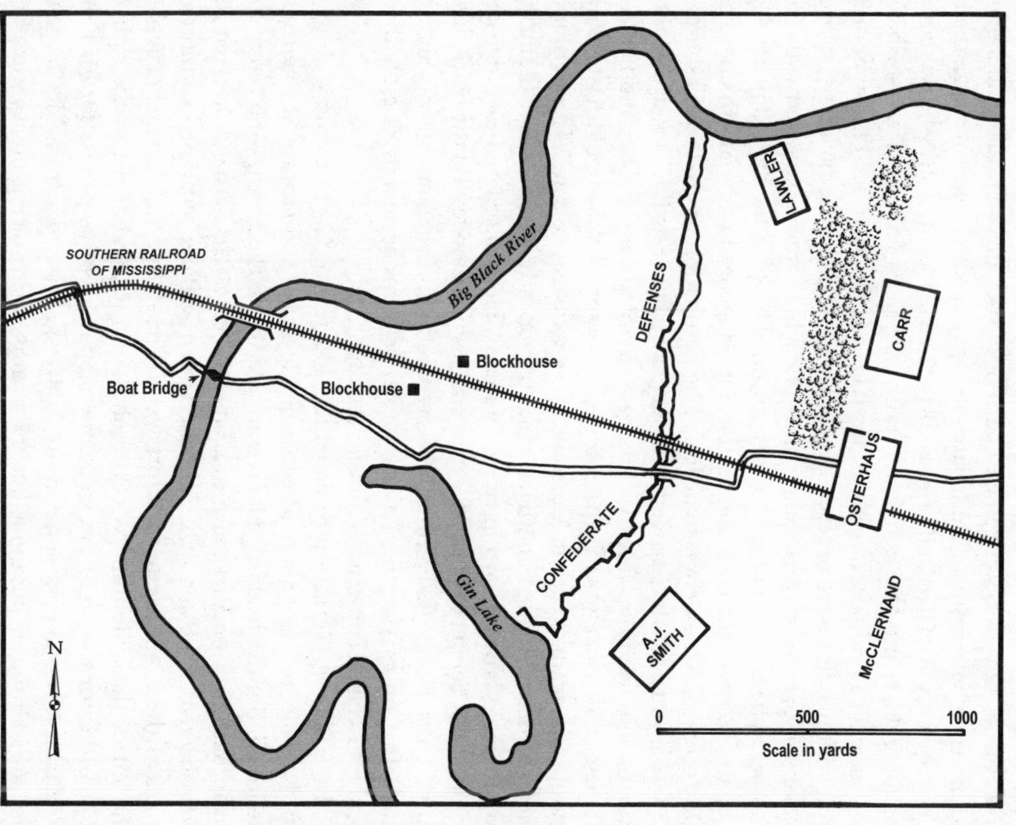

Battle of Big Black River Bridge, May 17, 1863

complained to Grant only after McClernand had left the command, sought to take advantage of the anti-McClernand sentiment at army headquarters and raise his stature with the army commander.[84]

Grant had hoped to capture the railroad bridge intact, and so had ordered his pontoon train, along with Blair's division, to meet Sherman at Bridgeport. The Rebels, however, were able to burn both the railroad bridge and a temporary span built from an old steamer before Union forces could seize them. Consequently, McClernand ordered Brig. Gen. Albert L. Lee, who was commanding the Ninth Division temporarily as a result of a wound to Osterhaus, to construct a bridge as quickly as possible over the obstacle. The other division commanders were ordered to camp in good defensive positions, set out pickets to prevent surprise, and ensure their lines were connected with one another. The corps commander then outlined his plan for the following day. Lee was to cross the river and establish a bridgehead while Smith and then Carr crossed. No time was to be lost. The destination was to be Vicksburg.[85]

Grant ordered McClernand to move "as early as possible" toward Mount Alban, only five miles from Vicksburg—an order that McClernand had anticipated. To Hovey the corps commander wrote: "You should hasten forward," and again, told him "to come up as soon as you can." The fiery former politician smelled another fight. At 7:00 A.M. he informed Grant he would begin crossing within twenty minutes. He also ordered each division to provide a detail to collect the arms and ammunition left on the battlefield. At 7:15 A.M. he notified Smith to be prepared to move momentarily. Shortly thereafter, on 18 May, the Thirteenth Army Corps began crossing the three bridges Lee had constructed during the night.[86]

In his order, Grant had directed the Thirteenth Corps to move along a road parallel to the main road between Vicksburg and Jackson, if one could be found. Smith's lead brigade, reconnoitering to the south, soon found the road that ran from Vicksburg to Baldwin's Ferry. McClernand diverted the corps to that road, and that night the Union soldiers encamped within two miles of the Confederate river fortress of Vicksburg. McClernand occupied the left of the Union line, McPherson the center, and Sherman the right.[87] The order for the night directed commanders to place pickets forward and to establish lateral communications. However, this order from McClernand had an addition: firing guns, beating drums, and blowing bugles were forbidden. To enhance security, fires could be built only in ravines, where they could not be observed. Finally, the soldiers were to be prepared to move forward at 4:00 A.M. the next day. McClernand had no desire for the Confederates to pinpoint his dispositions or determine his numbers. He would be prepared for any eventuality.[88]

In eighteen days the Thirteenth Corps had spearheaded victories at Port Gibson, Champion Hill, and Big Black River, and it was now poised to capture the final prize. McClernand's generalship had been more than adequate. He had handled his corps of four divisions well. His detailed orders had been superb, and he had maneuvered in accordance with the army commander's instructions. He had made mistakes, but none were so serious as to jeopardize the safety of the army. Certainly he could be criticized for his lack of aggressiveness at Champion Hill, but Grant's orders had undoubtedly instilled a cautious approach in his actions. Although he no longer commanded the Mississippi River expedition that he believed should have been his, he was convinced his corps would play a central role in the capture of Vicksburg. It would be the crowning accomplishment of his military career.

The Confederates had had almost a year to prepare the Vicksburg defenses. Engineers had designed a defense that took advantage of the many ravines, steep hills, and canebrakes that surrounded the city. By the time Grant's army arrived at the outskirts of the town, the Rebels had built a semicircular system that was anchored on both flanks by the Mississippi River and that incorporated a series of redoubts, redans, and rifle pits to protect the entrances to the city. Fort Hill and the Water Battery protected the river road; Stockade Redan defended the point in the line where the Graveyard Road entered; the 3d Louisiana Redan and Great Redoubt controlled the Jackson Road; the 2d Texas Lunette commanded the road to Baldwin's Ferry; the line of the Southern Railroad between Vicksburg and Jackson was protected by Railroad Redoubt; and the extreme southern end of the line was defended by Fort Garrott (also known as Square Fort), the Salient Work, and South Fort. Every strong point was connected by trenches and rifle pits, which concealed twenty-three thousand Confederates.

From Durden Creek, early on the morning of 19 May, McClernand observed the Confederate positions. Grant's messages of the previous day had urged haste, and the corps commander ordered his divisions forward from their bivouac sites. Smith deployed to the right of the Baldwin's Ferry Road, Osterhaus to the left, and Carr in reserve about four miles to the rear. Both forward divisions threw out skirmishers, began shelling the Confederate lines, and advanced a short distance to Two Mile Creek.[89]

Grant, "relying upon the demoralization of the enemy, in consequence of repeated defeats outside of Vicksburg," at about 10:30 A.M. directed his three corps commanders "to push forward carefully" and at two o'clock to launch a general attack all along the line. McClernand forwarded the order to his division commanders. Of Porter, Grant asked that he shell the city, to "demoralize an already badly beaten enemy." Clearly, Grant believed one giant push would crack the Confederate defenses. Porter, however, was pessimistic: Grant "will have the hardest fight ever seen during the war."[90]

At 2:00 P.M., at the signal of three artillery rounds being fired, the entire army moved forward. McClernand notified the army commander that he was advancing. At that time the infantry was on a line about a thousand yards from the Vicksburg fortifications. As they crossed the ridge along Two Mile Creek and then a smaller ridge known as Porters Chapel Ridge, they came under intense artillery and rifle fire from all along the Rebel line. They halted and hunkered down behind the protection of the small ridge to their front. The advance was able to get no closer than four to five hundred yards to the Vicksburg lines. The 13th United States Infantry, from Sherman's corps, reached the ditch in front of Stockade Redan, but was then forced to withdraw. One of McPherson's divisions reached Confederate entrenchments near 3d Louisiana Redan, but it too was driven back. Nightfall found his corps dug in between four hundred and eight hundred yards from the Vicksburg defenses. Grant's idea of a hasty attack against "the demoralized enemy" had failed. Over the ground lay 934 dead and wounded Union soldiers. Of those, a hundred were from the Thirteenth Corps, 129 from the Seventeenth, and 704 from Sherman's Fifteenth Army Corps.[91]

That evening Sherman wrote his wife, "Grant is off to the left with McClernand who did not push his attack as he should."[92] Had McClernand pushed the attack strongly? McClernand's personal reconnaissance had revealed the difficulty of the terrain to his front. From his vantage point, the commander knew his corps would have to cross a mile of ground covered with thick brambles and scored by innumerable gullies. Once his forces climbed out of the bottomland of Durden Creek, they would be exposed to cannon fire from twelve-pound Napoleons and other guns of the brigades of Brig. Gens. John Moore and Stephen Lee. From Durden Ridge McClernand's corps artillery would be firing at its maximum range. In the maze of ravines, it would be impossible to move the guns forward to support the advancing soldiers; the infantry would be on its own. On 19 May the two divisions thrown against the fortifications would be insufficient to achieve a breakthrough.

What about Carr? If McClernand had committed his reserve, might there have been a breakthrough? Generally, the purpose of a reserve is to exploit success, not to redeem failure. The two attacking divisions had not achieved success. They had suffered only a hundred casualties, but they had not gotten close to the Rebel defenses. Sherman's two divisions had gotten close, but at the cost of over seven hundred men. Throwing Carr's division into the melee would only have added to the mass of men thrashing through the canebrakes and attempting to climb out of the steep ravines. The entire Union army was executing a frontal assault with no attempt at finesse or probing for weak points. There was no designated main attack or supporting attack. Gen. J. F. C. Fuller later calculated that only one in eight frontal assaults during the Civil War succeeded.[93] There is little reason to believe that in this case one additional division would have caused the breakthrough to be achieved.

Neither Sherman's nor McPherson's soldiers had made significant gains against the dug-in Confederates. Each faced the same problem as McClernand—cleared ridge tops exposed to enemy fire and tangled gullies that impeded an orderly assault. Although their corps may have gotten closer to the Vicksburg entrenchments, neither was able to maintain his forward position. It should be noted that fault can be found with each of these attacks. Sherman had not ensured his attacking forces had scaling ladders; upon reaching the ditches in front of the forts, they were unable to climb out of them. Also, only one of McPherson's brigades reached its desired line of departure by the two o'clock attack time.[94] Failure cannot be laid at the feet of McClernand alone.

As the Thirteenth Corps took up defensive positions, several matters occupied the commander. Hovey was still at the Big Black River. McClernand, not knowing what the next day would bring, ordered him forward "as rapidly as possible." Hovey, however, was encumbered by four thousand prisoners and 3,400 stands of arms. He requested that McClernand allow him to start early on 20 May rather than continue to march toward Vicksburg the night of the 19th. Another concern was provisions. The army had existed on meager rations for several weeks, but now that Sherman's right was anchored on the Mississippi, supplies could be brought in by boat. Upon being notified by Grant that wagons were being made available, McClernand ordered his staff to see that supplies were drawn for the corps. Next, he addressed the details of establishing a defensive position. Stragglers were to be brought in; ammunition for infantry and artillery was to be distributed; defensive works were to be built; and, as previously, care was to be taken to prevent the enemy from learning their exact positions from bugles, drums, and fires. Lastly, he informed his divisions where he would be for the evening.[95] With that, the Thirteenth Corps, and the Army of the Tennessee, settled in for the night.

On 20 and 21 May Union forces consolidated their positions and reconnoitered to their front. Although Grant met with his three corps commanders on the 20th and directed that a coordinated attack be conducted on 22 May, apparently he issued no specific orders for actions to be taken in the interim. Each commander was to spend the meantime preparing for the upcoming assault.[96] The mistakes made during the hasty attack on 19 May would be rectified as the command prepared for the deliberate assault on the 22d. As with the first assault, however, the second would also be over a broad front.

McClernand did not agree with Grant's plan and submitted his objections in writing. The communique expressed great concern over the formidable earthworks to his front, and it was pessimistic that an attack along an extended front could carry them. Instead, he proposed concentrating the army against one or several points along the line thus overwhelming them with superior mass. A siege appeared the only realistic alternative to his plan.[97]

Grant disagreed and, consequently, McClernand began preparations for another attack. As he surveyed the ground, he recognized that Railroad Redoubt was the key position within his sector. That redoubt and the 2d Texas Lunette to its north protecting the Baldwin's Ferry Road guarded the only reasonably flat avenue of approach into the Confederate line. The remainder of the defenses were protected by the ravines and canebrakes, reinforced with abatis, that had stymied the army's advance on 19 May. It was not a great avenue of approach, but it was better than anything else available. To succeed, McClernand would have to move his forces closer to the Confederate lines prior to the attack. His men could not remain exposed to the fire that had engulfed them earlier and still gain the Rebel trenches.

A. J. Smith's division had occupied the ridge about four hundred yards from the 2d Texas Lunette after the hasty attack on 19 May. Unless McClernand could occupy its defenders, soldiers attacking the Railroad Redoubt would be exposed to continuous fire into their flank. Consequently, on 20 May he ordered Smith to attack at 2:00 P. M. and seize a position from which he could enfilade the Rebels in the lunette.[98]

Sherman and McPherson, too, adjusted their positions in front of the Rebel works, but there was little coordination among the three corps commanders or direction from Grant. McClernand notified McPherson, who was on his right, of his intention to attack and requested that McPherson's corps protect his flank "if the enemy should move out to attack." Grant told McPherson to inform Sherman, to his right, if he intended to attack so Sherman could protect his flank. As Smith advanced, McClernand notified Grant of his progress and requested McPherson's support. Grant wrote back that McPherson also was attacking and that he could see Smith. The implication of this was that McClernand need not worry about his flank.[99]

One of McClernand's messages to Grant during Smith's attack raised the question of the true objective of the assault. In this message he wrote: "I . . . am pressing for a sharp engagement up to the enemy's works." Brig. Gen.

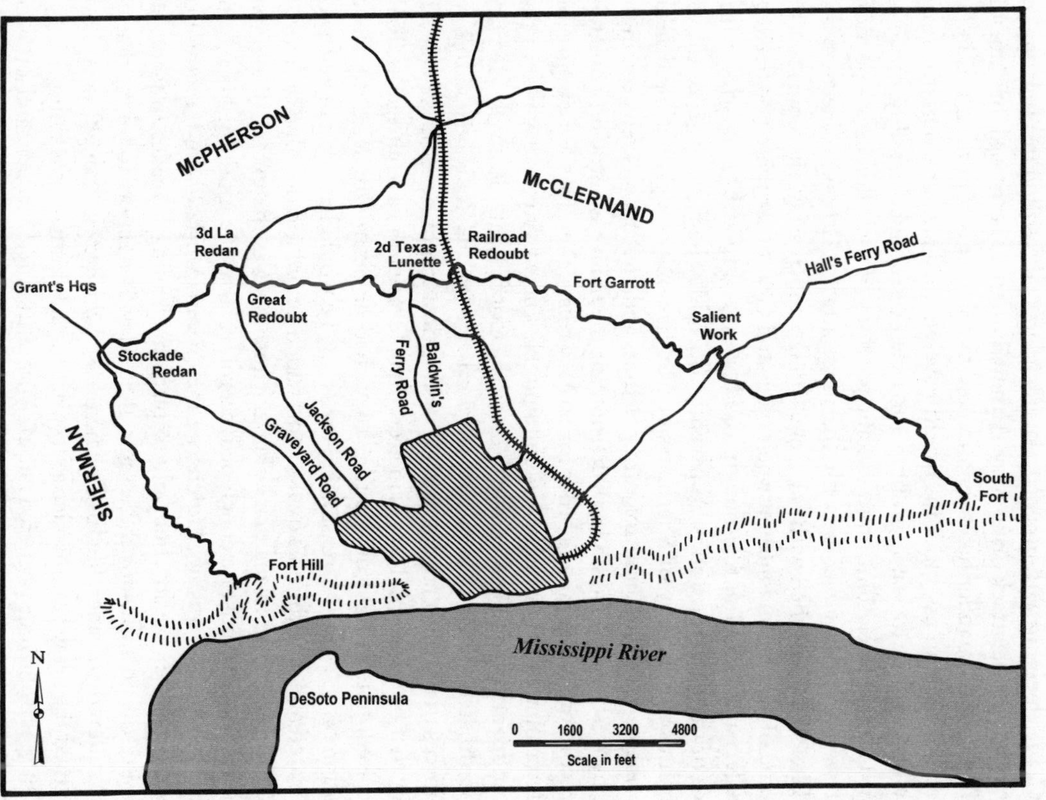

Vicksburg Defenses

Stephen G. Burbridge, whose brigade led the attack, stated in his report that he was ordered "to charge the enemy's works."[100] There is a considerable difference between a limited operation to gain favorable jumping-off positions and an attack on the enemy's works. What was the mission of Smith's attack?

Grant's meeting with his corps commanders had resulted in a warning order to renew the attack on 22 May. Although there is no record, presumably each corps commander had been directed to ensure his command was in position for such an assault. This would have entailed straightening the lines, moving artillery forward, probing for weaknesses, and, possibly, feints to draw Confederate attention to specific portions of their defenses—portions that would not be objectives for the main attack. Although Sherman and McPherson skirmished with the Rebels on 20 and 21 May, there was not the volume of correspondence between them and Grant that there was between McClernand and Grant, although McPherson did report being within fifty yards of the Rebel positions. Apparently, Burbridge had got closer to the entrenchments than any of Sherman's or McPherson's troops, but his brigade was unable to remain in its forward positions and, indeed, was replaced in the line by fresh troops from Carr's division for the main assault. Unfortunately, no record of McClernand's order for 20 May exists; therefore, it is impossible to determine exactly what he had in mind. He knew from the day before that the entire army had been unable to crack the Confederate defenses. He knew a coordinated attack was not planned until 22 May. He knew he had to have his forces in the most advantageous possible position prior to the assault. He knew that fire from 2d Texas Lunette would devastate an assault against Railroad Redoubt. In light of what he knew, had he desired to seize the Rebel position on 20 May, it is reasonable to assume he would have conducted a coordinated attack within his own sector, which he did not do. One of his staff officers even wrote in his diary that skirmishing was the extent of the two days' fighting. It must be concluded, therefore, that the intent of his actions on 20 and 21 May was not "to charge the enemy's works" with the intent of penetrating the position but only to place his leading brigades in favorable jumping-off positions for the assault of 22 May. His report to Grant that he had "suffered considerable loss" as he pressed the attack, though, must have mystified the army commander as to what his subordinate was doing.[101]

Only skirmishing occurred on 21 May. Although McClernand ordered Smith to continue his attack of the previous day, Smith, displaying the same lethargy he had exhibited at Champion Hill, "fooled around all day and finally didn't do it at all."[102]

Communications between Grant and McClernand continued to be strained as indicated by an incident that occurred on 20 May. The day before, Grant had directed Hovey, without informing McClernand, to guard the bridges over the Big Black River. He stated this order "was of the highest importance." Hovey received that message early 20 May, but he did not receive McClernand's 19 May message until after Grant's directive. Perhaps aware of previous disputes between his two higher commanders regarding orders, Hovey informed Grant that he had been ordered to the front, that the bridges would be unguarded, and that he was "bound to presume that this is in accordance with your orders." Grant immediately ordered Hovey to send one brigade back to guard the bridges.[103] With no orders to the contrary, McClernand had acted appropriately. The main fight would be at Vicksburg, and McClernand realized from the resistance on 19 May that he would need every available soldier for the next attempt to take the Confederate works. Hovey's confusion can only be attributed to Grant, who failed to keep McClernand informed of the army commander's intentions regarding the Twelfth Division. According to the diary of one soldier, this incident led to rumors that Grant had relieved McClernand from command.[104] Although the rumors were false, the acrimony between the two most senior officers in the Army of the Tennessee continued to increase.

McClernand continued to inform the army commander of his operations. So that the army was not surprised from the rear, McClernand dispatched cavalry patrols toward Hall's and Baldwin's Ferries, and he forwarded to Grant reports from Hovey's brigade near Big Black River bridge.[105] The Union left's rear would be protected.

On 21 May McClernand was summoned to army headquarters. There Grant issued an order to his corps commanders. At 10:00 A.M. the following day, the army would launch a simultaneous attack all along the line. Both Sherman and McClernand voiced concern over the concept of the operation. Sherman was concerned about losses, while McClernand again proposed massing the army against a few points rather than spreading it across the entire front. Grant, however, was confident that his course "would carry Vicksburg in a very short time." The Thirteenth Corps commander returned to his headquarters and issued the implementing order to his command. Each division commander was to select his most favorable axis of advance, but approval lay with the corps commander. Units would advance in column along those axes, rather than attempt to maintain a linear formation through the dense underbrush, ravines, and abatis. Although McClernand sought to encourage his troops with a reminder of the victories at Port Gibson, Champion Hill, and Big Black River, few soldiers were cheered. As he observed the Confederate fortifications, one wrote, "Our brigade and regimental officers look sad . . . and my heart is much depressed when meditating upon our duty for the morrow."[106]

9
End of the Line

Few soldiers in McClernand's corps slept the night of 21 May 1863. According to one participant, many "were busy divesting themselves of watches, rings, pictures and their keepsakes, which were being placed in the custody of the cooks, who were not expected to go into action." These would be sent to the loved ones of those who did not return.[1] Not only was there the usual tension before an attack, but Union pickets reported Confederates possibly preparing for a night attack. Grant ordered the Thirteenth Corps to be alert and prepared "to push immediately into the city and fall upon the rear of the enemy" should the opportunity arise. Pemberton did not attack, but the night was filled with the intermittent booming of artillery as the Union cannon sought to interrupt any massing of Confederates for an attack.[2]

For good reason, McClernand feared a Confederate attack between his left and the Mississippi. That portion of the Union line was thinly manned, and a strong attack might roll up the Union line. At Fort Donelson, his division had been victimized by just such a maneuver. To preclude that possibility, McClernand ordered the 2d Illinois Cavalry to cover the area with pickets and to build fires along the line to deceive the Rebels into thinking it was fully manned. McClernand also notified Grant of his concern about a Confederate attack upon his vulnerable left flank. What McClernand could not know was that Pemberton had no plan to assault that thinly held portion of the Union position.[3]

Grant too was concerned about the Union left. One brigade of McPherson's Sixth Division, commanded by Brig. Gen. John McArthur, was at Warrenton, south of Vicksburg. Grant ordered him to move up the river and attack the city. Such a movement would not only occupy the Confederates at South Fort but fill the gap on McClernand's left.[4]

McClernand arranged his Thirteenth Corps as follows: Hovey's one brigade was on the left (the other having been left to guard the Big Black

River crossings); next came Osterhaus's division, which faced Fort Garrott (or Square Fort); to his right Carr deployed his two brigades on line—Lawler to attack Railroad Redoubt, and Benton to attack 2d Texas Lunette; after Landrum's brigade from Smith's division was stacked behind Lawler; Smith's other brigade, commanded by Burbridge, occupied the extreme right of the corps line.[5]

At daybreak, 22 May, the Thirteenth Corps artillery batteries opened on the Confederate works that faced the Union divisions. For four hours the guns pounded gray-clad soldiers, who tried to hide behind the earthen embankments. Precisely at 10:00 A.M., the Union soldiers of McClernand's command rose from behind their covered positions and advanced toward the fortifications three to four hundred yards to their front. At the same time, Sherman's and McPherson's corps began their assault. Grant watched the attacks unfold from a position near the junction of Sherman's and McPherson's corps, a point from which he also could see a portion of McClernand's advance.[6]

Again two of Sherman's divisions attacked Stockade Redan, and again they were repulsed. His third division failed to reach the jump-off point on time and did not participate in the battle until midafternoon. McPherson's men planted one flag on the exterior of Great Redoubt, but the corps made little headway. Throughout the morning, only seven of McPherson's thirty-two infantry regiments were decisively engaged.[7]

When the Thirteenth Corps batteries ceased firing, Benton's brigade surged toward the 2d Texas Lunette. Cpl. Thomas J. Higgins, color bearer for the 99th Illinois, reached the works adjacent to the lunette, but he and the colors were captured as he stood atop the embankment. (In 1898 Higgins would receive the Medal of Honor for his valor that day.) To the right, Burbridge formed a line with Benton's brigade, but he did not have enough men to tie in with McPherson. This left his right unsupported and vulnerable to a Confederate counterattack.[8]

Burbridge then received orders from A. J. Smith to send two regiments to support Benton's attack. He protested, but Smith replied that Carr, who was senior in rank to Smith, had ordered it and that the order had to be obeyed. Burbridge then personally went to McClernand, but the corps commander referred him to Carr. Carr at first ordered the regiments to reinforce him, but then, shortly after they had been withdrawn from Burbridge's line, relented. The result was confusion within the Union ranks.[9]

Although Carr was senior to Smith and commanded a critical portion of the attack, McClernand should have made the decision whether to reinforce Carr's attack. It was his responsibility to know the effect of withdrawing two regiments from the right and of the gap between his corps and that of McPherson that would be aggravated thereby. He alone was responsible for coordinating the attack of his corps, for determining whether success was being achieved, and for determining the moment and the forces required for a final push to seize the key objectives. While it can be argued that the forward commander on the ground—Carr—was in the better position to know the situation, he knew only what was happening to his front. He also was embroiled in a thundering battle, which could easily cause him to misconstrue the actual situation. By deferring to Carr the decision to reinforce with Burbridge's regiments, McClernand failed to accept the responsibility that was his alone.

At Railroad Redoubt, Texans and Alabamians poured rifle fire into Lawler's advancing blue-coats. Despite the intense storm, soldiers from the 21st and 22d Iowa were able to reach the redoubt. Soon thereafter the colors of the 77th and 130th Illinois regiments were planted alongside those of the 22d Iowa. Later that day the colors of the 48th Ohio joined those earlier planted on the Rebel position.[10]

While this battle raged, Osterhaus deployed his two brigades in three columns but was able to get no closer than two hundred yards from the Confederate positions. Abatis, open ground, and intense musketry prevented his soldiers from advancing beyond that point. Sylvanus Cadwallader, correspondent for the *Chicago Times*, watched as the Union soldiers were "mercilessly torn to pieces by Confederate shot and shell." From their position the embattled troops exchanged fire with the Confederates until dark.[11]

On the extreme left Hovey's lone brigade, commanded by Col. William T. Spicely, remained unengaged throughout the day.[12]

At 11:15 A.M. the Thirteenth Corps commander began to send a series of messages that would be among the most controversial of the Civil War and that would be a major catalyst in determining the future of Maj. Gen. John Alexander McClernand.

His first message stated, "I am hotly engaged. If McPherson would attack it would make a diversion." Grant responded at 11:50 A.M. that McClernand should strengthen his advance by utilizing his own command rather than ask for assistance from another corps. At that time neither Quinby's division of McPherson's corps nor Spicely's brigade of McClernand's own corps were engaged. For some unknown reason, Grant did not order McPherson to move Quinby forward to create the diversion McClernand requested. Perhaps it was because from his vantage point he could see that Quinby was three hundred yards from the Confederate lines and would have to cross a hollow filled with downed trees to reach the entrenchments. To order him forward might have been foolhardy, but he made no effort to see that

McClernand was supported on his right. Instead of examining the situation personally, Grant left his headquarters and rode to meet Sherman near Stockade Redan.[13]

At noon McClernand sent a critical message to Grant: "We have part possession of two Forts, and the stars and stripes are floating over them. A vigorous push ought to be made all along the line."[14] In his memoirs Sherman was to remember the message differently. He would recall that the message said that "his troops had captured the rebel parapet in his front," that "the flag of the Union waved over the stronghold of Vicksburg," and that it requested Grant to order Sherman and McPherson to renew their attacks. In his official report Grant wrote that McClernand's message "stated positively and unequivocally that he was in possession of and still held two of the enemy's forts" and requested that Sherman and McPherson make a diversion to relieve the pressure on him.[15] There is a considerable difference between what McClernand sent and what Sherman thought, and Grant reported, he sent. The key point is whether McClernand reported that he possessed part, or possessed all, of the enemy forts.

In his official report, the Thirteenth Corps commander stated that Lawler's and Landrum's brigades "had carried the ditch, slope, and bastion of a fort." The bastion, however, is a projecting portion of a fortification, not the fortification itself. McClernand went on to state that he had reported at the time only that he was "in partial possession of two forts." The report, therefore, is consistent with McClernand's actual messages during the battle.[16]

According to Sherman's memoirs, Grant responded that he did not believe the message. In his official report Grant stated that he had been in a position to see what was occurring in the Thirteenth Corps sector and "could not see his possession of forts, nor necessity of reinforcements." At that time Grant was at least a mile and three-quarters from Railroad Redoubt, and his view of McClernand's sector would have been obstructed by the ridge along which ran the Jackson Road. Additionally, smoke would have obliterated any possibility of seeing exactly where McClernand's soldiers were. Furthermore, McClernand was not claiming to have possession of the forts, only to have "part possession."[17] Grant could clearly see that Sherman was making no progress, and he could probably see that McPherson was having minimal success. The only positive reports he had received were from McClernand, yet his initial response was not to believe them.

Sherman was with Grant when the army commander received the noon message from McClernand. He later wrote that he informed Grant that the message was official and that the army commander had to accept it as written. Grant, therefore, at 2:00 P.M., informed McClernand that Sherman and

McPherson "both are pressing the enemy" and that he should "concentrate with [McArthur] and use his forces to the best advantage." McClernand received this dispatch and immediately wrote back, "We have gained the enemy's entrenchments at several points, but are brought to a stand." He informed Grant that he had sent for McArthur. Again he suggested that Grant "concentrate the whole or a part of his Command on this point." He also stated that all his forces were committed, though in fact Spicely's brigade was not. Perhaps he forgot about that one brigade, assumed that it had been committed, or was concerned that if he pulled him out of the line, he would only increase the danger to his left. The exact reason for his error remains a mystery.[18]

At 2:30 P.M. Grant notified McClernand that he had ordered McPherson to send Quinby's division to reinforce him. Forty-five minutes later, McClernand replied that he had received Grant's messages in regard to McArthur and Quinby, and he added a report that indicated the precarious nature of his gains: "My men are in two of the enemy's forts but they are commanded by rifle pits in the rear. At this moment I am hard pressed."[19] These were not idle words. For several hours Lawler and Landrum had reported to McClernand and Smith that they were in a desperate situation and needed help. Landrum's message at 2:40 P.M. reiterated that he was "holding the flanks of the fort in our front."[20]

Grant must have noticed the critical words "in two of the enemy's forts" in this message, whereas the previous ones had stated that McClernand was in "part possession." McClernand obviously wanted Grant to believe that he was in a position to break through the Confederate lines if he was reinforced. Such a penetration could bring to culmination the Union effort to take Vicksburg, and much of the glory would undoubtedly fall upon the former Illinois politician. From his personal observation and the messages of his subordinates, McClernand must have had no doubt that he was on the verge of a breakthrough.

During this exchange of correspondence, Grant rode from Sherman's headquarters to that of McPherson, where, he believed, he had a good view of McClernand's situation. In his report Grant wrote that he had doubted the accuracy of McClernand's messages, but he never went to McClernand's headquarters to discuss the situation personally. He would claim to have been able to see that McClernand did not possess the enemy fortifications, but he sent him reinforcements anyway. Grant had repeatedly expressed reservations about McClernand's generalship, yet he failed to take any action personally to verify the accuracy of his corps commander's reports and requests for additional troops. He neither went himself to investigate nor sent a trusted staff officer to report the situation. On the afternoon of 22 May, the critical point in the entire Union attack was in McClernand's sector, but Grant chose to remain near McPherson rather than ride to the point where he could probably best influence the action. In his memoirs Sherman would write that Grant indicated "he would instantly ride down the line to McClernand's front," but he never reached his corps commander's location.[21] If Grant was certain that his subordinate's reports were inaccurate, he should have verified them for himself and should never have committed soldiers to a cause that had no chance of success.

Instead, the army commander ordered Quinby to reinforce McClernand, and Sherman and McPherson to renew their attacks. Neither of the latter two corps had any success. McClernand ordered one brigade of Quinby's division to reinforce Osterhaus in front of Fort Garrott. Upon their arrival, Osterhaus cancelled further attacks, because of the approaching darkness. This poor tactical decision by Osterhaus resulted in the waste of a brigade that could have been employed more effectively elsewhere.[22]

Although McClernand sent Quinby's other two brigades to reinforce Carr in front of 2d Texas Lunette and Railroad Redoubt, he allowed his subordinate to assign a brigade to each objective rather than massing them against one point. In another faulty decision, Burbridge withdrew as soon as his reinforcements arrived. In the resulting confusion, the Confederates were able to regroup and force Quinby's men back. Carr pointed Quinby's last brigade at the entrenchments that connected the two main positions to his front. As with other advances, the downed trees in the ravines caused confusion and misalignment, and the brigade had to stop to reform. The time lost allowed the Confederates to shift forces to meet the new threat. The attack was stopped cold.[23]

During the afternoon McClernand suddenly remembered Spicely and wrote Osterhaus that he would order that lone brigade to support Carr. According to Hovey, the division commander, the defenses prevented Osterhaus "from making a successful charge," and his brigade "was not seriously engaged."[24]

As the corps commander watched his soldiers retreat from the front of the Confederate positions, he realized he still faced several problems. First of all, he was concerned about the possibility of a Confederate counterattack, for a gap still remained between his right and McPherson's left. He notified the commander of the Seventeenth Corps that he would extend as far to the right as possible and would attempt to reduce the gap by the use of one of Quinby's brigades. After McClernand notified Grant of his concern, the army commander ordered Quinby's entire division into the gap. To protect his front,

McClernand prudently ordered his men to establish adequate guards, to dig rifle pits for protection, and to entrench the artillery to cover avenues of approach into his position. He also made certain that the soldiers were fed and supplied with ammunition.[25]

Second, he remained concerned about his left flank. He knew McArthur was to have marched from Warrenton that morning, but by that evening, as he informed Grant, he had heard nothing from him. Porter notified Grant that McArthur was "straggling" along the route. At 8:30 P.M. Grant countermanded his order and directed McArthur to hold the road between Warrenton and Vicksburg where it crossed Big Bayou south of the city. He informed McClernand of his decision and directed him to watch the roads between the city and the Big Bayou crossing.[26] Although this action did not complete the encirclement of the city, at least McArthur was in a position either to block a Confederate attempt to break out of the city or to fall on the flank of any force that tried to envelop McClernand's left.

Finally, McClernand again reiterated to Grant his belief that only by massing against one or two points could a breakthrough be achieved. Grant, however, had decided upon a siege.[27] There would be no more assaults.

Had McClernand been on the verge of a breakthrough? Had Union soldiers been either "in" or in "part possession of" the Confederate works? If McClernand had employed Spicely's brigade anywhere or massed Quinby's division against either 2d Texas Lunette or Railroad Redoubt, could a penetration have been achieved?

Cadwallader, who claimed he "was within plain view of the rebel earthworks," would write that McClernand had never "carried any part of the fortifications." The correspondent's reports were frequently incorrect and cannot be considered authoritative. Nevertheless, this report does contradict McClernand's report that he was in possession of part of the enemy's lines.[28]

Numerous accounts substantiated the fact that regimental colors were planted on the Confederate works that faced the Thirteenth Corps. As mentioned, Corporal Higgins would receive the Medal of Honor for placing his colors on the Confederate parapet. Several reports stated clearly that Sgt. Joseph E. Griffith and eleven privates from the 21st Iowa entered a Confederate work. This episode is repeated in the reports of the brigade commander, Lawler; the corps commander, McClernand; and even in that of the army commander, Grant. Grant went on to write, however, that the accomplishment had not been decisive, because the works to the left and right of the penetration had not been taken. Nevertheless, in his initial report to Halleck sent the day of the battle, Grant wrote, "We hold possession, however, of two of the enemy's forts, and have skirmishers close under all of them." He also informed Porter at 8:30 P.M. that the army had gotten into one or two of the enemy strongpoints.[29] Many other commanders claimed to have reached the ditch in front of the various works. These claims are substantiated by the number of Union flags emplaced along the Confederate position, among which were those of the 77th Illinois and 48th Ohio.[30]

Even Wilson accepted the possibility that McClernand had indeed taken part of the Confederate position. He too credited Griffith with breaking "through the enemy's line into a salient redan, capturing it and its guns for a time."[31]

Pemberton and his subordinates were alarmed by the gains made by McClernand's attack, and their reports substantiate the claims that Union forces had gained parts of the Rebel positions. At 11:45 A.M. Brig. Gen. Stephen D. Lee had informed his division commander that "they have made a lodgment in the ditch of left work, and they have a stand of colors in the work." In his later report Lee would write that Union forces carried "an angle of the work immediately to the right of the railroad" (Railroad Redoubt) and planted "two colors upon the parapet, which remained there for several hours." Pemberton himself wrote that Union troops had gained the parapet. Col. Thomas N. Waul, commander of Waul's Texas Legion, reported that Union forces "planted two flags upon the parapet, entered a breach made by their artillery . . . and [drove] the garrison from the angle of the fort." In the Confederate counterattack, about fifty Union soldiers, including the commander of the 22d Iowa, were captured.[32] The remainder of the Union soldiers in and around the Confederate forts withdrew at dark.

Two days later, Grant wrote Halleck about the attack. There was no doubt where Grant thought the blame for the heavy losses lay. In a telegram notably different from the one sent the evening of the attack, Grant reported that "Gen. McClernand's dispatches misled me as the real state of facts and caused much of this loss. He is entirely unfit for the position of Corps Commander both on the march and on the battle field. Looking after his Corps gives me more labor, and infinitely more uneasiness, than all the remainder of my Dept." In his view, the afternoon attacks had accomplished nothing except add to the army's casualty list.[33]

Rawlins, too, was convinced that McClernand alone was to blame for the failure to capture the Confederate positions and the resulting loss of life. At army headquarters he ordered Lt. Col. Theodore Bowers, the judge advocate, "to open the record book and charge a thousand lives to that —— McClernand."[34]

Dana added his voice to the storm of criticism. The day after the attack he telegraphed Stanton that Grant did not doubt the accuracy of McClernand's reports—an assertion that contradicted Grant's and Sherman's recollections. He wrote: "McClernand's report was false, as he held not a single fort, and the result was disastrous." He later modified his words slightly by adding, "although a few of his men had broken through in one place," but by then the damage to McClernand had been done.[35]

Years later, both Sherman and Wilson reassessed the reasons for failure of the attacks on 22 May. Although Sherman still believed McClernand had not reported his situation accurately, he now came to the conclusion that the attacks "had failed by reason of the great strength of the position and the determined fighting of the garrison." He went on to say that the Confederate defenses at Vicksburg were superior even to those of the Russians at Sevastopol during the Crimean War. McPherson also attributed the failure to "the strength of the works . . . and the determined character of the assailed."[36] Such a comparison and such comments, of course, would also excuse Sherman's and McPherson's lack of progress against the Vicksburg fortress. Wilson, in his postwar memoirs, was far more charitable toward McClernand. He observed "that McClernand's conduct [at Vicksburg] seems to have been no more blameworthy upon that occasion than Sherman's or McPherson's. The fact is that neither corps commander made the proper provision for the contingency of success in the attack."[37]

Wilson's assessment comes close to pinpointing the reasons for failure. Grant conducted a frontal assault all along the line rather than mass to achieve a breakthrough at a specific point, as proposed by McClernand. He also failed to provide for a reserve that could be used to exploit any success achieved by the attacks. Each corps commander, to include McClernand, also failed to designate a reserve to exploit success in the respective corps sectors. Because of the nature of fighting in the Civil War, commanders had little control over a battle after the forces had been committed. The most effective way they could then influence the outcome was through the employment of a reserve. These commanders cannot be criticized too heavily, however, for attacks into strong defenses rarely succeeded in the Civil War. Fredericksburg, Gettysburg, Cold Harbor, and Petersburg are only a few examples of failed attempts to dislodge well-protected soldiers. Although Union success at Missionary Ridge was an exception, it was a rare one. Nevertheless, the stage was set for Grant finally to rid himself of John McClernand.

On 6 May Stanton had written Dana in response to the envoy's 27 April dispatch, in which Dana castigated McClernand for the review held for Yates. This message to Grant, sent in a bizarre route through Dana, read, "General

Grant has full and absolute authority to . . . remove any person who, by ignorance in action or any cause, interferes with, or delays his operations. He has the full confidence of the Government, is expected to enforce his authority, and will be firmly and heartily supported, but he will be responsible for any failure to exert his powers. You may communicate this to him."[38] Grant received this message on or about 14 May, while at Jackson. On 24 May Dana reported to Stanton that Grant had decided to relieve McClernand because of the failed attack two days earlier but that Grant had changed his mind and decided to leave the Illinois general in command until Vicksburg fell. He would then ask McClernand to take a leave of absence. "Meanwhile he will especially supervise all of McClernand's operations, and will place no reliance on his reports unless otherwise corroborated."[39] McClernand's days as commander of the Thirteenth Corps, Army of the Tennessee, were numbered.

Union forces spent the remainder of May 1863 improving their defensive positions and conducting siege operations, which included digging approach trenches to the Confederate lines. Dana continued to provide to Stanton negative reports about what he perceived as McClernand's inactivity. On 24 May, Osterhaus with one brigade was posted at the Big Black River bridge to protect the rear of the Union army from attack by Joe Johnston's army, which still lurked north of Jackson in the vicinity of Canton and Vernon. He would continue to provide Grant information about Confederate movements until Pemberton surrendered. A supply base was opened at Warrenton, and the Thirteenth Corps had to garrison that depot and patrol in the vicinity of the town.[40]

Although McClernand's front remained comparatively quiet, the corps commander still worried about his left flank and the possibility of a Confederate attempt to break out of the city. He reported all indications of Rebel movements to Grant and suggested that the army and navy periodically fire shells into the city as well as near the parapets to break up formations that might attempt a sortie. Grant agreed and responded with an order for all corps commanders to picket roads to the rear and also for artillery fire into the city at periodic intervals. On 28 May Grant partially closed the gap with Brig. Gen. Jacob Lauman's division, and finally on 12 June, the division of Maj. Gen. Francis Herron completed the encirclement.[41]

Sherman's resentment of McClernand continued to manifest itself. In a letter to his wife written 2 June, he commented that McClernand was making less satisfactory progress in digging siege trenches than was his own Fifteenth Corps. Three days later, however, Dana, who undoubtedly would have recounted any lack of effort by McClernand, reported that "the siege works progress steadily." In mid-June, though, Dana asserted that McClernand's trenches were "mere rifle-pits," but McClernand's almost daily reports to Grant of his progress refute that observation. Also, McClernand's chief engineer, Lt. Peter Hains, was providing his commander detailed descriptions of the approaches, rifle pits, and trenches being dug within the corps sector. Grant, apparently, was satisfied with his corps commander's progress, for he expressed no displeasure with the digging. He only urged him to "make all advance possible in approaches."[42]

Although McClernand wrote Governor Yates about "the petty meanness which has permeated the army," he probably little appreciated the extreme depth to which his acceptance at Grant's headquarters had sunk when he unleashed an outburst early in June. Wilson carried an order from Grant for the Thirteenth Corps to strengthen the force that guarded the Big Black River crossings in the army's rear. According to Wilson, rather than accept the order, McClernand screamed, "I'll be God damned if I'll do it—I am tired of being dictated to—I won't stand it any longer, and you can go back and tell General Grant!" Wilson alleged that McClernand proceeded to curse him. McClernand then apologized: "I am not cursing you," he said. "I was simply expressing my intense vehemence on the subject matter." When this was reported to Grant, the army commander vowed to "get rid of McClernand the first chance I get." From then on, whenever Grant heard an officer curse, he would smile and say, "He's not cursing. He is simply expressing his intense vehemence on the subject matter."[43]

On 17 June Sherman launched a missive that exploded with the force of a bombshell at Headquarters, Department of the Tennessee. The evening prior he had read in the *Memphis Evening Bulletin* a general order from McClernand, dated 30 May, that congratulated his corps on their accomplishments during the Vicksburg campaign. The next day McPherson noted that the order had also been published in the *Missouri Democrat*, on 10 June. Issuance of such congratulatory messages was not unusual; indeed, both McClernand and Grant had issued several during the campaign. Yet this order was different. Although McClernand several times acknowledged that his corps had acted in support of those of Sherman and McPherson, several sentences cast aspersions on the efforts of those corps during the assault of 22 May, as well as on the army commander for developing a faulty plan.

> The Thirteenth Army Corps, acknowledging the good intentions of all, would scorn indulgence in weak regrets and idle recriminations. If, while the enemy was massing to crush it, assistance was asked for by a diversion at other

> points, or by re-enforcement, it only asked what in one case Major-General Grant had specifically and peremptorily ordered, namely, simultaneous and persistent attack all along our lines . . . and . . . by massing a strong force in time upon a weakened point, would have probably ensured success.[44]

Neither Sherman nor McPherson was impressed with McClernand's bombast or allegations that his corps had not been supported during the attack. Sherman cited War Department General Orders No. 151, dated 4 October 1862, forbidding publication of official letters and reports without authorization. The regulation did not specifically prohibit publication of orders, but McClernand's congratulatory "order" was not truly an order but a letter; thus, it had violated the general order. Sherman did not refer to the fact, but the letter also violated Grant's order issued in the aftermath of Shiloh that all official publications were to be routed through his headquarters. Sherman castigated his fellow general for "self-flattery," "vain glory," and "hypocrisy." In his view, the order was addressed "not to an army, but to a constituency in Illinois . . . who might innocently be induced to think General McClernand the sagacious leader and bold hero he so complacently paints himself." Complaining vehemently about McClernand's misstatements of facts in the order, he nevertheless repeated and expanded upon his own erroneous allegation that McClernand claimed to have "carried three of the enemy's forts."[45]

McPherson was equally furious, and he too believed the order was written primarily for public consumption in Illinois. He accused McClernand of being ungenerous and dishonorable. He went on to blame the Thirteenth Corps commander for the failure of his attack. His failure had not been the fault of any other corps commander, McPherson charged; it was each commander's responsibility to dispose his units so that any breakthrough could be exploited. Although that was true, Grant had himself designated no force to exploit a penetration, and McPherson had achieved less success in his sector than Sherman or McClernand.[46]

Upon receipt of Sherman's letter, Grant asked McClernand if the copy of the order he had received were correct. The following day McClernand replied that it was, but, apparently realizing that he had overstepped his bounds, he added: "I regret that my adjt [adjutant] did not send you a copy promptly as he ought & I thought he had."[47]

Whether the Illinois general had actually intended to send Grant a copy of his order, had intentionally ensured the order would be leaked to newspapers, or had written it primarily for political gain cannot be known for certain. McClernand knew that he was intensely disliked within the Army of the Tennessee, although he undoubtedly viewed that dislike as jealousy rather than disdain for his military abilities and personality. He knew he had enemies in Washington, but such was his ego that he probably believed that his political connections with the Illinois governor, the congressional delegation, and Lincoln himself would enable him to overcome any conspiracy against him. To Yates on 28 May he wrote of rumors that "would fix upon me the responsibility of the failure of the assault" and for "loss sustained by the other army corps." McClernand's counter was that success would have been achieved had the army been massed against a single point. Although he continued that it would be improper for him to impugn Grant's tactics for the attack, that clearly was what he was doing. He then indicated there should be an investigation of the entire campaign.[48]

The next day the Illinois general took his case to Lincoln. He outlined the rumors circulating in the army that he was responsible for the failure. To Lincoln he stated unequivocally that the plan of attack had been faulty and incapable of achieving success. In his view, "failure having resulted, indications of a disposition to shirk responsibility are becoming manifest." This was a direct attack on Grant. He then indicated again that an investigation would reveal "who led to failure, and who to success."[49]

Unfortunately, McClernand greatly exaggerated his support in the White House. The president had appointed him for strictly political reasons, but by June 1863 military considerations were at least equal to political calculations. Grant was besieging Vicksburg, and his stature was rising steadily in Lincoln's estimation. The president indicated clearly to his political appointee that he could not win a fight with Grant. McClernand, however, did not see clearly, and he continued to provoke Grant, his staff, and fellow corps commanders.

On 4 June McClernand vented his conspiracy theory to Grant: "What appears to be a systematic effort to destroy my usefulness and reputation as a commander, makes it proper that I should address you this note." He then enumerated the rumors circulating about the 22 May attack and added one that indicated he had been arrested. He called upon Grant for "a declaration as will be conclusive in the matter."[50] Grant ignored the request.

The climax to the struggle came on 18 June 1863. At 2:00 A.M., James Wilson arrived at McClernand's headquarters and asked that the general be awakened. Soon thereafter he was ushered in to meet the corps commander, who, in full uniform, was seated at a table with his sword lying across it. Wilson handed him a sealed envelope. As he read Special Orders No. 164,

McClernand exclaimed: "Well, sir! I am relieved! By God, sir, we are both relieved!" Wilson then informed the former commander that Maj. Gen. Edward O. C. Ord would immediately take command and that McClernand was to "proceed at your earliest convenience to your home in Illinois and there await the orders of the War Department." He then left McClernand alone to contemplate his future and the actions that had led to this moment.[51] While McClernand would be relieved from command, Grant would be relieved to have him gone.

McClernand wrote Grant that "having been appointed by the President . . . I might justly challenge your authority in the premises, but forbear to do so at present." He then suggested to Grant that any misstatements in his congratulatory order should be the subject of investigation. The next day he left for Memphis and Illinois.[52] Grant notified Halleck on 19 June that he had relieved McClernand and gave the publication of the congratulatory order as the reason. To Dana he wrote, "The change is better than 10,000 reinforcements."[53]

Wilson and Dana believed that the order had caused Grant to reach the end of his patience. Both later asserted that the real causes were disobedience, his relations with other officers in the Army of the Tennessee, his use of profanity, his order that created the Army of the Mississippi, and fear that should some tragedy befall Grant, McClernand would be left in command.[54]

Dana's regard for McClernand had diminished in the months since he first joined the army. He viewed McClernand as smart, but he characterized Sherman as a genius. Although he lacked any military experience whatsoever, Dana confidently judged McClernand as not having "the qualities necessary for commander even of a regiment." He criticized him for not being "a military man," although McClernand alone had supported Grant's plan to turn the southern flank of Vicksburg. In contrast, Dana lauded Sherman for having criticized the plan but then supported it during its execution. Unfortunately for McClernand, this lack of regard would continually manifest itself in Dana's dispatches to Stanton. The atmosphere at Grant's headquarters was decidedly anti-McClernand, and Dana admitted that he was on close terms with Wilson, Rawlins, and others who questioned McClernand's abilities and loyalties. Cadwallader, however, believed the closeness was actually an attempt by Grant's staff officers to ingratiate themselves with Dana to dampen any criticism that might be leveled at their commander. Although the two correspondents had their differences, Cadwallader characterized Dana as "an able, far-seeing public official," a characterization notably different from that of Henry Villard, who accused him of a "malignant bias."[55] Nevertheless,

Dana's role in McClernand's relief from command, particularly his dispatch that led to authorization from the War Department for Grant to relieve McClernand, must be considered as highly influential.

Cadwallader himself agreed with Grant's actions. He had little use for the likes of Banks, Butler, or McClernand, whom he viewed collectively as failures. Their fault was that they had gained their ranks as major generals through political influence rather than by first serving an apprenticeship at a lower rank among the soldiers. He determined that McClernand's particular fault was "his uncontrollable itching for newspaper notoriety." He had remained too long the politician and could not adjust either his ego or his actions to a military hierarchy. In the end, he had to go.[56]

The correspondent for the *Chicago Evening Journal* reported that McClernand's removal "was demanded by the best interests of the army." He went on to write that the announcement "was received with the greatest satisfaction by officers and men . . . of his own immediate command."[57]

Franc Wilkie, correspondent for the *Dubuque (Iowa) Herald*, had observed McClernand and characterized him as "fussy, irritable, and nervous. . . . I sometimes think there is a screw loose in his machinery." While Wilkie could not justify McClernand's conduct at Vicksburg, he had a different view of the relations between the general and his men: "The men of the 13th corps . . . believed religiously in their beloved corps commander. . . . His presence was always an inspiration to his men, many of whom did follow him to the death." That the political general could inspire such loyalty is testimony to his concern for his soldiers, his bravery, and his leadership.[58]

The generals were not so inspired. Kilby Smith wrote that he was "most thankful" that McClernand had been relieved, although he expected the action to "raise a good deal of a breeze." Sherman too exulted in McClernand's departure. To his wife he wrote that the army was sick of McClernand's "intense selfishness and lust of notoriety." He was a man of limited vision—"all was brilliant about him and dark and suspicious beyond." McClernand's "riddance was a relief to the whole army," he wrote his brother.[59] Although he did not say so, with McClernand gone the commanders of the Army of the Tennessee and its three corps were all West Point graduates.

McClernand's suspicion that Sherman was against him was reinforced by a letter he received in September from Capt. Ambrose A. Blount of the 17th Ohio Battery. Blount asserted that an officer on Sherman's staff had confided that "Genl. Sherman was no friend of [his]" and had been one of the principal proponents of McClernand's relief. McClernand became even more certain of Sherman's role in his relief when his fellow general published his memoirs in 1875. In a letter to his friend and former subordinate, George

W. Morgan, McClernand declared that Sherman was full of "abnormal ambition and egotism" and had used his memoirs maliciously to disparage and degrade his comrades.[60] Nevertheless, the combined effect of Grant, Sherman, McPherson, Dana, and Porter, plus his own shortcomings, had been too much to overcome. But John McClernand was not a man to accept his relief from command without a fight.

Upon his arrival at Cairo, Illinois, on 23 June McClernand sent a two-sentence telegram to Lincoln: "I have been relieved for an omission of my adjutant. Hear me." On the same day, he sent the president a seven-page report of his operations in Louisiana and Mississippi, with which he included a copy of his congratulatory order. In the report he reiterated his case that his adjutant, not he, had been responsible for the failure to provide Grant the order, but he neglected to mention how it had come into the hands of newspaper correspondents. In his view, the order's facts were true and its language respectful. Grant's motive had been personal hostility toward him, because the president had assigned him to an independent command and because of his subsequent success, in contrast to Grant's "previous failures and disasters." His plea was to be restored to command. At the end he appended a note that again accused "partisans intent only on exalting their chiefs" of misrepresenting and falsifying his deeds—a plea that Lincoln would not accept.[61]

Grant had his own version of McClernand's deeds, and they corresponded little to those of his former corps commander. He charged that his fellow Illinoisan's report "contains so many inaccuracies that to correct it, to make it a fair report to be handed down as historical, would require the rewriting of most of it. It is pretentious and egotistical." Rather than praise McClernand, the official report of 6 July castigated him for his performance at Port Gibson, Champion Hill, and Vicksburg.[62] By then Vicksburg had fallen, and Grant was the rising star of the Union cause.

John McClernand brooded at his home in Springfield. He did not intend to accept the disgrace that accompanied his relief from command of the Thirteenth Corps. The people of Springfield had greeted him as a hero. Bands serenaded him, and crowds gathered to hear him speak. He was a guest at a reception given by Governor Yates. The *Illinois State Journal* exclaimed that the "confidence of the people" in McClernand was "undiminished." In another column the paper editorialized that "it cannot and must not be that such a volunteer in the cause of our bleeding country, shall be stricken down by West Point prejudice and narrow-minded jealousy." A few days later the paper demanded a court-martial to clear the general's name and reveal those at the top of the military hierarchy who had plotted against him.[63]

For the next six months, General McClernand received and accepted invitations to address patriotic gatherings and fairs in Illinois, Wisconsin, Ohio, and New York. Despite his shortcomings, McClernand was a patriot. His speeches rang with entreaties to save the country, to suppress the rebellion, and "to keep alive the fires . . . of liberty." In Chicago he declared that the war must not end until the rebellion had been suppressed. At Janesville, Wisconsin, he spoke about readmission of states, but not "in a way that will permit traitors to overrule the loyal people." He called for settling the war in a manner that would ensure a lasting peace. "I don't want this war patched up so that it will break out again in eight or ten years," he declared. Although he expressed disagreement with Lincoln, who he believed was prolonging the war because of abolitionist fervor among Republicans, he continued to correspond with the president. He wrote of his concerns about the loyalty of Illinoisans and the prospects for violence by Confederate sympathizers in the Springfield area.[64]

McClernand also kept alive the fires of anger and resentment at his treatment by Grant and other members of the cabal that, he believed, had finally seen him removed from command. On 27 June he wrote General Halleck and Secretary of War Stanton to justify his failure to supervise the drafting of the congratulatory order, to charge Grant with "personal hostility" toward him, and to call for an investigation. Claiming "I have been deeply injured," on 16 July he appealed to the Secretary of the Interior, John Usher, as one "western man" to another. Usher forwarded the letter to Lincoln. McClernand attempted to conspire with Postmaster General Montgomery Blair to oust Stanton from office, but Blair refused to become involved. In a 3 August letter to Lincoln, McClernand cited a newspaper account that he was to be brought before a court-martial by "ribald and malicious foes." "More jealous of . . . honor than . . . life," he appealed to the president for an expeditious hearing and for Lincoln "to see that I am fairly dealt by." Lincoln wrote Stanton that he was unaware of "any charges being filed" against McClernand and asked him to look into the matter.[65]

Governor Yates, in several letters to the president, added his voice in support of his political friend. He extolled McClernand's accomplishments as a soldier and urged that he be returned to a command. As a politician, he communicated to Lincoln the mood of the Illinois people in regard to the matter. "He has been received by the people here with the greatest demonstrations of respect, all regretting that he is not now in the field," he wrote. "The popular verdict is irreversibly in his favor as a general."[66]

On 12 August Lincoln finally responded to McClernand's petitions. In a letter he expressed his gratitude for the general's "patriotic stand" and his anguish over the breach between him and Grant. Nonetheless, he could not intervene, he concluded, without forcing Grant to resign. He also had no command to give to the Illinois general. "Better leave it where the law of the case has placed it," he advised.[67]

Lincoln agonized over the McClernand-Grant affair. He was being pressed to give commands to other politically appointed generals and to professional soldiers who had fallen into disfavor—Franz Sigel, George McClellan, Joseph Hooker—but who had powerful constituencies or supporters. Yates and the Illinois congressional delegation fell into that latter category, and they were attempting to pressure the president to reinstate their political ally. John Hay, Lincoln's secretary, wrote that most people were "trying to keep out of the mess between McClernand and Grant."[68]

In late July, Dana arrived in Washington, and Lincoln questioned him at length. Perhaps sensing that Lincoln might reconsider, Grant sent Rawlins to Washington to meet with the president and the Cabinet. His purpose was to show McClernand to be "an impracticable and unfit man . . . an embarrassment, an obstruction to army operations." Secretary of the Navy Welles questioned Rawlins's objectivity but concluded, "There can hardly be a doubt McClernand is at fault." Rawlins's mission was successful, for although Welles wrote that "the President feels kindly towards McClernand," Lincoln would not undermine Grant's authority in the matter.[69] It would not do to second-guess the victor at Vicksburg.

John McClernand was a proud and ambitious man, and he would not let the matter lie. Because the War Department had directed him to await orders in Illinois, he could not travel to Washington to present his case personally to the president. Instead, upon receipt of Lincoln's August letter, he replied requesting an inquiry and defending his actions against new allegations that he had not prepared the siege works in his sector as efficiently and effectively as had been done by the other corps commanders. On the same day, he wrote Stanton to remind him that he had not responded to his letter of 27 June. On 29 August Stanton replied to both letters: "The President . . . instructs me to say that no charges against you have come to his knowledge. . . . An investigation therefore will not be ordered."[70]

McClernand then tried a different tack. His previous correspondence to Lincoln, Stanton, and Halleck had challenged Grant's conduct of the entire Vicksburg campaign and even as far back as Belmont. On 5 September he acknowledged to Stanton receipt of the 29 August missive, but he now asked instead for an investigation only of his own conduct and that it include all his actions since being appointed a brigadier general. As McClernand perceived the situation, Lincoln appeared to be stating that he would not order an investigation of Grant but that an investigation of his own conduct was still a possibility.[71]

In this hope McClernand was to be disappointed. On 14 September Stanton replied that Lincoln had directed that no court of inquiry be convened, because it would "withdraw from the field many officers whose presence with their commands is absolutely indispensable." Even this statement did not shut the door completely, for the letter concluded, "If hereafter it can be done without prejudice to the service, he will, in view of your anxiety upon the subject, order a court."[72]

While he was sending these pleas to Washington, McClernand was also sending letters to numerous former subordinates. He asked that they respond to several specific questions that concerned the assault on 22 May. He received at least twelve responses. They consistently stated that soldiers of the Thirteenth Corps had gained the Confederate works, that had they been supported promptly they could have achieved a breakthrough, that the corps commander had been in an excellent position from which to observe the assault, and that Grant's report was an injustice to McClernand.[73]

Stymied by Lincoln and Stanton, but with this new ammunition, McClernand fired a lengthy "official and responsible protest" to Halleck on 25 September. On 9 October he sent a copy to Lincoln. Four days later, he asked Governor Yates to intervene on his behalf. Just as Grant had challenged the accuracy of McClernand's reports, so McClernand challenged the accuracy of Grant's. As a lawyer, he knew how to fashion an argument—how to present evidence and how to refute his opponent's position. These skills were replete in the presentation of his case to the general in chief.

He began with an attack on Grant himself. His anger at his former commander spilled onto the nineteen pages, as he charged Grant with an attempt to "disparage" him through a "multitude of errors [and] inaccuracies." His personal assault reached new heights as he attacked his fellow Illinoisan's qualifications for command:

> How far General Grant is indebted to the forbearance of officers under his command for his retention in the public service so long, I will not undertake to state unless he should challenge it. Neither will I undertake to show that he is indebted to the good conduct of officers and men of his command . . . for the series of successes that have gained him applause rather than to his own merit as a commander, unless he should challenge it, too.[74]

Having laid the matter of qualifications before Halleck and Lincoln, it would then be up to Grant to challenge McClernand's assertions.

To each past assertion by Grant, McClernand countered either with copies of official communications during the battle or with accounts from the respondents to his inquiries after the battle. The crux of the argument was that the plan of attack had been flawed, in that Grant had ordered the army to make a frontal assault rather than mass against selected points; that soldiers from the Thirteenth Corps had indeed entered a portion of the Confederate works; that Grant had been in no position to observe the extent of McClernand's progress; that Grant's and Sherman's recollections about the extent of his progress and the nature of his reports did not represent the truth, as McClernand reported during the battle; that Grant should have ridden to see for himself if he doubted McClernand's reports; that the Army commander should have ordered reinforcements and supporting attacks promptly to complete the penetration of the Vicksburg defenses; and that Grant had allowed Sherman and McPherson to cease their attacks before McClernand had been able to employ the reinforcements sent to him. The final portion of his brief was a refutation of comments Grant had made in his report regarding McClernand's conduct at Port Gibson, Champion Hill, and Big Black River. He concluded by asking for "an impartial judgment of my military superiors and of my country and history."[75]

On 15 October Halleck notified McClernand that he had forwarded the "official protest" to Stanton.[76] Grant would not be called upon to refute McClernand's charges, and McClernand would not get the inquiry he so earnestly sought. Nor would he hear from Lincoln.

McClernand then turned to his old House colleague Andrew Johnson. On 23 October he wrote, "I have been greatly injured by Grant." He asserted that "success was the cause of [his] relief," and he asked that his "old friend" write back. As with Lincoln, he would hear nothing.[77]

Finally, in early December, McClernand wrote his friend Judge John Cowan for assistance. A few weeks later Cowan, who was Salmon Chase's personal secretary, replied that there was little prospect of another command for the general. His only friend in the cabinet was Chase, he said, but Chase "is powerless as far as the military part of the government is concerned." He ascribed ulterior motives to Lincoln's actions and claimed that he was "jealous of all Western men, unless they go for him, soul and body." He urged the Illinois politician to bide his time.[78]

McClernand also kept up a prolific correspondence with Illinois senator Lyman Trumbull. In December he asked the senator to shed light on "the

President's will and intention towards me." In an enclosure he stated that he had not resigned his commission because he believed that the president still supported him. If that were not the case, or if he could not be assigned to an active command, he would resign, but, concerned about his reputation and his political future, he requested that Lincoln "say to the people that I have done well." He urged Trumbull to propose, if Lincoln supported him, that a new department be created in Arkansas and Louisiana and that he be given command.[79]

He was right to be concerned about that future. In December Illinois politicians were discussing Democratic nominations for governor to oppose Yates. McClernand's name was mentioned but rejected, because he was "rather under a cloud."[80] That cloud had to be removed if he was to continue in politics.

Cowan's advice about biding his time was good, for on 21 December Senator Trumbull provided McClernand a glimmer of hope for a continuation of his military career. "I have had a conversation with the President," he wrote. "The President is aware that you have been unjustly treated, and . . . he would see what could be done for you."[81]

It is not known whether Lincoln read McClernand's September appeal, but it is difficult to believe that Stanton and Halleck did not discuss the matter with him. McClernand was still a powerful political figure in Illinois, he had many influential friends in Washington, and he could be either an ally or a foe in future political campaigns. Halleck certainly desired that Grant and the military viewpoint be well represented in any discussion regarding the feud with McClernand. Perhaps Lincoln actually believed that there was some substance to McClernand's complaints, but he would do nothing to jeopardize the future of the nation's only legitimate military hero. After a string of unsuccessful generals, Grant had been victorious. Maj. Gen. George Gordon Meade had defeated Lee at Gettysburg at the same time that Vicksburg surrendered, but the Union general had allowed Lee to escape to Virginia. In contrast, Grant had taken Pemberton's army captive. Nevertheless, Lincoln had to do something with his Democrat friend, John McClernand.

After Vicksburg, the four divisions of the Thirteenth Army Corps had been scattered from Algiers, Louisiana (near New Orleans), to Brownsville, Texas.[82] The corps commander was now Maj. Gen. Napoleon T. J. Dana. This region was in the Department of the Gulf, commanded by Maj. Gen. Nathaniel P. Banks—a political general who had failed in Virginia against Stonewall Jackson (as had many others) and had been banished to a backwater theater. Outside events, however, now had transformed this remote theater to one in which international affairs became primary.

On 7 June 1863, French troops had occupied Mexico City. This had prompted fears in Washington that the French might ally themselves with the Confederates and create great difficulties along the southern border of the divided United States. To preclude that possibility, in November Banks led an invasion of Texas that planted the Union flag over Brownsville. By January, Dana had occupied several isolated sandy islands along the southern Gulf of Mexico coast of that Confederate state.[83] Grant had opposed such a move, but Halleck made clear to him that the Texas operation had been undertaken "as a matter of political or State policy, connected with our foreign relations." The president himself had ordered the invasion.[84] Confederate troops had been too few and too widely scattered to offer effective resistance.

On 19 January 1864, Senator Trumbull sent his fellow politician a letter that would link events in faraway Texas to McClernand's hopes for redemption. He stated that he had seen the president twice within the past week, that he had conferred with Stanton, and that he was to see him again in a day or two. Trumbull wrote, "The President informed me that he would be glad to give you a command if it could be done without making trouble in some other quarter." The senator then suggested a return to the Thirteenth Corps, under Banks. Trumbull added that Halleck would oppose such a move but that Stanton and Lincoln "were for it." He concluded, "You have not been lost sight of."[85]

A week earlier McClernand had written Trumbull and threatened to resign. With the letter he enclosed a letter of resignation expressing his bitterness that his present status afforded him no "opportunity to combat the rebellion, nor to defend myself against the proscription and calumnies of . . . Maj. Genl. U. S. Grant." His hatred for Halleck also continued to be manifested: "Halleck would resort to any means to sacrifice me." Rather than await a reply, he also sent his letter of resignation to Lincoln and Stanton. On 20 January Judge Cowan again wrote him and advised against such a move. Three days later, Maj. Gen. John Alexander McClernand was ordered to report for duty to Banks. In a separate letter to Banks, Halleck left the specific assignment to him but strongly hinted at what that assignment should be: "If you think it advisable to restore him to the command of his former corps, your order will be confirmed by the President."[86] The day the order was published, Trumbull again wrote McClernand and stated that Stanton had received the request to resign, "written in rather a mean spirit," and had wanted to know whether he should accept it; Trumbull informed the Illinois general that he had told the secretary of war not to accept it.[87] McClernand's hasty actions and petulant attitude had almost cost him the opportunity to return to command.

McClernand was ecstatic. "You have rolled away a stone that was crushing me," he wrote Trumbull. Many of his former soldiers congratulated him on his return to active duty. Lt. Col. Thomas S. Bennett of the 69th Indiana had written the general in September that "there is not an officer or man in the Corps but has expressed opinions in your favor." Gov. William M. Stone of Iowa, who had served as a colonel under McClernand during the Vicksburg campaign, observed that his reinstatement was "the highest compliment that could have been paid" and was being "hailed with universal satisfaction" by Iowans who had served with him previously. Yates wrote Banks and, in a letter that was far more political than military, praised his constituent as a "sagacious Statesman," a "soldier, patriot, friend, and neighbor. Next after Senator Douglas [he was] the most influential gentleman in his party in the State."[88] Banks could hardly have failed to understand that the influential Illinois governor desired that McClernand be treated with the utmost courtesy.

Yates's influence, indeed, was significant. Wilson, who in January 1864 had been appointed chief of the Cavalry Bureau in Washington, wrote Grant about the developments regarding McClernand and stated that the president had reinstated him because "grave political considerations in Illinois had induced him to change his decision."[89] Republicans had lost control of the Illinois legislature in the 1862 elections. Democrats were initiating a significant peace movement, and the 1864 presidential elections were to be held within the year. Loss of his home state would be a significant embarrassment to Lincoln. Republican Yates and Democrat McClernand, each with considerable influence in their respective parties, perhaps could persuade the voters to support the president in his reelection bid. An assignment to the Gulf would accomplish several objectives. It would gain McClernand's and Yates's political support and possibly that of their state; it would reduce McClernand's ability to inject himself into national affairs, simply because of the distance from Texas to the East; it would separate McClernand from Grant; and it would concentrate two of the Union's most influential political generals—Banks and McClernand—in the same theater. Lincoln could only have seen such an assignment as a golden opportunity to put the McClernand-Grant affair behind him.

In this hope he was to be disappointed. On 12 February McClernand forwarded a letter to Lincoln through Senator Trumbull. In this letter he reiterated his desire to charge Grant with incompetence at Donelson and Shiloh. He also included a statement from an individual who said that on 6 July 1863 he had heard Pemberton state that "if McClernand had been reinforced in time, on the 22d of May, Vicksburg would have fallen in twenty minutes afterward." Although he stated that this quotation was offered as justification for Lincoln's faith in restoring him to command, it was clearly meant as ammunition to justify his complaint against Grant.[90] Lincoln did not respond to McClernand's letter.

After Vicksburg, Grant had been given command of the newly created Military Division of the Mississippi and had established his headquarters at Chattanooga. There he had atoned for the Union defeat at Chickamauga by driving the Confederates from Missionary Ridge and Lookout Mountain. Although Grant believed the Union forces should capitalize on their victories at Vicksburg and Port Hudson by the capture of Mobile, Lincoln was concerned about the situation in Mexico, and Halleck wanted to clear Louisiana of Confederates. These concerns had been the basis for Banks's invasion of southern Texas and now created the foundation for a spring movement by Banks up the Red River in Louisiana toward Shreveport. Although these operations were not in Grant's theater, there was the possibility that Halleck would order Sherman, who was in his theater, to accompany the Red River campaign. In a letter to his subordinate, Grant expressed his support for the expedition but also indicated his fear that Banks might place McClernand in command of it. The months had not tempered his feelings toward his former corps commander, and he confided to Sherman that "I have so little confidence in his ability to command that I would not want the responsibility of entrusting men with him." Sherman wrote back that McClernand had been "ingeniously disposed of."[91]

Major General Ord, who had replaced Dana as corps commander in early January (Dana took command of the corps's troops in Texas), learned of the possibility that McClernand would replace him and wrote directly to Grant about the matter on 18 February. He stated flatly that if McClernand took command, he, Napoleon Dana, Brig. Gen. Thomas Ransom, and Brig. Gen. Michael Lawler would "quit rather than serve under McClernand." He added that "all the Corps staff here will quit, at least so they say." A few days earlier, Dana had expressed to Ord his sentiments about the rumored change. "It will be a most cruel unkindness if you leave me in McClernand's hands," he wrote.[92] Ord and Dana would get their wish. Ransom would, for a while, be detached from McClernand and thus not be under the corps commander's direct influence. Lawler would continue to serve directly under McClernand and eventually would succeed him temporarily.

Despite McClernand's lack of popularity with some former associates, he was still highly thought of in Springfield. On 31 January a ceremony complete with bands, a glee club, and a speech by Governor Yates was held to send him back to the field. "The good will of the loyal people of this State will follow you . . . and we shall be glad to welcome you home again with new and brighter laurels upon your head," proclaimed one speaker.

On 2 February, after leaving a note for Governor Yates in which he expressed his "gratitude and admiration," McClernand departed Springfield, arriving in New Orleans on 15 February. Trumbull had prepared Banks for the general's arrival. He informed the former politician that "our people think well of him" and reminded Banks that men of the Thirteenth Corps also remembered him fondly. McClernand reported to Banks, who on 20 February authorized him to relieve Ord as commander of his old corps. Two days later he attended a party given by Mrs. Banks. The next day he met with Ord and officially assumed command.[93]

Apparently, McClernand had learned from his last experience with Grant's displeasure at the publication of a congratulatory order. Upon taking command, he forwarded to Banks an address that he proposed to publish to the corps. In the message he exhibited the same flamboyant language that had aroused the ire of past commanders and made several only slightly veiled references to the cause of his relief the past June. He recounted the corps's victories throughout the Vicksburg campaign and praised the valor of the assaults of 19 and 22 May. In a direct reference to the congratulatory order that had been the proximate cause of his relief, he exclaimed that it "stands unshaken by time and official scrutiny. Indeed, as the plain and simple truth, the contents of that order have become a part of the authentic history of the war." Apparently he felt very secure in his new position, for he continued with an attack on those who had caused him to be removed before the fall of Vicksburg: "My non-participation in that memorable event was involuntary and constrained, and is deeply deplored on my part."[94] There is no indication that Grant saw this general order after it was published, but if he had, he undoubtedly would have been amazed that McClernand had learned so little (aside from the administrative proprieties).

The idea of Texas becoming an active military theater was not new to McClernand. In early 1861, as a congressman, he had proposed to Lincoln that operations be conducted along the Texas coast. Ironically, in early 1864 he found himself commanding a corps along that coast. The first question McClernand had to address was how much of Texas the Thirteenth Corps could be expected to hold. In February the First Division had 4,421 men at Indianola; the Second, with attachments, had 3,330 at Brownsville; and other engineer and pioneer troops occupied Pass Cavallo, Matagorda Island, and Brazos Santiago. Spread as thinly as they were, each detachment could

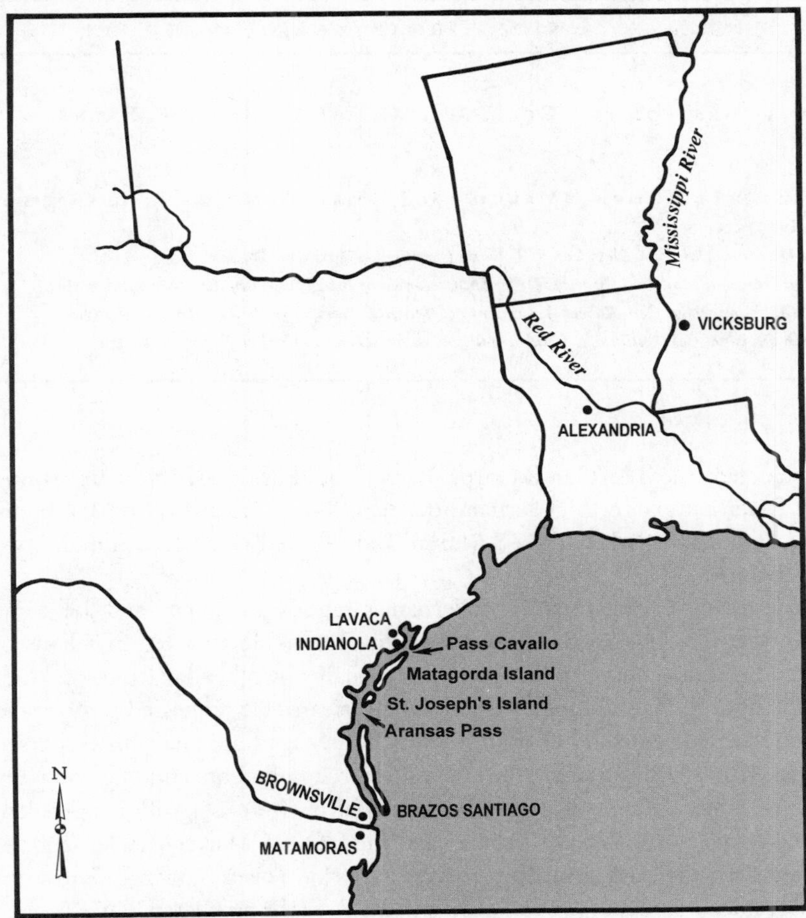

Louisiana–Texas Area of Operations

easily be defeated by a Confederate attack before aid could be provided. Dana was particularly concerned that he had an insufficient force on the mainland at Indianola to hold that position. As he had neither emplaced the forces himself nor inspected their positions, the corps commander wisely and humbly deferred to Dana's judgment. Banks directed that the First Division be withdrawn from Indianola.[95]

On 1 March, Banks ordered McClernand from New Orleans to Pass Cavallo, to "assume control of military affairs on the coast and frontier of Texas." Excluded from his immediate command were the Third and Fourth

Union Organization

Department of the Gulf, Maj. Gen. Nathaniel P. Banks

Thirteenth Corps (March 1864), Maj. Gen. John Alexander McClernand

First Division, Maj. Gen. Napoleon J. T. Dana (stationed at Pass Cavallo, Tex.)
Second Division, Maj. Gen. Francis T. Herron (stationed at Brownsville and Brazos Santiago, Tex.)
Third Division, Brig. Gen. Robert A. Cameron (detached for service in the Red River campaign)
Fourth Division, Col. William J. Landram (detached for service in the Red River campaign)

Divisions of the Thirteenth Corps. Banks would use these in the upcoming Red River campaign. McClernand departed New Orleans on 6 March, arrived at Matagorda Island on 8 March, and relieved Dana of command two days later.[96]

Energy had characterized McClernand's actions previously, and that same aggressiveness characterized his actions in Texas. He attacked problems of communications between his scattered posts, his own headquarters, and Department of the Gulf headquarters in New Orleans. He requested authority to raise, equip, organize, and train Texas volunteers to augment his dispersed corps. (Banks allowed him to fill only the three regiments and one company that were then being recruited.) Personnel levels were a significant problem for his corps, particularly in the artillery units. On 18 March McClernand reported that "the existing batteries of the corps have been rendered almost unserviceable, and must . . . soon cease to exist." Eight days later Banks replied that "immediate means will be taken to secure the efficiency of the batteries."[97]

To assist in the construction of defenses, he requested that an engineer officer be assigned, and he established a schedule and a priority for work on those defenses. To ensure compliance with his instructions, he directed his subordinates to report regularly on their progress. As he had done in Louisiana, he directed subordinate commanders to report their stocks of engineer tools and materials to preclude shortages that could affect the construction. Also, as he had done in earlier campaigns, he personally reconnoitered the area near his headquarters.[98]

Other details occupied his time. He demanded reports on the adequacy of clothing for the men, on quantities of ammunition, and types of artillery. He supervised emplacement of howitzers and field guns in the defensive positions. The evacuation of Indianola became a difficult issue, because of concerns about people who had declared allegiance to the United States. They would be at the mercy of Confederate partisans unless they too were evacuated. He also directed that bridges in the vicinity of Indianola be dismantled, not only to inhibit Confederate movements but also to serve as a source of building materials for the troops on Matagorda Island. By 14 March the mainland had been evacuated.[99]

There was little Confederate activity along the coast, but the Rebels did return to Indianola. Union sympathizers who had chosen not to evacuate were "harshly treated," and the town itself was burned. On 22 March, forty Confederates reconnoitered the Union defenses along the reef between the island and the mainland. No shots were fired, but two days later a small Union force was attacked near Aransas Pass. There were no Union losses, but the Rebels lost one killed and three wounded. Another small Rebel force was reported at Lavaca, near Indianola. Such reports prompted McClernand to warn his outposts of the necessity to be alert and to establish signals to warn of enemy approaches. Of particular concern was the southern end of Matagorda Island, where Cedar Bayou separated it from St. Joseph's Island. Not only were there numerous crossings from the mainland, but soldiers on the sand flats on Matagorda would be exposed as well to fire from the higher dunes on Saint Joseph's. McClernand would constantly concern himself with patrols and reports from this area.[100] The soldier in McClernand would not allow the Thirteenth Army Corps to be caught unawares.

Although McClernand's orders specified that he was responsible for military affairs, he found that there was an international component that he could not ignore. The previous August, Lincoln had written Grant that "in view of recent events in Mexico," he desired to reestablish a national presence in west Texas. Maj. Gen. Francis Herron, commander of the Second Division at Brownsville, reported that the Confederates were attempting to raise forces in the area and were conducting a thriving cotton trade with Mexicans in Matamoras. On 3 April, after a stop to inspect the fortifications at Brazos Santiago, McClernand arrived at Brownsville to assess the situation. The next day he inspected the Union soldiers there. Included in the reviewing party was His Excellency Juan N. Cortina, governor-general of the state of Tamaulipas, which encompassed Matamoras. The general hosted a banquet for the Mexican dignitaries at the Miller Hotel after the review. That afternoon Cortina reciprocated with a welcome that included an artillery salute, the ringing of church bells, and another formal dinner.

Cortina was a slippery character, known to be a cattle rustler, bank robber, extortionist, and murderer. In late 1863 he had killed the bandit ruler of the area and proclaimed himself governor. He continued to try to appease the Federals while selling cotton to the Rebels until a combination of French and Confederate pressure finally drove him out of Matamoras in September.[101]

McClernand was rightly concerned about Cortina's loyalties and the impact they could have on his forces isolated in southern Texas. His political skills were evident in his correspondence with the Mexican bandit-governor. The communication incorporated both praise and a veiled threat. He wrote the Mexican that Confederate access to Mexico "might, independently of the intention of the Mexican authorities, lead to the disturbance of the friendly relations subsisting between two sister and neighboring republics." He then asked the governor to close the border to Confederates.[102]

Cortina certainly was not anxious to agree, because of the fortune he was accumulating by extorting funds from the sale of cotton, so he replied that he would have to forward the Union general's request to President Benito Juarez. In the meantime, he would "do everything that tends to the good and prosperity of the American Union."[103]

McClernand read far more into that last sentence than was warranted and greatly exaggerated the role he had played in obtaining such a commitment. In his view, Cortina's reply amounted to "but little less than a declaration of war against the rebels." Obviously if Juarez were actually to make such a declaration, the credit would go to none other than John Alexander McClernand.[104]

In a private letter to Herron, McClernand explained his view of Cortina. He seemed to accept the governor's words that he supported the Union cause and believed that he and his "more devoted followers" would join the Federals if the French "[drove] him from his house and country" because of his sympathies. McClernand was not totally taken in by the Mexican; he had investigated Cortina, however, and believed "that he has been sinned against as well as sinning." Recognizing Cortina's base nature, he told Herron that "for comparatively small friendly returns by our Government," Cortina could be induced to close his border to the Rebels.[105] Other events, however, would soon divert McClernand from his foray into international affairs.

Upon his return to Pass Cavallo, McClernand again hinted to Trumbull that a separate department be established, this one to consist only of Texas. The state of "our delicate relations with Mexico and France" was his rationale. He warned that a French army along the Mexican border could have serious repercussions. He criticized Banks, whose army, he said, should have done more to prevent the deterioration of relations with Mexico and to destroy the few Confederate forces along the coast. However, in a sudden recognition of his subordinate military position, he added, "I am overstepping the privileges of my position. I must stop." Had such recognition come two years earlier, John McClernand's story might have been much different.[106]

One characteristic that had not changed was McClernand's concern for the soldiers. Perhaps, as a politician, he realized that people were his lifeblood. Soldiers have always needed words of praise and appreciation, and McClernand realized the influence a commander's declarations could have. Speeches came naturally to the politician, but it also had been a propensity for ill-chosen words that had gotten him removed from command. Nevertheless, while at Brownsville he addressed the troops. Herron was impressed and thanked him "for the words of cheer. It is the first time they have received encouragement . . . since in this department."[107] These comments were testimony to the good qualities McClernand possessed as a soldier.

What had interrupted McClernand's dabbling in international politics was a letter from Banks on 11 April requesting that he return to New Orleans with the infantry at Pass Cavallo and take command of the Thirteenth Corps units involved in the Red River campaign. On 8 and 9 April Banks had been severely beaten by Confederates at the Battles of Mansfield and Pleasant Hill, Louisiana, and had been forced to retreat to Alexandria. McClernand received the order on 17 April and departed from Pass Cavallo two days later. The command arrived at New Orleans late 21 April. McClernand issued the necessary embarkation directives and established the order of movement for the fleet. On 23 April he and his soldiers started for Alexandria.[108]

Upon arrival he informed Banks that he had brought 2,754 men with 150 rounds of ammunition each, and he provided him a brief report of the status of quartermaster, medical, and transportation items. The next day the corps deployed in line of battle, with instructions from Banks "to contest every inch of ground." Shortly thereafter, however, McClernand was ordered to fall back, even if it meant abandonment of camp items. McClernand obeyed, but he was able to save his equipment.[109]

On 26 April John McClernand again took command of the Thirteenth Army Corps in the field. Undoubtedly he felt vindicated. His protests, his belief that he had been wronged, his certainty that he was a victim of a cabal of West Pointers had resulted in a corps command in an active theater of operations. Earlier he had written Trumbull and asked him to see Grant on his behalf. He did not trust Grant and questioned "whether magnanimity or hostility will rule his conduct toward me." The senator had been unable to do so, but he had written McClernand that he did not believe Grant would "use his position to your disadvantage." At that time Grant and Halleck were discussing whether to replace Banks for his gross mismanagement of the Red

River operation. McClernand could not have known that he had at least two supporters for that job. Col. Marcus Spiegel, who had taken command of the 120th Ohio, retained total faith in McClernand. He wrote his wife that if McClernand took command, he could "look to the result as a Success, as almost foregone conclusion." Four days later, Spiegel wrote that he expected the Illinois general to "retrieve the great disaster" and hoped that McClernand would "command the Dept." A soldier who described himself as "an old Iowa veteran" wrote directly to Grant and proposed that the corps commander replace Banks. He urged the newly promoted lieutenant general to install "McClenard [*sic*]" in his stead. Grant's reaction to the letter is unknown, but it certainly would not have been favorable. Halleck was not going to appoint McClernand to replace Banks, for, in his words to Grant on 11 April, only Gen. David Hunter was "worse than McClernand in creating difficulties."[110]

Banks and his subordinate had lunch on 27 April and probably discussed the dire situation in which the army and the navy found themselves in his theater.[111] Porter's fleet had accompanied Banks's land expedition, and now, at Alexandria, it found itself trapped by low water. Loss of this fleet would be a devastating blow to the Union. The army would have to defend against Confederate attacks until a solution could be found for the navy's dilemma.

The Thirteenth Corps occupied the right of the defensive line, and a detachment from the Sixteenth Corps, commanded by the same A. J. Smith who had been McClernand's slow-moving subordinate at Champion Hill, occupied the left. McClernand ordered his command to entrench and be prepared for an attack by Confederates under Richard Taylor, former president Zachary Taylor's son. He also ordered, as he had during the winter and spring the year before, that commanders develop a training regimen for their units in both battalion and brigade drill. After a personal inspection of his line, he requested that Banks provide him an additional artillery battery to augment his defenses.[112]

Time had not lessened General McClernand's personal courage. He approached within four hundred yards of enemy pickets; his orderly was wounded by Rebel fire. His report on that occasion caused Banks to order him to move a brigade forward and occupy a ridge to his front. He executed this redeployment with Lawler's brigade, but McClernand was still nervous about the defensive posture of the entire army. He was particularly concerned that his left flank was not anchored, and he asked Banks to order A. J. Smith's command to tie in with him to support his left. So great was the concern for the safety of the entire army, that Banks ordered all forces to be alert and prepared to repel a Confederate attack from thirty minutes before dawn until 8:00 A.M. daily.[113]

Banks was greatly afraid that Taylor's six thousand Confederates would attack and defeat his thirty thousand Union soldiers entrenched around Alexandria. He was concerned only with retreat. His subordinate, however, had other ideas. In a private letter, McClernand implored his commander to allow him to concentrate the army and "go out, fight and beat the enemy." A victory was "a moral, political, and military necessity," he declared.[114] He probably also considered a victory to be a personal necessity. Were he able to reverse the fortunes of the defeated army, his star might again ascend. Such a victory would be ample rebuke to those who had slighted him, belittled him, conspired against him, and banished him. Banks, however, remained focused on improving his fortifications and repelling probes by the greatly outnumbered Rebels.

Halleck remained McClernand's bitter foe. On 29 April he wrote Grant and Sherman letters in which he deplored political generals and mentioned McClernand by name. Grant was considering removing Banks and combining the Department of the Gulf and several other commands into a Trans-Mississippi Department. Halleck reminded him that McClernand would be a senior officer in any department thus created. Although he expressed concern about Banks and his many political friends, who would demand an important command for him, the same held true for McClernand. To Sherman he wrote, "It seems but little better than murder to give important commands to such men as Banks, Butler, McClernand . . . and yet it seems impossible to prevent it."[115] Had McClernand learned of these letters, he would have considered them further evidence of the "clique of West Pointers" who were against him.

In fact, had McClernand known what was transpiring in Arkansas during this time, he would have harbored no doubts that West Pointers besides Grant, Sherman, and Halleck were against him. In March, Maj. Gen. Frederick Steele, a West Point classmate of Grant's, wrote Sherman that Brig. Gen. John W. Davidson had "attempted McClernand's game on me, and was also blown up by his own bombshell." Steele was convinced that Davidson was "going straight to Washington for the purpose of political intrigue," which he was. A letter written by Davidson that challenged a government policy had been published in the *Missouri Democrat.* He had been admonished, and then he had attempted to write directly to the president about the matter. As he did not have the political influence of McClernand, however, Halleck easily rebuffed his attempt.[116] Nevertheless, the incident is an indication of how widespread was the knowledge of the affairs of John McClernand.

For several days beginning in late April, McClernand was seriously ill with malaria. Finally, on 1 May, he placed Brigadier General Lawler temporarily in command of the Thirteenth Corps, although Lawler continued to issue orders in McClernand's name.[117]

On 2 and 5 May, the Thirteenth Corps made strong probes of Confederate positions to the front, but McClernand had little involvement with them. Finally, on 6 May, upon "the urgent entreaty of [his] physician," he requested that Banks allow him to move to a house in town. He expressed his expectation that it would be for only three or four days. Banks approved the request. The next day, however, McClernand informed Banks that "owing to the present state of health," he would place Lawler in command of the corps. This created a slight administrative problem, because Lawler was also assigned as corps chief of staff; Banks pointed out to his subordinate that Lawler could not simultaneously hold both positions. Finally, on 10 May 1864, Lawler assumed command of the Thirteenth Army Corps as his sole duty. In his letter to Banks McClernand expressed his hope "that improved health will enable me to rejoin my command at an early day."[118]

From Alexandria the next day McClernand wrote Brig. Gen. Fitz-Henry Warren, commander of the First Brigade, First Division, that he had "been desperately sick for seven or more days, but [was] getting better." The general was indeed very ill. A reporter for the *Chicago Tribune* reported that he had found McClernand "lying prostrate with chronic illness." He was not to return to his command as he hoped. The next month the Thirteenth Corps would be disbanded and its units scattered throughout the Department of the Gulf. In February 1865 it would briefly be resurrected, only to be disbanded again in July after the war ended.[119] John Alexander McClernand would not be present for those events.

10
The Final Years

An ailing John McClernand returned to Illinois that spring of 1864 to regain his health. He again practiced law, forming a partnership with fellow Springfield lawyers A. M. Broadwell and William M. Springer. In July he wrote Sen. Lyman Trumbull that his leave of absence from the army was about to expire and that he desired to visit Lincoln in Washington. Trumbull forwarded the request to the president, who responded only that the general's leave was "extended until further orders."[1]

He had not given up on the possibility of returning to an active military command. In July he proposed to Stanton that an independent command be created along the Mississippi from St. Louis to New Orleans and be manned by his old Thirteenth Corps. Apologetically, he offered his services and added that he desired "to be serviceable to my country in her present need." If not, he would resign, "rather than become a useless charge to the Government." He would not hear from Stanton.[2]

In the fall McClernand campaigned actively for the Democratic nominee, Maj. Gen. George Brinton McClellan (who had been at home in New Jersey "awaiting orders" since November 1862), against Lincoln. Harking back to his support for Douglas, McClernand proclaimed that McClellan "believes in the sovereignty of the people" and "would preserve the Union at all hazards."[3] The popular Lincoln, however, won an overwhelming victory.

The 1864 election raises the question of whether there was a more sinister reason than Lincoln gave for his unwillingness to pursue McClernand's demands for a court of inquiry. Is it conceivable that the general could have challenged Lincoln for the presidency rather than McClellan? Had the Thirteenth Corps broken the Confederate line on 22 May, much of the glory for the capture of Vicksburg would have gone to John McClernand. His record of military victories far surpassed that of McClellan. He was still a renowned figure in the Democratic party. Had he been instrumental in the fall of

Vicksburg, or had a court of inquiry determined that Grant—Lincoln's man—had not adequately supported him, would he have replaced McClellan on the ticket? By not supporting McClernand, Lincoln rid himself of a potential serious challenger in 1864.

On 23 November, Maj. Gen. John Alexander McClernand submitted his resignation from the army. He gave several reasons for that action. He stated he was unwilling to hold military office with no opportunity to exercise its functions; under those circumstances, he could do more for the war effort as a civilian. But the real reasons were reflected in his comments about his treatment at the hands of government officials: "The personal relations borne towards me by officers in the military service who are my superiors in rank and influence render my future usefulness in my military capacity contingent and uncertain. My retirement from the military service would relieve both them and me from any further embarrassment growing out of these actions."[4]

One government official, Lincoln's secretary John Hay, was delighted that McClernand was out of the picture. In his opinion, McClernand was "a vain, irritable, overbearing, exacting man who is possessed of the monomania that it was a mere clerical error which placed Grant's name and not his in the commission of the Lieutenant General."[5]

Neither Grant nor Sherman would elaborate on the resignation in their memoirs, but both welcomed his departure at the time. Grant added his official endorsement to McClernand's proposed resignation in a letter to Stanton. "I am satisfied the good of the service will be advanced by [his] withdrawal from service." Sherman left no doubt as to how he felt about the politician. He later wrote his father-in-law, Thomas Ewing, "McClernand is a mean, envious and impracticable fool that caused Grant and me more real trouble than any volunteer General we had to deal with."[6]

On 21 April 1865 the train carrying the body of the assassinated President Lincoln departed from Washington. On board were John McClernand and Richard Yates, who had been elected to the U.S. Senate in 1864. The train reached Springfield on 3 May. The funeral procession, divided into eight divisions, was held the following day. McClernand rode at the head of the second division, behind which came the hearse. Lincoln and McClernand had been political opponents, but both had believed in the Union. McClernand's eulogy stressed the "recuperative spirit" of the republic, which would "enable it to triumph over every vicissitude and every misfortune." He also declared his faith in the new president, Andrew Johnson, whom he had known since the two served together in Congress in 1848.[7]

Ironically, despite his antipathy toward West Pointers, in April 1866 McClernand requested Illinois senator Trumbull appoint his son Edward to the academy. Trumbull suggested that Edward request an "at large" appointment from President Johnson. In July the former general wrote the president, and later that month the secretary of war notified him that his son had received an appointment. Later that year Edward, who had accompanied his father during several Civil War campaigns, entered West Point; he would graduate in the class of 1870.[8]

McClernand continued his active involvement in Democratic politics. In February 1866, following Johnson's veto of the Freedman's Bureau bill, he wrote that "the people will adhere to him if necessary to the death." The stir resulting from the veto caused him to assure the president that he would do all in his power to oppose "the revolting schemes of your political opponents." In August he presided over the Illinois state Democratic convention and was elected chairman of the State Democratic Committee. On 17 September, the general attended a convention of former soldiers in Cleveland to demonstrate support for the administration. Among those attending was George Armstrong Custer. Back in Springfield, he attended a mass meeting of Democratic party enthusiasts and the next day wrote the president that "radicals of the Republican Party are making a fierce war upon you." He added that he expected Johnson to "triumph over all opposition." During September and October he addressed Democratic rallies throughout the state. He supported Lyle Dickey in his campaign for the House against McClernand's old subordinate, John Logan, who had switched to the Republican party. Logan, however, won decisively.[9]

In September, President Johnson, General Grant, Secretary of the Navy Welles, Secretary of State William Seward, now–Major General Rawlins, and a host of other dignitaries visited Springfield. McClernand was chairman of the arrangements committee and was part of the reception committee that traveled to Lincoln, Illinois, to meet the visitors. This was the first time the former general had encountered Grant and Rawlins since Vicksburg. Unfortunately, there is no record of the conversations during that meeting, but there must have been a chill in the fall air.[10]

McClernand supported President Andrew Johnson because he believed the nation should continue Lincoln's moderate reconstruction policies. Many radical Republicans in Congress opposed the Democrat Johnson on this issue and sought to impose a harsh settlement on the South. In a speech to the Democratic convention, McClernand decried those who desired to "treat the insurgents as prisoners of war, the states inhabited by them as territorial conquests, and their civil institutions as divested of all legitimacy." He urged the Democratic party to treat all states as "coequal, as members of the federal Union under the constitution."[11]

Nationally, the battle over Johnson's policies continued into 1867. The state elections that year would be critical to the survival not only of his policies but also of himself as president. McClernand viewed the prospects of a Democratic victory as "ominous." He offered to do whatever he could. After the results in Ohio (where Democrats lost by only a narrow margin) and Pennsylvania (which elected a Democrat as governor) were announced, McClernand wrote, "The long and cheerless night of misrule and violence is drawing to a close. We are transported with joy."[12]

The former general corresponded with Sen. Richard Yates, Secretary of the Interior Orville Browning, and with Illinois governor Richard Oglesby, with whom he had served in the war, on a variety of matters. His name was mentioned for ministerial posts in Berlin and Mexico. Illinois representative Samuel Scott Marshall assured McClernand that President Johnson supported his nomination for ambassador to Mexico, but now–Secretary of War Ulysses S. Grant actively worked against the nominations, as did his former colleague, John Logan. Unlike McClernand, Grant, a former Democrat, opposed Johnson's stance toward the former Confederacy. On 25 July 1868 the Senate rejected McClernand and instead confirmed West Point graduate and former Union general William S. Rosecrans as minister to Mexico.[13]

In 1868, as dissatisfaction with President Johnson increased, McClernand advised him that he needed to take strong action in defense of the Constitution to counter the Radical Republican offensive. He again offered his services to Johnson in whatever capacity he could be used: "Without seeking or even desiring prominence, I am willing to take any responsibility that patriotism and public duty may require." Johnson, though, was receiving other advice about McClernand's public duty. Thomas Ewing, who in addition to being Sherman's father-in-law was also an advisor to the president, had nothing good to say about the Illinoisan. Of the possibility of a cabinet post being offered to the former general, Ewing advised Johnson: "Do not give McClernand of Illinois a department. He is a blatherskite and withal a false man." No post was offered.[14]

In July of that year, in New York City, McClernand attended the National Convention of Soldiers and Sailors, called to express "the full harmony" of present and former military men "with the purposes and objects of the National Democratic Convention," meeting simultaneously in the city. McClernand was elected chairman of the first day's session. After adjournment he moved to the Democratic convention as a presidential elector. The Illinois delegation nominated him for vice president, but he declined, saying that his only ambition was "to assist is relieving the country from the thraldom which now binds her." He then assured the convention that the soldiers and sailors would support Horatio Seymour to oppose Grant. Seymour was subsequently nominated.[15]

McClernand's appearance at the Democratic convention caused quite a tumult in Springfield. The Republican-leaning *Daily State Journal* castigated him for the speech nominating him to the vice presidency; it had characterized the general as having been the brains behind the Vicksburg campaign but whose glory had gone to "a much inferior man." Although the *Journal* had supported McClernand immediately after his relief, in the politically charged atmosphere of 1868 it clearly favored the man who had taken the surrender of Vicksburg and then led the Union armies to Appomattox.[16]

A second controversy raised by the newspaper concerned a fellow attendee at the Democratic convention. In addition to blasting McClernand for opposing Grant, the *Journal* also took him to task for his "hand-shaking with Gen. Wade Hampton," a former Confederate. It had been natural that McClernand and his former enemy would meet, because Hampton, as did McClernand, supported President Johnson's lenient policies toward the South. In the month before the November election the paper several times raised the memory of that meeting and elaborated on what it believed to be the hypocrisy of McClernand. Once he had charged the Confederacy with having committed the "foulest crime in the history of the world since the crucifiction [*sic*] of our Saviour," but now he was inviting Hampton to Springfield to speak on political issues of the day. In a reexamination of McClernand's September 1863 speech in Janesville, Wisconsin, the *Journal* questioned whether he was now "guilty of shameful inconsistency" in forgetting "the principles he advocated during the war." In harsh terms, the paper urged the voters to reject the "sycophantic, fawning and disgusting attitude of the Democracy . . . toward the rebel chiefs." Hampton declined the invitation to Springfield, but the issue indicated how McClernand's almost undisputed popularity in his home town had changed since the war.[17]

Despite the *Journal*'s opposition, McClernand's popularity remained high among Democrats. In August McClernand spoke to a "grand democratic meeting" in Jacksonville, Illinois, and in September to a rally in Indianapolis. At home he served on the reception committee for, and introduced at a banquet, Sen. George H. Pendelton, who had been George McClellan's vice-presidential running mate in 1864. The next month, he served as master of ceremonies at a banquet to celebrate the laying of the cornerstone of a new statehouse. Presidential candidate Grant was in Springfield the day of the ceremony, but apparently he and McClernand did not meet. McClernand was then elected chairman of the Executive Committee of the Democratic State Central Committee. His oratorical skills had not lessened; he exhorted the faithful to go "once more to the breach," as "defeat and disasters are irresistibly closing upon [the Radicals] as the great waters close upon the depths of the dark, deep sea." Despite his efforts, Grant would capture the Illinois popular and electoral votes. Two years later the former general was elected to fill a vacancy on the court of the Thirteenth Judicial Circuit, and he would serve in that position for three years.[18]

Notwithstanding McClernand's intense dislike for Sherman, in July 1870 he wrote the recently appointed general in chief of the army to recommend that he visit Europe "for the purpose of acquiring information and making observations" about the approaching war between France and Prussia. Sherman replied that Grant also thought he should go, but that it would cost too much. He concluded, "I thank you for the confidence manifested by your letter."[19]

However, the publication of Sherman's memoirs in 1875 reopened the feud between the two former Union soldiers. The memoirs served only to reinforce McClernand's conclusion that Sherman had conspired to drive him from command. To a former subordinate at Arkansas Post, George Morgan, he wrote of his continued belief that Sherman had "inconsiderately hurried" the departure of troops from Memphis in December 1862 "to forestall my arrival to take command." In a fierce attack, he charged that "dignities, emoluments and homage are not sufficient to satisfy him." To McClernand, Sherman possessed "abnormal ambition and egotism"—a charge that many had levied against McClernand. In a reference to Sherman's relief from command in Kentucky in November 1861, McClernand asserted that the general was "lacking in mental equilibrium." Although in the letter to Morgan the former Illinois general praised Sherman's "March to the Sea" as "noble," he blasted his performance at Shiloh, Chickasaw Bayou, and Vicksburg. Unfairly and inaccurately, though, he also charged that Sherman had "inconsiderately wandered off" during the fighting at Arkansas Post.[20]

McClernand's feud with Sherman was revived not only upon publication of the latter's memoirs but also six years later, in a meeting of the Society of the Army of the Tennessee, held in Cincinnati. There he disputed Sherman's continuing claims that he had not been surprised at Shiloh. In his view, Sherman had been good at directing a "grand enterprise" (such as the march to the sea) but not at directing men in battle; his problem was his "natural excitability and disposition to exaggerate apparent difficulties." In another reference to Sherman's difficulties in the early stages of the war, when he had been charged with insanity, McClernand continued, "This excitability, combined with an abnormal egotism, sometimes interpreted as insanity, disqualified [him] to see men and things in a clear light."[21]

McClernand also continued to have low regard for Grant. In 1869 he attempted to correspond with the former Confederate general Stephen Dill Lee, who had commanded the forces at the point of McClernand's attack on 22 May 1863, but he was unsuccessful. Undoubtedly he wanted evidence to redeem his military reputation, at Grant's expense. He also corresponded with Stephen Burbridge, who had commanded a brigade in McClernand's Thirteenth Corps. Burbridge opposed Grant's renomination for president in 1872 and asked McClernand to supply whatever information he could to use against "the ignorant ambitious man who seeks to put himself at the head of the nation as dictator."[22] There is no record of a reply.

Although his son Edward was now a West Point cadet, time had not lessened his father's low opinion of academy graduates or the value of their training before and during the war. It had been Sherman's "technical education" that had "cramped and confined" his ability to succeed "in practical war." In McClernand's mind, the cost of that learning was "much valuable blood and treasure." For the remainder of his life he believed he had been treated unfairly by Grant, Sherman, and the "clique of West Pointers" who had driven him from command.[23]

In contrast, McClernand's conflicts with one West Pointer, Eugene Carr, had been forgotten by 1885. Carr, the general who in the summer of 1863 had complained to Grant that McClernand had not credited his division's role at the Big Black River battle, had remained in the army and was now seeking promotion to brigadier general. To Secretary of War William C. Endicott, McClernand wrote a warm letter of recommendation: "To say that he was an important factor in that remarkable [Vicksburg] campaign is but to say the simple truth and but to do him simple justice." Carr, though, would not be promoted until 1892.[24]

In 1872, McClernand again presided over the state Democratic convention, and in 1876 he chaired the national Democratic convention that nominated Samuel Tilden. McClernand traveled to New York, and on 11 July he officially notified Tilden of his nomination. Tilden lost in Illinois but won the popular vote nationally, with a margin of 247,448. In electoral votes, though, he had only 184 of the 185 votes required for election; Rutherford B. Hayes had garnered 165 electoral votes. Twenty votes were contested, nineteen of which were in the South. McClernand called for each state committee to meet in January to determine how to address the problem. Not until two days prior to the inauguration was a compromise reached, in which the Republicans agreed to withdraw troops from the South and appoint a Southern Democrat to the cabinet in exchange for the required electoral votes. Hayes was then inaugurated. That year also, McClernand returned to the Illinois House, to speak about the days when he and Lincoln had served together in that body.[25]

After the election McClernand continued his active role in national party affairs. In 1879 the Democrats in New York were split into two factions. Securing the governorship of that state was deemed critical to the party because of the impact such a victory could have on the national election the following year. McClernand urged Tilden to seek the governor's office. In his view, the split had caused the "diseased members of the party to fall off," and only Tilden—still referred to by many Democrats as president—had the stature to reunite the party to face the Republicans. Tilden declined to run, and the Republicans went on to victory in New York.

The following year McClernand urged Tilden to take another run at the presidency. "The old coach stands ready to be hitched to, and that done, a safe and prosperous journey lies ahead," he wrote. "Lead the way in a speech," he implored Tilden. The nomination, though, went to Winfield Hancock. The White House went to James Garfield. Again in 1884 McClernand urged Tilden to bear the standard for the Democratic party, referring to the 1876 election as a "crime which defeated the will of the people." In his view, only Tilden could save the Democrats. In poor health, he declined. The nomination and the presidency went to Grover Cleveland.[26]

Ironically, John Logan, who had served with McClernand, had campaigned for the 1884 Republican nomination, unsuccessfully. Much of his support had come from the Grand Army of the Republic, of which McClernand was a member. To counter that support, Democrats organized the National Veteran Association, which claimed to be the true friend of Union veterans. John McClernand represented Illinois on the national committee.[27]

In addition to his state and national political activities, John McClernand also maintained an active life in Springfield. He attended and gave a toast at the founding of the alumni association of Springfield High School, from which Edward had graduated in 1866. He was the grand marshal of a parade that transferred battle flags of Illinois regiments from the state arsenal to the newly constructed state capitol. He had an abiding interest in Union veterans and urged that a monument be erected in memory of the soldiers who died in the war. He also formed a new law partnership, with Charles A. Keyes, and he practiced in the town until 1886. He even had two horses, which he contracted with an individual in Dexter Park, Illinois, to train and race.[28]

In January 1886 McClernand's name was mentioned for the postmaster position in Springfield. He wrote Charles Lanphier of the *Illinois State Journal* that he "was not an applicant for any office" but that he would accept any position offered. He then wrote Illinois congressman and former law partner William M. Springer that he did not want the post office position, but that he did desire appointment as Commissioner for the Utah Territory.

McClernand had first become involved with Mormon interests during his Illinois legislature days of 1840. The year prior, Joseph Smith had arrived in the state after having been driven from Missouri. His group, known as "Mormons," had initially supported the Whigs, because it was the Democrats who had opposed them in Missouri. To curry favor, Democrats in the Illinois legislature, one of them John McClernand, had voted unanimously to charter a Mormon settlement, which soon became the largest town in Illinois. As a congressman in 1860, he had introduced a measure to repeal the organization of Utah as a separate territory, as provided for in the Compromise of 1850. His objective was to counter the growth of Mormonism and the practice of polygamy. Although he and Lincoln had agreed on the evil of polygamy, the two had disagreed on McClernand's proposal to counter its growth in Utah. On 19 April he received the appointment from Democratic President Grover Cleveland, and at month's end he arrived in Salt Lake City.[29]

Commissioner McClernand had left his wife Minerva and their children in Springfield. (Since their marriage in December 1862 prior to his departure for the Arkansas Post campaign, they had had three children—Rosalind, John, and Helen Chase. Unlike three of those born to John and Sarah, all would survive infancy and live into the 1900s.) The commission met about 170 days a year, in three or four sessions. Between sessions the commissioner would return to his home in Springfield.[30]

From Salt Lake City, McClernand wrote Lanphier of the extensive irrigation efforts that had led to great fertility in the area. He had found a mix of local and congressional laws that were often contradictory and made the resolution of legal questions difficult. "Everything . . . is substantially in the hands of the Mormons," he wrote. They held "absolute local dominion," and only action by the governor or the commission could override their decisions.[31]

Congress had created the Utah Commission in 1882, as a provision of the Edmunds Act. Republican President Chester Arthur had signed it into law on 22 March. Sen. George F. Edmunds of Vermont, who introduced the measure, had declared it the purpose of the commission to "put the political power of that Territory [Utah] . . . into the hands of those who are obedient to the law, and not to the hierarchy and the polygamists who are disobedient to it." The law required the appointment of five commissioners, no more than three of whom could be from one party. The main problems the commissioners faced were the polygamy question, the enfranchisement of women, and equitable political representation for non-Mormons. To resolve those questions, the commission sought to exclude polygamists from voting or holding office. To accomplish that, they needed to break the political power of the polygamists in the hierarchy of the Mormon church. Those issues were no farther toward resolution when McClernand arrived than they had been in 1882.[32]

In 1887 the commission recommended to Congress that Utah not be admitted as a state until the Mormons "have abandoned polygamy in good faith." That year Congress passed the Edmunds-Tucker Act, which required as a prerequisite to voting or holding office an oath that the applicant would obey all laws concerning polygamy. The following year, the commission recommended that all Mormons be disenfranchised. McClernand submitted a minority report, in which he disagreed with the recommendation. He argued that although polygamy was a ground for disenfranchisement, the practice of Mormonism was not, and that in fact disenfranchisement violated the Constitutional provision that allowed for free exercise of religion. He viewed polygamy as coming to an end, and he felt that any further efforts to impose sanctions on the practice amounted to persecution. Despite his argument, McClernand's minority position was not sustained. He submitted a second minority report in 1889, because the commission again recommended that all members of the Mormon church be disenfranchised. Maintaining the independence that had characterized his years in Congress, he refused in 1890 to sign the commission report, which recommended disenfranchisement.[33]

After the United States Supreme Court in February 1890 upheld an Idaho law allowing for disenfranchisement of Mormons, Sen. Shelby M. Cullum and Rep. Isaac C. Strubble introduced the Cullum-Strubble Bill to disenfranchise all members of the Mormon church. The issue was defused on 6 October 1890, when the General Conference of the Church of Jesus Christ of Latter-Day Saints approved a manifesto issued by church president Wilford Woodruff abolishing the practice of polygamy. The majority of the commission questioned the sincerity of Woodruff's manifesto, but, as reflected in his minority report of 1891, McClernand accepted it as genuine. In 1891 the Mormons also abandoned their People's party and began to affiliate with the Republican and Democratic parties. McClernand believed that this was evidence of the advances being made in Utah, and he urged that no more restrictions be placed upon the people of the territory. The majority of the commission disagreed, and in their 1892 report they expressed concern as to whether affairs in Utah had actually changed. McClernand's disagreement with that assessment is presumably why he refused also to sign the 1892 report.[34]

On 4 January 1893, President Benjamin Harrison issued an amnesty to all Mormons who had abstained from polygamy since 1 November 1890, a date that coincided with Woodruff's manifesto. Left unresolved was whether franchise privileges could be restored to those disenfranchised before Harrison's amnesty. The United States attorney general refused to issue an interpretation, and the decision was left to the commissioners. McClernand and two others maintained that the amnesty did not restore the right to vote. Because legal opinion in Utah was equally divided over the issue, they decided that voting rights should be restored to those previously disenfranchised if they swore that they had not practiced polygamy since 1 November 1890. The issue was finally resolved in September 1894, when President Cleveland issued an amnesty provision to that effect.[35]

McClernand retained his seat on the Utah Commission until 1894. As noted, the Edmunds Act had provided for no more than three members from one party. When the Republican Harrison was elected, he removed the Democratic chairman of the committee and replaced him with a Republican, in order to have three Republicans in the body. In 1893, Democrat Grover Cleveland removed the Republican chairman and replaced him with a Democrat. In March of that year, Congress determined that from that date forward, all members of the commission must be Utah residents. By April 1894 all members, to include McClernand, had resigned and been replaced as required by law. The former commissioner returned to Illinois.[36]

When in July 1888 Mary Todd Lincoln, a close friend of Sarah and widow of the slain president, died, McClernand had returned to Springfield from Salt Lake City to chair a citizen's committee to honor her memory. The group passed a resolution that recognized her as the wife of a man "whose name has become canonized in the hearts of all lovers of liberty."[37] The former general held no animosity toward his political foe. No words of disparagement would issue from him about his treatment by Lincoln. Never would he cast blame on him for his relief from command. Despite their political differences, he recognized the president's contribution to the maintenance of the Union.

In 1895, the Illinois legislature passed a resolution instructing the Illinois congressional delegation "to do all in their power" to obtain a pension for the aging Springfield general. The following year he received a grant, but in January 1900 another bill was introduced by Illinois congressman John G. Springer, to provide him a hundred dollars a month. Dan Sickles, a former Union general who had participated in the great Civil War battles in the East, rose in support: "Let us pass one good bill as an atonement for all the bad ones we have passed. A grateful country should not allow Gen. John A. McClernand to die in want." The bill passed.[38]

Citizen John A. McClernand was in ill health for several years. Springfield newspapers reported in February 1900 that he was confined to bed, and March that he had grown weaker. Finally, on 20 September, the old soldier crossed the river. Attired in the uniform of a United States Army major general, he lay in state in his home on Sixth Street. On the afternoon of 23 September he was laid to rest in Oak Ridge Cemetery, not far from the tomb of Abraham Lincoln.[39] In his will he left to his widow, Minerva, and his children a personal estate of eight hundred dollars and one piece of real estate. Minerva lived until 14 January 1931 and was buried in the family plot in Springfield.

John Alexander McClernand's military career spanned little more than three years. He commanded Union forces in numerous victories, but his relief from command outside the Vicksburg fortifications has sullied his legacy. In his 19 June 1863 letter to Halleck in which he informed the general in chief that he had relieved McClernand, Grant wrote, "I should have relieved him long since for general unfitness for his position."[40] Was John McClernand in fact unfit for his position? Does his military record accord with Grant's assessment?

McClernand entered military service on a par with many others who had no formal military education or little to no practical military experience. He rose from brigadier general commanding a brigade to major general commanding a corps. His initial appointment was a political expedient, but the record is clear that his subsequent promotion was a result of military success. Certainly, in his first major engagement at Belmont, he had made mistakes. He lost contact with one of his regiments, although the result was that the Confederate flank was enveloped by that regiment. He lost control of his men after the Rebel encampment was taken, but the same charge can be leveled against Grant. He again lost control of a regiment that failed to retreat with the main body. Despite those shortcomings, he was in the thick of the fighting. He personally sought the missing regiment, and his action to establish a defense at the landing site possibly saved the Union force from destruction.

At Fort Henry, although he made a personal reconnaissance, he failed to account for delays that could be caused by inclement weather, and he must bear responsibility for the escape of the Confederate garrison. At Fort Donelson he impulsively launched an ill-advised attack that served no purpose and resulted in numerous casualties. He also must bear some responsibility, along with Grant, for failure to perceive that the Confederates were massing for a breakout on his right flank. His reaction to that event, though, was superb: quickly he rallied and reformed his division to meet the onslaught. Recognizing the seriousness of the situation, he unhesitatingly sent for reinforcements. As at Belmont, he exposed himself to enemy fire and was conspicuous to his soldiers as he moved about the battlefield. His gallantry was recognized by promotion to major general.

Shiloh was a near disaster for the Union cause in the West. McClernand had learned a hard lesson at Fort Donelson, and he repeatedly questioned the security of the army deployed around Pittsburg Landing. Grant later wrote that he did not anticipate an attack. Despite his persistent denials, Sherman unquestionably was surprised by Johnston's assault. Much of the credit for stemming the Confederate tide on the first day of battle must go to John McClernand. As Sherman's division was crumbling, McClernand was deploying brigades to prevent Sherman's left flank from being enveloped and his command overrun. McClernand was able to keep his division reasonably in order despite the overwhelming force arrayed against him, was able to withdraw under intense enemy pressure, and was able to gain some success with dogged counterattacks. Had he not acted as promptly or as courageously as he did, the right of the Union line would have been smashed, Prentiss enveloped, and possibly the divisions of W. H. L. Wallace and Hurlbut destroyed before they had time to deploy into line of battle. There is little fault to be found with the generalship of John McClernand on that Sunday.

A critical question to be asked when assessing a general's performance is: "Did he accomplish his mission?" McClernand's mission at Arkansas Post was to destroy the Confederate garrison. Despite problems encountered soon after debarking, he reacted quickly, resolved the dilemmas, and captured the fort. The only controversy was whether its capture was a proper mission. Grant finally admitted that it was. At Port Gibson McClernand accomplished his mission of driving the Confederates from their defensive positions, although he can be faulted for not using his reinforcements properly. Had he done so, the victory might have been more complete, although such a conclusion is difficult because of the terrain over which he had to fight. At Champion Hill, the Union army succeeded in driving the Confederates back toward Vicksburg, but McClernand's leadership was not inspired. Had he followed Napoleon's admonition to "march to the sound of the guns," destruction of the Confederate army might have been possible. The fact that he did not, though, must be scrutinized in light of Grant's many admonitions to move cautiously. Despite his deliberateness, his actions were still far more aggressive than those of the West Pointer Andrew J. Smith, who commanded one of his divisions. The next day, at Big Black River, McClernand's corps, in the advance, smashed Confederate resistance in an aggressive attack by one of his brigades.

McClernand's first assault on Vicksburg failed, as did the assaults of the other corps commanders. McClernand had expressed his concern to Grant about the low probability of success due to the strength of the defensive position, but Grant nonetheless ordered the attack, and it failed. Perhaps Grant believed that the Rebel army was so weakened by Union successes of the past few days that resistance would easily crumble.

The most controversial event of McClernand's military career occurred on 22 May, and it was a major factor in his relief from command. His divisions entered the Confederate position, penetrating farther than the divisions of Sherman and McPherson. Obviously he believed he was on the verge of a breakthrough, on the basis of what he could observe from his position near the front. His failure to provide for a reserve, however, cost him the opportunity. Grant's failure to concentrate the attack, as recommended by McClernand, and to designate a reserve, and his failure to go personally to McClernand's position may have cost the army commander the opportunity to smash through the Confederate defenses. As later Confederate testimony would indicate, the situation was critical, but by the time Union reinforcements arrived, the Rebels had been able to stabilize their position.

This brief review of the major battles of McClernand's career indicates that he was, as Lew Wallace said, "rapidly acquiring the art of war." From November 1861 until 19 May 1863, McClernand had been part of victory after victory. He had made mistakes, but so had Grant, who was severely criticized for his absence at Fort Donelson and at Shiloh at the moment of Confederate attack. Sherman had been inexcusably unprepared at Shiloh and soundly defeated at Chickasaw Bayou. Sherman's and McPherson's assaults on 19 May, assaults directed by Grant, had also failed, as did their attacks on 22 May. John McClernand's record thus compares quite favorably with those of the luminaries of the western theater—luminaries whose stars would continue "ever in the ascendant."

The second critical question to be asked when assessing a general's leadership is: "Did he take care of his men?" With the exception of his failures to ensure his soldiers did not discard their overcoats and blankets prior to the Donelson and Shiloh campaigns, the answer is "yes." His initial concern was that his men be well armed. The variety of relics with which they were armed initially would be ineffective in battle. He used every means, to include his political connections with Yates, Lincoln, and Quartermaster General Meigs, to try to provide modern weapons for his soldiers. That he was not successful sooner is due to no fault of his own.

McClernand recognized that training led to victory as well as to survival on the battlefield. Details that distracted men from drill were abhorrent to him, and he pestered Grant to limit such distractions, usually unsuccessfully. His persistence could be vexing, but he recognized that the necessity to train his command was paramount.

To verify that his men were cared for, he conducted personal inspections of posts under his command while stationed at Cairo. On the march he was concerned about food, sanitation, and the care of equipment. Such details can make the difference between an army that is prepared to fight and one that is not.

Although it cannot be substantiated, there are allusions to McClernand being a "teetotaler." If true, that might explain partially his actions to restrict access to spirits during his command's stay in Cairo. In any event, he recognized the negative impact that drunkenness had on discipline. He realized that men who got drunk with officers could not be expected to exhibit respect for and obedience to those same officers. He also realized the detrimental effect of drinking on effective training. Although it was not a popular decision, he made the correct decision to close the drinking establishments in the town.

From his years of oratorical prowess as a politician, McClernand recognized the power of the spoken and written word. He did not hesitate to speak exuberantly to his soldiers of their exploits, to praise their accomplishments, and to exhort them to greater achievements. To do so after major victories was appropriate; to do so during a battle, such as at Port Gibson, was not. To extol their successes was laudable; to do so at the expense of other commands was base and could only lead to strained relations with other generals. Gustave Koerner recorded in his memoirs that McClernand's style was such that he did not try "to persuade, but to subdue."[41] Such a tone did not set well with Grant or Halleck. It was his inability to restrain his oratory that led eventually to his downfall.

Whether the publication of his congratulatory order at Vicksburg alone would have brought about McClernand's relief is problematical. Perhaps Grant would have overlooked it had it not been for a history of insubordinate behavior. Perhaps had Lincoln reprimanded McClernand for the numerous letters and complaints against other generals, as well as for his unsolicited advice, the general's future would have been different. As it was, Stanton clearly informed the political general that his letters to the secretary should be sent instead to Halleck, as general in chief. Halleck reminded him that a letter to the president violated army regulations. Despite that rebuke, McClernand continued to bombard Lincoln with missives about his accomplishments and his plights.

Although, as Shakespeare wrote in *Antony and Cleopatra*, ambition is the soldier's virtue, it is a virtue only so long as it is subordinated to the good of the army. John McClernand was certainly ambitious, but did he subordinate that virtue to the good of the army? Much of McClernand's difficulty in subordinating himself to military discipline can be attributed to his ambition, which Koerner described as "unbounded." His political career was one of ambition—the Illinois legislature, the United States House of Representatives, attempts to enter the Senate, a campaign for speaker. As Joseph Wallace, a fellow Illinoisan who knew him, wrote, "He would not be content with occupying an inferior position in any sphere of life." Sherman, Dana, and Badeau recognized the ambitious streak in the former politician and were convinced that his goal was to replace Grant and command the movement against Vicksburg. There may have been some truth to their suspicions. His actions to obtain command of the Mississippi River expedition and his continued attempts to obtain an independent department command are clear indicators that he had no desire to occupy "an inferior position."[42]

Unrestrained ambition can lead to disrespect and disloyalty. Although Napoleon called insubordination evidence of a strong mind, insubordination and strong-mindedness can destroy an army. Military insubordination was a decided character flaw in John McClernand. His profession of law and politics had provided little training in subordinating himself to higher authority. He had argued vehemently and often with political allies and opponents, and he had carried those arguments to the public through the newspapers. He had been accountable only to the electorate of his district, and it had continued to return him to the legislature and to Congress. He could be independent of politicians, including the great Stephen Douglas, with seeming impunity. As early as 1844 the editor of the *St. Clair Banner* had recognized the sterling qualities in the young politician but had added that he was "marked with true veteran independence."[43] He had been a party leader, but the military hierarchy was different. There were clear lines of authority to be obeyed, and chains of command to be recognized. Professional soldiers had little tolerance for those who ignored the rules of the profession and exercised "veteran independence." Loyalty, not independence, was required.

John McClernand gained a generalship through loyalty to the Union. While many Democrats opposed the war as Republican inspired, Democrat McClernand remained loyal to the cause; nonetheless, he could not remain loyal to his commanders. McClernand supported Grant when he was relieved by Halleck, but that soon changed. Halleck he charged with "utter incompetency," and Grant with owing his success to "the forbearance of [his] officers." He also reported to Lincoln rumors of Grant's drinking. Questions of rank were sure to cause him to bristle. Before Shiloh, he challenged Hurlbut's authority over transports and Smith's right to command him. After Shiloh, he challenged Halleck about his assignment as commander of the reserve and Grant about the geographical limits of his command. On numerous occasions, beginning after Arkansas Post, he challenged Grant's authority to command him. Both generals would become his enemies.[44]

Strong-mindedness can lead either to boldness, self-confidence, determination, and resoluteness, or to impulsivity, arrogance, willfulness, and inflexibility. Whether to Grant in regard to military operations or to Lincoln about perceived slights, he spoke his mind. In battle he was resolute. He fixed his mind on the objective and pushed relentlessly toward victory. His determination carried over to his men, who were infected with the same resoluteness. But his quality of a strong mind also had detrimental results. He was so sure of his own actions that he was given to bombast. He too quickly saw fault in others, and he was defensive and sensitive at perceived slights. His overestimation of his personal influence with Lincoln was such that he believed he could recommend strategy and condemn generals freely. A politician can succeed in a military environment only if he can control his ambition, his oratory, and his strong-mindedness.

Union major general Jacob Cox asserted that "self-command" was one of the chief qualities for a commander. McClernand, however, could not exercise the self-control necessary to constrain his spirit. The *New York Times* characterized his speeches as "temperately measured," yet he lost his temper with Wilson, which only reduced the low esteem in which he was held by members of Grant's staff. He had previously done the same with Warmoth and Jenney. He did not exercise self-control by limiting his correspondence with Lincoln or by tempering its content. James Wilson believed that this character flaw was the root cause of McClernand's ruin. "With an ordinary degree of self-control," he wrote, McClernand "would have come out of the war as one of its real heroes."[45]

McClernand had the potential to be a "real hero" because his dominant leadership characteristic was courage. Reports are replete with observations of his courage under fire and his presence at the front with his men. Even soldiers close to Grant who disliked the former politician granted him that much: Badeau—"he was a man of . . . courage," Wilson—"gallant," Rawlins—"an officer of undaunted courage." His post–Civil War political antagonist John Logan as late as 1887 still referred to him as "the gallant John McClernand."[46] John McClernand was able to put aside fear, expose himself to enemy fire, and lead his men to success on the battlefield. The strength of his own will and his confidence in his own ability and that of his soldiers allowed him to overcome fear of bodily harm. The politician McClernand had responded to challenges all of his professional life. The ultimate challenge for the soldier McClernand was combat. He had been stimulated by political difficulties, and his ability to overcome those difficulties had led to success. A personality that responded to the challenges and difficulties in the political arena was apt to accept those of the battlefield and respond similarly. Ambition, oratory, determination, confidence, and courage were John McClernand's heart and soul. Properly harnessed, those qualities can make a great politician or a great general. Unharnessed by self-control, they can lead to insubordination, inflexibility, and want of introspection.

Was there a hint of jealousy among professional soldiers at the success of a general with no military training and only very limited experience? Gideon Welles believed Grant hated McClernand and that he had a jealous streak that affected his judgment. He thought that Rawlins had been sent to Washington after McClernand was relieved specifically because Grant wanted to ensure that his own success would not be tainted by McClernand's charges. Franc Wilkie of the *Dubuque (Iowa) Herald* also wrote that Grant was jealous of McClernand.[47]

Neither Welles nor Wilkie offers evidence for their assertions. Although Grant had been far less successful before the war than had been McClernand, Grant still outranked him on the initial list of brigadier generals, and he continued to outrank him throughout the war. Grant had expressed confidence publicly in his fellow Illinoisan until McClernand wrote his report after Fort Donelson, which Grant referred to as "a little highly colored." Seemingly minor incidents, though, may have begun to affect Grant's opinion. McClernand's not taking command at Cairo and his renaming Fort Henry as Fort Foote, his long discourse on strategy before the movement to Fort Donelson, and the unauthorized attack on Maney's Battery may have caused Grant to wonder about the military aptitude of his subordinate. Grant's rush to judgment before he had the facts about the Arkansas Post campaign led to condemnation of McClernand by Halleck and cooled the relationship between the two Prairie State generals.

McClernand, too, may have had a jealous streak that affected his judgment and his actions. The Illinois politician Silas Noble observed in February 1863 that "there is a strong feeling of jealousy between Grant and McClernand." Surgeon Brinton believed McClernand to be jealous of Grant. An early biographer of Grant, Charles King, concluded that McClernand was "envious of Grant."[48] McClernand may have equated prewar political success as qualification for high command. In Grant he saw no evidence of prewar success in any endeavor. Perhaps McClernand could not bring himself to serve someone who had been on the lower fringes of society when he had been a leader of a major political party and had conversed freely and often with presidents. At Fort Donelson and at Shiloh, McClernand had been fighting Confederates while Grant was absent from the field, yet Grant continued to rise in prominence. The political general could not achieve distinction until he was out from under Halleck and Grant. An independent command would bring him unchallenged renown and the freedom to act without interference from others.

Despite his success on the battlefield and his character flaws, was McClernand's ultimate relief from command due to a conspiracy of West Pointers? Although Halleck had little regard for Grant, he had even less for political generals. When he took command in the field after Shiloh, McClernand was relegated to command of the reserve, while West Point officers commanded the forward corps. There can be no doubt that Grant and Sherman desired to seize Vicksburg before McClernand arrived. One of Grant's biographers, Robert McCormick, asserts that the primary reason was that they "feared that McClernand would . . . distinguish himself." He concludes that a conspiracy did exist against the Illinois general.[49]

Grant was vehemently opposed to the Arkansas Post expedition until he learned that fellow West Pointer Sherman had favored it. McClernand challenged Grant's order at Port Gibson to conserve ammunition and again in regard to outposts at Big Black River. Both challenges brought reactions from Rawlins and West Pointer Wilson that infected the atmosphere at Grant's headquarters. In May, near Raymond, the West Pointer McPherson not only defied an order from Grant and cursed at Wilson but also moved so slowly that Wilson believed he was responsible for Johnston's escape. This incident, however, apparently had no effect on the regard in which McPherson was held.[50]

Members of Grant's staff had long disliked McClernand. Rawlins after Belmont expressed his displeasure at the publicity the general received. Newspaperman Charles Dana clearly had little regard for the former politician and conveyed his opinions to Stanton. Because of the intimacy he enjoyed at Grant's headquarters, he undoubtedly was influenced by the opinions of the officers by whom he was surrounded. Even as late as July 1864, as assistant secretary of war, Dana wrote sarcastically to Rawlins that if Benjamin Butler were placed in overall command with McClernand and other discredited generals as subordinates, Washington would be safe.[51] Although Dana was not a graduate of West Point, the officers with whom he associated at Grant's headquarters—Grant, McPherson, Wilson, Sherman—were. Other key staff officers, such as Rawlins, who was intensely loyal to Grant and had no use for McClernand, and Brinton, who had clashed with McClernand, were outspoken in their criticism of the political general. Villard thought Dana's dispatches to be biased and reckless. Nevertheless, they were a source of information for Stanton and Halleck and had to have influenced their opinions of McClernand.[52]

John Logan, that other political general from Illinois, went on to a distinguished military career. After McPherson was killed near Atlanta in July 1864, Sherman appointed Logan to command the Army of the Tennessee, by virtue of seniority. Shortly thereafter, George Thomas, commander of the Army of the Cumberland and a West Point graduate, informed Sherman that he would not serve if Logan was given the command; he preferred West Pointer Oliver O. Howard. Sherman relented. Sherman wrote in his memoirs that Logan had taken command "and done well" but that "I regarded both Generals Logan and [Francis P.] Blair as 'volunteer soldiers,' that looked to personal fame and glory as auxiliary and secondary to their political ambition, and not as professional soldiers." Sherman realized criticism might ensue, so he added: "All these promotions happened to fall upon West Pointers, and doubtless Logan . . . had some reason to believe that we intended to monopolize the higher honors of the war for the regular officer. I . . . feel sure that I was not intentionally partial to any class."[53]

Logan, as did McClernand, would believe until he died that Sherman was partial and that he too had been a victim of a "clique of West Pointers." In a letter to his wife Mary he wrote, "Were I from West Point these two fights [battles near Atlanta] would make me more reputation that Sherman ever had before this campaign, but I do not expect it." A few days later he added, "West Point must have all under Sherman who is an infernal brute."[54]

There are similarities in the cases of McClernand and Logan. Both performed well on the battlefield. Both exhibited great personal courage. Both were used by Lincoln while in uniform. Both were politicians, and neither was a West Point graduate. The striking differences are in personality and desire for independence. Logan was more tolerant of his subordinate position, and even when replaced by Howard, he was willing to continue to serve under him and Sherman. McClernand had an overwhelming desire for independence, and his personality was such that he could not abide slights. Nevertheless, both were relieved by West Pointers and replaced by West Pointers.

It is impossible to state definitively whether a conspiracy existed by West Point graduates against non–West Point officers during the Civil War. The case of John McClernand, coupled with that of John Logan, provides cause to believe that such may have been the case. Sherman was defensive about the issue. So prevalent was the perception of favoritism that in a January 1865 letter to Grant, Sherman again addressed the question. The letter concerned Maj. Gen. Alfred H. Terry, a non–West Point officer who had captured Fort Fisher, North Carolina, earlier that month. Sherman wrote that he "rejoiced that Terry was not a West Pointer," because of allegations of conspiracy to ensure that military laurels were bestowed only on graduates of that institution.[55] Herman Hattaway and Archer Jones address the influence of West Point officers in their study *How the North Won.* Their conclusion is that a West Point education, in conjunction with service in the Mexican War, were the critical determinants for high rank in both the Union and Confederate armies. Of the forty-five highest ranking generals in both armies, forty-three (95 percent) had combat experience prior to the war. Twenty-eight (62 percent) met both criteria.[56]

Hattaway's and Jones's conclusion tends to dispel the charge of conspiracy in the aggregate, for non–West Point graduates with Mexican War experience rose to high rank in both armies. Yet the correspondence of Halleck, Sherman, and others suggests that there may have been prejudice against specific officers. Dislike by career officers of political appointees was only natural. To expect professional soldiers readily to accept politicians with little or no military background as superior or equal officers was unrealistic. One of those politicians was John McClernand. His arrival on the military scene undoubtedly was greeted with skepticism and disdain, even if it is not readily apparent in the written record. Grant's actions suggest that there may have been prejudice or jealousy toward McClernand. He had been severely criticized for absences at Fort Donelson and Shiloh, while McClernand had been lauded for his bravery. After Halleck took command in the field, Grant had been shunted aside, while McClernand at least had a command, albeit of the reserve. By mid-January 1863 Grant had been driven from Mississippi, but McClernand had won at Arkansas Post. McClernand knew and corresponded frequently with the president; Grant and Lincoln would not meet until March 1864. Nevertheless, newspapers reported that "Unconditional Surrender" Grant had won a string of victories in the West at a time when generals in other theaters were suffering defeat after defeat. He had earned the confidence of Lincoln and was in no danger of being replaced. After Vicksburg, McClernand was expendable.

McClernand's combat record of courage and success afforded no grounds for relief from command. His professional and personal conduct, however, did. Professional soldiers rightfully resented his insubordinate behavior and violations of the chain of command. His bombast, his attempts to garner glory for himself and his men, his disloyal missives about his superior officers, and his unbridled ambition fueled the resentment that met his arrival in the western theater. As Surgeon John Brinton wrote, the Illinoisan was unable to separate the politician from the soldier. Had he been able to do so, John McClernand, as Wilson wrote, "would have come out of the war as one of its real heroes."[57]

Although he served the citizens of the Prairie State faithfully for many years—in Vandalia, in Springfield, and in Washington—his legislative service is little known outside of Illinois. It was his lot to have lived in a state and in a time that featured the likes of Stephen Douglas and Abraham Lincoln. In Illinois he would always be in their shadow. On the national scene, he would not gain the prominence of Calhoun and Clay and Webster. His narrow defeat for speaker of the House of Representatives is evidence that John McClernand's star could not ascend beyond those of the more powerful and influential members of Congress.

Expansion and slavery were the critical issues of the day, and John McClernand was in the midst of both. His majestic oratory thundered through the House chamber, as he sought to persuade his colleagues to retain all United States territory south of 54°40' and to oppose the forces of disunion. His attempts to persuade the radicals and firebrands would fail, and secession would become a fact. When South Carolina seceded, John McClernand faced a crossroads in his life. Perhaps if he remained in the Congress he would acquire the mantle of Douglas. Yet he chose another path, and that was the way of the soldier. Why Lincoln appointed him is clear; why he accepted is much less so. No writings of his survive to provide insight into his motives. That he was ambitious is certain, but political ambition might have been achieved without the risk of death on the battlefield. Yet he chose the battlefield rather than the debate hall.

"Lawyer, Legislator, Soldier, Judge, Patriot" is the inscription on John Alexander McClernand's tombstone. His law practice had been successful, his legislative career remarkable. As a soldier he was brave, and as a judge, distinguished. He was influential, but his influence was overshadowed by the achievements of others. His accomplishments and his fame could not compete with those of Lincoln, Douglas, and Grant. In his lifetime he decried disunion; he fought to maintain the Union; and he served to expand the Union. As a patriot, he was their equal.

Notes

Preface

1. Russell F. Weigley, *History of the United States Army* (New York: Macmillan, 1967), 199, 216; Herman Hattaway and Archer Jones, *How the North Won: A Military History of the Civil War* (Urbana: Univ. of Illinois Press, 1983), 9.

2. T. Harry Williams, *Lincoln and His Generals* (New York: Random House, 1952), 191, 230; Bruce Catton, *The Army of the Potomac: A Stillness at Appomattox* (Garden City, N.Y.: Doubleday, 1953), 211; Bruce Catton, *This Hallowed Ground* (Garden City, N.Y.: Doubleday, 1956), 260; Robert Leckie, *None Died in Vain* (New York: Harper & Row, 1990), 245; Geoffrey Perret, *Ulysses S. Grant: Soldier & President* (New York: Random House, 1997), 163–64, 257–58; James McPherson, *Battle Cry of Freedom* (New York: Oxford Univ. Press, 1988), 400; Allan Nevins, *The War for the Union*, vol. 2, *War Becomes Revolution* (New York: Charles Scribner's Sons, 1960), 385; Shelby Foote, *The Civil War: A Narrative*, vol. 2, *Fredericksburg to Meridian* (New York: Random House, 1963), 373; Hattaway and Jones, *How the North Won*, 309–10.

1. From Congressman to General

1. [Joseph Wallace], "Biography of John A. McClernand," 1865[?], 1–5, Joseph Wallace Collection, Illinois State Historical Society; [Adolph Schwartz], "Biography of John Alexander McClernand," annotated by General Edward J. McClernand, 2 vols, 1863[?], 12, John Alexander McClernand Collection, Illinois State Historical Society; Alfred Orendorff, "General John A. McClernand," *Transactions of the Illinois State Historical Society* 6 (Springfield, Ill.: Phillips Bros., 1901): 80; Dumas Malone, ed., *Dictionary of American Biography*, 20 vols. and 8 supplements (New York: Charles Scribner's Sons, 1943–90), 7:587–88; handwritten manuscript by John Alexander McClernand in the possession of McClernand Crawford.

2. Orendorff, "General John A. McClernand," 81; John L. Satterlee, *The Black Hawk War and the Sangamo Journal* (Springfield, Ill.: John L. Satterlee, 1982[?]), 31–32, 73; Veterans' Records, National Archives, Washington, D.C.

3. Thomas M. Eddy, *The Patriotism of Illinois*, 2 vols. (Chicago: Clarke, 1865–66), 1:476; Orendorff, "General John A. McClernand," 81; Douglas C. McMurtie, "The First Printers of Illinois," *Journal of the Illinois State Historical Society* 26 (Oct. 1933): 211.

4. Wallace, "Biography of John A. McClernand," 6; Schwartz, "Biography of John Alexander McClernand," 14; David W. Lusk, *Politics and Politicians: A Succinct History of the Politics of Illinois from 1856 to 1884* (Springfield, Ill.: H. W. Rokker, 1884), 475. McClernand would be elected to the Illinois legislature in 1836, 1840, and 1842. He did not run in 1838 but chose instead to serve on the Canal Commission.

5. William H. Herndon and Jesse K. Weik, *Life of Lincoln* (Cleveland: World Publishing, 1942), 141; Josephine C. Chandler, "Dr. Charles Chandler: His Place in the American Scene," *Journal of the Illinois State Historical Society* 24 (Oct. 1931): 460–61; Rufus R. Wilson, ed., *Uncollected Works of Abraham Lincoln*, 2 vols. (Elmira, N.Y.: Primavera Press, 1947), 1:126; Usher Linder, *Reminiscences of the Early Bench and Bar of Illinois* (Chicago: Legal News, 1879), 71; Paul Simon, *Lincoln's Preparation for Greatness: The Illinois Legislative Years* (Urbana: Univ. of Illinois Press, 1971), 32, 156–57, 263.

6. Albert J. Beveridge, *Abraham Lincoln, 1809–1858*, 2 vols. (Boston: Houghton Mifflin, 1928), 1:189–95.

7. Wilson, *Uncollected Works of Abraham Lincoln*, 1:626–27; B. D. Monroe, "Life and Services of William Wilson, Chief Justice of the Illinois Supreme Court," *Journal of the Illinois State Historical Society* 11 (Oct. 1918): 393–94.

8. Eddy, *The Patriotism of Illinois*, 2:477; *Sangamo Journal*, 20 Sept. 1839, 2.

9. *Chicago Daily American*, 25 Apr., 2, 28 May 1839, 2; McClernand to Henry Eddy, 30 Oct. 1838, Henry Eddy Correspondence, Illinois State Historical Library.

10. *Sangamo Journal*, 3 May, 2, 7 June 1839, 2. "Colonel" was apparently an honorary title bestowed on McClernand for his service in the Black Hawk War.

11. Orendorff, "General John A. McClernand," 81; Robert W. Johannsen, ed., *The Letters of Stephen A. Douglas* (Urbana: Univ. of Illinois Press, 1961), 95–96; Cornelius J. Doyle, "Josiah Lamborn, Attorney General of Illinois," *Journal of the Illinois State Historical Society* 20 (July 1927): 191.

12. Simon, *Lincoln's Preparation for Greatness*, 243–44.

13. Wilson, *Uncollected Works of Abraham Lincoln*, 1:569; Clark E. Carr, *The Illini: A Story of the Prairies* (Chicago: A. C. McClurg, 1904), 367; *Sangamo Journal*, 23 Oct. 1840, 2; John Moses, *Illinois: Historical and Statistical*, 2 vols. (Chicago: Fergus Printing, 1895), 1:429, 431; *Galena (Illinois) Northwest Gazette and Advertiser*, 17 Feb. 1841, as quoted in Victor Hicken, "From Vandalia to Vicksburg" (Ph.D. diss., Univ. of Illinois, 1955), 30; Simon, *Lincoln's Preparation for Greatness*, 217, 221, 264

14. John Moses, *Illinois: Historical and Statistical*, 1:455; *Sangamo Journal*, 20 Sept. 1839, 2; Alexander Davidson and Bernard Stuvé, *A Complete History of Illinois from 1673 to 1873* (Springfield: Illinois Journal, 1874), 685; *Alton Telegraph*, 8 Apr. 1843, as quoted in Hicken, "From Vandalia to Vicksburg," 36.

15. Henry C. Whitney, *Life on the Circuit with Lincoln* (Boston: Estes and Lauriat, 1892), 419; Thomas J. McCormack, ed., *Memoirs of Gustave Koerner, 1809–1896*, 2 vols. (Cedar Rapids, Iowa: Torch Press, 1909), 1:483–84; Robert P. Howard, *Illinois: A History of the Prairie State* (Grand Rapids, Ill.: William B. Eerdmans Publishing, 1972), 103. Author Nathaniel Hughes surmised that the region was given the name "Egypt" as a result of its having sufficient grain to feed much of the area, which was

devastated by crop failures in the early nineteenth century. Nathaniel C. Hughes, *The Battle of Belmont: Grant Strikes South* (Chapel Hill: Univ. of North Carolina Press, 1991), 225 n.3.

16. *Alton Telegraph*, 20 May 1843, as quoted in Hicken, "From Vandalia to Vicksburg," 37; *Illinois State Register*, 21 July 1843, 2; Theodore C. Pease and James G. Randall, eds., *The Diary of Orville Hickman Browning*, 2 vols. (Springfield: Illinois State Historical Library, 1925), 1:25; Frank E. Stevens, "Life of Stephen Arnold Douglas," *Journal of the Illinois State Historical Society* 16 (Oct. 1923–Jan. 1924): 365; Johannsen, *Stephen A. Douglas*, 116.

17. *St. Clair Banner*, 23 Apr. 1844, 4; Beveridge, *Abraham Lincoln 1809–1858*, 2:311 n.

18. Hicken, "From Vandalia to Vicksburg," 43–44; *Congressional Globe*, 28th Cong., 1st sess., 6 Jan. 1844, 117–18. Judge Dominick Hall had fined Jackson for imposing martial law on New Orleans during the War of 1812.

19. *Sangamo Journal*, 5 Sept. 1844, 2; *Illinois State Register*, 27 Sept. 1844, 2; Schwartz, "Biography of John Alexander McClernand," 30; Theodore C. Pease, *Illinois Election Returns, 1818 to 1848* (Springfield: Trustees of the Illinois Historical Library, 1923), 143.

20. *Congressional Globe*, 29th Cong., 1st sess., 8 Jan. 1846, App. 273–79; 16 June 1846, 983; 11 May 1846, 795.

21. *Illinois Gazette*, 20 Aug. 1846, as quoted in Hicken, "From Vandalia to Vicksburg," 55; Stephen A. Douglas to Sidney Breese, 20 Oct. 1846, Sidney Breese Manuscript Collection, Illinois State Historical Library; Paul M. Angle, *Lincoln, 1854–1861: Being the Day-by-Day Activities of Abraham Lincoln from January 1, 1854 to March 4, 1861* (Springfield, Ill.: Abraham Lincoln Association, 1933), xviii; Paul M. Angle, *The Lincoln Reader* (New Brunswick, N.J.: Rutgers Univ. Press, 1947), 147–48.

22. *Congressional Globe*, 29th Cong., 2d sess., 15 Jan. 1847, 188, App. 103–4.

23. John S. Blum et al., eds., *The National Experience: A History of the United States*, 5th ed. (New York: Harcourt Brace Jovanovich, 1981), 289–90; McClernand to Charles H. Lanphier, 6 Jan. 1848, Charles H. Lanphier Papers, Illinois State Historical Library.

24. McClernand to Lanphier, 4 Mar., 30 May 1848, Lanphier Papers; *Congressional Globe*, 29th Cong., 2d sess., 15 Feb. 1847, 425.

25. James Dunlap to McClernand, 3 Jan. 1848; Charles Lanphier to McClernand, 13 Feb. 1848; F. D. Preston to McClernand, 22 Feb. 1848, all in McClernand Collection. Davidson and Stuvé, *A Complete History of Illinois*, 686–87; Moses, *Illinois: Historical and Statistical*, 2:563–64.

26. *Congressional Globe*, 31st Cong., 1st sess., 6 Dec. 1849, 8; 18 Dec. 1849, 43, 47; 28 Dec. 1849, 65–66. David M. Potter, *The Impending Crisis, 1848–1861* (New York: Harper & Row, 1976), 90.

27. Alexander H. Stephens, *A Constitutional View of the Late War between the States: Its Causes, Character, Conduct and Results*, 2 vols. (Philadelphia: National Publishing, 1870), 2:199–204; Orendorff, "General John A. McClernand," 82.

28. McClernand to Lanphier, 31 July 1850, McClernand Collection; George F. Milton, *The Eve of Conflict: Stephen A. Douglas and the Needless War* (Boston: Houghton Mifflin, 1934), 57; Joseph Wallace, "Biography of John A. McClernand," 35; *Congressional Globe*, 31st Cong., 1st sess., 10 June 1850, 696–701; McClernand to Augustus French, 4 July 1850, Augustus French Manuscript Collection, Illinois State Historical Library; Thomas Harris to Lanphier, 6 Feb. 1850, Lanphier Papers; Stephen A. Douglas to Lanphier, 7 Jan. 1850, Lanphier Papers; A. G. Sloo to McClernand, 14 May 1850, McClernand Collection.

29. McClernand to Lanphier, 31 July 1850, McClernand Collection. *Congressional Globe*, 30th Cong., 1st sess., 31 July 1848, 1015; 31st Cong., 1st sess., 24 July 1850, App. 944; 2d sess., 9 Dec. 1850, 16. Major L. Wilson, "Ideological Fruits of Manifest Destiny: The Geopolitics of Slavery Expansion in the Crisis of 1850," *Journal of the Illinois State Historical Society* 63 (Summer 1970): 133; Gerald M. Capers, *Stephen A. Douglas: Defender of the Union* (Boston: Little, Brown, 1959), 58–9; Allan Nevins, *Ordeal of the Union*, vol. 1, *Fruits of Manifest Destiny, 1847–1852* (New York: Charles Scribner's Sons, 1947), 353–54.

30. James Dunlap to McClernand, 19 May 1848, McClernand Collection; McClernand to Lanphier, 25 June 1850, Lanphier Papers; *Illinois State Register*, 1 Aug. 1850, 2.

31. Pease and Randall, *The Diary of Orville Hickman Browning*, 1:25.

32. *Illinois State Journal*, 20 Apr. 1852, 3; 21 Apr. 1852, 3. Roy F. Nichols, *Franklin Pierce* (Philadelphia: Univ. of Pennsylvania Press, 1931), 220, 228–29; Davidson and Stuvé, *A Complete History of Illinois*, 600; Milton, *The Eve of Conflict*, 97.

33. Milton, *The Eve of Conflict*, 118–19, 171–71; *Illinois State Journal*, 30 Sept. 1859, 2, reprint of speech quoted in full in *Alton Courier*, 16 Oct. 1854. President Pierce signed the Kansas-Nebraska Act into law on 30 May 1854. Most of the opposition in Illinois thus occurred after the bill was already law.

34. *Illinois State Register*, 17 Oct. 1854, 2; Carr, *The Illini*, 191–92, 200; reprint from *Alton Courier*, *Illinois State Journal*, 30 Sept. 1859, 2; Milton, *The Eve of Conflict*, 171–74.

35. Thomas Harris to Lanphier, 27 Jan. 1856, 6 Feb. 1856, Lanphier Papers. *Illinois State Journal*, 3 June 1856, 3; 3 July 1856, 3. Alonzo Rothschild, *"Honest Abe": A Study in Integrity* (Boston: Houghton Mifflin, 1917), 52–53, 105; Angle, *Lincoln, 1854–1861*, 159; Robert D. Holt, "The Political Career of William A. Richardson," *Journal of the Illinois State Historical Society* 26 (Oct. 1933): 239; Douglas to McClernand, 23 Dec. 1856, McClernand Collection.

36. Harris to McClernand, 10 Mar. 1857, McClernand Collection; *Illinois State Journal*, 24 Mar. 1857, 3; Johannsen, *The Letters of Stephen A. Douglas*, 375.

37. Roy F. Nichols, *The Disruption of American Democracy* (New York: Free Press, 1948), 129–32; Douglas to McClernand, 23 Nov. 1857, McClernand Collection; Broadside, "Col. McClernand's Letter to the People of Illinois," undated, Illinois State Historical Library, published in the *Illinois State Register*, 12 Feb. 1858, 1; Johannsen, *The Letters of Stephen A. Douglas*, 417.

38. *Illinois State Journal,* 18 Feb. 1858, 3; Douglas to McClernand, 21 Feb. 1858, McClernand Collection.

39. *Illinois State Journal,* 6 July 1858, 2; 3 Sept. 1858, 3. Paul M. Angle, *"Here I Have Lived": A History of Lincoln's Springfield* (Springfield, Ill.: Abraham Lincoln Association, 1935), 231.

40. *Illinois State Journal,* 11 Sept. 1858, 2.

41. Paul M. Angle, *Lincoln in the Year 1859: Being the Day-by-Day Activities of Abraham Lincoln during That Year* (Springfield, Ill.: Lincoln Centennial Association, 1927), 8, 35, 47; "The Centennial Anniversary of the Birth of Robert Burns," *Journal of the Illinois State Historical Society* 17 (Apr.–July 1924): 205–8. *Illinois State Register,* 29 Sept. 1859, 2; 1 Oct. 1859, 2. *Illinois State Journal,* 29 Sept. 1859, 3; 20 Oct. 1859, 2; 3 Nov. 1859, 2. Roy P. Basler, ed., *The Collected Works of Abraham Lincoln,* 9 vols. (New Brunswick, N.J.: Rutgers Univ. Press, 1953), 2:432–33.

42. Angle, *Lincoln in the Year 1859,* 49; *Illinois State Journal,* 21 Oct. 1859, 2; *Illinois State Register,* 15 Oct. 1859, 2.

43. Victor Hicken, "John A. McClernand and the House Speakership Struggle of 1859," *Journal of the Illinois State Historical Society* 53 (Summer 1960): 168–70; McClernand to Lanphier, 3 Jan. 1860, Lanphier Papers.

44. *Congressional Globe,* 36th Cong., 1st sess., 17 Jan. 1860, 492; 20 Jan. 1860, 513; McClernand to Lanphier, 22 Dec. 1859, Lanphier Papers. *Illinois State Register,* 6 Feb. 1860, 2; 15 Feb. 1860, 2; 29 Feb. 1860, 2. Hicken, "John A. McClernand and the House Speakership Struggle of 1859," 174.

45. Gustave Koerner to Lyman Trumbull, 23 Dec. 1859, Lyman Trumbull Manuscripts, Illinois State Historical Library; Alphonse B. Miller, *Thaddeus Stevens* (New York: Harper & Brothers, 1939), 137–38; McClernand to Lanphier, 11 Feb. 1860, Lanphier Papers; McClernand to Lanphier, 19 Jan. 1860, McClernand Collection; McClernand to Capt. John Henry, 14 Jan. 1860, McClernand Collection; Thomas Ford, *A History of Illinois from Its Commencement as a State in 1818 to 1847* (Chicago: S. C. Griggs, 1854), 289.

46. McClernand to Lanphier, 10 Jan. 1860, 4 Apr. 1860, Lanphier Papers; Johannsen, *Stephen A. Douglas,* 719.

47. Murat Halstead, *Caucuses of 1860: A History of the National Political Conventions of the Current Presidential Campaign* (Columbus, Ohio: Follett, Foster, 1860), 9.

48. Angle, *Here I Have Lived,* 240–41; Beveridge, *Abraham Lincoln 1809–1858,* 1:605, 2:308–9; *Illinois State Register,* 15 June 1860, 2.

49. *Illinois State Journal,* 9 July 1860, 2, 3; 27 Oct. 1860, 2; 10 Sept. 1860, 3; 3 Sept. 1860, 2. *Illinois State Register,* 4 Sept. 1860, 1, 2; 18 Oct. 1860, 1, 2; 5 Nov. 1860, 2. Justin G. Turner and Linda L. Turner, *Mary Todd Lincoln: Her Life and Letters* (New York: Alfred A. Knopf, 1972), 66. Owen Lovejoy was an Illinois Republican congressman who supported Lincoln and devoted his life to the cause of freeing the slaves.

50. David W. Lusk, *Eighty Years of Illinois Politics and Politicians* (Springfield, Ill.: D. W. Lusk, 1889), 103; McClernand to Lanphier, 3 Dec. 1860, Lanphier Papers;

Samuel S. Cox, *Three Decades of Federal Legislation, 1855 to 1885* (Freeport, N.Y.: Books for Libraries Press, 1970), 76; *Illinois State Register,* 11 Dec. 1860, 2.

51. Nichols, *The Disruption of American Democracy,* 393–94, 398–99.

52. Ibid., 402; McClernand to Lanphier, 21 Dec. 1860, 25 Dec. 1860, 27 Dec. 1860, Lanphier Papers; *New York Times,* 1 Jan. 1861, 1, as quoted in Hicken, "From Vandalia to Vicksburg," 144.

53. Lusk, *Eighty Years of Illinois Politics and Politicians,* 126–27; *Congressional Globe,* 29th Cong., 2d sess., 15 Jan. 1847, 188.

54. *Congressional Globe,* 36th Cong., 2d sess., 14 Jan. 1861, 367–72.

55. Joseph Wallace, "Biography of John A. McClernand," 45–51; J. M. Hofer, "Development of the Peace Movement in Illinois during the Civil War," *Journal of the Illinois State Historical Society* 24 (Apr. 1931): 115; Milton, *The Eve of Conflict,* 538–39; McClernand to Lanphier, 4, 8 Feb. 1861, Lanphier Papers; Carl Sandburg, *Abraham Lincoln: The Prairie Years,* 2 vols. (New York: Harcourt, Brace, 1926), 2:408.

56. Angle, *Here I Have Lived,* 263; McClernand speech, undated, McClernand Collection; *History of Sangamon County, Illinois* (Chicago: Inter-State Publishing, 1881), 110; McCormack, *Memoirs of Gustave Koerner,* 2:121; W. Jayne to Trumbull, 28 Jan. 1861, Trumbull Manuscripts; T. W. Kidd to McClernand, 29 Jan. 1861, McClernand Collection; William Herndon to Trumbull, 27 Jan. 1861, Trumbull Manuscripts.

57. *Illinois State Journal,* 4 Aug. 1860, 2; 1 Nov. 1860, 2. *Illinois State Register,* 11 Dec. 1860, 2; John G. Nicolay and John Hay, *Abraham Lincoln: A History,* 10 vols. (New York: Century, 1890), 7:135–36.

58. McClernand to Lincoln, 10 Apr. 1861, McClernand Collection; Schwartz, "Biography of John Alexander McClernand," 60–61; Yates to Lincoln, 15 May 1861, McClernand Collection.

59. *Congressional Globe,* 37th Cong., 1st sess., 9 July 1861, 33–35; Milton, *The Eve of Conflict,* 569. Douglas had been born in Brandon, Vermont.

60. Charles V. Darrin, "Your Truly Attached Friend, Mary Lincoln," *Journal of the Illinois State Historical Society* 44 (Spring 1951): 18; "Edward J. McClernand, Brigadier General," *Journal of the Illinois State Historical Society* 5 (Apr. 1912): 310–11; "Brigadier General Edward John McClernand, 1848–1926," *Journal of the Illinois State Historical Society* 19 (Apr.–July 1926): 266–67; Turner and Turner, *Mary Todd Lincoln: Her Life and Letters,* 57, 59, 61, 90. 2d Lt. Edward J. McClernand, 2d U.S. Cavalry, received the Medal of Honor for heroism at the Battle of Bear Paw Mountain, Montana, 30 September 1877.

61. Ulysses S. Grant, *Personal Memoirs of U. S. Grant* (New York: Smithmark Publishers, 1994), 145–46; Lloyd Lewis, *Captain Sam Grant* (Boston: Little, Brown, 1950), 428–30.

62. *Chicago Tribune,* 23 Apr. 1861, 1; 30 Apr. 1861, 1. *Cairo City Gazette,* 6 Dec. 1860, as quoted in James P. Jones, *"Black Jack": John A. Logan and Southern Illinois in the Civil War Era* (Carbondale: Southern Illinois Univ. Press, 1995), 67, 78, 84; Arthur C. Cole, *The Era of the Civil War, 1848–1870* (Springfield: Illinois Centennial Commission, 1919), 267; *Jonesboro Gazette,* 27 Apr., 25 May 1861, as quoted in

Hicken, "From Vandalia to Vicksburg," 153; Mary S. C. Logan, *Reminiscences of a Soldier's Wife* (New York: Charles Scribner's Sons, 1913), 88–89; Whitney, *Life on the Circuit with Lincoln*, 419–20.

63. Henry C. Hubbart, *The Older Middle West, 1840–1880* (New York: Russell & Russell, 1963), 73, 156; *Cincinnati Enquirer*, 22 Feb. 1861, as quoted in Edward C. Smith, *The Borderland in the Civil War* (New York: Macmillan, 1927), 99; Clark E. Carr, *Stephen A. Douglas: His Life, Public Services, Speeches and Patriotism* (Chicago: A. C. McClurg, 1909), 135–36.

64. James G. Robinson to McClernand, 27 Sept. 1875, McClernand Collection; *The War of the Rebellion: A Compilation of the Official Records of the Union and Confederate Armies*, 128 vols. (Washington, D.C.: GPO, 1880–1901), ser. 1, vol. 52:144 (hereafter cited as *OR*).

65. M. A. DeWolfe Howe, ed., *Home Letters of General Sherman* (New York: Charles Scribner's Sons, 1909), 198.

66. Pease and Randall, The *Diary of Orville Hickman Browning*, 1:xix, 474, 490–91; Charles King, *The True Ulysses S. Grant* (Philadelphia: J. B. Lippincott, 1914), 155–57; Basler, *The Collected Works of Abraham Lincoln*, 8:593–94. Prentiss was a Republican who had served in the Mexican War. There is no indication that McClernand lobbied for the appointment. Grant and McClernand both had dates of rank of 17 May 1861.

67. Ezra J. Warner, *Generals in Blue* (Baton Rouge: Louisiana State Univ. Press, 1964), passim.

68. Ibid., xx, 17–18, 36, 61, 97, 245, 423, 446, 448.

69. Basler, *The Collected Works of Abraham Lincoln*, 4:477; Whitney, *Life on the Circuit with Lincoln*, 421; Nicolay and Hay, *Abraham Lincoln: A History*, 7:136.

70. "A Statesman's Letters of the Civil War Period," *Journal of the Illinois State Historical Society* 2 (July 1909): 44–45; Bluford Wilson, "Southern Illinois in the Civil War," *Transactions of the Illinois State Historical Society* 16 (1911): 99; Frank L. Klement, *The Copperheads in the Middle West* (Chicago: Univ. of Chicago Press, 1960), 11, 206, 226; Frank L. Klement, "Copperhead Secret Societies in Illinois during the Civil War," *Journal of the Illinois State Historical Society* 48 (Spring 1955): 180; Carl Sandburg, *Abraham Lincoln: The War Years*, 4 vols. (New York: Harcourt, Brace, 1939), 2:52, 109; *OR*, vol. 17, 2:333.

2. A Taste of Battle

1. *Illinois State Journal*, 2 Aug. 1861, 2.

2. Pease and Randall, eds., *The Diary of Orville Hickman Browning*, 1:494; Thomas A. Scott to Richard Yates, 8 Aug. 1861, McClernand Collection.

3. John G. Nicolay and John Hay, *Abraham Lincoln: A History*, 10 vols. (New York: Century, 1890), 4:55–57; Allan Nevins, *The War for the Union*, vol. I, *The Improvised War, 1861–1862* (New York: Charles Scribner's Sons, 1959), 350.

4. Mark M. Boatner, *The Civil War Dictionary* (New York: David McKay, 1959), 266; Jack Coggins, *Arms & Equipment of the Civil War* (New York: Fairfax Press, 1983), 32; Claud E. Fuller, *The Rifled Musket* (Harrisburg, Pa.: Stackpole, 1958), 4.

5. McClernand to Messrs. Tellson and Shepherd, 10 Aug. 1861, McClernand Collection.

6. Pease and Randall, The *Diary of Orville Hickman Browning*, 1:495; Philip B. Fouke to McClernand, 12 Aug. 1861, McClernand Collection.

7. Special Orders No. 159, General Headquarters, State of Illinois, 20 Aug. 1861, McClernand Collection.

8. McClernand to Montgomery C. Meigs, 23 Aug. 1861, McClernand Collection; *Illinois State Journal*, 8 Feb. 1862, 2. Congress passed the act on 27 July 1861.

9. *OR*, vol. 51, 1:455; Boatner, *The Civil War Dictionary*, 314.

10. McClernand to John C. Frémont, 24 Aug. 1861, and Frémont to McClernand, 26 Aug. 1861, McClernand Collection.

11. Maj. Mason Brayman to McClernand, 27 Aug. 1861, McClernand Collection.

12. Frémont to McClernand, 27 Aug. 1861; McClernand to Col. Richard Oglesby, 27 Aug. 1861; McClernand to Col. James Reardon, 28 Aug. 1861; Capt. James Dunlap to McClernand, 29 Aug. 1861. All in McClernand Collection. *OR*, vol. 3: 141–42.

13. *OR*, vol. 3:52–3, 141–42.

14. Ibid., 144–47.

15. Grant, *Personal Memoirs*, 157; "Grant Takes Command at Cairo," *Journal of the Illinois State Historical Society* 38 (Mar. 1945): 242–43; Charles Wright Wills, *Army Life of an Illinois Soldier*, ed. Mary E. Kellogg (Washington, D.C.: Globe Printing, 1906), 25.

16. *OR*, vol. 3:143, 470; John Y. Simon, ed., *The Papers of Ulysses S. Grant*, 22 vols. (Carbondale: Southern Illinois Univ. Press, 1967–98), 2:184; McClernand to Frémont, 4 Sept. 1861; McClernand to Richard Oglesby, 4 Sept. 1861; Oglesby to McClernand, 4 Sept. 1861. All in McClernand Collection.

17. *OR*, vol. 4:181, 196–97; Simon, *The Papers of Ulysses S. Grant*, 2:194.

18. *Illinois State Journal*, 11 Sept. 1861, 2; Simon, *The Papers of Ulysses S. Grant*, 2:184.

19. *OR*, vol. 4:197.

20. Simon, *The Papers of Ulysses S. Grant*, 2:193–94, 198–99, 203–4; *OR*, vol. 3:480, 494–95; ibid., vol. 4:256; McClernand to Col. James D. Morgan, 4 Oct. 1861, McClernand Collection.

21. McClernand to Lincoln, 10 Sept. 1861; Oglesby to McClernand, 17 Sept. 1861; Capt. M. F. Wood, Lt. A. A. O'Seary, and Lt. G. J. Wood to McClernand, 24 Sept. 1861; Capt. Adolph Schwartz to McClernand, 29 Oct. 1861; McClernand to Oglesby, 18 Sept. 1861; General Orders No. 6, Headquarters, District of Southeast Missouri, 16 Sept. 1861. All in McClernand Collection. Simon, *The Papers of Ulysses S. Grant*, 2:346, 3:12, 391.

22. Basler, *The Collected Works of Abraham Lincoln*, 4:480, 517, 527; James H. Wilson, *Under the Old Flag*, 2 vols. (New York: D. Appleton, 1912), 1:1, 4; McClernand to Lincoln, 10 Sept. 1861, McClernand Collection.

23. Simon, *The Papers of Ulysses S. Grant*, 2:210–12; J. T. Dorris, "Michael Kelly Lawler: Mexican and Civil War Officer," *Journal of the Illinois State Historical Society* 48 (Winter 1955): 382; Adolph Schwartz to McClernand, 9 Oct. 1861, McClernand Collection; General Orders No. 5, Headquarters, First Brigade, 9 Oct. 1861, McClernand Collection; Lt. J. M. Eddy to McClernand, 29 Oct. 1861, McClernand Collection; General Orders No. 22, Headquarters, First Brigade, 24 Nov. 1861, McClernand Collection.

24. McClernand to Frémont, 2 Sept. 1861, McClernand Collection; Simon, *The Papers of Ulysses S. Grant*, 2:187.

25. McClernand to Col. John Loomis, 7 Sept., 22 Sept. 1861; McClernand to Col. Michael Lawler, 15 Sept. 1861; McClernand to Yates, 22 Sept. 1861; Col. Napoleon B. Buford to McClernand, 24 Sept. 1861. All in McClernand Collection. Dorris, "Michael Kelly Lawler," 382.

26. Simon, *The Papers of Ulysses S. Grant*, 2:277, 322; *OR*, vol. 3:507, 488–89; McClernand to Frémont, 30 Sept. 1861, McClernand Collection.

27. Fouke to McClernand, 1 Oct., 2 Oct. 1861; McClernand to Fouke, 6 Oct. 1861. All in McClernand Collection.

28. Fouke to McClernand, 14 Oct. 1861, McClernand Collection.

29. *OR*, ser. 3, vol. 1:89, 158–59; Basler, *The Collected Works of Abraham Lincoln*, 4:527.

30. McClernand to Col. W. H. L. Wallace, 8 Sept., 12 Sept. 1861; McClernand to Col. Richard Oglesby, 10 Sept., 12 Sept. 1861; McClernand to Frémont, 9 Sept. 1861. All in McClernand Collection. *OR*, vol. 3:169, 474–75. Wallace had served in the Mexican War and then had practiced law in Illinois. He returned to military service as commander of the 11th Illinois Infantry.

31. Col. C. Carroll Marsh to Capt. John A. Rawlins, 30 Sept. 1861; McClernand to Marsh, 30 Sept. 1861; Col. John A. Logan to McClernand, 28 Sept. 1861; McClernand to Logan, 29 Sept. 1861; Logan to McClernand, 3 Oct. 1861. All in McClernand Collection. This is the John Logan who had been an Illinois congressman.

32. *OR*, vol. 3:533–34; Simon, *The Papers of Ulysses S. Grant*, 3:39.

33. Dorris, "Michael Kelly Lawler: Mexican and Civil War Officer," 381. Lawler hailed from Shawneetown, Illinois, where he had become a large landowner. He had corresponded with McClernand while serving as a captain in the Mexican War.

34. Mary S. C. Logan, *Reminiscences of a Soldier's Wife*, 108; *Jonesboro (Illinois) Gazette*, 13 Sept. 1861.

35. Mary S. C. Logan, *Reminiscences of a Soldier's Wife*, 113.

36. Salmon P. Chase to Commandant, Port of Cairo, 3 Sept. 1861; McClernand to Capt. Robert S. Moore, 14 Oct. 1861; McClernand to Lt. Col. Elias S. Dennis, 21 Oct. 1861; McClernand to Col. Silas Noble, 18 Oct. 1861. All in McClernand Collection. *OR*, vol. 3:534.

37. Paddy Griffith, *Battle Tactics of the Civil War* (New Haven, Conn.: Yale Univ. Press, 1989), 99; William J. Hardee, *Rifle and Light Infantry Tactics for the Exercise and Manoeuvres of Troops When Acting as Light Infantry Or Riflemen* (Philadelphia: Lippincott, Grambo, 1855), passim; William S. Morris, J. B. Kuykendall, and L. D.

Harwell, *History 31st Regiment Volunteers, Organized by John A. Logan* (Evansville, Ind.: Keller Printing and Publishing, 1902), 20; Simon, *Papers of Ulysses S. Grant*, 3:406–7; *OR*, vol. 2:214–17, vol. 4:455; Henry W. Halleck, *Elements of Military Art and Science* (New York: D. Appleton, 1862), passim.; John Brinton, *Personal Memoirs of John H. Brinton* (New York: Neale Publishing, 1914), 52; T. W. Higginson, "Regular and Volunteer Officers," *Atlantic Monthly* 14 (Sept. 1864): 348. There is no record that McClernand requested the manuals, only of their receipt.

38. *OR*, vol. 3:480, 144; vol. 4:198. Grant himself had been reprimanded by Frémont on 6 September 1861 for having notified the Kentucky legislature of Polk's advance into that state. Frémont reminded his subordinate that such correspondence was more appropriate for Headquarters, Western Department, than for a district commander.

39. Simon, *The Papers of Ulysses S. Grant*, 2:327–28; Isabel Wallace, *Life and Letters of General W. H. L. Wallace* (Chicago: R. R. Donnelley & Sons. 1909), 139.

40. Simon, *The Papers of Ulysses S. Grant*, 3:98; Nicolay and Hay, *Abraham Lincoln*, 5:114–15.

41. Grant to McClernand, 23 Oct. 1861, McClernand Collection; *OR*, vol. 3:556–57.

42. McClernand to Frémont, 12 Sept. 1861, McClernand Collection.

43. Simon, *The Papers of Ulysses S. Grant*, 3:67.

44. John Brinton, *Personal Memoirs of John H. Brinton*, 103–5; Simon, *The Papers of Ulysses S. Grant*, 3:170–72. A similar conflict arose between Brinton and McClernand after the Battle of Belmont. In that case Grant endorsed McClernand's order and stated that "the Surgeon was evidently wrong in disobeying."

45. *OR*, vol. 3:145, 148, 151, 168–69, 507–8; Oglesby to McClernand, 16 Sept. 1861, McClernand Collection.

46. *OR*, vol. 3:273, 267; Simon, *The Papers of Ulysses S. Grant*, 3:113; Nathaniel Hughes, *The Battle of Belmont: Grant Strikes South*, 46. Hughes and Simon cast doubt on the validity of an order from Frémont to demonstrate against Columbus or to attack Belmont.

47. Maj. Gen. George B. McClellan to McClernand, 5 Nov. 1861; McClernand to McClellan (telegram), 5 Nov. 1861; McClernand to McClellan (letter), 5 Nov. 1861; Special Orders No. 1,496, 5 Nov. 1861, District of Southeast Missouri. All in McClellan Collection. Simon, *The Papers of Ulysses S. Grant*, 3:113.

48. *OR*, vol. 3:558, 277.

49. Ibid., 275, 269.

50. Simon, *The Papers of Ulysses S. Grant*, 3:125; *OR*, vol. 3:267, 278; *Daily Missouri Republican*, 14, 15 Nov. 1861; *Louisville Daily Journal*, 15 Nov. 1861; Brinton, *Personal Memoirs*, 73. Grant issued no written order to McClernand in regard to his intentions at Belmont. The force may have been en route before Grant actually decided to attack. For a complete discussion of the question see Hughes, *The Battle of Belmont*, 51–53.

51. *OR*, vol. 3:278, 283, 286–87.

52. Morris, Kuykendall, and Harwell, *History 31st Regiment Volunteers*, 23.

53. *OR,* vol. 3:279–89; Henry I. Smith, *History of the Seventh Iowa Veteran Volunteer Infantry* (Mason City, Iowa: E. Hitchcock, Printer, 1903), 19.

54. *OR,* vol. 3:288, 280; *Illinois State Journal,* 9 Nov. 1961, 2; [Adolph Schwartz], "Biography of John Alexander McClernand, 1863," Illinois State Historical Library, 67.

55. *OR,* vol. 3:280.

56. Ibid., 280, 293; John Seaton, "The Battle of Belmont," in *War Talks in Kansas: A Series of Papers Read before the Kansas Commandery of the Loyal Legion of the United States* (Wilmington, N.C.: Broadfoot Publishing, 1992), 313; Smith, *History of the Seventh Iowa Veteran Volunteer Infantry,* 19; Grant, *Personal Memoirs,* 163; *Chicago Evening Journal,* 8 Nov. 1861, 1; Albert D. Richardson, *A Personal History of Ulysses S. Grant* (Hartford, Conn.: M. A. Winter & Hatch, 1902), 193.

57. Grant, *Personal Memoirs,* 193; *OR,* vol. 3:284; Seaton, "The Battle of Belmont," 313–14; Morris, Kuykendall, and Harwell, *History 31st Regiment Volunteers,* 24.

58. *OR,* vol. 3:307.

59. Ibid., 3:280, 289.

60. Ibid., 280; Wills, *Army Life of an Illinois Soldier,* 43.

61. *OR,* vol. 3:271, 285.

62. Ibid., 281; Smith, *History of the Seventh Iowa Veteran Volunteer Infantry,* 260; Henry Walke, *Naval Scenes and Reminiscences of the Civil War in the United States* (New York: F. R. Reed, 1877), 37. In his report of the battle, Grant reported 224 missing; regimental reports, however, place the total at 205.

63. *OR,* vol. 3:276, 281, 285; *Official Records of the Union and Confederate Navies in the War of the Rebellion,* 30 vols. (Washington, D.C.: GPO, 1894–1922), ser. 1, vol. 22:401 (hereafter cited as *ORN*). Grant considered Buford's actions inexcusable. When in 1863 Buford was nominated for promotion to major general, Grant wrote Lincoln, "He would scarsely [*sic*] make a respectable Hospital nurse if put in petticoats, and certain is unfit for any other Military position. He has always been a dead weight." Simon, *The Papers of Ulysses S. Grant,* 7:301.

64. *Chicago Tribune,* 9 Nov. 1861, 2; *St. Louis Missouri Daily Democrat,* 8 Nov. 1861, 2; *OR,* vol. 3:271; ibid., vol. 53:507; *Congressional Globe,* 37th Cong., 2d sess., pt. 3:2036, quoted in Anna Maclay Green, "Civil War Public Opinion of General Grant," *Journal of the Illinois State Historical Society* 22 (Apr. 1929): 23.

65. Louis A. Coolidge, *Ulysses S. Grant* (Boston: Houghton Mifflin, 1917), 64; *New York Herald,* 19 Nov. 1861, 1; Charles A. Dana and James H. Wilson, *The Life of Ulysses S. Grant* (Springfield, Mass.: Gurdon Bill, 1868), 51–2; *Chicago Evening Journal,* 8 Nov. 1861, 1.

66. *OR,* vol. 3:271; ibid., vol. 53:507; *ORN,* vol. 22:399; Simon, *The Papers of Ulysses S. Grant,* 3:138.

67. Whitney, *Life on the Circuit with Lincoln,* 434; *Chicago Daily Tribune,* 9 Nov. 1861, 1, quoting from *Keokuk (Iowa) City Gate,* 8 Nov. 1861.

68. Simon, *The Papers of Ulysses S. Grant,* 3:238–39. This comment was in regard to a report in the *Burlington (Iowa) Daily Hawk-Eye,* 9 Nov. 1861, charging that Grant and McClernand were no closer to the battle than one and one-half miles and that Grant's horse was shot by straggling Confederates.

69. Helen Todd, *A Man Named Grant* (Boston: Houghton Mifflin, 1940), 29–30.

70. McClernand to McClellan, 8 Nov. 1861, McClernand Collection; *OR*, vol. 53:506.

71. Theodore H. Jansen, "Biography and Reminiscences of Matthew Jansen, 1905," 99, photocopy, Illinois State Historical Library.

72. Nicolay and Hay, *Abraham Lincoln: A History*, 5:114–15.

73. McClernand to Lincoln, 22 Nov. 1861, Robert Todd Lincoln Collection, microfilm, Illinois State Historical Library, and Combined Arms Research Library, Fort Leavenworth, Kansas.

74. *OR*, vol. 3:280; Hughes, *The Battle of Belmont*, 13; Capt. Alexander Bielaski to McClernand, 30 Oct. 1861; McClernand to Mrs. Alexander Bielaski, 8 Nov. 1861; Reverend L. P. Clover to McClernand, 8 Nov. 1861. All in McClernand Collection. *Illinois State Journal*, 9 Nov. 1861, 2; 27 Nov. 1861, 2. *Illinois State Register*, 11 Nov. 1961, 2.

75. Simon, *The Papers of Ulysses S. Grant*, 3:161–62, 170; Capt. W. J. Bruck to McClernand, 9 Nov. 1861; Special Orders No. 1,610, 13 Nov. 1861, Brigade Headquarters; McClernand to Col. John A. Logan and Col. Philip B. Fouke, 11 Nov. 1861; Col. Isham N. Haynie to McClernand, 16 Dec. 1861; Grant to McClernand, McClernand to Grant, 19 Dec. 1861. All in McClernand Collection. Robert J. Kerner, ed., "The Diary of Edward W. Crippen, Private, 27th Illinois Volunteers, War of the Rebellion, August 7, 1861, to September 19, 1863," *Transactions of the Illinois State Historical Society* 19 (Springfield, Ill.: State Journal, 1910): 224–230.

76. Brayman to McClernand, 11 Dec. 1861, McClernand Collection; McClernand to Grant, 14 Dec. 1861, McClernand Collection; Simon, *The Papers of Ulysses S. Grant*, 3:287–88.

77. Special Orders No. 1,934, 10 Dec. 1861, Headquarters, First Brigade, McClernand Collection; Report of Inspection of 18th Illinois Infantry Regiment, 31 Dec. 1861, McClernand Collection; Simon, *The Papers of Ulysses S. Grant*, 3:311–12.

78. Yates to McClernand, 9 Nov. 1861, McClernand Collection; McClernand to Yates, 19 Nov. 1861, McClernand Collection.

79. Fouke to McClernand, 20 Nov. 1861; Capt. James Dunlap to McClernand, 21 Nov. 1861; Fouke to McClernand, 24, 26, 28 Nov. 1861. All in McClernand Collection.

80. Capt. John C. Kelton to McClernand, 27 Nov. 1861, McClernand Collection.

81. Simon, *The Papers of Ulysses S. Grant*, 3:262.

82. Fouke to McClernand, 4 Dec. 1861; Mr. J. M. Wardwell to McClernand, 4 Dec. 1861; Wardwell to Illinois State Treasurer William Butler, date illegible; Butler to Wardwell, 3 Dec. 1861; McClernand to Wardwell, 3 Dec. 1861; McClernand to Dunlap, 18 Dec. 1861; Fouke to McClernand, 14 Jan. 1862. All in McClernand Collection. Judge William Thomas was an attorney in Jacksonville and had also served as a quartermaster in the Black Hawk War. Jesse K. Dubois held numerous state offices during his political career. Correspondence from Yates to Stanton is not available, but, from the sequence of events, it is likely that the governor notified the sec-

retary to ship the weapons. A discussion of efforts to obtain arms for the Union armies can be found in Nevins, *Ordeal of the Union,* vol 1, *Fruits of Manifest Destiny,* 342–69.

83. *Columbus (Ohio) Crisis,* 21 Nov. 1861, 6.

84. *OR,* vol. 3:567; Ulysses S. Grant, *Personal Memoirs of U. S. Grant,* 169; Benjamin P. Thomas and Harold M. Hyman, *Stanton: The Life and Times of Lincoln's Secretary of War* (New York: Alfred A. Knopf, 1962), 80–81, 183–84.

85. Warner, *Generals in Blue,* 183–85, 195–96.

86. Simon, *The Papers of Ulysses S. Grant,* 3:204–6; McClernand to Lincoln, 22 Nov. 1861, McClernand Collection.

87. Simon, *The Papers of Ulysses S. Grant,* 3:207; Logan to McClernand, 27 Dec. 1861, McClernand Collection; McClernand to Samuel S. Cox, 4 Dec. 1861, Samuel Sullivan Cox Papers, Rutherford B. Hayes Presidential Library, Frémont, Ohio.

88. McClernand to Representative John A. Logan, 5 Jan. 1862, Logan Papers, Library of Congress, quoted in Benjamin F. Cooling, *Forts Henry and Donelson: The Key to the Confederate Heartland* (Knoxville: Univ. of Tennessee Press, 1987), 76; Logan to McClernand, 14 Jan. 1862, McClernand Collection.

89. Hattaway and Jones, *How the North Won: A Military History of the Civil War,* 122–23; Boatner, *The Civil War Dictionary,* 96, 118, 367, 418, 448, 556, 590, 606, 614, 949; Weigley, *History of the United States Army,* 229; Marvin A. Kriedberg and Merton G. Henry, *History of the Military Mobilization in the United States Army, 1775–1945* (Washington, D.C.: Department of the Army, 1955), 116; James L. Morrison, *The Best School in the World* (Kent, Ohio: Kent State Univ. Press, 1986), 183–84; *Register of Graduates and Former Cadets of the United States Military Academy* (West Point, N.Y.: Association of Graduates, 1980), 253–55.

90. Simon, *The Papers of Ulysses S. Grant,* 3:214.

91. Sen. Orville Browning to McClernand, 23 Nov. 1861, McClernand Collection.

92. Grant to McClernand, 23 Nov. 1861; McClernand to Fuller, 27 Nov. 1861; McClernand to Grant, 30 Nov. 1861. All in McClernand Collection.

93. Grant, *Personal Memoirs,* 168; Simon, *The Papers of Ulysses S. Grant,* 3:184, 260–61, 328–29, 427; McClernand to Col. John Holt, 19 Nov. 1861, McClernand Collection; J. C. Swain to McClernand, 19 Nov. 1861, McClernand Collection; Capt. Augustus A. Willington to McClernand, 7 Dec. 1861, McClernand Collection.

94. McClernand to W. M. H. Osborn, 10 Nov. 1861; N. W. Mince to McClernand, 15 Nov. 1861; William Henry Barnes to McClernand, 21 Nov. 1861; Wallace Stockdale to McClernand, 21 Nov. 1861; Lyman Trumbull to McClernand, 16 Nov. 1861. All in McClernand Collection.

95. McClernand to Maj. Gen. Henry W. Halleck, 17 Dec. 1861; McClernand to Brig. Gen. Samuel D. Sturgis, 19 Dec. 1861; Col. John C. Kelton to McClernand, 24 Dec. 1861. All in McClernand Collection.

96. McClernand to Halleck, 7 Dec. 1861; John G. Nicolay to McClernand, 10 Dec. 1861; McClernand to Fouke and Logan, 14 Dec. 1861. All in McClernand Collection. McClernand to Lincoln, 3 Dec. 1861, Lincoln Collection. J. W. Vance,

Report of the Adjutant General of the State of Illinois, 8 vols. (Springfield, Ill.: H. W. Rokker, 1886), 2:503.

97. McClernand to the Hon. Samuel S. Cox, 4 Dec. 1861, McClernand Collection.

98. Henry Quigley to McClernand, 15 Oct. 1861, McClernand Collection; Mary Logan to John A. Logan, 5 Jan. 1862, John A. Logan Papers, Library of Congress, quoted in Cooling, *Forts Henry and Donelson*, 76.

3. Penetrating the Confederacy

1. Archer Jones, *Confederate Strategy from Shiloh to Vicksburg* (Baton Rouge: Louisiana State Univ. Press, 1961), 20.

2. *OR*, vol. 4:349.

3. Lew Wallace, *Lew Wallace: An Autobiography*, 2 vols. (New York: Harper & Brothers, 1906), 1:340–41; David W. Wood, *History of the Twentieth Ohio Veteran Volunteer Infantry Regiment* (Columbus, Ohio: Paul and Thrall, 1876), 47.

4. *OR*, vol. 7:450–52, 457–58, 487–88, 527–28.

5. William T. Sherman, *Memoirs of General William T. Sherman* (Westport, Conn.: Greenwood Press, 1972), 238.

6. *OR*, vol. 7:532–33.

7. Ibid., vol. 8:509.

8. Simon, *The Papers of Ulysses S. Grant*, 3:204.

9. Ibid., 3:88–89.

10. Grant to McClernand, 8 Jan. 1862, McClernand Collection; *OR*, vol. 7:533–34.

11. Special Orders No. 87, 8 Jan. 1862, Headquarters, First Brigade, McClernand Collection; Special Orders No. 117, 9 Jan. 1862, Headquarters, First Brigade, McClernand Collection; Peter Ripley, "Prelude to Donelson: Grant's January 1862 March into Kentucky," *Register of the Kentucky Historical Society* 68 (Oct. 1970): 314.

12. McClernand to Grant, 9 Jan. 1862, McClernand Collection; Grant to McClernand, 10 Jan. 1862, McClernand Collection; *ORN*, vol. 22:489–90.

13. *OR*, vol. 7:68; Field Order No. 6, 11 Jan. 1862, Headquarters, First Brigade, McClernand Collection.

14. Brinton, *Personal Memoirs*, 102.

15. McClernand to Grant, 11 Jan. 1862, McClernand Collection.

16. Edward H. Hagerman, "The Evolution of Trench Warfare in the American Civil War" (Ph.D. diss., Duke University, 1965), 13, 16, 19, 29; Dennis Hart Mahan, *A Complete Treatise on Field Fortifications* (New York: Wiley and Putnam, 1836), vii–viii.

17. William M. Polk, "General Polk and the Battle of Belmont," in *Battles and Leaders of the Civil War*, 4 vols, ed. Robert U. Johnson and Clarence C. Buel (New York: Castle Books, 1956), 1:348; Hagerman, "The Evolution of Trench Warfare in the American Civil War," 13; Halleck, *Elements of Military Art and Science*, 327, 437–38.

18. McClernand to Grant, 11 Jan., 12 Jan., 13 Jan. 1862, McClernand Collection.

19. *ORN*, vol. 22:499–500; McClernand to Cdr. William D. Porter, 12 Jan. 1862, McClernand Collection; Porter to McClernand, 12 Jan. 1862, McClernand Collection.

20. *OR*, vol. 7:71; McClernand to Grant, 12 Jan., 13 Jan. 1862, McClernand Collection.

21. *OR*, vol. 7:69–70.

22. Grant to McClernand, 18 Jan. 1862; *OR*, vol. 7:71; *New York Times*, 24 Jan. 1862, 2; *New York Herald*, 7 Feb. 1862, 1.

23. Grant, *Personal Memoirs*, 170; *OR*, vol. 7:68–72.

24. Grant, *Personal Memoirs*, 170.

25. McClernand to Lincoln, 28 Jan. 1862, Lincoln Collection.

26. *OR*, vol. 5:41.

27. Ibid., vol. 7:72, 561.

28. Bromfield L. Ridley, *Battles and Sketches of the Army of Tennessee* (Mexico, Mo.: Missouri Printing and Publishing, 1906), 65; Ezra J. Warner, *Generals in Gray* (Baton Rouge: Louisiana State Univ. Press, 1959), 74.

29. Ridley, *Battles and Sketches of the Army of Tennessee*, 65; Roy P. Stonesifer, "The Forts Henry-Heiman and Fort Donelson Campaign: A Study of Confederate Command" (Ph.D. diss., Pennsylvania State University, 1965), 5.

30. *OR*, vol. 4:404.

31. Ibid., 560; vol. 7:723–24.

32. Ibid., vol. 7:120–21; Grant, *Personal Memoirs*, 170.

33. *OR*, vol. 7:121–22, 571.

34. N. W. Mince to McClernand, 24 Jan. 1862; McClernand to Maj. John L. Loomis, 28 Jan. 1862; James W. Singleton to McClernand, 23 Jan. 1862. All in McClernand Collection.

35. *OR*, vol. 7:575, 577–78; Special Orders No. 353 and Special Orders No. 356, 1 Feb. 1862, Headquarters, First Division, McClernand Collection; Maj. Mason Brayman to Capt. Algernon S. Baxter, 1 Feb. 1862, McClernand Collection.

36. McClernand to Col. Allan C. Fuller, 27, 28, 30 Jan. 1862; Fuller to McClernand, 2 Feb. 1862. All in McClernand Collection. John G. Brown, "Historical Sketch of the 55th Reg. Ill. Vol.," in *Report of the Proceedings of the Association of the Fifty-fifth Illinois Veteran Volunteer Infantry at Their First Reunion* (Chicago: James Guilbert, 1885), 21.

37. Grant to McClernand, 2 Feb. 1862, McClernand Collection; General Orders No. 2, 2 Feb. 1862, Headquarters, First Division, McClernand Collection.

38. Grant to McClernand, 3 Feb. 1862; Field Order No. 5, 3 Feb. 1862, Headquarters, First Division; Field Orders Nos 8 and 9, 4 Feb. 1862, Headquarters, First Division. All in McClernand Collection.

39. Grant, *Personal Memoirs*, 92; Lew Wallace, *Lew Wallace: An Autobiography*, 1:366.

40. *OR*, vol. 7:126–27; Field Order No. 10, 4 Feb. 1862, Headquarters, First Division, McClernand Collection.

41. *OR*, vol. 7:127–28; Field Order No. 17, 4 Feb. 1862, Headquarters, First Division, McClernand Collection.

42. *OR*, vol. 7:127–28.

43. McClernand to Grant, 5 Feb. 1862, McClernand Collection.

44. Walke, *Naval Scenes and Reminiscences*, 55.

45. *OR*, vol. 7:585–86; Grant, *Personal Memoirs*, 172.

46. Field Order Nos. 14, 20, 43, 101, 5 Feb. 1862, McClernand Collection.

47. McClernand to Grant, 5 Feb. 1862, McClernand Collection.

48. *OR*, vol. 7:138.

49. Jesse Taylor, "The Defense of Fort Henry," in *Battles and Leaders of the Civil War*, 1:371; *OR*, vol. 7:138.

50. *OR*, vol. 7:122, 1229; John A. Logan, *The Volunteer Soldier of America* (Chicago: R. S. Peale, 1887), 631.

51. *OR*, vol. 7:129, 140, 143; Dana and Wilson, *The Life of Ulysses S. Grant*, 57.

52. Grant to McClernand, 6 Feb. 1862, McClernand Collection; *OR*, vol. 7:124. Tilghman had remained behind to cover the retreat.

53. *OR*, vol. 7:130.

54. McClernand to Yates, 6 Feb. 1862; McClernand to Allan G. Fuller, 8 Feb. 1862. Both in McClernand Collection.

55. McClernand to Lincoln, 8 Feb. 1862, Lincoln Collection.

56. *OR*, vol. 7:130; *ORN*, vol. 22:544.

57. Field Order No. 4, 7 Feb. 1862, Headquarters, First Division; McClernand to Grant, 7 Feb., 9 Feb. 1862. All in McClernand Collection.

58. Maj. Mason Brayman to Col. Richard Oglesby, 9 Feb. 1862, McClernand Collection.

59. McClernand to Grant, 9 Feb. 1862, McClernand Collection.

60. William S. Hillyer to McClernand, 10 Feb. 1862, McClernand Collection; Lew Wallace, *Lew Wallace: An Autobiography*, 1:376–77; Lew Wallace, "The Capture of Fort Donelson," in *Battles and Leaders of the Civil War*, 1:405.

61. Simon, *The Papers of Ulysses S. Grant*, 4:188–90. Smith's appointment was confirmed on 14 Feb. 1862.

62. *OR*, vol. 7:601, 605; *ORN*, vol. 22:583.

63. Field Order No. 116, 11 Feb. 1862, Headquarters, First Division, McClernand Collection; *OR*, vol. 7:605.

64. Field Order No. 125, 11 Feb. 1862, Headquarters, First Division; McClernand to Wallace, McClernand to Oglesby, 11 Feb. 1862. All in McClernand Collection.

65. Alfred D. Roman, *The Military Operations of General Beauregard in the War Between the States*, 2 vols. (New York: Harper and Brothers, 1883), 1:213–14; *OR*, vol. 7:861–64.

66. *OR*, vol. 7:267, 279, 383; Stonesifer, "The Forts Henry-Heiman and Fort Donelson Campaign," 203; Grant, *Personal Memoirs*, 176.

67. *OR*, vol. 7:170, 183; Wilbur F. Crummer, *With Grant at Fort Donelson, Shiloh, and Vicksburg* (Oak Park, Ill.: E. C. Crummer, 1915), 25–6; Lew Wallace, "The Capture of Fort Donelson," 410; J. E. Boos, "Civil War Diary of Patrick H. White," *Journal of the Illinois State Historical Society* 15 (Oct. 1922–Jan. 1923): 649.

68. *OR*, vol. 7:183, 192–93.

69. Ibid., 183, 383–84.

70. *OR*, vol. 7:171, 227; Henry G. Hicks, "Fort Donelson," in *Glimpses of the Nation's Struggle: Papers Read before the Minnesota Commandery of the Military Order of the Loyal Legion of the United States, 1892–1897*, ed. Edwin C. Mason, Ell Torrance, and David L. Kingsbury, 6 vols. (Wilmington, N.C.: Broadfoot Publishing, 1992), 4:445.

71. Simon, *The Papers of Ulysses S. Grant*, 4:213; *OR*, vol. 7:171–72, 184, 193.

72. Ibid., 172.

73. *OR*, vol. 7:172–73, 184, 212; Grant, *Personal Memoirs*, 177.

74. Carl von Clausewitz, *On War*, trans. and ed. Michael Howard and Peter Paret (Princeton, N.J.: Princeton Univ. Press, 1976), 359, 535; Baron Antoine Henri de Jomini, *The Art of War*, trans. G. H. Mendell and W. P. Craighill (Philadelphia: J. B. Lippincott, 1862; reprint, Westport, Conn.: Greenwood Press, 1971), 165–66, 201.

75. *OR*, vol. 7:367; William P. Johnston, *The Life of Gen. Albert Sidney Johnston* (New York: D. Appleton, 1878), 482.

76. Hagerman, "The Evolution of Trench Warfare in the American Civil War," 33.

77. Perry Jamieson, "The Development of Civil War Tactics" (Ph.D. diss., Wayne State University, 1979), 77, 80; Jacob D. Cox, *Atlanta* (New York: Charles Scribner's Sons, 1880), 129.

78. *OR*, vol. 7:173, 204, 206, 368; Stonesifer, "The Forts Henry-Heiman and Fort Donelson Campaign," 234.

79. *OR*, vol. 7:220, 227, 231; Grant, *Personal Memoirs*, 177.

80. Hicks, "Fort Donelson," 4:446; *OR*, vol. 7:613.

81. Grant, *Personal Memoirs*, 178; Lew Wallace, *Lew Wallace: An Autobiography*, 1:387–88.

82. *OR*, vol. 7:174, 185, 215, 217.

83. Henry Walke, "The Western Flotilla at Fort Donelson, Island Number Ten, Fort Pillow and Memphis," in *Battles and Leaders of the Civil War*, 1:433; *ORN*, vol. 22:586–87; Simon, *The Papers of Ulysses S. Grant*, 4:211.

84. *ORN*, vol. 22:612.

85. *OR*, vol. 7:263, 268–69, 317–18, 330–31, 360, 365.

86. Grant, *Personal Memoirs*, 180; Johnston, *The Life of Gen. Albert Sidney Johnston*, 481–82.

87. Grant, *Personal Memoirs*, 179.

88. *OR*, vol. 7:186, 218.

89. Lew Wallace, *Lew Wallace: An Autobiography*, 1:399–400. The exact Confederate strength at Fort Donelson has never been determined. The numbers used here are estimates derived by Cooling in *Forts Henry and Donelson: The Key to the Confederate Heartland*, 283; *OR*, vol. 7:269.

90. Lew Wallace, *Lew Wallace: An Autobiography*, 1:400.

91. *OR*, vol. 7:187, 189–90, 195, 216, 243, 373–74.

92. Ibid., 196, 244, 282.

93. Ibid., 237; Lew Wallace, *Lew Wallace: An Autobiography*, 1:403–4.

94. *OR*, vol. 7:178–79.

95. Lew Wallace, *Lew Wallace: An Autobiography*, 1:411–12; Bruce Catton, *Grant Moves South* (Boston: Little, Brown, 1960), 164; *Chicago Tribune*, 23 Sept. 1865, 3, in a reprint of a report in the *(Galena) Northwestern Gazette*, 18 Sept. 1865.

96. *OR*, vol. 7:180, 236; Lew Wallace, *Lew Wallace: An Autobiography*, 1:389.

97. Simon, *The Papers of Ulysses S. Grant*, 4:189; Lew Wallace to Susan Wallace, 11 Feb. 1862, Lew Wallace Papers, Indiana Historical Society, quoted in Stonesifer, "The Forts Henry-Heiman and Fort Donelson Campaigns," 200; *OR*, vol. 7:175; Lew Wallace, *Lew Wallace: An Autobiography*, 1:401.

98. *OR*, vol. 7:180, 332–33; vol. 52, 1:9; William P. Johnston, *The Life of Gen. Albert Sidney Johnston*, 482.

99. Master Plan Map No. 10, Fort Donelson National Military Park, prepared by Edwin C. Bearss, 17 Apr. 1959.

100. *OR*, vol. 7:275, 287, 293, 296–97, 302–3, 364, 386, 581; John Allan Wyeth, *That Devil Forrest: The Life of General Nathan Bedford Forrest* (New York: Harper and Brothers, 1950), 50. The exact number of prisoners taken at Fort Donelson cannot be determined. Various sources place the number between seven thousand and 14,623. Johnston, *The Life of Gen. Albert Sidney Johnston*, 474, 481–82) analyzed Confederate strength reports and Union reports of prisoners taken and estimated that about 1,200 men escaped capture.

101. Grant, *Personal Memoirs*, 183; *ORN*, vol. 22:596–97; *OR*, vol. 7:180.

102. *OR*, vol. 7:625–26.

103. *New York Tribune*, 22 Feb. 1862, 8; Catton, *Grant Moves South*, 181; *Cincinnati Commercial*, 22 Feb. 1862, sec. 2, 2; Simon, *Papers of Ulysses S. Grant*, 4:272. On 19 Jan. 1862 a force under Brig. Gen. George Thomas defeated a Confederate force at Logan Cross Roads, Kentucky. This cut the Rebel line in the eastern part of the theater. Instead of advancing into eastern Tennessee, Brig. Gen. Don Carlos Buell moved, on Halleck's orders, toward Forts Henry and Donelson.

104. *Chicago Times*, 18 Feb. 1862, 2; *Illinois State Journal*, 27 Feb. 1862, 2; Simon, *The Papers of Ulysses S. Grant*, 4:275–76.

105. James H. Wilson, *The Life of John A. Rawlins* (New York: Neale Publishing, 1916), 134; Dana and Wilson, *The Life of Ulysses S. Grant*, 65; Wallace, "The Capture of Fort Donelson," 405.

106. Field Order No. 145, 17 Feb. 1862, Headquarters, First Division, McClernand Collection.

107. McClernand to Lincoln, 18 Feb. 1862, Lincoln Collection.

108. Wallace, *Life and Letters of General W. H. L. Wallace*, 166.

109. *OR*, vol. 7:179; Lew Wallace, *Lew Wallace: An Autobiography*, 1:411–12.

110. *OR*, vol. 7:180.

111. McClernand to Lincoln, 27 Feb, 28 Feb. 1862, Lincoln Collection; *OR*, vol. 7:170.

112. Simon, *The Papers of Ulysses S. Grant*, 4:263–64, 274; *OR*, vol. 7:181.

113. *OR*, vol. 10, 2:24.

4. Into the Heartland

1. McClernand to Grant, 17 Feb. 1862; Grant to McClernand, 18 Feb. 1862. McClernand Collection.

2. General Orders No. 4, 18 Feb. 1862, District of West Tennessee; Field Orders Nos. 157, 160, 161, 18 Feb. 1862, Headquarters, First Division; Field Orders No. 183, 22 Feb. 1862, Headquarters, First Division. All in McClernand Collection. *OR*, vol. 7:629.

3. *OR*, vol. 8:381, 406; Grant to McClernand, 22 Feb. 1862; McClernand to Grant, 22 Feb. 1862. McClernand Collection.

4. Capt. John A. Rawlins to McClernand, 25 Feb. 1862, McClernand Collection.

5. McClernand to Grant, 26 Feb. 1862, McClernand Collection.

6. *OR*, vol. 7:637–38, 643, 648, 667.

7. McClernand to Col. W. H. L. Wallace, 28 Feb. 1862; McClernand to Grant, 1 Mar. 1862. McClernand Collection.

8. Mrs. James K. Polk to McClernand, 16 Mar. 1862, McClernand Collection; Isabel Wallace, *Life and Letters of General W. H. L. Wallace*, 171.

9. Simon, *The Papers of Ulysses S. Grant*, 4:301, 304.

10. Bruce Catton, *The Army of the Potomac: Mr. Lincoln's Army* (Garden City, N.Y.: Doubleday, 1962), 50–53; Mungo P. Murray to Father, n.d., Mungo P. Murray Letters, Civil War Times Illustrated Collection, U.S. Army Military History Institute, as quoted in Robert J. Dalessandro, "Morale in the Army of the Cumberland during the Tullahoma and Chickamauga Campaigns" (master's thesis, U.S. Army Command and General Staff College, 1995), 66.

11. *OR*, vol. 7:674.

12. Ibid., 678–79; Field Order No. 210, 2 Mar. 1862, Headquarters, First Division; Field Order (unnumbered), 3 Mar. 1862, Headquarters, First Division. McClernand Collection.

13. *OR*, vol. 7:676, 679–80, 682; vol. 10, 2:3–5, 22.

14. Simon, *The Papers of Ulysses S. Grant*, 4:322, 321; McClernand to Grant, 6 Mar. 1862, McClernand Collection; Charles King, *The True Ulysses S. Grant*, 155–57.

15. Simon, *The Papers of Ulysses S. Grant*, 4:338. On 3 March Lincoln wrote Secretary of War Stanton that he wanted McClernand and Smith, among others, promoted to major general. He also named several officers for promotion to brigadier general. Basler, *The Collected Works of Abraham Lincoln*, 5:142.

16. Simon, *The Papers of Ulysses S. Grant*, 4:338.

17. McClernand to Grant, 14 Mar. 1862, McClernand Collection.

18. McClernand to Col. Leonard F. Ross, 4 Mar. 1862; McClernand to Grant, 5 Mar. 1862; Field Order No. 230, 6 Mar. 1862, Headquarters, First Division; McClernand to Grant, 6 Mar. 1862. All in McClernand Collection. *OR*, vol. 10, 2:6.

19. *OR*, vol. 10, 2:7.

20. Ross to McClernand, 8 Mar. 1862; McClernand to Grant, 7 Mar. 1862. McClernand Collection.

21. McClernand to Maj. Gen. Charles F. Smith, 8 Mar. 1862; Field Order No. 237, 8 Mar. 1862, Headquarters, First Division; General Orders No. 2, 9 Mar. 1862, Headquarters, Expeditionary Corps. All in McClernand Collection.

22. Field Order No. 242, 10 Mar. 1862; Field Order (unnumbered), 10 Mar. 1862; Field Order No. 246, 10 Mar. 1862. All Headquarters, First Division. McClernand Collection.

23. McClernand to Smith, 11 Mar. 1862, McClernand Collection.

24. Hurlbut to McClernand, 12 Mar. 1862; McClernand to Hurlbut, 12 Mar. 1862. McClernand Collection; King, *The True Ulysses S. Grant*, 156–57.

25. Hurlbut to McClernand, 12 Mar. 1862, McClernand Collection.

26. Smith to McClernand, 13 Mar. 1862; Special Orders No. 20, 13 Mar. 1862, Headquarters, Expeditionary Corps; McClernand to Smith, 14 Mar. 1862. McClernand Collection.

27. Field Order No. 253, 14 Mar. 1862, Headquarters, First Division; McClernand to Capt. William M. Michael, 15 Mar. 1862; Col. W. H. L. Wallace to McClernand, 17 Mar. 1862. McClernand Collection. *OR*, vol. 10, 1:8–9.

28. Forest City Union Association to McClernand, 1 Mar. 1862; McClernand to Forest City Union Association, 14 Mar. 1862. McClernand Collection. Simon, *The Papers of Ulysses S. Grant*, 4:374–75.

29. McClernand to the Hon. James W. Singleton, 24 Mar. 1862, McClernand Collection.

30. *OR*, vol. 10, 2:40–42.

31. Ibid., 40, 42–43, 45–47.

32. Field Order No. 272, 17 Mar. 1862, Headquarters, First Division; McClernand to Ross, 18 Mar. 1862; McClernand to Grant, 20 Mar. 1862. McClernand Collection.

33. Adolph Schwartz to Thomas J. Newsham, 17 Mar. 1862, McClernand Collection.

34. *OR*, vol. 10, 2:52; McClernand to Grant, 21 Mar. 1862, McClernand Collection; Grant to McClernand, 21 Mar. 1862, McClernand Collection; McClernand to Ross, 21 Mar. 1862, McClernand Collection.

35. George B. Davis et al., *The Official Military Atlas of the Civil War* (Washington, D.C.: GPO, 1891–95), Plates 13–1, 78–6; *OR*, vol. 52, 1:230.

36. McClernand to Grant, 27 Mar. 1862, McClernand Collection.

37. *OR*, vol. 52, 1:559.

38. Simon, *The Papers of Ulysses S. Grant*, 4:429; Special Orders No. 36, 26 Mar. 1862, McClernand Collection; McClernand to Grant, 27 Mar. 1862, McClernand Collection; Letter of Appointment signed by President Lincoln and Secretary of War Stanton, 24 Mar. 1862, McClernand Collection. McClernand had been appointed brigadier general on 17 May 1861 and Smith on 31 August 1861. Both would be promoted to major general on 21 March 1862. Francis B. Heitman, *Historical Register and Dictionary of the United States Army*, 2 vols. (Washington, D.C.: GPO, 1903), 1:259, 470, 559, 657, 798, 882, 895, 954.

39. *OR*, vol. 10, 2:82, 84, 94; Ezra J. Warner, *Generals in Blue*, 293, 455.

40. Simon, *The Papers of Ulysses S. Grant*, 4:437–38; McClernand to Grant, 27 Mar. 1862, McClernand Collection.

41. McClernand to Grant, 29 Mar. 1862, McClernand Collection.

42. Gov. Richard Yates to McClernand, 26 Mar. 1862, Richard Yates Collection, Springfield State Historical Library.

43. McClernand to Lincoln, 31 Mar. 1862, Lincoln Collection.

44. *OR*, vol. 10, 1:385; 2:89; vol. 7:437–38.

45. Field Order No. 357, 2 Apr. 1862, Headquarters, First Division, McClernand Collection; McClernand to Brig. Gen. W. H. L. Wallace, 4 Apr. 1862, McClernand Collection; Olynthus Clark, ed., *Downing's Civil War Diary* (Iowa City: State Univ. of Iowa, 1916), 40.

46. *OR*, vol. 10, 1:83, 84, 89, 396; 2:94.

47. Ibid., 89, 567; 2:94; McClernand to Sherman, 5 Apr. 1862, McClernand Collection; McClernand to Grant, 5 Apr. 1862, McClernand Collection.

48. *OR*, vol. 10, 1:284–85; Robert Fleming, "The Battle of Shiloh as a Private Saw It," *Sketches of War History 1861–1865: Papers Prepared for the Commandery of the State of Ohio, Military Order of the Loyal Legion of the United States*, ed. Theodore F. Allen, Edward S. McKee, and J. Gordon Taylor, 9 vols. (Cincinnati: Monfort, 1908), 6:141.

49. *OR*, vol. 10, 1:143.

50. Ibid., 249–50.

51. Ibid., 278.

52. Ibid., 115, 139, 249; Sherman, *Memoirs*, 236. In his *Memoirs* Sherman includes a copy of his report of the battle, dated 10 April 1862. It is similar to that found in the *OR*s, with some exceptions. One is that in his memoirs Sherman says McClernand responded "promptly and energetically," while his report in the *OR* states that McClernand responded "promptly." Dana and Wilson, *The Life of Ulysses S. Grant*, 78. The brigade commander, Col. Leonard F. Ross, was on leave in Illinois due to the death of his wife. Adolph Engelmann to his wife, 17 Apr. 1862, Engelmann-Kircher Family Papers, Illinois State Historical Library. The acting brigade commander, Col. James S. Reardon, was ill.

53. *OR*, vol. 10, 1:115, 123–24, 133.

54. Ibid., 250. The time of the attack was determined from an examination of inscriptions on markers at Shiloh National Military Park.

55. Adam Badeau, *Military History of Ulysses S. Grant, from April 1861 to April 1865*, 3 vols. (New York: D. Appleton, 1868), 1:78. In assessing Badeau's comments it must be recognized that he did not join Grant's staff until February 1864. He wrote that his commentary prior to that time had been based on conversations with Grant and others who had accompanied him during the earlier period, but his observations must be weighed in the light of generally negative feelings toward McClernand among Grant's associates. Grant, *Personal Memoirs*, 203; *OR*, vol. 10, 1:278, 288; T. Worthington, *Shiloh: The Only Correct Military History of U. S. Grant and the Missing Army Records* (Washington City: M'Gill & Witherow, 1872), 153.

56. *OR*, vol. 10, 1:130, 423, 584.

57. Ibid., 220.

58. Ibid., 116, George Carrington, Diary 1862, Chicago Historical Society, entry for 6 Apr. 1862.

59. *OR*, vol. 10, 1:117, 250.

60. Wallace, *Life and Letters of General W. H. L. Wallace*, 193.

61. *OR*, vol. 10, 1:117, 250; Wallace, *Lew Wallace: An Autobiography*, 2:528; Committee of the Regiment, *The Story of the Fifty-fifth Regiment Illinois Volunteer Infantry in the Civil War* (n.p., 1887), 112.

62. *OR*, vol. 10, 1:130, 137, 145, 266, 288–89.

63. *Illinois State Journal*, 11 Apr. 1862, 1.

64. *OR*, vol. 10:117, 250; Grant, *Personal Memoirs*, 203.

65. Kenneth P. Williams, *Lincoln Finds a General*, vol. 3, *Grant's First Year in the West* (New York: Macmillan, 1952), 365.

66. Worthington, *Shiloh*, 153.

67. Badeau, *Military History of Ulysses S. Grant*, 1:79.

68. Howe, ed., *Home Letters of General Sherman*, passim; Rachel Sherman Thorndike, ed., *The Sherman Letters: Correspondence between General and Senator Sherman from 1837 to 1891* (New York: Charles Scribner's Sons, 1894), passim.

69. *OR*, vol. 10, 1:118, 134, 250, 265–66.

70. Ibid., 120, 323–24.

71. Henry Villard, *Memoirs of Henry Villard, Journalist and Financier, 1835–1900*, 2 vols. (Boston: Houghton, Mifflin, 1904), 1:244–45, 272; B. H. Liddell Hart, *Sherman: Soldier, Realist, American* (New York: Dodd, Meade, 1930), 129.

72. *OR*, vol. 10, 1:119, 205; Thomas Jordan and R. P. Pryor, *The Campaigns of Lieutenant General N. B. Forrest and of Forrest's Cavalry* (New York: DeCapo Press, 1996), 136–37.

73. *OR*, vol. 10, 1:119, 473.

74. Ibid., 119, 135, 251.

75. Ibid., 120, 145, 252, 308.

76. Ibid., 101, 108, 112; McClernand to Capt. John A. Rawlins, 8 Apr. 1862, McClernand Collection; McClernand to Grant, 9 Apr. 1862, McClernand Collection; *Illinois State Journal*, 28 Apr. 1862, 3.

77. McClernand to Capt. A. S. Martin, 9 Apr. 1862, McClernand Collection; *OR*, vol. 10, 1:144.

78. *OR*, vol. 10, 2:97; McClernand to Col. Marcellus M. Crocker, 8 Apr. 1862, McClernand Collection; McClernand to Col. C. Carroll Marsh, 11 Apr. 1862, McClernand Collection.

79. *OR*, vol. 10, 1:111–12.

80. Ibid., 2:100; McClernand to Grant, erroneously dated 8 Apr. 1862; Field Order No. 361, 8 Apr. 1862, Headquarters, First Division; Grant to McClernand, 9 Apr. 1862; Field Order No. 365, 10 Apr. 1862, Headquarters, First Division. McClernand Collection.

81. Grant, *Personal Memoirs*, 220; *OR*, vol. 10, 2:105–6.

82. McClernand to Grant, 11 Apr. 1862, McClernand Collection.

83. McClernand to Capt. Edward McAllister, 13 Apr. 1862; Special Orders No. 38, 16 Apr. 1862, Headquarters, First Division; Field Order No. 393, 16 Apr. 1862, Headquarters, First Division; unsigned letter to Capt. James Dunlap, 17 Apr. 1862; Special Field Order No. 12, 17 Apr. 1862, Headquarters, Department of the Mississippi; General Field Order No. 423, 19 Apr. 1862, Headquarters, First Division; Field Order No. 405, 17 Apr. 1862, Headquarters, First Division. All in McClernand Collection.

84. *Illinois State Journal*, 19 Apr. 1862, 2; *Illinois State Journal*, 24 Apr. 1862, 1, 2; Carr, *The Illini*, 408.

85. General Orders No. 37, 14 Apr. 1862, Headquarters, Army of the Tennessee; Field Order No. 387, 15 Apr. 1862, Headquarters, First Division. McClernand Collection.

86. *OR*, vol. 10, 1:113–14.

87. Simon, *The Papers of Ulysses S. Grant*, 5:19, 22–23; *OR*, vol. 10, 1:98.

88. *OR*, vol. 10, 1:110.

89. Ibid., 98.

90. Field Order No. 389, 15 Apr. 1862, Headquarters, First Division; A. S. Morton to Lt. Col. William McCullough, 21 Apr. 1862; Grant to McClernand, 22 Apr. 1862; McClernand to Grant, 22 Apr. 1862. McClernand Collection.

91. *OR*, vol. 10, 2:117–18, 138–39; Simon, *The Papers of Ulysses S. Grant*, 5:65–66. Field Order No. 433, 23 Apr. 1862, Headquarters, First Division; Field Order No. 443, 24 Apr. 1862, Headquarters, First Division; 24 Apr. 1862, McClernand to Brig. Gen. Leonard F. Ross. McClernand Collection.

92. McClernand to Grant, 23 Apr. 1862; McClernand to Grant, 24 Apr. 1862. McClernand Collection.

93. Special Orders No. 458, 26 Apr. 1862, Headquarters, First Division, McClernand Collection; *OR*, vol. 10, 1:753–54; Capt. William S. Hillyer to McClernand, 26 Apr. 1862, McClernand Collection; McClernand to Grant, 26 Apr. 1862, McClernand Collection.

94. *OR*, vol. 10, 1:652; Simon, *The Papers of Ulysses S. Grant*, 5:86–87.

95. *OR*, vol. 10, 2:138–39, 144–45, 182–83; Grant, *Personal Memoirs*, 224.

96. *OR*, vol. 10, 2:154, 182–83; Simon, *The Papers of Ulysses S. Grant*, 5:109.

97. *OR*, vol. 10, 1:754; 2:136; Field Order No. 470, 29 Apr. 1862, Headquarters, Reserve Army, McClernand Collection; McClernand to Brig. Gen. Stephen A. Hurlbut, 29 Apr. 1862, McClernand Collection.

98. *OR*, vol. 10, 1:755; *Illinois State Journal*, 15 May 1862, 2.

99. McClernand to Yates, 22 May 1862; Sen. Isaac Trumbull to McClernand, 24 May 1862. McClernand Collection.

100. General Orders No. 5, 2 May 1862, Headquarters, Reserve Army; Special Field Order No. 40, 3 May 1862, Headquarters, Department of the Mississippi. McClernand Collection.

101. General Orders No. 2, 2 May 1862, Headquarters, Reserve Army; General Orders No. 8, 2 May 1862, Headquarters, Reserve Army; Special Field Order No. 38, 2 May 1862, Headquarters, Department of the Mississippi. McClernand Collection.

102. Lew Wallace, *Lew Wallace: An Autobiography*, 2:573; *OR*, vol. 10, 1:762; General Orders No. 4, 2 May 1862, Headquarters, Reserve Army, McClernand Collection.

103. *OR*, vol. 10, 2:157, 159; Simon, *The Papers of Ulysses S. Grant*, 5:108–9.

104. Simon, *The Papers of Ulysses S. Grant*, 5:108–9; *OR*, vol. 10, 1:754.

105. Simon, *The Papers of Ulysses S. Grant*, 5:121; *OR*, vol. 10, 2:189.

106. *OR*, vol. 10, 1:755; 2:192–93; Simon, *The Papers of Ulysses S. Grant*, 5:121–23.

107. Simon, *The Papers of Ulysses S. Grant*, 5:129.

108. *OR*, vol. 10, 2:203, 214; Simon, *The Papers of Ulysses S. Grant*, 5:125–26.

109. *OR*, vol. 10, 2:230–31.

110. Grant, *Personal Memoirs*, 224.

111. *OR*, vol. 10, 2:240–41.

112. Ibid., 256–57.

113. Ibid., 244, 247; McClernand to Grant, 5 June 1862, McClernand Collection.

114. *OR*, vol. 10, 1:918; 2:261, 265, 267, 275; Simon, *The Papers of Ulysses S. Grant*, 5:141–42, 146–47. Ransom's appointment would not be approved until 15 April 1863. McClernand's orders to Wallace were to take "possession of Somerville and the Memphis and Ohio Railroad at the nearest and most commanding point west of Somerville." Wallace occupied Somerville, which was the terminus of a spur running north from Moscow. He also had a force along the line of the Mississippi Central Railroad between Grand Junction and Jackson. There is no indication that he was able to interrupt the Memphis and Ohio Railroad farther to the west.

115. *OR*, vol. 17, 2:6, 8, 14–15, 19; McClernand to Brig. Gen. John A. Logan, 18 June 1862, McClernand Collection.

116. *OR*, vol. 10, 2:288; vol. 17, 2:30–31.

117. Ibid., vol. 17, 2:38, 64; ibid., 1:67–69; Simon, *The Papers of Ulysses S. Grant*, 5:153–54; McClernand to Grant, 30 June 1862, McClernand Collection; McClernand to Grant, 3 July 1862, McClernand Collection. Existing records clearly indicate that Grant had divided his district into subdistricts. The order to do that, however, has not been found.

118. McClernand to Lincoln, 20 June 1862, Lincoln Collection.

119. *OR*, vol. 17, 2:25, 32, 37, 38, 40, 49.

120. Ibid., vol. 16, 2:76, 81–82; vol. 17, 2:52–53, 60–61; McClernand to Halleck, 1 July 1862, McClernand Collection.

121. *OR*, ser. 3, vol. 2:187–88; McClernand to Yates, 2 July 1862, McClernand Collection; McClernand to Grant, 7 July 1862, McClernand Collection.

122. Simon, *The Papers of Ulysses S. Grant*, 5:331; McClernand to Senators and Representatives of Illinois in Congress, 9 July 1862, McClernand Collection.

123. *OR*, vol. 17, 2:90, 101–2.

124. Ibid., 94–95, 99; Simon, *The Papers of Ulysses S. Grant*, 5:211–12.

125. Simon, *The Papers of Ulysses S. Grant*, 5:209, 211–12.

126. *OR*, vol. 17, 1:23–25; 2:124.

127. Ibid., 2:125; McClernand to Grant, 28 July, 5 Aug., 6 Aug. 1862, McClernand Collection; McClernand to Brig. Gen. Leonard F. Ross, 27 July 1862, McClernand Collection.

128. Simon, *The Papers of Ulysses S. Grant*, 5:236–37, 336–37; McClernand to Andrew Johnson, 26 July, 2 Aug., 12 Aug., 13 Aug., 20 Aug. 1862; Johnson to McClernand, 26 July, 3 Aug., 12 Aug. 1862. All in Andrew Johnson Papers, microfilm, Combined Arms Research Library.

129. *OR*, vol. 17, 2:128–30; McClernand to Logan, 27 July 1862, McClernand Collection; McClernand to Logan, 30 July 1862, McClernand Collection.

130. *OR*, vol. 17, 2:133–36, 138–39, 150–51; McClernand to Grant, 31 July 1862, McClernand Collection.

131. *Illinois State Journal*, 1 Aug. 1862, 2.

132. *OR*, vol. 17, 2:150–51.

133. Pease and Randall, *The Diary of Orville Hickman Browning*, 1:xix, 560.

134. Halleck to McClernand, 20 Aug. 1862, McClernand Collection.

135. Grant to Lincoln, 11 Aug. 1862, Lincoln Collection.

136. *OR*, vol. 17, 2:150; Benjamin F. Cooling, *Fort Donelson's Legacy: War and Society in Kentucky and Tennessee, 1862–1863* (Knoxville: Univ. of Tennessee Press, 1997), 74–75.

137. *OR*, vol. 17, 2:152–53, 166; McClernand to Grant, 6 Aug. 1862, McClernand Collection; McClernand to Grant, 10 Aug. 1862, McClernand Collection; Simon, *The Papers of Ulysses S. Grant*, 5:287.

138. McClernand to Grant, 11 Aug., 14 Aug., 16 Aug., 21 Aug. 1862. McClernand to Ross, 25 Aug. 1862. All in McClernand Collection. *Illinois State Journal*, 16 Aug. 1862, 2.

139. Simon, *The Papers of Ulysses S. Grant*, 5:406.

140. *OR*, vol. 17, 2:130; Simon, *The Papers of Ulysses S. Grant*, 5:412–14.

141. *OR*, vol. 17, 2:675–76, 687, 691; 1:51, 120.

142. McClernand to Grant, 13 Aug. 1862, McClernand Collection.

143. Simon, *The Papers of Ulysses S. Grant*, 5:299–300.

144. Ibid., 301–2; McClernand to Brig. Gen. Grenville M. Dodge, 18 Aug. 1862, McClernand Collection.

145. Simon, *The Papers of Ulysses S. Grant*, 5:403–4.

146. McClernand to Yates, 12 Aug. 1862, Yates Collection; Yates to secretary, 12 Aug. 1862, Yates Collection.

147. Yates to McClernand, 19 Aug. 1862, McClernand Collection.

148. *OR*, ser. 3, vol. 2:293–94; ser. 3, vol. 4:1264–65; ser. 1, vol. 17, 2:187; Grant to McClernand, 25 Aug. 1862, McClernand Collection; Special Orders No. 174, District of West Tennessee, 27 Aug. 1862, McClernand Collection.

5. Return to Illinois

1. General Orders No. 15, Headquarters, District of Jackson, 28 Aug. 1862; McClernand to Halleck, 1 Sept. 1862; McClernand to Yates, 28 Aug., 1 Sept. 1862. All in McClernand Collection.

2. Aretas A. Dayton, "The Raising of Union Forces in Illinois during the Civil War," *Journal of the Illinois State Historical* Society 34 (Dec. 1941): 410; *Illinois State Journal*, 16 Aug. 1862, 2.

3. McClernand to Yates, 1 Sept. 1862, McClernand Collection; McClernand to Yates, 2 Sept. 1862, McClernand Collection; Yates to McClernand, 5 Sept. 1862, McClernand Collection. The authorized strength of a Union regiment was 1,037, but rarely did a regiment have so many men.

4. CoL. M. D. Leggett to McClernand, 24 Sept. 1862, McClernand Collection; Newton Bateman to McClernand, 9 Sept. 1862, McClernand Collection; Col. Adolph Engelmann to McClernand, 8 Sept. 1862, McClernand Collection; McClernand to Lincoln, 13 Sept. 1862, McClernand Collection.

5. Maj. E. S. Jones to McClernand, 13 Sept. 1862, McClernand Collection.

6. McClernand to Yates, 12 Sept. 1862, McClernand Collection; McClernand to Yates, 15 Sept. 1862, McClernand Collection.

7. Chicago Tribune, 3 Sept. 1862; *Illinois State Journal*, 6 Sept. 1862; *Chicago Tribune*, 8 Sept. 1862; quoted in Victor Hicken, *Illinois in the Civil War* (Urbana: Univ. of Illinois Press, 1962), 86–87.

8. Basler, ed., *The Collected Works of Abraham Lincoln*, 5:484.

9. Yates to McClernand, 22 Sept. 1862, McClernand Collection; McClernand to Maj. Warren Stewart, 22 Sept. 1862, McClernand Collection.

10. John Cowan to McClernand, 25 Sept. 1862, McClernand Collection; David Donald, ed., *Inside Lincoln's Cabinet: The Civil War Diaries of Salmon P. Chase* (New York: Longmans, Green, 1954), 161–62; John Niven, ed., *The Salmon P. Chase Papers*, 4 vols. (Kent, Ohio: Kent State Univ. Press, 1993), 1:402.

11. *OR*, vol. 17, 2:849–53.

12. Ibid., vol. 10, 1:671; vol. 16, 2:14, 62–63; Robert Means Thompson and Richard Wainwright, eds., *Confidential Correspondence of Gustavus Vasa Fox*, 2 vols. (New York: DeVinne Press, 1920), 2:101–2.

13. Catton, *Grant Moves South*, 325; U.S. Congress, House, Historical Manuscripts Commission, "Diary and Correspondence of Salmon P. Chase," in *Annual Report of the American Historical Association for the Year 1902*, 2 vols., 57th Cong., 2d sess. (Washington, D.C.: GPO, 1903), 2:55.

14. Donald, *Inside Lincoln's Cabinet*, 169–70; Stephen W. Sears, ed., *The Civil War Papers of George B. McClellan* (New York: Ticknor & Fields, 1989), 488. There is no record of what transpired between Lincoln and McClernand during the trip to Antietam.

15. Donald, *Inside Lincoln's Cabinet*, 98, 162–63; Gideon Welles, *Diary of Gideon Welles*, 3 vols. (New York: Houghton Mifflin, 1911), 1:217; Wilson, *Under the Old Flag*, 1:120–21.

16. *OR*, vol. 17, 2:274–75, 277–78; Edwin M. Stanton to Henry W. Halleck, 11 Oct. 1862, McClernand Collection; McClernand to Halleck, 16 Oct. 1862, McClernand Collection.

17. Klement, *The Copperheads in the Middle West*, 3–4, 11; *New York Times*, 30 Oct. 1862, 1.

18. Hicken, *Illinois in the Civil War*, 91; Frank L. Klement, "The Democrats as Sectionalists," in *Lincoln and Civil War Politics*, ed. James A. Rawley (New York: Holt, Rinehart and Wilson, 1969), 96–97; *OR*, vol. 17, 2:849–50, 333, 308–9.

19. *New York Times*, 30 Oct. 1862, 1.

20. David Dixon Porter, *Incidents and Anecdotes of the Civil War* (New York: Appleton, 1885), 14.

21. Ibid., 122–23.

22. Welles, *Diary of Gideon Welles*, 1:167; Richard S. West, *The Second Admiral: A Life of David Dixon Porter* (New York: Coward-McCann, 1937), 170; Nicolay and Hay, *Abraham Lincoln: A History*, 7:135–36; *Chicago Tribune*, 22 Nov. 1862, 1.

23. Welles, *Diary of Gideon Welles*, 1:88.

24. Ibid., 3:559, 562.

25. *OR*, vol. 17, 2:282.

26. Basler, ed., *The Collected Works of Abraham Lincoln*, 4:468–69.

27. *OR*, vol. 17, 2:401–2.

28. Ibid., 332; McClernand to Gov. Samuel D. Kirkwood, 27 Oct. 1862, McClernand Collection.

29. *OR*, vol. 17, 2:300.

30. McClernand to Maj. Walter B. Scates, 28 Oct. 1862, McClernand Collection; Col. Allen C. Fuller to McClernand, 28 Oct. 1862, McClernand Collection; Maj. Adolph Schwartz to Fuller, 29 Oct. 1862, McClernand Collection.

31. *OR*, vol. 17, 2:302.

32. Fuller to McClernand, 30 Oct. 1862, McClernand Collection; McClernand to commanders, 82d, 95th, 103d, 111th, and 119th Regiments, 30 Oct. 1862, McClernand Collection; McClernand to Morton, 30 Oct. 1862, McClernand Collection.

33. McClernand to Kirkwood, 3 Nov. 1862, McClernand Collection. Porter notified Welles on 29 Oct. that the fleet was ready. Welles did not officially pass this information to Stanton until 5 November. As Porter claimed not to be in communication with McClernand, it is unclear how McClernand would have known on 3 November that the fleet was ready. *OR*, vol. 17, 2:320–21. McClernand to Stanton, 3 Nov. 1862, McClernand Collection; McClernand to Stanton, 5 Nov. 1862, McClernand Collection; McClernand to Capt. W. H. Bailhache, 5 Nov. 1862, McClernand Collection; McClernand to Col. Nathaniel Niles, 5 Nov. 1862, McClernand Collection; McClernand to Stanton, 6 Nov. 1862, McClernand Collection.

34. *OR*, vol. 17, 2:278, 344–45.

35. Ibid., 307–8.

36. *Illinois State Journal*, 17 Nov., 1862, 1; 20 Nov. 1862, 2. *New York Times*, 30 Oct. 1862, 1.

37. Wilson, *Under the Old Flag*, 1:120–21, 144–45.

38. Ibid.; Wilson, *The Life of John A. Rawlins*, 103.

39. Simon, *The Papers of Ulysses S. Grant*, 6:279.

40. Ibid., 6:285.

41. *OR*, vol. 17, 1:469.

42. Ibid., 2:347–48.

43. Thorndike, ed., *The Sherman Letters: Correspondence between General and Senator Sherman from 1837 to 1891*, 169.

44. Porter, *Incidents and Anecdotes*, 125; *Missouri Republican* and *Chicago Tribune*, 22 Nov. 1862, as cited in Simon, *The Papers of Ulysses S. Grant*, 6:341; West, *The Second Admiral*, 181.

45. Thompson and Wainwright, *Confidential Correspondence of Gustavus Vasa Fox*, 2:143.

46. *ORN*, vol. 23:458, 484; David Dixon Porter, *The Naval History of the Civil War* (Secaucus, N.J.: Castle, 1984), 283.

47. *ORN*, vol. 23:495–96, 501.

48. Ibid., 535, 538, 542–44; Thompson and Wainwright, *Confidential Correspondence of Gustavus Vasa Fox*, 2:150.

49. Welles, *Diary of Gideon Welles*, 1:387.

50. *OR*, vol. 17, 2:347–48; *ORN*, vol. 23:496–97.

51. Simon, *The Papers of Ulysses S. Grant*, 6:407; *OR*, vol. 17, 1:474, 601; 2:347–48.

52. *OR*, vol. 17, 1:474–75.

53. Wilson, *Under the Old Flag*, 1:138.

54. Grant, *Personal Memoirs*, 253.

55. *OR*, vol. 17, 1:475; vol. 52, 1:313–14.

56. Grant, *Personal Memoirs*, 255.

57. Thorndike, *The Sherman Letters*, 174; Badeau, *Military History of Ulysses S. Grant*, 1:136.

58. Sherman, *Memoirs*, 285–86.

59. *OR*, vol. 17, 2:300, 302.

60. *Illinois State Journal*, 18 Nov. 1862, 3; Col. Allen C. Fuller to Maj. Walter B. Scates, 10 Nov. 1862, McClernand Collection; McClernand to Stanton, 12 Nov., 14 Nov., 15 Nov., 22 Nov., 28 Nov., 29 Nov. 1862, McClernand Collection; McClernand to Morton, 28 Nov. 1862, McClernand Collection; McClernand to Col. N. B. Baker, 28 Nov. 1862, McClernand Collection; Baker to McClernand, 18 Nov. 1862, McClernand Collection; *OR*, vol. 17, 2:332–35, 866–67.

61. *OR*, vol. 17, 2:332–34.

62. Ibid., 345.

63. McClernand to Yates, 20 Nov. 1862, McClernand Collection; *Chicago Tribune*, 22 Nov. 1862, 1.

64. McClernand to Sen. Lyman Trumbull, 26 Nov. 1862, McClernand Collection; Trumball to McClernand, 1 Dec. 1862, McClernand Collection.

65. McClernand to Sen. Orville H. Browning, 26 Nov. 1862, McClernand Collection; Browning to McClernand, 2 Dec. 1862 McClernand Collection; *OR*, vol. 17, 1:371–72.

66. McClernand to Gov. O. P. Morton, 5 Dec. 1862, McClernand Collection.

67. *OR*, vol. 17, 2:401, 413, 415.

68. McClernand to Browning, 16 Dec. 1862, McClernand Collection.

69. *OR*, vol. 17, 2:420.

70. Ibid., 432–33; ibid., 1:476; Grant, *Personal Memoirs*, 256; *OR*, vol. 17, 2:461.

71. *OR*, vol. 17, 2:425, 461–62; Foote, *The Civil War: A Narrative*, vol. 2, *Fredericksburg to Meridian*, 65.

72. McClernand to Stanton, 24 Dec. 1862, McClernand Collection.

73. Welles, *Diary of Gideon Welles*, 1:217.

74. *OR*, vol. 17, 2:446, 435–36.

75. Ibid., vol. 22, 1:793.

76. Ibid., vol. 17, 1:471, 474.

77. Samuel Carter, *The Final Fortress: The Campaign for Vicksburg*, 1862–1863 (New York: St. Martin's Press, 1980), 104; *OR*, vol. 17, 1:474, 605; J. W. Vance, ed., *Report of the Adjutant General of the State of Illinois*, 1:145–51.

78. Welles, *Diary of Gideon Welles*, 1:217

79. Ibid., 1:273, 369; 3:247, 384.

80. Ibid., 1:36, 259.

81. McClernand to Yates, 1 Sept. 1862, McClernand Collection; *OR*, vol. 17, 2:282, 332; McClernand to Maj. Walter B. Scates, 28 Oct. 1862, McClernand Collection.

82. *OR*, ser. 3, vol. 4:1264–65; Frederick H. Dyer, *A Compendium of the War of the Rebellion*, 2 vols. (Dayton, Ohio: Press of Morningside Bookshop, 1979), 1:1021–1103.

83. Unpublished manuscript biography of John Alexander McClernand, probably produced in October or November 1863, possibly written by Adolph Schwartz, annotated by Gen. Edward J. McClernand, 2 vols, 1:162; Carter, *The Final Fortress*, 92–93, 104; *ORN*, vol. 23:658.

84. Kenneth P. Williams, *Lincoln Finds a General*, vol. 4, *Iuka to Vicksburg* (New York: Macmillan, 1956), 189; Carter, *The Final Fortress*, 95; Simon, *The Papers of Ulysses S. Grant*, 7:109.

85. *OR*, vol. 17, 1:604; Carter, *The Final Fortress*, 94–95.

86. Simon, *The Papers of Ulysses S. Grant*, 7:108–9, 135–36; Edwin C. Bearss, *Decision in Mississippi* (Jackson: Mississippi Commission on the War between the States, 1962), 130.

87. *OR*, vol. 17, 2:501–3.

88. McClernand to Lincoln, 29 Dec. 1862, McClernand Collection.

6. Victory in Arkansas

1. *OR*, vol. 17, 1:701.

2. Roger E. Coleman, *The Arkansas Post Story* (Santa Fe, N. Mex.: Southwest Cultural Resources Center, 1987), 63, 81, 93, 119.

3. Ibid., 95.

4. Ibid., 103; Edwin C. Bearss, "The Battle of the Post of Arkansas," *Arkansas Historical Quarterly* 18 (Autumn 1959): 237; Thomas L. Snead, "The Conquest of Arkansas," in *Battles and Leaders of the Civil War,* 3:450.

5. *ORN,* vol. 23:491–92; Bearss, "The Battle of the Post of Arkansas," 243.

6. *OR,* vol. 22, 1:855; Thomas A. Belser, "Military Operations in Missouri and Arkansas, 1861–1865" (Ph.D. diss., Vanderbilt University, 1958), 477 n.

7. *ORN,* vol. 24:93; William W. Heartsill, *Fourteen Hundred and 91 Days in the Confederate Army,* ed. Bell I. Wiley (Jackson, Tenn.: McCowat-Mercer Press, 1953), 86, 88.

8. Porter, *Incidents and Anecdotes,* 129; *ORN,* vol. 23:608; *OR,* vol. 17, 1:610.

9. McClernand to Sherman, 3 Jan. 1863, McClernand Collection; Gorman to Sherman, 2 Jan. 1863, McClernand Collection; Sherman, *Memoirs,* 296; *ORN,* vol. 13:605–6; Howe, *Home Letters of General Sherman,* 235.

10. Porter, *Incidents and Anecdotes,* 131, 123; Sherman, *Memoirs,* 297.

11. On 31 December 1862, Col. N. P. Chipman, Curtis's chief of staff, wrote the Department commander from Helena that McClernand "thinks it highly important that Old Post be reduced at the very earliest. . . . I am glad to know that General McClernand has a practical illustration of the insecurity of his rear . . . and that he fully appreciates the necessity of dislodging the enemy at Old Post, and driving him away from his communications." *OR,* vol. 22, 1:887.

12. *ORN,* vol. 23:606; William T. Sherman, "Vicksburg by New Years," *Civil War Times Illustrated* 16 (Jan. 1978): 48.

13. *ORN,* vol. 23:602–3.

14. *OR,* vol. 17, 2:528.

15. Howe, *Home Letters of General Sherman,* 235, 237; Hart, *Sherman: Soldier, Realist, American,* 165; Thorndike, *The Sherman Letters,* 182; Sandburg, *Abraham Lincoln: The War Years,* 2:114; Jean Powers Soman and Frank L. Byrne, eds., *A Jewish Colonel in the Civil War: Marcus M. Spiegel of the Ohio Volunteers* (Lincoln: Univ. of Nebraska Press, 1994), 210.

16. Welles, *Diary of Gideon Welles,* 1:220, 249; 2:235; 3:13; Pease and Randall, *The Diary of Orville Hickman Browning,* 2:25.

17. *OR,* vol. 17, 1:700–701, 2:562; Thomas L. Livermore, *Numbers and Losses in the Civil War in America, 1861–65* (Boston: Houghton, Mifflin, 1900), 140.

18. *OR,* vol. 17, 1:612; Thorndike, *The Sherman Letters,* 179–80.

19. Sherman, *Memoirs,* 295.

20. *OR,* vol. 17, 1:709–10.

21. *ORN,* vol. 24, 136; Robert L. Kerby, *Kirby Smith's Confederacy: The Trans-Mississippi South, 1863–1865* (New York: Columbia Univ. Press, 1972), 28–29.

22. Grant, *Personal Memoirs,* 260.

23. Ibid.; Howe, *Home Letters of General Sherman,* 237; *Illinois State Journal,* 12 Jan. 1863, 2.

24. *OR,* vol. 15:820; Thomas L. Connelly and Archer Jones, *The Politics of Command: Factions and Ideas in Confederate Strategy* (Baton Rouge: Louisiana State

Univ. Press, 1973), 101, 108; *OR*, vol. 17:2:757–58, 787. Pemberton was promoted to lieutenant general on 13 October 1862.

25. Dunbar Rowland, ed., *Jefferson Davis, Constitutionalist: His Letters, Papers, and Speeches*, 10 vols. (Jackson: Mississippi Department of Archives and History, 1923), 5:386–89.

26. *OR*, vol. 22, 1:898; vol. 17, 2:768, 783–84, 786–88, 793.

27. Connelly and Jones, *The Politics of Command*, 89; Rowland, *Jefferson Davis—Constitutionalist*, 425–26.

28. Kerby, *Kirby Smith's Confederacy*, 30, 32, 35, 37, 42, 53.

29. *OR*, vol. 17, 2:570–71.

30. Grant, *Personal Memoirs*, 264.

31. Ibid., 262.

32. *OR*, vol. 17, 2:536. Although McClernand had appointed Sherman and Morgan corps commanders, only Sherman's correspondence is available. In his report of the campaign, McClernand stated he sent orders to both corps commanders. The orders to Sherman are extant, but those to Morgan are not.

33. Naval History Division, *Civil War Naval Chronology* (Washington, D.C.: Department of the Navy, 1971), 3:5; *ORN*, vol. 24:100; *OR*, vol. 17, 1:701; Edwin C. Bearss and Leonard E. Brown, *Arkansas Post National Memorial* (Washington, D.C.: Office of History and Historic Architecture, 1971), 2–3; Foote, *The Civil War: A Narrative*, vol. 2, *Fredericksburg to Meridian*, 135.

34. *OR*, vol. 17, 2:537–38; 1:702.

35. Porter to McClernand, 7 Jan., 8 Jan. 1863, McClernand Collection; *ORN*, vol. 24:100.

36. Porter to McClernand, 7 Jan. 1863, McClernand Collection.

37. *OR*, vol. 13:653; vol. 17, 2:278.

38. Ibid., vol. 13:778–79; vol. 17, 2:545–46; vol. 17, 2:542.

39. Ibid., vol. 22, 2:32.

40. *ORN*, vol. 24, 99–103; General Orders No. 30, Headquarters, Army of the Mississippi, 8 Jan. 1863, McClernand Collection.

41. McClernand to Lincoln, 7 Jan. 1863, Lincoln Collection.

42. *OR*, vol. 17, 2:546–47.

43. *ORN*, vol. 24, 149; *OR*, vol. 17, 2:551.

44. *OR*, vol. 22, 2:31.

45. Walter G. Smith, ed., *Life and Letters of Thomas Kilby Smith, Brevet Major-General, United States Volunteers, 1820–1887* (New York: G. P. Putnam's Sons, 1898), 256.

46. *Illinois State Journal*, 12 Jan. 1863, 3; Soman and Byrne, eds. *A Jewish Colonel in the Civil War*, 206, 220, 294. By late June Spiegel would change his opinion of Sherman and refer to him as "the most accomplished General in this Army."

47. *OR*, vol. 17, 2:553–54.

48. Ibid., 553.

49. Ibid., 552.

50. Heartsill, *Fourteen Hundred and 91 Days in the Confederate Army*, 90.

51. Ibid., 90–91.

52. Bearss and Brown, *Arkansas Post National Memorial,* 2–5; *OR,* vol. 17, 1:705.

53. *OR,* vol. 17, 1:702, 704, 780.

54. Committee of the Regiment, *The Story of the Fifty-fifth Regiment Illinois Volunteer Infantry in the Civil War,* 199.

55. *OR,* vol. 17, 1:703, 719, 754–55, 722; *ORN,* vol. 24:104.

56. *OR,* vol. 17, 1:703, 722, 755.

57. Ibid., 764–69; Morgan to McClernand, 13 Jan. 1863, McClernand Collection; Heartsill, *Fourteen Hundred and 91 Days in the Confederate Army,* 91; Foote, *The Civil War: A Narrative,* vol. 2, *Fredericksburg to Meridian,* 135.

58. Porter, *The Naval History of the Civil War,* 289.

59. *OR,* vol. 17, 1:765; *ORN,* vol. 24:107.

60. *OR,* vol. 17, 1:704, 723, 755.

61. Ibid., 755; McClernand to Sherman, McClernand to Morgan, McClernand to Porter and Morgan, 11 Jan. 1863, McClernand Collection.

62. McClernand to Porter, Morgan to McClernand, McClernand to Porter, 11 Jan. 1863, McClernand Collection.

63. *OR,* vol. 17, 1:706, 723, 755.

64. Ibid., 706, 756; *ORN,* vol. 24:105; McClernand to Porter, 11 Jan. 1863, McClernand Collection.

65. Sherman, *Memoirs,* 298; Bearss and Brown, *Arkansas Post National Memorial,* Historical Base Map.

66. *OR,* vol. 17, 1:723.

67. Ibid., 719; vol. 53:866–67; Bearss, "The Battle of the Post of Arkansas," 274; Sherman, *Memoirs,* 303; *ORN,* vol. 24:106–7.

68. Thomas Yoseloff, *Confederate Military History,* 12 vols. (New York: Thomas Yoseloff, 1962), 10:100.

69. Sherman, *Memoirs,* 301.

70. Thorndike, *The Sherman Letters,* 181–82.

71. *OR,* vol. 17, 1:708.

72. Ibid., 763.

73. Porter, *Incidents and Anecdotes,* 131; Porter, *Naval History,* 292.

74. Thompson and Wainwright, *Confidential Correspondence of Gustavus Vasa Fox,* 154.

75. *OR,* vol. 17, 2:570–71.

76. Porter, *Incidents and Anecdotes,* 131; Grant, *Personal Memoirs,* 260.

77. *OR,* vol. 17, 1:700–710.

78. *ORN,* vol. 24:114–15, 163–64, 194.

79. Ibid., 113–14.

80. *OR,* vol. 17, 1:699.

81. Ibid., 710; *ORN,* vol. 24:117–18; *OR,* vol. 22, 2:41; McClernand to Porter, 11 Jan. 1863, McClernand Collection.

82. McClernand to Porter, 11 Jan. 1863, McClernand Collection; *ORN*, vol. 24:120, 151–52.

83. McClernand to Sherman, 12 Jan. 1863, McClernand Collection.

84. General Orders No. 44, 12 Jan. 1863; McClernand to Sherman, 12 Jan. 1863; Special Orders No. 58, 12 Jan. 1863. All in McClernand Collection. Heartsill, *Fourteen Hundred and 91 Days in the Confederate Army*, 98; Porter to McClernand, 12 Jan. 1863, McClernand Collection; *ORN*, vol. 24:154, 165.

85. McClernand to Morgan, 13 Jan. 1863; McClernand to Col. George W. Clark, 13 Jan. 1863; McClernand to Stewart, 14 Jan. 1863; McClernand to Morgan, 14 Jan. 1863. All in McClernand Collection.

86. Gorman to McClernand, 13 Jan. 1863; Sherman to McClernand, 14 Jan. 1863. All in McClernand Collection. *OR*, ser. 2, vol. 5:176; ibid., vol. 17, 2:562–64; ibid., vol. 22, 2:41.

87. *OR*, vol. 17, 2:551, 558, 561; McClernand to Fisk, undated (probably 14 Jan. 1863), McClernand Collection.

88. *OR*, vol. 17, 2:553, 555; Simon, *The Papers of Ulysses S. Grant*, 7:210. Rawlins wrote "not sent" on the message to relieve McClernand.

89. Ibid., 559, 560.

90. *OR*, vol. 17, 2:566–67.

91. Ibid.

92. Basler, *The Collected Works of Abraham Lincoln*, 6:70.

93. McClernand to Jonathan Baldwin Turner, 16 Jan. 1863, Jonathan Baldwin Turner Papers, Illinois State Historical Library; S. Noble to Lyman Trumbull, 24 Feb. 1863, Lyman Trumbull Transcripts, Illinois Historical Survey.

94. *OR*, vol. 17, 2:425, 432–33, 534–35, 556, 562–63; Sherman to McClernand, 14 Jan. 1863, McClernand Collection.

95. Sherman to Ellen Boyle Sherman, 16 Jan. 1863, Sherman Family Papers, University of Notre Dame; Sherman to John Sherman, 17 Jan. 1863, William T. Sherman Papers, Library of Congress. Quoted in John F. Marszalek, *Sherman: A Soldier's Passion for Order* (New York: Free Press, 1993), 210; Sherman, "Vicksburg by New Years," 48.

96. Sherman to McClernand, 16 Jan. 1863, McClernand Collection; Grant, *Personal Memoirs*, 261; Frank H. Mason, *The Forty-second Ohio Infantry: A History* (Cleveland: Cobb, Andrews, 1876), 179; Smith, *Life and Letters of Thomas Kilby Smith*, 31.

97. *OR*, vol. 17, 2:570–71; Naval History Division, *Civil War Naval Chronology*, Part 3, 8; Grant, *Personal Memoirs*, 260.; Sherman, *Memoirs*, 302; Thorndike, *The Sherman Letters*, 183; *ORN*, vol. 13:401.

98. *Illinois State Journal*, 19 Jan. 1863; *New York Herald*, 21 Jan. 1863; Yates to McClernand, 20 Jan. 1963, McClernand Collection.

99. *OR*, vol. 17, 1:710; Yates to McClernand, 17 Jan. 1863, McClernand Collection.

7. PRELUDE TO VICKSBURG

1. General Orders No. 11, 17 Jan. 1863, Headquarters, Army of the Mississippi, McClernand Collection; *OR*, vol. 17, 2:570; McClernand to Morgan and Sherman, 19 Jan. 1863, McClernand Collection.

2. *OR*, vol. 17, 2:574.

3. Col. Warren Stewart to McClernand, 18 Jan. 1863; McClernand to Grant, 18 Jan. 1863. Both in McClernand Collection.

4. Special Orders No. 130, 21 Jan. 1863, Headquarters, Army of the Mississippi, McClernand Collection.

5. Grant to McClernand, 18 Jan. 1863; Special Orders No. 120, 18 Jan. 1863, Headquarters, Army of the Mississippi, McClernand Collection; *OR*, vol. 24, 3:5.

6. *OR*, vol. 17, 2:573.

7. *Vicksburg Whig*, 9 Jan. 1863, as quoted in Carter, *The Final Fortress*, 110.

8. Grant, *Personal Memoirs*, 262; Wilson, *Under the Old Flag*, 1:158–59.

9. Richard B. Irwin, "Military Operations in Louisiana in 1862," in *Battles and Leaders of the Civil War*, 3:582–83.

10. *OR*, vol. 24, 1:8–9; Grant, *Personal Memoirs*, 264–65.

11. *ORN*, vol. 24:181.

12. *OR*, vol. 24, 1:10.

13. Grant, *Personal Memoirs*, 264.

14. Ibid.

15. *OR*, vol. 24, 3:7–8; Walter Scates to Capt. James P. Foster, 21 Jan. 1863, McClernand Collection; McClernand to Sherman, 22 Jan. 1863, McClernand Collection.

16. *OR*, vol. 24, 3:6.

17. Ibid., 8; McClernand to Col. Warren Stewart, 23 Jan. 1863, McClernand Collection; McClernand to Sherman, 23 Jan. 1863, McClernand Collection.

18. *OR*, vol. 24, 3:9–10, 12–13; Sherman to McClernand, 24 Jan. 1863, McClernand Collection; Brig. Gen. George W. Morgan to Lt. Col. Walter B. Scates, 25 Jan. 1863, McClernand Collection; McClernand to Sherman and Brig. Gen. John McArthur, 26 Jan. 1863, McClernand Collection; *OR*, vol. 24, 1:10; Col. L. B. Parsons to McClernand, 28 Jan. 1863, McClernand Collection.

19. *OR*, vol. 24, 1:10.

20. Capt. Sidney Lyon, Acting Topographic Engineer, Thirteenth Corps, to Brig. Gen. Morgan, 27 Jan. 1863; Victor Vifquain to McClernand, 27 Jan. 1863; McClernand to Sherman, 27 Jan. 1863; McClernand to Porter, 28 Jan. 1863. All in McClernand Collection. *ORN*, vol. 24:204. A tug was a small steam-powered screw-driven vessel that could produce only a small wake that would be inefficient for this task.

21. *ORN*, vol. 24:204–5.

22. *OR*, vol. 24, 3:19.

23. Ibid., 17–18; McClernand to McArthur, 30 Jan. 1863, McClernand Collection.

24. Parsons to McClernand, 25 Jan. 1863; McClernand to Porter, 25 Jan. 1863. Both in McClernand Collection.

25. *ORN*, vol. 24:209–10.

26. *OR*, vol. 24, 3:10–11; McClernand to Maj. Jones, Army Transport Commander, Morgan, and Sherman, 25 Jan. 1863, McClernand Collection; McArthur to McClernand, 28 Jan. 1863, McClernand Collection.

27. McClernand to Sherman, 27 Jan. 1863; McClernand to Porter, 26 Jan. 1863; Special Orders No. 155, Headquarters, Army of the Mississippi, 29 Jan. 1863. All in McClernand Collection.

28. McClernand to Morgan, 28 Jan. 1863, McClernand Collection; *OR*, vol. 24, 3:13–14; McClernand to Gov: Richard Yates, 26 Jan. 1863, McClernand Collection. Stewart was buried in New York.

29. Paul H. Hass, ed., "The Vicksburg Diary of Henry Clay Warmouth," *Journal of Mississippi History* 31 (Nov. 1969): 344, 346; W. L. B. Jenney, "Personal Recollections of Vicksburg," in *Military Essays and Recollections*, 4 vols. (Chicago: Dial Press, 1899), 3:253.

30. Yates to McClernand, 20 Jan. 1863; Maj. Gen. Samuel R. Curtis to McClernand, 20 Jan. 1863; W. D. Sanders to McClernand, 22 Jan. 1863; Lt. Harl Christie to McClernand, 20 Jan. 1863; N. W. Mince to McClernand, 30 Jan. 1863; Sen. Lyman Trumbull to McClernand, 13 Feb. 1863. All in McClernand Collection. *OR*, vol. 22, 2:72–73.

31. *OR*, vol. 17, 2:528–30.

32. McClernand to Lincoln, 7 Jan. 1863, Lincoln Collection.

33. *OR*, vol. 17, 2:579.

34. Ibid., vol. 24, 1:8, 11; vol. 17, 2:446; Simon, *The Papers of Ulysses S. Grant*, 7:233. On 18 Dec. 1862 the War Department had ordered McPherson to command the Seventeenth Corps, but Grant did not forward the order to McPherson until 22 December.

35. Simon, *The Papers of Ulysses S. Grant*, 7:234.

36. *OR*, vol. 22, 2:65.

37. Ibid., vol. 24, 3:5–7.

38. Col. Lewis B. Parsons to Lt. Col. Walter B. Scates, 28 Jan. 1863, Lewis B. Parson Papers, Illinois State Historical Library.

39. *OR*, vol. 24, 1:12.

40. Special Orders No. 157, Headquarters, Army of the Mississippi, 29 Jan. 1863, McClernand Collection.

41. McClernand to Stanton, 25 Jan. 1863, McClernand Collection.

42. *OR*, vol. 24, 3:18–19.

43. Ibid., 1:11.

44. Ibid., 12; Grant, *Personal Memoirs*, 261.

45. McClernand to Yates, 4 Feb. 1863, Richard Yates Papers, Springfield State Historical Library.

46. *OR*, vol. 17, 2:555; vol. 24, 1:13; vol. 24, 3:39, 122–23; McClernand to Grant, Grant to McClernand, 28 Mar. 1863, McClernand Collection.

47. *OR*, vol. 24, 1:13–14.

48. Ibid., 11.

49. General Orders No. 20, 31 Jan. 1863, Headquarters, Thirteenth Army Corps, McClernand Collection.

50. McClernand to Lincoln, 1 Feb. 1863, Robert Todd Lincoln Papers, CI, 21431–2, 21488, 21489.

51. Curtis to McClernand, 21 Jan. 1863, McClernand Collection.

52. McClernand to Grant, 1 Feb. 1863, McClernand Collection; McClernand to Lincoln, 2 Feb. 1863, Lincoln Papers.

53. McClernand to Lincoln, 14 Feb. 1863. McClernand Collection.

54. *OR*, vol. 24, 3:54, 56–57; McClernand to Prentiss, 19 Feb. 1863, McClernand Collection.

55. Prentiss to McClernand, 24 Feb. 1863, McClernand Collection; *OR*, vol. 24, 3:73; *OR*, vol. 22, 2:66, 871.

56. *OR*, vol. 22, 2:107–8, 113.

57. McClernand to Grant, 19 Mar. 1863, McClernand Collection. The idea of another operation along the Arkansas River was still being considered as late as 19 May, while Grant was moving against Vicksburg. In a telegram from Halleck to Welles on that date, the former stated that the War Department was considering such an operation and asked for Navy cooperation. *OR*, vol. 24, 3:331.

58. McClernand to Lincoln, 2 Feb. 1863, McClernand Collection.

59. Grant, *Personal Memoirs*, 270; Sherman, *Memoirs*, 305.

60. Col. Thomas S. Mather to McClernand, 2 Feb. 1863; McClernand to Grant, 2 Feb. 1863; Grant to McClernand, 2 Feb. 1863; Special Orders No. 179, Headquarters, Thirteenth Army Corps, 2 Feb. 1863. All in McClernand Collection.

61. Special Orders No. 174, Headquarters, Thirteenth Army Corps, 2 Feb. 1863; Scates to Osterhaus and Smith, 17 Feb. 1863. All in McClernand Collection.

62. Scates to John A. Rawlins, 2 Feb. 1863; Letter of Appointment, 11 Feb. 1863; Brashear to Scates, 15 Feb. 1863; Special Orders No. 240, Headquarters, Thirteenth Army Corps, 17 Feb. 1863; Brashear to Scates, 17 Feb. 1863; Brashear to Scates, 19 Feb. 1863; Brashear to Scates, 26 Feb. 1863. All in McClernand Collection.

63. Scates to Rawlins, 11 Feb. 1863; McClernand to David Tod, O. P. Morton, Richard Yates, Edward Salaman, James F. Robinson, 25 Feb. 1863; Salaman to McClernand, 11 Mar. 1863. All in McClernand Collection.

64. Scates to Rawlins, 2 Feb. 1863, 5 Feb. 1863; Special Field Orders, Headquarters, Department of the Tennessee, 11 Feb. 1863. All in McClernand Collection.

65. Special Orders No. 167, Headquarters, Thirteenth Army Corps, 3 Feb. 1863, McClernand Collection.

66. Special Orders No. 210, Headquarters, Thirteenth Army Corps, 9 Feb. 1863; Col. George W. Neeley to Col. William J. Landrum, 8 Feb. 1863; Neeley to Lincoln, 8 Feb. 1863. All in McClernand Collection.

67. General Orders No. 25, Headquarters, Thirteenth Army Corps, 12 Feb. 1863; Lt. Samuel Caldwell to McClernand, 1 Apr. 1863. In McClernand Collection.

68. *ORN*, vol. 24:359–60; *OR*, vol. 24, 3:52–54; Headquarters, Tenth Division to Scates, 14 Feb. 1863, McClernand Collection.

69. *OR*, vol. 24, 3:76; vol. 52, 1:337.

70. Ibid., vol. 24, 3:89–90; Grant to McClernand, 7 Mar. 1863, McClernand Collection; McClernand to Brig. Gens. A. J. Smith and Peter J. Osterhaus, 7 Mar., 8 Mar. 1863, McClernand Collection.

71. General Orders No. 40, Headquarters, Thirteenth Army Corps, 13 Mar. 1863; J. S. Bobbs to McClernand, 14 Mar. 1863; Lt. Samuel Caldwell to McClernand, 27 Mar. 1863, 28 Mar. 1863; Caldwell to Scates, 30 Mar. 1863; John Schenk to McClernand, 29 Mar. 1863. All in McClernand Collection. John H. Moore, *The Horizon and Zenith of the Great Rebellion*, 2 vols. (Cincinnati: Elm Street Printing, 1870), 2:327; Jacob W. Wilkin, "Personal Reminiscences of General U. S. Grant," *Transactions of the Illinois State Historical Society* 12 (Springfield, Ill.: Phillips Bros., 1908): 132.

72. General Orders No. 5, Headquarters, Fourteenth Division, Thirteenth Corps, 31 Mar. 1863, McClernand Collection.

73. McClernand to Lt. Col. John J. Mudd, 18 Mar. 1863, McClernand Collection; *OR*, vol. 24, 3:119.

74. *OR*, vol. 24, 3:119.

75. McClernand to Grant, 19 Mar. 1863; Grant to McClernand, 22 Mar. 1863. All in McClernand Collection.

76. Issac H. Elliott, *History of the Thirty-third Regiment Illinois Veteran Volunteer Infantry in the Civil War, 22nd August 1861 to 7th December 1865* (Gibson City, Ill.: Regimental Association, 1902), 35; Benjamin P. Thomas, ed., *Three Years with Grant as Recalled by War Correspondent Sylvanus Cadwallader* (Westport, Conn.: Greenwood Press, 1980), 50.

77. Williams, *Grant Moves South*, 394–95. These letters were printed in the *Chicago Tribune* on 28 Sept. 1885.

78. Murat Halstead to Salmon P. Chase, 1 Apr. 1863; Chase to Lincoln, 4 Apr. 1863. All in Lincoln Collection.

79. Carter, *The Final Fortress*, 150–51; *OR*, vol. 20, 2:297; vol. 24, 1:25; ser. 3, vol. 3:62.

80. *OR*, vol. 24, 1:46, 151–52, 495–96; Scates to Lt. Col. John J. Mudd, 30 Mar. 1863; McClernand to Osterhaus, 31 Mar. 1863. All in McClernand Collection.

81. Col. Thomas W. Bennett to Scates, Scates to Carr, 31 Mar. 1863, McClernand Collection.

82. Lt. Col. James Dunlap to McClernand, 30 Mar. 1863; McClernand to Dunlap, 31 Mar. 1863, McClernand Collection.

83. *OR*, vol. 24, 3:76, 118–19; Scates to Mudd, 28 Mar. 1863; McClernand to Bennett, 30 Mar. 1863; Mudd to McClernand, 1 Apr. 1863; McClernand to Osterhaus, 2 Apr. 1863; Grant to McClernand, 3 Apr. 1863. All in McClernand Collection.

84. McClernand to the Hon. John Van Buren, 22 Feb. 1863; Lucian B. Chase to McClernand, 10 Mar. 1863; McClernand to Yates, 16 Mar. 1863; Yates to McClernand, 2 Apr. 1863. All in McClernand Collection.

85. Sherman, *Memoirs*, 315.

86. *OR*, vol. 17, 2:446; Wilson, *The Life of John A. Rawlins*, 105–6; Wilson, *Under the Old Flag*, 1:138.

87. Howe, *Home Letters of General Sherman*, 237, 256–57; Sherman to Ellen Boyle Ewing Sherman, 3 Apr. 1863, Sherman Family Papers, University of Notre Dame, as quoted in Marszalek, *Sherman*, 216; *OR*, ser. 3, vol. 3:65–66.

88. Smith, *Life and Letters of Thomas Kilby Smith*, 269.

89. Charles A. Dana, *Recollections of the Civil War* (New York: D. Appleton, 1898), 20–21.

90. Villard, *Memoirs of Henry Villard*, 1:ix, 2:188–89.

91. Dana, *Recollections of the Civil War*, 33; *OR*, vol. 24, 1:75, 78–79.

92. *OR*, vol. 24, 3:152–53.

93. McClernand to Robert Halsey, 20 Mar. 1863, McClernand Collection.

94. Adolph Schwartz to McClernand, 4 Apr. 1863, McClernand Collection.

95. McClernand to Lincoln, 15 Mar. 1863, Lincoln Collection.

96. McClernand to Yates, 15 Mar. 1863, Chicago Historical Society, as quoted in Hicken, *Illinois in the Civil War*, 164.

97. Howe, *Home Letters of General William Sherman*, 237–39, 248; Wilson, *The Life of John A. Rawlins*, 116–17; *OR*, vol. 24, 3:179–80; Sherman, *Memoirs*, 315–17; J. F. C. Fuller, *The Generalship of Ulysses S. Grant* (New York: Dodd, Mead, 1929), 135.

98. Howe, *Home Letters of General Sherman*, 254.

99. *OR*, vol. 24, 1:496; Col. Thomas W. Bennett to McClernand, 1 Apr. 1863; Maj. D. B. Bush to Scates, 1 Apr. 1863. All in McClernand Collection.

100. Lt. F. H. Mason to Scates, 1 Apr. 1863; Capt. W. T. Patterson to McClernand, 1 Apr. 1863. All in McClernand Collection. *OR*, vol. 24, 3:98.

101. Rawlins to McClernand, 1 Apr. 1863; Special Orders No. 423, Headquarters, Thirteenth Army Corps, 1 Apr. 1863. All in McClernand Collection. *OR*, vol. 24, 3:164; 1:125. McClernand to Lt. F. H. Mason, 2 Apr. 1863; Mason to McClernand, 3 Apr. 1863; McClernand to Brig. Gens. A. J. Smith and Eugene A. Carr, 3 Apr. 1863. All in McClernand Collection.

102. *OR*, vol. 24, 3:170–71; Hass, "The Vicksburg Diary of Henry Clay Warmouth," 338.

103. McClernand to Col. Lionel A. Sheldon, 5 Apr. 1863; McClernand to Osterhaus, 5 Apr. 1863 (two letters). All in McClernand Collection.

104. Grant to McClernand, 6 Apr. 1863; McClernand to Grant, 6 Apr. 1863. In McClernand Collection. Hass, ed., "The Vicksburg Diary of Henry Clay Warmouth," 340.

105. *OR*, vol. 24, 3:198.

106. Capt. James Leeper to Col. Theophilus T. Garrard, 5 Apr. 1863; Garrard to Scates, 5 Apr. 1863; Osterhaus to McClernand, 6 Apr. 1863. All in McClernand Collection. *OR*, vol. 24, 3:173, 730; vol. 15:1044.

107. Special Orders No. 28, Headquarters, Thirteenth Army Corps, 6 Apr. 1863, McClernand Collection; *OR*, vol. 24, 3:186, 190.

108. *OR*, vol. 24, 3:186, 197; Scates to Rawlins, 13 Apr. 1863; Scates to Brig. Gen. Alvin P. Hovey, 15 Apr. 1863. In McClernand Collection.

109. *OR*, vol. 24, 3:187; Thompson and Wainwright, *Confidential Correspondence of Gustavus Vasa Fox*, 2:170; Adolph Schwartz to McClernand, 27 Mar. 1863, McClernand Collection.

110. *OR*, vol. 24, 3:188–89, 205.

111. Ibid., 204–5, 207, 222.

112. Ibid., 205, 211–12

113. Ibid., 204–5, 207, 211–12; McClernand to Osterhaus, 19 Apr. 1863; McClernand to Alvin P. Hovey, 17 Apr. 1863; McClernand to A. J. Smith, 17 Apr. 1863; McClernand to Eugene A. Carr, 18 Apr. 1863; McClernand to James B. McPherson, 20 Apr. 1863. All in McClernand Collection.

114. *OR*, vol. 24, 3:222; *ORN*, vol. 24:605–6.

115. *ORN*, vol. 24:603; *OR*, vol. 24, 3:222, 226–27; McClernand to Osterhaus, 23 Apr. 1863, McClernand Collection.

116. *OR*, vol. 24, 3:227–28, 231.

117. Ibid., 1:497; 3:200–201, 215–16; Hass, "The Vicksburg Diary of Henry Clay Warmoth," 341.

118. McClernand to Carr, 23 Apr. 1863, McClernand Collection.

119. *OR*, vol. 24, 1:80–81; Grant, *Personal Memoirs*, 279.

120. *OR*, vol. 24, 3:229–30, 234.

121. Thompson and Wainwright, *Confidential Correspondence of Gustavus Vasa Fox*, 2:173; Porter, *The Naval History of the Civil War*, 313.

122. *OR*, vol. 24, 3:212–14; Scates to Osterhaus, 22 Apr. 1863, McClernand Collection.

123. *OR*, vol. 24, 1:80.

124. Ibid., 31.

125. Grant, *Personal Memoirs*, 275.

126. *OR*, vol. 24, 3:188–89, 221, 230.

127. Wilson, *Under the Old Flag*, 1:174; *OR*, vol. 24, 1:80–81; Edgar Erickson, ed., "With Grant at Vicksburg: The Diary of Charles E. Wilcox," *Journal of the Illinois State Historical Society* 30 (Jan. 1938): 465; Jack Nortrup, "Richard Yates: A Personal Glimpse of the Illinois Soldiers' Friend," *Journal of the Illinois State Historical Society* 56 (Summer 1963): 131.

128. *OR*, vol. 24, 1:142.

129. McClernand to Osterhaus and Smith, 26 Apr. 1863, McClernand Collection; *OR*, vol. 24, 1:80–81.

130. *OR*, vol. 24, 1:81.

131. Ibid., 3:237–40; Special Orders No. 447, Headquarters, Thirteenth Army Corps, 27 Apr. 1863, McClernand Collection; Carr to McClernand, 27 Apr. 1863, McClernand Collection.

132. *OR*, vol. 24, 1:571–72; 3:239; McClernand to A. J. Smith, 27 Apr. 1863, McClernand Collection.

133. *ORN*, vol. 24:607–28.

134. *OR*, vol. 24, 3:188; 1:81; Wilson, *Under the Old Flag*, 1:170.

135. *OR*, vol. 24, 3:229.

136. *ORN*, vol. 24:605–6; Thompson and Wainwright, *Confidential Correspondence of Gustavus Vasa Fox*, 2:175.

137. *OR*, vol. 24, 3:242.

138. Ibid., 1:32; 3:246; *ORN*, vol. 24:611, 615; McClernand to Carr, 28 Apr. 1863, McClernand Collection.

139. *OR*, vol. 24, 1:142.

140. Edwin C. Bearss, The *Campaign for Vicksburg*, vol. 2, *Grant Strikes a Fatal Blow* (Dayton, Ohio: Morningside Press, 1986). 318; Simon, *The Papers of Ulysses S. Grant*, 8:126; *OR*, vol. 24, 1:83; Grant, *Personal Memoirs*, 284.

8. SPRINGTIME IN MISSISSIPPI

1. John C. Taylor diary, Apr. 2–July 7, 1863, Apr. 27 entry, Henry Baylor Taylor Papers, University of Virginia Library; Michael B. Ballard, *Pemberton: A Biography* (Jackson: Univ. Press of Mississippi, 1991), 137–39.

2. *OR*, vol. 24, 3:808; 1:663–64.

3. Ibid., 1:257; 3:808.

4. Ibid., 1:142, 615; Bearss, *Grant Strikes a Fatal Blow*, 295, 318–19.

5. *OR*, vol. 24, 3:248.

6. Ibid., 1:83.

7. Williams, *Lincoln Finds a General*, vol. 4, *Iuka to Vicksburg*, 346.

8. This conclusion was reached in a discussion on 14 November 1994 with Mr. Edwin C. Bearss, former Chief Historian of the Vicksburg National Military Park and Special Assistant to the Director of the National Park Service. *OR*, vol. 24, 1:601.

9. *OR*, vol. 24, 1:615, 672; Bearss, *Grant Strikes a Fatal Blow*, 356.

10. Hass, "The Vicksburg Diary of Henry Clay Warmouth," 64; *OR*, vol. 24, 1:143.

11. *OR*, vol. 24, 1:143, 625, 664, 678–79; Bearss, *Grant Strikes a Fatal Blow*, 405.

12. *OR*, vol. 24, 1:144–45, 601, 615, 664, 674, 682.

13. Grant, *Personal Memoirs*, 286; *OR*, vol. 24, 1:49.

14. *OR*, vol. 24, 1:32.

15. Ibid., 603; Hass, "The Vicksburg Diary of Henry Clay Warmouth," 65; Bearss, *Grant Strikes a Fatal Blow*, 385; Erickson, "With Grant at Vicksburg: The Diary of Charles E. Wilcox," 473..

16. *OR*, vol. 24, 1:664, 668, 673, 675; Bearss, *Grant Strikes a Fatal Blow*, 387–89.

17. Grant, *Personal Memoirs*, 286; *OR*, vol. 24, 1:145, 652; Bearss, *Grant Strikes a Fatal Blow*, 389.

18. *OR*, vol. 24, 1:653, 666, 676.

19. Ibid., 69, 673, 679, 681; James R. Arnold, *Grant Wins the War: Decision at Vicksburg* (New York: John Wiley & Sons, 1997), 114.

20. Committee of the Regiment, *The Story of the Fifty-fifth Regiment*, 233.

21. Grant, *Memoirs*, 285–86.

22. Wilson, *The Life of John A. Rawlins*, 125; Wilson, *Under the Old Flag*, 1:174–76.

23. *OR*, vol. 24, 3:260.

24. Ibid., 1:594; Haas, "The Vicksburg Diary of Henry Clay Warmouth," 66.

25. *OR*, vol. 24, 1:128–29, 635; Richardson, *A Personal History of Ulysses S. Grant*, 308–9.

26. Ballard, *Pemberton*, 141; *OR*, vol. 24, 1:636, 656; 3:265–67.

27. *OR*, vol. 24, 3:266–67; Simon, *The Papers of Ulysses S. Grant*, 8:150; Bearss, *Decision in Mississippi*, 218.

28. *OR*, vol. 24, 1:81; 3:266.

29. Grant, *Personal Memoirs*, 284, 290.

30. *OR*, vol. 24, 3:125–26, 192, 204; 1:75; Badeau, *Military History of Ulysses S. Grant*, 1:181; Fred Harvey Harrington, *Fighting Politician: Major General N. P. Banks* (Westport, Conn.: Greenwood Press, 1948), 54.

31. Grant, *Personal Memoirs*, 290; *OR*, vol. 24, 1:33.

32. *OR*, vol. 24, 1:50; 3:267–68; Grant, *Personal Memoirs*, 284.

33. Badeau, *Military History of Ulysses S. Grant*, 1:225; Grant, "The Vicksburg Campaign," in *Battles and Leaders of the Civil War*, 3:495.

34. Simon, *The Papers of Ulysses S. Grant*, 8:156, 172; *OR*, vol. 24, 3:269–70, 277; General Orders No. 18, 7 May 1863, Headquarters, Thirteenth Army Corps, McClernand Collection.

35. *OR*, vol. 24, 1:84–85.

36. McClernand to Lincoln, 6 May 1863, Lincoln Collection.

37. *OR*, vol. 24, 3:277, 279–80; 1:753.

38. Ibid., 3:280.

39. Simon, *The Papers of Ulysses S. Grant*, 8:177, 182; *OR*, vol. 24, 3:282–83; Hass, "The Vicksburg Diary of Henry Clay Warmoth," 68; Bearss, *Grant Strikes a Fatal Blow*, 462.

40. *OR*, vol. 24, 3:282–83.

41. Ibid., 1:595, 259; 3:283–84; Simon, *The Papers of Ulysses S. Grant*, 8:182–83.

42. *OR*, vol. 24, 3:289.

43. Ibid., 3:292; 1:35; Simon, *The Papers of Ulysses S. Grant*, 8:194, 198; Badeau, *Military History of Ulysses S. Grant*, 1:233.

44. *OR*, vol. 24, 3:292–93.

45. Ibid., 296–97.

46. Ibid., 3:294–95.

47. Ibid., 1:146; 2:40; 3:299; Bearss, *Grant Strikes a Fatal Blow*, 472.

48. *OR*, vol. 24, 2:31.

49. Ibid., 1:50.

50. *OR*, vol. 24, 3:300–301; Simon, *The Papers of Ulysses S. Grant*, 8:207–8.

51. Badeau, *Military History of Ulysses S. Grant,* 1:231; Grant, *Personal Memoirs,* 293–94.

52. *OR,* vol. 24, 3:306–7.

53. Ibid., 3:305–7; Grant, *Personal Memoirs,* 295; Bearss, *Grant Strikes a Fatal Blow,* 563–64.

54. *OR,* vol. 24, 1:147; 2:41; Hass, "The Vicksburg Diary of Henry Clay Warmouth," 69.

55. *OR,* vol. 24, 3:305–8; Ulysses S. Grant, "The Vicksburg Campaign," in *Battles and Leaders of the Civil War,* 3:504–5.

56. *OR,* vol. 24, 3:310–11.

57. Ibid., 1:147.

58. Ibid., 24, 1:240, 638, 753, 785; Grant, *Personal Memoirs,* 296–97.

59. *OR,* vol. 24, 3:310.

60. McClernand to Carr, 14 May 1863, McClernand Collection; *OR,* vol. 24, 2:12–13; 3:310–11.

61. *OR,* vol. 24, 1:148; Grant, *Personal Memoirs,* 300; Badeau, *Military History of Ulysses S. Grant,* 1:253.

62. Hass, "The Vicksburg Diary of Henry Clay Warmouth," 2:70; *OR,* vol. 24, 1:616; 2:12–13, 41, 255; 3:249.

63. Grant to McClernand, 15 May 1863, McClernand Collection; *OR,* vol. 24, 1:646–47, 730.

64. *OR,* vol. 24, 3:313–14.

65. Ibid., 1:263; 3:313–14, 320.

66. Ibid., 1:51–2; 3:318; Simon, *The Papers of Ulysses S. Grant,* 8:224; Grant, *Personal Memoirs,* 301.

67. *OR,* vol. 24, 1:148, 639; 3:320.

68. Ibid., 2:87, 134, 255; 3:316.

69. Ibid., 1:149; 2:101; 3:316–17, 319.

70. Ibid., 3:317–18.

71. Bearss, *Grant Strikes a Fatal Blow,* 587; *OR,* vol. 24, 1:263.

72. *OR,* vol. 24, 1:52; 2:32.

73. Ibid., 2:66, 315, 718.

74. Ibid., 2:14; 3:318–19.

75. Ibid., 2:52; 3:318; Grant, "The Vicksburg Campaign," 510.

76. *OR,* vol. 24, 1:150; 2:15, 32, 80.

77. Ibid., 1:53; Grant, *Personal Memoirs,* 304–5; Wilson, *Under the Old Flag,* 1:177, 204.

78. Nicolay and Hay, *Abraham Lincoln,* 7:189–90; *OR,* vol. 24, 1:150. Much of this analysis resulted from conversations with Mr. Edwin C. Bearss on November 14, 1994, and with Mr. Warren C. Grabau on 13 October 1994.

79. Grant, *Personal Memoirs,* 305.

80. *OR,* vol. 24, 2:7–9.

81. Ibid., 96.

82. Ibid., 1:151, 266; 3:318; Simon, *The Papers of Ulysses S. Grant,* 8:228.

83. *OR*, vol. 24, 1:640, 152; 3:321–22.

84. Ibid., 1:137–157, 623–24.

85. Ibid., 3:322; McClernand to Brig. Gen. Albert L. Lee, 17 May 1863; McClernand to Division Commanders, 17 May 1863; McClernand to A. J. Smith, 17 May 1863. All in McClernand Collection.

86. *OR*, vol. 24, 3:324; Grant, "The Vicksburg Campaign," 515; Special Orders 461, Headquarters, Thirteenth Army Corps, 18 May 1863; McClernand to A. J. Smith, 18 May 1863; McClernand to Brig. Gen. Alvin P. Hovey, 5:15 A.M., 18 May 1863; McClernand to Hovey, 18 May 1863. All in McClernand Collection.

87. *OR*, vol. 24, 3:324; Grant, "The Vicksburg Campaign," 517.

88. McClernand to division commanders, 18 May 1863, McClernand Collection.

89. *OR*, vol. 24, 1:153, 617.

90. Ibid., 54; 3:325–27, 329; McClernand to division commanders, 19 May 1863, McClernand Collection.

91. *OR*, vol. 24, 1:154; 2:33; 3:327; Edwin C. Bearss, *The Campaign for Vicksburg*, vol. 3, *Unvexed to the Sea* (Dayton, Ohio: Morningside Press, 1986), 770–71, 773–778.

92. Howe, *Home Letters of General Sherman*, 261.

93. Fuller, *The Generalship of Ulysses S. Grant*, 57.

94. Bearss, *Unvexed to the Sea*, 765, 769.

95. McClernand to Hovey, 19 May 1863; Lt. Col. G. I. Taggert to McClernand, 19 May 1863; Grant to McClernand, 19 May 1863; Hovey to McClernand, 19 May 1863; Special Orders No. 462, Headquarters, Thirteenth Army Corps, 19 May 1863. All in McClernand Collection.

96. Sherman, *Memoirs*, 325–26.

97. *OR*, vol. 24, 3:332.

98. Ibid., 2:33.

99. Ibid., 3:331–32; *Simon, The Papers of Ulysses S. Grant*, 8:239.

100. *OR*, vol. 24, 2:33; 3:332.

101. Ibid., 3:332; Hass, "The Vicksburg Diary of Henry Clay Warmouth," 72.

102. Hass, "The Vicksburg Diary of Henry Clay Warmouth," 72.

103. Simon, *The Papers of Ulysses S. Grant*, 8:241–42; *OR*, vol. 24, 3:331–32.

104. Diary, Owen Francis, Vicksburg National Military Park, as quoted in Bearss, *Unvexed to the Sea*, 804.

105. *OR*, vol. 24, 3:333, 336.

106. Ibid., 333–34; General Field Order No. 1, 21 May 1863, Headquarters, Thirteenth Army Corps, McClernand Collection; Erickson, "With Grant at Vicksburg," *Journal of the Illinois State Historical Society* 30:478.

9. End of the Line

1. Osborn H. Oldroyd, *A Soldier's Story of the Siege of Vicksburg* (Springfield, Ill.: Privately published, 1885), 31–32.

2. Simon, *The Papers of Ulysses S. Grant*, 8:247–48.
3. *OR*, vol. 24, 1:171–72, 274.
4. Ibid., 3:334.
5. Ibid., 2:20, 33, 140, 240.
6. Ibid., 1:55, 154; 2:19; Grant, *Personal Memoirs*, 311.
7. Bearss, *Unvexed to the Sea*, 815–18, 836.
8. Letter, Higgins to C. A. Hobbs, 7 Dec. 1878, as quoted in Bearss, *Unvexed to the Sea*, 829; *OR*, vol. 24, 2:34; George Lang, Raymond L. Collins, and Gerard F. White, *Medal of Honor Recipients 1863–1994*, 2 vols. (New York: Facts on File, 1995), 1:602.
9. *OR*, vol. 24, 2:34.
10. Ibid., 140–41, 238.
11. Ibid., 20–21; Sylvanus Cadwallader, *Three Years with Grant*, 90.
12. *OR*, vol. 24, 2:240.
13. Ibid., 1:172, 55.
14. Ibid., 172.
15. Sherman, *Memoirs*, 327; *OR*, vol. 24, 1:55.
16. *OR*, vol. 24, 1:154.
17. Sherman, *Memoirs*, 327; *OR*, vol. 24, 1:56.
18. *OR*, vol. 24, 1:172–73.
19. Simon, *Papers of Ulysses S. Grant*, 8:252; *OR*, vol. 24, 1:178.
20. *OR*, vol. 24, 1:177.
21. Sherman, *Memoirs*, 327.
22. *OR*, vol. 24, 1:56, 777.
23. Ibid., 1:732; 2:67–68.
24. Ibid., 2:240; 3:340.
25. Ibid., 3:339–40.
26. Ibid., 337–39, 343; Simon, *Papers of Ulysses S. Grant*, 8:256–57.
27. *OR*, vol. 24, 1:37.
28. Thomas, *Three Years with Grant*, 92.
29. *OR*, vol. 24, 1:37; 3:337.
30. Ibid., 1:55, 154–55; 2:142, 243; William H. Bentley, *History of the 77th Illinois Volunteer Infantry* (Peoria, Ill.: Edward Rink, Printer, 1888), 152; John A. Bering and Thomas Montgomery, *History of the Forty-eighth Ohio Vet. Vol. Inf.* (Hillsboro, Ohio: Highland News Office, 1880), 87.
31. Wilson, *Under the Old Flag*, 1:179.
32. *OR*, vol. 24, 1:275; 2:349, 351, 357.
33. Ibid., 1:37; Grant, *Personal Memoirs*, 311.
34. Jenney, "Personal Recollections at Vicksburg," 261–62.
35. *OR*, vol. 24, 1:86–7; Dana, *Recollections of the Civil War*, 56.
36. Sherman, *Memoirs*, 327–28; *OR*, vol. 24, 1:164.
37. Wilson, *Under the Old Flag*, 1:180–81.
38. *OR*, vol. 24, 1:84.

39. Badeau, *Military History of Ulysses S. Grant*, 1:364; *OR*, vol. 24, 1:87.

40. *OR*, vol. 24, 1:242, 348, 88–89; 2:209; Simon, *Papers of Ulysses S. Grant*, 8:264.

41. Simon, *Papers of Ulysses S. Grant*, 8:277, 281; *OR*, vol. 24, 3:333, 356–57, 368, 375, 401.

42. Howe, *Home Letters of General Sherman*, 266; *OR*, vol. 24, 1:93, 107; 3:387; Dana, *Recollections of the Civil War*, 89; Simon, *The Papers of Ulysses S. Grant*, 8:358–59, 370–71; Janet B. Hewitt et al., eds., *Supplement to the Official Records of the Union and Confederate Armies*, 63 vols. (Wilmington, N.C.: Broadfoot Publishing, 1994–98), vol. 4, part 1:396–400.

43. McClernand to Yates, 29 May 1863, McClernand Collection; Wilson, *Under the Old Flag*, 1:182–83.

44. *OR*, vol. 24, 1:159–63.

45. Ibid., 1:162–63; vol. 3, 2:649.

46. Ibid., vol. 24, 1:163–64.

47. Ibid., 102–3.

48. McClernand to Yates, 28 May 1863, McClernand Collection.

49. McClernand to Lincoln, 29 May 1863, Lincoln Collection.

50. *OR*, vol. 24, 1:165–66.

51. Wilson, *Under the Old Flag*, 1:185–86; *OR*, vol. 24, 1:103. Ironically, in September 1861 McClernand had petitioned Lincoln to have Wilson assigned to his staff. Because of the shortage of engineers, however, the War Department denied the request. George D. Ruggles to McClernand, 7 Oct. 1861, McClernand Collection.

52. *OR*, vol. 24, 1:103, 105.

53. Ibid., 43; Grant to Dana, 5 Aug. 1863, as quoted in Bernarr Cresap, *Appomattox Commander: The Story of General E. O. C. Ord* (San Diego: A. S. Barnes, 1981), 100.

54. Cresap, *Appomattox Commander*, 103; Wilson, *Under the Old Flag*, 1:217.

55. Thomas, *Three Years with Grant as Recalled by War Correspondent Sylvanus Cadwallader*, 224; Dana, *Recollections of the Civil War*, 29, 57–9; Villard, *Memoirs of Henry Villard*, 2:188–89.

56. Thomas, *Three Years with Grant as Recalled by War Correspondent Sylvanus Cadwallader*, 92–93.

57. *Chicago Evening Journal*, 30 June 1863, 1.

58. Franc B. Wilkie, *Pen and Powder* (Boston: Tickner, 1888), 138, 212–13.

59. Smith, *Life and Letters of Thomas Kilby Smith*, 306–7; Howe, *Home Letters of General Sherman*, 272; Sherman to John Sherman, 20 June 1863, William T. Sherman Papers, Library of Congress, as quoted in Marszalek, *Sherman*, 228–29.

60. Capt. Ambrose A. Blount to McClernand, 2 Sept. 1863, McClernand Collection; McClernand to George W. Morgan, 30 Nov. 1875, William T. Sherman Letters, Western Reserve Historical Society.

61. McClernand to Lincoln, 23 June 1863, Lincoln Collection.

62. *OR*, vol. 24, 1:44–59, 157.

63. Anna Ridgely, "A Girl in the Sixties," *Journal of the Illinois State Historical Society* 22 (Oct. 1929): 428. *Illinois State Journal*, 25 June 1863, 2; 27 June 1863, 2; 30 June 1863, 2; 1 July 1863, 2.

64. R. F. Stevens to McClernand, 25 July 1863; Lyman Trumbull to McClernand, 5 Aug. 1863; Clark E. Carr to McClernand, 7 Sept. 1863; Hon. William Flagg to McClernand, 13 Dec. 1863. All in McClernand Collection. *OR*, vol. 52, 1:414–15; *Chicago Times*, 26 Nov. 1863, as quoted in Holt, "The Political Career of William A. Richardson," 258; *(Springfield, Illinois) Daily State Journal*, 29 July 1868, 2.

65. *OR*, vol. 24, 1:165–67; McClernand to Secretary of the Interior John Usher, 16 July 1863; McClernand to Lincoln, 3 Aug. 1863. All in Lincoln Collection. Capt. Wright Rives to McClernand, 16 July 1863, as cited in Thomas and Hyman, *Stanton: The Life and Times of Lincoln's Secretary of War*, 268; John G. Nicolay and John Hay, *Abraham Lincoln: Complete Works Comprising His Speeches, Letters, State Papers, and Miscellaneous Writing*, 2 vols. (New York: Century, 1894), 2:385.

66. *OR*, vol. 24, 1:167–68; vol. 52, 1:431.

67. Ibid., vol. 52, 1:437–38.

68. Tyler Dennett, *Lincoln and the Civil War in Diaries and Letters of John Hay* (New York: Dodd, Meade, 1939), 69.

69. Fletcher Pratt, *Stanton: Lincoln's Secretary of War* (New York: W. W. Norton, 1953), 315; Welles, *Diary of Gideon Welles*, 1:387.

70. *OR*, vol. 52, 1:439–40; vol. 24, 1:168; Stanton to McClernand, 29 Aug. 1863, McClernand Collection.

71. *OR*, vol. 24, 1:168.

72. Ibid., 169.

73. Ibid., 177–81; Capt. F. H. Mason to McClernand, 18 Aug. 1863; Col. W. M. Stone to McClernand, 26 Aug. 1863; P. C. Koscialowski, 31 Aug. 1863; Cpl. J. P. Black to McClernand, 1 Sept. 1863; 2d Lt. N. C. Messenger to McClernand, 1 Sept. 1863; Col. Don Pardee to McClernand, 2 Sept. 1863; Col. Richard H. Ballinger to McClernand, 4 Sept. 1863; Lt. Col. Lysander R. Webb to McClernand, 22 Sept. 1863. All in McClernand Collection.

74. *OR*, vol. 24, 1:169–70; McClernand to Yates, 13 Oct. 1863, McClernand Collection.

75. Ibid., 169–86.

76. Halleck to McClernand, 15 Oct. 1863, McClernand Collection.

77. McClernand to Johnson, 24 Oct. 1863, Johnson Papers.

78. McClernand to J. F. Cowan, 11 Dec. 1863; Cowan to McClernand, 29 Dec. 1863. All in McClernand Collection.

79. McClernand to Trumbull, 15 Dec., 18 Dec. 1863, McClernand Collection.

80. George T. Palmer, *A Conscientious Turncoat: The Story of John M. Palmer, 1817–1900* (New Haven, Conn.: Yale Univ. Press, 1941), 130.

81. Lyman Trumbull to McClernand, 21 Dec. 1863, McClernand Collection.

82. List of Locations, Thirteenth Army Corps, Jan. 1864, McClernand Collection.

83. Alvin M. Josephy, *The Civil War in the American West* (New York: Alfred A. Knopf, 1991), 179, 186–87.

84. *OR*, vol. 34, 2:46.

85. Trumbull to McClernand, 19 Jan. 1864, McClernand Collection.

86. McClernand to Trumbull, 14 Jan. 1863; John F. Cowan to McClernand, 20 Jan. 1864, McClernand Collection; *OR*, vol. 34, 2:134, 123; McClernand to Lincoln, 14 Jan. 1864, McClernand Collection.

87. Trumbull to McClernand, 23 Jan. 1864, McClernand Collection.

88. McClernand to Trumbull, 30 Jan. 1864; Gov. William M. Stone to McClernand, 29 Mar. 1864; Capt. Wright Rives to McClernand, 28 Jan. 1864; Capt. Edgar to McClernand, 28 Jan. 1864; Col. Grantham Taggart to McClernand, 30 Jan. 1864; Capt. A. J. Lusk to McClernand, 31 Jan. 1864; Lt. Col. Thomas W. Bennett to McClernand, 14 Sept. 1863; Yates to Maj. Gen. Nathaniel P. Banks, 28 Jan. 1864. All in McClernand Collection. Gov. William M. Stone to McClernand, 25 Mar. 1864, Trumbull Manuscripts.

89. Simon, *The Papers of Ulysses S. Grant*, 10:37–38; Wilson, *Under the Old Flag*, 1:326.

90. McClernand to Trumbull, 12 Feb. 1864; McClernand to Lincoln, 12 Feb. 1864. All in McClernand Collection.

91. *OR*, vol. 32, 2:424–25; 3:40–41.

92. Simon, *The Papers of Ulysses S. Grant*, 10:142–43; Napoleon J. T. Dana to Edward O. C. Ord, 10 Feb. 1864, as quoted in Cresap, *Appomattox Commander*, 112.

93. McClernand to Yates, 2 Feb. 1864, McClernand Collection; *OR*, vol. 34, 2:378, 392, 400; 1864 Order Book, McClernand Collection; James Tucker to McClernand, 20 Feb. 1864, McClernand Collection; Trumbull to Banks, 6 Feb. 1864, Nathaniel P. Banks Papers, Illinois State Historical Library; *History of Sangamon County* (Chicago: Inter-State Publishing, 1881), 343.

94. *OR*, vol. 34, 2:400–401.

95. Ibid., 335, 409, 418, 469.

96. Ibid., 474, 545; 1864 Order Book, McClernand Collection.

97. *OR*, vol. 34, 2:482, 643–44, 737.

98. Ibid., 425, 495, 585, 630, 637–38.

99. Ibid., 503, 585, 587, 599, 771.

100. Ibid., 701, 692, 757, 727–28, 783–84; 1:653; 3:74.

101. Lincoln to Grant, 9 Aug. 1863, Lincoln Collection; *OR*, vol. 24, 2:475; 1864 Order Book, McClernand Collection; Kerby, *Kirby Smith's Confederacy*, 15, 180, 192, 371; unsigned letter, 7 Apr. 1864, McClernand Collection; James W. Daddysman, *The Matamoras Trade: Confederate Commerce, Diplomacy, and Intrigue* (Newark: Univ. of Delaware Press, 1984), 181–82.

102. *OR*, vol. 34, 3:73.

103. Ibid., 73–74.

104. Ibid., 87–88.

105. McClernand to Maj. Gen. Francis Herron, 7 Apr. 1864, McClernand Collection.

106. McClernand to Trumbull, 16 Apr. 1864, Trumbull Manuscripts.

107. *OR*, vol. 34, 3:176.

108. Ibid., 128, 245, 269–70; 1864 Order Book, McClernand Collection.

109. 1864 Order Book, McClernand Collection; *OR*, vol. 34, 3:296.

110. *OR*, vol. 34, 3:295, 322–23, 331; Trumbull to McClernand, 14 Apr. 1864, McClernand Collection; Simon, *The Papers of Ulysses S. Grant*, 10:351–52; McClernand to Trumbull, 24 Mar. 1864, Lyman Trumbull Manuscripts; Soman and Byrne, eds., *A Jewish Colonel in the Civil War*, 329, 334.

111. Banks to McClernand, 27 Apr. 1864, McClernand Collection.

112. *OR*, vol. 34, 3:317–19, 334.

113. Ibid., 334–36, 373–74.

114. Ibid., 1:590; 3:369. McClernand to Banks, 30 Apr. 1864, McClernand Collection.

115. *OR*, vol. 34, 3:331–33.

116. Ibid., 2:105, 403, 427, 433, 523.

117. Ibid., 373–75; Hicken, *Illinois in the Civil War*, 332.

118. *OR*, vol. 24, 3:392, 430, 457–58, 475–76, 519–20, 533.

119. Ibid., 546; 4:479–80; *Illinois State Journal*, 27 May 1864, 2, as quoted from the *Chicago Tribune;* Boatner, *The Civil War Dictionary*, 194.

10. The Final Years

1. Undated manuscript, McClernand Collection; Basler, *The Collected Works of Abraham Lincoln*, 7:473.

2. McClernand to Stanton, 15 July 1864, Lincoln Papers.

3. *Illinois State Register*, 7 Oct. 1864, 1.

4. McClernand to Trumbull, 23 Nov. 1864, Trumbull Manuscripts; McClernand to Brig. Gen. Lorenzo Thomas, (no day indicated) Nov. 1864, McClernand Collection.

5. Dennett, *Lincoln and the Civil War in Diaries and Letters of John Hay*, 229.

6. Simon, *The Papers of Ulysses S. Grant*, 13:16; James M. Merrill, *William Tecumseh Sherman* (Chicago: Rand McNally, 1971), 227.

7. Edward L. Merritt, "Recollections of the Part Springfield Bore in the Obsequies of Abraham Lincoln," *Transactions of the Illinois State Historical Society* 14 (Springfield, Ill.: State Journal, 1910): 182; Sandburg, *Abraham Lincoln: The War Years*, 4:270, 394; undated manuscript, McClernand Collection.

8. Trumbull to McClernand, 17 Apr. 1866, McClernand Collection; McClernand to Johnson, 7 July 1866, 18 July 1866, Johnson Papers.

9. McClernand to Samuel S. Marshall, 24 Feb. 1866, McClernand to Johnson, 24 June 1866, McClernand to G. D. Patterson, 26 Oct. 1866, Johnson Papers; Cox, *Three Decades of Federal Legislation*, 398. *Illinois State Register*, 29 Aug. 1866, 1; 12 Sept. 1866, 1; 22 Sept. 1866, 3. McClernand to T. Lyle Dickey, 5 Sept. 1866, W. H. L. Wallace–Lyle Dickey Papers, Illinois State Historical Library; Jones, "*Black Jack*,"

283; *Illinois State Register,* 18 Sept. 1866, 1; George F. Milton, *The Age of Hate: Andrew Johnson and the Radicals* (New York: Coward-McCann, 1930), 356.

10. Broeck N. Oder, "Andrew Johnson and the 1866 Illinois Election," *Journal of the Illinois State Historical Society* 73 (Autumn 1980): 190. *Illinois State Register,* 5 Sept. 1866, 1; 8 Sept. 1866, 1.

11. *Illinois State Register,* 3 Sept. 1866, 1.

12. Milton, *The Age of Hate,* 468; McClernand to David T. Patterson, 11 Oct. 1867, Johnson Papers; McClernand to Johnson, 5 Sept. 1867, Johnson Papers.

13. McClernand to Yates, 29 Mar. 1867; McClernand to Richard Oglesby, (no day indicated) Mar. 1867; William H. Seward to Browning, 31 May 1867; Samuel S. Marshall to McClernand, 15, 21 July 1867. All in McClernand Collection. Pease and Randall, *The Diary of Orville Hickman Browning,* 2:73; James P. Jones, *John A. Logan: Stalwart Republican from Illinois* (Tallahassee: University Presses of Florida, 1982), 2, 9; *Daily State Journal,* 27 July 1868, 1.

14. Thomas Ewing, Sr., to Johnson, 12 Oct. 1867; McClernand to Johnson, 14 Jan. 1868, All in Johnson Papers. Milton, *The Age of Hate,* 736.

15. Lusk, *Politics and Politicians,* 207. *Illinois State Register,* 20 Sept. 1900, 2; 14 Oct. 1868, 3. *Daily State Journal,* 6 July 1868, 1; 10 July 1868, 1.

16. *Daily State Journal,* 10 July 1868, 1; 27 Aug. 1868, 2. *Illinois State Register,* 13 Oct. 1868, 1.

17. *Daily State Journal,* 22 July 1868, 2; 29 July 1868, 2; 9 Sept. 1868, 2; 15 Oct. 1868, 2. Manly Wade Wellman, *Giant in Gray: A Biography of Wade Hampton of South Carolina* (New York: Charles Scribner's Sons, 1949), 210, 222.

18. *History of Sangamon County,* 73. *Illinois State Register,* 12 Aug. 1868, 1; 12 Sept. 1868, 1; 17 Sept. 1868, 1; 5 Oct. 1868, 1; 14 Oct. 1868, 1; 10 Oct. 1868, 1; 19 Oct. 1868, 1; 4 Nov. 1868, 1. Arthur M. Schlesinger, Jr., ed., *History of Presidential Elections, 1789–1968,* 4 vols. (New York: Chelsea House Publishers, 1971), 2:1300.

19. McClernand to Sherman, 20 July 1870; Sherman to McClernand, 29 July 1870. In McClernand Collection.

20. McClernand to Morgan, 30 Nov. 1875, Sherman letters, Western Reserve Historical Society. For information of Sherman's relief from command see Marszalek, *Sherman: A Soldier's Passion for Order,* 162–63.

21. Fellman, *Citizen Sherman* (New York: Random House, 1995), 320; *Illinois State Register,* 13 Apr. 1881, 2.

22. James M. Bourne to McClernand, 22 Oct. 1869; Stephen Burbridge to McClernand, 16 Mar. 1872. In McClernand Collection.

23. McClernand to Morgan, 30 Nov. 1865, Sherman letters, Western Reserve Historical Society.

24. McClernand to W. C. Endicott, 23 May 1885, as quoted in James T. King, *War Eagle: A Life of General Eugene A. Carr* (Lincoln: Univ. of Nebraska Press, 1963), 236.

25. Alexander C. Flick, *Samuel Jones Tilden: A Study in Political Sagacity* (New York: Dodd, Mead, 1939), 296–97; McCormack, *Memoirs of Gustave Koerner,* 2:560, 605,

617–18; Blum, *The National Experience*, 413–15; Simon, *Lincoln's Preparation for Greatness*, 303; Schlesinger, *History of American Presidential Elections, 1789–1968*, 2:1399.

26. Flick, *Samuel Jones Tilden*, 444–46, 451; John Bigelow, *The Life of Samuel J. Tilden*, 2 vols. (New York: Harper & Brothers, 1895), 2:405–6,

27. Mary R. Dearing, *Veterans in Politics: The Story of the G. A. R.* (Westport, Conn.: Greenwood Press, 1974), 292, 295.

28. *History of Sangamon County*, 122, 422–25, 591; Richard J. Oglesby to McClernand, 15 May 1886, McClernand Collection; McClernand to Harry Van Siewo, 2 Aug. 1876, copy of letter in possession of McClernand Crawford, great-great-great-grandson of John McClernand, New Palestine, Indiana.

29. McClernand to Lanphier, 18 Jan. 1886; Lanphier to William R. Morrison, 18 Jan. 1886; Morrison to Lanphier, 24 Jan. 1886. All in Lanphier Papers. Notation in McClernand Collection, 19 and 30 Apr. 1886. *History of Sangamon Country*, 122; Basler, *The Collected Works of Abraham Lincoln*, 4:41–2; George R. Gaylor, "The Mormons and Politics in Illinois: 1839–1844," *Journal of the Illinois State Historical Society* 49 (Spring 1956): 51–2; Simon, *Lincoln's Preparation for Greatness*, 266–69.

30. Information on tombstones is available in the cemetery office, Oak Ridge Cemetery. Stewart L. Grow, "A Study of the Utah Commission, 1882–96" (Ph.D. diss., University of Utah, 1954), 228–29.

31. McClernand to Lanphier, 19 May 1886, Lanphier Papers.

32. Grow, "A Study of the Utah Commission," 1, 32, 28–29, 191; *Congressional Record*, 47th Cong., 1st sess., 1882, 13, pt. 2:1156.

33. Grow, "A Study of the Utah Commission," 48–49, 75.

34. Gustive O. Larson, *The "Americanization" of Utah for Statehood* (San Marino, Calif.: Huntington Library, 1971), 98, 100, 245, 263–64; "Annual and Special Reports of the Utah Commission to the Secretary of Interior, 1882–1887," as quoted in Larson, *The "Americanization" of Utah*, passim; Grow, "A Study of the Utah Commission," 76–77, 241–42, 265. The manifesto was issued by Woodruff on 24 September, but it was not approved by the church Saints until 6 October.

35. Grow, "A Study of the Utah Commission," 133, 135–36.

36. Ibid., 218–19.

37. *Illinois State Journal*, 18 July 1888, 6; 19 July 1888, 6; 20 July 1888, 4.

38. Resolution, State of Illinois, 39th General Assembly, 23 Jan. 1895; McClernand to John G. Springer, 21 Jan. 1896; untitled newspaper clippings, 11 Jan. 1900, 3 Mar. 1900. All in McClernand Collection.

39. John A. McClernand, "In Memory of John McLean," *Transactions of the Illinois State Historical Society* 36 (Springfield, Ill.: Phillips Bros., 1904): 198–99; untitled newspaper clippings, 25 Feb., 3 Mar. 1900, McClernand Collection; *Illinois State Register*, 23 Sept. 1900, 1. "Last Will and Testament of John A. McClernand," 11 Oct. 1899; "Inventory of Real and Personal Estate," all in Sangamon County Courthouse, Springfield, Illinois.

40. *OR*, vol. 24, 1:43.

41. McCormack, *Memoirs of Gustave Koerner*, 1:480.

42. Ibid.; Joseph Wallace, "Biography of John A. McClernand," 73; Badeau, *Military History of Ulysses S. Grant,* 1:128; Dana, *Recollections of the Civil War,* 32; Sherman, *Memoirs,* 339; William Shakespeare, *Antony and Cleopatra,* act 3, scene 1, lines 22–23.

43. *(Belleville, Ill.) St. Clair Banner,* 23 Apr. 1844, 4.

44. McClernand to Lincoln, 7 Jan. 1863, Lincoln Collection; *OR,* vol. 24, 1:169–70.

45. Jacob D. Cox, *Military Reminiscences of the Civil War,* 2 vols. (New York: Charles Scribner's Sons, 1900), 1:167; *New York Times,* 24 Dec. 1859, 1; Wilson, *Under the Old Flag,* 1:186.

46. Badeau, *Military History of Ulysses S. Grant,* 1:128; Wilson, *The Life of John A. Rawlins,* 105, 135; Logan, *The Volunteer Soldier of America,* 568.

47. Welles, *Gideon Welles,* 1:387, 2:283; Wilkie, *Pen and Powder,* 211–12.

48. Silas Noble to Lyman Trumbull, 24 Feb. 1863, Lyman Trumbull Transcripts, Illinois Historical Survey, as quoted in Hicken, *Illinois in the Civil War,* 162; King, *The True Ulysses S. Grant,* 213–14; Brinton, *Personal Memoirs of John H. Brinton,* 13–15.

49. Robert R. McCormick, *Ulysses S. Grant: The Great Soldier of America* (New York: Bond Wheelwright, 1950), 95.

50. Wilson, *Under the Old Flag,* 1:198–200.

51. Simon, *The Papers of Ulysses S. Grant,* 11:210. In July 1864 Washington was threatened by Confederate forces commanded by Jubal Early. The city was defended by several discredited Union generals.

52. Villard, *Memoirs of Henry Villard,* 2:189.

53. Sherman, *Memoirs,* 558–59.

54. Logan to Mary Logan, 31 July, 6 Aug. 1864, John A. Logan Manuscripts as quoted in Jones, *"Black Jack,"* 224.

55. *OR,* vol. 47, 2:154.

56. Hattaway and Jones, *How the North Won,* 503.

57. Brinton, *Personal Memoirs of John H. Brinton,* 103; Wilson, *Under the Old Flag,* 1:186.

Bibliography

Manuscript Collections

Nathaniel P. Banks Papers. Illinois State Historical Library. Springfield, Ill.

Sidney Breese Manuscript Collection. Illinois State Historical Library. Springfield, Ill.

Samuel Sullivan Cox Papers. Rutherford B. Hayes Presidential Library. Fremont, Ohio.

Henry Eddy Correspondence. Illinois State Historical Library. Springfield, Ill.

Engelmann-Kircher Family Papers. Illinois State Historical Library. Springfield, Ill.

Augustus French Manuscript Collection. Illinois State Historical Library. Springfield, Ill.

Andrew Johnson Papers. Microfilm. Combined Arms Research Library. Fort Leavenworth, Kans.

Charles H. Lanphier Papers. Illinois State Historical Library. Springfield, Ill.

Robert Todd Lincoln Collection. Microfilm. Illinois State Historical Library. Springfield, Ill.

John Alexander McClernand Collection. Illinois State Historical Library. Springfield, Ill.

Lewis B. Parson Papers. Illinois State Historical Library. Springfield, Ill.

William T. Sherman Papers. Western Reserve Historical Society. Cleveland, Ohio.

Elizabeth Simpson Letters. Illinois State Historical Library. Springfield, Ill.

Henry Baylor Taylor Papers. University of Virginia Library. Charlottesville, Virginia.

Lyman Trumbull Manuscripts. Illinois State Historical Library. Springfield, Ill.

Jonathan Baldwin Turner Papers. Illinois State Historical Library, Springfield, Ill.

Joseph Wallace Collection. Illinois State Historical Library. Springfield, Ill.

W. H. L. Wallace–Lyle Dickey Papers. Illinois State Historical Library. Springfield, Ill.

Richard Yates Papers. Illinois State Historical Library. Springfield, Ill.

Newspapers

Chicago Daily-American.

Chicago Evening Journal.

Chicago Tribune.

Illinois State Journal. This newspaper underwent several name changes that included *Illinois Daily Journal*, *Illinois Journal (Daily)*, and *Illinois Daily State Journal.*
Illinois State Register.
New York Daily Tribune.
New York Times.
St. Clair (Illinois) Banner.
St. Louis (Missouri) Weekly Democrat.
Sangamo Journal.

PUBLISHED PRIMARY SOURCES

Badeau, Adam. *Military History of Ulysses S. Grant, from April 1861 to April 1865.* 3 vols. New York: D. Appleton, 1868.
Basler, Roy P., ed. *The Collected Works of Abraham Lincoln.* 9 vols. New Brunswick, N.J.: Rutgers Univ. Press, 1953.
Bentley, William H. *History of the 77th Illinois Volunteer Infantry.* Peoria, Ill.: Edward Rink, Printer, 1888.
Bering, John A., and Thomas Montgomery. *History of the Forty-eighth Ohio Vet. Vol. Inf.* Hillsboro, Ohio: Highland News Office, 1880.
Boos, J. E. "Civil War Diary of Patrick H. White." *Journal of the Illinois State Historical Society* 15 (Oct. 1922–Jan. 1923): 640–63.
Brinton, John. *Personal Memoirs of John H. Brinton.* New York: Neale Publishing, 1914.
Broadside. "Col. McClernand's Letter to the People of Illinois." 18 Feb. 1858. Illinois State Historical Library. Springfield, Ill.
Broadside. "The Record of Hon. John A. McClernand." To the Voters of the Sixth Congressional District. 13 October 1860. Illinois State Historical Library. Springfield, Ill.
Brown, James G. "Historical Sketch of the 55th Reg. Ill. Vol." In *Report of the Proceedings of the Association of the Fifty-fifth Illinois Veteran Volunteer Infantry at Their First Reunion.* Chicago: James Guilbert, 1885.
Cadwallader, Sylvanus. *Three-Years with Grant.* New York: Alfred A. Knopf, 1955.
Carr, Clark E. *Stephen A. Douglas: His Life, Public Services, Speeches and Patriotism.* Chicago: A. C. McClurg, 1909.
Carrington, George. "Diary, 1862." Chicago Historical Society. Chicago, Ill.
Clark, Olynthus, ed. *Downing's Civil War Diary.* Iowa City: State Univ. of Iowa, 1916.
Clausewitz, Carl von. *On War.* Translated and edited by Michael Howard and Peter Paret. Princeton, N.J.: Princeton Univ. Press, 1976.
Committee of the Regiment. *The Story of the Fifty-fifth Regiment Illinois Volunteer Infantry in the Civil War.* N.p. 1887.
Congressional Globe. 29th Cong., 31st Cong., 36th Cong., 37th Cong.
Congressional Record. 47th Cong.
Cox, Jacob D. *Atlanta.* New York: Charles Scribner's Sons, 1882.

———. *Military Reminiscences of the Civil War.* 2 vols. New York: Charles Scribner's Sons, 1900.

Crummer, Wilbur F. *With Grant at Fort Donelson, Shiloh, and Vicksburg.* Oak Park, Ill.: E. C. Crummer, 1915.

Dana, Charles A., and James H. Wilson. *The Life of Ulysses S. Grant.* Springfield, Mass.: Gurdon Bill, 1868.

Dana, Charles A. *Recollections of the Civil War.* New York: D. Appleton, 1898.

Darrin, Charles V. "Your Truly Attached Friend, Mary Lincoln." *Journal of the Illinois State Historical Society* 44 (Spring 1951): 7–25.

Davis, George B., Leslie J. Perry, Joseph W. Kirkley, and Calvin D. Cowles. *The Official Military Atlas of the Civil War.* Washington, D.C.: GPO, 1891–1895.

Dennett, Tyler. *Lincoln and the Civil War in Diaries and Letters of John Hay.* New York: Dodd, Meade, 1939.

Donald, David, ed. *Inside Lincoln's Cabinet: The Civil War Diaries of Salmon P. Chase.* New York: Longmans, Green, 1954.

Elliott, Isaac H. *History of the Thirty-third Regiment Illinois Veteran Volunteer Infantry in the Civil War, 22nd August 1861 to 7th December 1865.* Gibson City, Ill.: Regimental Association, 1902.

Erickson, Edgar, ed. "With Grant at Vicksburg: From the Civil War Diary of Charles E. Wilcox." *Journal of the Illinois State Historical Society* 30 (Jan. 1938): 441–503.

Fleming, Robert. "The Battle of Shiloh as a Private Saw It." *Sketches of War History 1861–1865: Papers Prepared for the Commandery of the State of Ohio, Military Order of the Loyal Legion of the United States.* 9 vols. Cincinnati: Monfort, 1908.

Grant, Ulysses S. *Personal Memoirs of U. S. Grant.* New York: Smithmark Publishers, 1994.

———. "The Vicksburg Campaign." In *Battles and Leaders of the Civil War,* 4 vols. Edited by Robert U. Johnson and Clarence C. Buel, 3:493–538. New York: Castle Books, 1956.

Halleck, Henry W. *Elements of Military Art and Science.* New York: D. Appleton, 1862.

Halstead, Murat. *Caucuses of 1860: A History of the National Political Conventions of the Current Presidential Campaign.* Columbus, Ohio: Follett, Foster, 1860.

Hardee, William J. *Rifle and Light Infantry Tactics for the Exercise and Manoeuvres of Troops When Acting as Light Infantry Or Riflemen.* 2 vols. Philadelphia: Lippincott, Grambo, 1855.

Hass, Paul H., ed. "The Vicksburg Diary of Henry Clay Warmoth." *Journal of Mississippi History* 31 (Nov. 1969): 334–47; 32 (Feb. 1970): 60–74.

Heartsill, William W. *Fourteen Hundred and 91 Days in the Confederate Army.* Edited by Bell I. Wiley. Jackson, Tenn.: McCowat-Mercer Press, 1953.

Hewitt, Janet B, Noah A. Trudeau, Bryce A. Suderow, Gary W. Gallagher, eds. *Supplement to the Official Records of the Union and Confederate Armies.* 63 vols. Wilmington, N.C.: Broadfoot Publishing, 1994–98.

Hicks, Henry G. "Fort Donelson." In *Glimpses of the Nation's Struggle: Papers Read before the Minnesota Commandery of the Military Order of the Loyal Legion of the United*

States, 1892–1897. Ed. Edwin C. Mason, Ell Torrance, David L. Kingsbury. 6 vols. Wilmington, N.C.: Broadfoot Publishing, 1992.

Higginson, T. W. "Regular and Volunteer Officers." *Atlantic Monthly* 14 (Sept. 1864): 348–57.

Howe, M. A. DeWolfe, ed. *Home Letters of General Sherman*. New York: Charles Scribner's Sons, 1909.

Irwin, Richard B. "Military Operations in Louisiana in 1862." In *Battles and Leaders of the Civil War*. 4 vols. Edited by Robert U. Johnson and Clarence C. Buel, 3:582–84. New York: Castle Books, 1956,

Jansen, Theodore H. "Biography and Reminiscences of Matthew Jansen, 1905." Photocopy. Illinois State Historical Library. Springfield, Ill.

Jenney, W. L. B. "Personal Recollections of Vicksburg." In *Military Essays and Recollections*. 4 vols. Chicago: Dial Press, 1899.

Johannsen, Robert W., ed. *The Letters of Stephen A. Douglas*. Urbana: Univ. of Illinois Press, 1961.

Jomini, Baron Antoine Henri de. *The Art of War*. Translated by G. H. Mendell and W. P. Craighill. Philadelphia: J. B. Lippincott, 1862; reprint, Westport, Conn.: Greenwood Press, 1971.

Kerner, Robert J., ed. "The Diary of Edward W. Crippen, Private 27th Illinois Volunteers, War of the Rebellion, August 7, 1861, to September 19, 1863." *Transactions of the Illinois State Historical Society* 14 (1910): 220–82.

Linder, Usher. *Reminiscences of the Early Bench and Bar of Illinois*. Chicago: Legal News, 1879.

Logan, John A. *The Volunteer Soldier of America*. Chicago: R. S. Peale, 1887.

Logan, Mary S. C. *Reminiscences of a Soldier's Wife*. New York: Charles Scribner's Sons, 1913.

Lusk, David W. *Eighty Years of Illinois Politics and Politicians*. Springfield, Ill.: D. W. Lusk, 1889.

———. *Politics and Politicians: A Succinct History of the Politics of Illinois from 1856 to 1884*. Springfield, Ill.: H. W. Rokker, 1884.

McClernand, John A. "In Memory of John McLean." *Transactions of The Illinois State Historical Society* 36 (1904): 198–99.

McCormack, Thomas J., ed. *Memoirs of Gustave Koerner, 1809–1896*. 2 vols. Cedar Rapids, Iowa: Torch Press, 1909.

Mahan, Dennis H. *A Complete Treatise on Field Fortifications*. New York: Wiley and Putnam, 1836.

Mason, Frank H. *The Forty-second Ohio Infantry: A History*. Cleveland: Cobb, Andrews, 1876.

Morris, William S., J. B. Kuykendall, and L. D. Harwell. *History 31st Regiment Volunteers, Organized by John A. Logan*. Evansville, Ind.: Keller Printing and Publishing, 1902.

Nicolay, John G., and John Hay. *Abraham Lincoln: A History*. 10 vols. New York: Century, 1890.

———. *Abraham Lincoln: Complete Works Comprising His Speeches, Letters, State Papers, and Miscellaneous Writings.* 2 vols. New York: Century, 1894.

Niven, John, ed. *The Salmon P. Chase Papers.* 4 vols. Kent, Ohio: Kent State Univ. Press, 1993.

Official Records of the Union and Confederate Navies in the War of the Rebellion. 30 vols. Washington, D.C.: GPO, 1894–1922.

Oldroyd, Osborn H. *A Soldier's Story of the Siege of Vicksburg.* Springfield, Ill.: Privately published, 1885.

Pease, Theodore C., and James G. Randall, eds. *The Diary of Orville Hickman Browning.* 2 vols. Springfield: Illinois State Historical Library, 1925.

Polk, William M. "General Polk and the Battle of Belmont." In *Battles and Leaders of the Civil War,* 4 vols. Edited by Robert U. Johnson and Clarence C. Buel, 1:348–57. New York: Castle Books, 1956.

Porter, David Dixon. *Incidents and Anecdotes of the Civil War.* New York: Appleton, 1885.

———. *The Naval History of the Civil War.* Secaucus, N.J.: Castle, 1984.

Ridgely, Anna. "A Girl in the Sixties." Edited by Octavia R. Corneau. *Journal of the Illinois State Historical Society* 22 (Oct. 1929): 401–46.

Rowland, Dunbar, ed. *Jefferson Davis, Constitutionalist: His Letters, Papers, and Speeches.* 10 vols. Jackson: Mississippi Department of Archives and History, 1923.

Schwartz, Adolph (?). Unpublished manuscript biography of John Alexander McClernand. Probably written in October or November 1863. Annotated by Gen. Edward J. McClernand. 2 vols. Illinois State Historical Library. Springfield, Ill.

Sears, Stephen W., ed. *The Civil War Papers of George B. McClellan.* New York: Ticknor & Fields, 1989.

Seaton, John. "The Battle of Belmont." In *War Talks in Kansas: A Series of Papers Read before the Kansas Commandery of the Loyal Legion of the United States.* Wilmington, N.C.: Broadfoot Publishing, 1992.

Sherman, William T. *Memoirs of General William T. Sherman.* Westport, Conn.: Greenwood Press, 1972.

———. "Vicksburg By New Years." *Civil War Times Illustrated* 16 (Jan. 1978): 44–48.

Simon, John Y., ed. *The Papers of Ulysses S. Grant.* 22 vols. Carbondale: Southern Illinois Univ. Press, 1967–98.

Smith, Henry I. *History of the Seventh Iowa Veteran Volunteer Infantry.* Mason City, Iowa: E. Hitchcock, Printer, 1903.

Smith, Walter G., ed. *Life and Letters of Thomas Kilby Smith, Brevet Major-General, United States Volunteers, 1820–1887.* New York: G. P. Putnam's Sons, 1898.

Snead, Thomas L. "The Conquest of Arkansas." In *Battles and Leaders of the Civil War,* 4 vols. Edited by Robert U. Johnson and Clarence C. Buel, 3:441–61. New York: Century, 1887–88.

Soman, Jean Powers, and Frank L. Byrne, eds. *A Jewish Colonel in the Civil War: Marcus M. Spiegel of the Ohio Volunteers.* Lincoln: Univ. of Nebraska Press, 1994.

"A Statesman's Letters of the Civil War Period." *Journal of the Illinois State Historical Society* 2 (July 1909): 43–50.

Stephens, Alexander H. *A Constitutional View of the Late War between the States: Its Causes, Character, Conduct and Results.* 2 vols. Philadelphia: National Publishing, 1870.

Taylor, Jesse. "The Defense of Fort Henry." In *Battles and Leaders of the Civil War.* 4 vols. Edited by Robert U. Johnson and Clarence C. Buel, 1:368–72. New York: Castle Books, 1956.

Taylor, John C. Diary, 2 April–7 July 1863. 27 April entry. Henry Baylor Taylor Papers, University of Virginia Library, Charlottesville.

Thomas, Benjamin P., ed. *Three Years with Grant as Recalled by War Correspondent Sylvanus Cadwallader.* Westport, Conn.: Greenwood Press, 1980.

Thompson, Robert Means, and Richard Wainwright, eds. *Confidential Correspondence of Gustavus Vasa Fox.* 2 vols. New York: DeVinne Press, 1920.

Thorndike, Rachel Sherman, ed. *The Sherman Letters: Correspondence between General and Senator Sherman from 1837 to 1891.* New York: Charles Scribner's Sons, 1894.

Turner, Justin G., and Linda L. Turner. *Mary Todd Lincoln: Her Life and Letters.* New York: Alfred A. Knopf, 1972.

U.S. Congress. House. Historical Manuscripts Commission. "Diary and Correspondence of Salmon P. Chase." In *Annual Report of the American Historical Association for the Year 1902.* 2 vols. 57th Cong., 2d sess. Washington: GPO, 1903.

Vance, J. W. *Report of the Adjutant General of the State of Illinois.* 8 vols. Springfield, Ill.: H. W. Rokker, 1886.

Villard, Henry. *Memoirs of Henry Villard, Journalist and Financier, 1835–1900.* 2 vols. Boston: Houghton, Mifflin, 1904.

Walke, Henry. "The Gun-boats at Belmont and Fort Henry." In *Battles and Leaders of the Civil War,* 4 vols. Edited by Robert U. Johnson and Clarence C. Buel. 1:358–67. New York: Castle Books, 1956.

———. *Naval Scenes and Reminiscences of the Civil War in the United States.* New York: F. R. Reed, 1877.

———. "The Western Flotilla at Fort Donelson, Island Number Ten, Fort Pillow and Memphis." In *Battles and Leaders of the Civil War,* 4 vols. Edited by Robert U. Johnson and Clarence C. Buel. 1:430–52. New York: Castle Books, 1956.

Wallace, Isabel. *Life and Letters of General W. H. L. Wallace.* Chicago: R. R. Donnelly & Sons, 1909.

[Wallace, Joseph]. "Biography of John A. McClernand." Unpublished manuscript. Joseph Wallace Collection. Illinois State Historical Library. Springfield, Ill.

Wallace, Lew. "The Capture of Fort Donelson." In *Battles and Leaders of the Civil War,* 4 vols. Edited by Robert U. Johnson and Clarence C. Buel. 1:398–428. New York: Castle Books, 1956.

———. *Lew Wallace: An Autobiography.* 2 vols. New York: Harper & Brothers, 1906.

The War of the Rebellion: A Compilation of the Official Records of the Union and Confederate Armies. 128 vols. Washington, D.C.: GPO, 1880–1901.

Welles, Gideon. *Diary of Gideon Welles.* 3 vols. Boston: Houghton Mifflin, 1911.

Whitney, Henry C. *Life on the Circuit with Lincoln.* Boston: Estes and Lauriat, 1892.

Wilkie, Franc B. *Pen and Powder.* Boston: Ticknor, 1888.

Wilkin, Jacob W. "Personal Reminiscences of General U. S. Grant." *Transactions of the Illinois State Historical Society* 12 (1908): 131–40.

Wills, Charles Wright. *Army Life of an Illinois Soldier.* Edited by Mary E. Kellogg. Washington, D.C.: Globe Printing, 1906.

Wilson, James H. *The Life of John A. Rawlins.* New York: Neale Publishing, 1916.

———. *Under the Old Flag.* 2 vols. New York: D. Appleton, 1912.

Wilson, Rufus R., ed. *Uncollected Works of Abraham Lincoln.* 2 vols. Elmira, N.Y.: Primavera Press, 1947.

Wood, David W. *History of the Twentieth Ohio Veteran Volunteer Infantry Regiment.* Columbus, Ohio: Paul and Thrall, 1876.

Published Secondary Sources

Angle, Paul M. *"Here I Have Lived": A History of Lincoln's Springfield.* Springfield, Ill.: Abraham Lincoln Association, 1935.

———. *Lincoln, 1854–1861: Being the Day-by-Day Activities of Abraham Lincoln from January 1, 1854 to March 4, 1861.* Springfield, Ill.: Abraham Lincoln Association, 1933.

———. *Lincoln in the Year 1859: Being the Day-by-Day Activities of Abraham Lincoln during That Year.* Springfield, Ill.: Lincoln Centennial Association, 1927.

———. *The Lincoln Reader.* New Brunswick, N.J.: Rutgers Univ. Press, 1947.

Arnold, James R. *Grant Wins the War: Decision at Vicksburg.* New York: John Wiley & Sons, 1997.

Ballard, Michael B. *Pemberton: A Biography.* Jackson: Univ. Press of Mississippi, 1991.

Bearss, Edwin C., and Leonard E. Brown. *Arkansas Post National Memorial.* Washington, D.C.: Office of History and Historic Architecture, 1971.

Bearss, Edwin C. "The Battle of the Post of Arkansas." *Arkansas Historical Quarterly* 18 (Autumn 1959): 237–45.

———. *The Campaign for Vicksburg.* Vol. 1, *Vicksburg Is the Key.* Dayton, Ohio: Morningside Press, 1986.

———. *The Campaign for Vicksburg.* Vol. 2, *Grant Strikes a Fatal Blow.* Dayton, Ohio: Morningside Press, 1986.

———. *The Campaign for Vicksburg.* Vol. 3, *Unvexed to the Sea.* Dayton, Ohio: Morningside Press, 1986.

———. *Decision in Mississippi.* Jackson: Mississippi Commission on the War between the States, 1962.

Belser, Thomas A. "Military Operations in Missouri and Arkansas, 1861–1865." Ph.D. diss., Vanderbilt University, 1958.

Beveridge, Albert J. *Abraham Lincoln, 1809–1858.* 2 vols. Boston: Houghton Mifflin, 1928.

Bigelow, John. *The Life of Samuel J. Tilden.* 2 vols. New York: Harper & Brothers, 1895.

Biographical Dictionary of the American Congress, 1774–1996. Alexandria, Va.: CQ Staff Directories, 1997.

Black, Robert C. *The Railroads of the Confederacy.* Chapel Hill: Univ. of North Carolina Press, 1952.

Blum, John S., et al., eds. *The National Experience: A History of the United States.* 5th ed. New York: Harcourt Brace Jovanovich, 1981.

Boatner, Mark M. *The Civil War Dictionary.* New York: David McKay, 1959.

"Brigadier General Edward John McClernand, 1848–1926." *Journal of the Illinois State Historical Society* 19 (Apr.–July 1926): 266–67.

Capers, Gerald M. *Stephen A. Douglas: Defender of the Union.* Boston: Little, Brown, 1959.

Carr. Clark E. *The Illini: A Story of the Prairies.* Chicago: A. C. McClurg, 1904.

Carter, Samuel. *The Final Fortress: The Campaign for Vicksburg, 1862–1863.* New York: St. Martin's Press, 1980.

Catton, Bruce. *The Army of the Potomac: Mr. Lincoln's Army.* Garden City, N.Y.: Doubleday, 1962.

———. *The Army of the Potomac: A Stillness at Appomattox.* Garden City, N.Y.: Doubleday, 1953.

———. *Grant Moves South.* Boston: Little, Brown, 1960.

———. *This Hallowed Ground.* Garden City, N.Y.: Doubleday, 1956.

"The Centennial Anniversary of the Birth of Robert Burns." *Journal of the Illinois State Historical Society* 17 (Apr.–July 1924). 205–9.

Chandler, Josephine C. "Dr. Charles Chandler: His Place in the American Scene." *Journal of the Illinois State Historical Society* 24 (Oct. 1931): 369–552.

Coggins, Jack.. *Arms & Equipment of the Civil War.* New York: Fairfax Press, 1983.

Cole, Arthur C. The *Era of the Civil War, 1848–1870.* Springfield: Illinois Centennial Commission, 1919.

Coleman, Roger E. *The Arkansas Post Story.* Santa Fe, N. Mex.: Southwest Cultural Resources Center, 1987.

Conger, Arthur L. *The Rise of Ulysses S. Grant.* New York: Century, 1931.

Connelly, Thomas L., and Archer Jones. *The Politics of Command: Factions and Ideas in Confederate Strategy.* Baton Rouge: Louisiana State Univ. Press, 1973.

Coolidge, Louis A. *Ulysses S. Grant.* Boston: Houghton Mifflin, 1917.

Cooling, Benjamin F. *Fort Donelson's Legacy: War and Society in Kentucky and Tennessee, 1862–1863.* Knoxville: Univ. of Tennessee Press, 1997.

———. *Forts Henry and Donelson: The Key to the Confederate Heartland.* Knoxville: Univ. of Tennessee Press, 1987.

Cox, Samuel S. *Three Decades of Federal Legislation, 1855 to 1885.* Freeport, N.Y.: Books for Libraries Press, 1970.

Cresap, Bernarr. *Appomattox Commander: The Story of General E. O. C. Ord.* San Diego: A. S. Barnes, 1981.

Daddysman, James W. *The Matamoras Trade: Confederate Commerce, Diplomacy, and Intrigue*. Newark: Univ. of Delaware Press, 1984.

Dalessandro, Robert J. "Morale in the Army of the Cumberland during the Tullahoma and Chickamauga Campaigns." Master's thesis, U.S. Army Command and General Staff College, 1995.

Davidson, Alexander, and Bernard Stuvé. *A Complete History of Illinois from 1673 to 1873*. Springfield: Illinois Journal, 1874.

Dayton, Aretas A. "The Raising of Union Forces in Illinois during the Civil War." *Journal of the Illinois State Historical Society* 34 (Dec. 1941): 401–38.

Dearing, Mary R. *Veterans in Politics: The Story of the G. A. R.* Westport, Conn.: Greenwood Press, 1974.

Dorris, J. T. "Michael Kelly Lawler: Mexican and Civil War Officer." *Journal of the Illinois State Historical Society* 48 (Winter 1955): 366–401.

Doyle, Cornelius J. "Josiah Lamborn, Attorney General of Illinois." *Journal of the Illinois State Historical Society* 20 (July 1927): 185–200.

Dyer, Frederick H. *A Compendium of the War of the Rebellion*. 2 vols. Dayton, Ohio: Press of Morningside Bookshop, 1979.

Eddy, Thomas M. *The Patriotism of Illinois*. 2 vols. Chicago: Clarke, 1865–66.

"Edward J. McClernand, Brigadier General." *Journal of the Illinois State Historical Society* 5 (Apr. 1912): 310–11.

Fellman, Michael. *Citizen Sherman*. New York: Random House, 1995.

Fiske, John. *The Mississippi Valley in the Civil War*. Boston: Houghton, Mifflin, 1901.

Flick, Alexander C. *Samuel Jones Tilden: A Study in Political Sagacity*. New York: Dodd, Mead, 1939.

Foote, Shelby. *The Civil War: A Narrative*. Vol. 2, *Fredericksburg to Meridian*. New York: Random House, 1958–74.

Ford, Thomas. *A History of Illinois from Its Commencement as a State in 1818 to 1847*. Chicago: S. C. Griggs, 1854.

Fuller, Claud E. *The Rifled Musket*. Harrisburg, Pa.: Stackpole, 1958.

Fuller, J. F. C. *The Generalship of Ulysses S. Grant*. New York: Dodd, Mead, 1929.

Gaylor, George R. "The Mormons and Politics in Illinois: 1839–1844." *Journal of the Illinois State Historical Society* 49 (Spring 1956): 48–66.

"Grant Takes Command at Cairo." *Journal of the Illinois State Historical Society* 38 (Mar. 1945): 242–43.

Green, Anna Maclay. "Civil War Public Opinion of General Grant." *Journal of the Illinois State Historical Society* 22 (Apr. 1929): 1–64.

Griffith, Paddy. *Battle Tactics of the Civil War*. New Haven, Conn.: Yale Univ. Press, 1989.

Grow, Stewart L. "A Study of the Utah Commission, 1882–96." Ph.D. diss., University of Utah, 1954.

Hagerman, Edward H. "The Evolution of Trench Warfare in the American Civil War." Ph.D. diss., Duke University, 1965.

Harrington, Fred Harvey. *Fighting Politician: Major General N. P. Banks*. Westport, Conn.: Greenwood Press, 1948.

Hart, B. H. Liddell. *Sherman: Soldier, Realist, American.* New York: Dodd, Meade, 1930.

Hartje, Robert G. *Van Dorn: The Life and Times of a Confederate General.* Nashville: Vanderbilt Univ. Press, 1967.

Hattaway, Herman, and Archer Jones. *How the North Won: A Military History of the Civil War.* Urbana: Univ. of Illinois Press, 1983.

Hearn, Chester G. *Admiral David Dixon Porter: The Civil War Years.* Annapolis, Md.: Naval Institute Press, 1996.

Heitman, Francis B. *Historical Register and Dictionary of the United States Army.* 2 vols. Washington, D.C.: GPO, 1903.

Herndon, William H., and Jesse K. Weik. *Life of Lincoln.* Cleveland: World Publishing, 1942.

Hicken, Victor. "From Vandalia to Vicksburg: The Political and Military Career of John A. McClernand." Ph.D. diss., University of Illinois, 1955.

———. *Illinois in the Civil War.* Urbana: Univ. of Illinois Press, 1962.

———. "John A. McClernand and the House Speakership Struggle of 1859." *Journal of the Illinois State Historical Society* 53 (Summer 1960): 163–78.

History of Sangamon County. Chicago: Inter-State Publishing, 1881.

Hofer, J. M. "Development of the Peace Movement in Illinois during the Civil War." *Journal of the Illinois State Historical Society* 24 (Apr. 1931): 110–28.

Holt, Robert D. "The Political Career of William A. Richardson." *Journal of the Illinois State Historical Society* 26 (Oct. 1933): 222–69.

Howard, Robert P. *Illinois: A History of the Prairie State.* Grand Rapids, Ill.: William B. Eerdmans, 1972.

Hubbart, Henry C. *The Older Middle West, 1840–1880.* New York: Russell & Russell, 1963.

Hubbell, John T. "McClernand, John Alexander." In *Dictionary of Military Bibliography.* 3 vols. Edited by Roger J. Spiller. Westport, Conn.: Greenwood Press, 1984.

Hughes, Nathaniel. *The Battle of Belmont: Grant Strikes South.* Chapel Hill: Univ. of North Carolina Press, 1991.

Jamieson, Perry. "The Development of Civil War Tactics." Ph.D. diss., Wayne State University, 1979.

Johanssen, Robert W. *Stephen A. Douglas.* New York: Oxford Univ. Press, 1973.

Johnston, William P. *The Life of General Albert Sidney Johnston.* New York: D. Appleton, 1878.

Jones, Archer. *Confederate Strategy from Shiloh to Vicksburg.* Baton Rouge: Louisiana State Univ. Press, 1961.

Jones, James P. *"Black Jack": John A. Logan and Southern Illinois in the Civil War Era.* Carbondale: Southern Illinois Univ. Press, 1995.

———. *John A. Logan: Stalwart Republican from Illinois.* Tallahassee: Univ. Presses of Florida, 1982.

Jordan, Thomas, and R. P. Pryor. *The Campaigns of Lieutenant General N. B. Forrest and of Forrest's Cavalry.* New York: DeCapo Press, 1977.

Josephy, Alvin M. *The Civil War in the American West.* New York: Alfred A. Knopf, 1991.

Kerby, Robert L. *Kirby Smith's Confederacy: The Trans-Mississippi South, 1863–1865.* New York: Columbia Univ. Press, 1972.

King, Charles. *The True Ulysses S. Grant.* Philadelphia: J. B. Lippincott, 1914.

King, James T. *War Eagle: A Life of General Eugene A. Carr.* Lincoln: Univ. of Nebraska Press, 1963.

Klement, Frank L. *The Copperheads in the Middle West.* Chicago: Univ. of Chicago Press, 1960.

———. "Copperhead Secret Societies in Illinois during the Civil War." *Journal of the Illinois State Historical Society* 48 (Spring 1955): 152–80.

———. "The Democrats as Sectionalists." In *Lincoln and Civil War Politics.* Edited by James A. Rawley. New York: Holt, Rinehart and Wilson, 1969.

Kriedberg, Marvin A., and Merton G. Henry. *History of the Military Mobilization in the United States Army, 1775–1945.* Washington, D.C.: Department of the Army, 1955.

Lang, George, Raymond L. Collins, and Gerard F. White. *Medal of Honor Recipients 1863–1994.* 2 vols. New York: Facts on File, 1995.

Larson, Gustive O. *The "Americanization" of Utah for Statehood.* San Marino, Calif.: Huntington Library, 1971.

Leckie, Robert. *None Died in Vain.* New York: Harper & Row, 1990.

Lewis, Lloyd. *Captain Sam Grant.* Boston: Little, Brown, 1950.

Livermore, Thomas L. *Numbers and Losses in the Civil War in America, 1861–65.* Boston: Houghton, Mifflin, 1900.

Longacre, Edward G. "Congressman Becomes General." *Civil War Times Illustrated* 21 (Nov. 1982): 30–39.

McCormick, Robert R. *Ulysses S. Grant: The Great Soldier of America.* New York: Bond Wheelwright, 1950.

McMurtie, Douglas C. "The First Printers of Illinois." *Journal of the Illinois State Historical Society* 26 (Oct. 1933): 202–21.

McPherson, James B. *Battle Cry of Freedom.* New York: Oxford Univ. Press, 1988.

Malone, Dumas, ed. *Dictionary of American Biography.* 20 vols plus 8 supplements. New York: Charles Scribner's Sons, 1943–1990.

Marszalek, John F. *Sherman: A Soldier's Passion for Order.* New York: Free Press, 1993.

Master Plan Maps. Fort Donelson National Military Park. Prepared by Edwin C. Bearss. 17 Apr. 1959.

Merrill, James M. *William Tecumseh Sherman.* Chicago: Rand McNally, 1971.

Merritt, Edward L. "Recollections of the Part Springfield Bore in the Obsequies of Abraham Lincoln." *Transactions of the Illinois State Historical Society* 14 (1910): 179–83.

Miller, Alphonse B. *Thaddeus Stevens.* New York: Harper & Brothers, 1939.

Milton, George F. *The Age of Hate: Andrew Johnson and the Radicals.* New York: Coward-McCann, 1930.

———. *The Eve of Conflict: Stephen A. Douglas and the Needless War.* Boston: Houghton Mifflin, 1934.

Monroe, B. D. "Life and Services of William Wilson, Chief Justice of the Illinois Supreme Court." *Journal of the Illinois State Historical Society* 11 (Oct. 1918): 391–99.

Moore, John H. *The Horizon and Zenith of the Great Rebellion.* 2 vols. Cincinnati: Elm Street Printing, 1870.

Morrison, James L. *The Best School in the World.* Kent, Ohio: Kent State Univ. Press, 1986.

Moses, John. *Illinois: Historical and Statistical.* 2 vols. Chicago: Fergus Printing, 1895.

Naval History Division. *Civil War Naval Chronology.* Washington, D.C.: Department of the Navy, 1971.

Nevins, Allan. *Ordeal of the Union.* Vol. 1, *Fruits of Manifest Destiny, 1847–1852.* New York: Charles Scribner's Sons, 1947.

———. *The War for the Union.* Vol. 1, *The Improvised War, 1861–1862.* New York: Charles Scribner's Sons, 1959.

———. *The War for the Union.* Vol. 2. *War Becomes Revolution.* New York: Charles Scribner's Sons, 1960.

Nichols, Roy F. *The Disruption of American Democracy.* New York: Free Press, 1948.

———. *Franklin Pierce.* Philadelphia: Univ. of Pennsylvania Press, 1931.

Nortrup, Jack. "Richard Yates: A Personal Glimpse of the Illinois Soldiers' Friend." *Journal of the Illinois State Historical Society* 56 (Summer 1963): 121–38.

Oder, Broeck N. "Andrew Johnson and the 1866 Illinois Election." *Journal of the Illinois State Historical Society* 73 (Autumn 1980): 189–200.

Orendorff, Alfred. "General John A. McClernand." *Transactions of the Illinois State Historical Society* 6 (1901): 80–85.

Palmer, George T. *A Conscientious Turncoat: The Story of John M. Palmer, 1817–1900.* New Haven, Conn.: Yale Univ. Press, 1941.

Pease, Theodore. *Illinois Election Returns, 1818 to 1848.* Springfield: Trustees of the Illinois Historical Library, 1923.

Pemberton, John C. *Pemberton: Defender of Vicksburg.* Chapel Hill: Univ. of North Carolina Press, 1942.

Perret, Geoffrey. *Ulysses S. Grant: Soldier & President.* New York: Random House, 1997.

Potter, David M. *The Impending Crisis, 1848–1861.* New York: Harper & Row, 1976.

Pratt, Fletcher. *Stanton: Lincoln's Secretary of War.* New York: W. W. Norton, 1953.

Register of Graduates and Former Cadets of the United States Military Academy. West Point, N.Y.: Association of Graduates, 1980.

Richardson, Albert D. *A Personal History of Ulysses S. Grant.* Hartford, Conn.: M. A. Winter & Hatch, 1902.

Ridley, Bromfield L. *Battles and Sketches of the Army of Tennessee.* Mexico, Mo.: Missouri Printing and Publishing, 1906.

Ripley, Peter. "Prelude to Donelson: Grant's January 1862 March into Kentucky." *Register of the Kentucky Historical Society* 68 (Oct. 1970): 311–18.

Roman, Alfred D. *The Military Operations of General Beauregard in the War Between the States.* 2 vols. New York: Harper and Brothers, 1883.

Rothschild, Alonzo. *"Honest Abe": A Study in Integrity.* Boston: Houghton Mifflin, 1917.

Sandburg, Carl. *Abraham Lincoln: The Prairie Years.* 2 vols. New York: Harcourt, Brace, 1926.

———. *Abraham Lincoln: The War Years.* 4 vols. New York: Harcourt, Brace, 1939.

Satterlee, John L. *The Black Hawk War and the Sangamo Journal, 1832.* Springfield, Ill.: John L. Satterlee, (1982?).

Schlesinger, Arthur M., Jr., ed. *History of American Presidential Elections, 1789–1968.* 4 vols. New York: Chelsea House Publishers, 1971.

Shakespeare, William. *Antony and Cleopatra.* Act 3. Scene 1. Lines 22–23.

Simon, John Y. "Grant at Belmont." *Military Affairs* 45 (Dec. 1981): 161–66.

Simon, Paul. *Lincoln's Preparation for Greatness: The Illinois Legislative Years.* Urbana: Univ. of Illinois Press, 1971.

Smith, Edward C. *The Borderland in the Civil War.* New York: Macmillan, 1927.

Stevens, Frank E. "Life of Stephen Arnold Douglas." *Journal of the Illinois State Historical Society* 16 (Oct. 1923–Jan. 924): 243–673.

Stonesifer, Roy P. "The Forts Henry-Heiman and Fort Donelson Campaign: A Study of Confederate Command." Ph.D. diss., Pennsylvania State University, 1965.

Thomas, Benjamin P., and Harold M. Hyman. *Stanton: The Life and Times of Lincoln's Secretary of War.* New York: Alfred A. Knopf, 1962.

Todd, Helen. *A Man Named Grant.* Boston: Houghton Mifflin, 1940.

Warner, Ezra J. *Generals in Blue.* Baton Rouge: Louisiana State Univ. Press, 1964.

———. *Generals in Gray.* Baton Rouge: Louisiana State Univ. Press, 1959.

Weigley, Russell F. *History of the United States Army.* New York: Macmillan, 1967.

Wellman, Manly Wade. *Giant in Gray: A Biography of Wade Hampton of South Carolina.* New York: Charles Scribner's Sons, 1949.

West, Richard S. *The Second Admiral: A Life of David Dixon Porter.* New York: Coward-McCann, 1937.

Williams, Kenneth P. *Lincoln Finds a General.* Vol. 3, *Grant's First Year in the West.* New York: Macmillan, 1952.

———. *Lincoln Finds a General.* Vol. 4, *Iuka to Vicksburg.* New York: Macmillan, 1956.

Williams, T. Harry. *Lincoln and His Generals.* New York: Random House, 1952.

Wilson, Bluford. "Southern Illinois in the Civil War." *Transactions of the Illinois State Historical Society* 16 (1913): 93–103.

Wilson, Major L. "Ideological Fruits of Manifest Destiny: The Geopolitics of Slavery Expansion in the Crisis of 1850." *Journal of the Illinois State Historical Society* 63 (Summer 1970): 132–57.

Worthington, T. *Shiloh: The Only Correct Military History of U. S. Grant and the Missing Army Records.* Washington City: M'Gill & Witherow, 1872.

Wyeth, John A. *That Devil Forrest: The Life of General Nathan Bedford Forrest.* New York: Harper and Brothers, 1950.

Yoseloff, Thomas. *Confederate Military History.* 12 vols. New York: Thomas Yoseloff, 1962.

Index

Index